A
Guide
to the
Historic
Architecture
of
Eastern

North

Carolina

A Guide to the Historic Architecture of
Eastern North Carolina

CATHERINE W. BISHIR *&* **MICHAEL T. SOUTHERN**

The
University of
North Carolina
Press
Chapel Hill
& London

Publication of this work

has been made possible by

generous grants from the

Kellenberger Historical

Foundation and the North

Carolina Department of

Cultural Resources.

© 1996
The University of North Carolina Press
All rights reserved
Manufactured in the United States of America
The paper in this book meets the guidelines for
permanence and durability of the Committee on
Production Guidelines for Book Longevity of the
Council on Library Resources.
Set in Garamond and Franklin Gothic by
G & S Typesetters
Printed by Thomson-Shore
Designed by Richard Hendel

Library of Congress
Cataloging-in-Publication Data
Bishir, Catherine W.
A guide to the historic architecture of Eastern
North Carolina / Catherine W. Bishir and
Michael T. Southern.
p.   cm.
Includes bibliographical references and index.
Contents: v. 1. The East.
ISBN 0-8078-2285-x (cloth: alk. paper).—
ISBN 0-8078-4594-9 (pbk.: alk. paper)
1. Architecture—North Carolina—Guidebooks.
I. Southern, Michael T.   II. Title.
NA730.N8B49   1996
720′.9756—dc20   95-50149
CIP

00 99 98 97   5 4 3 2

Contents

Maps

Preface

This book, a guide to historic architecture in eastern North Carolina, is the first in a three-volume series that will also include volumes on western North Carolina and piedmont North Carolina. The series is part of the educational and outreach program of the State Historic Preservation Office, North Carolina Division of Archives and History. Each book is intended as a field guide and reference for the traveler, resident, student, and preservationist with an interest in North Carolina's historic architecture. Although too large for a coat pocket, it is meant to fit in a backpack, bike basket, or glove compartment, to accompany the traveler and visitor in the field as well to rest on a bookshelf.

Originally the guide was envisioned as a single volume to cover the entire state, but at the suggestion of the University of North Carolina Press, the three-volume format was adopted as offering a more convenient and portable size for region-by-region use. This approach has also proved to offer a greater opportunity for focusing on the regions that delineate the state's varied landscape and shape its architectural, cultural, economic, and social history. For it is not so much the grandeur or fame of its individual landmarks that defines North Carolina's architectural heritage, but its intensely regional and local character, the sense of place, which captivates the traveler and sustains the residents in this old state. And it is that same local and regional character that seems most at risk in the late twentieth century, as strip developments and megastores and endless suburbs reach out into the landscape, and traditional landscapes of farming and small-town life vanish almost overnight.

NORTH CAROLINA REGIONS

The three regional guides follow a familiar division of the state that reflects differences in topography, history, and architectural patterns. North Carolina is a large state—some 500 miles wide. Its three principal regions run roughly parallel to the diagonal line of the coast. The eastern 40 percent of the state is a gently rising, level land of tidewater and coastal plain dominated by sandy or loam soils and predominantly pine forests. This section was the first to be settled by Europeans: beginning in the late seventeenth century, people of mainly British and African stock developed a maritime subsistence and commercial agriculture and established small port towns. The Piedmont—"foot of the mountain"—is a rolling country across the central portion with chiefly clay soils and mixed hardwood and pine forests. In the eighteenth century a tide of settlers came from the mid-Atlantic area and Virginia and created a society of smaller farms

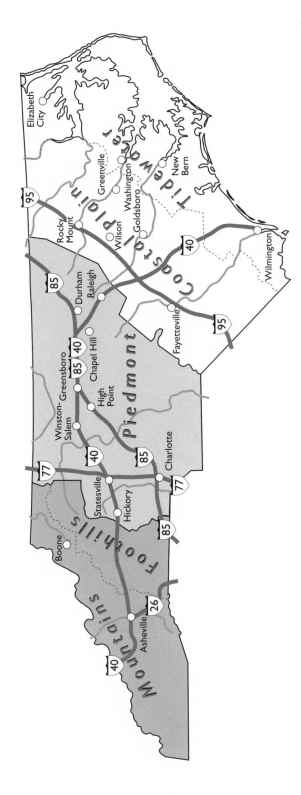

FIGURE 1. Map of N.C. showing principal regions, cities, routes, and regions. I-95, built during the 1970s, skirted the western edge of the eastern region, while I-77, and I-40 fortified trade in the Piedmont. By 1990 the first interstate highway in eastern N.C. was completed—I-40 from Raleigh to Wilmington. Only in this decade, too, have the main roads of the east been made into multilane highways.

distant from markets; here, in the nineteenth century, waterpower and railroad networks supported industrial and urban development. In the west, where the mountains rise against and beyond the Blue Ridge—the Eastern Continental Divide—the ancient, timeworn slopes are cloaked in hardwood and evergreen forests. This zone remained the domain of the Cherokees until after the American Revolution. Difficulties of transportation kept the region one of isolated rural communities until railroads and highways spurred lumbering and resort development in the late nineteenth and early twentieth centuries.

North Carolina's topography intensified the economic and cultural differences among the regions. The coastline is a treacherous one, where the long barrier islands known as the Outer Banks hampered oceangoing trade and prevented the development of a port metropolis. Without a principal city, and with the rivers and other natural arteries of trade leading from the backcountry into neighboring states rather than into a North Carolina port, the sections of the state remained distinct and isolated from one another. By 1810 a Raleigh journalist found that "between the Eastern and Western parts of this State there is as great dissimilarity in the face of the country, productions, and means of subsistence as usually exists between different and widely separated nations."[1]

Even after rail networks developed and industrialization worked its changes, the population remained predominantly rural and dispersed, and regional differences persisted. Amid the urban growth of the late nineteenth and early twentieth centuries, little towns and cities of roughly equal size combined intense localism with spirited competition for growth. The makeup of the population also strengthened the sense of localism, for the state received scant in-migration after the eighteenth century. While thousands of people left the state, few came in, so that for many years the proportion of native-born residents was among the highest in the nation. The late twentieth-century sunbelt boom brought the first infusion of immigration from other states and countries. Today North Carolina ranks tenth among the states in population, but it is still one of the least urbanized states in the nation. Only toward the end of the twentieth century has there been an urban majority in population. This recent urbanization has continued the old dispersed pattern among many small towns and cities rather than coalescing into a dominant metropolis. Although changes are blurring some boundaries, the long-standing sense of localism and regional identity still persists.

1. Thomas Henderson and Co., "Circular Letter," March 30, 1810, quoted in A. R. Newsome, "Twelve North Carolina Counties in 1810–1811," *North Carolina Historical Review* 5, no. 4 (October 1928): 416.

We imagine this guide serving as a friend might do when introducing a visitor to the region and its communities—sketching a brief history of the place and the patterns of life its architecture depicts, then pointing out and relating a story or two about the famous landmarks, strolling through the oldest neighborhoods, and discovering some of the special places that make each community itself. Our purpose is to present selected examples of common and uncommon architectural traditions, styles, and forms that define the particular character of each place and that compose broader regional and state patterns. This field guide is meant to complement existing studies. For fuller treatment of localities, the reader is encouraged to refer to the several published local surveys; for analysis of architectural practice and the state's architectural development, the reader may turn to *Architects and Builders in North Carolina, North Carolina Architecture*, and other works cited in the bibliography.

No guidebook can include every important landmark in each community and county. Selection and presentation of entries have followed several rules of thumb. Because the guide is aimed at the traveling public, the entries are generally restricted to those that may be seen reasonably well from a public thoroughfare. Illustrations represent buildings as they appear in the landscape or townscape rather than depicting interiors or architectural details. In a few rare instances, descriptions but no locational information are provided for exceptionally important properties that are not visible or accessible to the public. These are cited only in cases where the understanding of the region's architecture would be incomplete without acknowledging these places.

In choosing selections from many representative local building types, particularly farmhouses and farmsteads, we have focused on those that are located on readily accessible rather than remote roads and on those that are convenient to other properties cited. (The selections are *not* intended to represent a list of properties worthy of preservation, which are far more numerous than can be included here.) Preference is also given to places that are occupied and in reasonably good condition. Many important properties have been omitted because they are in ruinous or vulnerable condition, drastic alterations have taken place, or vegetation or distance shields them from public view. Over the period of this project, conditions have changed for many properties. Some originally included have fallen into disuse or decay, while others that were in dire straits ten years ago have been rescued for new life. In this respect, we have tried to make the book as up to date as possible; however, circumstances are always changing, and we welcome updated information.

Several other factors affected the choice of properties. Different levels of architectural survey fieldwork and research from town to town and county to county are reflected by more or less complete representation and information for various towns and counties. So, too, some examples were selected over others when a strong history was available that illustrated trends in the region, or where a good story captured the spirit of the time or place. We have also focused attention on communities and areas with unusually rewarding concentrations of historic architecture accessible to public view.

On the other hand, it has not been feasible to treat some kinds of buildings as fully as they deserve within the entries. The state's architectural history has been defined by the prevalence of very simple, often rudimentary and short-lived buildings that have stood by the thousands, from the log and earthfast frame houses and barns of the eighteenth and nineteenth centuries to the log and frame tobacco barns, sheds and outbuildings, and modest workers' and tenant houses of the late nineteenth and early twentieth centuries. Today, because of the late twentieth-century revolution in agriculture, these are rapidly vanishing; particular examples are too fragile to cite reliably. Hence we have discussed these as important types in the introduction and mentioned their previous or continued presence in the landscape in counties where they are especially important. Travelers who keep an eye open for them will see scores of tobacco barns, small farmhouses, and myriad outbuildings along the back roads—and even in view of interstate highways.

PRIVATE AND PUBLIC PLACES

In using this guide, especially in rural areas, the reader is urged to remember that unless otherwise specified, the properties presented are *private and not open to the public.* Where private properties are easily visible from a public thoroughfare, attention is called to them as parts of the architectural landscape. This does not constitute an invitation to visit or trespass! Users of this book are strictly enjoined to respect the privacy of residents and owners—to remain on the public right-of-way, not to set foot or wheel upon private property uninvited, and to admire and learn from afar.

Where places are open to the public, this status is indicated. For the most part, detailed descriptions of interior features are restricted to properties that are open to the public in some fashion. As opening hours may vary markedly, visitors are advised to call local chambers of commerce for information on local sites open to the public, bed and breakfast inns, and other businesses operating in historic buildings. The North Carolina Department of Travel and Tourism as well as state visitors' centers on principal highways offer flyers and other information about places open to the public. The nonprofit statewide preservation organization, Preservation North Carolina, has published the *Complete Guide to*

North Carolina's Historic Sites, listing hours and telephone numbers for selected historic properties open to the public. State-owned state historic sites are normally open during business hours seven days a week, though some of these are closed on Mondays during the winter. Several communities, such as Beaufort, Edenton, New Bern, Wilmington, and others, hold annual or biennial home tours of selected private houses, and local chambers of commerce generally have information on their schedules.

ORGANIZATION OF THE GUIDE

The guidebook is organized by regional clusters of counties, an arrangement that is meant to assist in organizing a visit and in understanding regional architectural patterns. As in most southern states, North Carolina's principal geographical and political unit traditionally has been the county, which encompasses urban as well as rural places. The county unit is the building block for this guide. Map and entry codes (such as PQ 1, NH 2, etc.) employ the county code system used for the statewide architectural survey program.

The guide begins in the northeastern corner of the state, in the northern tidewater where European and African settlement first began in the seventeenth century. Subsequent sections proceed south along the coastline in the tidewater zone, then turn to the northern counties of the inner coastal plain and run southward through that region.

Most county units begin with the county seat. Following the section on the county seat, entries are arranged in geographical order—typically clockwise from the north to the east, south, and west—around the county. In a few cases, the shape of the county or the distribution of entries requires a different treatment. Within the county seat and other towns, the presentation usually begins either with the courthouse or, in some maritime cases, with the waterfront and then proceeds around the town core and then outward to outlying properties. Town properties are generally presented in clockwise or linear order, depending on the layout of the community. Properties are treated either as individual entries or as components of group entries, depending on the density of the area and relationships among buildings in a community or neighborhood. Cross-references to properties treated elsewhere in the volume are denoted with an asterisk.

MAPS

Simplified county maps are grouped together following the Introduction; selected town maps appear within the text. These are necessarily much-reduced depictions of complex places, showing only a few of the many roads and streets that weave through the landscape. Four-digit SR numbers indicate secondary roads, which are part of the state-maintained highway system along with N.C. and U.S. highways. These roads have designated names as well as numbers, but for rural roads only the numbers are employed in this guide, for purposes of brevity and correlation with standard maps.

Serious travelers in the countryside are encouraged to acquire county-by-county road maps. These are available in commercially published atlases and individually from the Department of Transportation. These detailed maps complement the official state transportation map, available free from the Department of Transportation. Currently in North Carolina many changes are under way in the road system, including new construction and widespread renumbering, rendering even the most current maps outdated. We have striven to make the locations clear and accurate, but we expect that readers, like the authors, will sometimes get lost and find something even more interesting down a winding back road.

ACKNOWLEDGMENTS

In the early 1980s, the North Carolina State Historic Preservation Office (Division of Archives and History, Department of Cultural Resources) began the project to produce a guide to the historic architecture of the state, based primarily on the existing fieldwork and research in the Survey and Planning Branch of the Historic Preservation Office. The first phase of the project was completed in 1984–85 by the Historic Preservation Office with assistance from a 1983 grant from the National Endowment for the Humanities (RS-20386-83) to the Federation of North Carolina Historical Societies, a nonprofit affiliate organization of the Division of Archives and History. During subsequent years, additional fieldwork has been conducted, the format has been modified, and much new information gained from recent county and town surveys and National Register of Historic Places nominations has been incorporated.

The principal source of historical, architectural, and locational information is the extensive collection of survey site files and National Register of Historic Places nomination files of the Survey and Planning Branch. These files reflect fieldwork and research conducted since the late 1960s as part of the ongoing statewide architectural survey and National Register of Historic Places programs in North Carolina. Many individuals—too numerous to list in full—have contributed to this growing body of information as staff members and consultants, and their contributions are gratefully acknowledged.

For this volume we have depended upon the fieldwork and research from town and county surveys conducted by many architectural historians. Several of these individuals have also assisted by recommending properties for inclusion, drafting entries, reviewing the text, and answering endless questions. These include the following:

Bradley Barker—Chowan County;
Angela Barnett—Pamlico County;
David and Allison Black—Halifax County towns including Roanoke Rapids, Scotland Neck, Weldon, and Halifax;
Claudia Brown—Hyde, Currituck, and Dare counties;
Thomas Butchko—Gates, Johnston, Pasquotank, Sampson, and Scotland counties, and also Edenton, Elizabeth City, Weldon, Williamston, and Wilson;
Donna Dodenhoff—Martin County;
Barbara Hammond—Goldsboro;
Davyd Foard Hood—Plymouth and New Hanover County;
Robbie Jones—Lenoir County;
Diane Lea—Lumberton;
Philip Letsinger—Ahoskie and Maxton;
Ruth Little—Bladen County;
Ruth Little and Thomas Hanchett—New Bern African American sites;
Carl Lounsbury—Southport;
Christopher Martin—New Hanover County;
Jennifer Martin—Duplin County;
Richard Mattson—Nash County, Rocky Mount, and East Wilson;
Kate Ohno—Rocky Mount, Wilson, and Wilson County;
Daniel Pezzoni—Manteo, Columbia, and Onslow County;
Scott Power—Greenville and Pitt County;
Peter Sandbeck—New Bern and Craven County;
Janet Seapker—New Bern and Wilmington;
Mary Shoemaker—Hamilton and Smithfield;
Henry Taves—Halifax and Edgecombe counties;
Edward Turberg—Wilmington and New Hanover County;
Nicholas Wilson—Red Springs;
Tony Wrenn—Beaufort, New Bern, and Wilmington;
Dru Haley York—Cumberland and Perquimans counties.

The surveys that have been published are cited in the bibliography. Thomas Butchko drafted entries for Johnston, Sampson, and Scotland counties, and Peter Sandbeck drafted entries for Craven County.

Most of the photographs in this volume come from the photographic collection of Archives and History. The majority of these were made over the years by field surveyors and Archives and History staff members, including staff photographers. The excellent work of these staff photographers, including Tony Vaughan, JoAnn Sieburg-Baker, Randall Page, and Bill Garrett, is acknowledged with special thanks. Several photographs in the Archives and History collection were donated by photographer Elizabeth Matheson, whose work is likewise acknowledged with appreciation. Expert and patient assistance in locating photographs was provided by Steve Massengill, Archives and History's iconographic archivist. Additional photographs (see photo credits) were obtained from the Division of Travel and Tourism, the Duke University Special Collections Library, and the North Carolina Collection, University of North Carolina at Chapel Hill; thanks go to William Erwin and Jerry Cotten at the latter two collections for their assistance.

The preparation of this guide has also relied on the help of innumerable other individuals, organizations, and institutions. The late Robert M. Kelly of Greensboro gave important and timely assistance through his solicitation and coordination of several generous private donations to the Federation of North Carolina Historical Societies on behalf of the project. These gifts permitted the purchase of a computer, printer, and software compatible with the system used by the publisher. Contributors were Mr. and Mrs. Robert M. Kelly of Greensboro, Boren Clay Products Company of Pleasant Garden (Dean L. Spangler), the Dillard Fund of Greensboro (John H. Dillard), W. L. Burns of Durham, and Mr. and Mrs. A. P. Hubbard of Greensboro, whose gift was made in memory of Thomas Turner. These gifts are acknowledged with thanks.

In the initial stages of the project, Christi Dennis served as field and research assistant. She also prepared the original draft county maps that became the basis for the county maps used in this guide. Mark Mathis helped convert the text from one computer operating system to another, and Virginia Oswald assisted with word processing. The county, municipal, and regional maps were prepared with computer graphics software by Michael Southern, with advice and assistance from Heidi Perov.

Throughout the project, staff at Archives and History have provided essential assistance, including technical help, architectural and historical expertise, and moral support and encouragement. Key among these are David Brook, William Price, and Betsy Buford, as well as Jeff Adolphsen, Jerry Cashion, Lloyd Childers, Jerry Cross, Diane Filipowicz, Paul Fomberg, Brent Glass, Renee Gledhill-Earley, Terry Harper, Michael Hill, Al Honeycutt, Davyd Foard Hood, Rick Jackson, Peter Kaplan, Bill McCrea, Linda McRae, Peter Sandbeck, Beth Thomas, Sondra Ward, Mitch Wilds, and Dru Haley York.

The information in this volume has been enhanced by new data from the "History through Timber" dendrochronology project. This study was conducted in 1993–94 by Archives and History staff in cooperation with Preservation North Carolina and funded by grants from the Weyerhaeuser Foundation. By taking samples of timbers and comparing them with a "key year" data base of tree-ring variations over the years, dendrochronologist Herman J. Heikkenen provided tree-ring-based dates for the cutting of the timbers—and thus, presumably, the construction dates—for a number of early buildings. These dates—some differing considerably from previous estimates—are used in entries in this volume.

For this volume, we have also relied on the knowledge and generous assistance of Dr. Margaret Battle, Millie Barbee, Robert Boykin, Watson Brown, Michael Cotter, Randy Davis, Mary Grady, Meade Horne, Collin Ingraham, Sam Johnson, Meg Kluttz, Stanley Little, Lu-Ann Monson, William Murphy, Margaret Phillips, T. E. Ricks, Leon Sikes, Barbara Snowden, R. S. Spencer Jr., Glenn Suttenfield, John Tyler, and others who reviewed various sections. Research assistants Michele Michael and Anna Tilghman, along with Scott Power, Robin Stancil, and Reid Thomas of the Eastern Office of Archives and History, provided essential help in fieldchecking sites. John Bishir, Jerry Cashion, Michael Hill, and Kate Hutchins provided critical readings of the Introduction. Claudia Brown supplied unflagging moral support and leadership. Chandrea Burch and Bill Garrett were heroically patient in production of photographs.

Among the many friends and colleagues who have given guidance and support to this endeavor over the years are John Bishir, Charlotte Brown, Robert Burns, Al Chambers, Ed Chappell, Dan Chartier, Elizabeth Cromley, Bernard Herman, Myrick Howard, John Larson, Ruth Little, Carl Lounsbury, Michelle Michael, Gray Read, Orlando Ridout, Margaret Supplee Smith, Kathleen Southern, Dell Upton, and Camille Wells. We are especially grateful for the encouragement and expertise of the staff of the University of North Carolina Press, particularly David Perry, Heidi Perov, Pamela Upton, and Rich Hendel.

In assembling this guide, we have sought to make it as accurate as possible, but inevitably errors will have crept in undetected. Readers are encouraged to provide any corrections, particularly on property locations and factual information, to the authors at the Survey and Planning Branch, Division of Archives and History, Department of Cultural Resources, 109 E. Jones St., Raleigh NC 27601-2807. Inevitably, too, we know we have left out some wonderful places, some of everyone's—including our own—favorite spots. For this we ask readers' forgiveness. We hope that for every place that does appear in the book, you will visit and delight in many, many more.

Catherine W. Bishir
Michael T. Southern
November 1995

Introduction

EASTERN NORTH CAROLINA

LAND & ARCHITECTURE

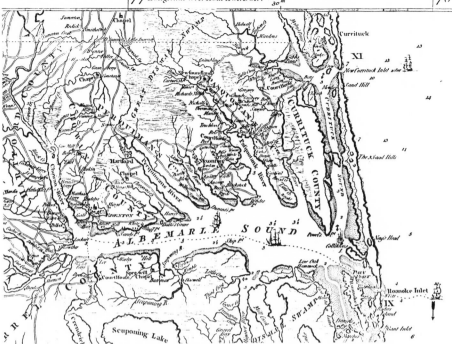

FIGURE 3. *Detail of "An Accurate Map of North and South Carolina," by Henry Mouzon, 1775. Eastern N.C.'s tidewater and coastal plain zones compose an intricate patchwork of land and water. The barrier islands are part of an ever-moving system of land and water. Over the eons, the waters have risen and fallen. In recent centuries, inlets have opened, shoaled up, and closed. From the first maps drawn, the image of the land was densely studded with Indian and English names for every waterway and natural feature.*

LAND AND WATER

In eastern North Carolina the flat land stretches out for miles across the horizon. Fields of dark purple-black loam or creamy white sand gleam between stands of tall pines and oaks. Water is everywhere. The tidewater zone, running 300 miles west and south along the Atlantic coast, encompasses a series of broad sounds created by the Outer Banks, the great bent arm of slender islands that stretches far out to sea. Broken only by a few narrow, shallow, and changeable inlets, the Outer Banks compose a continually shifting barrier that shields the mainland from Atlantic storms. Except for the Cape Fear River at the southeastern corner of the state, the rivers from the mainland—with the nutrients and vessels they carry—empty into the sounds rather than into ocean harbors.

FIGURE 4. *Bennett's Pond, Chowan Co. The tidewater section of eastern N.C. includes many areas of swamp and other wetlands, and much of the land is arable only if it is drained.*

These conditions make the wide and shallow sounds and their tributaries nurseries for fish and shellfish, while making seagoing trade extremely difficult.[1]

The tidewater terrain, with elevations from 3 or 4 feet above sea level in some areas, 30 or 40 in others, is a fecund wetland web with patches of arable land interspersed among sounds, bays, inlets, shoals, rivers, creeks, marshes, and swamps. The latter range from the vast cypress depths of the Great Dismal Swamp to the raised swamps known by the Indian name *pocosin*, "swamp on a hill." When adequately drained, the soils adjacent to the sounds are among the richest in the world, especially the deep peat deposits of the Pamlico peninsula, which have attracted ventures since the eighteenth century.

West of the tidewater, the inner coastal plain rises gently to elevations of 100 to 200 feet, where occasional slight mounds are celebrated by names such as Snow Hill and Rocky Mount. In this inner coastal plain between the tidewater and the fall line, swaths of well-drained loam or sandy soil create a prolific agricultural zone, but here too the terrain is interlaced with slow-moving rivers, creeks, lakes, swamps, and pocosins. Some of the lakes and swamps are oval depressions called Carolina bays, which dot the southern coastal plain.

This mosaic of land and water is young in geological terms. In contrast to the older crystalline rocks that begin at the fall line and underlie North Carolina's Piedmont and mountain regions, the tidewater and inner coastal plain are formed of sediments laid down eons after the westward formations were in

1. For emphasis on the interplay of water and land in the region—"water is everywhere"—the authors are indebted to Thomas Butchko, "Welcome to the Albemarle," presented at the Preservation North Carolina annual meeting, Edenton, September 29, 1995.

place. (For this reason, the east lacks the good building stone so abundant from the fall line westward.) At intervals the inner coastal plain was covered by ancient seas that lapped at the present fall line, and at other times the ocean withdrew to expose beaches that reached many miles east of the present coastline. This migration of the seas also formed the Outer Banks; some believe they were sand dunes formed when the coastline lay farther east, and when the sea rose again, water filled the sounds.

For the people who came to live in eastern North Carolina, nature's bounty of fish, game, fertile land, abundant water and forests, and a long growing season punctuated by mild winters promised a new Eden. But for those who sought an El Dorado, the lay of the land ordained another story. The Outer Banks and other barriers restricted trade and limited prosperity. One generation after another found that this "inconvenient geography" inhibited the accumulation of wealth and prevented the creation of a dominant metropolis, while encouraging dispersed rural communities and small towns. So strong was this influence that even after railroads and highways crisscrossed the region in the twentieth century, an ingrained sense of localism and regional identity maintained its power.

PEOPLE AND ARCHITECTURE

Across this broad land of promise and challenge, the historic architecture of eastern North Carolina depicts the story of a people and the world they created at the edge of the North American continent. There are many threads to this story—some unique to the region, others that connect to the world beyond—and they intertwine across the generations.

Distinctive landmarks recall familiar and celebrated sagas. Towering lighthouses on barrier islands warn of shoals that have menaced sailors since the first European explorers peered from their vessels toward the low, distant shoreline. Lifesaving stations on those same windswept banks witnessed acts of great heroism on stormy seas. Stout little houses and public buildings in small port towns evoke the struggles to transplant British culture to an unfamiliar land. Scattered plantation houses reflect the wealth a few great landowners accrued from fields, forests, and rivers with the labor of African slaves. Along with townhouses in the old ports they evoke a genteel society whose webs of kinship, trade, political power, and taste linked localities to one another and to distant urban centers. Forts and battlefields once echoed with the thunder of battles fought for control of the land and the people. Rambling white frame houses with deep porches on quiet, shady streets suggest the charms of life in small southern towns.

Other threads expand the tale of how people shaped a culture on the land.

FIGURE 5. *Courthouse Green and Water St., Edenton, across Edenton Bay* (CO 1–3). *By the late nine-teenth century, amid growing tourism and attention to historic landmarks, travel writers marveled at "North Carolina's brilliant constellation of historic towns," calling Edenton a "museum-like little city . . . rich in her history, wealthy in the retention of her old landmarks, and double fortunate in her pastoral beauty and picturesque glimpses of land and water"* (George I. Nowitzky, Norfolk and the Marine Metropolis of Virginia, and the Sound and River Cities of North Carolina: A Narrative *[Norfolk and Raleigh: George I. Nowitzky, 1888]*).

Modest farmhouses of many eras reflect the subsistence that self-reliant farming and fishing families garnered from the fields and the water. Tenant houses reveal a cycle of farming life, now all but ended, that for over a century tied thousands of families to the rhythm of crops and debts. Barns and outbuildings depict an ever changing agricultural economy: smokehouses, mule barns, and stables, rapidly vanishing legions of flue-cure tobacco barns, and their successors for new crops and technologies. In shady groves and at crossroads, country churches proclaim a strong and independent if sometimes contentious faith. Small towns and cities with main streets lined by sturdy commercial buildings and proud public edifices embody hopeful times of economic vitality and earnest boosterism fed by riverboats, railroads, and highways. Compact neigh-borhoods of houses and gardens, churches, businesses, and fraternal lodges show the determination of black citizens to establish community and identity within an often inimical larger society. In a few places, textile mills and workers' hous-ing, tobacco factories and warehouses, and lumber mills and peanut factories show local entrepreneurs' struggles to bring an agricultural society into the industrial age.

For many eastern North Carolinians, it is this still-abundant and unpretentious architecture built between the Civil War and World War II that most powerfully evokes the character of the region. In their simplicity and their numbers these places make up a landscape of subtle beauty. The popular image of the region's history often concentrates on the vestiges of the colonial past or the high points of antebellum prosperity. Today's pursuit of prosperity and modernization is generating a stream of new buildings across the land. Much of the rural past has been lost from the landscape within the last few years. Yet despite the overwhelming transformations at work, at the end of the twentieth century it is still the pragmatic, now often poignant architecture of the interwar years—the white frame houses nestled beneath big trees; dark, weathered sheds and tobacco barns; Cola-painted country stores; little white frame country churches; and small towns with a clump of brick stores facing a railroad track and a few blocks with shade trees and deep porches—that makes eastern North Carolina look like home.

In this region of old mixed with new, rural neighborhoods and small towns weave a complex and often baffling pattern, where invincible individuality ties into neighborliness and intimate community, and where old issues of wealth and poverty, race and class, change and conservatism run deep. In one community after another, the architecture embodies old hierarchies that do not always demand separation or display; eccentricity flourishes amid conformity; and

FIGURE 6. *Daughtridge Farm, Edgecombe Co.* (ED 59). *The inner coastal plain has supported productive agriculture for many years, yielding crops of grains, cotton, tobacco, and vegetables. Farmsteads like this one, with a frame farmhouse beneath large shade trees and a series of frame barns and other outbuildings among broad, flat fields, define much of the region's agrarian landscape.*

civility covers conflict as well as camaraderie. A slow pace and a love of tradition intermix with insistent boosterism and hustling after progress. And a powerful sense of family, local, and regional identity combines pride and defensiveness, love and hate, old stories and new hopes, all in generous measure.

Despite the illusion of the region as a place slow to change, the architectural landscape of eastern North Carolina depicts an endless series of often wrenching transformations. In a land where nature offered immense promise coupled with daunting obstacles, one little town after another saw booms and busts with national and international trade patterns. Hard-won canals, railroads, and highways channeled prosperity into some communities while siphoning it away from others. Farmers contended with the powerful shifts in market, methods, and crops as well as the implacable cycles and whims of nature that require a resilient faith and fatalism to "take the good with the bad."

SETTLEMENT AND DEVELOPMENT, 1580S–1860S

It was on North Carolina's coast, on Roanoke Island, that the first attempts at permanent English settlement in North America took place. But the two colonies planted in 1585 and 1587 by Sir Walter Raleigh failed, and the men, women, and children who arrived in 1587 had vanished from history by 1590, leaving only the mystery of the "Lost Colony."

The settlers entered a land where Algonkian, Siouan, and Iroquoian people had been hunting, farming, and fishing along the sounds and rivers for centuries, and indeed where their predecessors had hunted game, fished, and gathered shellfish and edible plants for nearly 10,000 years. During the seventeenth century, while English settlements struggled, then thrived in Virginia and New England, North Carolina was still the domain of these Native Americans. Although the Algonkians' villages and farms were numerous when Raleigh's colonists arrived in the 1580s, by the time renewed efforts at English colonization began in the 1650s, the Algonkians were much reduced by disease, and the Iroquoian Tuscarora had emerged as the most populous and powerful tribe in eastern North Carolina.

In the middle 1600s, adventurers from Virginia began to move "to the southward" to establish Indian trading posts and take up cheap and fertile land in northeastern North Carolina. In 1663 the newly enthroned and grateful Charles II chartered Carolina as a proprietary colony, which was duly named in his honor. The Carolina proprietors focused their attention on the profitable southern portion, which became South Carolina after 1712, leaving the scattered settlers of the northern section to manage pretty much on their own, contending with pirates, Indian wars, and erratic government. For a time the colonists

FIGURE 7. *"Village of Secoton," engraving by Theodor deBry from John White drawing. Little remains of the architecture of the native people of eastern N.C. Roanoke colonist John White's watercolors, probably made during the 1585–86 expedition, depict the local Algonkian villages and their barrel-roofed longhouses. Post-hole patterns of such longhouses have been discovered in several coastal counties, but no aboveground remains of early Indian habitations survive. The legacy of the Indians lives in the agricultural skills and crops they passed to the colonists, especially corn and tobacco, and in beautiful place-names, such as Currituck, Pasquotank, Perquimans, Chowan, Roanoke, Pamlico, Contentnea, Mattamuskeet, and Waccamaw.*

and the natives lived alongside one another in relative peace on the fringes of Tuscarora territory. But as the settlements expanded, tensions built up that exploded in war in 1711. After the Tuscarora attacked the new Swiss colony around New Bern and other English settlements along the coast, they were countered and eventually defeated in 1715 with the aid of colonial and Yemassee troops from South Carolina.

After the proprietors turned the colony over to royal control in 1729, royal governors strove to achieve greater order and growth. North Carolina's population soared from 35,000 in 1730 to 70,000 in 1750 and 250,000 in the 1770s. Although the most dramatic population growth occurred in the piedmont frontier country, settlement also thickened rapidly in the east as settlers arrived from Britain, Virginia, Barbados, South Carolina, and other colonies. Growing numbers of North Carolinians brought in African slaves, chiefly to eastern counties. From fewer than 500 in 1700, the number of black slaves had increased to 100,000 by 1790. Old communities expanded in the Albemarle and Pamlico regions, towns and plantations took root along the Lower Cape Fear, and settlement reached up the rivers into the inner coastal plain.

Along the sounds and streams, amid towering forests of longleaf pines and hardwoods, settlers cleared land and established farms and plantations. Small farms were the predominant unit of the landscape and the economy. The majority of North Carolina's free population owned no slaves, and of the third who did own slaves, most held fewer than five. Learning from the Indians how to farm in the forest, settlers girdled towering trees and cut fields into the forests and between the swamps. They planted crops of corn and wheat, beans and tobacco, in clearings among the tree stumps and set their cattle and hogs to feed and multiply in the woods. Most landholders, small or large, cleared and "improved" and fenced only a fraction of their land for crops, leaving the remainder in forest: woodlot, potential for fresh fields when old ones wore out, and grazing for livestock. Free range prevailed until the late nineteenth century. Fence laws required farmers to build fences to keep animals out of fields or house yards, not to keep them in an enclosed pasture.

In some areas, fishing was as important as farming. Whalers from New England established colonies near Beaufort and around Cape Lookout, and all along the coast fishermen harvested an astonishing bounty from the ocean, the streams, and the sounds. In this "good poor man's country," thousands of families obtained a generous sufficiency from the sounds and streams, forests and fields, and produced occasional surpluses for export.

By the mid-eighteenth century, eastern North Carolina also possessed a small but powerful planter and merchant class, whose wealthiest members rivaled those elsewhere in the South. Most of these were ambitious new arrivals from

Britain, Barbados, or other colonies. During the early and mid-nineteenth century, consolidation of landholding and ownership of slaves increased. In some sections of eastern North Carolina, especially along the Lower Cape Fear River in the southeast and the Roanoke River to the north, a few planter families assembled thousands of acres. Some owned 100 or 200 slaves, who cultivated rice, corn, and tobacco fields; cut timber and tapped pine rosin; and, at several coastal plantation fisheries, hauled in nets full of fish. In these locales African slaves constituted the majority of the population. Tied by trade networks between town and country and between North Carolina and distant urban marketplaces, the region's colonial planters and merchants developed local and supralocal oligarchies that wielded lasting social, political, and economic power in the region and the state.

Commercial plantation agriculture varied, for North Carolina lies in a transitional zone for staple crop cultivation: at the northern limits for cotton and rice and at the southern limits for tobacco. Large planters and small farmers alike raised a variety of food and fibers to supply their own needs. For the market planters produced a variety of crops: tons of corn nearly everywhere; wheat and tobacco and some cotton in the Albemarle area and in the inner coastal plain; and rice along the Lower Cape Fear River. In the 1840s and especially the 1850s, cotton production soared as rising cotton prices, improved cotton gins, and better access to market made the crop vastly more profitable. By the late

FIGURE 8. *Driving a wagonload of cotton to market. Along with naval stores, grains, tobacco, and other crops, cotton became increasingly important to the expansion of commercial agriculture and plantation slavery in the mid-19th c. Slaves worked in the fields, operated cotton presses (seen in the background here; see also Norfleet Cotton Press,* [ED 21]*), and drove wagonloads of produce to markets.*

antebellum period, cotton was the state's most important money crop for large and small growers, and its cultivation expanded slaveholding and commercial agriculture across the coastal plain and into the Piedmont.

From the colonial period well into the nineteenth century, North Carolina's main exports came from the naval stores and timber industries. Throughout the region, slave and free workers tapped the seemingly limitless longleaf pines for the tar and pitch used as preservatives for the wooden ships and hemp ropes of British and, later, American fleets. Indeed, North Carolina's leadership in naval stores exports earned it the nickname "Tar Heel State." From the pine and hardwood forests, workers also cut vast quantities of lumber, barrel staves, and shingles (especially from the cypress swamps) and sent them downriver bound for markets in New England, the Caribbean, and elsewhere.

With all this bounty, North Carolinians found that the inconvenient geography of the coast hampered trade and town growth. The barrier islands prevented development of a major port in the Albemarle or Pamlico areas served by the Roanoke, Tar, and Neuse river basins. Even at the mouth of the Cape Fear, the only major river opening into the ocean, treacherous shoals endangered shipping and limited trade. In the absence of a superior deepwater harbor into which to channel trade, a series of small ports sprang up. Each in turn enjoyed a period of prominence, then receded into quieter times. Bath, the colony's first incorporated town in 1705, remained a village on the Pamlico River. Edenton on the Albemarle Sound became a colonial trade and political center, but it and other Albemarle ports languished after Roanoke Inlet, which had opened by 1657, shoaled up and eventually closed about 1795, forcing ships to make a long and arduous journey through Albemarle and Pamlico sounds and Ocracoke Inlet to reach the open sea. Frustrated in attempts to have Roanoke Inlet reopened, Edentonians saw their prospects plummet when the Dismal Swamp Canal diverted trade to Elizabeth City and Norfolk. New Bern, located on the Neuse River near the Pamlico Sound, emerged as capital and a leading port in the late colonial period. Even after the capital was moved to Raleigh in the 1790s, New Bern continued as the state's largest town into the early nineteenth century. But, despite efforts to improve its competitiveness with a canal to route trade to the ocean harbor at Beaufort, New Bern's trade and status declined in the 1820s and 1830s. The maritime communities of Elizabeth City, Washington, and Beaufort all had periods of modest advancement in the eighteenth and nineteenth centuries, as their fortunes waxed and waned with currents of trade.

On the Cape Fear River, Brunswick thrived briefly in the mid-eighteenth century but dwindled to a ghost town while Wilmington, which had been established in 1740 at a more favorable site upstream, emerged as the chief port. Developing as a hub of rail as well as steamship connections, Wilmington grew by 1840 into North Carolina's largest city, a status it maintained until it was eclipsed in the early twentieth century by fast-growing industrial cities in the Piedmont.

Inland trade centers developed at ferry crossings or near the heads of river navigation at the fall line. Halifax emerged as a center of the Roanoke River plantation economy, and Murfreesboro arose by the Meherrin River. In the central coastal plain, Tarboro, Greenville and other towns developed along the Tar, and Kingston (later Kinston) and Smithfield were small market towns on the Neuse. As the center of the Highland Scots settlements on the Cape Fear and the head of navigation on the river, Fayetteville (initially called Cross Creek), emerged as the largest inland river town and was considered as possible capital for the new state in the 1790s. Throughout the region, even smaller settlements operated as local political and trade centers—still illustrated today by communities such as Camden and Currituck—with a courthouse, a tavern, a few houses, and perhaps a store or a fraternal lodge clustered at a rural clearing. The region's towns and villages developed more as a network of equals than as satellites around a single star, a pattern that has persisted to the present.

FIGURE 9. *Wilmington waterfront. The state's chief port in the 19th c., Wilmington became an export center for naval stores, rice, and cotton and an entrepôt for a large region, with ships arriving from other American ports, the West Indies, and Europe.*

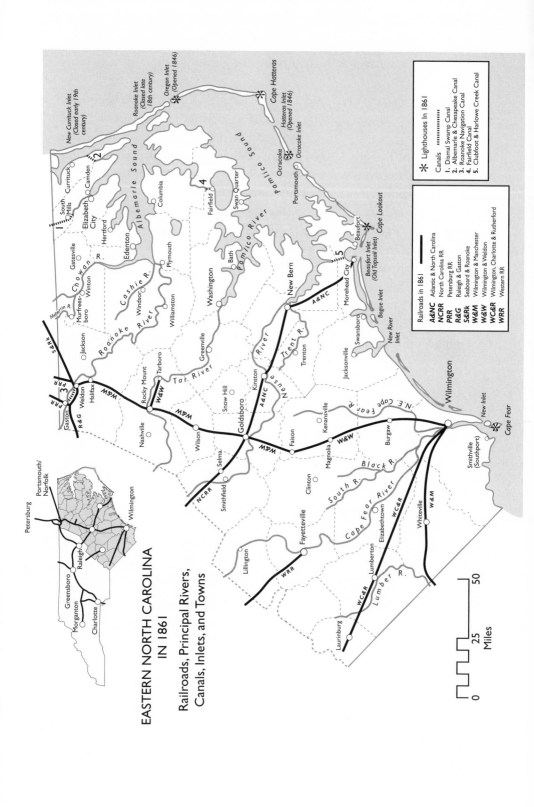

EASTERN NORTH CAROLINA
IN 1861

Railroads, Principal Rivers,
Canals, Inlets, and Towns

Lighthouses In 1861

Canals
1. Dismal Swamp Canal
2. Albemarle & Chesapeake Canal
3. Roanoke Navigation Canal
4. Fairfield Canal
5. Clubfoot & Harlowe Creek Canal

Railroads In 1861

A&NC	Atlantic & North Carolina
NCRR	North Carolina RR
PRR	Petersburg RR
R&G	Raleigh & Gaston
S&Rk	Seabord & Roanoke
W&M	Wilmington & Manchester
W&W	Wilmington & Weldon
WC&R	Wilmington, Charlotte & Rutherford
WRR	Western RR

During the American Revolution, leaders from Edenton, New Bern, Halifax, Brunswick, and Wilmington figured prominently in the patriot cause. They also took principal roles in creating the new state and nation, promoting ratification of the U.S. Constitution and serving as early governors and in other key offices. After recovering from the war, towns and plantations thrived for a time. Triangular trade routes connected them with the Caribbean, New England, and New York. New Bern and other ports enjoyed renewed prosperity, and although planters continually complained about low prices and high shipping costs, their profits were sufficient to allow expansion of their holdings in land and slaves.

The second quarter of the nineteenth century brought economic and social change to the region and the state. Immigration had tapered off in the late eighteenth century, and there was no further significant in-migration until the mid-twentieth century. Problems of trade and transportation worsened as competition from other ports and manufacturing centers intensified. Although some state and local leaders pressed for investment in internal improvements to boost commercial agriculture, trade, and manufacturing—and a few projects succeeded, such as the *Roanoke Navigation System and the *Dismal Swamp Canal—many of the region's dominant planters and legislators resisted public investment in such endeavors. The economy stagnated, ports often stood empty of ships, and in the 1820s and 1830s, promising new plantation lands in Alabama and Mississippi drew thousands of eastern North Carolinians westward.

FIGURE 10. (Opposite) Eastern N.C. in 1861, showing railroads, principal rivers, canals, inlets, and towns. After Roanoke Inlet silted up and closed in the late 18th c., Ocracoke Inlet was the chief natural outlet for waterborne trade for the Tar, Neuse, and Roanoke hinterlands. Beginning in the late 18th c., canals were built to link N.C. rivers and sounds with ocean ports. These were followed in the mid-19th c. by rail lines.

The building of railroads expanded commercial agriculture and boosted trade and growth in coastal plain towns. The Wilmington and Weldon Railroad (originally the Wilmington and Raleigh) came first, a 161-mile north-south route completed in 1840 as the longest railroad in the world at the time. The Wilmington and Weldon was intersected in the 1850s by the east-west N.C. Railroad, which tapped the piedmont hinterlands and was augmented by the Atlantic and N.C. Railroad, which reached east to the port of Morehead City and boosted trade in New Bern.

The railroad network linked coastal plain towns to one another and to the outside world. These links reinforced their roles as regional markets and stimulated growth and new construction, roughly in equal measure from town to town. Rail and steamboat routes transformed Wilmington into a bustling city, which in 1840 surpassed New Bern and Fayetteville to become the largest town in the state. Waynesboro literally picked up and moved; it was reincarnated as Goldsboro at the junction of the Wilmington and Weldon and the N.C. Railroad. New and old towns blossomed as cotton markets and trade centers. Wilson, on the N.C. Railroad, developed into one of the region's busiest cotton markets. Faison, one of a string of depots on the Wilmington and Weldon, boomed as a stylish little market town. Tarboro, at the head of the Tar River's steamboat navigation, flourished as a cotton plantation market town and gained a branch line of the Wilmington and Weldon shortly before the Civil War.

FIGURE II. *Boyette House, Johnston Co.* (JT 5). *From the earliest years of settlement into the early 20th c., eastern North Carolinians built small, often short-lived wooden structures. Many of these were constructed of horizontal logs joined at the corners. As William Byrd observed near Edenton in 1728, "most of the Houses . . . are Log-houses, covered with Pine or Cypress shingles" and built entirely of wood; such houses were typically placed directly on the ground or on pine blocks and had wooden chimneys of sticks or logs daubed inside with clay. Similar descriptions of typical housing stock recurred in travelers' accounts throughout the 18th and 19th centuries. Wooden chimneys lined with clay were built throughout the 19th c., though only a handful still stand. A few examples of eastern N.C. log buildings survive in areas open to public view, such as the 19th-c. log houses moved from remote sites to *Harmony Hall in Bladen Co. and the *John Blue Farm in Scotland Co.*

Plank buildings like the Boyette House shown here, constructed with sawn planks laid horizontally and dovetailed together, also became part of the region's repertoire, both for houses and for smokehouses and jails, where security was needed. Examples have been moved to public sites at *Hope Plantation in Bertie Co. and the *John Wheeler House, Murfreesboro, in Hertford Co.

Also common in eastern N.C. were frame structures built without masonry foundations. As in Virginia and other Chesapeake colonies, in the 17th and early 18th centuries builders erected many houses, barns, and chapels by setting vertical posts directly into the ground, building a light frame around these, and covering the frame with split clapboards and the roof with wooden shingles. Although a number of archaeological sites of such structures have been investigated, no early examples are known to stand. Farm buildings were constructed with posts in the ground well into the 20th c. and the use of wood blocks for foundations continued in rural areas through most of the 19th c.

By the late 1830s a few modernizing steps had begun, and by the 1850s the economy was rebounding. Railroads along with growing steamboat trade brought new prosperity to towns and counties along their routes. In the countryside, commercial agriculture expanded as better access to markets boosted profits, planters accumulated larger holdings in land and slaves, and cotton production soared. Old towns blossomed, and new towns sprang up. Many

FIGURE 12. *Newbold-White House, Perquimans Co.* (PQ 3). *The Newbold-White House site shows the 18th-c. transition to durable housing. On one part of the farm patented in 1684, post-hole marks and late 17th-c. pottery shards may indicate the location of the first house. East of that site, toward the river, stands the 1½-story, brick dwelling built ca. 1730 with two main rooms per floor. This well-built house was one of the most substantial buildings of its time and place. Confronted with a scarcity of good building stone and high costs for making brick and obtaining lime, eastern North Carolinians restricted masonry construction to the very finest houses and public buildings. In a typical 18th-c. treatment, the masons who built the Newbold-White House used glazed headers to emphasize the checkerboard pattern of the Flemish-bond brickwork. Also typical, they employed English bond below the molded water table.*

supported a new level of social and cultural life: new colleges and academies, new churches of many denominations, agricultural fairs, and even theaters. For many North Carolinians by 1860 it seemed that the efforts spent on building canals, dredging harbors, constructing railroads, and promoting education had at last gained the region the prosperity and vitality they had sought so long.

ARCHITECTURAL TRADITIONS

The early architecture of eastern North Carolina delineates the complex story of making farms and towns amidst a coastal forest. All the buildings that served the first generations of British and African settlers in North Carolina—the thousands of little wooden dwellings and agricultural buildings erected from the 1660s through the 1710s—have vanished, along with nearly all of the dwellings,

FIGURE 13. *Caleb Grandy House, Camden Co.* (CM 4). *The frame house with big brick chimneys exemplifies the type built for prospering planters in the mid-18th c. During the 18th and 19th centuries, frame construction was far more common than brick. In the best early frame houses, carpenters erected structures with heavy mortise-and-tenon frames and covered them with weatherboards. The house typically sat on piers or foundations of brick and was heated by brick chimneys. Sometimes the chimneys rose within the house, but more often they stood at the gable ends. The roof was typically covered in wood shingles. Status was communicated by the display of skilled craftsmanship in a well-made frame, molded or beaded weatherboards, a stout brick chimney, and well-finished interior work, where techniques embodied familiar English traditions of workmanship. The *Palmer-Marsh House (1750–51) in Bath and the *Cupola House (1758) in Edenton are accessible examples of large, colonial period frame houses.*

farm buildings, churches, and public buildings eastern North Carolinians built during the remainder of the colonial period. The oldest standing buildings date from the 1720s and 1730s, and only a handful of the sturdiest structures built before 1780 have survived to the present.

Construction of simple, short-lived frame and log structures suited North Carolina conditions, where skilled labor was scarce and difficult transportation made materials such as glass, nails, hardware, brick, and stone costly and hard to obtain. For nearly everyone, a building adequate to last a few years or a generation was a sufficient and suitable investment. Although the buildings themselves seldom lasted long, the building techniques and the attitude toward building they represented persisted well into the twentieth century.

By the middle of the eighteenth century, some members of the emerging upper class of merchants and planters invested in more substantial, elaborate, and costly buildings. Regarding good building as a sign of order and prosperity, they

FIGURE 14. *McNider House, Perquimans Co.* (PQ 7). *One form of 2-story house became especially prevalent in N.C. during the 19th c.: the 2-story house two or more rooms wide and one room deep, a house type seen in many regions of the nation and later dubbed the "I-house" by geographer Fred Kniffen. Built initially for wealthy planters in the late 18th and early 19th centuries, during the 19th and early 20th centuries this house type was favored by middling farmers and townspeople. Various kinds of porches and rear extensions expanded the house form, including the shed porch and shed rooms typical of the earlier phases, and the hip-roofed porches and long rear ells that grew more numerous in the later 19th c.*

employed carpenters, bricklayers, and joiners to erect well-crafted buildings that were dramatic improvements over their predecessors.

The first generations of durable building erected in the eighteenth century set patterns of form and plan that continued for years. Public buildings such as courthouses, jails, churches, and chapels were typically plain, wooden structures without architectural pretension; only a few were constructed of brick. Nearly all houses were built one story high with only one or two main rooms and perhaps a sleeping chamber above. The A-shaped gable roof was most common, though a number of eighteenth-century houses employed the double-sloped gambrel roof to provide more space in the upper chambers. In the eighteenth century very few families built two-story houses, but by the early nineteenth century such houses grew more numerous.

A few basic floor plans shaped life in most dwellings. Whether the house had one, two, or three main rooms per floor, typically the main room was entered directly from outdoors. Until the mid-nineteenth century, few North Carolinians built houses with passages—as hallways were called—opening from the front door or separating the rooms. Gradually in the nineteenth century such passages—in side-passage-plan townhouses and in symmetrical houses with

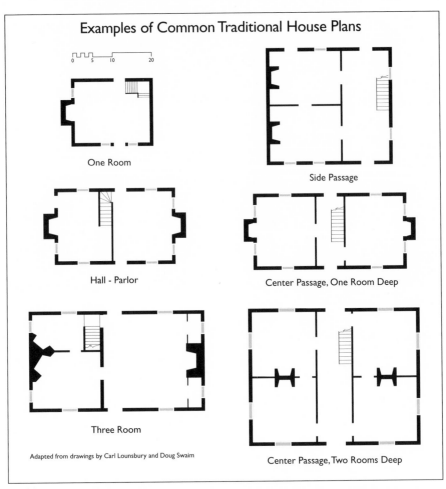

Examples of Common Traditional House Plans

One Room

Side Passage

Hall - Parlor

Center Passage, One Room Deep

Three Room

Adapted from drawings by Carl Lounsbury and Doug Swaim

Center Passage, Two Rooms Deep

FIGURE 15. *Common early house plans. During the 18th and 19th centuries, most houses in the region were built along a few basic plans. One-room houses were the most numerous, though few survive to the present. The 2-room "hall-parlor" plan was especially prevalent in the 18th and early 19th centuries. In this plan, the front door opened into the slightly larger room known as the "hall," an all-purpose room for socializing. From the hall one entered the "parlor," a more formal sitting room also used as a bed-chamber, and from the hall the stair rose to the upper sleeping chambers. A commonly used 3-room plan (sometimes called the "Quaker plan" because it was commended to Pennsylvania settlers in a document attributed to William Penn) has the space opposite the hall subdivided into two small rooms.*

Several plans with passages, employed in a few houses in the 18th c., became increasingly popular in the 19th c. The side-passage plan, with a passage on one side and one or two heated rooms on the other, was used most frequently in towns, particularly in New Bern, but the plan also appeared in rural areas. This plan continued in use in the region into the early 20th c., especially in relatively modest urban houses. By the mid-19th c. many houses had a central passage separating two main rooms, plus a rear shed or ell. In the 18th c. only a few especially large houses contained four main rooms per floor divided by a central passage, but in the 19th c. this layout was often employed for substantial dwellings, par-ticularly for Greek Revival houses of the mid-19th c. Even when irregular plans became popular dur-ing the later 19th c., these basic plans persisted, either unchanged or with slight variations in response to current styles.

FIGURE 16. *Jacob Henry House, Beaufort* (CR 2). *Porches, usually called piazzas, provided shaded outdoor living space in front and sometimes in back of traditional house plans. Rear shed rooms—extending the slope of the roof often in a pendant form to the porch—added bedchambers. Carpenters often built porches and sheds as structural extensions of the main house rather than as appendages, with porches either inset under the main rafters of the house or engaged with a second set of rafters beginning midway up the roof slope as seen here. Among such houses open to the public, the *David Bell House in Beaufort is a side-passage-plan house with 2-tier, engaged porch; *Harmony Hall in Bladen Co. is a 2-story house with piazzas, one of which contains the sole stair; and the *Pender Museum in Tarboro exemplifies the small coastal cottage with hall-parlor plan, engaged front porch, and balancing rear shed.*

center passages—grew more popular among prosperous families who sought greater privacy and formality.

In houses of every form and plan, eastern North Carolinians expanded their living space with porches and sheds. Early dwellings often had only small entrance stoops, but by the mid-eighteenth century, residents of the region had adapted architecture to suit the climate and were regularly building piazzas, which they found to be in "this hot Climate . . . essentially necessary to the Health and convenience of the Inhabitants."[2]

2. Petitions, 1790, Legislative Papers, Archives and Records, Division of Archives and History, Raleigh, quoted in Catherine W. Bishir, *North Carolina Architecture* (Chapel Hill, University of North Carolina Press, 1990), 114.

FIGURE 17. *Somerset Place, Washington Co. (WH 9). Exemplary of the largest plantations, at Somerset Place a cluster of neatly finished antebellum domestic outbuildings stands in an orderly compound near the owner's house. Foundations remain of the long row of slave houses that extended back from this house; there are plans to reconstruct these dwellings. The plantation also had a large barn and other agricultural buildings, which no longer stand.*

FIGURE 18. *Kitchen, Iredell House, Edenton (CO 36). A few types of buildings usually constituted the domestic complex. In a pattern common throughout the South, the kitchen was typically a separate structure with a large fireplace for cooking. It stood close enough to the house for convenience but far enough away to remove heat, smells, and the threat of fire. Not far away stood the smokehouse, essential in a region where pork was a dietary staple, a square or rectangular building perhaps 10 to 16 feet on a side, tightly built to smoke ham and bacon and secure the hanging meat. A corncrib, where farmers stored the other mainstay of the diet, might stand within the domestic complex or near the agricultural buildings; usually these were built with openings for ventilation.*

FIGURE 19. *Dairy, Fletcher-Skinner Farm, Perquimans Co. (PQ 12). On some farms a freestanding dairy—built with deep eaves for shade, vents beneath the eaves, and sometimes with insulated walls— housed milk, cheese, and butter, serving a similar purpose to the springhouses seen in some areas.*

FIGURE 20. *Slave House, Fayetteville. Slave houses varied from 1-room log cabins or crude frame dwellings to neatly finished frame or brick houses of two or more rooms. Two-room slave quarters with center chimneys were especially common in the antebellum period. Like this building, which evidently had four rooms, most of the region's slave houses no longer stand.*

FIGURE 21. *Barn and sheds, Boyd Farm, Beaufort Co.* (BF 25). *With open range and mild climates, large barns and stables were rare in eastern N.C., though a few antebellum planters took pride in erecting large-scale agricultural structures. Barns were usually built to store crops; stables, to shelter animals. Several forms of barns were constructed in the region. Especially numerous are single-crib barns, which have the entrance in the gable end. Some have flanking sheds extending the roofline on each side. Less common are English barns, which have the entrance on the long side.*

From earliest times the farmhouse and its agricultural buildings constituted the dominant architectural unit of the landscape. Travelers repeatedly compared southern farmsteads with small villages because of the multitude of separate, specialized outbuildings. The household-oriented dependencies—on substantial farms these included a kitchen, a smokehouse, a laundry, and a dairy—usually clustered near the main dwelling, within a fenced house yard to keep out free-ranging farm animals.

Plantations also included houses built for slaves. Eighteenth- and early nineteenth-century accounts indicate that on most farms both owner and slave occupied small frame or log houses. In the mid-nineteenth century, while the scale of the planters' own houses increased and a few especially progressive planters erected more substantial dwellings for slaves, most slave houses continued to be small, crude buildings. Few of these still stand in the region.

Located beyond the domestic compound, agricultural buildings commonly included sheds, corncribs, stables, and barns. These might be arranged in rows, open squares, or informal clusters, but nearly all exemplified the tendency toward small, separate structures distributed across the land. Seldom did eastern Carolina farmers focus their pride in the creation of massive barns or pack their farm buildings into tightly organized farmyard units.

FIGURE 22. *Cupola House, Edenton* (CO 8). *In this ambitious and unique house, exuberant interiors probably adapted from William Salmon's* Palladio Londinensis *fit tightly into the low-ceilinged rooms. This house was unusually elaborate. Most of the finest 18th-c. houses had much simpler Georgian moldings and paneled wainscoting, paneled mantels, and stairs with turned balusters. A few featured a modillion or dentil cornice and a piazza or entrance portico with simple posts or classically inspired columns, depending on the taste and budget of the client and the skill of the artisan.*

CHANGING ARCHITECTURAL STYLES

The building traditions established during the eighteenth century formed the backbone of the region's architecture. The basic forms, the plans, the craftsmanship, and the ideas of what constituted appropriate building lasted for generations. Into this conservative and resilient framework a few taste-conscious planters and merchants introduced elements of national and international architectural trends. From the mid-eighteenth century onward, North Carolina's most ambitious buildings showed a range of involvement in broader architectural currents, as some clients and designers participated in the most advanced developments, while many more partook selectively and conservatively of national patterns.

By the mid-eighteenth century, members of the American colonial elite were building in the English Georgian style, a conservative version of late Renaissance classicism shaped by architect James Gibbs and others in England. As North Carolina's emerging elite sought to improve their colony's status, they exhibited the prevailing genteel taste. Their approach was to erect buildings of

FIGURE 23. *St. Philip's Church, Brunswick Co.* (BW 6). *Anglican parish churches in N.C. had simple, rectangular plans oriented to a service focused on preaching and the prayer book. St. Philip's, now a ruin, was the grandest church in colonial N.C. Of other colonial churches in the region, *St. Paul's Episcopal in Edenton and *St. Thomas in Bath still stand, and foundations remain of the first *Christ Church in New Bern. Dissenting denominations such as Presbyterians, Quakers, Baptists, and Methodists typically built simple log or frame meetinghouses; none survive from the colonial period.*

FIGURE 24. *"The Elevation of the Governor's House" (Tryon Palace), New Bern, drawing by John Hawks* (CV 21). *When Gov. William Tryon established New Bern as the capital, he employed John Hawks, an English-trained architect, to build a governor's residence there, a public building that established a new level of monumentality and taste in the colony. Hawks, the first full-fledged professional architect in the colonies, drew on English architectural books and examples to design the Palladian-inspired, five-part composition, with central block featuring a pedimented pavilion and flanked by curved colonnades and wings. Hawks may have also designed other sophisticated Georgian buildings in the region, such as the *Chowan County Courthouse in Edenton and the *John Wright Stanly House in New Bern. The palace burned in 1798 and was reconstructed in the 1950s.*

FIGURE 25. *St. John's Masonic Lodge and Theater, New Bern* (CV 46). *In New Bern ambitious clients and highly skilled artisans produced a superb collection of Federal period architecture, in which Palladian forms established by the palace were combined with Adamesque details. English-born architect William Nichols, who lived in New Bern ca. 1800–1806, may have had a hand in designing its principal buildings, but only his later works in Edenton, Fayetteville, and Raleigh have been documented.*

simple and conservative form and to enrich them with English Georgian architectural elements. A few clients had their best rooms adorned with elaborate woodwork adapted from English architectural books, but most restricted themselves to simplified Georgian moldings, mantels, and wainscoting.

In the leading towns, colonial leaders strove to improve the quality of public architecture as well. Replacing the makeshift wooden buildings of earlier years, they erected substantial brick government buildings and parish churches much like those in Virginia and provincial England. These were usually symmetrical in form and executed with fine craftsmanship and simple, robust classical detail. The epitome of this movement took form in the governor's residence and government house known as *Tryon Palace. In New Bern in 1767–70, the new royal governor and his architect created an "elegant and noble structure" in "pure English taste." Considered by some to "excel for Magnificence & architecture any edifice on the continent," the palace interjected a new level of ambition and sophistication into North Carolina's architecture.[3]

3. John Whiting of Rhode Island and Francisco de Miranda of South America, quoted in Alonzo T. Dill Jr., *Governor Tryon and His Palace* (Chapel Hill: University of North Carolina Press, 1955), 114, 118.

FIGURE 26. *Oval Ballroom, Fayetteville* (CD 11). *The elegant interior of the freestanding ballroom, adorned with attenuated Ionic pilasters and delicate classical moldings, epitomizes the urbane, Adam-influenced Federal style.*

FIGURE 27. *Wilkinson-Dover House, Edge-combe Co.* (ED 48). *Throughout the region, especially in newly elaborate plantation houses, Federal period artisans reveled in the possibilities offered by the designs presented in builders' guides by William Pain, Owen Biddle, Asher Benjamin, and others, often rendering classically derived Adamesque motifs with great individuality.*

After the American Revolution, eastern North Carolina participated in a nationwide building boom. First came a surge of building in the wake of the war, which had slowed or stopped construction for several years. This was followed in the early nineteenth century by a conscious effort to improve and update the state's architecture in keeping with national trends. Despite the economic problems the state suffered, the Federal period was an era of widespread building and rebuilding.

Most of the new buildings were plain and functional, from the sturdy lighthouses along the coastline to the frame and brick warehouses that lined the waterfronts and the austere wooden meetinghouses built in small towns and rural clearings. But as eastern North Carolina merchants and planters engaged in renewed trade, they showed a growing interest in stylish and pretentious architecture. Artisans created local clusters of distinctive architecture, which initially continued the familiar Georgian style and then in the early decades of the nineteenth century began to show the influence of the delicate, Roman-inspired Neoclassicism shaped by Scots architects Robert and James Adam. Patternbooks by English and American designers popularized the attenuation of forms, intricate surface decoration, and emphasis on curved spaces and motifs.

In New Bern, trade with the Caribbean and New England supported the construction of the state's premier collection of stylish Federal period architecture. In other towns and in the wealthiest plantation sections, increasingly elaborate plantation houses, townhouses, and public buildings showed the growing taste for fine building. Town and rural gentry employed artisans to continue old forms and traditional hall-parlor and three-room plans but to adjust the proportions and incorporate new motifs in keeping with current styles. During the early nineteenth century, more and more wealthy families built houses with center passages and side passages, while planters along the Virginia border especially favored houses in a symmetrical villa form with pedimented center block. Throughout the region, carpenters and joiners adorned the best houses with intricate, imaginative carving in free renditions of Adamesque bookplates—classically derived porches, airy stairs, delicate moldings and gougework, and mantels enriched with slim pilasters, sunbursts, and fans.

Beginning in the late 1830s, and increasing in the 1840s and 1850s, as railroad building and improvements expanded trade and prosperity, rebuilding in "modern" styles became a watchword in communities tied to the growing market economy. As counties built new courthouses and congregations erected new churches, and as newly wealthy planters replaced their old log dwellings or hall-parlor-plan frame houses, almost universally they selected the nationally popular Greek Revival style. This version of Neoclassicism—with bold and massive forms derived from the ancient Greek and occasionally Roman prototypes—

FIGURE 28. *Philadelphus Presbyterian Church, Robeson Co.* (RB 8). *In the Upper Cape Fear River valley, where the evangelism of the Great Revival movement had expanded the congregations of the old, mostly rural Highland Scots Presbyterians, one congregation after another erected handsome, temple-form, wooden churches, in which local carpenters melded the frame meetinghouse tradition with the simplified classicism of the Greek Revival. Many other congregations, especially Methodists, erected frame churches with pedimented front gables, broad corner boards simulating classical pilasters, and simplified Grecian detail. Prominent examples include *Old Bluff Presbyterian Church in Cumberland Co., *First Presbyterian Church in Goldsboro, *White Rock Presbyterian Church in Kinston, *Rehoboth Methodist Church in Washington Co., and *Elizabeth Methodist Church in Johnston Co. Of the many Greek Revival courthouses built in the region, surviving examples include the *Northampton County Courthouse and the *Camden County Courthouse.*

FIGURE 29. *Bracebridge Hall, Edgecombe Co.* (ED 52). *Regional builders incorporated the Greek Revival style into customary house forms. The symmetrical, center-passage plan, one or two rooms deep, became the dominant form among the newly prosperous planters of the inner coastal plain in the 1840s and 1850s. Shallow roofs, broad forms, and porches with columns—often the still-popular full-width piazza—were complemented by bold Greek Revival carpentry details of corner pilasters and door and window frames with cornerblocks, motifs adapted from popular architectural books. Greek Revival houses appeared throughout the region, with variations identifying the work of individual artisans in different localities.*

FIGURE 30. *Calvary Church, Tarboro, perspective drawing by architect William Percival* (ED 5).
*Episcopal parishes were the first to adopt the Gothic Revival style for their churches, with pointed windows and steep roofs intended to lend an inspiring sense of the medieval past. Some commissioned plans from urban architects such as Thomas U. Walter of Philadelphia, who designed *St. James Episcopal Church in Wilmington; Richard Upjohn of New York, who provided a design for *Grace Episcopal Church in Plymouth; and J. Crawford Neilson of Baltimore, who designed *Christ Episcopal Church in Elizabeth City. Others employed a resident architect or builder to design their churches. Architect William Percival, who designed Calvary Church, lived briefly in N.C. and planned both Gothic Revival and Italianate buildings. In the late 1840s and especially the 1850s, other denominations began to employ the style. *First Baptist Church in New Bern was evidently the region's first non-Episcopal church in the Gothic Revival style.*

FIGURE 31. *Zebulon Latimer House, Wilmington* (NH 57). *In areas closely tied to the market economy, a few merchants and planters built villas and cottages in the picturesque style. Some took designs from the popular architectural books of Andrew Jackson Downing and William Ranlett; others had artisans drape traditional building forms with brackets and lacy sawnwork to give a stylishly picturesque aura.*

Wilmington engaged most fully in national architectural trends, a pattern that paralleled its trade with New York, Philadelphia, Baltimore, and other urban centers. Wilmingtonians commissioned works from the growing ranks of the American architectural profession from New York and Philadelphia. Many of the city's resident builders were immigrants from northern cities, such as Robert and John Wood and James F. Post, who constructed the Latimer House in opulent Italianate style. The city's Gothic Revival churches, Italianate and Greek Revival townhouses, and eclectic public buildings gave clear evidence of its growing size and prosperity as a railroad hub and port. *St. James Episcopal Church, *First Baptist Church, *City Hall–Thalian Hall, and the *Bellamy Mansion, all open to the public, demonstrate the range of stylish architecture in the antebellum city.

was modeled in North Carolina by the State Capitol, completed at the same time as the state's first railroads in 1840. The magnificent building, emblem of renewed state pride, was well known to eastern North Carolinians who made the trip west to Raleigh on politics or business.

Greek Revival courthouses and churches often followed a temple form with pedimented front and portico. Simplified wooden versions of this form were especially popular as Presbyterians, Baptists, and Methodists flourished during the great revival movements of the nineteenth century. As they grew more numerous and prosperous, they replaced the plain, small chapels in which they had begun. The Greek Revival style was equally popular in domestic architecture, but for their houses, North Carolinians eschewed the temple form in favor of traditional house forms. Spacious and symmetrical center-passage dwellings were built by local and regional carpenters who adapted their proportions to the new style and installed simplified renditions of the robust Greek Revival mantels, doorways, moldings, and classical orders depicted in current architectural books.

A smaller, specialized clientele—a few merchants, planters, and professionals tied to national networks of business and ideas—adopted the picturesque Italianate and Gothic Revival styles promoted in national architectural literature. Beginning in the late 1830s, eastern North Carolina Episcopalians commissioned the state's first Gothic Revival churches from distant urban architects; by the 1850s urban congregations of other denominations had adopted the style as well. During the 1840s and 1850s, as Wilmington's mercantile elite strove for a "city-like" image, they commissioned designs from New York and Philadelphia architects for big, classical, public buildings and towering Gothic Revival churches. At the same time they employed local builders to erect Italianate residences in popular villa and cottage styles inspired by current patternbooks. In towns such as Edenton and Tarboro a wealthy and venturesome individual might commission a stylishly picturesque villa or cottage, but these were exceptional cases. For most eastern North Carolinians, the continuation of traditional forms best suited local norms and needs, and once adopted in the early nineteenth century, the symmetry and restrained classicism of the Greek Revival maintained its hold on the region's public and private architecture.

TRANSFORMATIONS, CIVIL WAR TO WORLD WAR II

Although North Carolina resisted secession until it seemed unavoidable, the state contributed heavily to the Confederacy and suffered tremendously during the war. The eastern section of the state saw more military action than any other region. Early in the war, Union forces occupied the central and northern areas of the coast. The town of Winton was burned, and Plymouth and Washington sustained heavy losses. Wilmington, defended by the great Confederate earthworks at Fort Fisher, remained the last major Confederate port open to world markets. When Fort Fisher fell to overwhelming Union firepower in early 1865, it was the death knell of the Confederacy.

The war's lasting impact was chiefly economic and social. Many North Carolinians had been reduced to poverty during the war, and thousands of families had lost fathers and sons. The transition from slave to free labor, and especially the development of the tenant farming system, redefined agriculture and transformed the landscape. Thousands of black citizens left the region for opportunities in the North and West; others, seeking to establish a new, free way of life nearer home, moved into towns to find work.

FIGURE 32. *Fort Fisher (1865), New Hanover Co.* (NH 101). *Until it fell to Union attack on Jan. 15, 1865, after days of intense bombardment, the large fortification defended the mouth of the Cape Fear River and permitted Wilmington to remain open to blockade-runners that supplied Confederate armies. Fort Fisher is one of several Civil War sites preserved in eastern N.C. A smaller earthworks, *Fort Branch in Martin Co., was constructed to protect the upper Roanoke River. Union victories early in the war put the central and northern coast in Union hands—New Bern and Beaufort were occupied by Union troops during the rest of the war. Many residents of the New Bern, Beaufort, and Albemarle regions refugeed inland. With most of the rest of the state remaining within Confederate lines through- out the war, N.C. became a major supplier of men and goods to the Confederacy. During the last months of the war the state became the scene of key battles. Not long after the siege of Fort Fisher, on Mar. 19–21, 1865, *Bentonville Battleground in Johnston Co. became the site of one of the last battles of the war, when Confederate forces under Gen. Joseph Johnston engaged Gen. William T. Sherman's troops on their way north from South Carolina.*

The economic power base of the state shifted westward to the emerging in- dustrial towns and cities of the Piedmont, where cotton and tobacco factories drew thousands of people to Charlotte, Greensboro, Winston-Salem, and Durham. Leaders in eastern North Carolina communities strove to renew the economy, but it was a difficult task. Success came most readily in the towns along the railroads where old and new entrepreneurs boosted lumbering, tur- pentine distilling, and cotton sales. The volume of farm production rebounded quickly after the war, but falling crop prices and other problems plagued farm- ers and sent many into debt. Some old plantation sections, including those that had once been the wealthiest, never fully recovered from the war. Slowly, in a period of bitter conflict as well as high hopes and determination, former slaves and former planters and yeomen made their way into a new era.

On the Farm

For more than a century after the Civil War, eastern North Carolina remained overwhelmingly agricultural. In contrast to patterns of urbanization elsewhere in the state and nation, as late as the mid-twentieth century most of the people of eastern North Carolina lived on farms. Beginning soon after the war, farming in the region shifted away from the old diversity of crops toward a single cash crop—first cotton, then tobacco.

Although many farm families continued to cultivate their own land with the help of hired hands, the system of farm tenancy, sharecropping, and crop-lien credit grew to dominate much of the region. Black and white farm families worked landowners' fields either as cash renters or commonly as sharecroppers who received a share of the crop at harvest time. Without sufficient cash, both landowners and sharecropping farmers were often forced to depend on credit, generally available only from merchants who would "carry" the farmer's purchase of supplies, including fertilizer, seed, and household necessities, backed by a lien on the future crop sales. Farm tenancy was not a new system when cash-poor landowners and emancipated blacks without land turned to it as an expedient after the war. But the system expanded as dropping crop prices, rising costs, and a general agricultural depression sent more and more farm families into debt. The tenant system continued to expand throughout the nineteenth and early twentieth centuries, especially in the old plantation belt of the coastal plain. By 1930—after two decades when farm tenancy increased in the inner coastal plain faster than anywhere in the nation—almost 70 percent of all farms in the inner coastal plain were operated by tenants.

The new economy altered farm life in many different ways. In the late nineteenth century, the old range laws were reversed, as large landholders passed legislation that required farmers to fence in their livestock rather than their crops. The new laws meant that families could no longer feed themselves on pigs or cattle that had fattened in others' woods and fields. At the same time, lenders' insistence that borrowers grow a cash crop to satisfy their debts encouraged a shift from diverse crops to a single staple. Focusing on producing a cash crop, farm families spent less time raising their own necessities, and thus depended more on store-bought supplies and hence on the market economy, whose ups and downs brought boom and bust.

"King Cotton," which demanded ever more costly fertilizers and brought ever declining prices—dropping from 25 cents a pound in the late 1860s to 12 cents in the 1870s—reigned throughout much of eastern North Carolina in the 1870s and 1880s. In the 1890s, however, after suffering from plummeting cotton prices—which fell to 5 cents a pound in the depression after 1893—eastern North Carolina businessmen, aided by tobacconists from the tobacco-growing and -marketing areas of the Piedmont, successfully promoted tobacco

FARMHOUSES AND FARMSTEADS

Thousands of small houses were built for small landowners, tenant farmers, and farm laborers. As the tenant system took hold in old plantation districts, the rows or clusters of slave dwellings gave way to separate small farmsteads dispersed across the land. Their occupants might change continually as black and white families moved to find work, or a single family might occupy and maintain a house for generations. There was no specific difference in form or plan among these types of habitation, though a landowner's farmhouse was likely to be more substantial and have more outbuildings than the tenant farmer's.

Old forms of modest housing continued, whether in rudimentary log houses and farm buildings or weatherboarded frame structures. Well into the 20th c. many tenant farm families occupied crudely built log houses with wooden chimneys of the same type that had been built in the region since the 18th c. (Fig. 33). Most of these have disappeared since World War II.

As the industrialization of construction materials swept across the state, small frame houses and farm buildings began to supplant the last generation of log building. Many dwellings are little 2-room-plan houses with chimneys, doors, and windows in familiar arrangements. Others are small L-plan dwellings. On one farm after another, the weatherboarded, 2- or 3-room house sits on brick or stone piers, with well-spaced, big-paned windows; a broad porch, a kitchen

FIGURE 33. *Tenant house, New Bern vicinity*

wing out back, maybe a bit of gable decoration, a swept yard, and a big, old tree or two making a strong, plain little place. A shed or two, a privy, and perhaps a chickenhouse cluster nearby, and a few tobacco barns stand in the distance. Some are the centers of small farms; some string along a stretch of road, connected to a large farming operation. Some few are still tended, but many are vacant; and those that survive are only a fragment of the thousands that once stood (Fig. 34).

Landowning farmers also planned their houses along customary lines, even as they built them with new, mass-produced framing, weatherboards, flooring, doors, and windows. One- and 2-story houses with a center passage between two main rooms continued as the mainstay, usually with a rear shed or, more often, an ell. The kitchen was now more likely to be attached to the house, either in the ell or linked by a breezeway. The I-house was built until the early 20th c., its tall form

proud as ever, typically adorned with a decorative porch and wide eaves returning in the gable ends. From the 1870s into the 1910s the most ubiquitous token of modernity appeared in the form of a central gable breaking through the front roofline of otherwise familiar house forms, large and small (Figs. 35, 36).

FIGURE 34. *Williams Farm, Nash Co.*

FIGURE 35. *Roberson Farm, Martin Co.*

FIGURE 36. *Coley House, Nash Co.* (NS 19)

cultivation in eastern North Carolina. By the early twentieth century, tobacco had swept all else before it, again transforming the landscape and becoming the region's principal money crop in the twentieth century.

The late nineteenth and early twentieth centuries were a period of tremendous rebuilding. Difficult as farming was, thousands of new houses and farm buildings were erected, as old dwellings required replacement or expansion and as large farms were broken into smaller ones. Throughout much of the region, a few building types epitomize this last era of labor-intensive family farming: the small farmhouse with its outbuildings, the tobacco barn, and the country church. These are so abundant and yet individually so ephemeral in the landscape that they cannot appear singularly in this volume in the numbers they deserve. As types, however, they define much of the landscape. They appear along nearly every roadside today and may be gone tomorrow.

TOBACCO BARNS

Tobacco barns still define the landscape created by the early 20th-c. shift from cotton to tobacco. Although tobacco had been cultivated in eastern N.C. in the colonial period, it was in the piedmont region during the 19th c. that growers perfected the growing and curing of the light-bodied, yellow, "bright-leaf" tobacco that became the foundation of the modern tobacco industry. Its curing process required small, tight barns heated with interior flues that permitted regulation of temperatures. Prompted by falling cotton prices and

FIGURE 37. *Tobacco barn, Ellington-Ellis Farm, Johnston Co.* (JT 24)

FIGURE 38. *Tobacco barns, Martin Co.*

boll weevil infestations in the late 19th c., eastern N.C. farmers found that the light, sandy soils of the coastal plain, if properly fertilized, were excellent for tobacco. The demand for bright-leaf tobacco, boosted by marketing strategies of the Duke and Reynolds manufacturing companies, guaranteed strong sales.

The introduction of tobacco transformed the landscape. In 1898 a Pitt Co. farmer wrote, "Go to the old cotton counties of Edgecombe, Greene, Pitt, and a number of others, and you will find the gin houses gone down and tobacco barns erected in every direction, the farmers paying off their old cotton mortgages and moving forward with new life and vigor!" Because tobacco offered an excellent return on a small acreage, even small landowners and tenants could profit from its cultivation, and the crop sustained a large rural population. In the 1930s a government system of acreage allotments tied to individual farms helped curtail overproduction and reinforced the vitality of the small tobacco farm.

By the mid-20th c. there were tens of thousands of tobacco barns in eastern N.C., standing in small groups or long rows behind farmhouses or at the edge of the woods, usually with generous lean-to sheds to protect workers from the summer sun. The traditional barn is a windowless structure about 16 to 18 feet on a side, with a small door on one side and some means for ventilation through the gables or roof. Most eastern N.C. barns are frame, though some were built of pole logs, and a few experimental barns were of ceramic block. Inside are rows of horizontal "tier" poles and flues leading from a furnace fueled by wood, oil, kerosene, or gas.

In the curing season from July through Sept., as the tobacco ripened gradually from the lower leaves upward, workers pulled ripe leaves individually from the tobacco plants and tied them to sticks, which were then laid across the tier poles in the barn. The farmer heated the barn in carefully controlled stages over a period of days, with the temperature at times approaching 200 degrees. The cure took about a week. As the tobacco ripened over a period of several weeks, workers made successive passes through the fields, then filled the barns and repeated the curing process. Tobacco harvest was a great social event, with "city cousins" often going out to the country to help with the work, and with men, women, and children, black and white, often working together under the sheds.

The tobacco barns that advanced across the land in such great numbers in the early 20th c. are now receding at an equally fast pace at the century's end. Tobacco is still grown, if in somewhat reduced quantities: N.C.'s 1992 tobacco production was just over two-thirds of the peak production of almost 900 million pounds grown in 1964, and in 1992 eleven of the fifteen top tobacco-producing counties in the nation were located in eastern N.C. But automation in the harvesting and cure of the leaf, using modern bulk barns—metal curing containers that resemble small trailers—has made traditional barns obsolete, and few are still used for curing. In addition, changes in the acreage allotment system now permit farmers to transfer allotments from farm to farm and county to county, so that production has moved away from the small family farm into the hands of fewer but bigger producers. The number of tobacco farms in N.C. has dropped from a high of 150,000 in 1954 to 17,000 in 1992. As a result, the familiar rows of tobacco barns are vanishing. By early in the 21st c. the building form will be extinct except for a few adapted by their owners for storage or other uses, or those in museum settings, such as the *Tobacco Farm Life Museum in Johnston Co. Its century-long era as the region's defining building type has come to an end.

COUNTRY CHURCHES

FIGURE 39. *London's Primitive Baptist Church, Wilson Co.* (WL 6). *Many country congregations continued to build austerely plain, gable-ended buildings that maintained a tradition unbroken since early settlement. The essence of simplicity appears among the Primitive Baptist churches that are especially numerous in Martin, Pitt, and Wilson counties. Having broken with other Baptists over issues of predestination and evangelism in the early 19th c., Primitive Baptists established a strong presence in the coastal plain and erected simple churches that display an unswerving conservatism in building as in faith.*

FIGURE 40. *Parker's Methodist Church, Gates Co.* (GA 16). *Landmarks in the rural life and land-scape, country churches were built by the score throughout the region. Agricultural profits and lowered construction costs permitted old congregations to replace worn log or frame buildings and the many new congregations to erect their first churches. A few built in brick, but most devoted their hard-earned re-sources and often their own labors to erecting small, weatherboarded frame churches. Although some rural congregations have dispersed, many continue to flourish, often building larger, brick churches on the old site, sometimes updating old churches with brick veneer, aluminum, or vinyl, and sometimes maintaining the old church as well as its traditions.*

Like townsfolk, many rural congregations obtained church designs from denominational publica-tions. Using these sources, Methodists often built small, Gothic Revival churches with corner towers and broad, dominant gables, often set at angles to accommodate an auditorium-plan sanctuary. As Episco-palians established missions in country villages, they continued their penchant for the Gothic Revival with picturesque chapels of board and batten with fanciful trim. More often, congregations adopted the tower and the Gothic pointed arch as two universal symbols in even the simplest churches—1-room, gable-fronted buildings sometimes adorned with a tower or spire. Like their urban counterparts, many rural black congregations built twin-towered facades with a dynamic antisymmetry provided by differ-ences between the two towers.

Town Boom Times

From the late nineteenth century onward, much of the energy of the region concentrated in towns. Despite economic problems and regional outmigration, the towns became the focus of recovery and new trade in the 1870s and 1880s. From the 1890s into the 1920s, towns across the region enjoyed an unprecedented building boom. As one economic analyst explained in 1929, "The cream of the wealth produced in this area is skimmed off by the town traders and bankers. The towns are unusually attractive looking and give evidence of the profits to be made."[4]

New transportation networks undergirded hopes for the prosperity that had eluded the region. Railroad construction proliferated in the 1880s and 1890s, and in the twentieth century, the automobile age brought yet another transformation.

The new routes encouraged establishment of new industries amid the fields and forests. Late in the nineteenth century, big lumber mills opened in Wilmington, near New Bern, and in Elizabeth City and Edenton. Wilmington became a major cotton shipping center with a huge cotton compress. Roanoke Rapids was founded as a cotton manufacturing town, and several other eastern North Carolina towns gained new cotton mills. As rail and highway connections encouraged some farmers to try truck farming, Chadbourn, Faison, and Mount Olive emerged as marketing or processing centers. From the 1890s onward, the businessmen who advocated tobacco cultivation also invested in tobacco factories and tobacco sales warehouses in railroad towns throughout the region.

From the 1890s through the 1920s, eastern North Carolina towns experienced an extraordinary building boom. Every town's newspaper spouted hopeful booster slogans—"Come to Rocky Mount, go into business and get wealth!" "A new era for Kinston! Our businessmen are united and enthusiastic for making Kinston a great tobacco town." Towns doubled or tripled in size, and nearly every one rebuilt its main street with sturdy brick buildings—stores, warehouses, hotels, and even little skyscrapers in a few small cities by the 1920s. Hundreds of new houses were built on block after block of newly platted street grids, while on the edges of the largest towns, developers laid out fashionable new suburbs.

These neighborhoods embodied social as well as economic changes. In the 1870s and 1880s, as black and white families moved into town, old patterns of

---

4. Samuel Huntington Hobbs Jr., *North Carolina: Economic and Social* (Chapel Hill: University of North Carolina Press, 1930), 76.

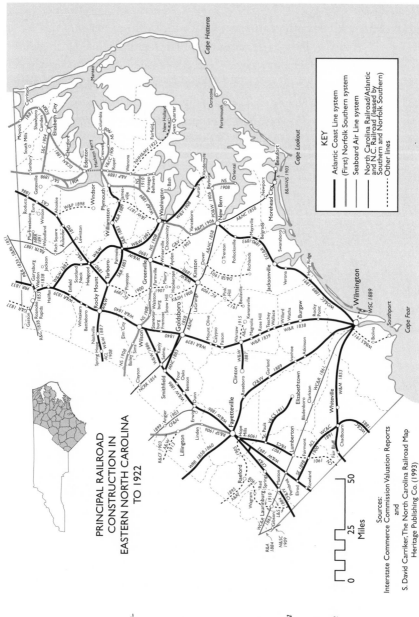

FIGURE 41. Principal railroad construction in eastern N.C. to 1922. Hundreds of miles of track were built during the late 19th c., with spurs to scores of small towns. The newly dense railroad network of many different lines spawned growth throughout the region, permitting large-scale timbering, boosting manufacturing, and stimulating commercial agriculture. The Wilmington and Weldon system, with headquarters in Wilmington, acquired small lines as well as building new ones during the late 19th c. At the end of the 19th c., national corporations began to consolidate myriad lines into north-south interstate networks. In eastern N.C. the Atlantic Coast Line gained dominance: headquartered in Wilmington, it was formed from a merger of the Wilmington and Weldon and other companies in neighboring states. Railroad construction continued to expand in the early 20th c.

PRINCIPAL RAILROAD
CONSTRUCTION IN
EASTERN NORTH CAROLINA
TO 1922

KEY

Atlantic Coast Line system
(First) Norfolk Southern system
Seaboard Air Line system
North Carolina Railroad/Atlantic and N.C. Railroad (leased by Southern and Norfolk Southern)
Other lines

Miles
0   25   50

Sources:
Interstate Commerce Commission Valuation Reports
and
S. David Carriker, The North Carolina Railroad Map
Heritage Publishing Co. (1993)

FIGURE 42. *Weldon Union Station, Weldon* (HX 30). *The 1-story station with broad eaves typifies many built during the railroad expansion years of the late 19th and early 20th centuries. Today, Amtrak passes through Weldon on the old Wilmington and Weldon route, here elevated to approach the bridge over the Roanoke River.*

FIGURE 43. *Billy's Grocery No. 2, Nash Co. In the 1920s state leaders inaugurated a "Good Roads" movement intended to conquer the inconvenient geography and carry new prosperity to town and countryside. Thousands of miles of paved and unpaved roads brought long-isolated farms and villages into new contact with the outside world and boosted trade in small as well as large towns. Country stores with gas pumps quickly became a fixture along highways throughout the rural landscape.*

FIGURE 44. *Rocky Mount Mills, Rocky Mount* (NS 32). *Cotton manufacturing had begun in eastern N.C. in the early 19th c.: early mills were founded at waterpower sites at *Rocky Mount Mills on the Tar River and *Hope Mills and Fayetteville on the Cape Fear, and these were expanded in the later 19th c. But, without many reliable waterpower sites, until the advent of electrification, widespread textile manufacturing was slow to develop in the region. The textile mill movement was in full swing in the Piedmont when investors established mills in eastern N.C. towns such as Tarboro, Wilson, Wilmington, and Edenton.*

FIGURE 45. *Roanoke Rapids Mill Village* (HX 28). *Roanoke Rapids, named for its advantageous location on one of the state's principal rivers, was founded in 1893 as a textile mill site. With its several mills and attendant mill villages, it grew into one of the leading manufacturing towns of the region.*

FIGURE 46. *Tobacco Warehouse and Manufacturing District, Wilson* (WL 2). *After curing their tobacco, farmers carried their leaf to market in a nearby town—first by wagon, later by truck. During the early 20th c., tobacco sales warehouses were built in virtually every county seat and market center in the inner coastal plain. Wilson developed into one of the world's largest tobacco markets.*

FIGURE 47. *Tobacco warehouse during sales, Wilson. Tobacco sales warehouses, usually brick, sheltered cavernous expanses of open floor space where scores of farmers could unload and display their crops for sale to tobacco company representatives. Market days during the autumn sales season were exciting times punctuated by chants of the auctioneers. The prices farmers received could make or break a long year of labor. The money they received reverberated through the community as they repaid loans and bought goods and services.*

FIGURE 48. *Portsmouth Village Lifesaving Station* (CR 25). *Federal construction projects were among the most ambitious of the late 19th c., especially the great lighthouses erected along the Outer Banks. There had been lighthouses along the coast since the late 18th c., but in the mid-19th c. the U.S. government began a sequence of much taller and more brilliant lighthouses, of which *Cape Lookout Lighthouse, built in the 1850s, was the first. Those built in the 1870s included *Currituck Beach Lighthouse and *Cape Hatteras Lighthouse. The government also established a series of lifesaving stations along the banks to reduce the cost in lives of frequent shipwrecks. The small, picturesque stations were built at close intervals along the Outer Banks during the 1870s and 1880s, and beginning around the turn of the century, they were followed by a second generation of shingled, often towered stations. The advent of motor-powered rescue boats in the 20th c. reduced the need for the closely spaced stations required when men rowed lifeboats into the sea, and many of the stations were eventually closed.*

"salt and pepper" residential occupation persisted, as large and small houses, homes of blacks and whites, and indeed commercial and residential structures often stood as neighbors. Toward the end of the century, industrial sectors developed, and residential patterns shifted toward a "checkerboard" arrangement, with small concentrations of housing and institutions for blacks and whites interspersed. Increasingly in the 1910s and 1920s as populations grew and racial segregation solidified in the Jim Crow era, certain areas of town were defined by greater concentrations of black or white residents. As the century continued, in some cities entire sectors came to be exclusively occupied by one race.[5]

Architectural Developments

In the difficult decades immediately after the Civil War, town architecture remained modest and conservative, and even the most ambitious buildings

---

5. On these phases of urban racial living patterns, see Thomas W. Hanchett, "Sorting Out the New South City," Ph.D. diss., University of North Carolina, 1993.

FIGURE 49. *Craven County Courthouse, New Bern* (CV 40). *This eclectic edifice was one of the few large public buildings erected in the late 19th c. in the region. Designed by the Philadelphia architect Samuel Sloan, it is one of eastern N.C.'s few examples of the Second Empire style, with characteristic Mansard or "French" roof, a style widely popular in thriving cities throughout the nation.*

FIGURE 50. *W. Center St., Goldsboro* (WY 1). *The Italianate stores of brick, with heavy, bracketed cornices and arched windows, typified the commercial buildings erected along the main streets of towns recovering their prosperity and prospects in the late 19th c. Railroad trading towns such as Goldsboro were among the first to rebound after the Civil War.*

FIGURE 51. *Evans Metropolitan A.M.E. Zion Church, Fayetteville* (CD 6). *Almost immediately after emancipation, black church members established their own congregations—African Methodist Episcopal and African Methodist Episcopal Zion, Baptist, Presbyterian, Episcopal, and others. As soon as possible, they focused their efforts on building substantial new churches, often relying on the skills and labor as well as the donations of their members. This form, with twin towers—usually subtly differentiated—flanking a broad gable and finished in Romanesque or Gothic Revival style, was especially favored by black congregations.*

represented greatly simplified renditions of national trends. There was little money for the monumentality or extravagance seen in northern industrial cities and thriving midwestern towns. Among the few important public works of the 1870s and 1880s were scattered federal government projects such as post offices and, along the Outer Banks, a series of lighthouses and lifesaving stations.

New technologies, however, were making building cheaper, faster, and more accessible than ever before. Beginning in the 1870s and 1880s, huge lumber mills founded throughout the region processed millions of feet of eastern North Carolina timber. Steam-powered sash-and-blind factories proliferated along the thickening web of rail connections, churning out miles of ornamental millwork as well as framing, roofing, and flooring. Rail connections that linked the region's towns with brick manufacturers in the piedmont region enabled downtowns to build or rebuild in brick.

FIGURE 52. *Fifth Ave. Methodist Church, Wilmington* (NH 79). *Baptist and Methodist congregations made frequent use of denominational publications that popularized the auditorium-plan sanctuary, with sloping floor and curving pews focusing on the pulpit. This church was designed by Philadelphia architect Benjamin Price, a national leader in Methodist church plans.*

As towns recovered and grew, thousands of new buildings were erected. Many were rough railroad shacks or barnlike warehouses, to be sure, but each town pointed with pride to the completion of substantial brick stores and public buildings and churches built for black and white congregations.

Town residents also built row after row of frame houses, for wood was still the predominant material for dwellings. These ranged from thousands of simple dwellings built for working people to large and "tasty" residences decorated with millwork in the current styles. The Italianate and Gothic cottage styles saw renewed popularity in the 1870s and 1880s, but by the 1890s the more ornate Queen Anne style had gained tremendous popularity for large and small houses.

New trends began around the turn of the century, as eastern North Carolina towns entered an era of unprecedented growth and prosperity and local leaders adopted new ideas that were reshaping architectural taste and practice nationwide. Throughout America by the end of the nineteenth century, a reaction had set in against the picturesque and ornate architecture expressive of industrialized mass production. A growing group of professional architects and

FIGURE 53. *Weil Houses, Goldsboro* (WY 4). *In towns where trade recovered quickly in the 1860s, 1870s, and 1880s, residents built houses in the Italianate style, which became far more popular, as well as more ornate, than it had been in the antebellum era. Mass-produced trim was displayed in the deep, bracketed cornices, decoratively framed doors and windows, and ornamented porches.*

FIGURE 54. *Dennis Jones House, Elizabeth City* (PK 2). *In the urban building boom of the 1890s into the 1910s, many townspeople built in the nationally popular Queen Anne style, which celebrated the possibilities of mass-produced millwork. These residences ran the gamut from towered and turreted mansions built for leading merchants and lawyers to the small but clearly stylish residences of the growing middle class of shopkeepers, clerks, teachers, and artisans, who filled the towns. The Queen Anne style, built in large and small houses, featured asymmetrical forms with tall hip roofs, front-facing gables, and wide porches adorned with turned, sawn, shingled, and especially after 1900, classical decorations as seen here.*

the architectural press, influenced by France's École des Beaux Arts and by the Progressive movement's advocacy of simple living, urged a revival of classicism and other simpler architectural styles, complemented by new urban planning ideals that defined different sectors of cities for different purposes. In eastern North Carolina these ideas coincided with town growth and long-awaited prosperity and suited local political and business leaders' growing emphasis on civic order and greater separation of races and uses in living patterns. From Elizabeth City to Wilmington, from Rocky Mount to Red Springs, national architectural concepts and planning ideas were translated into local realities.

SMALL-TOWN FORMS

By the 1910s and 1920s the region's small towns assumed a typical form, which many have maintained to the present. In the smaller towns, a business core of 2 to perhaps 4 or 5 blocks centers on the railroad and depot or on the columned courthouse in the green. The streets were paved in the 1920s and concrete sidewalks installed, about the same time that power lines were run. The commercial buildings built from the 1890s to the 1920s to replace old frame buildings consist of 1- and 2-story brick blocks with plate-glass windows and simple, corbeled brick cornices. A few brick stores have pressed-metal fronts. The bank, with its vault-like entry, has the only columned facade on the street. Lawyers, doctors, and dentists have offices in second-floor rooms or in small, freestanding office structures near the courthouse.

In the largest towns a small skyscraper of 6 or 8 stories rises above it all, and a 4- or 5-story hotel near the railroad promises first-class, modern accommodations. Along intersecting or parallel streets stand a variety of service and commercial operations, a former livery stable perhaps converted to an automobile dealership, a tobacco sales warehouse, and a machine or repair shop.

FIGURE 55. *Queen St. Commercial District, Kinston* (LR 1)

The region's dispersed urban building boom spurred the development of a lively regional architectural practice, with architects in small firms operating in many towns and crisscrossing the region by rail and then by automobile. Although some important commissions went to major national architects with headquarters in New York or Philadelphia, by the 1910s and 1920s many eastern North Carolina buildings were designed by architects with offices in Wilmington, Goldsboro, Wilson, and New Bern as well as Raleigh, Charlotte, and Greensboro. This was a golden age of the small architectural firm, as architects took a hand in designing every building type from city halls and banks to middle- and upper-class houses.

The revival of classicism, which coincided with the demand and prosperity to build new public buildings, also fit harmoniously with local antebellum

Brick churches occupying prominent corners house the principal white congregations: the Baptist and Methodist churches may have a columned portico and a dome, or, like the Presbyterian and Episcopal churches, are restrained Gothic or Romanesque Revival compositions. The principal thoroughfare extending from the town center—typically N. Main St.—is lined by the houses of leading merchants and lawyers. Conservative but handsome frame houses in the late Queen Anne, Colonial Revival, and bungalow styles stand in spacious yards beneath shade trees. Flanking the main avenue are grids of streets with middle-class houses in similar styles. Along the side streets or in a section of the lowest-lying topography stand clusters or rows of houses, large and small, that compose the oldest black neighborhood, and brick and frame churches and small frame stores and barber shops mark the community's corners.

On a prominent site on the main street nearest the neighborhood is a small business district and a movie theater and a sturdy, 2-towered brick church built for the Baptist, A.M.E., or A.M.E. Zion congregation. At an edge of town near the railroad stand tobacco warehouses, a feed mill, or a textile mill and a few rows of mill housing, and from there roads make their way into the countryside.

FIGURE 56. *E. Branch St., Spring Hope* (NS 41)

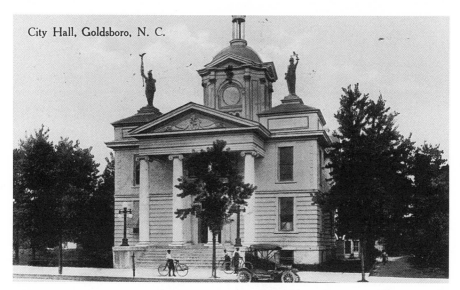

City Hall, Goldsboro, N. C.

FIGURE 57. *Goldsboro City Hall* (WY 2). *Designed by New Bern architect Herbert W. Simpson, this is one of many classically treated municipal buildings and courthouses built during the early 20th c.*

In the early 20th c., professional architectural practice developed rapidly in eastern N.C. Leading architects included Charles C. "Colonial" Benton and Frank Benton (Benton & Benton) and D. J. Rose in Wilson; John C. Stout in Rocky Mount; Herbert Simpson in New Bern; and Henry Bonitz, Joseph F. Leitner (architect for the Atlantic Coast Line Railroad), Burett Stephens, Charles McMillen, Leslie Boney, and others in Wilmington. At the same time, architects from piedmont cities also gained commissions in eastern N.C., including William P. Rose, Charles Barrett, and, especially, Charles E. Hartge of Raleigh; Charles Hartmann and Harry Barton of Greensboro; and C. C. Hook and J. M. McMichael of Charlotte. Several important projects went to more distant urban architects such as Frank Milburn (Milburn & Heister) of Washington, D.C., and Alfred Bossom, Carrere and Hastings, Kenneth Murchison Jr., and, especially, Hobart Upjohn of New York City.

precedents. During the 1910s and 1920s county after county commissioned designs for economical but clearly classical courthouses and city halls, with symmetrical forms dignified by porticoes, domes, and cupolas. Urban congregations continued their preference for Gothic and Romanesque Revival churches, while a new classical spirit produced churches with domed sanctuaries and classical porticoes. Businessmen who were opening unprecedented numbers of banks in the region's large and small towns employed the classical temple form to convey a sense of permanence and reliability. And entrepreneurs in the leading towns erected small, classically detailed skyscrapers as declarations of the urban status or ambitions of their communities.

Eastern North Carolinians also embraced the revival of "colonial" forms in residential architecture. For families of the old plantation elite as well as the new magnates of cotton, tobacco, and lumber, images of a glorious antebellum past wielded special power. The Colonial Revival in various guises emerged as the

FIGURE 58. *Atlantic Trust and Banking Co., Wilmington* (NH 26). *Several eastern N.C. towns, including Wilmington, Goldsboro, and Elizabeth City, joined the ranks of towns across the nation that saw a skyscraper as a declaration of urban status and ambitions. When he saw Goldsboro's 6-story "skyscraper" in 1915, New York politician Al Smith compared it to "a baby's first tooth." In this typical example, Wilmington architect Joseph F. Leitner employed a popular, classically derived skyscraper composition with base, shaft, and cap. These skyscrapers of the 1920s (in contrast to their contemporaries in piedmont cities, which were dwarfed by their successors) remained the triumphant spikes of their skylines throughout the 20th c.*

FIGURE 59. *W. Nash St., Wilson* (WL 5). *Around 1900 the "Southern Colonial" house, with a tall portico and lower, flanking porch or terrace, was especially popular. Though described as Colonial, it more vividly recalled the myth of the antebellum Old South. These houses—such as the white house at the center of this postcard view—appeared in town after town and were often built for leaders of local industrial booms. New Bern architect Herbert W. Simpson designed "Colonial" mansions for New Bern's new lumber magnates, and Charlotte architects C. C. Hook and J. M. McMichael planned residences for cotton and lumber dealers in Red Springs in Robeson Co., which became known as "The Town of Handsome Homes." The Georgian Revival style grew popular in the 1910s and 1920s, as exemplified in the house seen on the right, in the form of frame or brick houses with details and proportions copied from specific American Colonial examples. Many were built along a town's most prestigious residential avenues. Among the specialists in the style were C. C. Benton of Wilson and Harry Barton of Greensboro. Although the houses pictured here have been lost, comparable ones still line Wilson's W. Nash St.*

FIGURE 60. *Lucas Ave., Wilson* (WL 5). *The bungalow, unlike revival styles, was a "modern" house type without specific historical references. Originating out of the Craftsman movement and developing into a popular house form on the West Coast, the bungalow was disseminated nationwide through the popular print media in the 1910s and 1920s. The simple, easily built house with its open, informal plan, natural materials, and low-slung silhouette with deep porch suited North Carolinians' need for simple, convenient housing at a time of vast demand. Built large in elite suburbs or small in working-class neighborhoods, the frame bungalow with its distinctive, tapered porch posts and angular roof brackets multiplied across the state. Especially in its smallest, usually gable-end form, the so-called Southern bungalow took its place as the period's principal contribution to the tradition of common dwellings.*

dominant taste for the region's most substantial residential architecture. Far more numerous, however, were two less pretentious, nationally popular small house types: the bungalows and shotgun houses erected by the thousands for the middle- and working-class families moving into town.

The Progressive movement also produced other changes. As reformers pressed for improvements in education to better the prospects for the region and the state, hundreds of schoolhouses were built, including small, wooden, one- or two-teacher rural schools—the predominant type for both races—and growing numbers of big, brick, consolidated schools with expanded facilities for white students. Educators and local boosters also established colleges, as the state placed new emphasis on the normal colleges needed to educate future schoolteachers. A simultaneous emphasis on health and recreation, aided by improved transportation, began the transformation of the Outer Banks from its old isolation to a popular resort area.

By 1929, when the stock market crash came, determined city boosters and resilient farmers had remade both the region and its landscape. Farmers, who had

FIGURE 61. *Harvey St., Kinston* (LR 5). *The shotgun house is typically one room wide with a gable front and has a single rank of rooms extending back from the front entrance, each one opening into the next. The plan is believed to trace back to African traditions by way of New Orleans and the Caribbean. Although some were built in the 19th c., shotgun houses became most numerous in N.C. during the early 20th-c. burst of town growth and construction of thousands of small, closely placed houses as new working-class housing, especially for black families. Rows of shotgun houses, along with gable-sided and L-plan dwellings and small bungalows, were built in nearly every community as workers expanded the urban population.*

FIGURE 62. *Selma Graded School, Johnston Co.* (JT 3). *The early 20th c. saw a boom in schoolhouse building that produced hundreds of small 1- or 2-room schools. This was followed by a movement to improve and consolidate schools, resulting in larger masonry buildings with auditoriums and other facilities. The N.C. Department of Public Instruction provided standardized designs for schoolhouses by type and size, and each community took pride in building a modern and progressive schoolhouse.*

FIGURE 63. *Elizabeth City State University, Elizabeth City* (PK 6). *Like the expansion of primary and secondary education, the establishment of teachers' training schools was a high priority in N.C. in the late 19th and early 20th centuries. State-supported normal colleges for blacks were established at Elizabeth City and Fayetteville, successors to schools founded by local black residents. In this era of normal school expansion, a state-supported normal school for whites was established at Greenville; it later became East Carolina University. The Elizabeth City college also received some assistance from the Julius Rosenwald Foundation, which aided in building 5,300 schoolhouses for black students throughout the South, including over 800 schools in N.C.*

prospered briefly during the 1910s, were already troubled by an agricultural depression that had begun in the 1920s. For many town residents the Great Depression brought an abrupt end to an era of promise and prosperity. Rural poverty worsened. Gradually during the 1930s a series of New Deal federal programs bolstered the economy, providing work to the unemployed and supporting institutions that had long-lasting effects on the region, from the construction of post offices and municipal water plants to the stabilization of the tobacco economy.

The advent of World War II brought full employment and renewed prosperity. Farmers raised bumper crops of cotton, tobacco, and food to meet new wartime demands. Rapid construction of military facilities brought a vast new presence into the region. Proximity to the Atlantic Ocean and north-south rail arteries combined with eastern North Carolina's flat terrain and cheap land made the region suitable for Army and Marine bases. A Coast Guard base was installed at Elizabeth City, and just south of Elizabeth City two enormous blimp hangars were built for Lighter Than Air surveillance vessels. Facilities at Fort Bragg near Fayetteville and several other installations were quickly expanded,

FIGURE 64. *Pier at Nags Head* (DR 11). *New transportation improvements and emphasis on health and recreation expanded interest in seaside resorts. One of the region's best-known resorts was Nags Head, where regular steamboat service from Elizabeth City increased the popularity of the longtime summer community established by planter and merchant families from northeastern N.C. Northern industrialists established hunting clubs on Currituck Sound and elsewhere along the Outer Banks, and the old maritime village of Beaufort attracted growing numbers of summer tourists. At Wrightsville Beach local Wilmington developers created a commuter beach resort in the 1890s.*

FIGURE 65. *Federal Building, New Bern* (CV 41). *Construction of this post office was but one among the many National Recovery Act and Works Progress Administration projects that brought eastern N.C. towns new municipal facilities such as swimming pools, post offices, armories, city halls, and schools. Establishment of the perennially popular outdoor drama "The Lost Colony" in 1937 was also aided by the Civilian Conservation Corps, the Civil Works Administration, the WPA, and the Federal Theatre Project in cooperation with state and local sponsors.*

and new bases were established. Advantages of location and terrain also brought important new facilities to the region soon after the war. Isolated Topsail Island became an important missile testing site, "Operation Bumblebee," and a Voice of America broadcasting facility was constructed near Washington, as the nation and the region prepared for a new balance of power.

THE LATE TWENTIETH CENTURY

The powerful changes of the last half of the twentieth century have yet again transformed the landscape of eastern North Carolina. The Civil Rights movement ended legal segregation of schools and public facilities and reopened the political process to the black citizens who composed majorities or substantial minorities in much of the region. Electricity and air conditioning redefined domestic and business life and, together with improved highways, opened the region, like the rest of the South, to the new possibilities that generated the "Sun Belt" economic boom. Yet for much of eastern North Carolina, the old problems of isolation and poverty persisted. Many in the region believed that it had

been ignored and left behind in the state's pursuit of progress and prosperity—
even as they saw the region's traditional way of life under siege.

In the late twentieth century the building block of the region's history, the
family farm, is rapidly vanishing. In 1950 about 25 percent of North Carolina
workers were reported as engaged primarily in agriculture; by 1970 the figure
had dropped to under 5 percent; by 1990 less than 3 percent were so employed.
Mechanized agriculture and chemical weedkillers radically reduced the labor involved in farming. The tenant farm system died out during the middle years of
the century. Migrant farm laborers from Mexico and other Latin American
countries come to work the fields at harvest time. Crops are changing: tobacco,
still a high-income producer, is on the wane, while mass production of livestock—chickens, turkeys, and most recently, hogs—has become the most
profitable rural industry, with eastern North Carolina becoming one of the nation's leading producers. Soybeans are planted among the tobacco barns. Cotton, with the help of new strains and new technology, is making a dramatic
comeback. In many areas, large-scale, mechanized agriculture has cleared fields
on a vast scale, wiping away all trace of past farming life. The new farming demands investment in big machinery, not in laborers, and the huge planters and
harvesters are housed in metal sheds that create a new architectural presence in
the landscape.

The region's quest for prosperity continues. Economic development leaders
extol the friendly business climate, low taxes, and low wages to attract manufacturers to establish plants on old fields, from light bulb and computer component factories to chicken processors and pig packers. The children and grandchildren of farmers compete for manufacturing and service jobs. Tourism has

FIGURE 66. *Farm structures, Gates Co. Architecture accommodates labor-saving, mechanized methods of planting, cultivating, harvesting, and storing crops, including these trapezoidal equipment sheds
and cylindrical storage bins.*

FIGURE 67. *"Williamsburg" designs, Standard Homes. This Raleigh home-designing firm is one of many sources of late Colonial Revival residential architecture in the region.*

mushroomed along the Outer Banks, bringing a new population and new jobs and threatening old ways of life. The fishing industry is under tremendous threat, as pollution from farms, towns, and factories pouring into the streams and sounds has reduced fish, crab, shrimp, and oyster populations precipitously. Everywhere, ingrained rural ways adapt to new circumstances as people maintain their traditional focus on locality, church, and family, holding fast to a conservative outlook in politics, social roles, and religion while learning to work and live in entirely new settings.

In the late twentieth century the architecture of the region has been pulled ever more uniformly into the national mainstream. The small log and frame houses of the last century have dwindled in numbers. During the 1940s and 1950s new, small house types appeared on the rural landscape as both the Farmers Home Administration and private designers developed standard plans intended to satisfy the needs expressed by the region's families, and provided plans that generated thousands of neat, convenient, modern houses. For many in the region the mobile home—of which North Carolina is a major manufacturer—has provided the most recent generation of an affordable, practical dwelling sufficient to raise a family.

The public and ambitious private architecture of the last half-century has generally displayed trends similar to those evolving elsewhere, with some accommodation to local needs and preferences. The modernist movement in North Carolina, which found its principal expression in the cities of the Piedmont, exerted less appeal in eastern North Carolina communities. For the most part public officials, developers, and individual clients show a continuing preference for a colonial flavor and classical motifs as refracted through the Williams-

FIGURE 68. *"B's" Barbecue & Grill, Pitt Co. The sense of tradition is strong in eastern N.C. even amidst the vast changes of recent years. Communities in the region sponsor celebrations and dramas— some old, some new—to commemorate historical events and cultural traditions. One of the region's strongest traditions is eastern N.C. barbecue—pig slowly roasted over hickory coals and laced with a vinegar and pepper sauce. The taste for barbecue transcends class and racial lines and has a definite regional identity. East of I-95—the highway that delineates the region for many—residents universally regard eastern N.C. barbecue as infinitely superior to the red-sauced variety of the piedmont region.*

FIGURE 69. *House under restoration, Beaufort Co. Historic preservation has had a widespread impact in eastern N.C., though successes have been more numerous in towns than in rural areas, where many houses suffer from vacancy and neglect, victims of complex and deep-seated changes in the society and the economy. Many local preservation organizations have worked steadily to help preserve community landmarks. Edenton, New Bern, Beaufort, Wilmington, Wilson, Tarboro, and Fayetteville, to name but a few, have long-established preservation initiatives. In recent years other towns and counties have begun efforts to preserve their historic character. Several of the region's architectural firms are focusing on renewal of historic buildings and new designs intended to harmonize with traditional settings. On a statewide basis, the State Historic Preservation Office works with local citizens, organizations, towns, and counties to develop preservation efforts. Through its revolving fund, Preservation North Carolina has rescued and found new owners for endangered buildings across eastern N.C. such as this long-vacant plantation house, Rosedale in Beaufort Co.*

burg phenomenon. In the last decades of the century this preference has blended with the stylized revival of historical precedents promoted by the postmodern movement to produce some conscious gestures toward a new regional architecture. New coastal resort developments sometimes draw on themes from the region's vernacular architecture as well as from historic lifesaving stations, and several house designers reproduce traditional porch and roof forms.

Like much of rural and small-town America, eastern North Carolina faces paired threats of economic stagnation on one hand and uncontrolled development on the other. As one commentator on the region expressed it in 1985, "The critical question is whether in the long term Coastal Plain residents will balance satisfactorily their need for employment and living space with a respect for the land and their historic endowment." Amid the pressure for economic survival, "the danger, of course, is that this diverse, historic region, once proud of its regional flavor—the flavor of grits and greens, salt air and soft summer nights—will be homogenized into a land and people with vague identity and little memory."[6]

6. Joel Arrington, "From the Ocean's Bed—a Vast and Sandy Plain," *Raleigh News and Observer*, July 14, 1985.

Much the same could be said of many other parts of rural America. Eastern North Carolina shares issues with rural communities elsewhere. Social and economic changes have left many old farmsteads to the elements, with the small farmhouses, barns, sheds, and tobacco barns of the recent past vanishing most rapidly. Yet there is evidence of a growing historical consciousness and newly energized efforts by local and state organizations to preserve historic buildings, neighborhoods, and rural districts. Most important, thousands of eastern North Carolinians, oldtimers and newcomers alike, maintain old places because they love them. Although time, the elements, and the bulldozer will take their toll as the years go by, many of eastern North Carolina's historic places, grand and modest, famous and obscure, will survive and will continue to tell their parts of the story of this extraordinary region.

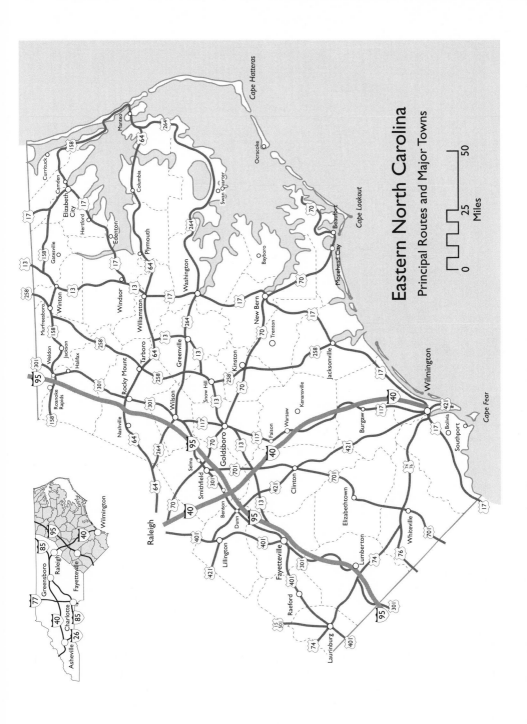

Eastern North Carolina
Principal Routes and Major Towns

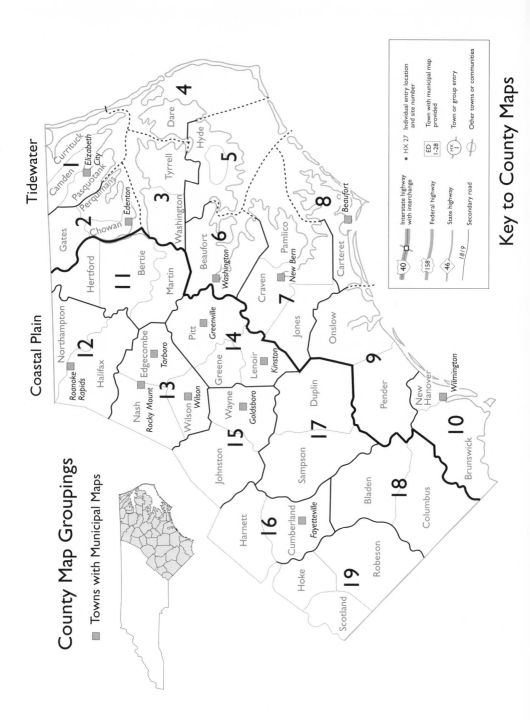

Key to County Maps

County Map Groardings

■ Towns with Municipal Maps

Tidewater

Coastal Plain

Currituck
Camden
1
Elizabeth City
Pasquotank
Perquimans
Gates
2
Chowan
Edenton
Hertford
Bertie
11
Northampton
12
Halifax
Roanoke Rapids
Nash
Rocky Mount
13
Wilson
Wilson
Edgecombe
Tarboro
Pitt
Greenville
14
Greene
Lenoir
Kinston
Wayne
Goldsboro
15
Johnston
16
Harnett
Cumberland
Fayetteville
Hoke
19
Scotland
Robeson
18
Bladen
Columbus
Sampson
17
Duplin
Pender
9
New Hanover
Wilmington
10
Brunswick
Jones
Craven
7
New Bern
Pamlico
Carteret
Beaufort
Beaufort
Washington
6
Washington
Martin
Beaufort
Tyrrell
3
Washington
Hyde
5
Dare
4
Onslow
8

Interstate highway
with interchange
Federal highway
State highway
Secondary road

• HX 27   Individual entry location
          and site number
ED   Town with municipal map
1-28   provided
HX   Town or group entry
1-1
          Other towns or communities

68

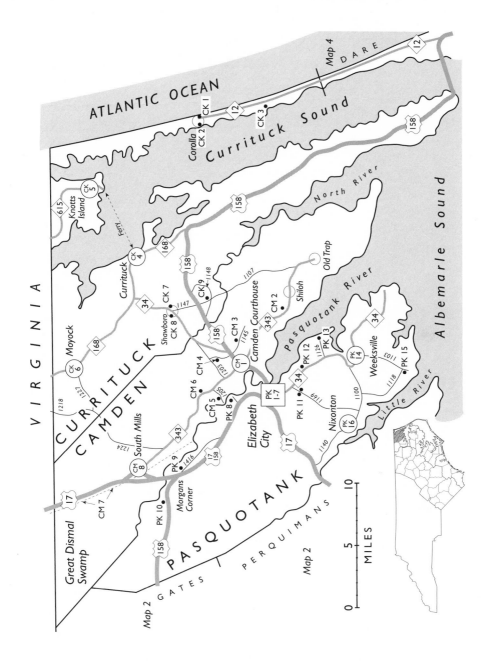

I.

Currituck Co. (p. 90),
Camden Co. (p. 94),
and Pasquotank Co.
(p. 98)

69

2. *Perquimans Co. (p. 111), Gates Co. (p. 119), and Chowan Co. (p. 126)*

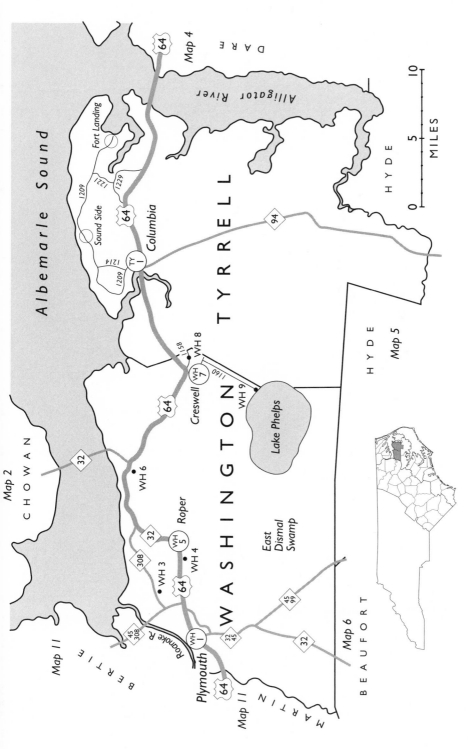

3. *Washington Co. (p. 148), and Tyrrell Co. (p. 153)*

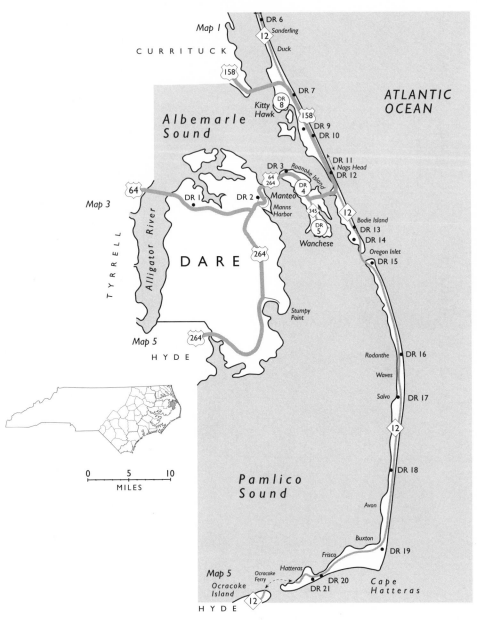

Map 1

C U R R I T U C K

158

Albemarle
Sound

64

Map 3

DR 1

DR 2

T Y R R E L L

Alligator River

D A R E

264

Stumpy
Point

Map 5

264

H Y D E

DR 6

12   Sanderling

Duck

DR 7

DR
8

Kitty
Hawk

158

DR 9

DR 10

DR 11

Nags Head

DR 12

DR 3   Roanoke Island

64
264

DR
4

Manteo

Manns
Harbor

345

DR
5

Wanchese

12   Bodie Island

DR 13

DR 14

Oregon Inlet

DR 15

ATLANTIC
OCEAN

Pamlico
Sound

Rodanthe   DR 16

Waves

Salvo   DR 17

12

DR 18

Avon

Buxton

Frisco   DR 19

Map 5   Hatteras

Ocracoke   Ocracoke Ferry   DR 20

Ocracoke
Island   DR 21   Cape
Hatteras

12

H Y D E

0   5   10
MILES

4. *Dare Co. (p. 154)*

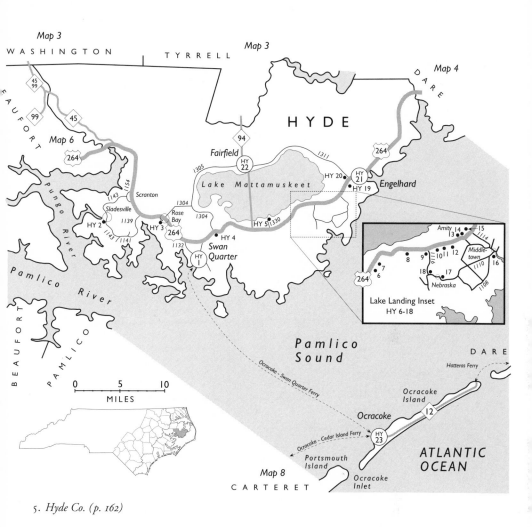

5. *Hyde Co. (p. 162)*

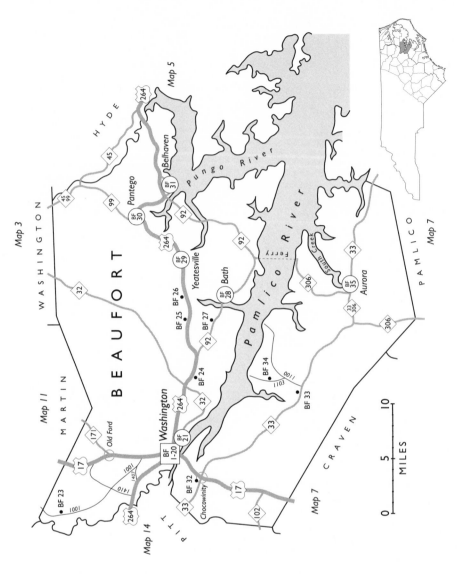

6. Beaufort Co. (p. 171)

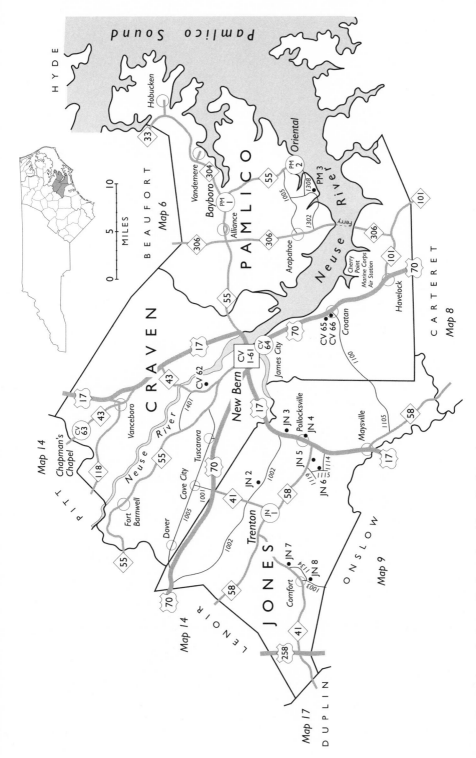

7. *Pamlico Co. (p. 184), Craven Co. (p. 186), and Jones Co. (p. 210)*

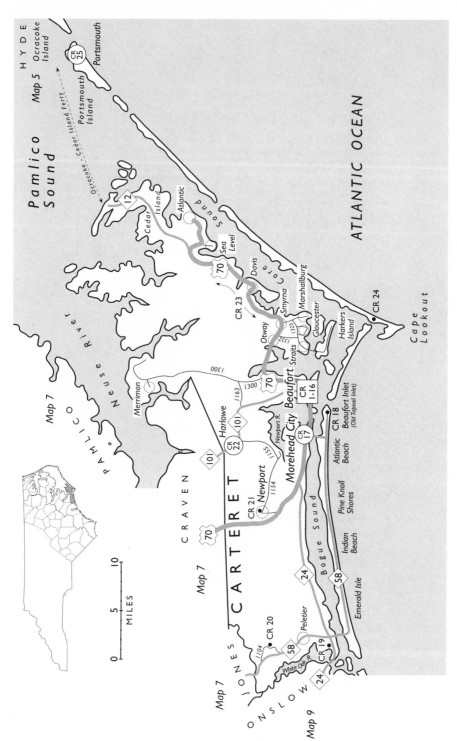

8. *Carteret Co. (p. 213)*

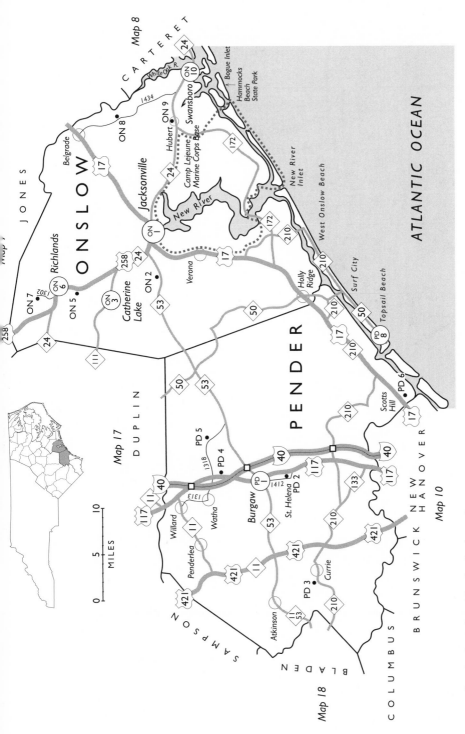

9. *Onslow Co. (p. 225) and Pender Co. (p. 229)*

10. *New Hanover Co. (p. 233) and Brunswick Co. (p. 262).*

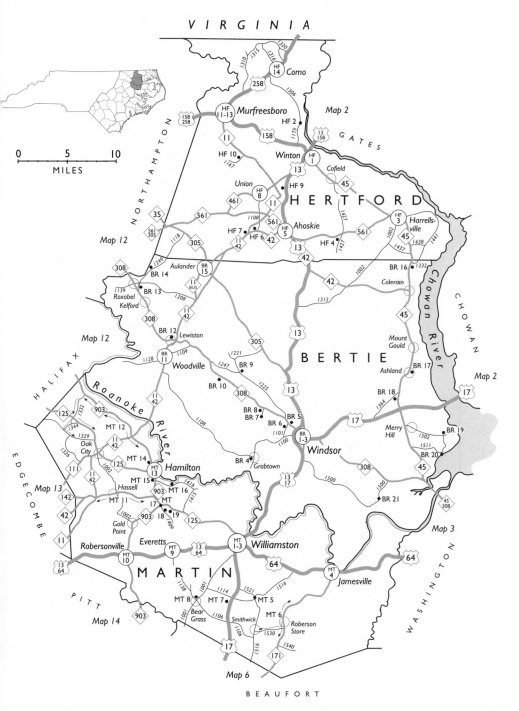

11. *Hertford Co. (p. 269), Bertie Co. (p. 276), and Martin Co. (p. 283)*

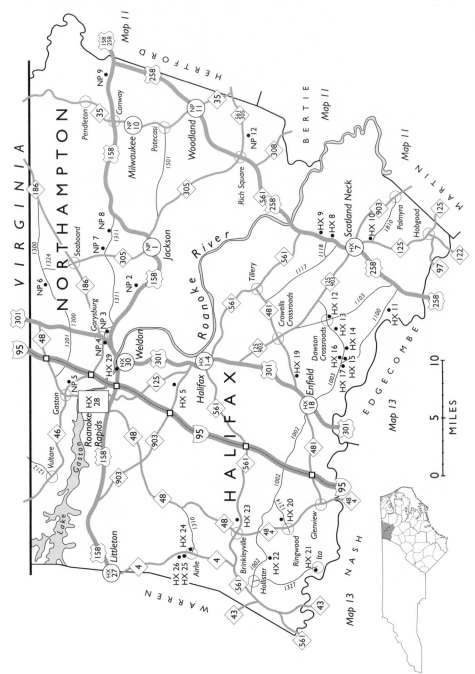

12. *Northampton Co. (p. 200) and Halifax Co. (p. 204)*

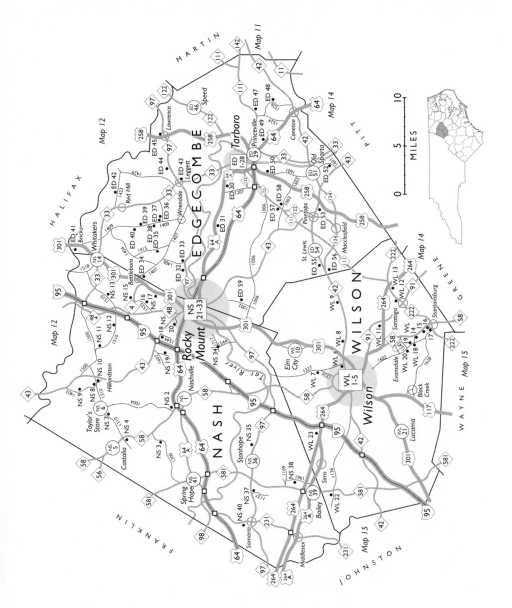

13. *Edgecombe Co.
(p. 311), Nash Co.
(p. 327), and
Wilson Co. (p. 340)*

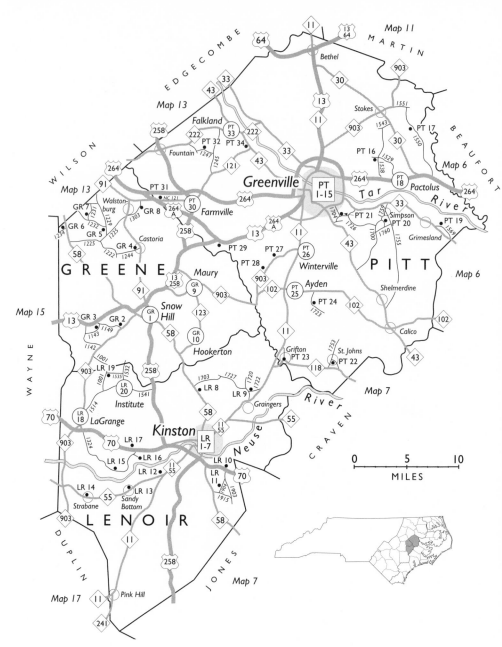

14. *Pitt Co. (p. 354), Greene Co. (p. 366), and Lenoir Co. (p. 369)*

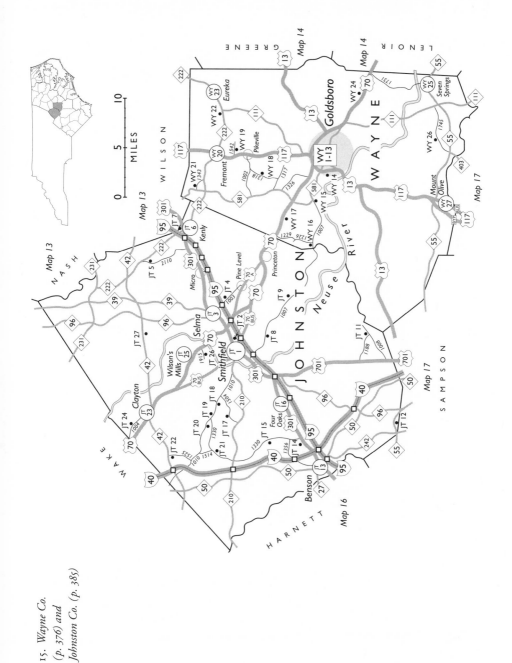

15. Wayne Co.
(p. 376) and
Johnston Co. (p. 385)

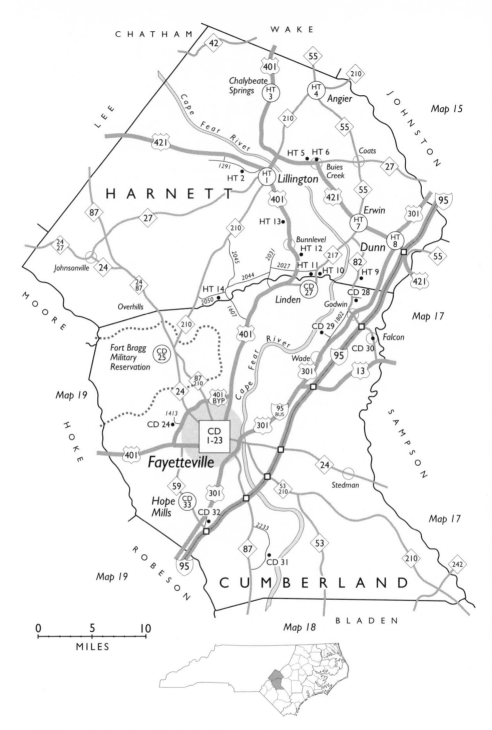

CHATHAM

WAKE

42

401

55

210

JOHNSTON

Chalybeate
Springs

HT
3

HT
4

Angier

Map 15

LEE

Cape Fear River

421

210

55

HT 5   HT 6

Coats

27

1291

Buies
Creek

H A R N E T T

HT 2

HT
1

Lillington

401

421

55

Erwin

301

95

87

27

210

HT 13

HT
7

55

24
27

24

2045

2031

Bunnlevel
HT 12

217

HT
8

55

Johnsonville

HT 11

Dunn

421

24
87

HT 14

2044

2027

HT 10

82

HT 9

CD 28

MOORE

Overhills

2050

1607

CD
27

Linden

Godwin

1802

Map 17

210

CD
25

401

Cape Fear River

CD 29

CD 30

Falcon

Fort Bragg
Military
Reservation

Wade

95

Map 19

87
210

301

13

24

401
BYP

95
BUS

1413

CD 24

CD
1-23

301

24

Stedman

Map 17

HOKE

401

Fayetteville

59

53
210

Hope
Mills

CD
33

301

CD 32

2233

Map 19

95

87

53

210

242

CD 31

ROBESON

Map 18

C U M B E R L A N D

SAMPSON

BLADEN

0   5   10

MILES

16. *Harnett Co. (p. 393) and Cumberland Co. (p. 397)*

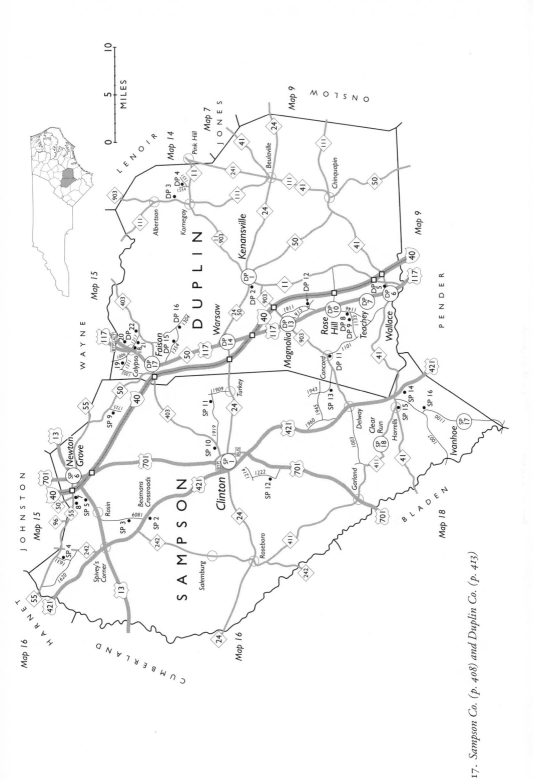

17. *Sampson Co. (p. 408) and Duplin Co. (p. 413)*

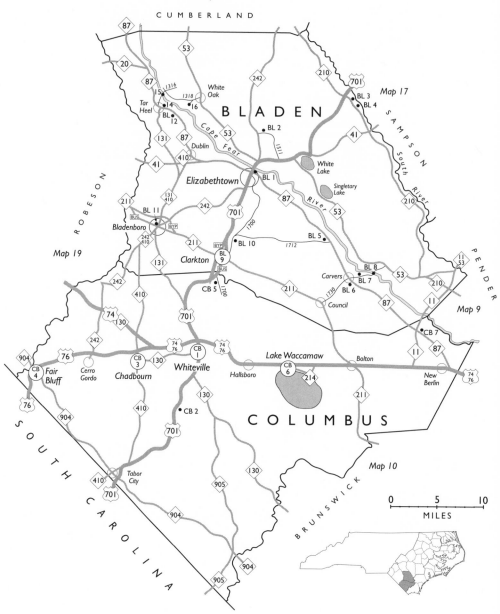

18. *Bladen Co. (p. 420) and Columbus Co. (p. 424)*

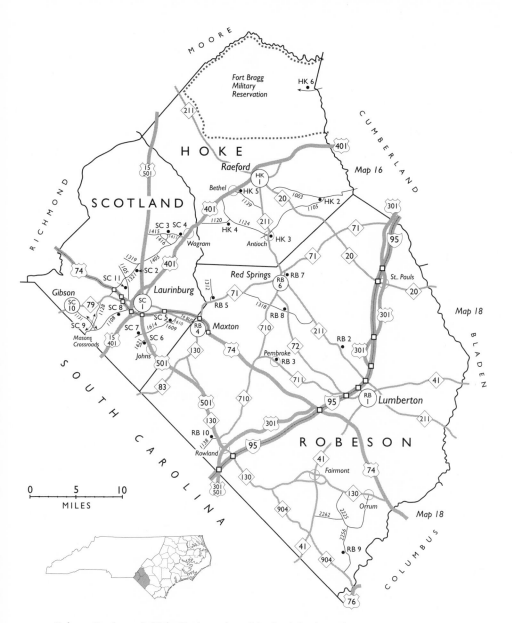

19. *Robeson Co. (p. 427), Hoke Co. (p. 433), and Scotland Co. (p. 435)*

Catalog

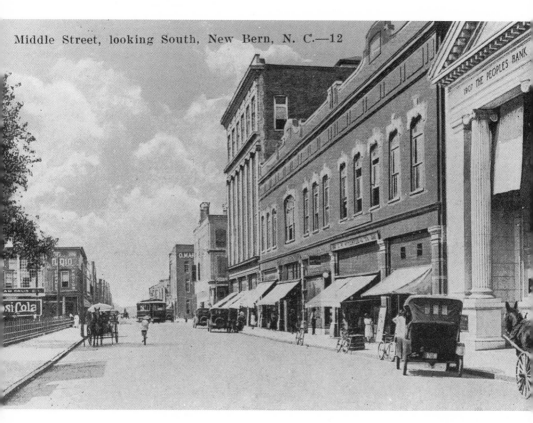

Middle Street, looking South, New Bern, N. C.—12

Currituck County (CK)

Currituck Banks (CK 1–3)

Long famed as a haven for migrating water-fowl and the sportsmen who hunt them, until the 1980s the barrier island separating Currituck Sound from the Atlantic Ocean remained a hunting preserve reached only by boat from the mainland or by private road from Dare Co. State acquisition of the road opened the area to the public, and although sections of the beach and soundside wetlands are in the hands of environmental organizations or hunting clubs, intensive beach resort development has transformed the landscape since 1985. Construction has centered on the old community of Corolla, which was known as Currituck Beach until a post office was established here in 1895.

CK 1 Currituck Beach Lighthouse and Keeper's Residences

1875; NC 12, Corolla; open to public, May–Oct.

The 158-foot, red brick tower was the last of the great 19th-c. beacons constructed by the Federal Lighthouse Board to guide mariners along the treacherous shoals of the Outer Banks. The 1875 first-order Fresnel lens—the largest size, used in the largest seacoast lighthouses—remains in place. The low, flat coastline made tall lighthouses a necessity along the banks, and the undifferentiated, oft-changing landscape required each tower to be boldly marked to enable sailors to distinguish one location from another. The Currituck lighthouse was left unpainted to

CK 1 *Currituck Beach Lighthouse and Keeper's Residences*

distinguish it from the black-and-white-patterned daymarks of the *Bodie Island, *Cape Hatteras, and *Cape Lookout lighthouses farther south, all of similar design. Even in this remote outpost, federal design standards combined function and ornament in fine Victorian fashion, ringing the lantern with an ornate, bracketed iron gallery and executing the brick **Oil House**, frame **Double Keeper's Residence**, and frame **Single Keeper's Residence** as picturesque cottages with corbeled chimneys and king-post gable decorations. Even the original **Privy**, returned to the site and restored in 1994, emulates a picturesque cottage in its cruciform design with board-and-batten walls and gable decorations. On NC 12 just north of the lighthouse is the former **Kill Devil Hills Lifesaving Station** (1870s), a board-and-batten Gothic Revival building dating from the first phase of lifesaving station construction on the Outer Banks, moved to this site from Dare Co. in 1986 for use as an office.

CK 2 Whalehead Club

1922–25; architect unknown; Mr. Carr, head carpenter; W side NC 12, Corolla; under restoration as Currituck Wildlife Museum; tours offered to public in summer

CK 2 *Whalehead Club*

The grandest and most elegant of the Currituck Co. shooting clubs and lodges was built under the supervision of Edward C. Knight Jr. and his wife, Amanda Marie Louise LeBel, as their private hunting retreat. Tradition reports that the couple built the lodge after Amanda Knight, an avid

sportswoman, was excluded from local all-male hunting clubs. Edward Knight, whose father developed the sleeping car and sold the patent to Pullman in 1868, had employed Philadelphia architect Horace Trumbauer for two Rhode Island residences, but no evidence links any architect's name with the lodge at Corolla. Local tradition credits the Knights with the design, an opulent combination of Arts and Crafts and Art Nouveau detail with a water lily motif selected by Mrs. Knight. The exterior walls are sheathed with flush vertical boards, and the sweeping gable roof is covered with molded copper strips imitating shingles. The lodge is part of a dramatic ensemble including a bridge and a boathouse. After years of decay, it was stabilized and in 1992 was acquired by the county for restoration and public use as the Currituck Wildlife Museum.

CK 3 Currituck Shooting Club

1857, 1879–82; W side NC 12, 4.5 mi. N of Dare Co. line, Corolla vic.; private, visible at a distance from road (no public access)

Established in 1857 by northern businessmen and sportsmen, this is the oldest of the exclusive hunting clubs of the Currituck Banks. The late 19th-c. complex centers on the clubhouse of three intentionally austere and rustic shingled buildings linked by 1-story passageways. Other buildings include boathouses, outbuildings, and watchtowers. Much of the club's extensive landholdings have been sold to private developers.

Currituck County Mainland (CK 4–9)

CK 4 Currituck

The village on the western shore of Currituck Sound had its beginnings as a 17th-c. port of entry, and a courthouse was established in 1722. The slow silting of Currituck Inlet and its closure by the early 19th c. ended the town's port status. Like *Camden Courthouse, the community is a rare example of the small size and basic components of early county seats, with a courthouse, a jail, and a few dwellings and stores.

Of principal interest is the **Currituck County Jail** (ca. 1820), a 2-story building of brick laid in 1:3 and 1:4 bond, one of the earliest jails still standing in the state (cf. *Chowan County Jail, *Carteret County Jail, and *Halifax County Jail). With its pedimented and parapeted gable roof, corbeled cornice, and tooled stone sills and lintels, the building has no surviving counterparts in the state. It is attached to the brick **Currituck County Courthouse**, which encompasses a small, pre-1869 brick core and enlargements of 1897 and 1952.

Opposite the courthouse is the handsome, Italianate style **Walker House** (ca. 1875; private) and the related frame store (1898). The frame **Currituck Teacherage** (1923; NC 168, W side of town) is the only survivor of three identical Colonial Revival style teachers' dormitories, all with engaged, 2-story porches, donated to the county by philanthropist Joseph Palmer Knapp of New York, a frequent hunter on Currituck Banks and a benefactor of local education.

CK 5 Knotts Island
Accessible by ferry from Currituck

The quiet, isolated community located on a peninsula extending into Currituck Sound maintains its maritime character, with small farmsteads flanking NC 615 and a fringe of roads reaching to the water. Known as Knots Island by 1657, the area was settled late in the 17th c. Though the border run in 1728 gave it to N.C., it continues close linkages with Virginia. A place of fishermen and subsistence farmers, the rural landscape is dotted with modest houses and outbuildings dating from the late 19th and early 20th centuries. Typical are compact versions of traditional forms—1- and 2-story, gable-roofed dwellings and the occasional L-shaped dwelling—seen in many tidewater areas. The principal landmark is the **Knotts Island Methodist Church** (1911; SR 1256), a well-preserved frame edifice, with corner entrance tower and broad gables enclosing the sanctuary. A plaque notes the congregation was established in 1811, and the church was built by members in 1911.

CK 6 Moyock
NC 168, 2 mi. S of Virginia line

CK 6 *Poyner Store, Moyock*

In 1880 the Elizabeth City and Norfolk Railroad reached the village that had existed on Shingle Landing Creek by 1753—the name *Moyock* is probably an Indian one. The new line (which later became the Norfolk and Southern) stimulated construction of the late 19th-c. frame houses along Oak St. and Tulls Creek Rd. (SR 1222). The chief landmark along the railroad is the **Poyner Store** (ca. 1903; Oak St. at Shingle Landing Rd.), a frame commercial building with a robustly stepped, curved, and bracketed parapet front.

CK 7 Shaw House
1880s; NE corner NC 34 and SR 1203, Shawboro; private, visible from road

An anomaly amid the county's conservative rural architecture, this stylish if eccentric Italianate villa with bracketed cornices and front tower is also known as the Cupola House. It was built for attorney William B. Shaw, son of Henry Shaw, Civil War hero for whom Shawboro was named. As is true of many other frame structures in this and nearby counties, vinyl or aluminum siding covers its walls.

CK 8 Twin Houses
Ca. 1800; W side NC 34 opp. SR 1147, Shawboro; private, visible from road

The pair of 2-story, hall-parlor-plan houses, joined by a passage, was evidently completed after the death of planter John Perkins in 1797 to accommodate his widow and son, who occupied the property jointly.

CK 9 Culong

1812 (date brick); E side SR 1147, 0.6 mi. S of NC 158, Shawboro vic.; private, visible from road

The gable-fronted Federal style house with a 1-story entrance portico, cross-hall plan, and Federal finish was built for planter and politician Thomas Cooper Ferebee. One of several of this form that once stood in the neighborhood, it is a simplified version of a type built for planters along the Virginia border counties, including the *Hinton-Morgan House in Pasquotank Co., *Shelton in Chowan Co., and *Oakland in Halifax Co. Tradition ascribes the name to an Indian chief whose domain included the surrounding lands.

Camden County (CM)

CM 1 Camden Courthouse

The little community on the Pasquotank River evokes the character of 19th-c. county seats where a few essential institutions and homesteads gathered around the courthouse, in the midst of farmland and forests. Known as Plank Bridge by 1740 and serving as a port for a time, the village was incorporated as Jonesborough in 1792 and called Camden by the 1840s. It is the seat of a small rural county, which was settled early and remains sparsely populated.

CM 1 *Camden County Courthouse*

The **Camden County Courthouse** (1847; w side NC 343), a jewel among the state's Greek Revival public buildings, is one of the few antebellum courthouses still serving its original function. The building, of brick laid in Flemish bond, exemplifies a prevalent mid-19th-c. form with the courtroom occupying the second-story piano nobile above a raised basement containing offices. The pedimented central portico, with its simplified Doric columns of brick standing on tall brick piers, reiterates the hierarchy. Large 12/12 sash windows, heavy stone lintels and sills, and a broad, simple frieze unify the courthouse. Despite its modest size appropriate to a small county, the building's consistent sense of scale and proportion, combined with the bold, simple portico, give it remarkable dignity and monumentality.

Immediately south stands the 2-story brick **Camden County Jail** (1910; Stewart Jail Works [Cincinnati, Ohio], contractors), a 2-story brick building with hip roof, built

to replace an earlier jail burned by the inmates. The Stewart Jail Works specialized in jail building as well as manufacture of ironwork jail fittings (and was an affiliate of the Stewart Iron Works, prolific fencemakers.) A Stewart agent, the Southern Jail Building Company of Baltimore, erected the building and installed Stewart's iron doors, iron barred openings, and a formidable high-security, iron-walled cellblock on the second floor.

The **Widow's Son Masonic Lodge #75** (1856; E side NC 343) across the road presents a contrasting face of the Greek Revival style. The boxy wooden temple with a full-height portico carried by tapered, squared pillars demonstrates the enthusiasm with which builders embraced the spirit, if not the letter, of the Greek Revival. The building has served as a school as well as a fraternal lodge. South of the courthouse, the **Noah Burfoot House** (ca. 1840) is an L-plan Greek Revival farmhouse with pedimented gable ends, a full-width shed porch, and a complement of contemporary outbuildings. Its proximity to the courthouse emphasizes the rural character of the county seat.

CM 2 Godfrey-Burgess House
Early 19th c.; NE side NC 343, 5.7 mi. SE of US 158, Shiloh vic.; private, visible from road

Several 19th-c. farmhouses of varying form and condition stand along NC 343 between Camden and Shiloh. This 1½-story frame house near the road is a well-maintained example of the hall-parlor-plan coastal cottage form, with a full-width front porch and rear shed rooms inset beneath the slope of the roof. Looking west from this road, the *Blimp Hangar may be seen across the river in Pasquotank Co.

CM 3 Sanderlin-Prichard House
1851; N side SR 1145, 1 mi. SE of US 158, Belcross; private, visible from road

The 2-story, frame house with hall-parlor

plan exemplifies a classic regional type, here with a 1-story shed porch and kitchen wing.

CM 4 Caleb Grandy House

Late 18th c.; W side SR 1145, 0.8 mi. N of US 158, Belcross vic.; private, visible from road

The 1½-story frame dwelling typifies the modest size and careful workmanship of substantial houses of the 18th c. The asymmetrical facade reflects the hall-parlor plan. Massive chimneys of brick laid in irregular English bond with paved, double shoulders stand at the gable ends. The house was built for Caleb Grandy during the second half of the 18th c. and was expanded with rear shed rooms in 1787 (date brick). Owner of more than 1,200 acres, Grandy was among the richest planters in Camden Co. and served as commissioner to establish the new county, as county sheriff, and as state legislator. (See Introduction, Fig. 13.)

CM 5 Milford (Grice House)

1744–46 (date brick, 1746); NW side SR 1205, 0.5 mi. SW of NC 343, Spence's Corner vic.; private, visible from road.

CM 5 *Milford (Grice House)*

Evidently the oldest 2-story brick house standing in N.C., the imposing dwelling is also unique in the state for masonry details shared with the early architecture of the Delaware River Valley, most visibly the deep, plastered cove cornice. Splayed door and window openings reveal the thickness of the walls, and the Flemish-bond brickwork with glazed headers, fine flat arches, tumbled

brickwork in the gables, and a projecting belt course display the mason's virtuosity. The interior followed a center-passage plan, one room deep; the original interior finish was removed in the 20th c. Little is known of the early history of the house or of its builders' links with the mid-Atlantic region.

CM 6 Grandy House

1816; E side NC 343, 0.7 mi. N of SR 1205, Lambs Corner vic.; private, visible from road

The farmhouse near the road epitomizes the 2-story dwelling one room deep, often called an I-house, which was built repeatedly by moderately prosperous planters and farmers for over a century. Like most early 19th-c. examples, this frame house is three bays wide with a hall-parlor plan, exterior end chimneys, and rear shed rooms. It is finished in restrained Federal style. "April, 1816 rote by John Nash" (perhaps a carpenter) is penciled in a closet. Outbuildings include a 19th-c. schoolhouse and a large, gable-roofed barn, ca. 1900, with a gabled hood similar to several in the Albemarle region.

CM 7 Dismal Swamp Canal

Running for 22 miles through Virginia and N.C., the Dismal Swamp Canal is the oldest canal in the United States still in active use. Its construction from 1793 to 1805 was the largest of N.C.'s ambitious internal improvement projects of the early national period, when state leaders strove to better transportation networks and prospects for trade.

The swamp, a forested peat bog with tannin-dark waters, once occupied some 600 to 1,000 square miles. Though now reduced by lumbering and draining to about 30 by 10 miles, it remains a primeval refuge. Marked as "a swampy wilderness" on a 1657 map, it was identified as the Great Dismal Swamp on the Moseley map of 1733. Its tangled cypress and juniper depths filled with game provided a haven for runaway slaves who established maroon colonies within its borders. Slave and free workers extracted endless quantities of timber and got shingles from its ancient cypresses. Because the swamp impeded trade between the

Albemarle region and Virginia seaports, from the early 18th c. onward entrepreneurs such as William Byrd and George Washington envisioned a north-south waterway through it.

After several false starts, the Dismal Swamp Company was chartered by Virginia in 1787 and by N.C. in 1790. In 1793 the company began construction at both ends of the canal, which was dug by slave workmen, to connect the Elizabeth River near Norfolk with the Pasquotank River and thence the Albemarle Sound. The final cut came in 1805. A toll road was built simultaneously along the eastern bank.

Various improvements included the early installation of locks, including those at *South Mills, because the swamp was not as flat as first thought; widening and deepening of the canal well beyond its original 15-foot width; and cuts and feeders to supplement the water supply. Vast quantities of shingles, staves, timber, corn, beans, meat, fish, and manufactured goods were shipped through the canal. During the early 19th c., landings, sawmills, and rambunctious hostelries grew up on the banks, but these settlements have vanished, except for South Mills. A key carrier of supplies to the Confederacy, the canal was captured in 1862 by Union troops, and it suffered from neglect during and after the war.

In 1892 the canal was acquired by the Lake Drummond Canal and Water Com-

pany, which rebuilt it and revived trade. In 1929 the U.S. government purchased the canal for inclusion in the new toll-free Intracoastal Waterway, and the U.S. Army Corps of Engineers began improvements: dredging a channel 50 feet wide and 9 feet deep within the 100-foot-wide canal; installation of new drawbridges; and replacement of the locks. After a late 20th-c. threat of closing, the canal continues in service. Like the old toll road, us 17 runs along its length—a 4-lane expressway in N.C., but in Virginia it narrows and is again enveloped by the overhanging forest. The placid juniper water of the canal stretches like a gleaming brown satin ribbon through flat farmlands and the shadowy cypress depths of the Great Dismal Swamp.

CM 8 South Mills

Of the villages and landings where cargo from nearby farmlands was loaded onto vessels plying the Dismal Swamp Canal, only South Mills persists. First called New Lebanon for the abundant cedars, the village developed in the early 19th c. at the locks near the southern end of the canal and was renamed by 1839 for its mills powered by the canal waters. In 1941 the **Locks** on the southern edge of town were rebuilt, producing the present locks, 300 feet long and 52 feet wide with a concrete floor and steel sides.

The town's modest prosperity through

CM 7–8 *Dismal Swamp Canal, with Baxter-Mullen House in background*

the 19th c. produced 2-story frame dwellings oriented to the canal. The best-preserved early 19th c. house is the **Baxter-Mullen House** (108 Mullen Dr.), a large, 5-bay, Federal style residence east of the canal and north of the Old US 17 drawbridge. The **Drawbridge** (1933–34) is a steel bascule structure built by the U.S. Army Corps of Engineers to replace a wooden bridge. Northwest of the bridge stand several unpretentious frame stores of the early 20th c. Mid-19th-c. houses facing the canal from the eastern bank south of the bridge include the **Col. Ferebee House** and the **Dr. Mul-** len House (Joy's Creek Rd.), neighboring 2-story houses with tapered, Greek Revival porch pillars. Late 19th- and early 20th-c. houses appear in the small residential section west of the canal.

A short distance north rises the **William Ira Halstead Bridge** (1982; Bridge #44, US 17 over the Dismal Swamp Canal), a towering construction 2,132 feet long, with a 75-foot vertical clearance. Built with a concrete slab on prestressed concrete and steel plate girders carried on tall cylindrical pylons, the bridge offers a panoramic view of the canal and countryside.

Pasquotank County (PK)

See Thomas R. Butchko, On the Shores of the Pasquotank: The Architectural Heritage of Elizabeth City and Pasquotank County, North Carolina *(1989).*

Elizabeth City (PK 1–7)

The metropolis of the Albemarle (pop. 15,000), Elizabeth City boasts a 30-block core of handsome 19th- and early 20th-c. urban architecture, plus important outlying residential areas. The town was founded as Redding in 1793 below the south terminus of the newly begun *Dismal Swamp Canal. Its location at the narrows of the Pasquotank River was that of an old ferry and mill site, but the town's raison d'être was its position on the canal. By the time the canal opened to traffic in 1805, the community had been designated as county seat and renamed Elizabeth City.

The town grew slowly at first, but improvements to the Dismal Swamp Canal in the 1820s, complemented by new steamboat and stagecoach lines, boosted its trade sufficiently that by 1831 community leaders were trumpeting Elizabeth City as the "Eastern Emporium of North Carolina." Residents of the old port of Edenton, meanwhile, grumbled in 1830 that the canal was "to North Carolina, a blood-sucker at her very vitals." Shipyards, warehouses, fisheries, tanneries, sawmills, and other manufactories flourished along with commission merchants, artisans, and navigators who traded with Norfolk, the West Indies, New England, New York, and Charleston. Slaves and free blacks, who constituted about half the population, worked as mariners and construction artisans as well as digging the canal, working in fisheries, and toiling as servants and laborers. The town's population grew from about 400 in 1830 to nearly 1,800 in 1860.

Early in the Civil War, Union troops captured Elizabeth City, Norfolk, and the canal. Postwar recovery came slowly, and traffic on the neglected canal was only sluggishly renewed. Meanwhile, Elizabeth City was transforming itself as local newspapers preached the New South gospel of progress and industrial development. By 1870 northern lumbermen and other entrepreneurs were leading an industrial revolution. Prominent among these was Daniel Steigerwalt Kramer, who came in 1870 as a pioneer lumberman from Pennsylvania. He began making windows and fish boxes and soon established Kramer Brothers, a lumber mill and sash-and-blind factory that traded with regional as well as northern markets, sending building materials by boat to Outer Banks communities from Kitty Hawk to Hatteras. The company also developed into a major regional contracting firm. With the 1881 arrival of the Elizabeth City and Norfolk Railroad (which within months reached Hertford and Edenton), the local *Economist* proclaimed that the city had been "baptized into the family of railroad communities" and anticipated "a new departure in our business prosperity." To the chagrin of Elizabeth City boosters, the railroad's name was changed to the Norfolk Southern in 1883. (The company was reorganized in 1891 as the Norfolk and Southern, but the name then returned to Norfolk Southern [1910–82]. The route is now part of the present Norfolk Southern Railroad, which, confusingly enough, was formed in 1990 from the old Norfolk and Western and the Southern Railway Company.)

"Energetic, enterprising, and progressive" Elizabeth City took pride in its variety of businesses and industries: six big sawmills that filled rail cars and steamboats; its 100 stores, five hotels, and three newspapers; and private and public schools that included teacher training colleges for whites and for blacks. Building on a strong tradition of African American schools begun soon after the war, the State Normal School was established by the General Assembly in 1891 and

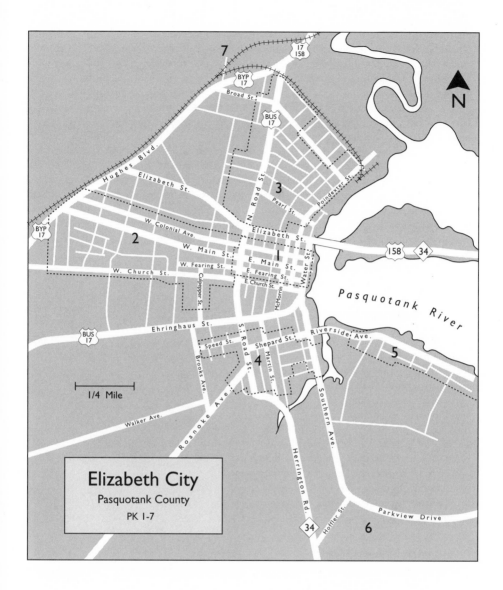

Elizabeth City
Pasquotank County
PK 1-7

subsequently evolved into *Elizabeth City State University.

The town grew quickly from 2,300 people in 1880 to nearly 4,000 in 1885, and to 6,348 in 1900. By 1893 the updated city plan showed newly enlarged limits encompassing five wards fanning out from the curve in the river. By 1915 boosters proclaimed that the town had "sufficient river frontage to meet the demands of several hundred thousand people," as well as "flattering prospects of becoming the largest city in the State within the next quarter of a cen-

tury—and why not?" Construction of imposing public buildings, and especially the completion of a modern water plant in 1925 and the 9-story Virginia Dare Hotel and Arcade in 1927—celebrated as the "Albemarle's first skyscraper"—asserted the town's status as metropolis of northeastern N.C.

After a boost from the 1938 establishment of a Coast Guard air base and wartime projects, town growth tapered off with the decline of the forest industry and increasing competition from Norfolk. Today the riverside town looks to a diverse economy based on Intracoastal Waterway travel, the Coast Guard facility, several manufacturing plants, and colleges, including Elizabeth City State University, Roanoke Bible College, and the College of the Albemarle.

Like Asheville in western N.C., Elizabeth City took form in the great 1880s–1920s era of American city building, then saw little growth. In keeping with its New South sense of a city "destined to become an important trade and social centre," Elizabeth City has an urban flavor and compact density unusual in the region. Its principal downtown buildings designed by an array of regionally prominent architects are complemented by grid-plan neighborhoods with close-knit rows of frame houses. In contrast to towns where each generation of houses fit among and around the preceding ones, here the principal neighborhoods date from a brief span of late 19th- and early 20th-c. development. Because developers typically platted subdivisions with an urban template of 25-foot lots (some were double), houses tended to be narrow and closely placed. The dominant Elizabeth City house type of this era stands two stories tall with a front-gabled facade and a side-passage plan. Many were Italianate, Queen Anne, or Colonial Revival versions for middle-class residents, while others were constructed more simply for working-class families—all part of a townscape evoking an era of "city-like" hopes and accomplishments.

PK 1 Central Business District

E. Main St. and nearby streets, extending west from Pasquotank River, from Water St. to Road St.

The heart of the city comprises several blocks extending west from the recently revitalized waterfront, where the old wharf area now welcomes boaters on the Intracoastal Waterway. The area encompasses essentially the original city limits, which covered 37 blocks flanking Main St. between the river and Road St.—the old road southward that separates east and west street designations. Early in the 19th c. two discrete business centers emerged, one at Main and

Water beside the river, the other at Main and Road; between them stood the courthouse and residences. This core area includes the principal antebellum buildings as well as commercial and institutional buildings from the turn-of-the-century boom era.

The **McMullen Building** (ca. 1891, 1896, 1908; 117 N. Water St.), with its ornate, 3-story, pressed-metal facade, is among the best preserved of its type in the state. The facade, installed by 1896, was manufactured by the Mesker Brothers "Front Builders" of St. Louis. The building was erected for physician and druggist Oscar McMullen and retains a remarkably intact drugstore on the first floor.

PK 1 *McMullen Building*

Towering over downtown is the **Virginia Dare Hotel and Arcade** (1927; William L. Stoddart [New York], architect; J. E. Beamon [Raleigh], builder; 507–9 E. Main St.). Built 9 stories tall as a first-class hotel and symbol of civic pride, it is still the only "skyscraper" in the Albemarle region. The brick structure, with classical stone and terra-cotta detail typical of popular hotel architect Stoddart, covers most of the block and encompasses a 2-story, skylit shopping arcade.

PK 1 *Christ Episcopal Church, Parish House, and Virginia Dare Hotel*

The commercial district consists of solid rows of 2- and 3-story brick buildings with Italianate and Neoclassical detail. The **Lowry-Chesson Building** (1897; 514–16 E. Main St.), built for Dr. Freshwater Lowry, housed a department store below and opera house and offices above. Its 3-story mass is dramatized by the 2-story brick arcade framing the windows beneath an Italianate cornice. The **Kramer Building** (1909; Joseph Kramer, contractor; 500–512 E. Main St.), built as a commercial rental property by the Kramer family and designed by Joseph Kramer, the architect-builder son of company founder Daniel Kramer, features free classical motifs in contrasting brickwork. Across the street is the **Selig Building** (1926; Rudolf, Cook, and Van Llewen [Norfolk], architects; Lord Byron Perry [Elizabeth City], contractor; 513 E. Main St.), an elegant little jewelry store and office building with a polychrome terra-cotta facade with stylized classical motifs. Just south of Main on Poindexter is the former **Citizens Bank** (1899; 200 S. Poindexter St.), a rich blend

of Romanesque and chateauesque motifs, including an oriel window with a foliated sandstone console accentuating the corner bay that once carried a tower.

A prime architectural landmark is **Christ Episcopal Church and Parish House** (1856–57; J. Crawford Neilson [Baltimore], architect; Thomas H. Coats, builder; 200 S. McMorrine St.). Its almost Germanically muscular rendition of the Gothic Revival style contrasts with the predominant sedateness of the denomination's Gothic Revival churches in the state. The brownstone-trimmed brick church is an early work and the only known N.C. commission by the prominent Baltimore architect. Beside the gabled nave, a robust corner belltower rises from a square, buttressed base, with broad chamfered corners emphasizing the transition to an octagonal, crenellated belfry. Expressive brickwork with strong corbel tables reinforces the energetic forms. The sanctuary with hammerbeam ceiling features fine stained glass. The adjoining **Parish House** (1925–26; Benton & Benton [Wilson], architects; Lord Byron Perry [Elizabeth City], builder) is in harmonizing Tudor Revival style.

A cluster of landmarks flanks Main St. east of Road St. The **U.S. Post Office and Courthouse** (1906; 306 E. Main St.) presents a suavely Italianate monument of governmental Beaux Arts classicism in limestone, with a rusticated first story, heavy pedimented window caps, and a slate-covered hip roof. Its classically detailed courtroom in polished mahogany is a splendid public chamber. The **Pasquotank County Courthouse** (1882; A. L. West [Richmond], architect; Daniel S. Kramer [Elizabeth City], builder; 206 E. Main St.), despite massive new wings and an interior remodeling (1979), retains its symmetrical facade with its Corinthian portico set on an arched, rusticated basement—a perennially popular classical formula from the Renaissance onward.

PK 1 *Charles O. Robinson House*

Across the street looms the **Charles O. Robinson House** (1913; Herbert W. Simpson [New Bern], architect; Joseph Kramer, builder; 201 E. Main St.), one of the state's most magnificent examples of the Southern Colonial style residence. Lumberman William B. Blades of New Bern erected the opulent frame dwelling with towering Corinthian portico for his daughter Ivy on her marriage to Charles O. Robinson, president of the Elizabeth City Cotton Mill. New Bern architect Simpson, prolific master of the style, had erected similar houses for Blades family members who led New Bern's lumber boom, and this residence symbolized the joining of two families who had come south and become leaders in the region's industrial development.

Recalling the 19th-c. mercantile focus at the junction of Main and Road Sts. is a cluster of antebellum commercial buildings— some of the earliest surviving in the region. Probably the oldest is the **Cluff-Pool Store** (ca. 1819, ca. 1858, ca. 1895; 100 S. Road St.), a 2-story brick building occupied in the 1820s by Matthew Cluff, shipowner. Later 19th-c. renovations brought the arch-topped double windows, ornate metal cornice, and 2-tier rear porch. The **Cobb House and Store** (1840s; 111 S. Road St.) presents an unusual survival of an adjoining house and store, of brick with stepped parapet gables. The second story served as courthouse from the burning of the old one in 1862 until the new one was completed in 1882. The delectably bold **Farmers Bank Building** (1855; 108 E. Main St.) is a tiny Gothic Revival style bank, recently restored to reinstate its facade with Gothic-arched roofline and openings. The exterior was originally painted, reported the local newspaper, "under the cunning hand of Benjamin Richardson [in] an admirable counterfeit presentment of beautiful marble."

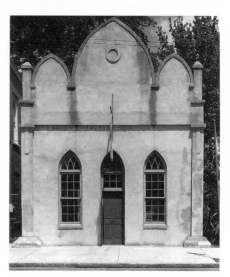

PK 1 *Farmers Bank Building*

Two antebellum residences built for merchants near the old town edge show the locally favored side-passage plan. The **Grice-Fearing House** (ca. 1800, 1840, 1885; 200 S. Road St.) began with a side-passage-plan house one room deep, built for Pennsylvania-born merchant Francis Grice, who bought the lot in 1798. His widow, Mary, married merchant Isaiah Fearing, who enlarged the house and added the 2-story engaged porch. The **Pool-Lumsden-Peters House and Office** (ca. 1840, ca. 1895; 204 S. Road St.), the town's most intact antebellum house, has a side-passage plan two rooms deep with Greek Revival detail. It was was built for Lovey Taylor Pool, who, as widow of merchant and planter Thomas Pool, moved to town and carried on her husband's shipping business. The small freestanding brick office in the yard was built in 1895 for William J. Lumsden, longtime local physician.

PK 1 *First United Methodist Church*

Across Road St. the **First United Methodist Church** (1919–22; James M. McMichael [Charlotte], architect; Joseph Kramer, builder; 205 S. Road St.), successor to an 1857 Greek Revival church that stood on Church St., shows architect McMichael's popular Protestant Neoclassicism in which Roman-inspired motifs—large porticoes, shallow dome, and spacious auditorium-plan sanctuary with fine stained glass—suited prosperous congregations throughout the state.

West, north, and south of the old town limits, predominantly residential areas recall the rapid expansion of the late 19th and early 20th centuries.

PK 2 W. Main St. Area

W of Road St. on W. Main, W. Fearing, W. Church, and nearby streets

In the late 19th c. several firms such as the West End Land and Improvement Company began platting and developing residential lots west of town. The resulting neighborhood centering on W. Main St. contains a remarkably solid, varied, and intact grouping of closely placed late 19th- and early 20th-c. houses. In the 400 block, for example, a rhythmic row of multigabled Queen Anne dwellings nearly abuts the sidewalk. Examples of foursquare houses and bungalows—many built by Joseph Kramer—are abundant and varied. As throughout the city, 2-story, gable-fronted houses with side-passage plans make their appearance on the narrow single lots.

Key buildings illustrate the neighborhood's variety. The **Dr. Isaiah Fearing House** (ca. 1905; George F. Barber [Knoxville], architect; 203 W. Main St.) is one of a number of houses built in Queen Anne style from designs by the mail-order architect Barber. The area is punctuated by substantial Gothic Revival churches in red brick, including the **First Baptist Church** (1889; 302 W. Main St.). In the 300 block of W. Main, various Colonial Revival compositions appear, such as the Southern Colonial style **Judge Isaac Meekins House** (1903; William P. Rose [Raleigh], architect; 310 W. Main), with symmetrical facade and Ionic portico, and the **Dennis M. Jones House** (1902; Arnold Eberhard [Norfolk], architect, John W. Martin, builder; 312 W. Main St.; see Introduction, Fig. 54), which combines classical detail with the irregular roofline and flowing plan of the late Queen Anne style. The 400 block has an especially fine sequence of narrow Queen Anne houses, and there are a few antebellum dwellings built before development thickened, notably the **Charles-Harney House** (ca. 1853–63; 400 W. Main St.), a brick, side-hall-plan house, and the **Overman-Sheep House** (ca. 1859; 401 W. Main St.), a big frame Greek Revival house with a full-height Doric portico.

The 500 block continues the prevalent Queen Anne mode, including the **Lilly Grandy House** (1897; George F. Barber, architect; 504 W. Main St.), another documented Queen Anne style design from the Tennessee mail-order architect Barber. The

PK 2 *400 Block of W. Main St.*

William T. Culpepper House (1935; 609 W. Main St.; B&B) is the town's prime example of the Georgian Revival style, in red brick with symmetrical facade focused on a small curved entrance portico, built during the depression by a local businessman, postmaster, and state legislator.

Parallel and cross streets likewise have rows of late 19th- to early 20th-c. residential architecture punctuated by churches. **Church St.** and **Fearing St.** to the south and **Colonial Ave.** on the north have especially strong collections. The predominant type is the 2-story, gable-fronted narrow house, but there are Queen Anne and Colonial Revival residences and many bungalows as well. Two antebellum Greek Revival dwellings include the **Charles-Hussey House** (1849, ca. 1910; 1010 W. Colonial Ave.), a house with massive Doric-order porch, once the seat of a plantation that bordered the town, and the **Richardson-Pool House** (1850s; 301 Culpepper St.) with a double portico with hefty, tapered pillars of distinctive local type.

A landmark in regional church history is **Mount Lebanon A.M.E. Zion Church** (1905; J. W. Hines, minister and designer; Elisha Overton, chief mason; 320 Culpepper St.), a late Gothic Revival brick edifice with a broad, gabled facade flanked by a pair of dramatically unequal corner towers. Its dis-

tinguished history as the oldest known separate black congregation in the Albemarle region—and possibly in eastern N.C.—began with its organization in 1850 as a religious society that met in the basement of the First Methodist (Elizabeth City Methodist) Church. In 1855 the congregation built a large frame church here—then the largest in town—on land bought by the Elizabeth City Methodist Church for the purpose. Along with others in the region, the church became an African Methodist Episcopal Zion church following a visit by Rev. J. W. Hood soon after the Civil War. The congregation erected the present brick church during the city's turn-of-the-century building boom, when many congregations built new facilities. Across the street stands the **Whitmel Lane House** (ca. 1870; 315 Culpep-

PK 2 *Mount Lebanon A.M.E. Zion Church*

per St.), a 2-story frame house built for Lane, a carpenter, who was born a free black in Chowan Co.; as a builder in Elizabeth City, he acquired considerable property and prominence. Lane's son-in-law, Elisha Overton, was chief brickmason for Mount Lebanon Church. When Lane bought this property in 1857, the street was called African Church St.

At the end of Main St., the **Norfolk Southern Passenger Station** (1914; 109 S. Hughes Blvd., opp. w end of Main St.) is a brick depot with a tile-covered, hip roof with deep overhang. It replaced an 1881 facility located near the river.

PK 3 Northside

1880s–1910s; N. Road St., N. Poindexter, Broad, and Pearl Sts.

PK 3 *N. Road St.*

With the arrival of the railroad in 1881, the sparsely settled area around the depot and railyard was transformed into a neighborhood where residents ranged from the mercantile elite to railroad hands and laborers. The area contains dense rows of late Victorian houses, from imposing residences to simple cottages. Along N. Poindexter St., for example, stretches a row of Queen Anne style houses whose lively rooflines and or-nate porches create a staccato streetscape. Along N. Road St. are nearly uniform, 2-story, gable-end, side-passage dwellings, each in line with its decorated front porch. Churches dominate key corners. **City Road Methodist Church** (1900–1902; 511 N. Road St.) is a forcefully asymmetrical, Romanesque Revival red brick church with the Methodists' favored auditorium plan entered from a large corner tower. **Blackwell Memorial Baptist Church** (1904; 700 N. Road St.) repeats the Romanesque Revival style and corner tower with spire and bartizan.

PK 4 Shepard St.–S. Road St. Area

S of E. Ehringhaus St. to Charles Creek on S. Road, Shepard, and nearby streets

The first major expansion of Elizabeth City's boundaries in 1851 stretched south to encompass the area flanking S. Road St., the old road southward, including the "Race tract," site of a horse-racing track. Black and white residents soon established homes here, a pattern that continued after the Civil War. Proximity to Kramer Brothers' sawmill on Charles Creek and other factories attracted many working families. In the late 19th c. the neighborhood drew growing numbers of black residents, a trend reinforced when the State Colored Normal School opened here. Nearly all of the town's leading black churches concentrated here. As Jim Crow laws and social segregation intensified in the 20th c., the area became increasingly identified as a black neighborhood, home to business and educational leaders who owned substantial residences as well as families who rented or owned smaller dwellings.

PK 4 *S. Martin St.: Corner Stone Baptist Church (center) and St. Phillips Episcopal Church (right)*

The architecture repeats local patterns of density, with many narrow, 2-story, gable-fronted, side-passage houses interspersed among houses of diverse forms and popular styles—a few mid-19th-c. Greek Revival and Italianate houses, and several Queen Anne, Colonial Revival, and Craftsman examples. The **Elisha Overton House** (ca. 1880; 517 S. Road St.), a multigabled, side-passage-plan house with ornate millwork, was built for leading bricklayer Overton soon after he married Mary Virginia Lane, daughter of carpenter Whitmel Lane. A foursquare house with Craftsman motifs is the **Henry C. Hargraves House** (ca. 1923; 108 Speed St.), built for Hargraves, a businessman who was a barber by trade but also owner of the Blue Duck Inn on E. Ehringhaus St., the town's best-known black night spot in its day, as well as Hargraves Beach in Currituck Co., one of the few beaches for blacks on the Outer Banks in the first half of the 20th c. Corner stores and other small commercial concerns enliven many blocks.

Churches are the most prominent landmarks. **St. Phillips Episcopal Church** (1893; 512 S. Martin St.), built as a mission chapel for the black community, exemplifies the Episcopal preference for Carpenter Gothic architecture among its late 19th-c. mission churches, with board-and-batten walls, lancet windows, and a bellcote topping the gabled front. Within, walls scored to imitate stone rise to a scissors truss roof. **Corner Stone Missionary Baptist Church** (1889; brick veneered 1942; 507 S. Martin St.) features two contrasting corner towers flanking the broad central gable, enlivened by polychrome brickwork. **Antioch Presbyterian Church** (ca. 1900; 518 Shepard St.) is a simple frame building with front tower and spire, now a community center. Important in educational history is the former **State Colored Normal School** (1880s; 708 Herrington Rd.), a hip-roofed frame building that initially housed the school established in 1870 "for Freedmen and Children irrespective of color" and then the State Colored Normal School from ca. 1894 to 1912. It has been expanded over the years for various uses.

PK 5 Riverside

1890s–1960s; S side of town along the Pasquotank River, on Riverside and adjoining streets

PK 5 *Beveridge House*

The suburb along the river developed on the old Fearing plantation. Among the few houses erected in the 1890s is the **Preyer-Cropsey-Outlaw House** (1891; 1109 Riverside Ave.), a Queen Anne style residence that by 1901 had become the home of the Cropsey family. It was from this house that on Nov. 20, 1901, young Nell Cropsey vanished after a spat with a suitor and either drowned or was murdered. The subsequent sensational murder trial focused national attention on Elizabeth City. After 1900 residential subdivision proceeded under the Riverside Land Company, with architecture in bungalow and period revival styles, the latter best represented in the fine Tudor Revival style **Foreman House** (1935; 1116 Riverside Ave.). The standout of the Riverside neighborhood is the **Beveridge House** (1926; Lord Byron Perry [Elizabeth City], contractor; 1006 Riverside Ave.), a uniquely sited 1½-story, wood-shingled bungalow. Built on piers over the water, with a little bridge linking the porch to land, it was designed by a Norfolk architect (unnamed) for George and Nellie Grice Beveridge to emulate her parents' cottage at Nags Head and to satisfy George's desire to live in a houseboat—and avoid mowing grass.

PK 6 Elizabeth City State University

1910–present; Parkview Dr.

When the State Colored Normal School outgrew its home on Herrington Rd., property was acquired for a new campus at the edge of town beginning in 1903. The earliest buildings are simple red brick ones: **Lane Hall** (begun 1910, remodeled 1955) and **Symera Hall** (begun 1911). At the end of the first school year in 1913, principal Peter W. Moore marveled at the "almost undescribable" contrast between the former dilapidated wooden buildings and the "beautiful, well ventilated, modernly finished brick building," in which "the school took on new life, more dignity and self-respect." The small frame **Practice School** (1921–23) was built as a "model practice school" with assistance from the Rosenwald Foundation, which aided education for blacks throughout the South. During the 1920s and 1930s the campus grew to include several buildings in red brick Georgian Revival style. Renamed Elizabeth City State Teachers College in 1939, since 1969 the school has been Elizabeth City State University. (See Introduction, Fig. 63.)

PK 7 Elizabeth City Water Plant

1926; William C. Olsen (Raleigh), engineer; 1978 annex, J. N. Pease (Charlotte), engineers; N end of Wilson St., 1100 block

PK 7 *Elizabeth City Water Plant*

The handsome facility embodies the Progressive era's civic pride in providing for health and sanitation, rendered, as the local newspaper reported, "in attractively ornamental fashion, the main building to be of Spanish architecture, flanked by huge concrete reservoirs and settling tanks . . . fronted by a small park." In keeping with the ambitions of the era, the plant reportedly had capacity for twice the city's population. Engineer Olsen was a leading designer of municipal water plants. The 160-foot-long building is symmetrically planned with a central 3-story office pavilion. Great round-arched windows light the flanking pump and filter rooms. The green tile roof complements the walls of red brick and white stucco. A 1978 annex to the east, connected by an overhead passage, matches the original. Still in use, the building is surrounded by a series of tanks and basins.

PK 8 Old Brick House

Mid-18th c.; end of SR 1345 (Brick House Lane), Elizabeth City vic.; private, no public access

PK 8 *Old Brick House*

The ancient riverside dwelling is one of the key early houses in the Albemarle region, though its legendary association with the pirate Blackbeard (d. 1718) is strictly myth. It is one of a small number of 1½-story 18th-c. houses with weatherboarded front and rear facades with brick gable ends that contain interior-end chimneys; here the brick ends are of Flemish bond with glazed headers. The house, among the finest of its time and place, follows a center-hall variation of the 3-room plan. Its spectacularly idiosyncratic Georgian woodwork, inspired by plate 74 of Batty Langley's *The Builder's Jewel* (1746), was removed to a house in Delaware in the 1930s.

North of Elizabeth City

PK 9 Hinton-Morgan House

1826 (date brick); N side SR 1416, 100 yds. E of US 17/158, Morgans Corner; private, visible from road

The beautifully detailed frame house is one of the finest of several pediment-front houses built in the Federal era near the Virginia border. The main pediment and the entrance portico are outlined by dentil and modillion cornices that, like the large fanlight, recall *Elmwood in Gates Co. and *Mulberry Hill in Chowan Co. Typical of this house form, the plan has a transverse

PK 9 *Hinton-Morgan House*

stair hall across the front and two large parlors behind. The house was built for planter William Smith Hinton and his wife, Mary, shortly before his death in 1827.

PK 10 Mount Carmel Baptist Church

Ca. 1910, late 1940s; N side US 158, 2.3 mi. W of US 17, Morgans Corner vic.

Built for the oldest rural black congregation in the county, which was begun in 1861 as Harvey's Chapel and met in a brush arbor, the prominent church with its pair of contrasting towers was constructed in frame in the early 20th c. After World War II it was neatly veneered in brick, retaining the original form.

South of Elizabeth City

PK 11 Pitts Chapel A.M.E. Zion Church and School

1890, ca. 1880; both sides SR 1169, 0.8 mi. SW of NC 34, Elizabeth City vic.

The pair of rural institutional buildings served as a focus of community life. On the

northwestern side of the road, the symmetrical frame church with lancet windows and central entrance tower was built in 1890, successor to a church erected on land that C. W. Hollowell of *Bay Side donated in 1870 to the African Methodist Episcopal Church. Across the road, the gable-fronted frame schoolhouse with its delicate gable ornament was erected about 1880 for black children. A portion of the former Brothers School was appended to it in 1923.

PK 12 Bay Side

1856; E side NC 34, 1.4 mi. S of SR 1169, Elizabeth City vic.; private, visible from road

The big Greek Revival plantation house is the grandest of its era in the county. The symmetrical house with double-pile plan features robust woodwork in the spirit of Asher Benjamin's *Practical House Carpenter* (1830). The Doric-order porch was rebuilt in the 1910s. Planter Christopher W. Hollowell, who had the house built about the time of his marriage to Alpine Bodine, had come from Perquimans Co. in the 1840s to manage the plantations of James C. Johnston of *Hayes near Edenton and John Hollowell, a cousin, who left him land and slaves in 1855. From this Hollowell built up a plantation of some 2,000 acres, where he practiced scientific farming.

PK 13 Blimp Hangar (U.S.N. "Lighter Than Air" Airship Dock)

1941–42; end of SR 1126, 1.1 mi. E of NC 34, Weeksville vic.; private, visible from road

A spectacular and memorable sight, the huge metal blimp hangar from World War II looms 300 feet above the flat countryside. Its scale is inestimable except by comparison with normal-sized objects. This hangar was one of a pair built here, part of a series of Naval Air Stations erected along the Pacific and Atlantic coasts to house the surveillance blimps that the U.S. Navy deployed as a network of submarine patrols to warn against enemy submarines offshore. The navy chose the site on the Pasquotank River for its proximity to the Outer Banks, where U-boats were wreaking havoc on shipping.

PK 13 *Blimp Hangar*

The great rounded, metal-clad **Dock Number One**, 960 feet long, was designed with curved "clamshell" folding doors at each end. Until it was destroyed by fire in 1995, Dock Number Two stood nearby, 1,048 feet long, with full-height sliding doors between great concrete pylons and a wood truss system—Douglas fir was used because of wartime steel shortages—believed to be the largest in the world. Construction of the two docks was completed in just nine months at a cost of $11 million. Vestiges of the original landing areas survive. Dock One is now owned by a private business.

PK 14 Weeksville

Known as Newbegun (Newbeggin) Creek from the 1770s until it was renamed for a local family in the 1890s, the community around the creek includes a grouping of 19th- and early 20th-c. frame buildings from its years as a rural trading and manufacturing center. In "Old Weeksville" at the western end is the **Newbegun Methodist Church** (1827; SR 1100), the best preserved of several large, gable-fronted frame churches built by county Methodists during the revival movement of the early 19th c. Alterations in the 1920s shifted the entrance from front to side. One of the oldest houses, the **Knox-Davis-Sherlock House** (1820s; SR 1100) repeats the locally popular side-passage plan with a pair of double-shouldered chimneys and a 2-tier front porch. Recalling the mercantile growth of "New Weeksville" in the late 19th c., the **John H. Sawyer House** (ca. 1892; NC 34), built for a leading merchant, combines the familiar gable-fronted, side-passage main block into a stylishly asymmetrical composition with decorated porch and corner pavilion. The **Weeksville Ginning Company** (ca. 1908; NC 34) at the creek is the last of a breed once essential to the economy, a plain, weatherboarded building that stands alongside a gable-fronted country store with 2-tier porch.

PK 15 Shannonhouse House

1836; 1992, Shurley Vann, architect; SW corner SR 1118 and SR 1103, Weeksville vic.; private, visible from road

Visible across the open fields, the big plantation house of transitional Federal–Greek Revival style is the most elaborate of several side-passage-plan plantation houses in the area. Double-shouldered chimneys in common-bond brick serve two large parlors on the eastern side. The house was built for Robert and Mary Whedbee Shannonhouse on land he acquired in 1835 from the Markham family, who had held it since the 1680s. After a long period of vacancy, the house has been restored by a Markham descendant and gained a large rear addition with late 20th-c. amenities.

PK 16 Nixonton

Only fragments remain of the important Quaker settlement that flourished at the

Little River landing in the early and mid-18th c. Here stood the Lane House cited by Thomas Waterman in *The Early Architecture of North Carolina* (1947) as an early example of the 3-room plan promoted by William Penn. Its paneling was removed in the 1940s and installed in the Wilson Library at UNC in Chapel Hill. The most visible early house is the **Pendleton-Morris House** (late 18th c.; mid-, late 19th c.; NE side SR 1140, 0.1 mi. NW of SR 1100), a small, gambrel-roofed dwelling with a side passage and rear shed rooms, plus a 2-story gabled addition to the side.

PK 14 *Weeksville*

Perquimans County (PQ)

See Dru Gatewood Haley and Raymond A. Winslow, The Historic Architecture of Perquimans County, North Carolina *(1982).*

PQ 1 Hertford

The pleasant town beside the Perquimans River is the seat of a county settled in the late 17th c. by immigrants from England, northern colonies, and Virginia, including a large number of Quakers. The county was formed by 1679 as Berkeley precinct and subsequently named after the Indians in the vicinity—spelled Pequaimings, Wiquemans, and Paquinous on 17th-c. maps. Hertford, incorporated in 1758, honored Gov. Arthur Dobbs's patron, the Earl of Hertford. Market and Church Sts. are the principal arteries, and other street names such as Hyde Park, Covent Garden, and Grubb St. bespeak London influence. Located on a point projecting into the river where the stream suddenly broadens, the town is seen to best advantage when approached from the north on US 17 BUS on the **S-Shaped Bridge**. This 1928 concrete bridge, which is interrupted by a pivoting Warren steel truss to permit boat traffic, occupies the site of bridges since the late 18th c. and offers an excellent river view.

PQ 1 *S-Shaped Bridge, Hertford*

The **Perquimans County Courthouse** (1823–25; John Gatling, builder; 1832; 1890s; early 20th c.; Church St.) stands on its green at the town center. Praised by a local citizen in 1824 as a "fine large Brick court house the Majestick appearance of which when it is finish [*sic*] will add a considerable degree of Splendor to Hertford," the 2-story brick

building replaced an early 18th-c. frame structure. The symmetrical, austere courthouse is one of only three Federal period courthouses surviving in the state; the others stand in Gates and Beaufort counties. A simplification of the Palladian format with a pediment over the central three bays, the building has brick walls laid in Flemish bond, fanlights over the entrance and in the pediment, and a small (ca. 1832) classical porch. Additions and changes were made in the late 19th and early 20th centuries.

PQ 1 *Perquimans County Courthouse*

In the **Commercial District** opposite the courthouse, a row of 2-story brick storefronts enriched with corbel tables and quoins maintains a character established between 1895 and 1920. Churches embody various styles and eras. The **Church of the Holy Trinity** (1849–50; tower, 1894, T. W. Watson [Elizabeth City], contractor; 207 Church St.) recalls antebellum Episcopalians' use of simplified Gothic Revival forms. In 1894 Watson expanded it with a belltower, narthex, and other enrichments. **Hertford Baptist Church** (ca. 1854, 1900, 1923; 124–26 W. Market St.), built for a congregation formed in 1854, began as the large, brick sanctuary with Italianate, round-arched windows and bracket cornice, then gained a classical portico in the 1920s. **Hertford Methodist Church** (1901; Hill C.

Linthicum [Durham], architect and builder; 201 W. Market St.) typifies the denomination's sturdy brick churches of the turn of the century, with a crenellated corner tower, auditorium plan, and Gothic Revival details.

Hertford's tree-lined streets preserve a village feeling, punctuated by well-preserved 19th-c. houses, mostly of frame and painted white, many with side-passage plans. There are nearly a dozen 2-story antebellum houses with engaged double-tier porches, a common Albemarle type. Among the most prominent of these are the **Edward Wood House** (ca. 1818, 1829; 208 N. Church St.), home of a tavern owner and clerk of court; the **Lewis H. Richardson House** (ca. 1851; 310 N. Church St.), built for a prosperous blacksmith; the **Alfred Moore House** (ca. 1825; 119 W. Market St.), home of a local merchant; and the **Creecy-Skinner-Whedbee House** (early 19th c.; 101 Punch Alley).

PQ 1 *Creecy-Skinner-Whedbee House*

Popular styles of later eras appear in large and small dwellings. The Queen Anne style **Penelope McMullan House** (ca. 1900; attributed to Hill C. Linthicum [Durham], architect; 308 N. Church St.); the Queen Anne–Colonial Revival style **Lewis Norman House** (1894; 132 W. Market St.); and the Southern Colonial style **Thomas Nixon House** (1917; 314 N. Church St.) typify the major turn-of-the-century residences.

In the 17th c. Quakers settled in Perquimans Co., established farms, and formed the first religious organizations in N.C., making the county an important center of the Quaker faith. Although Quakers held slaves in the colonial period, the Society of Friends discouraged the practice after 1776, leading many local Quakers to depart for free states in the early 19th c. Many of their farms were purchased by slaveholding planters, including some former Quakers, and landholding grew more consolidated. All but one of the Perquimans meetings closed. South of Hertford, two peninsulas, created by rivers opening into the Albemarle Sound, were sites of the earliest settlements, and the names at their ends, "Harvey's Neck" and "Durant's Neck," recall early colonial landowners. The latter was named for George Durant, whose 1661 deed recording acquisition of a tract from Kilcocanen, chief of the Yeopim Indians, is the oldest land title recorded in N.C. Along rural roads the traveler may see, usually at a distance, some of the state's oldest buildings—small, gable- or gambrel-roofed frame farmhouses. Also evident is the 19th-c. emergence of larger dwellings with double porches. Many early farm buildings, including barns, dairies, smokehouses, and sheds, survive along with later tenant houses and small country churches.

PQ 2 John O. White House

1890s; Mr. Hudgins, attributed carpenter; W corner US 17 BYP-BUS fork, Hertford vic.; private, visible from road

PQ 2 *John O. White House*

This prominently located house exemplifies a perennial 19th-c. farmhouse type, the 5-bay I-house with center-passage plan and rear ell, here with the front cross-gable roofline and elaborate porch trim that give it a fashionable demeanor. It was built for John O. White shortly after he purchased the farm in 1891, and family tradition attributes its construction to a black carpenter named Hudgins. Whitewashed fences complement a full set of outbuildings.

PQ 3 Newbold-White House

Ca. 1730; NE side SR 1336, 1.3 mi. SE of US 17 BYP, Hertford vic.; open regular hours

The compact, glittering brick house epitomizes the first generation of long-lasting architecture in the Albemarle and Chesapeake regions. (See Introduction, Fig. 12.) British colonists built in ways that adapted forms derived from postmedieval English traditions to accommodate New World conditions. The steep, parapeted gable roof, tiny arched windows, hall-parlor plan, and vividly patterned Flemish-bond brick walls with glazed headers recall the early English Renaissance tradition not yet transformed by the Georgian classicism of Christopher Wren and James Gibbs.

Located near the Perquimans River in the heart of the old Quaker settlement, the property was granted to Joseph Scott in 1684 and passed through several hands before the farm, known as "Vineyard," was bought in 1727 by Abraham Sanders. After Sanders's death in 1751, the place stayed in the family into the mid-19th c., but it has been named for later owners. The construction date of the house has been variously estimated from 1684 to the 1730s; however, recent dendrochronology indicates the timbers were cut in 1730, thus placing its construction early in the occupancy of Abraham and Judith Pricklove Sanders. (Archaeological evidence parallels this dating and also indicates 17th-c. post-hole structures elsewhere on the property.) Abraham was a Quaker who had come from Virginia ca. 1715 and in 1716 married Judith, probably the granddaughter of Samuel Pricklove, a Quaker leader and one of the county's first settlers. With a small number of slaves the Sanderses worked the 633-acre farm, which produced wheat, corn, and other provisions. Over the years the brick house was altered—including insertion of a partition to create a center-passage plan—but its basic structure remained intact. Details of the extensive 1970s restoration, including the reconstructed first-floor interiors, were based on early Chesapeake precedents. Interior finish in the upper chambers is largely original. Nearby is the **David Newby House**, an early 19th-c. frame house moved from across the river and restored as a caretaker's house.

PQ 4 Isaac White House

Late 18th c., early 19th c.; SE side SR 1339, just SW of SR 1347, Bethel vic.; private, visible from road

PQ 4 *Isaac White House*

The house probably began in the 18th c. as a 2-room, 1½-story dwelling, and like many in the area it was enlarged in the early 19th c. to create a 2-story house with 2-tier engaged porch. The English-bond chimney on the western end is unusually massive with steep shoulders. Frame outbuildings include a dairy, a smokehouse, and the originally detached kitchen now connected to the house. The oldest part of the house may have been built for Thomas Long, who held the property from 1729 to 1773, or for William White, a Quaker leader, who bought it in 1786. His son Isaac White owned the farm by 1794 and may have raised the house to 2 stories. The farm has remained in the White family.

PQ 5 Myers-White House

Mid-18th c.; S side SR 1347, 0.8 mi. SE of SR 1339, Bethel vic.; private, visible at distance from road

The combination of the gambrel-roof form with brick ends is found in only two houses

in the state, this and the *King-Bazemore House in Bertie Co. The English-bond brickwork and T-stack chimneys with steep, herringbone-patterned shoulders recall contemporary Virginia masonry practices. The hall-parlor-plan house was evidently built for Thomas Long Jr., who inherited his father's land in 1721, acquired an adjoining farm in 1730, and died in 1781.

PQ 6 Richard Pratt House

Late 18th c., early 19th c.; NW side SR 1339, 0.2 mi. NE of SR 1340, Bethel vic.; private, visible from road; B&B

The 2-story house with shed porch, hall-parlor plan, and Georgian finish was moved here in 1974 and restored. The oldest part of the house was built for Pratt, a brickmason and farmer who operated a sawmill and gristmill. Several early outbuildings, collected from the region and moved here, display a variety of construction methods and building types now increasingly rare. Most unusual is the "lock room" from the Edward Blount Skinner Plantation, a tiny, frame building constructed with tightly spaced studs and a small window with iron crossbars. There are also a dovetailed plank smokehouse and a small, weatherboarded dairy structure.

PQ 7 John McNider House

Ca. 1800; E side SR 1340, 0.9 mi. N of SR 1339, Bethel vic.; private, visible from road

An exemplary version of the house type dominant in the landscape from the late 18th c. to the early 20th, and from the coast to the Blue Ridge. Sometimes called the "Carolina I-house," it is a 2-story gable-roofed frame dwelling, one room deep with

balancing shed porch and rear shed rooms and exterior brick chimneys rising at the gable ends. Typical of the best early examples, the chimneys are in Flemish-bond brick, the finish is of restrained Federal character, and the interior follows a hall-parlor plan. A contemporary frame smokehouse and other outbuildings also survive. The house was probably built for planter McNider soon after he acquired the property in 1803. (See Introduction, Fig. 14.)

PQ 8 Thomas Nixon Plantation

Ca. 1848; S side US 17, 1.3 mi. E of US 17 BUS-BYP fork, Hertford vic.; private, visible from road

One of the most complete plantation complexes in the county, with cedar-lined drive leading to a picket fence. Planter Thomas Nixon received the property from his father, Francis, member of an old Quaker family in the county. Dependencies include a smokehouse and a dairy, a large antebellum grain barn and livestock barn, and a windmill. The frame dwelling features a 2-story engaged front porch that was altered under the Mount Vernon mystique with the removal of the upper floor. A double-tier porch survives along the rear ell.

PQ 9 Francis Nixon House

Early 19th c.; S side SR 1300, 0.5 mi. E of US 17 BYP, Old Neck; private, visible from road

The 3-part, "telescope" form depicts the continued enlargement of an early dwelling to meet a family's changing needs. The earliest portion is the 1½-story coastal cottage nearest the road. Simple Federal style detail characterizes the two additions of successively taller, 2-story, gable-roofed form. All three sections were built for Francis Nixon, who inherited the property from his father, Samuel, a planter and former Quaker who was disowned by the meeting over the issue of slaveholding. The place has remained in the family.

PQ 10 William Jones House

Early 19th c., mid-19th c.; S side SR 1301, 0.2 mi. E of SR 1300, Old Neck; private, visible from road

A center-hall plan Federal period dwelling was enlarged in the Greek Revival era to form a T-plan plantation house with 2-story piazzas. The tall-columned front portico is unusual and probably shares a builder with *Cove Grove.

PQ 11 Fletcher-Skinner House

Ca. 1814–20; N side SR 1301, 0.4 mi. E of SR 1300, Old Neck; private, visible from road; B&B

PQ 11 *Fletcher-Skinner House*

The prominently sited plantation house features a 2-tier engaged porch with chamfered posts across the 5-bay front. The house is two rooms deep with a center passage. The front two chimneys, evidently the earliest, are built of Flemish-bond brick with double shoulders; the rear ones are of 1:5 common bond with single shoulders. The Federal period interior work is quite fine. The notable early and mid-19th-c. outbuildings include an unusual stuccoed brick dairy (ca. 1820; see Introduction, Fig. 19), a frame smokehouse, and a large frame barn. The house was built for William and Sarah Nixon Fletcher, members of Quaker families long established in the county. William Fletcher

(d. 1827) was one of the first North Carolinians to provide in his will for his slaves to be freed and transported to Liberia, Haiti, or another free state of their choice. After his death, the 391-acre plantation was owned by members of the prominent Skinner family, a family that had been among the earliest Quaker settlers in Perquimans but had become Baptists, Presbyterians, and Episcopalians by the 19th c. James Leigh Skinner, son of Benjamin and Elizabeth Leigh Skinner of *Cove Grove, owner from 1849 to 1897, expanded the plantation to more than 700 acres and built one of the largest (60 by 55 feet) frame barns in the county about 1860.

PQ 12 Cove Grove

Ca. 1830; SW side SR 1301 opp. SR 1302; private, visible from road

With *Land's End and others, the columned frame plantation house is a member of an important group of houses related by architectural features and family connections. Its great scale, elaborate detail, and dramatic multislope gable roof extending over broad porticoes create a house of great presence. The Ionic portico is one of the state's few antebellum examples of a 2-story porch without an intervening gallery; the rear porch repeats the Ionic order but has two tiers. The double-pile plan has a central passage divided by a transverse arch, echoing the fanlit entrance. The finish combines Federal and Greek Revival motifs. The house was built for planter Benjamin Skinner and his wife, Elizabeth Leigh, daughter of James Leigh of *Land's End. Leigh may have been involved in construction.

PQ 12 *Cove Grove*

PQ 13 Sutton-Newby House

Early to mid-18th c.; private, no public access or visibility

One of the region's small group of 18th-c. frame houses with brick ends. The surviving brick end features glazed header patterns similar to work at the *Newbold-White House. Joseph Sutton I patented the house site in 1713, but the house was probably built for his son Joseph Sutton II, who inherited the farm in 1724 and gave it to his son in 1765.

PQ 14 James Whedbee House

Ca. 1790; end of SR 1316, N side SR 1300, 3.1 mi. SE of SR 1303; private, visible from road

A well-kept example of the traditional 2-story house with shed porch, here with double-shouldered chimneys of Flemish bond. The unusual arrangement of five bays on the first floor and three on the second is a local pattern.

PQ 15 Land's End

1830–37; W side SR 1300, 11.6 mi. SE of SR 1303; private, visible from road

PQ 15 *Land's End*

The flat landscape of Durant's Neck provides a dramatic setting for one of coastal N.C.'s most spectacular houses. The regional form of the two-tier piazza engaged under a double-sloped roof is rendered in robust Greek Revival style, creating great front and rear porticoes with tall Tuscan columns. These emphasize the mass of the 2½-story house on a full raised basement. The entrance with Greek key trim and other Greek Revival details are taken from Asher Benjamin's *Practical House Carpenter* (1830). The

materials and execution are of first quality throughout, from the Flemish-bond brick walls to the molded stone steps and expertly rendered woodwork. As at *Cove Grove, a spacious double-pile plan has a central passage with transverse arch framing the stair. Outbuildings include a dairy and a smokehouse, but the great antebellum frame barn has been lost. James Leigh, a son of Chowan Co. joiner Gilbert Leigh, became one of the county's wealthiest planters as well as a building contractor and evidently built this house in the 1830s.

PQ 16 Stockton

1840s; W side SR 1329, 0.5 mi. S of SR 1367, Woodville; private, visible from road

PQ 16 *Stockton*

The epitome of the stylish patternbook plate grafted onto a vernacular building tradition. The 3-part facade was probably copied from the "Design for a Country Villa" in Minard Lafever's *The Modern Builder's Guide* (1833). The full prostyle tetrastyle portico is rare in the state's domestic architecture, as are the proportions of the facade. Bookishness stops with the facade, for the interior finish is plain Greek Revival, and the irregular plan and rear elevations suggest difficult compromises. The house was built for Josiah Thomas Granberry, a planter with mercantile and fishing interests.

PQ 17 Winfall

NC 37 at SR 1218 and SR 1219

The crossroads community blossomed with the arrival of the Elizabeth City and Norfolk Railroad (later Norfolk and Southern) in 1881. Tradition traces the name to a windstorm that toppled a store at the junction. Winfall's collection of late Victorian frame buildings illustrates the period's penchant for sawn and turned work. Among them are the **J. D. White House** (ca. 1890; private), with richly embellished 2-story porch, and the highly decorative late Gothic **Epworth United Methodist Church** (1903). The commercial block has mostly frame, gable-fronted stores dominated by the **U.S. Post Office** (ca. 1890), whose origin as a combination general store and dwelling is recalled by its 2-story porch with exterior stair. West of town, **Poplar Run A.M.E. Zion Church** (1891; s side NC 37) exemplifies the frame, double-towered churches erected by many rural black congregations.

PQ 18 Belvidere
NC 37 between SR 1118 and SR 1200

Located in an especially pleasant rural area of well-tended farmsteads, this handsome village contains an unusually strong collection of ambitious frame buildings. It began as Newby's Bridge, a trading center on the upper Perquimans River associated with Quaker planter and merchant Thomas Newby's Belvidere Plantation. On the western edge of the community, Newby's house, **Belvidere** (late 18th c., N side NC 37 opp. SR 1118; private), has an unusual hip on gambrel roof, a central-passage plan, and restrained Georgian detail.

The Quaker presence associated with *Piney Woods Friends Meetinghouse led to the establishment of local academies. As the village grew, frame stores and houses clustered around the intersection of present-day

NC 37 and SR 1200. The community includes two of the best rural Queen Anne houses in the region. The **Francis H. Nicholson House** (ca. 1891; private) is dominated by a cylindrical tower with turret. At the **Elihu A. White House** (mid-1890s; private), a square central tower and a decorated porch emphasize the long, irregular volumes of the facade. There are several 2-story houses of more traditional form, some with decorated porches, and 1-story coastal cottages of various periods.

PQ 19 Piney Woods Friends Meetinghouse
1854, 1884, 1927; NE side SR 1119, 0.1 mi. N of SR 1118, Belvidere vic.

A venerable center for the Quakers important to Perquimans Co. history from the 17th c. onward, the modest frame meetinghouse began as a plain gabled structure in 1854, with partitions separating men's and women's sections. In 1927 the congregation removed the partitions, added lancet windows, and added the portico on the long side. Piney Woods became a monthly meeting in 1794 but traces its origins to a local meeting established in 1724 and a monthly meeting begun in the 1670s. As Quakers moved away from Perquimans Co. to free states, six of the county's seven congregations were discontinued, leaving only this one for several years, until *Up River Friends Meeting was formed from it in 1866. Several Belvidere Quakers took the Union side during the Civil War and were Republican leaders in the postwar period.

PQ 20 Riddick's Grove Baptist Church and Weeping Mary Burial Society
1880s, early 20th c.; E side SR 1202, 1.3 mi. N of SR 1200, Belvidere vic.

Two important rural institutions were built by black community organizations here. The simple Gothic Revival frame church was probably standing when the trustees of Riddick's Grove Baptist Church purchased the land in 1884, and it gained a front vestibule and tower some years later. Associated with the church is the **Weeping Mary

PQ 18 *Francis H. Nicholson House*

Burial Society Hall, a gabled 2-story frame building of domestic form, one of the few surviving examples of the halls built by the local societies formed to assure proper burial of their members.

PQ 21 Up River Friends Meetinghouse

1914; W side SR 1208, 0.5 mi. S of SR 1001, Nicanor vic.

Established in 1866 from *Piney Woods Monthly Meeting, Up River Meeting served the farming community in the northern portion of the county. The picturesque frame meetinghouse in its grove of trees was built in 1914 from plans from an Elizabeth City lumber mill, probably Kramer Brothers. A pedimented front pavilion is flanked by corner entrances and accented by triangular and lozenge-shaped windows.

Gates County (GA)

See Thomas R. Butchko, Forgotten Gates: The Historical Architecture of a Rural North Carolina County *(1991).*

Gates is a rural county long isolated by the Chowan River on the west and the Great Dismal Swamp on the east. Swamplands still occupy much of the county, including Merchants Mill Pond State Park. Drainage ditches thread through the broad, flat farmland. With little industrialization except lumbering, Gates Co. has maintained an agrarian economy of small and medium-sized farms, which compose one of the most satisfying and unspoiled rural landscapes in the tidewater. The sites noted here are but a sampling along principal routes. Many of the county's roads are lined with broad fields, crossroads villages, country churches, and working farmsteads of many eras. A high proportion of the old farmsteads stand near the road and retain traditional as well as modern outbuildings of many types, from antebellum kitchens, smokehouses, dairies, and barns to big 20th-c. metal equipment sheds and storage bins.

GA 1 Gatesville

GA 1 *Old Gates County Courthouse*

Gatesville is a quiet courthouse town with well-kept frame buildings and shaded green spaces. First called Bennett's Creek Landing, the community became Gates Court House when the county was formed in 1779 and named for Gen. Horatio Gates, who had defeated Burgoyne at Saratoga in 1777. In 1830 it was incorporated as Gatesville. The principal edifice is the **Old Gates County Courthouse** (1836; John B. Baker, contractor; expanded 1904; N side Court St.; open regular hours as public library). One of three surviving Federal style courthouses in the state (cf. Beaufort Co. and Perquimans Co.), the austere 2-story brick building repeats an essentially domestic building form, dignified by a central entrance pavilion with a large fanlight. It illustrates the persistence of the Fed-

eral style during the ascendancy of the Greek Revival.

Among Gatesville's most appealing features are the 1-story, 1-room frame stores built ca. 1880 near the courthouse—a type once common but now seldom seen. Their decorated gable fronts feature broad windows flanking recessed doors, framed by bracketed cornices and pilasters: the **Parker Store** and the **Rufus Riddick Store** (s and N sides Court St.) and the **Cowper Eason Store** (Main St. at Court St.). Dating from the early 20th c. are the **Bank of Gates** (ca. 1904; Court St.), a narrow, 2-story brick block with corbeled decoration, and the **Gatesville Baptist Church** (1916–17; Court St.), a small, Gothic Revival brick church with crenellated corner tower and auditorium plan.

Main St. is lined by frame houses in a conservative sequence from Federal to Greek Revival, Queen Anne, and Colonial Revival themes. Probably the oldest is the **Lemuel P. Hayes House** (early 19th c.; E side Main St., N of Court St.), a simply finished, 2-story, side-passage dwelling with original shed rooms. Several late 19th-c. houses feature lavish sawn porch ornament, and some incorporate earlier dwellings. Two Queen Anne style frame houses with high hip roofs, gabled bays, and wraparound porches exemplify the far-flung use of Sears, Roebuck, and Company prefab houses, here "The Clyde" model: the **Adolphus Pilston Godwin House** (1911; High St.), documented by the contractor's agreement, and the **William R. Cowper House** (1908; Main St.), which reverses the plan. Gatesville also retains an important collection of frame domestic outbuildings in yards—smokehouses, sheds, stables, and the like.

GA 2 Reid's Grove School

1927–28; E side NC 37, at N town limit of Gatesville; open business hours

GA 2 *Reid's Grove School*

Built with financial assistance and standard plans provided by the Julius Rosenwald Foundation, Reid's Grove typifies Rosenwald designs for efficient, well-lighted schoolhouses. This was one of seven Gates Co. schools erected as part of the foundation's program to improve public education for blacks in the South. It follows the "Type 3" two-teacher arrangement published in *Community School Plans* (1924). Two large classrooms combine into a single large space by raising overhead doors in the partition; the center front pavilion typically housed industrial education. The schoolhouse now serves as county offices.

GA 3 Harrells Methodist Church

1883; S side SR 1116, 2 mi. S of US 158 BUS, Gatesville vic.

The best-preserved 19th-c. church in the county, the beautifully proportioned, straightforward little frame structure epitomizes the longevity of the simple gable-end sanctuary in an era when more elaborate

forms were popular. Tall 9/9 sash windows—three on each side, two flanking the central entrance—light the sanctuary. The congregation began early in the 19th c., and this church was built on land given in 1883 by neighboring families. Local families maintain the church for an annual May homecoming and special services.

GA 4 Ballards Grove Missionary Baptist Church

Ca. 1890, 1916; S side NC 137, 3.8 mi. W of NC 37, Gatesville vic.

The frame country church embodies the simplified Gothic Revival style, with plain lancet openings and a slightly later corner tower. It is one of the best preserved of several late 19th-c. churches built for black congregations in the county. The land was given in 1890 by two neighboring landowners, the Eures and the Ballards, and named for the latter, a black farming family. Nearby stands the **Ballard-Eure-Mullen House** (ca. 1850, 1920s), a big L-shaped frame house seven bays wide, with an early 20th-c. porch replacing an original Greek Revival portico. It was built for Richard and Mary Ballard, among the largest antebellum planter families in the county. Later it was the home of Nathaniel Eure, who gave the land for the church and became a leading merchant in nearby *Eure.

GA 5 Eure

NC 137, 1.8 mi. E of US 13/158

GA 5 *Streetscape, Eure*

Begun in the late 1880s (inc. 1915), the picturesque whistle-stop at a bend in the road is one of scores of villages whose birth, life, and decline were tied to the railroad.

Nathaniel and Adminta Baker Eure moved here from Ballards Crossroads about the time of the arrival of the Chowan and Southern Railroad (later a branch of the Atlantic Coast Line) in 1886. Nathaniel opened a general store and soon became postmaster of the village, which was named after him. The tracks were pulled up in 1981, but a cluster of stores and substantial frame houses recalls Eure's railroad heyday. **Charlie Sawyer's Store** (1927; Dick Hofler, builder) a 1-story, 3-part brick store, and **Jack Harrell's Store** (early 20th c.), a gable-end frame store, stand at the crossroads, both featuring arched canopies added in 1947, when they were moved back when the road was upgraded. The **Nathaniel Eure House** (ca. 1890; N side NC 137), with its ornate 2-story entrance porch, and the **J. Paul Hale House** (ca. 1911; N side NC 137), an L-shaped house with 2-tier porch, built for a local blacksmith, are the most striking of several frame houses. Among the Eure family homesteads in the neighborhood is the **Henry A. Eure House** (1860s, 1914; SR 1114), childhood home of Thaddeus "Thad" Eure, who served as N.C. secretary of state from 1936 to 1988 and called himself "the oldest rat in the Democratic barn."

GA 6 Story Farmstead

Mid-19th–early 20th c.; W side US 13/158, opp. NC 137, Storys; private, visible from road

The extensive rural agricultural and industrial complex of some twenty buildings centers on a 2-story Italianate house with bracketed double porch built for James and Frances Cross Story in 1887. Near the house are two smokehouses, a washhouse, an icehouse, and a potato house. A little distance north stand a newer dwelling, an implement shelter, a mule and horse stable, a corn barn, and a 3-story cow barn with silo built in 1916 by carpenter Walter J. Felton. Over the years the Story family operation grew to include a steam-powered planing mill, a saw and grist mill, and a water-powered cotton gin. Two sons built and operated a small steamboat, the *Tadpole*, on the nearby Chowan River. The farmstead, still in the family, suggests the complexity of many rural family operations now lost or radically reduced.

GA 7 Roduco Depot

Ca. 1900; SR 1224, just N of US 158, Roduco

Bereft of its track, the picturesque frame depot retains its characteristic board-and-batten walls, angular brackets, and contrasting trim. The only remaining depot in the county, it was the focus of a village on the Atlantic Coast Line, with several neatly trimmed I-houses and bungalows. Originally Greene's Siding, it was renamed in 1905 after the local Roberts Drug Company. In the 1930s six regularly scheduled passenger trains plus two locals chugged through Roduco.

GA 8 Lassiter Riddick House

1851; N side US 158 BYP, 0.6 mi. E of NC 37; private, visible from road

GA 8 *Lassiter Riddick House*

This is among the most visible of the county's many farmsteads with barns and trees gathered around a substantial farmhouse. The frame I-house displays a local variation on the hall-parlor plan: two adjoining front doors open to a pair of main rooms sharing an enclosed central stair. Detail is simple Greek Revival work. Following a prevalent local pattern, the rear ell is an earlier (ca. 1810) house 2 stories tall with a 1-room plan. The 19th-c. farm buildings include a 2-room frame dairy and brandy house, a smokehouse, and a grain barn. In the antebellum period this was the 510-acre farm of Lassiter and M. Jane Riddick. With thirty-four slaves in 1860 the farm produced a variety of grains and livestock.

GA 9 Buckland

1795; W side NC 37, 2.7 mi. N of US 158 BYP, Buckland; private, visible from road

The massive frame plantation house is an anomaly in the generally unpretentious architecture of the county. It is one of the state's earliest examples of the full-blown Georgian form, 2 stories high with a center-passage plan and four big rooms on each floor. Despite removal of its interiors, its great scale and four tall chimneys make it a powerful presence in the landscape. The modillion cornice and Flemish-bond brickwork of the double-shouldered chimneys (one dated 1795) attest to the quality of its workmanship. It was built for William Baker, a planter who owned some 3,000 acres and 108 slaves by 1805. In 1778 legislator Baker had introduced the bill to create Gates Co. Since 1847 Buckland has been in the Smith family.

GA 10 Pipkin-Savage Farm

Ca. 1800, ca. 1830, ca. 1850; NE corner US 13 and SR 1202, Gates vic.; private, visible from road

Like many in the county, the well-kept and prominent farm complex reflects several building campaigns during the 19th c. The 5-bay frame farmhouse with broad 2-tier porch follows a center-passage plan. It was built for Hening and Martha Pipkin Smith as an addition to a 2-story, 1-room-plan dwelling (now the rear ell), which was probably built for Martha's parents ca. 1800. By the 1850s this was part of a 1,583-acre plantation. Important 19th-c. frame outbuildings include a kitchen (ca. 1800), a smokehouse, and a large antebellum barn. To the west along SR 1202 are several more handsome farmsteads with 2-story frame farmhouses and collections of 19th-c. outbuildings.

GA 11 Thomas B. Riddick House

Late 18th c.; E side US 13, 0.3 mi. N of NC 37, Gates vic.; private, visible from road

This is the most visible of four gambrel-roofed dwellings in the county. Typical of late 18th-c. usage in the region, the gambrel half-story is so broad as to constitute almost a full second story. Also typical, the house has simple Georgian detailing and follows a hall-parlor plan with shed rooms and shed porch, with an enclosed stair rising from the shed. Its orientation was reversed (front porch and shed rooms switched) in response to the realignment of the road, present US 13, in the early 1940s.

GA 12 Joseph Freeman House

1820; Gates vic.; private, no public visibility or access

The small, late Georgian farmhouse, erected by cabinetmaker and carpenter Joseph Freeman as his own residence, exemplifies the 2-story, 1-room plan form prevalent in the county's architecture until the 1840s. The asymmetrical facade has great presence, and its craftsmanship is of the first order, with chamfered porch posts, molded window frames, and weatherboards. The rear shed rooms are original; the upper floor is divided into two chambers. Freeman, the son of Bertie Co. carpenter Solomon Freeman, came to Gates as a youth to live with relatives after his father's death.

GA 13 Freeman House (State Line House)

Late 18th c. and later; E side US 13 at N.C.-Va. line; private, visible from road; B&B

The house began ca. 1815 as a side-passage plan dwelling on the Virginia side of the state line, with a ca. 1800 1-room dwelling pulled up to it as a rear ell. In the 1830s a tier of rooms extending into N.C. created a center-passage-plan house. The position of the house—with the state line running down the center passage—created a colorful history as a site of interstate gatherings and friendly rivalries. Around 1900 its owner Edmund "Ned" Freeman, grandson of cabinetmaker Joseph Freeman, was justice of the peace in both states concurrently. His house was the scene of marriages of couples eloping from both directions. The large assem-

blage of 19th-c. outbuildings includes an antebellum stable, a barn, a wagon shelter, and
others.

GA 14 Red Oak Grove A.M.E. Church
*1882, 1899; E side SR 1300, 0.1 mi. SE of
US 13*

GA 14 *Red Oak Grove A.M.E. Church*

Crisp simplicity emphasizes the careful proportions of the small country church, where
a corner entrance tower slightly precedes the
gable-fronted nave. Its form dates from the
1899 remodeling of a simpler building of
1882. The land was provided to the congregation by neighboring property owner Edmund Freeman.

GA 15 Riddick-Whedbee Farm
*Ca. 1836, later 19th c.; W side SR 1318, 1.2 mi.
N of SR 1320; private, visible from road*

The large farm centers on a side-passage-
plan plantation house with transitional
Federal–Greek Revival finish. An unusual
brick pent links the pair of tall brick chimneys. Farm buildings are of many types
and eras: a washhouse, a dairy on stilts, a
kitchen, a smokehouse, and a commissary as
well as four tenant houses, a barn, a shed,
and more recent bins and elevators for
current operations. Known as the "Cypress
Pond" farm and containing about 580 acres
in 1860, it has been in the Whedbee family
since 1850. Across the road stands **Middle
Swamp Baptist Church** (1903), a modest

frame Gothic Revival gable-end church
built for the county's oldest Baptist congregation (1806).

GA 16 Parker Farm and Parker's Methodist Church
*Early 19th c., ca. 1840, 1911; SR 1327 at
SR 1328, Corapeake vic.; private, visible
at distance from road*

The extensive farmstead comprises several
exemplary buildings: an oft-expanded, 2-
story, hall-parlor-plan dwelling; a frame
dairy and a smokehouse; a large English-
type antebellum barn; and several big barns
and sheds of the 20th c. Jordan and Penelope Walton Parker, for whom the house
and antebellum outbuildings were constructed, had a middle-sized farm where
160 of 484 acres were improved for crops.
Parker's Methodist Church nearby on
SR 1328 is a well-kept frame country church,
with its 1813 establishment date and 1911
construction date emblazoned in stained
glass. The corner entrance tower links intersecting, gabled blocks with large, pointed-
arched windows, and the auditorium-plan
sanctuary has concentric curving pews—
a form promoted by denominational publications and seen also in *Philadelphia
Methodist Church in Sunbury. (See Introduction, Fig. 40.)

GA 17 John R. Lassiter Farm
*1880s–1890s; both sides NC 32, 0.5 mi. S of
SR 1327, Corapeake vic.; private, visible from
road*

Late in the 19th c., John and Missouri Jarvis
Lassiter expanded an older house into this
2-story, foursquare, hip-roofed farmhouse
with decorated porch. To the rear extends a
kitchen-dining ell with its own porch. The
well-kept farmstead has a series of big barns
for hay and corn and a fine stock barn
flanked by large sheds and other outbuildings, complemented by neat board fences
and mature trees. Across the road, the Las-
siters built a small frame **Tenant House**
(1890s) that enabled them to employ one
family to work on the farm. The 1-story
dwelling has a symmetrical facade and shed

porch opening into a hall-parlor plan with rear ell.

GA 18 Sunbury
US 158 at NC 32

The crossroads village begun early in the 19th c. comprises a good selection of frame architecture from the late 19th and early 20th centuries. One- and 2-story houses of various styles are unified by broad porches, white-fenced yards, and assorted outbuildings. Especially striking is the **Costen-Nixon House** (ca. 1840, ca. 1910) at the crossroads, which began as the tripartite Greek Revival house of early merchant and tavern owner James Costen. About 1910 William Nixon added a Colonial Revival front section. The domestic compound—dwelling, smokehouse, shed, washhouse, chickenhouse, and others—is defined by a picket fence, which follows a tradition of linking the outbuildings to form the enclosure.

A pair of late 19th-c. 2-story frame country stores stands north of the crossroads: the **Benton-Hill Store** and the **Harrell-Rountree & Riddick Store**, the latter still in business. **Philadelphia Methodist Church** (1911), a near twin to *Parkers Methodist Church, features broad, shingled gables on two sides linked by an inset corner tower with open belfry. Large Gothic Revival windows light an auditorium-plan sanctuary, an arrangement promoted by Methodist publications.

GA 19 Hunter-Norfleet-Cross Farm
1870–1930s; W side NC 32, 0.5 mi. S of Sunbury; private, visible from road

The extraordinarily complete ensemble illustrates the diverse farming operations of the decades after the Civil War. Farmer and merchant John F. Cross and his family developed the complex at Hunters Mill Swamp, the site of Jacob Hunter's 18th-c. farm, gristmill, and sawmill. The T-shaped house built in 1870 reused an old hall-parlor dwelling as the rear ell. Nearby stand a smokehouse and icehouse from the earlier 19th-c. farm, a latticed wellhouse, a Delco plant, and a garage. Dominating the scene is a tremendous gambrel-roofed barn built in the 1930s with a prominent hood over the opening into its vast loft. The Crosses' 2-story, gable-fronted general store faces the road. There are also warehouses and the remains of a cotton gin and sawmill as well as traces of the old Suffolk and Carolina Railroad that ran through here in the 1890s, boosting local business.

GA 20 Elmwood
Ca. 1822; W side SR 1400, 0.6 mi. N of NC 37, Gatesville vic.; private, visible from road

The elegant frame plantation house follows a side-passage plan and is graced with Federal style detail including delicate corner pilasters, a modillion cornice, and a great gable lunette with sunburst center akin to that in the *Gates County Courthouse. Tradition claims it was built for David and Sarah Hinton Parker on a plantation he inherited from his father. By 1860 with twenty-one slaves Parker was farming 700 of his 1,200 acres. To the rear is a tiny, earlier gambrel-roofed dwelling (perhaps the home of David's grandfather Jesse Parker), long used as a kitchen and dwarfed by its great chimney, from which extends an unusual brick potato house. The big antebellum frame barn has a center aisle entered from the gable end. The farm remains in the family.

GA 21 *Rountree-Blanchard Farm*

GA 21 Rountree-Blanchard Farm

1840s, 1913; both sides NC 37, 1.5 mi. N of jct.
w/NC 37/32; private, visible from road

Among the most complete of the many old farmsteads along NC 37, the 275-acre family farm typifies the middling rank of agricultural operations in the antebellum county. Seth Alphonsa and Lavinia Rountree probably built the simply finished, side-passage-plan house ca. 1844. Their descendant Elisha Alphonsa Blanchard and his wife, Lula, expanded the residence to a symmetrical, hip-roofed dwelling in 1913. The outbuildings flanking the road include a plank smokehouse, a 19th-c. frame cotton house, and a privy, washhouse, barn, stable, and other agricultural structures from the early 20th c.

GA 22 Sumner-Winslow House

1748 (date brick), 19th-c. alterations; W side
NC 32/37 at Gates/Chowan county line;
private, visible from road

At first this appears to be a mid-19th-c. frame house, but the northern brick end visible from the road reveals its mid-18th-c. origin as a 1½-story brick-ended dwelling. Here survives the 1748 brick end of Flemish bond with glazed headers and a chevron pattern delineating the steep gable roofline of the earlier house. This is a rare remnant of an important 18th-c. tradition of patterned brickwork in northeastern N.C. There were once other examples in the county, such as the 1755 Walton House, but they have been lost.

Chowan County (CO)

See Thomas R. Butchko, Edenton: An Architectural Portrait *(1992).*

Edenton (CO 1–56)

An architectural treasurehouse, the old port on Edenton Bay combines buildings of remarkable range and quality with an idyllic atmosphere of well-tended gentility. (See Introduction, Fig. 5.) The small, pedestrian-scale town of 5,400 offers an ensemble of architecture from over 250 years. Its best-known landmarks—the *Chowan County Courthouse, the *Cupola House, and *St. Paul's Episcopal Church—compose the state's most important group of English colonial buildings, but these are part of a richer whole and a more complex history than first meets the eye.

Settlement in the vicinity began as early as 1665, and St. Paul's parish was organized in 1701. In 1712 "the town on Queen Anne's Creek" was established as a courthouse. It was incorporated as Edenton in 1722 in honor of Gov. Charles Eden, and it served as metropolis and de facto capital of the colony until 1746, when the governor moved to New Bern. Situated in a sheltered bay on the Albemarle Sound, Edenton prospered as a port of entry for trade with England and the West Indies as well as headquarters of the land agent of Lord Granville, the lord proprietor who retained property rights across the northern half of the colony. Ships passed through the barrier islands at Roanoke Inlet (near present-day Nags Head), a crucial aperture for trade that, until it closed in 1795, provided relatively direct access between the Albemarle Sound and the Atlantic Ocean.

As depicted in C. J. Sauthier's map of 1769, Edenton was laid out as a grid extending north from the waterfront along the road to Virginia. Settlement concentrated near the bay, and much of the grid remained sparsely occupied for years. Attracting ambitious and talented individuals from Britain and other colonies, by the mid-18th c. Edenton bustled with merchants and lawyers, laborers and sailors, a silversmith and a wigmaker, carpenters, cabinetmakers, and bricklayers. About half the residents were slaves who worked as artisans, watermen, fishermen, laborers, and servants. By the eve of the American Revolution, the town of about 1,000 had developed a merchant-planter aristocracy with ties throughout the region.

Edenton merchants and lawyers took leading roles in N.C.'s Revolutionary and Federal period history. Merchant Joseph Hewes was a signer of the Declaration of Independence. The learned merchant and physician Hugh Williamson was a signer of the U.S. Constitution. Lawyer and planter Samuel Johnston served as governor of the young state. Lawyer James Iredell Sr. became a Federalist political leader and justice of the first U.S. Supreme Court. A 1774 resolution, signed by fifty-one women from Edenton and the Albemarle region in support of the First Provincial Congress's protest of British taxation policies, was caricatured in a London newspaper. The women's action gained fame as the "Edenton Tea Party," a mainstay of local and state patriotic lore from the late 19th c. onward.

During the Revolution, ships slipping past the British fleet into the Albemarle Sound boosted Edenton's trade so much that "the inhabitants wished peace away." Trade dwindled after the war, and two subsequent blows worsened Edenton's troubles: a 1795 storm closed the already silt-choked Roanoke Inlet, forcing seagoing trade to make the arduous journey via Ocracoke Inlet; and the *Dismal Swamp Canal, begun in 1793, diverted Albemarle area trade to Elizabeth City and Norfolk. Although local planter-entrepreneurs invested in such enterprises as rope manufacturing and large fisheries, Edenton's economy stagnated. Efforts to obtain rail connections were stymied by local

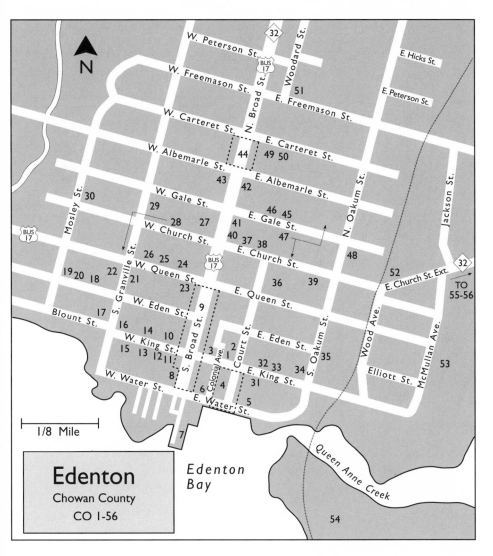

W. Peterson St.

32

BUS 17

Woodard St.

E. Hicks St.

W. Freemason St.

E. Freemason St.

51

E. Peterson St.

W. Carteret St.

N. Broad St.

E. Carteret St.

W. Albemarle St.

44

49 50

E. Albemarle St.

43

42

Mosley St.

30

W. Gale St.

29

46 45

E. Gale St.

N. Oakum St.

Jackson St.

BUS 17

28 27

W. Church St.

41

40 37 38

47

E. Church St.

48

26 25 24

S. Granville St.

19 20 18

22

21

BUS 17

W. Queen St.

23

36

39

52

E. Church St. Ext.

32

TO 55-56

Blount St.

17

W. Eden St.

9

E. Queen St.

16 14 10

S. Broad St.

W. King St.

15 13 12 11

Colonial Ave.

3

2

1

Court St.

E. Eden St.

S. Oakum St.

35

Wood Ave.

53

McMullan Ave.

8

6 4

31

32 33 34

E. King St.

Elliott St.

W. Water St.

E. Water St.

5

7

1/8 Mile

Edenton

Chowan County

CO 1-56

*Edenton
Bay*

Queen Anne Creek

54

refusal to support any route that carried trade to Virginia, coupled with insistence that "the reopening of Roanoke Inlet is the only work of Internal Improvement that will meet our wishes or answer our wants."

Antebellum Edenton remained a quiet town, where the population stood at about 1,500—roughly 60 percent black and 40 percent white—from 1790 to 1860. When *Harper's Monthly* journalist "Porte Crayon" visited in 1856, he found the town "queen-like, one might say, but in a small way." Most citizens lived in "neat, old fashioned residences," though a few new houses "would figure handsomely in the environs of

New York." Edenton was "all the prettier" for the absence of "those forests of shipping which usually mar the appearance of seaport towns."

Early in the Civil War, Edenton came under Union control in 1862, and many local families refugeed elsewhere. After the war, residents strove to rebuild the economy, improving the harbor, forming a new steamship company, and expanding fisheries into big waterfront operations. But by 1877 the population was only 1,200, down 300 from 1860.

In 1881 the town finally gained rail connections with the arrival of the Elizabeth

City and Norfolk Railroad, a link in what was to become the Norfolk Southern system. The waterfront was transformed into a railyard, with a 750-foot pier accommodating the *John W. Garrett*, a vessel that carried twenty-seven rail cars on three parallel tracks across the Albemarle Sound to and from Plymouth. Tons of local fish, vegetables, cotton, grain, and forest products went out, and general merchandise came in. Industrial development followed apace, boosted by the local *Fisherman and Farmer*, as first newcomers and then established families invested in manufacturing. In the 1880s, big sawmills were built along the waterfront, including the Branning Manufacturing Company's saw and planing mill. In 1898 local investors formed the *Edenton Cotton Mill, followed by the *Edenton Peanut Company in 1909, both near the railroad at the eastern edge of town.

Between 1880 and 1900 the population more than doubled—from 1,200 to 3,000. The commercial district was quickly rebuilt after a fire in 1893. New houses, churches, and schools filled out the old grid, and old buildings were replaced, renovated, or expanded. An array of local millwork celebrated the potential of the industrial age of building. For a time settlement patterns continued the scattered racial distribution of the antebellum era, but from the 1890s onward, working people's housing and black neighborhoods coalesced on the edges of the grid, especially on the east near the railroad and factories. In the early 20th c., as the town grew to some 3,500 people, the first expansion beyond the old plan produced modest suburbs.

Amid the national and regional interest in patriotic and historical pursuits, late 19th-early 20th-c. Edentonians led in celebrating colonial heritage, from the Lost Colony on Roanoke Island to the Edenton Tea Party. Historic preservation began early with the rescue of the ancient *Cupola House in 1918. In 1927 completion of a bridge across the Chowan River provided a new link to the rest of the state. Beginning in 1940, Edenton's colonial image gained cachet from the best-selling historical novels of Inglis Fletcher, who set several colonial sagas in the Edenton area and for a time lived at nearby Bandon Plantation. During the late 20th c., growth has been gradual, and the economy has remained diverse. Most vestiges of the waterfront railyard and manufacturing have disappeared, as Edenton burnished its image as a colonial capital.

As a result of Edenton's early prominence and subsequent stability, the scale and density of its architectural townscape remain remarkably intact. The proximity of waterfront, institutional, commercial, and residential uses continues long-standing town patterns, where dwelling and working are but a few steps apart. Blocks contain a lively mix of periods, with colonial buildings standing alongside late 19th and early 20th-c. structures.

In the 18th c., modest, gambrel-roofed, frame dwellings and a few gable-roofed houses, typically with side-passage or hall-parlor plans, were common; several survive as cores of later enlargements. With a few spectacular exceptions, architecture of the 19th and 20th centuries exemplifies conservative renditions of popular national styles. Side-passage plans continued in use from Federal townhouses to the 2-story, front-gabled form seen in late 19th and early 20th-c. dwellings. Throughout the town, and especially in the neighborhoods on the edges and northwestern and northeastern quadrants of the old grid, many small, traditional houses still stand, some with 1- and 2-room plans, built from the late 18th into the early 20th c. for artisans, entrepreneurs, and laborers. Unifying the town's domestic architecture over time is the perennially popular piazza, particularly the double piazza, rendered in a variety of treatments from simple classicism to exuberant Victorian millwork.

Identities of an unusual number of Edenton's builders are known. Mid-18th-c. house carpenter Gilbert Leigh is the earliest with a corpus of surviving work. English-born architect-carpenter William Nichols practiced in Edenton from 1806 to 1817, then went on to become state architect in N.C., Alabama, and Mississippi. In the post–Civil War era, several black house carpenters—including Hannibal Badham Sr. and Jr., John Page, Kellis Murphy, and Joseph and Robert Price (father and son)—took prominent roles. In the late 1880s, Theo Ralph, a white builder from Pasquotank Co., dominated local building, working in Italianate and Queen Anne styles. He was succeeded by German-born builder Frank Fred Muth, who arrived in 1905 from Atlantic City, N.J., and excelled in the Colonial Revival style. The industrial era pulled in out-of-town architects, such as mail-order architect George F. Barber of Knoxville, church specialist J. M. Mc-Michael of Charlotte, and Colonial Revival devotees Charles C. and Frank Benton of Wilson. Post–World War II work drew on the Standard Homes Company of Raleigh (whose house design book was available at the Edenton Building and Loan Association), and Williamsburg-influenced architects J. Everette Fauber Jr. of Lynchburg, Va., and Jack Pruden of Edenton.

The spine of the town is Broad St., which begins with the commercial district near the waterfront and proceeds north as a residential avenue. Flanking it are grid-plan neighborhoods. Generally, the oldest and grandest buildings predominate in the earliest settled southwestern and southeastern quadrants between the waterfront and Church St. Remarkably intact middle- and working-class neighborhoods from the industrial era concentrate in the northwestern and northeastern sections of the grid. The town retains such a great concentration of historic architecture from every era that only a small selection can be cited here.

Courthouse Green area

CO 1 Chowan County Courthouse

Begun 1767; attributed to John Hawks; E. King St., head of Courthouse Green; National Historic Landmark; open to public (from visitors' center)

One of the finest Georgian public buildings in the southern colonies, the courthouse combines serenely confident proportions and excellent craftsmanship in a superb setting overlooking the Courthouse Green and Edenton Bay. The symmetrical form with central pedimented pavilion recalls English patternbooks of James Gibbs and others. Its

CO 1 *Chowan County Courthouse*

similarity to the contemporary *Tryon Palace in New Bern has suggested English architect John Hawks as possible designer, but there is no construction documentation. Walls are of brick laid in Flemish bond above an English-bond water table.

Carrying out the spatial relationships expressed by the exterior, the first-floor courtroom occupies the full depth of the 3-bay pavilion. The front entrance opens directly into the large chamber, facing the paneled, curved apse at the rear, which contains the curved judges' platform dominated by the magnificent chief magistrate's chair. The floor is paved with stone. The unfluted Doric columns were installed in the antebellum period. The great assembly room above the courtroom—measuring 30 by 45 feet, with 13-foot ceilings—is said to have been the largest fully paneled room in colonial America. It has simply framed fireplaces on east and west walls, and tall raised panels below and above a robust chair board. Flanking bays contain the simple turned stair on the west and offices on the east. The courthouse served its original function until the 1978–79 construction of a new courthouse on Broad St.

CO 2 Chowan County Jail

1825; Ebenezer Paine, contractor; S. Court St., N of courthouse

The austere brick building is among the oldest jails in the state. Although architect John Hawks drew plans for a 2-story brick prison in 1773, and another plan was obtained in 1786, these remained unbuilt. A wooden jail was built by William Nichols ca. 1810. After it burned in 1824, the present structure, of brick laid in English bond, was built at a cost of nearly $4,000. Next to the jail stands the simplified Italianate style brick **Jailer's Residence** (1905; M. B. Brown Company, contractors; 115 E. King St.).

CO 3 Leary Law Office
Ca. 1882; 105 E. King St.

The little 1-story, gable-fronted brick office, its pediment adorned with brackets, was built for attorney William L. Leary. It is one of several late 19th-c. office and commercial buildings near the courthouse, such as the small brick building across the street that began as the first **Bank of Edenton** (1895; 106 E. King St.) and the 2-story **Wood Building** (1890s; 114–16 E. King St.), built at the rear of the *Homestead property for law offices.

CO 4 Courthouse Green

The rectangular green stretching from the courthouse to the waterfront was laid out as public land in 1718. A drill ground during the Revolution, by the late 19th c. it had diagonal paths crossing at a cast-iron fountain. In 1904 a Confederate memorial was placed at the northern end; but in 1961 that was moved to the southern end of Broad St., and the green was terraced. The **Joseph Hewes Memorial**, celebrating the Edenton merchant who was one of three N.C. signers of the Declaration of Independence, was erected at the southern end in 1932.

Houses from various eras frame the green and flank it along Water St. At the northeastern corner, the **Skinner Law Office** (ca. 1810, attributed to William Nichols; 1920s, Frank Fred Muth; 401 Court St.) was built as a small law office for Joseph Blount Skinner and finished with early Greek Revival details; it was later expanded into a Colonial Revival residence. The **Skinner-Bond House** (ca. 1790, ca. 1810s, 1840s; 405 Court St.) began as a side-passage-plan dwelling, was expanded to a center-passage-plan residence with double piazzas for attorney Joseph Blount Skinner and his wife, Maria Lowther Skinner, and was reworked in Greek Revival style for Henry and Mar-

garet Manning Bond. The **James Woodard House** (1910s; Frank Fred Muth, builder; 407 Court St.) is an especially handsome bungalow whose form with deep inset porch fits easily into the local traditions. It was built for merchant James A. Woodard and his wife, Annie Bond Woodard, who had grown up in her grandfather's house next door. The big, frame **Julien Wood House** (ca. 1890; 409 Court St.) at the southeastern corner blends Queen Anne massing with Colonial Revival classical detail. Wood was a leading farmer and president of the Bank of Edenton.

CO 5 William Leary House
1897; George F. Barber (Knoxville), architect; Theo Ralph, contractor; 203 Water St.

For their fashionable house in the Queen Anne style, William and Emma Woodard Leary obtained plans from the prolific mail-order architect George F. Barber of Tennessee. The contract with local builder Ralph specified various items to be "like Mrs. Dixon's," citing Ralph's recently completed *Dixon-Powell House across town in an age-old pattern of reference to existing buildings. East along Water St., several other 2-story frame houses from the late 18th through the early 20th centuries create a handsome ensemble overlooking Edenton Bay.

CO 6 The Homestead
1770s; 101 E. Water St.

co 6 *The Homestead*

Just west of the green, the house overlooking the bay presents an unusual example of the double piazza carried around all four sides. The porches are finished with a scalloped cornice board. Side and rear porches have been enclosed to expand the hall-parlor plan. Evidently built for merchant Robert Smith, the house was purchased in 1786 by Josiah Collins I, a native of Somerset, England, who became a leading merchant trading with Europe and the West Indies and owner of the huge *Somerset Place across the sound. Called "The Homestead" since the 1840s, it has continued in family ownership. In 1895 Frank Wood appended a big Queen Anne style residence facing the green. This section was removed in 1956 when the older house was renovated by J. Everette Fauber Jr. for Wood's daughter Rebecca and her husband, the Reverend Dr. Frederick Blount Drane.

In the yard stands a tiny Edenton landmark: the **Edenton Teapot** (1906; Frank Baldwin), erected by the history-minded Frank Wood to commemorate the Edenton Tea Party amid the early 20th-c. efflorescence of historical and patriotic activity. Local lore celebrated the signing of the 1774 resolution by fifty-one area women as having occurred at a "tea party" led by Edentonian Penelope Barker. Some stories placed the party at a house that stood here. Wood had the bronze teapot cast as a copy of a Johnston family teapot that descended in the Wood family, and he had it set atop a Revolutionary era French cannon, one of several pulled out of Edenton Bay and installed at the foot of the green and on Union Square in Raleigh.

CO 7 Barker-Moore House

1782, early 19th c.; S terminus of Broad St.

Moved here from the 200 block of S. Broad St. in 1952, the frame house with its double rear piazza overlooking the bay creates an evocative if recent panorama, part of a waterfront that was once dominated by wharves, warehouses, a railyard, and fish factories but now has a parklike character. Like many Edenton houses, this began as a smaller dwelling, the home until 1796

of Thomas and Penelope Barker—she of Edenton Tea Party fame. It was enlarged and given its piazza in the 19th c. by Augustus and Susan Moore, whose family lived in the house from 1832 to 1952 and included distinguished lawyers, judges, and community leaders.

CO 8 Cupola House

1758–59; 408 S. Broad St.; National Historic Landmark; open to public (from visitors' center)

CO 8 *Cupola House*

This extraordinary house, one of the state's prime examples of colonial architecture, has long been a focus of local pride. As memorialized on the front gable finial— "FC/17/58"—the house was built for Francis Corbin, who came to N.C. from England in 1747 as Lord Granville's land agent. In 1777 Samuel Dickinson, Connecticut-born physician and businessman, bought the house from Corbin's estate. His heirs occupied the Cupola House until 1918, celebrating its antiquity with such events as a 150th anniversary tea in 1908. In 1918 the first-story woodwork was acquired by the Brooklyn Museum; Edentonians rallied to keep the stair and upper interiors and save the house as a library. In 1965–66, craftsman Wilbert M. Kemp replicated the first-floor woodwork.

Embodying a unique combination of architectural elements, the 2½-story frame house is evidently the only dwelling in the South with the second-story "jetty" or overhang characteristic of Jacobean English and 17th- and 18th-c. New England architecture. Why Corbin desired such an old-fashioned feature in the mid-18th c. is unknown. The slightly asymmetrical facade rises to a front cross gable and features an early 19th-c. gabled entrance porch. The massive cupola emerges from a rusticated wooden base. Continuing the traditional English decoration of framing members, acanthus carving adorns the rafter ends of the cupola and purlin tips at the gable ends of the house.

The framing was executed in idiosyncratic fashion, as the carpenter evidently adapted familiar construction methods to accommodate Corbin's unfamiliar demands for a house with jetty and cupola. Especially unusual is the jetty: rather than cantilevering or hewing out the jetty, as was traditional in New England and England, the carpenter riveted a jetty girder to the main front girder of the house and supported the jetty girder with heavy brackets bolted to the posts. Massive chimneys of Flemish-bond brick heat the two front rooms; the northwest chimney was added in an early 19th-c. renovation.

The interior presents a unique and stunning amalgam of 18th-c. architectural concepts. (See Introduction, Fig. 22.) The asymmetrical plan has a central stair passage flanked by two large, unequal front rooms and much smaller rear chambers. Framing members project into the rooms and are neatly boxed. The bold classical forms and rich foliated carving, probably inspired by plates in the second (1738) edition of William Salmon's *Palladio Londinensis*, gain a baroque energy from being compressed into the low-ceilinged rooms. Elaborate classical pilasters and pediments frame the doors from the central passage into the front rooms. The largest room is the fully paneled east room, with its exuberant pedimented mantel and a barrel-backed built-in cupboard. The smaller room opposite has wainscoting and a pedimented mantel. The robust stair has a heavy railing, turned balusters, and ornate foliated brackets. The upper rooms retain original paneling and mantels

with overmantels. From the attic a barrel stair leads to the cupola.

CO 9 Central Business District
400–200 blocks, S. Broad St.

The eastern side of the 400 block from Water St. to King St. was the old "Cheapside" until a fire in 1893 destroyed "an entire block of old English buildings of pre-revolutionary origin." Prompt rebuilding produced "fireproof" masonry and metal-front structures. The most striking is the **Josephine Napoleon Leary Building** (1894; Theo Ralph, contractor; 421–25 S. Broad St.), with its rich and intact metal facade by "Mesker Bros. Front Builders, St. Louis, Mo.," adorned with columns, sunbursts, foliage, and on the parapet, "J. N. Leary, 1894." It was erected by local contractor Theo Ralph for Josephine Napoleon Leary, a businesswoman who had been born into slavery in Williamston and came with her husband, Sweety Leary, of Petersburg, Va., to Edenton by the mid-1870s. Beginning in the barbering trade, Mrs. Leary invested in several commercial and residential properties and rebuilt on her Cheapside lots immediately after the fire. The adjacent **Rogerson Building** (1894; 417–19 S. Broad St.), features a similar pair of Mesker facades. The 400, 300, and 200 blocks contain several simple Italianate brick stores. Corbeled brickwork and an original storefront enrich the 2-bay **J. N. Leary Barbershop** (1904–10; 317 S. Broad St.), which Mrs. Leary built to replace the old frame barbershop she bought in 1881.

Early 20th-c. prosperity added a series of classical buildings as the business district grew northward. The **Bank of Edenton** (1911; 400 S. Broad St., at King St.) is a tan

CO 9 *Josephine Napoleon Leary Building*

brick temple-form building with stone and metal trim. Corinthian columns carry the front pediment, and corresponding pilasters recur along the side. A grander version of banker's classicism appears in the former **Citizens Bank** (1924; Charles C. Benton [Wilson], attributed architect; 216 S. Broad St.), with Doric columns and pilasters at the first story and Ionic ones above, complementing a columned and coffered banking room. The **Taylor Theatre** (1925; Charles C. Benton [Wilson], attributed architect; 206–10 S. Broad St.) is a quietly splendid movie theater with a creamy terra-cotta facade featuring Corinthian pilasters, enriched entablature, and classical balustrade with urns carrying the neon "Taylor" sign.

CO 9 *Bank of Edenton*

W. King St. and adjoining sites:
The 100 block of W. King St., adjoining the central business district, is among the most impressive residential streets in the state. At the corner of W. King and S. Granville Sts. stand two antebellum mansions—doubtless those compared favorably with New York in 1856—that carry the double-piazza house into the height of antebellum grandeur and fashion.

CO 10 Wagner-Wood House
1851; 106 W. King St.

The big, austere rendition of the double-piazza house in Greek Revival style takes an unusual form, with its porches inset under the deep hip roof.

CO 11 Disbrowe-Warren House
1756, William Luten, carpenter; early, mid-19th c.; 105 W. King St.

A good number of Edenton houses contain vestiges of 18th-c. dwellings at their core. Here traces remain of an early house documented in the account book of carpenter William Luten, who erected it for George Disbrowe in 1756. Subsequent owners expanded and reworked the house, added the rear ell with double piazzas in the 19th c., and made further changes in the 20th c.

CO 12 Elliott House
1895; 107 W. King St.

Illustrating the longevity of the double-piazza house, the single-pile frame dwelling has an ornate 2-tier porch across the front and another along the 2-story rear ell. It was built for rental by merchant W. O. Elliott.

CO 13 Skinner-Paxton House
Ca. 1820s; 115 W. King St.

Edenton's prime example of the side-passage-plan townhouse, this large, 2-story frame house has Federal style detail, a new entrance portico, and a double piazza across the rear.

CO 14 Beverly Hall
Ca. 1810; 114 W. King St.

The most elaborate Federal era house in Edenton, the 2-story brick residence five bays wide was built for John Bonner Blount, whose private bank here later became the State Bank of N.C. William Badham—the richest merchant in town—enlarged the house and added Gothic Revival embellishments in the 1850s, including an arched doorway on the east. In the late 19th c. this was the home of Dr. Richard Dillard and his wife, Mary Louisa Beverly Cross Dillard (thus the name Beverly Hall). Their son, Dr. Richard Dillard Jr., a physician and local history buff, created the elaborate garden.

CO 15 Pembroke Hall
1850; 121 W. King St.

CO 15 *Pembroke Hall*

Set in spacious, romantically landscaped grounds, this grand and stylish version of the familiar double-piazza house has a broad hip roof sheltering porches facing both the land and the water, executed in patternbook Greek Revival style. The lower columns follow a Doric order, and the upper ones feature a waterleaf order from Minard Lafever's *Beauties of Modern Architecture* (1835). The interior, likewise enriched with stylish Greek Revival detail, follows a center-passage plan two rooms deep, with the stair in a side passage. The 2-story kitchen wing stands recessed to the east. The house was built for Virginia-born physician Matthew Page and his second wife, Henrietta Collins Page (daughter of planter and merchant Josiah Collins Jr.), shortly after their marriage in 1848.

CO 16 Wessington

1850–51; 120 W. King St.

CO 16 *Wessington*

The massive brick house, standing on a large, lushly planted lot, takes the honors as the most opulent residence in Edenton. It was built for one of the richest men in the county and state—Dr. Thomas D. Warren, a Virginia-born physician who married two heiresses: in 1840, Penelope Skinner, only daughter of lawyer and fishery owner Joseph Blount Skinner; and in 1843, Margaret Coffield, only child of planter James Coffield. By 1860 Warren owned $300,000 in real estate and $657,000 in personal property, a startling sum in an era of local depression. Warren lost the house after the Civil War, and in 1886 it entered a long period of ownership by the Cameron family, who named it Wessington. For his house, which stands 2½ stories atop a raised basement and has four main rooms per floor flanking a broad center passage, Warren chose "A Villa in the French Style" from William Ranlett's *The Architect* (1847) and modified it to local custom with 2-tier front porches and side balconies of iron. The great scale of the house and its lavish ironwork evoke the spirit of the Deep South. In the yard are a pergola, several outbuildings, and a great vaulted cistern.

CO 17 Dixon-Powell House

1895; Theo Ralph, contractor; 304 S. Granville St.

CO 17 *Dixon-Powell House*

Edenton's grandest Queen Anne style house is this 2½-story frame residence with gabled bays emerging from its high hip roof and a wraparound porch sweeping into a pavilion. In 1895 the *Fisherman and Farmer* predicted after viewing drawings for the residence of merchant Milton Dixon and his wife, Sallie Dillard Dixon, "We are safe in saying that when completed it will be the finest dwelling in the city."

CO 18 Charlton House
1760s; 206 W. Eden St.

The gambrel-roofed house prevalent in the 18th c. appears here with a center-passage plan and original full-width shed porch. Showing a local pattern among early houses standing at the fronts of their lots, the porch is entered by steps at either end—emphasizing its sociable orientation. The house was built for Jasper and Abigail Charlton; he was a lawyer active in Revolutionary politics, she the first signer of the "tea party" resolves. In back stands a 1-room plank house moved here from the Harvey's Neck section of Perquimans Co.

CO 19 Littlejohn House
Ca. 1790; 218 W. Eden St.

The typical 2-story, center-passage-plan house with engaged double piazza was executed in neat Federal style for William Littlejohn, commissioner of the port of Roanoke, and his wife, Sarah Blount Littlejohn.

CO 20 Byrum House
1896; 216 W. Eden St.

Illustrating a century's continuity, the neighboring 2-story house repeats the center-passage plan and double piazza, here an attached porch rich with local millwork. It was built for farmer and fishery owner Octavius Coke Byrum and his wife, Sarah Basnight Byrum.

CO 21 Goodwin-Leggett House
Ca. 1884; 205 S. Granville St.

The Italianate brick house, a local anomaly in its asymmetry and bold quoins and brackets, reflects the ambitions of Edenton's industrial boom era pioneers. It was built for sawmill and gristmill owner Silas Goodwin, who sold it to John A. Wilkinson, a manager for the Branning Manufacturing Company.

CO 22 Edenton Baptist Church
1916–20; James M. McMichael (Charlotte), architect; 206 S. Granville St.

A prominent rendition of the domed, cruciform-plan classical church designs popularized in N.C. by McMichael, the church has a Tuscan portico leading to a fan-shaped auditorium beneath the tall dome. Characteristic of the era, slatted wooden doors roll up between side pillars to open the adjoining Sunday school space for large services. This is the third church of the congregation, which was organized in 1817.

W. Queen St. and adjoining sites

CO 23 Mitchell-Wozelka House
Ca. 1877; 105 W. Queen St.

Illustrating the postwar popularity of the picturesque Gothic cottage mode, particularly among those who moved to town to generate new enterprises, the cross-plan dwelling features a central front pavilion with a kingpost gable ornament and bay window. It was built for Robert Mitchell, an Englishman who came here from Baltimore and became a merchant, fishpacker, and co-owner of the *Fisherman and Farmer*.

CO 24 Bond-Lipsitz House
Late 19th c., ca. 1900; 112 W. Queen St.

Houses with double piazzas appear in many forms on this street. This one combines a conservative 2-story form with an ornate 2-tier porch and corner tower. The adjoining **Skinner-Chappell House** (1890s; 116 W. Queen St.) has a sawnwork-trimmed double piazza stretching across a symmetrical, double-pile house.

CO 25 Leigh-Hathaway House
Ca. 1759 (Gilbert Leigh, carpenter), early 19th c.; 120 W. Queen St.; B&B

Carpenter Gilbert Leigh evidently built for his own family the small gambrel-roofed house with side-passage plan—repeating a form and size typical of colonial houses. In the early 19th c. the Hathaway family added the 2-story, gable-roofed east section with

CO 25 *Leigh-Hathaway House*

simple Federal detail. With the house standing near the front lot line, the shed porch across both sections repeats the traditional local usage of steps at the ends.

CO 26 Leigh-Bush House

Ca. 1759 (Gilbert Leigh, carpenter), early 19th c., 1880s; 126 W. Queen St.

One of Edenton's many time-capsule houses, a small side-passage house built by Leigh in the mid-18th c. was overbuilt in the 19th c. into a double-pile dwelling with ornate 2-tier porch.

W. Church St. and adjoining sites

CO 27 St. Paul's Episcopal Church

Begun 1736, 1806–9 (William Nichols), 1848 (Frank Wills), 1949–50; W. Church St. at Broad St.

Described by Thomas Waterman as "an ideal in village churches, unrivaled in this country except perhaps by Christ Church, New Castle, Delaware," St. Paul's is the second oldest church building in N.C. and the state's only colonial church still in regular parish use. The parish was established in 1701, the first in N.C., and a little wooden church was built at the site of the present *Hayes plantation. After the town was founded, construction of a more conveniently located "large, handsome brick church with steeple" began in 1736 and proceeded in fits and starts. The church stood unfinished and open to livestock and the weather for years at a time. It was completed sufficient for use in 1760, but the windows were not glazed until 1767, and woodwork was installed in 1774. The Flemish-bond brick building, rectangular in plan, is akin to contemporary Virginia and English parish churches. Characteristic features include the large arched windows, rusticated entrances in the spirit of James Gibbs located on the northern and southern sides, and the square entrance tower at the western end. Unusual is the semicircular apse at the eastern end, which is laid in all-header bond.

In 1806, after a post-Revolutionary period of decline, the parish employed English-born carpenter-architect William Nichols, who came from New Bern to Edenton to renovate the church. He added the spire and remodeled the interior in simple Neoclassical taste in 1806–9. In 1848 new chancel fittings, designed by Ecclesiologist architect Frank Wills, accommodated new liturgical emphasis on the chancel, with round arched motifs harmonizing with the old building. In 1949, during a renovation that had removed much of the woodwork from the church for safekeeping, fire swept through the church. The roof was rebuilt in steel, and the church was restored from Historic American Building Survey drawings. The surrounding churchyard contains many old gravestones—including some early 18th-c. ones moved from eroding sites by the sound—as well as elaborate imported markers from Philadelphia and Baltimore.

CO 27 *St. Paul's Episcopal Church*

CO 28 W. Church St. Houses

As Edenton grew in the industrial age, the outer blocks of the old grid filled in. The 100 and 200 blocks of W. Church St. display a collection of the multifaceted Colonial Revival work of Frank Fred Muth, the German builder who came to Edenton in 1905 from Atlantic City, N.J. The **Edmund R. Conger House** (1910; 110 W. Church St.) is a massive frame residence with dramatic gambrel roof, pedimented entrance pavilion, and wraparound porch. At the **William D. Pruden Sr. House** (ca. 1883, ca. 1910; 116 W. Church St.), Muth transformed an Italianate residence into a distinctive Colonial Revival dwelling, asymmetrically composed with a great curved cornice and wraparound porch. Muth also reworked the **Bond-McMullan-Elliott House** (1860, 1890s, ca. 1910; 200 W. Church St.) by erecting a massive Colonial Revival portico beneath the double-slope roof. Across Church St., the **Paine House** (ca. 1844; 100 S. Granville St.) is a coastal cottage of the antebellum era, with double-pile plan, engaged porch, and simple, Greek Revival details. Muth's rendition of the Southern Colonial style with heroic portico and wraparound, 1-story porch appears in the **Dr. Henry Cason House** (1907; 108 S. Granville St.; B&B), built for a physician and Ford dealer. Houses on nearby W. Queen St. likewise show Muth's talents.

CO 29 Williams-Flury House
Ca. 1779, 1790s; 108 N. Granville St.

Sea captain Willis Williams built the first section of this house in a form favored by 18th-c. Edentonians, a small, gambrel-roofed dwelling with a 1-room plan. It was expanded for Henry Flury with a center passage and an additional room under the gambrel, plus a shed porch and rear shed rooms.

CO 30 Providence Baptist Church
1893; 214 W. Church St.

Home of the oldest black congregation in Edenton, organized in 1868 by black members of Edenton Baptist Church, the brick edifice in late Gothic Revival style features the characteristic front gable flanked by a pair of contrasting towers, one with a spire, the other with a dome.

E. King St. and adjoining sites

CO 31 Hatch-Bruer-Davis House
Ca. 1744, 1780s–1804; 200 E. King St.

The core of the house may be the oldest in Edenton, a 1½-story, side-passage-plan dwelling built for André Richard, a French barber, who in 1745 sold the house "lately Erected and built" to his son-in-law, Edmund Hatch. Later in the 18th c. it was expanded to 2 stories with a center passage beneath a hip roof. Changes in the chimney brickwork indicate the sequence of development.

CO 32 Haywood Privott House
1900; 205 E. King St.

The "elegant brick residence" in Queen Anne style was built for Haywood and Georgia Byrum Privott. Businessman Privott, a director of the Edenton Cotton Mill, bought 20,000 bricks left from the mill to build his house. He had previously built the **Privott-Jones House** (1892–98; 208 E. King St.), a decorated 2-story L-plan frame house that, like several in the neighborhood, served as rental housing.

CO 33 James Coffield House
Late 18th c., ca. 1830s; 209 E. King St.

Like many Edenton dwellings, a small 18th-c. house stands at the core of the large 19th-c. structure with double piazzas across the front. Delicate tracery fills the elaborate Greek Revival entrance, which opens into a center passage.

CO 34 Jane C. Page House
Ca. 1881; 306 S. Oakum St.

Simplified renditions of the picturesque gabled cottage were especially popular among prominent members of Edenton's black community in the late 19th c., particularly among leading builders and their families. This symmetrical, 1½-story frame house, with a pair of peaked dormers enlivening the roof, is the best preserved. It was built for the widow of carpenter John R. Page.

CO 35 John R. Wheeler House

Ca. 1901; 215 S. Oakum St.

CO 35 *John R. Wheeler House*

Built and supposedly designed by Wheeler, superintendent at the Branning Manufacturing Company, the 2-story house displays the mill's full potential in the double porch exuberant with spindles, pendants, scrolls, and drilled work, including panels featuring cosmic sawnwork with sun, moon, planet, and comet motifs.

CO 36 Edenton Graded School (Swain School)

1916; 101 Court St.

The big brick public school building, proclaiming the importance of education in the community, typifies the period's incorporation of Colonial Revival classicism and Flemish-bond brickwork in a modern classroom building following progressive educational norms of the time. It was built on the former site of the Edenton Academy. Wings of ca. 1926 and an auditorium of the 1930s expanded the facility. Vacated in 1985, the school has been renovated and preserved in a new use for apartments and a community center.

CO 37 Iredell House

1800, 1827; 105 E. Church St.;
state historic site, open to public through
visitors' center

The house and its large lot full of outbuildings illustrate the character of town domestic establishments. A dwelling stood here—probably a 1½-story gambrel-roofed house—when James Iredell Sr. bought the property in 1778. Iredell, an English-born attorney who had married Hannah Johnston (sister of his mentor, Samuel Johnston of *Hayes), became a distinguished Federalist political leader and justice of the first U.S. Supreme Court. Recent dendrochronology indicates that the eastern section, a simply finished, late Georgian style structure with its gable end to the street, was built for Hannah Iredell in 1800 (the year after James's death) as an addition to the older house. After Hannah's death in 1826, the old western section was razed and replaced in 1827 with a rental house that provided income for their daughter Helen. This 2-story Federal style structure facing the street features a 2-tier porch entered from the end and adorned with a delicate sheaf-of-wheat balustrade and pierced cornice molding inspired by Asher Benjamin's *American Builder's Companion* (1806ff.).

CO 37 *Iredell House*

Frame outbuildings original to the site include a very early kitchen (1756), which has been restored (see Introduction, Fig. 18); a privy sheathed with flush boards and topped by a pyramidal roof; and a small, gable-roofed carriage house or barn with flanking sheds typical of the region. The early 19th-c. plantation office (furnished as a schoolhouse) was moved from Bandon Plantation, as was the small, frame dairy, which displays the pyramidal roof, wide eaves, and sawn grille frieze typical of the region's early dairy structures.

CO 38 Edenton Academy

1800 (Joe Welcome, mason), 1895; 109–11 E. Church St.

The pair of 2-story, gable-fronted, side-passage houses appear to date from the early 20th-c. popularity of that form, but in fact they are the separated portions of the former Edenton Academy, a simply finished frame building that probably had two classrooms flanking a passage on each floor. Brick and plaster work was executed by Joe Welcome, a leading mason in the Albemarle area, and other slave workmen, as recorded by Welcome's owner Josiah Collins I.

CO 39 St. John the Evangelist Episcopal Church

1885–87, 1910–20, 1901; 212 E. Church St.

CO 39 *St. John the Evangelist Episcopal Church*

The asymmetrical frame church, featuring broad, gabled facades filled with triangular-headed windows and joining at the crenellated corner entrance tower, reflects a long construction history. The congregation of black members organized in 1881 from *St. Paul's Episcopal Church, and with support of Herbert Page (of *Pembroke Hall), dedicated their new church at the same time. After an 1884 tornado demolished that building, its frame was reused in rebuilding in 1885–87. The church was enlarged and re-

oriented in the 1910s. The sanctuary features a dramatic truss roof and ornate rood screen as well as a chancel window dedicated to Jane R. and John R. Page, the latter a prominent local builder born a slave of Herbert Page's parents, Matthew and Henrietta Collins Page.

North Broad St.:

The area from Church St. northward, which remained sparsely settled until after the Civil War, developed rapidly from the 1880s onward. It presents a remarkable spectrum of late 19th- and early 20th-c. architecture. The principal artery, N. Broad St., presents a sampler of popular 19th- and early 20th-c. architecture, including Italianate works by builder Theo Ralph and Colonial Revival examples by Frank Fred Muth.

CO 40 U.S. Post Office

1931; James A. Wetmore, supervising architect of the Treasury; 100 N. Broad St.

The restrained Georgian Revival style building rendered in red brick typifies post offices erected in many small towns during the Great Depression.

CO 41 Louis Ziegler House

Ca. 1892 (Theo Ralph, builder), 1990 (Burnstudio, Raleigh, architects); 108 N. Broad St.; open as visitors' center

Exemplary of late 19th-c. Edenton houses, the familiar 2-story frame dwelling with center-passage plan partakes of "artistic, ornate" taste with the asymmetry of a front ell and abundant millwork on the porch and in the gables. Local contractor Theo Ralph evidently built the house for undertaker Louis F. Ziegler and his wife, Ella. It has been restored and expanded as the Historic Edenton visitors' center.

CO 42 A. H. Mitchell House

Ca. 1890; Theo Ralph, builder; 208 N. Broad St.

Typical of several local examples of Ralph's Italianate work, the residence features a pair of 2-story front bays accented by a bracket cornice. It was built for A. H. Mitchell, publisher of the newspaper *Fisherman and Farmer*, indefatigable New South booster of industrial progress, who moved with his paper to Elizabeth City in 1897.

CO 43 St. Ann's Catholic Church

1858, 1898; L. L. Long (Baltimore), architect; Richard Keogh and Joseph Godfrey, contractors; 209 N. Broad St.

One of the state's very few antebellum Romanesque Revival churches, this is the only antebellum Catholic church in N.C. still in regular parish use. Begun in 1858, construction on the rectangular brick church stalled with the front entrance tower unfinished for lack of funds. In 1898 its crenellated parapet was completed. When the church was built in 1858, it stood on the northern edge of town, as *St. Paul's Church had done when it was built only a block south a century earlier.

CO 44 300 Block, N. Broad St.

This block offers an array of 19th- and early 20th-c. domestic architecture. The **Henry Bond House** (ca. 1872; 301 N. Broad St.) is a Carpenter Gothic cottage with sawnwork enriching the steep gables, twin front wall dormers, and porch. Across the street the **Fred White House** (ca. 1902; 300 N. Broad St.; B&B) typifies the turn-of-the-century blend of Queen Anne massing with Colonial Revival classical detail in a large brick residence. Builder Frank Fred Muth's multi-faceted work in the Colonial Revival style appears prominently in the **Charles N. Griffin House** (1910s; Frank Fred Muth; 304 N. Broad St.), with its Southern Colonial style portico and flanking 1-story porches, and in the exuberant, shingled **John W. Branning House** (ca. 1907; Frank Fred Muth; 305 N. Broad St.), where a robust gambrel expands the roof into a third story. Branning, locally lauded as "that Prince of Northern Capitalists," was a Pennsylvania lumber manufacturer who transformed the local lumber business. The dramatic Queen Anne style **Oatman-White House** (ca. 1890; 306 N. Broad St.) features a high roof that swoops down to engage a deep porch. Other houses in this and subsequent blocks continue Queen Anne and Colonial Revival motifs, complemented by bungalows and foursquare dwellings.

Northeast and Northwest Neighborhoods: The blocks flanking N. Broad St.—E. and W. Gale, Albemarle, Carteret, and Freemason Sts.—along with blocks adjoining to the south constitute one of N.C.'s most complete, diverse, and well-preserved late 19th- and early 20th-c. neighborhoods developed principally by and for African Americans. During the post–Civil War era of industrial development, as black and white families moved to town to find work, the demand for housing increased and the community expanded. Filling out the colonial town plan, the streets continue the grid, and houses stand in close proximity to one another and to the street. Black and white residents often lived in the same blocks in late 19th-c. Edenton, as had been the pattern in earlier years, but in the 20th c., residential segregation increased.

A variety of 1- and 2-room-plan houses is mixed with larger structures, including many houses that were expanded over the years. Nearly every regional vernacular house form appears, from 1-room and hall-parlor-plan dwellings to center-passage-plan I-houses, gabled cottages, bungalows, and many 2-story, gable-end houses with side-passage plans—a form frequently built in eastern N.C. towns in the industrial era. Larger and more fashionable residences display a range of styles, from simplified picturesque cottages with paired dormers to Queen Anne, foursquare, and bungalow houses. Typical of other similar neigh-

borhoods now lost, owner-built houses and rental dwellings coexisted in the neighborhood. Corner stores and tiny groceries and barber-shops—often associated with the proprietors' dwellings—punctuate the blocks, along with churches and lodges. As an ensemble, these streets compose a remarkable survival of the scale and quality of late 19th- and early 20th-c. urban life, a townscape once familiar but often effaced in the state's larger towns and cities.

CO 45 Bennett's Inn
Ca. 1765; 129 E. Gale St.

The tiny house evidently incorporates the 1-room dwelling shown on the 1769 Sauthier map, when settlement of the northeastern section of the grid was still sparse and scattered. Here John and Sarah Bennett opened an inn in 1765. Long a rental property, it was expanded ca. 1910 and features an engaged porch and shed rooms.

CO 46 Kadesh A.M.E. Zion Church
1897; Hannibal Badham Sr., builder; 119 E. Gale St.

CO 46 *Kadesh A.M.E. Zion Church*

The frame church, built by congregation member and carpenter Hannibal Badham Sr., has a front gable flanked by two contrasting entrance towers, one rising to a tapered peak, the other taller but devoid of the spire that was struck by lightning ca. 1955. The congregation began in 1866 from Edenton Methodist Church; Kadesh refers to an oasis where the Israelites camped on their journey out of bondage. Next door, the **Parsonage** (ca. 1900; 121 E. Gale St.) exemplifies Badham's work in the Queen Anne style, a 2-story residence with projecting polygonal bay and wraparound porch with turned decoration and corner pavilion.

CO 47 Badham Family Houses
1880s–1910s; 100–200 blocks, E. Gale and E. Church Sts.

CO 47 *Hannibal Badham Jr. House*

An important concentration of buildings on E. Gale and E. Church Sts. was erected by Hannibal Badham Sr. and Jr.—late 19th-c. house carpenters who were descendants of Miles Badham, a carpenter emancipated by the will of James C. Johnston of *Hayes. Part of a larger African American neighborhood, the buildings recall both the importance of the Badham family as late 19th-c. builders and the role of the extended family in establishing the neighborhood and community. They built several houses for their families and others on land that Hannibal Badham Sr. and his siblings had inherited from Miles Badham. These houses illustrate a variety of popular forms and styles.

The most striking of the family residences is the **Hannibal Badham Jr. House** (ca. 1900; 116 E. Gale St.), which Hannibal Badham Sr. built for his son—an eclectic combination of conservative, 2-story form with a fantastically exuberant porch and corner pavilion with spire. Next door is another delectably ornate **Badham House** (1890s; 114 E. Gale St.), a small, symmetrical, gable-roofed cottage with elaborate porch and trim, built by Badham and his sons Miles and Hannibal Jr. The elder Badham also erected the **Evelina Badham School** (1880s; 137 E. Gale St.), a 1-story, hip-roofed schoolhouse, for his wife, Evelina Williams Badham, a native of New York and graduate of present-day Hunter College, who came with the Freedmen's Bureau as a schoolteacher to Edenton. She later served as dean of girls at the Edenton Industrial and Normal School. Next door to it stands the **Hannibal Badham Sr. House** (ca. 1880; 133 E. Gale St.), which the builder constructed for his own family as a 2-story, L-plan frame house (since veneered in brick).

Related family residences also stand on Church St., immediately to the south within the same town blocks. Among these is the **Miles Badham (II) House** (ca. 1896; 117 E. Church St.), which Hannibal Badham Sr. erected on land he had given his son Miles, a carpenter with the Norfolk and Southern Railroad. The house displays the popular 2-story, gable-fronted, side-passage form, adorned with shingles, brackets, and 2-tier porch. For his sister, Badham built the **Elijah and Hellen Blair House** (1897; 125 E. Church St.), a 2-story, single-pile dwelling. It was built on a lot that Hellen Badham Blair had received from her siblings to "carry out and perform the oral directions of [their father] Miles Badham, dec'd, from whom the lands hereinafter descended."

CO 48 John R. Page Masonic Lodge
Ca. 1890; 116 N. Oakum St.

The 2-story frame fraternal lodge building, featuring a parapeted facade and peaked hoods over the windows, was built, probably by Hannibal Badham Sr., as an Odd Fellows hall for the Pride of the South Lodge. In 1968 it was sold to the John R. Page Masonic Lodge, a fraternal group named for local carpenter Page, which had occupied other halls since its establishment in 1892.

CO 49 Rev. N. S. Harris House
1942; 108 E. Carteret St.

The asymmetrical, brick bungalow was built from the "San Lois" model in *Better Homes at Lower Cost* (1940), a plan book published by the Standard Homes Company of Raleigh, a copy of which was owned by the Edenton Building and Loan Company. Nathaniel and Cornelia Harris chose the design and had it built by local carpenters. A graduate of Tuskegee Institute, Howard University, and Livingstone College, the Reverend Mr. Harris was pastor of A.M.E. Zion churches, including *Kadesh in Edenton and *Mount Lebanon in Elizabeth City.

CO 50 Capehart Rental Houses
Ca. 1875; 112, 114 E. Carteret St.

Important survivors of the houses built by landowners for working people who moved to town after the Civil War, these are two diminutive versions of the traditional coastal cottage form with 2 main rooms and engaged porch and shed rooms. They were built ca. 1875 for William R. Capehart, a physician, farmer, and fishery owner.

CO 51 Hicks Field
1939; E. Freemason St.

Located on the site of the 18th-c. town common and 19th-c. fairgrounds, the ballfield is among the state's best examples of the modest baseball parks vital to American life in the early 20th c. In 1939 a WPA project renovated the "old and dilapidated" field and installed a new grandstand for baseball and bleachers for football. The wooden grandstand and fence still stand. Baseball had flourished in Edenton since the late 19th c. Like many southern towns it had both a black team—the Quick Steps, who played on another diamond (builder Hannibal Badham Jr. was pitcher)—and a white team—the Colonials, who played at Hicks Field. In the 1930s and 1940s Hicks Field hosted spring training for several minor league teams from other states, and into the 1950s Edenton fielded teams in the Class D Virginia and Coastal Plain leagues.

CO 52 Edenton Peanut Factory
1909; E. Church St. Ext. at head of Wood Ave.

The county's most imposing industrial building is this starkly handsome brick

co 52 *Edenton Peanut Factory*

structure with corbeled and chamfered brickwork subtly emphasizing its height, mass, and strength. Like the cotton mill, the factory was organized by local businessmen, lawyers, and agriculturists to keep profits in the community. Peanut growing had developed rapidly in the region, but there was no processing plant in northeastern N.C. The organizers hired an experienced peanut factory manager, W. H. Clark, from Franklin, Va., and began operation with the fall harvest of 1909. The big brick building was divided into sections by functions, in which some 100 workers—most of them women and all black, except managers, foremen, and office workers—accomplished the different tasks. After the peanuts were shelled by machine, the women cleaned, sorted, and graded them by hand and packed them into bags for shipment by cars on the adjoining rail spur. The first floor was for storage, the second for picking, the third and fourth for polishing, and the fifth for hoppers. By 1927 annual sales had reached nearly $1 million. After World War II, changing peanut marketing regulations eventuated closing of the plant. It has been vacant for years while the local peanut industry it began thrives in a new facility.

CO 53 Edenton Cotton Mill and Village

1899–1920s; E. King St. extended and nearby streets

The Edenton Cotton Mill and its village constitute one of the best preserved such plants in eastern N.C. It was established in 1898 by nineteen local businessmen who sought to keep profits in the community. The company bought 30 acres of the old Collins rope manufacturing property in 1899 and hired the firm of C. R. Makepeace and Company of Providence, R.I., a nationally prominent textile mill engineer and architect. To build the plant, a million bricks were made on-site with machinery leased from W. O. Speight of the Edenton Brick Works. The mill was almost immediately doubled in size, then expanded again, from Makepeace plans. The steam-powered factory was processing 2,000 bales of local farmers' cotton a year in 1909, 3,000 by the late 1910s, and more than 4,000 by the mid-1920s. Despite heavy losses during the depression, the firm survived under the management of John Augustus Moore, son of an old Edenton family, who had managed the Patterson Mills in Roanoke Rapids and returned to Edenton in 1931. The mill ceased operations in 1995.

co 53 *Edenton Cotton Mill and Village*

The **Edenton Cotton Mill** (1899, 1904, 1913, and later; C. R. Makepeace and Company) is a typical brick mill of restrained Italianate design with a campanile-like entrance tower. The company also constructed the compact mill village with the amenities that had become customary: a baseball field, vegetable gardens, and seventy neat, plain workers' "cottages" with good-sized yards. There was no company store, but businesses developed on nearby Oakum St. to trade with mill employees.

Operatives' houses, built from 1899 onward, stand in even rows along E. King, Elliott, Queen, Church, and McMullan

Sts. Most are 1-story, gable-sided frame dwellings with front shed porches and rear ells, typically "three-room tenements" with two rooms flanking center chimneys and another in the ell. Many have two front entrances, enabling them to serve as either duplexes or single-family dwellings. Some are 2-story houses, also one room deep with a center chimney and rear ell. Other types include the gable-fronted, shingled cottages at 410–12 Elliott St., which came from Sears, Roebuck, and Company in 1921.

More individualized residences were built for upper personnel: the **Engineer's House** (1908; 310 E. King St.), a multi-gabled, frame house built as "a very good dwelling for our engineer, Mr. Bean"; the **Supervisor's House** (1921; 312 E. King St.), a gable-fronted, 2-story house; the **Superintendent's House** (1909; 400 E. King St.), a 1½-story Queen Anne–Colonial Revival house with front gambrel ell; the **Spinning Overseer's House** (1914; 410 E. King St.), a 2-story Colonial Revival house with wraparound porch; and the **Carder's House** (1916; 403 E. King St.), a foursquare residence—"a comfortable house for the carder."

CO 54 *Hayes*

CO 54 Hayes

1814–17; William Nichols, architect and house carpenter; Joe Welcome, bricklayer; National Historic Landmark; private, no public visibility or access

One of the state's most important plantation houses of the Federal period, Hayes was built for James C. Johnston and his sisters on the plantation left to him by his father, Gov. Samuel Johnston. To plan the house and superintend construction, James employed the English-born architect and carpenter William Nichols. He created a unique and heady blend of conservative and progressive architectural influences. In a 5-part Palladian composition, the main house is flanked by curved, colonnaded hyphens that lead to small, temple-form wings containing the kitchen and the library. The 2-story central block, capped by a belvedere, features a small, curved entrance portico on the land side, while a tall, colonnaded portico with

double piazza overlooks the sound. In finishing the house, Nichols introduced remarkably early Greek Revival motifs along with Gothic Revival touches in the library. He commissioned the iron balustrade, stone steps, and mahogany handrail from New York suppliers. Dependencies include a coach house and a smokehouse. Also on the plantation are an old dwelling known as the gatehouse, early 20th-c. tenant houses of shingled bungalow form, and barns and other agricultural buildings. Hayes has descended through the heirs of Edward Wood, to whom James Johnston willed Hayes in 1865.

CO 55 Strawberry Hill

Late 1780s, later expansions; S side E. Church St. Ext. at SR 1105; private, visible from road

CO 55 *Strawberry Hill*

An unsullied early example of the region's 2-story, double-pile house with a 2-tier engaged porch. Like many others, it was begun as a side-hall-plan house and was expanded to its present form in the early 19th c.

CO 56 Speight House and Cotton Gin

1900–1902; N side E. Church St. Ext. at SR 1105; private, visible from road

The full-blown Queen Anne style brick house, a rarity in rural N.C., was built for Will Oscar Speight, founder of the Edenton Brick Works, providing a prominent showcase for brick construction. The complex includes a big, 2-story brick cotton gin with arched entrance, a brick smokehouse, an octagonal frame chicken coop, frame laborers' quarters, and storage sheds.

East of Edenton, from roads along the Albemarle Sound (NC 32, SR 1114, SR 1108) one may see at a distance a series of 18th- and 19th-c. plantation houses oriented to the sound and linked by long-standing family ties. Several others lie beyond the view of public thoroughfares. A sense of the maritime plantation landscape persists despite extensive new residential development.

CO 57 Mulberry Hill

Ca. 1810; end of SR 1113, Edenton vic.; private, visible from road

CO 57 *Mulberry Hill*

An elegant rural version of the Federal period side-passage-plan house. Clement Blount, a bachelor who built the house to share with his mother and sisters, probably erected this house in emulation of his brother Frederick's fashionable new residence in New Bern. Flemish-bond brickwork combines with Adamesque woodwork, including an intricately carved fanlight in the gable. The reconstructed entrance portico is copied from a New Bern model. The soundside plantation, home of the Blount family from the 17th c., came into Wood family ownership in the 19th c.

CO 58 Sandy Point

Ca. 1815, ca. 1830; end of SR 1118, 0.8 mi. S of SR 1114, Edenton vic.; private, visible from NC 32 Albemarle Sound bridge

The soundside plantation house began as a side-passage-plan dwelling and received an additional bay to create a double-pile house with center passage, sheltered by a full-width engaged double piazza. The simple, well-crafted finish is of late Federal and Greek Revival character. The house was evidently built for James Sutton and expanded for Thomas Benbury; both were prosperous planters. The plantation was known as Sandy Point by 1864.

CO 59 Poplar Neck

1853; S side NC 32, 0.25 mi. W of NC 37, Edenton vic.; private, visible from road

A Greek Revival rendition of the double-porch house, with simple pillars carrying the engaged piazzas front and back. It follows a central-passage plan, with pairs of double parlors. The house was built for Susan Moore, who moved her family here from Edenton after the death of her husband, Judge Augustus Moore.

CO 60 Locust Grove A.M.E. Zion Church

Ca. 1895; S side SR 1100, 0.3 mi. W of SR 1108, Somer vic.

Located near the soundside plantations, the little weatherboarded church shares the eloquent simplicity of many country churches of its era. It is one of several built for small, rural black congregations in the late 19th c., when railroad-based industrial growth provided new wage jobs to rural workers. The gable-fronted church is symmetrically composed, with a central entrance, lancet windows, and a bull's-eye window in the gable. Locust Grove, located on land donated by Frank Wood of Greenfield, cites a founding date of 1865 and is considered mother church to several churches in the area.

CO 61 Yeopim Baptist Church

1851; E. side SR 1102, 0.3 mi. S of SR 1100, Yeopim

The simply finished, temple-form country church was built for a congregation whose church minutes go back to 1791, when itinerant ministers served the congregation. After the 1847 church burned in 1850, the present church was erected—one of the oldest Baptist church buildings in the region.

CO 62 Shelton

Ca. 1820; W side NC 32, 1.0 mi. N of US 17 BYP, Edenton vic.; private, visible from road

One of a handful of pediment-front houses built for planters near the Virginia line during the Federal period, this prominent example features a modillion cornice and fanlit pediment. Characteristically, the plan has a lateral hall across the front and two parlors behind. The plantation's history stretches back to the mid-18th-c. ownership of Clement Hall, priest of the colonial parish of *St. Paul's Church. The stylish house was built for planter Baker Hoskins and his wife, Martha Ann Skinner.

CO 63 Warren Grove Baptist Church and Warren Grove School

Ca. 1892, 1914; E side NC 32, 0.2 mi. N of SR 1222, Valhalla vic.

A landmark along the old "Virginia Road" is this archetypal pair of frame community buildings—a church and a school—built by African Americans at the turn of the century. The church, built on land donated in 1886, has a subtly asymmetrical facade with a pair of slightly differentiated corner towers flanking the recessed gable. The

schoolhouse, with its projecting center bay and flanking rooms, reverses the format. The county advertised in 1914 for contractors to build the school—the "two-room type," to be built "according to plan 2B in Plans for Public School Houses, 1911," with certain modifications.

CO 64 Waff-Felton-Hollowell House

Early 19th c., late 19th c.; E side SR 1222, 2.0 mi. N of NC 32, Rockyhock vic.; private, visible from road

The highly visible plantation house embodies a typical sequence of building phases. It began as a side-passage-plan Federal era dwelling—a popular form among middling planters in the Albemarle section. It was expanded to a central-passage-plan house with double porch in the 1840s and received a wraparound porch and other Victorian embellishments in the 1890s. A nursery operates on the site.

CO 65 Cullen Jones House (Ferry Road Farm)

Early 19th c.; SE corner SR 1224 and SR 1222, Rockyhock vic.; private, visible from road

The small house with engaged porch exemplifies the regional coastal cottage type, here with massive, hewn porch posts. Most notable, the oldest portion of the dwelling is of round log construction—one of the few known examples in eastern N.C., though log building was described as common in the 18th c. The house is also an unusual survival of the small farmer's dwelling. With only 20 acres under cultivation, Jones's farm was more typical than the big plantations whose buildings have more often survived to the present.

CO 66 Tyner (Center Hill)

Though its railroad depot is gone, the village on the old Suffolk and Carolina route retains a country store, Gothic Revival style Methodist church, and frame houses with decorated porches. Called Center Hill in the 1880s, it was renamed for former postmaster general James Tyner but continues use of the old name.

CO 67 Happy Home Pentecostal Holiness Church and Arbor

1919, 1920s, 1950s; E side SR 1303, 2.3 mi. N of SR 1002, Icaria vic.

Happy Home is a 20th-c. version of a long-lived form of religious architecture—the arbor and surrounding tents used for annual camp meetings. The congregation, established in 1915, built a small frame church in 1918. Probably during the 1920s the large, open frame "arbor" was erected, along with wooden "tents" to house worshipers during the weeks of summer camp meeting. The tents were rebuilt as small concrete block duplex units in the 1950s. Camp meetings flourished throughout the state in the 19th c., and several campgrounds survive in the Piedmont, but few in eastern N.C.

Washington County (WH)

WH 1 Plymouth

Apparently named for the Massachusetts port with which the Albemarle region had early trade connections, Plymouth began in the early 18th c. as a landing on the southern side of the Roanoke River near its mouth on Albemarle Sound. The town was laid out in 1787, incorporated in 1807, and made county seat in 1823, succeeding Lee's Mill—present-day *Roper. Gaining a U.S. customhouse in 1830, antebellum Plymouth flourished as a prime regional shipping point for agricultural and forest products and a shipbuilding community. During the Civil War, its strategic position on the Roanoke River made Plymouth the site of three fierce battles contesting control of the region. Bombardments in 1864 destroyed much of the town. Postwar rebuilding of the town and its economy came slowly, delayed by devastating downtown fires in 1881 and 1898, but despite these setbacks, local entrepreneurs strove to "build up Plymouth" as a business center. Key to their success were the railroads: the Albemarle and Raleigh Railroad (later the Atlantic Coast Line), which entered Plymouth in 1889, and the Norfolk and Southern Railroad, which came in 1891. These made Plymouth a maritime railhead and invigorated shipping and manufacturing. In the 20th c., major wood products factories bolstered the economy of the town and the region.

The principal public building is the **Washington County Courthouse** (1918–19; Benton & Benton [Wilson]; NE corner Adams and Main Sts.), a conservative Neoclassical brick building with Ionic portico and stone trim. The bracketed, brick **Plymouth Passenger Station** (1927; 612 Washington St.), built as a union station, stands at its original location just north of US 64, adapted as a bank. At the eastern end of the brick commercial district, the **Atlantic Coast Line Railroad Station** (1923; 302 E. Water St.), also brick with a bracketed, hip roof, has been renovated as the Port of Plymouth Museum, recalling the maritime rail trade that revitalized the community.

Plymouth has two churches of special distinction. **Grace Episcopal Church** (1860–61; Richard Upjohn [New York]; 1892–93, Charles E. Hartge [Rocky Mount and Raleigh]; 107 Madison St.) was originally built to designs that Upjohn provided long-distance, as documented in the New York architect's correspondence from rector Francis W. Hilliard and contractor Nehemiah J. Whitehurst. The unfinished Gothic Revival brick building was damaged during the bombardment of 1864, and though it was repaired and used for nearly three decades thereafter, by 1892 it had weakened to the point that the congregation decided to replace it. Hartge deftly incorporated Upjohn's 2-stage corner tower and 5-sided apse into a design for a new 5-bay nave, with the compact, buttressed, and steeply gabled structure of dark red brick punctuated by the tower with spire. The cemetery contains fine gravestones and iron fencing dating to the mid-19th c.

WH 1 *Grace Episcopal Church*

New Chapel Baptist Church (1924; Rev. S. C. Copeland [Marion, S.C.], architect and pastor; Madison and E. 3rd Sts.) is an edifice of extraordinary power and presence. Among the region's most architecturally imposing churches, the red brick cruciform building stands on a high basement, with tall, twin towers rising at the eastern facade. Subtly differing caps distinguish the towers, which flank a dramatic portico with two great, stylized columns set in antis. Built for a congregation of freedmen established by 1867, the church was designed by the minister. Tradition reports that the plan, with multiple entrances and principal portico reached by seven exterior staircases, is based on the biblical description of Solomon's temple.

WH 1 *New Chapel Baptist Church*

A few traditional, 2-story frame houses that survived the war are mixed among the late 19th- and early 20th-c. frame dwellings on the shaded streets leading out from the riverside commercial district. Least altered is the original block of the **Clark-Chesson House** (early 19th c.; 219 Jefferson St.), a 2-story, 3-bay frame house with gable-end chimneys and a shed porch. The principal antebellum landmark is the **Latham House** (ca. 1850; 311 E. Main St., under museum development), a 2-story Greek Revival frame house with a later 19th-c. cross-gable roof and front porch. The raised basement is said to have sheltered local citizens during the Civil War bombardment. A notable cluster on W. Main St. includes the picturesque, 2-story **Hornthall House** (ca. 1880; 109 W. Main St.; B&B), with steep roof, bargeboard trim, and cross gables, built for Louis Henry Hornthal, an early business leader in rebuilding the community; the **Hampton Academy** (1902, 1905; 110 W. Main St.), a brick building with arched windows; and the **David O. Brinkley House** (1914; 114 W.

Main St.), a unique, 2-story house of rusticated concrete block with a conical corner tower, built for a leading businessman. Outstanding among several examples of the picturesque style is the 1½-story **Perry-Spruill House** (ca. 1883; 326 Washington St.), a Gothic cottage in the spirit of A. J. Downing, with high hip roof dramatized by steep gables, decorative bargeboards, finials, and recently restored porch trim.

WH 2 Garrett's Island Home
Mid-18th c.; private, no public access

The gambrel-roofed frame house may be the oldest surviving house on the southern shore of Albemarle Sound. Its small size, double-shouldered exterior brick chimneys, and hall-parlor plan typify the first durable houses of the region. The "island" refers to its location on an oval of high ground encircled by an arm of the East Dismal Swamp, which occupies much of the county.

WH 3 Westover Plantation
Mid-19th c., early 20th c.; S side NC 308, 1.2 mi. E of NC 45/308, Plymouth vic.; private, visible from road

Approached by a road embowered with moss-hung live oaks, this is one of the agricultural county's most extensive plantation complexes. The farmstead centers on a 2-story Greek Revival house enlarged in the early 20th c. Especially notable are the many frame outbuildings, including an enormous frame barn with gambrel roof.

WH 4 Homestead Farm (Hassell House)
Mid-19th c.; S side US 64, 1.5 mi. W of Roper; private, visible from road

The 5-bay, 2-story frame house is the most prominent and best preserved of several Washington Co. plantation houses visible along US 64. Its clean, sharp profiles are created by the flush gable ends, strong gable-end chimneys, and full-width shed porch, typical of the I-house as built from the late Georgian to the early Greek Revival eras.

The large collection of outbuildings and barns is among the best in the county.

WH 5 Roper

A small place with a long history. The site on Kendricks Creek was settled in 1706 by Thomas Blount, member of a large and influential family in N.C. Thomas Lee, who married Blount's widow, built a mill here about 1709, which was noted on the Moseley map of 1733 as "S. Lee, Saw Mills." The community known as Lee's Mill was county seat in the early 19th c. It was renamed Roper in 1889 after a large lumber business was established here by John L. Roper. The small commercial district and much of the surrounding residential fabric dates from the late 19th- and early 20th-c. lumber boom. Near the site of the old mill, which operated from 1709 until 1921, is the **Harrison-Blount House** (early and late 19th c.; NE corner SR 1119 and SR 1122; private), a 2-story, Federal style house with Victorian enrichments. **Hebron Methodist Church** (1842, 1887; N side Buncombe Ave. opp. Bank St.) began in the antebellum period as a simple, gable-fronted frame building. **St. Luke's Episcopal Church** (early 20th c.; E side Bush St.) is a small, Gothic Revival frame church with a corner tower.

WH 6 Rehoboth Methodist Church

1853; S side US 64/NC 32, 0.5 mi. W of US 64/NC 32 fork, Skinnersville vic.

A memorable and evocative landmark along a well-traveled highway, the simple, digni-

WH 6 *Rehoboth Methodist Church*

fied frame church has a quiet presence enhanced by its grove of trees draped with Spanish moss. Among the finest of the state's simple Greek Revival churches of the antebellum period, the weatherboarded building has a pedimented gable front with double entrance, and large, clear windows of 16/16 sash that make the sanctuary a bright, essentially transparent space. The church is said to have been constructed by slaves of Joseph H. Norman, a member who donated the land.

WH 7 Creswell

Creswell's commercial district—the 100 blocks of E. and W. Main St., just south of US 64—contains probably the state's best collection of 19th-c. wooden store buildings, most with gable fronts, many plain, but some embellished with brackets and other simple ornamentation. Several mid- and late 19th-c. houses show Greek Revival and Victorian influences, including a number of steep-gabled, picturesque cottages. Begun as Cool Spring by 1826, the community was renamed for John Creswell, U.S. postmaster general in the late 19th c.

WH 8 Belgrade and St. David's Church

Ca. 1797, 1803, 1857; N and S sides SR 1158, 0.4 mi. E of US 64, Creswell vic.; private, visible from road

WH 8 *Belgrade*

The modest frame house and church are associated with Episcopal priest and planter Charles Pettigrew, rector of *St. Paul's Episcopal Church in Edenton during the Revolution, who settled in this area after the war.

WH 7 *E. Main St., Creswell*

In 1794 Pettigrew was elected bishop of the reconstituted Episcopal Church in N.C. but never made the journey to Philadelphia for consecration. His progressive farm operation here was considered among the state's most efficient. Pettigrew built the simple, 1½-story frame house, with paired chimneys of Flemish-bond brick. His son later commented that it was better than any house his father had previously occupied, attesting to the quality of local architecture in the 18th c. In 1803 Pettigrew established the chapel across the road, which was expanded in 1857 and became a parish church, St. David's. The starkly simple frame structure takes a cruciform plan with a central entrance tower and spire.

WH 9 Somerset Place

Late 18th c., house ca. 1838–40; N side Lake Phelps, end of SR 1160, Creswell vic.; state historic site, open regular hours

One of N.C.'s greatest coastal plantations, Somerset began in 1784 when three Edenton businessmen formed the Lake Company to drain the rich swampland around Lake Phelps for the cultivation of rice and other crops. For this massive undertaking they imported large numbers of slaves directly from Africa; by 1788 they had completed a canal between the lake and the Scuppernong

River. This was one of the northernmost locations for the successful production of rice. By 1816 Edenton merchant-planter Josiah Collins had bought out other interests in the Lake Company and named the plantation "Somerset" after his native English county. In 1820 the operation was described as "the finest estate in North Carolina," with "thousands of acres of land in one body as rich as the banks of the Nile." On the isolated plantation the slaves retained many aspects of their African culture, including language, religion, and agricultural practices. Though rice production was eventually abandoned, under Josiah Collins II and III as many as 300 slaves produced corn and other crops through the antebellum period.

It was for Josiah Collins III that the mansion house was built, in a sequence of construction that began after his 1829 marriage to Mary Riggs of New Jersey. With double porches on three sides, the house combines regional coastal features with simplified Greek Revival detail. The T-plan has a center passage and a transverse arch framing a cross stair passage, with the dining room in the rear ell—a plan seen in a few other Albemarle region houses. Cypress timber was used extensively in construction.

Half a dozen buildings survive of more than thirty structures that formed a plantation village around a 4-acre garden. (See

WH 9 *Somerset Place*

Introduction, Fig. 17.) Located near the mansion house, these include an old dwelling known as the "Colony House," a smokehouse, a dairy, a kitchen-laundry, and an icehouse. Several other structures have been reconstructed. Foundations remain of other buildings, including the slave hospital and the long row of more than twenty slave quarters along the old lakeshore. Drainage ditches, the canal, and Lake Phelps, along with the broad fields and quiet woods, create a setting evocative of the distant past. After decades of decline following the Civil War, the property was acquired by the state in 1939 as part of Pettigrew State Park; in 1967 the house and outbuildings were developed as a state historic site. In recent years the interpretation has placed new emphasis on African heritage and life during slavery, and the plantation has been the scene of "Somerset Homecomings" for the descendants of the black and white families who lived there. In 1985–87 low water in Lake Phelps revealed twenty-six prehistoric canoes in the lake bottom, including dugout canoes up to 4,000 years old—the oldest boats in eastern North America by more than 1,000 years.

Tyrrell County (TY)

TY 1 Columbia

TY 1 *Tyrrell County Courthouse*

Though settlement began in Tyrrell Co. by the early 18th c., little architecture survives even from the first half of the 19th c. Until recent swampland reclamation, much of the county was not arable, and Tyrrell remains the state's least populous county. Columbia, the county seat and the only incorporated town, is a pleasant community on the eastern bank of the Scuppernong River, established in the late 18th c. as a trading post. Its chief landmark is the **Tyrrell County Courthouse** (1903; B. F. Smith Construction Company [Washington, D.C.]; sw corner Main and Broad Sts.). The red brick building, the most intact of four similar courthouses built in eastern N.C. by the Washington firm, has a square plan under a pyramidal roof and features parapeted gable wall dormers, Italianate arched windows and doors, and a Colonial Revival porch. The 2-story brick jail to the rear was built shortly afterward.

West of the courthouse the business district of early 20th-c. commercial buildings with corbeled brickwork reaches along Main St. to the river. A good collection of turn-of-the-century frame houses typical of the re-

gion's small towns extends east down Main St. and along the narrow, shaded side streets north of Main. The **Combs-Hussey House** (1890s; 415 Main St.) is a 2-story frame house with a fanciful wraparound porch with corner pavilion. Churches of varied Gothic Revival character mingle with the residential fabric: the frame **Columbia Baptist Church** (1905 with additions; NW corner Road and Bridge Sts.), dominated by a 3-stage corner tower with pinnacled belfry; **Wesley Memorial Methodist Church** (1909–12; NE corner Main and Church Sts.), brick with a crenellated corner tower and arcaded entrance loggia; and **Columbia Christian Church** (ca. 1905; 602 Bridge St.), frame with low flanking twin towers. **St. Andrews Episcopal Church** (1909; Thomas Swain, builder; near SE corner Main and S. Road Sts.), frame with a steep gable roof, has a front entrance tower with an octagonal open belfry under an ogee cap and a hammerbeam ceiling. In 1859 New York architect Richard Upjohn provided plans, now lost, for an Episcopal chapel in Columbia that was never built; it is not known whether builder Swain had knowledge of that design. The Gothic Revival altar rail was carved by German immigrant Johann Frederick Schlez, owner of the town's early movie house.

An anomaly among the town's frame domestic architecture is the **Steanie C. Chaplin House** (1928; Jim and Joe Alexander, builders; 107 N. Broad St.), a buff brick house of Mediterranean inspiration with an arcaded front porch and Spanish tile pent roof above the second-floor windows. It was built for the town's doctor and founder of the local hospital by the Alexander brothers, accomplished masons who also erected several buildings in Columbia's commercial district during the 1920s.

Dare County (DR)

Mainland:

Covered mostly in maritime forests and wetlands, the Dare Co. mainland has always been sparsely populated, and much of its land area is now in the hands of the U.S. Fish and Wildlife Service as the Alligator River Preserve. The only towns are two small fishing settlements, Stumpy Point and Manns Harbor. The chief landmarks are the rural churches that have been the focal points of community life.

DR 1 East Lake Methodist Church

Ca. 1900; N side US 64, 3.6 mi. E of Alligator River, East Lake vic.

The simple, handsome, frame country church makes effective use of a single decorative motif—round arches—in its windows, doors, and fanlit entrance gable.

DR 2 Mount Carmel Methodist Church

Early 20th c.; W side US 64/264, Manns Harbor

The frame country church was built on an L-plan with a 4-stage belltower capped with a pinnacled spire. The triangular heads over the windows and doors complement the diamond-shaped windows in the gable ends and the tower.

Roanoke Island:

Although the 25-square-mile island between the mainland and the Outer Banks was the site of the first attempted English settlement in the New World, permanent settlement was late in coming and remained scattered until the late 19th c. The two communities are Manteo (the county seat) and Wanchese, named for the two Indians from the island who accompanied explorers Amadas and Barlowe to England in 1584.

DR 3 Fort Raleigh National Historic Site

1585; reconstructed early 1950s (Jean C. Harrington, archaeologist); N end Roanoke Island off US 64, 1.0 mile E of Umstead Memorial Bridge; open to public

This reconstruction of the oldest identifiable English-built structure on the North American continent stands on its original site and is based on archaeological evidence. The earthwork was built by Sir Walter Raleigh's first contingent of colonists in the New World, led by Ralph Lane. About 130 feet on its longest dimension, the small fort, shaped roughly like a star, was planned around a square with bastions along the sides. This type of earthwork predated the use of firearms, though military engineers continued to use the form after the introduction of gunpowder. (The colonists were equipped with muskets and small cannon). The fort was abandoned in 1586 when the company returned to England. A second colony, led by John White, came in 1587 and, unlike the first, included women and children. White returned to England for additional supplies but was prevented from returning by England's war with Spain. The colonists had disappeared by the time help arrived in 1590. The fate of this "Lost Colony" has never been ascertained.

The mystery and the place have long attracted attention. By the late 19th c., history-minded individuals from the Albemarle region and elsewhere were holding celebrations on Roanoke Island, with special attention to Virginia Dare, the first child born of English parents in America. In 1921 a set was built and the *Lost Colony* movie was filmed using many local cast members. The outdoor drama *The Lost Colony*, produced each summer at the Waterside Theater, is the oldest outdoor symphonic drama in the nation: by famed author Paul Green, it began production in 1937 as a Federal Theatre Project of the WPA. The adjacent **Elizabethan Garden** (private; open to public), a 10½-acre interpretation of a 16th-c. Elizabethan pleasure garden, was established in 1951 by the Garden Club of N.C. as a memorial to the first colonists. It was designed by M. Umberto Innocenti and Richard Webel.

DR 4 Manteo

Manteo's location on US 64 has brought intense commercial development in recent years. During much of the 20th c., the town has emphasized the Lost Colony saga in attracting tourism. In the 1960s Manteo's streets were renamed for characters and places associated with the Lost Colony drama, and the first of many buildings were remodeled or built new with half-timbering and other "Elizabethan" effects. Commemoration of the 400th anniversary of the colony included construction of the *Elizabeth II*, built locally in 1982–84 and docked at Manteo. The vessel, a representative of the type used by the Roanoke colonists to sail to America, is a popular tourist attraction.

Several buildings recall earlier times in Manteo. Facing Queen Elizabeth Ave. and the waterfront between Sir Walter Raleigh St. and Budleigh St., the red brick **Dare County Courthouse** (1903; B. F. Smith Construction Company [Washington, D.C.]; w side Queen Elizabeth St. at Budleigh St.) originally resembled the *Tyrrell County Courthouse erected the same year by the same builder. It has lost its raised gables and gained a ca. 1970 porch, but the Italianate arched openings and decorative brickwork remain. The **Theodore S. Meekins House** (1910–12; Joe Dailey and John Wilson, builders; 319 Sir Walter Raleigh St.) is an ebullient late Queen Anne style residence with shingled gables and rounded corner tower with conical roof. Meekins was contractor for the *Chicamacomico Lifesaving Station. Carpenters Dailey and Wilson had previously built lighthouse keeper's dwellings and lifesaving stations, and the materials reportedly came from the Kramer Brothers Lumber Company in Elizabeth City. The **George Washington Creef Jr. House** (late 19th c.; 304 Budleigh St.), built

DR 4 *Theodore S. Meekins House*

for a prominent family of boat builders, is a cruciform-plan, board-and-batten house with shingled gables and sawn and turned ornament akin to the lighthouse keepers' quarters of the era. Creef is best known as builder and owner of the *Hattie Creef* (1889–1968), a sailboat named for his daughter, which carried the Wright Brothers to Kitty Hawk.

DR 5 Wanchese

Bypassed by US 64 and its associated tourist-oriented strips, Wanchese on the southern end of Roanoke Island thus far retains the character of a turn-of-the-century fishing village, with white frame houses and community buildings scattered among the live oaks.

Outer Banks:

The Outer Banks, a series of barrier islands lined by shoals dangerous to shipping, include alternating sections of intense development and protected national seashore. Principal architectural landmarks from the years of isolation before bridge construction include vestiges of resort and fishing communities, lighthouses, and lifesaving stations. (See Introduction, Fig. 48.)

*Nine lifesaving stations survive in Dare Co. in various conditions and ownership, some still in Coast Guard hands, others moved and converted to private uses. *Chicamacomico is the best known, most accessible, and most dramatic architecturally. Others are* noted here for travelers with special interest. The U.S. Lifesaving Service and later the Coast Guard erected stations of two main architectural eras: first a picturesque style in the 1870s, then a shingled mode that began at the turn of the century. Both types presented nationally popular styles considered suitable to a coastal location and easy to build on remote locations.

Established in 1870, the Lifesaving Service built seven stations along the N.C. coast in 1874, plus additional facilities in 1878 and in the 1880s. Constructed in a standard format along with stations in other states, these first stations were 1½-story, steep-gabled buildings in a picturesque cottage style, finished with shingles, board and batten, and sawnwork ornament. Each accommodated the lifeboat and a crew living room at the first level and crew quarters above, plus a watchtower atop the roof. Six surfmen and a keeper, usually of local families, originally manned each station.

A second construction campaign began in the 1890s, with a new shingled and towered prototype called the Quonochontaug type, and several variations developed after 1900, including one that was first built at *Chicamacomico in 1911, with front porch and square tower. This type was the last generation of stations before the Lifesaving Service was incorporated into the Coast Guard in 1915. The Coast Guard continued along similar lines for some years. Typically, when new stations were built alongside old ones, the original buildings were converted to boathouses.

By the mid-20th c., many of the stations were sold to private owners, as improvements in shipping and rescue technology eliminated the need for the many closely placed stations. Several have been moved to new sites; loca-tions given here may be subject to change. Recently both types have become the models for postmodern beach architecture on the banks. Sites are listed north to south along the 100-mile stretch of Dare's banks from Caffey's Inlet to Hatteras Inlet. See Joe A. Mobley, Ship Ashore! (1994).

DR 6 Caffey's Inlet Lifesaving Station
1897; E side NC 12, 0.8 mi. S of Currituck Co. line; private restaurant open to public

A well-preserved example of the early 20th-c. wood-shingled lifesaving stations. Atypical is the combination hip and gable roof, with the cupola at the peak of the hip.

DR 7 First Kitty Hawk Lifesaving Station
1875; W side US 158 BUS (E of US 158 BYP) at SR 1206; private restaurant open to public

The Kitty Hawk Lifesaving Station is represented by structures from both building periods that formerly sat side by side on the oceanfront and were moved in recent years due to the eroding shoreline. Now directly across the road from its original site, the original board-and-batten station displays decorative gable ends amidst modern expansions. South 0.2 mi. stands the **Second Kitty Hawk Lifesaving Station** (1911; Richard C. Evans [Manteo], builder; w side US 158 BUS, 0.2 mi. s of SR 1206; private), which typifies the second generation of stations, a shingled building with hip-roofed dormers on its steep gable roof and a hip-roofed cupola at one end.

DR 8 Kitty Hawk Village
SR 1206 (W. Kitty Hawk Rd.) and SR 1208, W of US 158 BYP

Settled before 1790, the village of Kitty Hawk is one of the largest and most intact Outer Banks communities, despite recent commercial development. Older buildings dot the length of W. Kitty Hawk Rd. as it meanders across the widest stretch of the barrier islands through woods and marsh and over creeks to the sound. Late 19th- and early 20th-c. dwellings include small coastal cottages and compact I-houses with rear sheds or side wings; 1920s and 1930s bungalows are scattered throughout. **Providence Primitive Baptist Church** (early 20th c.; SE corner SR 1208 and SR 1207) exemplifies the plain, gable-fronted buildings favored by the denomination. Near the eastern end of SR 1208 the picturesque **Austin Cemetery** occupies a prominent tree-shaded rise.

DR 9 Wright Brothers National Memorial

Monument, 1928–32, Rodgers and Poor; Visitors' Center, 1960, Mitchell/Giurgola (Philadelphia); W side US 158 at milepost 7; open regular hours

The first self-propelled airplane flight in history was made here by Ohioans Orville and Wilbur Wright on Dec. 17, 1903. This is the event celebrated on N.C. automobile license plates with the motto "First in Flight." The towering 60-foot pylon of Mount Airy, N.C., granite, erected by the federal government to commemorate the flight, is carved with a stylized wing design of Art Deco character and stands atop a 90-foot dune. A reconstruction (1953) of the brothers' 1903 camp lies at the base of the hill near the "first flight" area. The **Visitors' Center** (1960) is an early work by the Philadelphia firm of Mitchell/Giurgola, which has since achieved international recognition. The concrete structure is elevated slightly above the flat terrain, and the dome over the assembly room echoes the rise of nearby dunes.

DR 9 *Wright Brothers National Memorial*

DR 10 Kill Devil Hills Lifesaving Station

1910; E side US 158 at milepost 9; private, visible from road

The 2-story shingled station has a pyramidal roof pierced by a large, glassed observation tower. It replaced an 1870s station that was then converted to a boathouse. The older building was moved in 1986 to *Corolla in Currituck Co.

DR 11 Nags Head Beach Cottage Row

Between US 158 and Atlantic Ocean, mileposts 12.5–13.5

DR 11 *Nags Head Beach Cottage Row*

Amid the onslaught of new beach development, vestiges of a quieter time remain. Most striking is the row of starkly handsome, wood-shingled frame beach cottages extending nearly a mile along the beach overlooking the Atlantic Ocean. The cottages with their outbuildings compose a remarkable and evocative survival of the late 19th- and early 20th-c. lifestyle of this once-isolated summer coastal resort. Long accessible only by boat, Nags Head was a fashionable antebellum resort that built up on the sound side. Construction of summer cottages along the ocean side began after the Civil War. Families of merchants, planters, and professional men of northeastern N.C., especially the Albemarle, owned their own cottages and returned summer after summer, generation after generation, contending occasionally with storms that forced the whole community to move back from the sea. Houses were simply built, of frame covered with weatherboards or shingles, set up on piers, and without heat. During the early 20th c., the oceanside development expanded from the dozen or so pioneer cottages, with most of the 1920s and 1930s construction done by Elizabeth City builder

S. J. Twine. His big, sturdy cottages, distinguished by swooping roofs and expansive dormers in a wood-shingled bungalow idiom, blend with the earlier cottages and provide much of the character of the district. Highly functional, characteristic details include "lean-out" benches set into porch balustrades, awning-type batten shutters, and hurricane doors outside screen doors. **St. Andrew's by the Sea** (w side US 158, milepost 12.5), combines the Gothic Revival style with wood shingles in a chapel suited to the cottage community.

DR 12 First Colony Inn
1932; Willis Leigh, designer; Frank Benton, builder; 6720 S. Virginia Dare Trail, Nags Head; B&B

DR 12 *First Colony Inn*

The last traditional beach hotel left in Nags Head is this H-shaped, shingled frame building composed of three 25-by-60-foot sections joined by breezeways. Like an oversized beach cottage, the 2½-story building is dominated by a capacious hip roof, which reaches out over the deep, 2-tier porches that surround the building. Nags Head style, lean-out benches are fitted into the porch railings. The inn was built by Henry and Marie LeRoy as LeRoy's Seaside Inn during a period of growth of Nags Head as the "summer capital of the Albemarle," when the resort's popularity was boosted by the 1930 completion of the Wright Memorial Bridge. Willis Leigh, an employee of Kramer Brothers in Elizabeth City (he later married the LeRoys' daughter Marguerite), designed the inn in traditional Nags Head fashion. The lumber arrived by boat from Elizabeth City's Kramer Brothers Lumber Company. Frank Benton, also of Elizabeth City, con-

structed the inn within four months for $16,000 and had it ready to open in June 1932, complete with running water and electricity. In 1937 the inn was sold to Capt. C. P. Midgett and Ernest Jones, who in the spirit of the new Lost Colony drama changed the name to First Colony Inn. After service as apartments and threats of demolition, in 1988 it was moved here from its original oceanfront site 3.5 miles north, then carefully restored in 1990–91 for renewed use as a first-class inn.

DR 13 Bodie Island Lifesaving/ Coast Guard Station
1878, 1903, 1925; E side NC 12, 5.3 mi. S of US 64; visible from road, no public access

The original cottage-style station with decorative gable ends is now a ranger's residence, and a 1903 boathouse survives. The main building is a 2-story frame structure with gable-on-hip roof erected in 1925 by the U.S. Coast Guard. It continued in service through the early 1950s.

DR 14 Bodie Island Lighthouse and Keeper's Quarters
1872; Dexter Stetson, contractor; E side Park Rd., 0.9 mi. from entrance at W side NC 12, 5.8 mi. S of US 64; open to public

DR 14 *Bodie Island Lighthouse and Keeper's Quarters*

The conical brick lighthouse, 163 feet high on a granite foundation, is painted with a daymark of wide horizontal stripes to distinguish it from other lighthouses of similar design. It replaced towers built in 1848 and 1859 (the latter destroyed during the Civil War) on the southern side of Oregon Inlet. The small brick oil house at the base is like that at *Currituck Beach Lighthouse. The facility was converted from oil to electric light in 1932. The first-order Fresnel lens—the largest, brightest type, used for principal seacoast lighthouses—was installed in 1872 and is still in place. The 2-story brick keeper's quarters (1872) is now a visitors' center.

DR 15 Oregon Inlet Lifesaving/ Coast Guard Station

1897, 1933; E side SR 1257, 0.3 mi. N of NC 12; visible from road, no public access

The station was among those established in 1874 and remains in service as the oldest active lifesaving and Coast Guard station in the state, though the original building has not survived. The present building retains its 1897 form with sweeping roofline, deep porches, and shingled surfaces. In 1933 additional dormer windows were added, and the large observation tower was rebuilt. Part of the endless saga of change along the Outer Banks, Oregon Inlet opened as a result of a hurricane in 1846 and was named for the first vessel that passed through it, the *Oregon*. The inlet has moved steadily southward.

DR 16 Chicamacomico Lifesaving Station

1874, 1911; Victor Mindeleff, architect; Theodore S. Meekins (Manteo), builder; E side NC 12 at SR 1247, Rodanthe; open limited hours

The most intact and best known of the state's lifesaving stations is an evocative and popular attraction at the beach. One of the original seven built in N.C. by the Lifesaving Service, the 1874 board-and-batten station was converted into a boathouse when a new shingle-style station with lookout tower was constructed in 1911. Designed for the Lifesaving Service by architect Victor Mindeleff, the 1911 Chicamacomico station with columned porch and dormers became a prototype for other stations. The stations from both eras, plus supporting structures such as water tanks and storage buildings, survive as the state's most complete lifesaving station complex, with museum and exhibits tracing an exciting era in the history of the Atlantic coast. Crews of Chicamacomico took part in some of the most daring rescues along the coast. The most famous came in 1918:

DR 16 *Chicamacomico Lifesaving Station*

after a German U-boat torpedoed the British tanker *Mirlo*, Chicamacomico surfmen braved seas aflame with oil to rescue the British seamen. The crewmen were awarded gold medals of honor by the British and U.S. governments for their heroism.

DR 17 Salvo Post Office

Ca. 1910; Lafayette Douglas, builder; W side NC 12, 0.1 mi. S of Park Rd., Salvo; open to public

The tiny (8 by 12 feet) gable-fronted frame building was erected at a time when most Outer Banks post offices were located in stores or houses. After taking office in 1908, Salvo postmistress Marcie Douglas operated the post office out of her kitchen, but within a short time her husband, a fisherman and carpenter, built her the small separate post office structure near their house. After Mrs. Douglas retired in 1946, the post office was moved—once on skids, once on a boat hitch—to the yards of the subsequent postmistress and postmaster. U.S. Postal Service efforts to relocate the facility brought strong local resistance, and in 1988 the Postal Service officially recognized the Salvo Post Office as the second smallest post office in the nation (Ochopee, Fla., has a smaller one, but it was not purpose-built). A fire in 1992 damaged the building and ended over 80 years of nearly continuous service, but the community rallied to restore the building as a local landmark.

DR 18 Little Kinnakeet Lifesaving Station

1874, 1904; W side NC 12, 2.6 mi. N of Avon; private, visible from road

Little Kinnakeet is the southernmost of the original seven lifesaving stations on the Outer Banks. The board-and-batten building with sawnwork trim housed surfboats below and crew quarters above. The larger, 1904 structure is a 1½-story wood-shingled building with a 2-tier hip observation tower.

DR 19 Cape Hatteras Lighthouse

1870; Dexter Stetson, contractor; S side NC 12, Buxton; site open to public

The tallest brick lighthouse in the United States rises 208 feet and is painted with a daymark of black-and-white spiral stripes. The towering beacon stands at Cape Hatteras, one of the most dangerous points along the Outer Banks, where clashing air and water currents, the extensive Diamond Shoals, and the absence of natural landmarks made sea travel perilous. The frequent shipwrecks in the area gained this zone the title of "Graveyard of the Atlantic." The first lighthouse here was completed in 1803, an octagonal structure of stone and brick 90 feet tall plus a 12-foot lantern; it was blown up in 1870 when this lighthouse was completed. When the U.S. government began to improve shipping safety along the coast after the Civil War, construction of a new lighthouse at Hatteras was a top priority. It was completed in 1870 and painted with its spiral striping in 1873. Originally the lighthouse had a first-order Fresnel lens in keeping with its importance as a major coastal beacon. The present DCB 24 optic was installed in 1972. With its modern electric beacon still in use, the Hatteras light serves as the primary navigational aid for mariners rounding the

DR 19 *Cape Hatteras Lighthouse*

treacherous Diamond Shoals. Other buildings remain from its long history, including a small brick oil house, brick keeper's quarters (1871), and a 2-story frame keeper's quarters (1854), now a visitors' center. The lighthouse is threatened by beach erosion. Alternate schemes for its preservation include a technically difficult move to safer ground and the construction of protective berms, which would leave the lighthouse on an island by the 21st c.

DR 20 Creed's Hill Lifesaving Station
1918; S side NC 12, 1.9 mi. E of SR 1246, Hatteras village vic.; private, visible from road

The 2-story, weatherboarded structure represents the second generation of lifesaving stations, with a gable-on-hip roof, interior chimneys, and a hip-roofed porch.

DR 21 Durant's Lifesaving Station (formerly Hatteras Lifesaving Station)
1879; S side NC 12 E of Hatteras village; private, visible from road

One of the first generation of lifesaving stations, the small building has a central gabled lookout tower and a cross gable on the ocean side, decorated with bargeboards and pendants.

Hyde County (HY)

In 1863, Hyde Co. planter William S. Carter wrote to Gov. Zebulon Vance, "Our granaries are full of the old crops and our prolific earth is groaning under the abundance of the new." Much of the county is given to marsh, but vast fields of arable land, drained by an extensive system of ditches, are indeed prolific, even in years when drought afflicts crops further inland. A long history of agricultural abundance is written in a collection of rural architecture spanning two centuries. The absence of large towns, high-speed four-lane highways, or commercial strips make the county a good place for a leisurely road tour of 19th-c. plantations, farms, rural churches, and country stores. Twenty miles across Pamlico Sound but also part of Hyde Co., the maritime village of Ocracoke still provides a sense of the seagoing life of another era. Here as in other areas of the Outer Banks the distinctive "hoi-toid" accent recalls the long isolation of early British settlers and their descendants.

HY 1 Swan Quarter

The unincorporated town has been county seat since 1836. The romantic name apparently derives from early landowner Samuel Swann, not the bird, though the nearby Swan Quarter National Wildlife Refuge on Pamlico Sound is in fact a haven for swan, geese, and other waterfowl. Set amid a cluster of early 20th-c. frame commercial buildings, the **Hyde County Courthouse** (1850s, 1878, 1908; at the town center) is one of seven antebellum courthouses in N.C. still in use by the courts. The compact, stuccoed, 2-story brick building has been modified by later remodelings and additions, though the corbeled mousetooth cornice and ornate gable-end brackets suggest its 19th-c. character.

Four churches of the late 19th and early 20th centuries stand near the courthouse. **Swan Quarter Christian Church** (1882; SR 1132), **Swan Quarter Baptist Church** (1912; SR 1129), and **Calvary Episcopal Church** (1925; SR 1129) are simple country Gothic Revival churches executed in frame. **Providence Methodist Church** (1912; SR 1129), the town's largest church, is brick with entrance towers of unequal height at the front corners. The congregation's first simple frame sanctuary of 1876 is attached to the rear as a fellowship hall. Tradition recalls that shortly after the little building's construction, storm-driven high water lifted it from its foundation at a less desirable site and floated it to the present location, where it was allowed to stay because it was considered to have been moved by the hand of Providence.

HY 2 St. John's Episcopal Church
1875; H.B. Fortiscue, builder; SW side SR 1143, 0.15 mi. S of SR 1142, Sladesville

A few late 19th- and early 20th-c. houses, stores, and churches survive of the community of Sladesville, once an incorporated trading center. The central landmark is St. John's, a well-tended Carpenter Gothic church retaining its original furnishings and sawnwork decoration. The church was moved in 1908 from nearby Makleyville, where a church had been established in the mid-18th c. The 1875 construction contract specified that carpenter Fortiscue reuse sound timbers from the earlier church and that the building have "ten windows Pointed of suitable size."

HY 3 Rose Bay Missionary Baptist Church and School
Church ca. 1923; school ca. 1913; S side SR 1138, 0.2 mi. SE of US 264, Rose Bay

HY 3 *Rose Bay Missionary Baptist Church and School*

A fanlight in the pedimented front gable, molded and decorated eaves and window hoods, and a small open belfry enrich the weatherboarded country church, which contains a simple, 1-room, 2-aisle-plan sanctuary. Adjacent is the 1-story frame **Rose Bay School** of a decade earlier, now used as a community center, with a central pavilion flanked by recessed porches and topped with a tiny belfry.

HY 4 Swindell House and Store

House ca. 1850, 1903; store ca. 1890; S side US 264 opp. SR 1304, Swindell Fork; private, visible from road

HY 4 *Swindell House and Store*

Hyde Co. abounds in small frame country stores, virtually all now empty, that served a widely dispersed rural population before the automobile age. The small, gable-fronted store at Swindell Fork was built about 1890 by Albin B. Swindell to house the retail business he had established in 1875. The store also contained the post office and the first telephone in the community. The 2-story frame house nearby is Swindell's 1903 enlargement of a mid-19th-c. house he bought in 1877. A 1-story kitchen wing is attached to the southwestern corner, and

a smokehouse, washhouse, and other outbuildings create a small domestic compound.

HY 5 Lake Mattamuskeet Pump Station

1926; end of SR 1330 on Lake Mattamuskeet; grounds have public access; building under development as a research facility and visitors' center

HY 5 *Lake Mattamuskeet Pump Station*

Lake Mattamuskeet is the largest natural inland lake in N.C. Generations of planters dreamed of draining its 30,000 acres to expose the rich bottom soil for farming. John White's 1585 map showed it as Paquippe, from an Indian word for "shallow lake," but by 1733 maps called it Mattamuskeet, from an Indian word meaning "moving swamp." As early as 1789 drainage projects were undertaken, and in the 1840s gravity-flow canals dug by slaves partially lowered the lake level. In 1915 the New Holland Corporation began work on canals and a pump station, but the project had limited success until New York entrepreneur August Heckscher took over the venture in 1925. When completed shortly thereafter, the pump station with four centrifugal steam pumps was said to be the world's largest pumping plant. Heckscher successfully drained and farmed the lake bed, achieving extraordinary yields of corn, sweet potatoes, beans, wheat, flax, oats, and soybeans. After the project was abandoned in 1933 due to pumping difficulties, excessive rainfall, and agricultural pests, the lake soon refilled. In 1934 the federal government bought the property for a wildlife refuge. The Civilian Conservation Corps converted the 3-story brick pumping station into a hunting lodge, and the 120-foot chimney became an observation tower. The building is under development by the Fish and Wildlife Service for an estuarine resource center.

Lake Landing Plantations District:
Several thousand acres of rich farmland south of Lake Mattamuskeet comprise a historic rural landscape of exceptional character. In the early 19th c. agriculturalist Edmund Ruffin marveled, "I have never seen such magnificent growths of corn, upon such large spaces."

The flat terrain is punctuated by farmsteads established in the 18th and 19th centuries and linked by drainage ditches, canals, and creeks that were once the primary transportation arteries to New Bern and other markets. The expansive openness and dramatic vistas of the landscape reflect the recent introduction of large-scale farming machinery that eliminated the tall hedgerows that once girded the fields. Clusters of vacant frame commercial buildings at Middletown and Nebraska—ghosts of once-bustling trading towns—and elsewhere recall a past era of water transportation. The architecture of the district includes stylish antebellum plantation houses—some with New Bern influenced features such as exposed face chimneys—as well as characteristic vernacular domestic, agricultural, and commercial rural architecture. Visitors are encouraged to take a leisurely drive around the loop formed by US 264, SR 1114, SR 1108, SR 1110, and SR 1116 as marked by the Hyde Co. Historical Society. A few landmarks are noted below.

HY 6 Jennette Farm
Ca. 1852, 1902; S side US 264, 3.4 mi. E of SR 1330; private, visible from road

One of the most complete 19th-c. farms in the area is situated on land owned continuously by a single family since 1772. Sited in a grove of pecan trees, the house, with its proliferation of decorative gables, is a 1902 expansion made for Thomas Henry Jennette Jr. of his father's simple, mid-19th-c. dwelling. The large complex of red-painted outbuildings includes a small barn that may have been the original farmhouse.

HY 7 Hugh Credle House
Ca. 1902; S side US 264, 3.7 mi. E of SR 1330; private, visible from road

The unusually robust Queen Anne farmhouse features projecting gables with lacy ornamental bracing, sawn porch spandrels, and sawtooth shingles in the front gable.

HY 8 Riley Murray House
Ca. 1821–26; Caleb Brooks, attributed builder; S side US 264, 0.7 mi. W of SR 1116; private, visible from road

HY 8 *Riley Murray House*

The largest of the plantation houses on the southern side of Lake Mattamuskeet, the 2½-story dwelling has interior gable-end chimneys with exposed faces, a chimney type seen frequently in New Bern. The finish is of restrained, well-crafted Federal style, including an entrance with fluted pilasters. Riley Murray was a county clerk of court and state senator. This is one of several Hyde Co. houses attributed to local builder Caleb Brooks.

HY 9 Jones-Mann-Ballance House

Early 19th c.; Caleb Brooks, attributed builder; S side US 264, 0.1 mi. W of SR 1116; private, visible from road

Bordered on the east by a major drainage and transportation artery called the Great Ditch, the 2-story, single-pile, 5-bay dwelling is among the handsomest of the county's early 19th-c. houses. Built for Dr. Hugh Jones, a planter with New Bern connections, it shows New Bern influence in its interior end exposed-face chimneys and flush door panels. The broad eaves and latticework porch date from the later 19th c., and the rear ell replaces an earlier shed. Across the highway is the **John Edward Spencer Store** (1880s), a frame country store, which housed the Lake Landing Post Office for many years.

HY 10 Wallace-Mann-Clarke House

Early 19th c.; S side US 264, 0.5 mi. E of SR 1116; private, visible from road

The 2-story, side-passage-plan house reiterates the New Bern influence on early 19th-c. Hyde Co. building in the plan, the two exposed-face, Flemish-bond brick chimneys in the eastern gable end, and the restrained Federal style woodwork. An early kitchen and milkhouse remain.

HY 11 Octagon House

1850s; S side US 264, 1.4 mi. E of SR 1116; open limited hours

Known locally as the Ink Well or the Ink Bottle House, the 2-story, octagonal house was built for Dr. William T. Sparrow and his wife, Elizabeth, in the 1850s. It is one of only two known antebellum examples in N.C. of the form made popular by New York phrenologist Orson S. Fowler in his book *A Home for All* (1848) (cf. *Octagon House, Carteret Co.). The stuccoed walls are constructed of overlapping horizontal timbers, a method suggested by Fowler. Local tradition holds that Dr. Sparrow believed that the octagon form would provide superior protection from the frequent local

HY 11–12 *Octagon House, with Bell-Jennette Farm in distance*

storms, but as a physician, he also may have subscribed to Fowler's claims of the form's healthfulness. The house has been restored as a museum and chamber of commerce office.

HY 12 Bell-Jennette Farm

1808 (date brick); S side US 264, 1.6 mi. E of SR 1116; private, visible from road

The 2-story, 5-bay frame house has a highly unusual plan: a single-pile, side-passage arrangement, with two rooms extending left of the passage separated by a large, off-center interior chimney. An early 19th-c. frame smokehouse survives among later outbuildings.

HY 13 Amity Methodist Church and Cemetery

1850–52, early 20th c.; NW side US 264 at SR 1107, Amity

HY 13 *Amity Methodist Church and Cemetery*

Visible for miles across the open countryside, the Greek Revival country church is a community landmark. The gable-fronted church has large, 12/12 sash windows and a balcony on three sides of the interior. In the early 1900s the congregation added the portico with fluted metal columns and an open belfry. The Greek Revival interior remains unchanged, with symmetrically molded door and window surrounds and Tuscan balcony columns. Especially notable is the Neoclassical altar topped with a pediment with sunburst and finial. Stairs similar to plate 22 of Asher Benjamin's *Country Builder's Assistant* (1797ff.) rise in the narthex. A large 19th-c. cemetery surrounds the church.

HY 14 Chapel Hill Academy

Ca. 1850; NW side US 264, just N of SR 1107, Amity

The 2-story frame meeting hall is typical of rural public buildings of the mid-19th c.: plain and boxy under a low hip roof, with simple Greek Revival finish and one large room on each floor. This building has been used by various schools and the local Masons over the years.

HY 15 St. George's Episcopal Church

1874−75; William Walling (Beaufort Co.), builder; NW side US 264, N of SR 1107, Amity

The fanciful Gothic Revival frame church shares with *Fairfield Methodist Church, also built by Walling, such features as paneled cornerboards, lancet arch windows, scrolled bargeboards, and drop pendants. The interior features exposed trusswork, brilliant colored glass, and stained beaded boards in a zigzag pattern. A cemetery with late 19th- and early 20th-c. markers is adjacent.

HY 16 Gibbs House

Ca. 1815; SE side SR 1108, 0.15 mi. NE of SR 1110, Middletown vic.; private, visible from road

The 2-story frame house, one of the oldest dwellings in the county, features fine Federal details. It rests on ballast stone piers and follows a single-pile, center-passage plan with original rear shed rooms flanking a recessed porch that was later enclosed. Beneath the gabled entrance porch, traces of the original cream and green paint highlight the Federal entrance with fluted pilasters. The earliest known owners were Henry and Frances Burrus Gibbs.

HY 17 Swindell-Barber-Ballance Farm (Shorewind Farms)

Ca. 1840 and later; N side SR 1110, 1.0 mi. E of SR 1116, Nebraska; private, visible from road

The main house, domestic outbuildings—washhouses, smokehouse, toilet, milkhouse, and cistern—and adjoining agricultural buildings form a complex characteristic of an evolving Lake Landing farm. The 2-story, side-passage-plan house, its shed porch now enclosed, was probably built for Joseph Swindell by 1840. The Ballance family established Shorewind Farms here and has added a hog parlor, fertilizer house, and other modern agricultural structures.

Within view on SR 1110 are three turn-of-the-century frame **Commercial Buildings** that were the center of the town of Nebraska. Just to the west of the stores is the **James Riley McKinney House** (ca. 1900), a 1-story house with rear shed wing and detached kitchen-dining room, an excellent example of a simple vernacular house of the turn of the century.

HY 18 Watson Family Complex

NE corner SR 1116 and SR 1110, Nebraska vic.; private, visible from road

Two houses and a store mark the long presence of the Watson family here. The **Fulford-Watson House** (ca. 1800; N side SR 1110, E of SR 1116), which was acquired by William Watson in 1831, is one of the oldest dwellings in the county, a small, story-and-a-jump house with an asymmetrical facade and heavy, double-shouldered chimneys. Built a century later, the **George Israel Watson House** (1896−98; NE corner SR 1110 and SR 1116) is an unusually full-blown rural version of the Queen Anne style, featuring complex rooflines, a polygonal corner tower, and tall decorative interior chimneys. It is said to have replicated a house the contractor, remembered only as a Mr. Kirk of New Bern, built for Watson relatives in that city. Included in the complex are a 2-story stock barn, a detached kitchen that was a dwelling on a nearby farm, a smokehouse, a woodhouse, a shop, and a buggy house.

The nearby **Watson Store** (mid-19th c.; NE corner SR 1116 at SR 1110), a gable-fronted frame building that is one of the oldest country store buildings in the state, retains its large chamfered interior posts, horizontal flush sheathing, and sawn decorative trim along the top of the office partitions. It served as the Wysocking Post Office early in the 20th c.

HY 19 Wynne's Folly

1840s; E side US 264, 1.0 mi. S of 1311, Engelhard vic.; private, visible from road

The 2-story Greek Revival plantation house is one of the most ambitious antebellum buildings in the county, measuring 40 feet square. Each elevation features a central entrance, reflecting the unusual plan with four rooms and a T-shaped hall arrangement. Shallow pediments accent windows and doors. The house is said to have been built by planter Richard Wynne to impress a young woman he was courting, but she married another.

HY 20 Anson Gibbs House II

1901; W corner SR 1311 and US 264, Engelhard vic.; private, visible from road

The distinctive T-plan house blends Queen Anne and Colonial Revival elements, with sunburst panels above the attic windows, sawnwork gable inserts, delicate bargeboards, and corbeled and paneled chimney stacks. A contemporary small frame store building stands near the highway.

HY 21 Engelhard

Among the commercial buildings at the center of this fishing, farming, and trading village is the **Gibbs Store** (ca. 1905; N side US

264, just W of SR 1101), a large frame store with an unusual stepped parapet cascading down the front of the 1-story shed addition to the right of the 2-story main block. On the approach into town from the west is the **Israel B. Watson House** (1850s, enlarged 1870s; S side US 64, 0.3 mi. W of SR 1103), two small houses linked by a broad lattice porch and ornamented with sawn bargeboard and gable ornaments similar to decorative work seen at *Fairfield. Also reflecting Fairfield-type craftsmanship, the **Anson Gibbs House** (late 19th c.; W side US 264 opp. SR 1100) on the other side of town boasts fleur-de-lis cresting on the roof ridges of both the main house and the small kitchen wing, complemented by bargeboards and bracketed window hoods. Merchant Gibbs later built a larger house outside Engelhard (see *Anson Gibbs House II).

HY 22 Fairfield

The village on the northern shore of Lake Mattamuskeet presents an unexpectedly rich collection of picturesque Carpenter Gothic and Italianate architecture. The completion of the Fairfield Canal about 1860 under the leadership of planter David Carter Jr. connected Hyde Co. to Albemarle Sound and Chesapeake markets, and for three decades after the Civil War Fairfield thrived as a shipping center for the county's agricultural bounty. Several buildings are attributed to master carpenter Cason Emery Swindell, whose own modest residence survives in Fairfield, but William Walling of Beaufort Co. also erected some key structures. One or both men probably made use of such popular patternbooks as A. J. Bicknell's *Village Builder* (1870) and other volumes, whose "tasty and convenient" designs inspired the jauntily ornate carpentry that adorns many local buildings. Since the decline of canal traffic in the early 20th c., Fairfield has experienced little subsequent growth or change.

The centerpiece of the village is **Fairfield Methodist Church** (1877; William Walling, builder; W side NC 94 at SR 1309), an extraordinarily fine country church in Gothic Revival style accented with Italianate touches;

HY 22 *Fairfield Methodist Church*

E side NC 94, S of SR 1305; private), an un-usual cruciform Italianate house, also displays millwork probably adapted from Bicknell's *Village Builder*: bracketed cornices, scrollwork, and fluted pilasters with diminutive sawn brackets. Dr. Simmons moved to Hyde Co. from his native Currituck Co. in 1861 to treat slaves suffering from typhoid and smallpox epidemics. Several other 19th-c. houses in town display similar motifs, as do two gable-fronted, 1-room frame stores, the **Brown-Mann Store** and **O'Neal and Sons Store** next door (N side SR 1305, just W of NC 94).

sawn and turned ornament enriches the whole church from the central belltower to the cove-ceilinged sanctuary in "elegant modern style." When the bell was rung in the belfry, it could be heard "all over Mattamuskeet Lake." The 1-story, cross-gable **Parsonage** next door (private) is decorated with scroll brackets, ornamental bracing, and bargeboards with icicle-like pendants, motifs that recur elsewhere in Fairfield.

Similarly picturesque motifs adorn Fairfield's oldest house, the **Laura Blackwell House** (late 1850s, Cason Emery Swindell, attributed builder; N side SR 1305, 0.2 mi. W of NC 94; private), which Fairfield's founder, David Carter Jr., commissioned Swindell to build for his daughter Laura upon her marriage to Edward L. Blackwell, a leading local merchant. The 2-story house and 1-story entrance porch are adorned with bracketed cornices and fluted pilasters and posts with bracketed caps. The unusual plan features a front transverse hall with two rooms and a rear center chimney. An original smokehouse and a warehouse moved from the Fairfield Canal for use as a barn stand in the yard.

In the **Fairfield Cemetery** (late 19th c.; S side SR 1305, 0.3 mi. W of NC 94), across the road from the Blackwell House, stands the picturesque Gothic Revival style latticed **Pavilion** (1890) with a bellcast pyramidal roof, surrounded by fine marble and granite markers. **All Saints Episcopal Church** (1885–90; N side SR 1305, W of NC 94) is a small Gothic Revival church with an octagonal steeple and decorative shingles.

The **Dr. Patrick Simmons House** (1877; Cason Emery Swindell, attributed builder;

HY 22 *Dr. Patrick Simmons House*

HY 23 Ocracoke Village

NC 12 at S end of Ocracoke Island; accessible by ferries from Hatteras, Swan Quarter, and Cedar Island

Though challenged in recent times by modern resort development, Ocracoke Village remains the best-preserved traditional maritime village on the Outer Banks. Even with the changes wrought by growing tourism, it is a place of unique and compelling beauty. The village lies at the southern end of Ocracoke Island, a 16-mile strip between Hatteras and Portsmouth Islands, 20 miles from the Hyde Co. mainland across Pamlico Sound. The name Ocracoke probably derives from the Indian name spelled as Wococon on John White's 1585 map. The island's early history is colored with legends of pirates. The notorious Edward Teach, known as Blackbeard, was captured and killed near Ocracoke Inlet in 1718.

Especially after Currituck and Roanoke inlets shoaled up, Ocracoke Inlet was long the principal access for vessels to the central

HY 23 *Ocracoke Village*

and northern port towns of N.C. The village was settled by the mid-18th c. as a base for pilots who guided ships through the inlet and across the sound to mainland ports. By the late 19th c., as the inlet grew shallower, the economy of the village turned to fishing. The establishment of lifesaving stations at both ends of the island provided employment for some villagers.

The island remained isolated until 1959, when regular ferry service for cars began and NC 12 was paved the length of the island. Much of the island was acquired by the National Park Service in the mid-20th c. as part of the Cape Hatteras National Seashore, and today Ocracoke village is the only inhabited portion. It lies on the sound side at the mouth of Cockle Creek, which was dredged first in the 1930s and again during World War II to create a circular harbor, popularly known as Silver Lake, about ¼ mile in diameter. About 650 people live in the village year-round, and vacationers swell the population between late spring and early fall.

For generations, isolation and a harsh environment fostered a tradition of simple wooden buildings erected in clearings within the low, dense maritime forest canopy of windswept scrub pines, live oaks, and yaupon that provide a measure of protection from steady winds and frequent storms. The dense, informal layout of houses and yards bespeaks generations of self-reliant community life and the interrelationships of a few families. The story-and-a-jump, or 1-story house with raised attic, is the most common traditional house form, though there are also I-houses, foursquares, and bungalows. Most houses have front porches, and many have kitchens and dining rooms located in a rear ell or detached rear building. A number of the older houses were built from materials salvaged from shipwrecks.

Several of the streets have no recorded names and are simply lanes that began as footpaths. The best example of a traditional path is **Howard Street**, a sandy lane winding beneath old live oaks and bordered by small homesteads. Here and along the network of lanes that thread through the village, in the small, shaded yards enclosed by picket fences, the utilitarian elements of island life form intricate patterns: a cistern to collect rainwater, one or two small frame net houses, crab pots, fishnets, boats, a fish-cleaning bench near a pump or spigot, a washhouse, and a family graveyard.

Rising above the village is **Ocracoke Lighthouse** (1823; Noah Porter, builder; N side SR 1326 [Lighthouse Rd.]), its white

HY 23 *Ocracoke Lighthouse*

shaft above the tree canopy visible for miles. The sturdy, 69-foot, stuccoed, conical brick tower is the oldest active lighthouse in N.C. and second oldest standing after *Bald Head Lighthouse in Brunswick Co. It replaced a beacon erected in the 1790s on Shell Castle Island, just inside the inlet, and was built at a cost of over $11,000 by Noah Porter of Massachusetts, who also constructed the adjacent **Keeper's Quarters**. The lighthouse walls taper from 5 feet thick at the base, and a cast-iron dome and finial tops the structure. The lens is a fourth-order Fresnel type—a relatively small lens—installed in 1899. Now under the jurisdiction of the Coast Guard, the lighthouse operates with an automatic light visible 14 miles at sea.

The **U.S. Coast Guard Station** (ca. 1942; at the mouth of Silver Lake Harbor) is an important island institution. The current building, which replaced a 1904 lifesaving station that burned, is a Colonial Revival structure with a 5-story square observation tower presiding over the harbor and inlet. The only surviving traditional inn is the **Island Inn** (1901 and later; SR 1326 [Lighthouse Rd.] at NC 12). Its 2-story, gable-fronted block was built as an Oddfellows Lodge and school and later expanded by Ocracoke native Robert Stanley Wahab as a tourist hotel.

Two of the village's most distinctive buildings were erected in the mid-20th c. by Norfolk industrialist Sam Jones for the use of his vacationing family and occasional tourists and sportsmen who then visited the island in relatively small numbers. **Berkley Manor** (1951; N end of Harbor Loop Rd.) and **Berkley Castle** (1950s; Harbor Loop Rd. on the S side of Silver Lake) are both gray, shingle-clad buildings of Colonial Revival character with gable-roofed wings, dormers, and towers.

Beaufort County (BF)

Washington (BF 1–20)

Washington is one of the state's most distinctive coastal towns, with a strong collection of architecture from its 19th- and early 20th-c. heyday as the chief port on the Pamlico River. The Pamlico, which feeds into Pamlico Sound, becomes the Tar River west of Washington and drains a large agricultural hinterland. The community on the northern side of the river began as a landing on the property of James Bonner, who laid off and sold lots in 1775. An entry in the Journal of the Council of Safety of N.C. dated Sept. 27, 1776, refers to the new town as "Washington"—evidently the first town in America named after George Washington. During the Revolution, Washington supplied patriot forces while other southeastern ports were under British control or blockade, and privateers based their operations here.

Incorporated in 1782, Washington replaced *Bath as county seat in 1785. Commerce expanded steadily. Washington became a port of entry in 1790 and gained a customhouse in 1815. Mercantile firms, several of them founded by New Englanders who settled here, prospered in trade with New England and the Caribbean, dealing mainly in naval stores, corn, staves, tobacco, pork, and furs. Churches, academies, banks, hotels, and newspapers were established. By 1857 *Harper's Monthly* reporter David Strother found Washington "a flourishing place" that "drives a smart trade in the staples of the State—turpentine, cotton, and lumber." From a distance, he observed, "the town presents nothing but a few steeples, peering out from a thick grove of trees, and the street views only continuous archways of verdue. In fact, its modest white wooden houses are completely buried in trees; and when the weather is hot the effect is highly pleasing."

Along with *Plymouth (in Washington Co.) and *Winton (in Hertford Co.), Washington endured more Civil War destruction than any other N.C. town. Union forces occupied Washington in 1862 soon after the fall of New Bern. After the Confederates recaptured Plymouth in 1864, the Union garrison evacuated Washington, and much of the town was burned in the wake of their retreat. After the war, businessmen rebuilt the town and its commerce, trading in regional farm products and growing supplies of timber. In 1877 the Jamesville and Washington Railroad and Lumber Company ran a rail line into Washington from its timberlands in Beaufort and Martin counties. Sawmills and other lumber businesses were soon established. In 1892 the Wilmington and Weldon built a branch to Washington, which further stimulated business and construction. But in 1900 another fire destroyed much of the commercial district along Main and Water Sts., and Washingtonians rebuilt again, erecting imposing business houses on the burned blocks and entering a period of busy railroad and river trade. Later in the 20th c., however, as rail and river traffic dwindled, the port's commercial importance diminished, though the lumber businesses continued as mainstays of the economy. In recent years diversified businesses along with maritime and heritage tourism have revitalized the waterfront downtown and brought new energy to a town that is one of the most pleasant in the region.

The downtown beside the river possesses one of the state's most impressive commercial districts, with boldly handsome commercial and public buildings expressing the renewal of the town after the 1900 fire, along with a few earlier structures that escaped war and fire. In the residential areas that stretch back from the water, handsome churches punctuate a shaded grid plan with houses from every era, a few survivors from early years, and many more from the town's successive eras of growth, including 19th- and early 20th-c. dwellings in the Queen Anne, Gothic Revival, Colonial Revival, and Neo-

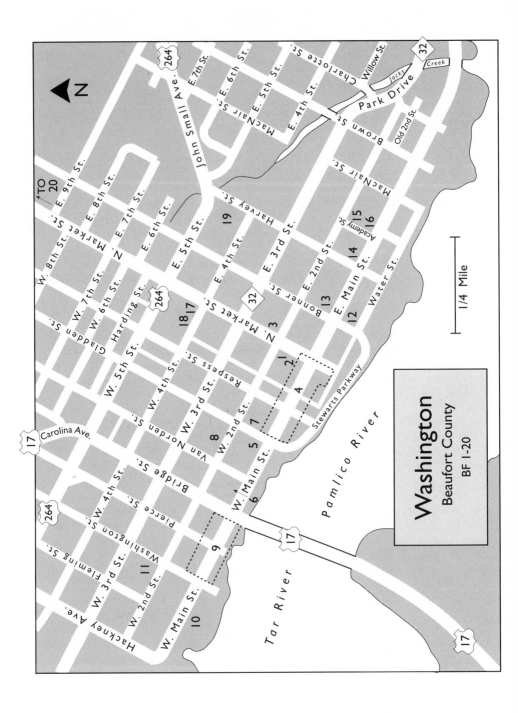

Washington
Beaufort County
BF 1-20

classical styles. Main St., which runs parallel to the river, and Market St., perpendicular to Main, contain the compact commercial district and major public buildings.

BF 1 Old Beaufort County Courthouse
Ca. 1820; SW corner Market and W. 2nd Sts.

One of the state's oldest courthouses, the 2-story, Flemish-bond brick edifice was built after the county advertised in 1819 for bidders to erect a brick courthouse 32 by 37 feet. Initially a simple, gabled square three bays on a side, it was later extended two bays to the rear and gained the square clock tower with pilasters. The large lunette in the front gable recalls those at the *Gates County and *Perquimans County courthouses, the only other surviving Federal era courthouses in the state. The building, now a library, served its original purpose until 1971, when a large, Neocolonial replacement was built. Next door on the south, the former **Beaufort County Jail** (late 19th c.) is a 2-story, brick building with a gabled entrance pavilion and segmental arched windows, adapted for local government offices. Across 2nd St. stands the **Mayo Law Office** (ca. 1830; 102 W. 2nd St.), a little, 1-story, brick building with parapeted gable front, representative of the small, freestanding law offices that once clustered around courthouses.

BF 2 Washington Municipal Building and Firehouse
1884; W side N. Market St.

In contrast to the simplicity of the early 19th-c. courthouse, the chief public edifice from Washington's post–Civil War rebuilding features an exuberant facade of corbeled brick with arched openings, hood molds, a pedimented frontispiece on brackets, and a latticed cupola.

BF 3 U.S. Post Office and Courthouse (now Municipal Building)
1913; James Knox Taylor, supervising architect of the Treasury; 102 E. 2nd St.

One of N.C.'s finest early 20th-c. federal buildings, the Beaux Arts classical landmark is the most imposing public building in town. Beautifully proportioned and opulently detailed, the massive structure features a typical Beaux Arts palazzo composition rendered in brick and stone. The upper two floors of brick laid in Flemish bond rise from a ground story of rusticated stonework pierced with arched openings. Dominating

BF 1 *Old Beaufort County Courthouse*

BF 3 *U.S. Post Office and Courthouse*

the main facade, a loggia rising through the second and third floors features Corinthian columns and pilasters and an ornate, coffered ceiling. A full entablature and a classical balustrade cap the building. Within, the large courtroom behind the loggia is a splendidly appointed chamber with pilasters and paneling rising to a coved and coffered ceiling.

BF 4 W. Main St. Commercial District

The two long commercial blocks along W. Main St. between Market and Gladden Sts. constitute one of the region's prime concentrations of early 20th-c. commercial architecture. The predominant character is established by the 2- to 4-story buildings of red or gray brick erected in a burst of rebuilding

after the 1900 fire. A spectrum of Romanesque, Italianate, and classical facades features ornate corbeled trim, granite lintels and sills, arched door and window openings, and varied and vivid classical features. Many retain original wood and plate-glass storefronts.

A contrast to the predominant brick character appears in the (second) **Bank of Washington Building** (ca. 1920; Benton & Benton [Wilson], architects; 192 W. Main St.), a 4-story, stone and gray brick composition, with heavy Doric columns in antis marking the lower 2 stories. On the opposite corner, the **S. R. Fowle and Son General Merchandise Building** (ca. 1905; 201 W. Main St.) is a 3-story building with corbeled cornice, ornamental hood molds, and stuccoed walls scored like masonry. To the rear it connects to the **Fowle Warehouse** (early to mid-19th c.), built by an earlier generation of the mercantile family and, along with the *Havens Warehouse, a rare example of an important early building type. The 2-story, gable-end warehouse of commonbond brick rests on a raised basement of ballast stone. Before the waterfront was filled in, the river came within 10 feet of the building, permitting loading and unloading of cargoes.

The (first) **Bank of Washington** (1854; 216 W. Main St.), with its 4-columned,

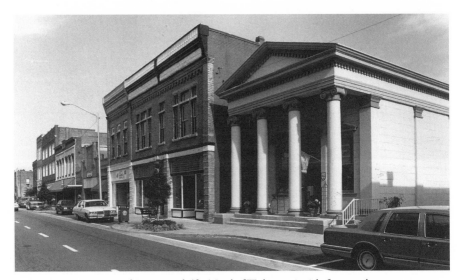

BF 4 *W. Main St. Commercial District, with (first) Bank of Washington in right foreground*

Ionic portico, is the state's finest small Greek Revival commercial building. In 1854 bank directors advertised "for the erection of a banking house. . . . The front gable is to extend so as to form a Portico supported by four columns. Walls of brick, stuccoed to resemble stone, with fire proof roof"—a feature that helped the bank survive the fires of 1864 and 1900.

BF 6 *Havens Warehouse*

BF 5 Washington Passenger Station and Freight Warehouse
Ca. 1904; Gladden St. at W. Main St.

BF 5 *Washington Passenger Station and Freight Warehouse*

One of the largest and best-preserved railroad stations in eastern N.C., the 2-story depot of gray brick is sheltered under a hip roof with metal cresting along the ridgeline. A deep pent roof supported by heavy brackets shields the first floor. The long, red brick freight house has arched openings along each side and is topped by a clerestory. The buildings are preserved as a civic and community arts center.

BF 6 Havens Warehouse
Early 19th c.; SE corner W. Main and Bridge Sts.

The big, 2-story brick building is similar in form but slightly larger than the *Fowle Warehouse to the east. The two buildings represent a class of early mercantile facility that has not survived in other N.C. port towns. This well-built, utilitarian structure features sandstone lintels and sills, iron shutters at the splayed openings, and a corbeled

cornice. It now houses a marina with a harmonizing addition to the west.

Across the street two houses illustrate an important maritime pattern in which mercantile families erected their houses within sight of their warehouses on the waterfront: the **Havens House** (ca. 1820, early 20th c.; 404 W. Main St.; B&B), a 2-story, Federal style house, was expanded and gained its porch in the early 20th c., while the neighboring **Fowle House** (ca. 1816, ca. 1890; 412 W. Main St.) is likewise an early 19th-c. house, remodeled in the late 19th c. with an elaborate curving porch.

BF 7 First Presbyterian Church
1824, 1871, later alterations and additions; SE corner Gladden and W. 2nd Sts.

The 1824 brick church that first housed Washington's Presbyterians was destroyed during the Union evacuation in 1864, but the congregation rebuilt soon after the war. The Flemish-bond brick walls may date from the original building. The present church developed from a simple, Greek Revival style building to include a heavy portico and a tall, Colonial Revival steeple.

BF 8 First Methodist Church
1899; Charles E. Hartge, architect; 304 W. 2nd St.

Epitomizing German architect Hartge's impressive church architecture in eastern N.C., the energetically composed, Gothic Revival church displays fine materials and craftsmanship throughout. Deep red, pressed, molded, and corbeled brick emphasizes the heavy buttresses, lancet windows, and crenellation. Two entrance towers flank a

broad gabled ell, with the taller of the pair mounting dramatically from a rectangular, buttressed base through deep chamfers to a polygonal, then cylindrical, shaft topped by a polygonal open belfry. The auditorium-plan sanctuary is richly finished in dark wood beneath a deep coffered ceiling.

W. Main St./W. 2nd St. Area:
Now separated from the downtown by strip development along Bridge St., W. Main and W. 2nd Sts. west of Bridge St. retain notable 19th- and early 20th-c. residential architecture.

BF 9 500 and 600 blocks of W. Main St.

These two blocks west of the business area are especially impressive and varied. The **Rodman House** (mid-19th c.; 520 W. Main St.), a 2-story, Italianate style house with Doric posts and cast-iron balustrade, was the home of William B. Rodman, N.C. Supreme Court justice. The **Dumay House** (1901–4; 603 W. Main St.) is the town's finest Queen Anne house, lively with gables and bay windows and enhanced by a cast-iron fence and fountain. A row of three houses associated with the locally prominent Warren family includes the **Warren House** (Greenhill) (mid-19th c.; 612 W. Main St.), a frame, Greek Revival cottage on a raised brick basement; the **Lindsay Warren House** (late 19th c.; 624 W. Main St.) in a Gothic

Revival mode, built for a congressman and U.S. comptroller general; and the **Charles Warren House** (mid-19th c.; 626 W. Main St.), a 2-story, frame house with Greek Revival and Italianate features and sawnwork porch. Notable among many imposing Colonial Revival and eclectic houses of the early 20th c. is the **Beverley Moss House** (ca. 1920; 621 W. Main St.), built for the founder of the Moss Planing Mill, an especially rich blend of Colonial Revival and Spanish motifs, including a green tile roof.

BF 10 Elmwood
Early and mid-19th c., early 20th c.; 731 W. Main St.; private

Washington's largest and finest antebellum residence began as the Federal style home of the Grist family, evidently as a tripartite house, as sketched by *Harper's Monthly* correspondent David Strother in 1857. By ca. 1860 it was greatly enlarged to a 2-story, double-pile, Italianate residence. Still later Colonial Revival embellishments were added, including the wraparound porch with central 2-story portico. Originally located at the western terminus of Main St. facing downtown, the house was moved to the south side of the street ca. 1911 by its owner, buggy manufacturer George Hackney, to make way for the extension of W. Main St. and development to the west.

BF 11 Hollyday House
Mid-19th c.; NW corner W. 2nd and Washington Sts.; private

On its large corner lot amid dense plantings and brick outbuildings, the large, 2-story frame Italianate house retains the qualities of an in-town antebellum estate.

BF 12 Water St.

BF 12 *Water St.*

Just east of the commercial district, a trio of houses built for leading merchant families in the late 18th or early 19th c. face Water St. and the river. The **Marsh House** (ca. 1795; 210 Water St.), the **Myers House** (ca. 1780; 214 Water St.), and the **Hyatt House** (ca. 1785; 218 Water St.) are substantial, 2-story frame houses with center-passage plans that share features such as double-shouldered chimneys, Flemish-bond brickwork, and molded weatherboards. The Hyatt House was altered in the early 20th c. with a clipped gable roof and new porch. The Marsh House is believed to have been constructed for brothers Jonathan and Daniel Marsh, Rhode Island merchants who also purchased the *Palmer-Marsh House in Bath.

E. Main St./E. 2nd St. Area:
The residential blocks east of the downtown retain a dense collection of late Victorian and early 20th-c. houses—including large numbers of bracketed, 2-story frame houses and bungalows and a few imposing Colonial Revival residences—with key corners punctuated by landmark churches.

BF 13 St. Peter's Episcopal Church
1868–73, 1893 (Charles E. Hartge, architect); NE corner Bonner and E. Main Sts.

The Gothic Revival, brick building with lancet windows and corbeled detail is domi-

nated by an off-center, 4-stage tower. Like the Presbyterians, Washington's Episcopalians lost their first church to fire in 1864 but rebuilt quickly. In 1893 the church was remodeled by architect Charles Hartge, with robust and lively corbeled brickwork and an impressive entrance tower. The lovely churchyard contains many early markers and graves of prominent residents. Landscaping of the grounds in exotic trees and shrubs was carried out by Miss Patsy Blount in the 1870s with the assistance of the Reverend Joseph Blount Cheshire, who also planted churchyards upriver at *Calvary Episcopal Church in Tarboro and at *Trinity Episcopal Church in Halifax Co.

BF 14 First Baptist Church
1917; NE corner E. Main and Harvey Sts.

The prominent Neoclassical brick church displays a shallow Ionic portico and a large dome on an octagonal drum. The design is believed to have been provided by the Southern Baptist Convention.

BF 15 First Christian Church
1921–26; James M. McMichael (Charlotte), architect; SE corner E. 2nd and Academy Sts.

Another eastern N.C. example of the robust Neoclassicism of the popular church architect McMichael of Charlotte, the church of buff brick has a cruciform plan on a high basement with a wide terrace on the street side reached by double stairs.

BF 16 (Former) Episcopal Rectory (Pamlico House)
1906; 400 E. Main St.; B&B

One of the town's largest residences, the 2½-story, hip-roofed Colonial Revival style house features a spacious porch with Ionic columns, built by St. Peter's Episcopal Church as the rectory.

BF 17 Griffin House
Early 19th c.; NW corner N. Market and W. 4th Sts.; private

Located on N. Market St. among later 19th- and early 20th-c. residences, the frame house is a prominent vestige of Washington's early days, though its early history is not known. Like other homes of early merchants along *Water St., the 2-story, 5-bay structure has Flemish-bond brick chimneys, a center-passage plan, and Georgian-Federal finish.

BF 18 Metropolitan A.M.E. Zion Church
1909; W. 4th St.

BF 18 *Metropolitan A.M.E. Zion Church*

The brick edifice has a forceful facade composed of a central gabled section, a castellated entrance pavilion, and flanking towers of unequal height emphasized by tall, tapering buttresses.

BF 19 John Small School
1923–24; G. Lloyd Preacher & Company (Atlanta and Raleigh), architect; NW corner Harvey and E. 4th Sts.

The handsome brick school reflects community pride during the great 1920s era of public school consolidation and construction, with Tudor Gothic style details emphasizing the entrance pavilion.

BF 20 N. Market St.

As Washington grew in the early 20th c., development extended the original town grid northward. The most exclusive section lay along N. Market St. between 9th and 15th Sts., where several Colonial Revival houses were built for leading business families. The **Bowers-Tripp House** (1921; Benton & Benton [Wilson], architects; Miller Construction Company, contractor; 1040 N. Market St.) is a massive and symmetrical residence of tan brick from the region's Colonial Revival specialists. Its near twin, the **Litchfield House** (1001 N. Market St.), with green tile roof and matching garage, was also designed by the prolific Wilson firm about the same time. The **Gerard House** (ca. 1915; 1036 N. Market St.) is the town's most resplendent house in Southern Colonial style. Parallel to N. Main St., Bonner St. to the east and Respess St. to the west continue the theme on a more modest scale, with bungalows and a few stuccoed, Spanish Mission Revival houses interspersed among simpler variations of the Colonial Revival.

BF 21 Washington Park
S side NC 32 (River Rd.), SE of Washington

The residential suburb along the northern bank of the Pamlico was laid out prior to World War I on a farm owned by John H. Small, but few houses were built before its incorporation in 1923. It exemplifies the early automobile suburb, with a homogeneous collection of frame and brick residences, most in informal renditions of the Colonial Revival style, in a tranquil riverside setting. The three main thoroughfares running parallel to the river—Riverside Dr., Isabella Ave., and College Ave.—are divided by medians planted with crepe myrtle and shaded by cedars, pines, and live oaks draped in Spanish moss.

BF 22 Belfont
Late 18th c.; private, no public access

The frame plantation house is most notable for its double chimney, which, like that at the *Palmer-Marsh House in Bath, consists of a pair of double-shouldered chimneys joined by a 2-story pent rising to the stacks. The base is of English bond, the body is of Flemish bond, and the shoulders are narrow. After 1797 this was the home of Reading Blount, an officer under George Washington.

BF 23 Voice of America Site A

Early 1960s; 2 mi. along E side SR 1001, S of Martin Co. line; public visitation permitted; call Greenville VOA office in advance

Looking to the first-time visitor like something out of a science fiction world—and known locally as "the antenna farm"—the 3,000-acre assemblage of shortwave radio antennae was created by the U.S. Information Agency (USIA), the public relations arm of the federal government, to broadcast news and information from the American point of view worldwide. Considered together with another site of equal size (Site B) and a third, smaller one (Site C), both in Pitt Co., the facility was the largest and most powerful of its type in the world when built, and it remains the principal VOA transmission facility in the United States. Factors influencing the selection of eastern N.C. for the site included the availability of sufficient level land near the edge of the continent and the reflective qualities of the moist soil. Program transmissions from this site originally targeted the Soviet Union and eastern Europe; today they are directed primarily to Latin America and Africa. Programming originating in Washington, D.C., is transmitted to this site by satellite or microwave and then broadcast via shortwave to be re-

ceived directly by individual radio sets or by local stations for retransmission. Under the leadership of two native North Carolinians who headed the USIA during the planning and building of this facility, George Venable Allen (1957–60) and Edward R. Murrow (1961–64), the VOA outgrew its World War II and early Cold War role, expanded its programming, and developed a broad, worldwide audience based on the integrity of its news and information services.

BF 24 Zion Episcopal Church

1856; S side US 264, 1.0 mi. E of NC 32

The simple, frame country church has a gabled vestibule, a small octagonal belfry, and original blinds on the 3-bay sides. Shaded by magnolias and fir trees behind a white picket fence, the cemetery adjoins the church building and contains a fine collection of mid-19th-c. stones. The church, founded in the 18th c. and admitted to the diocese in 1823, is one of several small, rural, Episcopal churches in the county.

BF 25 Boyd Farm

Late 19th–early 20th c.; N side US 264, 4.4 mi. E of NC 92, Everetts Crossroads vic.; private, visible from road

A remarkably complete farm complex of the late 19th and early 20th centuries, showing traditional outbuilding construction and farm layout. The farmhouse is an I-house with a full-width shed porch and rear ell. The array of unpainted frame outbuildings set out informally to the east of the house includes several barns, sheds, and cribs, among

BF 25 *Boyd Farm*

them a transverse crib barn with flanking sheds. Like many farmers in the region, the Boyds made the transition from cotton to tobacco in the early 20th c., and several tobacco barns stand under the trees at the rear of the complex. The farm remains in the family. (See also Introduction, Fig. 21.)

BF 26 John H. Oden Store and Hunters Bridge Church of Christ

Store 1904, church ca. 1920; N side US 264, 6.0 mi. E of NC 92, Everetts Crossroads vic.

A prominent example of an important rural institution, this frame country store with a stepped parapet gable housed a general merchandise operation founded in 1896. The building was moved from its original location closer to Bath Creek upon construction of the new highway about 1920. The vernacular Gothic frame church to its rear has an unusual, four-stage central tower ascending in telescope form.

BF 27 Athens Chapel Church of Christ

1891 and later additions; N side NC 92, 3.5 mi. E of US 264, Bath vic.

A landmark on a main highway, the large frame church has a projecting portico and a tall belfry with a cross-gable cap. It was built for a Disciples of Christ congregation founded in 1850 and later became an independent Church of Christ. The Disciples, Church of Christ, and related independent Christian churches rose out of the Restoration movement of the early 19th c. led by Thomas Campbell and others and evolved into the largest American-born fellowship of churches. The movement was especially strong in east-central N.C. through the 19th c.; this is one of the largest such country churches in the region.

BF 28 Bath

Incorporated in 1705 as N.C.'s first town, Bath occupies a point on Bath Creek where it formed a sheltered bay off the Pamlico River. In the early years Edward Teach, the notorious pirate Blackbeard, frequented the area and terrorized coastal shipping. Bath's

tiny size belies its great importance to the young colony. Early 18th-c. political leaders resided in or near the town, and the governor's council and the colonial assembly met here several times. Yet Bath never became more than a village; in the late 18th c. *Washington, a few miles west on the Pamlico, supplanted it as county seat and trade center. Today the quiet waterside village with its 18th- and early 19th-c. historic sites maintained by the state lies almost entirely within the boundaries of the original town plan laid out by John Lawson, explorer and first surveyor-general of the colony.

Surrounded by old plantings and gravestones, **St. Thomas Episcopal Church** (1734; s side Craven St. near Harding St.) is the oldest church building in N.C. and a cherished landmark. It was a major accomplishment for its time and place, its small size and simplicity reflecting the challenges of building well in the colony in the early 18th c. In 1734 the vestry reported that the parishioners were building a small church at their own expense, and it was apparently completed the following year. The rectangular brick building is laid up in glazed header Flemish bond, with vestiges of decorative brickwork in the front gable. The single-room plan is original, but no original interior fabric survives.

BF 28 *St. Thomas Episcopal Church*

The **Palmer-Marsh House** (1750; E side Main St., near Carteret St.; National Historic Landmark; open regular hours), is one of the principal mid-18th-c. dwellings standing in N.C., notable for its unusual size and plan and its spectacular chimney. The

BF 28 *Palmer-Marsh House*

weatherboarded, 2-story house was built for Michael Coutanche, a French merchant who moved to Bath via Boston. In the late 1750s Robert Palmer, who had come from Scotland in 1753 as surveyor-general of the colony, acquired the house. In 1802 it was purchased by Jonathan and Daniel Gould Marsh, shipowners and merchants from Providence, R.I.

The colossal English-bond chimney on the eastern gable end is one of the state's greatest expressions of the 18th-c. brickmason's craft. Measuring 17 feet wide and 4 feet thick at its base, it consists of two chimneys joined with a 2-story pent. A Flemish-bond chimney, also massive, stands on the northern wall. The southern entrance opens into a large, unheated central room—an enlarged hall with stair and doorways into the flanking rooms. On the eastern side are two chambers, with fireplaces served by the big double chimney, and small closets in the chimney pent. To the west is a single, large room, which has its own entry at the gable end facing the street and may have served as a business office. The heavy house frame is exposed on the interior, with planed and beaded cornerposts, plates, and door frames projecting into the rooms, as well as the

summer beam measuring more than 50 feet in length. Much of the first-floor finish including the mantels dates from the 1960s restoration, but the turned stair and the Georgian woodwork and mantels of the second floor are original, as is the unusually early weighted window sash. A small burial ground contains Marsh and Coutanche family graves.

The **Van der Veer House** (w side Harding St.) is a late 18th-c. example of the gambrel-roofed form, moved here for restoration as part of the state historic site. Also open to the public is the **Bonner House** (ca. 1835; Front St.), a 2-story, side-hall-plan house with a 1-story wing and a double-shouldered, Flemish-bond chimney.

Notable private buildings include the **Williams (Glebe) House** (ca. 1830; e side Main St.), a simple, 2-story frame dwelling acquired in 1847 by Dr. John F. Tompkins, agricultural reformer and founder of the state fair, and **Swindell's Store** (late 19th c., w side Main St.), a typical brick commercial building. Early 20th-c. frame houses, several of the regionally prevalent 2-story gable-fronted form; simple frame churches; and an early 20th-c. brick school contribute to the ambience of the village.

BF 29 Yeatesville

Now a quiet, rural crossroads community, Yeatesville was populous enough in the late 19th c. to warrant its incorporation in 1881. A small cluster of well-kept 19th-c. houses focuses on **St. Matthews Episcopal Church** (1899; sw corner us 264 and sr 1718), a tiny frame church with lancet arch windows. A former 1-room frame school building from the community has been attached to the rear of the church. The sign identifying "Iglesia Episcopal de San Mateo" reflects the growing presence of Spanish-speaking agricultural workers in the region.

BF 30 Pantego

The small farming and milling community on Pantego Creek was settled by the early 19th c., with a post office at the site as early as 1828. It retains a good collection of late

19th- and early 20th-c. houses and public buildings. The chief landmark is **Pantego Academy** (1875, early 20th c.; Academy St., just N of US 264), an important regional institution founded as a private school. The original 2-story frame building was enlarged in the early 20th c. to its present 9-bay, hip-roof form with 2-story rear ell, one of the state's largest and best-preserved wooden school buildings of the period. Sheltered by the 2-story porch of slender columns is a striking double stair of wishbone form with solid balustrade rising to a second-story entrance. The academy became part of the public school system in 1907, and a 2-story brick school was built next door about 1931. The older building is preserved by an alumni association.

Behind the academy is **Hebron Methodist Church** (late 19th c.; Church St. just N of US 264), a Gothic Revival frame church with a corner entrance tower. Nearby on the main highway, the **Credle House** (mid- and late 19th c., N side US 264, just E of NC 99) is a Queen Anne style enlargement of an older house, with sawn ornament in the porches and gables. Along SR 1704 on the southern side of town are several late 19th- and early 20th-c. buildings, including the **P. H. Johnson House** (early 20th c., E side SR 1704, 0.2 mi. S of US 264), a Colonial Revival house with central entrance pavilion featuring a Palladian window.

BF 31 Belhaven

The town at the confluence of Pantego Creek and the Pungo River was first settled in the 1880s as Jack's Neck, renamed Belle Port in 1891 and Belhaven in 1893. Belhaven became a center of the county's booming lumber industry in the early 1890s with the arrival of the Roper Lumber Company and a branch of the Norfolk and Southern Railroad. Within a few years a half-dozen lumber companies were established, each employing hundreds of workers. The largest was the Interstate Cooperage Company, a subsidiary of the Standard Oil Company, which produced barrels and boxes for the shipment of oil and oil products until 1940.

Ruins of the sprawling complex lie between US 264 BUS and Pantego Creek on the western side of town.

The principal downtown landmark is the **Belhaven City Hall** (1911; W. T. Kirk, designer and carpenter; C. F. Doughty, brickmason; N side Main St.), a multipurpose municipal facility designed by local carpenter Kirk. The 2-story brick building has a shingled belfry, bracketed cornices, and arched openings for the fire department and market that originally occupied the first floor. City offices still use the lower level, and the second floor auditorium houses the Belhaven Memorial Museum. This memorably eclectic collection, the core of which was assembled by a local resident before 1918, opened here in 1967 and includes antique furniture and clothing, 30,000 buttons, a preserved 8-legged pig, a wedding party of dressed fleas (visible through a magnifying glass), and thousands more items of interest.

Belhaven retains large groupings of houses erected between the 1890s and 1920s for plant managers and workers. Choice sites along Front St. south of Main St. were reserved for the finest houses, Queen Anne and Colonial Revival style residences enjoying vistas across the Pungo. Simpler, traditional 1- and 2-story frame houses line the shady streets north of Main St. The most elaborate of several frame churches is **Belhaven Missionary Baptist Church** (1906; Edward St. near Front St.), with an unusual corner entrance tower containing a large open belfry.

The grandest house is **River Forest Manor** (1899–1904; SE corner E. Main St. and Riverview; B&B), an imposing Southern Colonial frame residence with a monumental curving portico carried by Ionic columns. The interior features elaborate woodwork, frescoes, and other appointments befitting the status of its first owner, John Aaron Wilkinson, president of Roper Lumber Company and vice-president of the Norfolk and Southern Railroad. Local tradition says that Italian and other immigrant craftsmen were brought in to complete the interiors. Today the house is a popular inn,

BF 31 *River Forest Manor*

restaurant, and marina serving recreational boat traffic on the Intracoastal Waterway.

BF 32 Trinity Episcopal Church

Ca. 1774 (Giles Shute and John Harrington, carpenters), later alterations; N side NC 33, 0.2 mi. NW of US 17, Chocowinity

The early date ascribed to the original portion of this tiny, gable-fronted church is supported by the presence of a few sections of hand-riven weatherboards with overlapping feathered butt joints, a rare survival of the treatment in the state. Nathaniel Blount, a native of the area, was ordained an Anglican priest in England in 1773, and this little chapel is traditionally said to have been built upon his return. Blount served the parish until his death in 1816. The church originally stood a few miles west on the road to Greenville, where its associated cemetery remains today, and was moved to Chocowinity in 1939. The building was enlarged in the early 19th c., and the gabled vestibule and rear additions date from about the time of the move.

BF 33 Warren Chapel Methodist Church

Late 19th c.; N side NC 33, 0.3 mi. W of SR 1100, Cox's Crossroads vic.

The simple, neatly kept frame country church is sheltered in a grove of tall pines, with triangular window heads and a diagonally sheathed triangular panel over the

front entrance providing a Gothic touch. In the yard stands a stone memorial to William Warren, Revolutionary soldier for whom the church was named.

BF 34 Ware Creek Community School

1919; E side SR 1103, 2.0 mi. N of SR 1100, Cox's Crossroads vic.

The Julius Rosenwald Foundation assisted construction of schools for rural blacks in the South between 1915 and 1948. Over 800 Rosenwald schools were erected in N.C., more than in any other state, typically following standard plans supplied by the foundation. The Ware Creek School is a 3-room, frame Rosenwald school with a gabled and bracketed central section flanked by hip-roof wings. Having served as the public school for the surrounding area's black children from elementary through high school from 1920 to 1954, it is now the focus of local efforts to preserve it as a community center.

BF 35 Aurora

The town on South Creek flourished through the late 19th and early 20th centuries as a shipping point for potatoes, corn, cotton, and timber produced in southern Beaufort Co. At its peak Aurora had several stores, two banks, two hotels, a private telephone company, several physicians, and a town concert band and ball team. Passenger and freight boats plied South Creek to and from points all along the Pamlico River, and the town was served by a branch of the Atlantic Coast Line Railroad. Aurora's era of prosperity is reflected in a long **Main St. Commercial District** of 1- and 2-story buildings with decorative brickwork, several substantial churches, and surrounding neighborhoods of 19th- and early 20th-c. frame houses. The town declined after World War II. In recent decades vast phosphate mining operations along the southern side of the Pamlico River have dominated the local economy.

Pamlico County (PM)

See Angela Barnett, Pamlico County Imagery *(1980).*

   Pamlico County, formed in 1872 from parts of Craven and Beaufort counties, occupies a marshy peninsula on Pamlico Sound between the Pamlico and Neuse rivers. A few plantations were established here along the northern bank of the Neuse River below New Bern, but little has survived from the county's early history. Only one major landmark, *China Grove plantation house, dates from the early 19th c. The county remained a thinly populated domain of isolated farmers and fishermen until the turn of the 20th c., when lumber companies and the railroad stimulated the growth of several small towns. Especially numerous in the county are small, frame, story-and-a-jump dwellings of the late 19th and early 20th centuries, accompanied by frame out-buildings. Many North Carolinians know the county as the site of popular summer camps and small resort beaches on the Neuse.

PM 1 Bayboro

Centrally located in the county on the Bay River between two vast, uninhabitable po-cosins (an Indian word meaning "swamp on a hill")—Light Ground Pocosin on the south and Bay City Pocosin to the north—Bayboro became the county seat in 1876, four years after Pamlico Co. was formed from parts of Craven and Beaufort counties. The present **Pamlico County Courthouse** (1938; Raymond Fuson, architect; N side NC 55 at town center) shows the WPA Colonial Revival reduced to the essentials: a brick rectangle with a simple portico. The former **Register of Deeds Office** behind the court-house (1905; B. F. Smith Construction Company) is a small, gable-fronted brick building with a corbeled brick cornice and segmental-arched windows, constructed by the Wash-ington, D.C., firm that built several eastern N.C. courthouses.

PM 2 Oriental

The community at the mouth of Smith Creek on the Neuse River is a leisurely mar-itime village with unpretentious, early 20th-c. architecture. Oriental's shaded streets are lined with frame and occasionally brick buildings in simple Victorian, Colonial Revival, and bungalow styles. The commu-nity's appeal lies in its cumulative ambience rather than the presence of individual land-marks. Though the surrounding area had been settled by the 18th c., the town was founded about 1870 when Louis Midgett brought his family to the site. Tradition re-calls that the community was known as Smith's Creek until Midgett's wife, Rebecca, found washed ashore the nameplate of the *Oriental*, a Federal transport that had sunk near Bodie Island in 1862. The major impe-tus for growth was the 1907 arrival of the Roper Lumber Company and the subse-quent construction of a branch of the Nor-folk and Southern Railroad. During the Great Depression, commercial fishing be-came the principal source of income. Today the town is enjoying a resurgence as a recre-ational sailing center.

   Oriental is laid out in a broken grid within the wedge formed by the Neuse River and Smith Creek. The largest building in town is the 2-story brick **Oriental School** (ca. 1915; SW side Church St., s of Broad St.), with a 7-bay front marked by segmental-arched windows, adapted for apartments. A historical marker recalls that the state's first motorized school bus delivered children to this school in 1917. The main residential area lies south of Broad St. toward the Neuse River. **South Ave.**, beside the river, was a fa-vored building site for leading lumbermen and merchants during the early 20th-c. boom. The **W. J. Moore House** (ca. 1905; s

PM 3 *China Grove*

side South Ave. at King St.) is a simply detailed, 2-story house with a high hip roof and a 2-story porch sheltering the front and river side. The **Will Moore House** (ca. 1910; s side South Ave. at Neuse St.), built next door for W. J. Moore's son, is a 1-story Colonial Revival house with wraparound porch.

PM 3 China Grove

Early 19th c.; S side SR 1302, 1.5 mi. S of SR 1308, Oriental vic.; private, visible from road

Overlooking the wide Neuse River near the mouth of Dawson's Creek, China Grove is one of the state's most dramatically sited plantation houses, best viewed from the river. It is a magnificent example of the coastal double-piazza form with a full-width porch inset beneath the broad, dormered gable roof. The 4-bay width reflects the off-center hall plan; Federal style interiors indicate a New Bern influence. The house was probably built for William and Harriet Sparrow after their marriage in 1813. Sparrow profited from a large plantation, a lumber and gristmill, and turpentine production. Following his death in 1827 his widow retained the plantation until after the Civil War.

Craven County (CV)

See Peter B. Sandbeck, The Historic Architecture of New Bern and Craven County, North Carolina *(1988).*

New Bern (CV 1–61)

N.C.'s leading port and largest town from the mid-18th c. until the 1820s, New Bern is a compact little city with a distinguished collection of architecture from three centuries. The riverside town possesses the state's prime assemblage of urban Federal period architecture, as well as important buildings from the late colonial period and from an early 20th-c. lumber-based boom. When arriving by highway, the most dramatic approach is across the Trent River bridge (Tryon Palace exit off US 70), which offers a river vista of the dense town center, canopied in trees and punctuated by cupolas and spires of many eras. (A huge new bridge carrying US 17 will provide new views of the city.)

Located at the confluence of the Neuse and Trent rivers, near the Pamlico Sound, New Bern was settled in 1710 by a colony of Swiss and German Palatines organized by Baron Christoph von Graffenried and took its name from Bern, Switzerland. The settlement was virtually abandoned in 1711 following a devastating attack by Tuscarora Indians, but by 1720 the end of the Tuscarora War permitted renewed settlement by English-speaking immigrants from Virginia, Maryland, and the Middle Atlantic colonies.

In 1765, attracted by the growing town's central coastal location, Gov. William Tryon chose New Bern for the site of N.C.'s first permanent capital. Between 1767 and 1770 Gov. Tryon and English architect John Hawks erected an imposing capitol and governor's residence on the western edge of town overlooking the Trent River. The project

CV 20–22 *600 Block, Pollock St., New Bern*

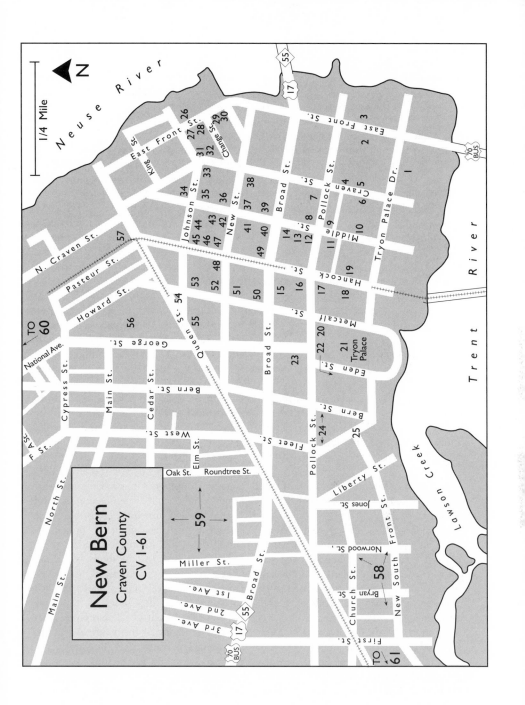

New Bern
Craven County
CV 1-61

N

1/4 Mile

Neuse River

Trent River

Lawson Creek

East Front St.
King St.
Broad St.
Craven St.
Pollock St.
Middle St.
Hancock St.
Metcalf St.
Tryon Palace Dr.
Eden St.
Bern St.
Johnson St.
New St.
Change St.
Tryon Palace
N. Craven St.
Pasteur St.
Howard St.
George St.
Queen St.
Cypress St.
Main St.
Cedar St.
Bern St.
West St.
Elm St.
Fleet St.
Pollock St.
Liberty St.
Jones St.
Norwood St.
Front St.
New South Front St.
Bryan St.
Church St.
First St.
Miller St.
3rd Ave.
2nd Ave.
1st Ave.
Broad St.
Oak St.
Roundtree St.
North St.
National Ave.
E. F St.

59
58

TO 60
TO 61

generated an efflorescence of sophisticated late Georgian architecture, and its influence persisted even after the palace burned in 1798.

Despite the removal of the state's capital to Raleigh in the 1790s, New Bern flourished as the state's largest town and leading mercantile center until the 1820s, exporting lumber products, naval stores, and crops from the Neuse and Trent river basins. New Bern merchants—many of them new arrivals from Britain and other American cities—profited from a triangular trade route with the West Indies and northern ports (especially New England, New York, and Philadelphia). The town grew from about 1,000 in 1775 to about 2,500 in 1800 and over 3,600 in 1820. The merchant-lawyer gentry, along with planter families who frequented the town, created a lively and fashionable society. A strong artisan class included highly skilled craftsmen, both black and white, in the building trades. Black residents—artisans, watermen, entrepreneurs, servants, and laborers—made up over half of the town's population. Although most of New Bern's blacks were slaves, a substantial number were free blacks, some of whom were among the wealthiest free blacks in the state.

Early 19th-c. mercantile prosperity supported construction of exceptional Federal style public buildings, churches, and dwellings, from elegant townhouses to modest artisans' houses, a remarkable number of which still stand. New Bern townhouses were often built with a side-passage plan, and some had a formal drawing room on the second story in keeping with urban precedents elsewhere. New Bernians also favored piazzas of 1 or 2 stories, often with the ends enclosed to form a sheltered outdoor room.

Several local construction features are peculiar to the New Bern sphere of influence: exposed face chimneys—interior end chimneys with the lower portion of the chimney face exposed by a tall, rectangular opening in the weatherboarding—and 6-panel doors made with the upper 4 panels raised or flat, and the bottom 2 panels solid or flush paneled. These features are seen in other Ameri-can seaboard towns, and the door treatment is also common in England; but they do not appear elsewhere in N.C. Excellent craftsmanship and intricate classical detail characterize the principal buildings of the era, testament to the skills of the town's close-knit artisan community.

An enigma in New Bern's Federal era architecture is the role of William Nichols, the architect and carpenter from Bath, England, who was in New Bern from 1800 to 1806, but for whom no New Bern works are documented. Similarities between New Bern buildings and later Nichols projects—such as *New Bern Academy in New Bern and *Hayes near Edenton—raise tantalizing possibilities.

New Bern's fortunes began to decline in the late 1820s. Growth of the port was limited as the increasing size and draft of ships intensified the hazards of Ocracoke Inlet and the Pamlico Sound. Although the *Clubfoot and Harlowe Creek Canal was chartered in 1813 to remedy the problem by providing a direct route from New Bern to the ocean harbor at *Beaufort, its halting construction during the 1810s and 1820s delayed its completion too long to bring the anticipated benefits. During the 1830s the town was beset by a period of economic decline and outmigration—a depression that lifted with the 1840s resurgence of local naval stores and turpentine industries. Trade expanded with the completion of the Atlantic and N.C. Railroad in 1858, which linked New Bern to Goldsboro, Morehead City, and the larger rail network. In the antebellum years local builder Hardy B. Lane and others erected a series of handsome buildings in current Greek and Gothic Revival styles, many of them executed in the still-favored Flemish-bond brickwork, accentuated with brownstone trim.

Early in the Civil War, on Mar. 14, 1862, New Bern was peacefully taken over by Union forces, and it remained occupied until the war's end. Many blacks were attracted to the federally occupied city during the war and established a refugee camp known as James City just across the Trent River. Although most of the refugees departed after the war, the black population of New Bern increased substantially between 1860 to 1870. Continuing traditions from antebellum days, in the late 19th c., New Bern developed a strong black professional class who established businesses—more than in any other N.C. town—schools, and churches, including one of the first A.M.E. Zion congregations in the South.

From the 1880s until the 1920s, rapid expansion of the region's lumber industry brought New Bern the greatest prosperity of its history. There had been sawmills in New Bern earlier in the 19th c., but with the "advent of Northern capitalists . . . and the construction of modern mills . . . creating values in our timber forests," the industry's growth made New Bern one of the South's leading lumber centers. It was during these same years that New Bern pharmacist Caleb D. Bradham invented "Brad's Drink," a carbonated beverage that was marketed after 1898 as Pepsi-Cola. The lumber and commercial boom manifested itself in construction of large Italianate, Queen Anne, and Colonial Revival dwellings, as well as public buildings in Romanesque and Beaux Arts styles. Prominent at the height of the boom years was New Bern architect Herbert Woodley Simpson, who designed boldly in popular styles, from Romanesque and Neoclassical Revival churches and public buildings to Southern Colonial mansions of lumber magnates. The town grew from about 6,000 people in 1870 to 9,000 in 1900 to 12,000 in 1920.

The layout of the older section of the city, reaching from the Neuse to the Trent, shows important vestiges of the 18th- and 19th-c. pattern of proximity of workplace and residence. The merchants' houses included business offices and overlooked their wharves. Neighborhoods had both large and small houses and black and white residents. The late 19th- and early 20th-c. shift toward greater segmentation of use and population appears in subtle changes within the old town. It is clearer still in later settled areas. At the turn of the century, with the grid within the original town boundaries fully occupied, developers began to lay out new

residential sectors on old farmland to accommodate the town's burgeoning population of working-class and middle-class families, typically segregated by race. Among the largest extensions westward were the predominantly black neighborhoods north of Queen St., now known as *Greater Duffyfield, and the white suburbs of *Riverside (on the Neuse) and *Ghent (beside the Trent). In 1914 the chamber of commerce reported that "until a few years ago everybody [was] trying to get houses downtown," but the electric streetcar lines brought "a wonderful spreading out, and hundreds of families who for years remained in cramped quarters and the congested section of the city, now reside outside of the corporation."

In the mid-20th c., New Bern developed a growing sense of its historic identity, epitomized by the monumental reconstruction of *Tryon Palace, funded largely by a former resident of the town. Over the years, history-minded citizens steadily enhanced New Bern's position as an attractive small city and tourist attraction. The orientation of its waterfront has shifted from shipping to leisure boating, as a popular stop on the Intracoastal Waterway.

Downtown New Bern:

During the 20th c., the old waterfront lost status with the emphasis on railroad and highway travel, but the central business district still recalls the focus on the converging Neuse and Trent rivers that were the city's lifeblood in the 18th and 19th centuries. Tryon Palace Dr. (originally South Front St.) and East Front St. run along the old waterfront area, which has been transformed by landfill but has new vitality with tourist and leisure boats docking here. The dense commercial blocks along Craven, Pollock, Middle, and Broad Sts. contain a variety of late 19th- and early 20th-c. commercial architecture, two important churches, and a surprising number of Federal period townhouses and stores.

CV 1 Harvey Mansion

Ca. 1798; 219 Tryon Palace Dr. (formerly S. Front St.); restaurant

Built for English-born merchant John Harvey during the optimistic early years of New Bern's Federal period mercantile heyday, the big, 3-story, 5-bay, Flemish-bond brick structure evidently combined elegant residential quarters on the east with office and warehouse space at the west end. Originally an arched passageway extended through the center bay at ground level to provide street access to Harvey's Trent River wharves. This feature remains visible on the riverfront, though fill has obscured the original relationship to the water. Academic Adamesque interiors, particularly the elaborate second-floor drawing room, are among the finest of the period in New Bern and the state.

CV 2 John Justice House

1846; 221 E. Front St.

The brick townhouse exemplifies the persistence of the side-passage plan, in a simply detailed Greek Revival version. The stepped gable-end parapets, slate roof, and masonry window surrounds suggest a concern with fire prevention. The tooled brownstone lintels and sills were probably imported from New York or Connecticut. A running bond facade contrasts with 1:5 bond side and rear walls. The house was built for John R. Justice, a merchant with a "large country trade," on the site of a dwelling probably destroyed by an 1841 fire that swept this Union Point area.

CV 3 Thomas Sparrow House

Ca. 1843; 222 E. Front St.

The side-passage plan takes another form in this tall, 3½-story, brick townhouse in Greek Revival style, here with a central chimney, Flemish-bond brickwork, and brownstone trim. Sparrow, a shipbuilder, also built his brick house with parapeted gable roof in the wake of the Union Point fire.

cv 4 *Isaac Taylor House*

CV 4 Isaac Taylor House

Ca. 1792; 228 Craven St.

Rising 3 full stories above a full basement, the imposing brick side-passage-plan townhouse—the oldest in town—was built for Scots-born merchant Taylor. Its urban siting with the door opening onto the sidewalk and its conservative, fire-resistant detailing reflect precedents in larger cities. Notable details include the Flemish-bond brickwork with rubbed-brick flat arches, an open pediment entrance enriched with fluted pilasters and carved sunbursts, and a Diocletian-style attic window in the southern gable. Restrained Adamesque interiors illustrate the use of English architectural books by local craftsmen.

CV 5 Stephens' Brick Block (Old City Hall)

1816–18, ca. 1905; 220–26 Craven St.

Although the row of four, 3-story brick stores was remodeled ca. 1905, vestiges remain of its early 19th-c. character as the "Brick Block" built for rental purposes by Marcus Cicero Stephens. It is a unique example in the state of an early 19th-c. commercial block. After financial difficulties, the four units were sold to separate owners. By

1888 the city had purchased the entire block and made it into a city hall, then renovated it ca. 1905 with a new facade. It has seen various uses since the city hall moved out in 1936.

CV 6 James Riggs House
Ca. 1830s; 223 Craven St.

The simply finished, 3-story brick house was built for Riggs, the town's hatter. In his shop in *Stephens' Brick Block across the street he manufactured hats from beaver, otter, mink, and raccoon pelts. Of brick laid in Flemish bond, the house repeats the parapet gable ends and Greek Revival detail of the *Thomas Sparrow House.

CV 7 New Bern City Hall (U.S. Post Office, Courthouse, and Customhouse)
1895–97 (Charles E. Kemper and William Martin Aiken, architects, U.S. Treasury Dept.), 1910–11 (tower); 300 Pollock St.

Built by the U.S. Treasury Department, the eclectic combination of the Romanesque Revival and High Victorian Gothic styles reflects a national rather than a local idiom. The contrasting colors and textures of stone

cv 7 *New Bern City Hall*

and brick, coupled with its dramatic massing and roofline, make the building a distinctive landmark in the architecturally conservative downtown. The tower with its illuminated, 4-faced clock was added at the behest of local citizens. The copper bears emblematic of Bern, Switzerland, projecting above the entrances were bought by the city in 1913 or 1914 and mounted on the old city hall, then were moved here in 1936 when the building became the city hall upon completion of the new *Federal Building.

CV 8 Christ Church
1822–24 (Martin Stevenson and Thomas S. Gooding, builders), rebuilt and enlarged 1871–85 (George Bishop, contractor, and others); 320 Pollock St.

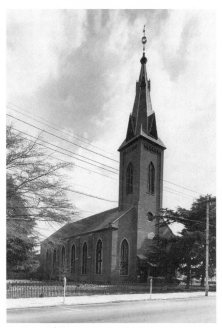

cv 8 *Christ Church*

Christ Church bears the appearance of a late Gothic Revival structure at first glance, but the Flemish-bond brick walls and lancet window openings of the nave survive from the 1822–24 church gutted by fire in 1871. This notably early Gothic work was embellished during the rebuilding of the 1870s and the 1880s, when the present tower was built, with its corbeled brickwork, slate-covered spire and Stick-style porch. The churchyard, a shady oasis in the heart of the commercial district, contains fine 18th-c. slate and brownstone tombstones from New England makers. The foundations of the colonial Christ Church, a 30-by-70-foot brick building with an apsidial chancel, give form to a quiet outdoor chapel.

CV 9 Baxter's Jewelry Store

Ca. 1915; 323 Pollock St.

Typical of many downtown commercial blocks, the 2-story brick building with its curved gable reflects the early 20th-c. interest in eclectic revivals. Baxter's, a local institution, has been here since 1920. **Baxter's Clock**, a street clock built by the Seth Thomas Company and shipped here in 1920, is a characteristic early 20th-c. jewelry store advertising feature. It was rebuilt after a 1977 truck accident.

CV 10 Hotel Albert

1887; 226 Middle St.

The only survivor of New Bern's three major downtown hotels, the 3-story structure dominates the streetscape with its Italianate detailing and pressed-brick ornament. Its mansard-roofed cupola, visible from a distance, adds a Second Empire accent to the skyline.

CV 11 First Baptist Church

1848; Thomas and Sons (New York), architects; Hardy B. Lane, builder; 239 Middle St. (at Church Alley)

With its pointed windows, crenellated central tower, and pinnacles, this was evidently the state's first thoroughgoing Gothic Revival church built for a non-Episcopal congregation. The gable-fronted building with central entrance tower is handsomely executed in Flemish-bond brick with brownstone trim. Tradition claims that church members traveled to New York to obtain the design from Thomas and Sons, specialists in

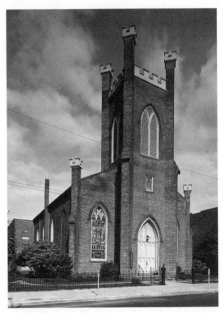

CV 11 *First Baptist Church*

Baptist churches. Builder Lane was prominent in New Bern's antebellum resurgence.

CV 12 Elks Temple

1908; William P. Rose (Raleigh), architect; 400 Pollock St.

The 5-story office building, the city's tallest, dates from the early 20th-c. lumber boom; like other lodge buildings of the era, it contained commercial and civic space—a department store and public library as well as the lodge rooms on the top floor. Architect Rose employed the period's characteristic classical detail in terra-cotta and yellow brick.

CV 13 Peoples Bank Building

1913; Burett H. Stephens (Wilmington), architect; 317 Middle St.

The granite-faced bank, with Ionic columns in antis framing an arched entrance beneath a full pediment, is the downtown's prime example of Beaux Arts classicism. When built for a locally organized bank, it was touted as "the city's most beautiful and imposing edifice," to be equipped "in strict accordance to modern ideas of banking."

CV 14 Stanly Building

1912; George Eubanks, attributed architect; 335 Middle St.

Built for Lucinda Stanly, a black business-woman and real estate owner, the 2-story brick commercial block was also known as the Eubanks building and may have been designed or built by George Eubanks, who appears in city directories of the day as the city's only black architect. Upon the building's completion, the first floor was leased to the Bradham Drug Company, which opened a soda fountain described as "one of the handsomest in the South," where the most famous offering was the Pepsi-Cola that Caleb Bradham had invented several years earlier. Much of the drugstore interior survives subsequent uses, including mosaic tile floor and pressed tin ceiling.

CV 15 Attmore-Oliver House

Ca. 1790, enlarged ca. 1834; 513 Broad St.; open regular hours

The 2½-story, double-pile frame house attained its present configuration ca. 1834, when a small, late Georgian house was enlarged by merchant Isaac Taylor for his daughter Mary and her new husband, George Attmore. The 5-bay facade shows the early local use of Greek Revival elements, including a Doric-order entrance portico, fluted door and window surrounds, and full-length, first-floor windows opening onto cast-iron balconies. A traditional 2-story piazza reaches across the back of the house. In the backyard stands a ca. 1834 brick smokehouse, one of the few early outbuildings to survive in New Bern.

CV 16 Edward R. Stanly House

Ca. 1848; 502 Pollock St.

Built for Stanly, a prominent manufacturer and one of the first directors of the Atlantic and N.C. Railroad, the townhouse displays the persistent side-passage plan, rendered in Greek Revival style. The Flemish-bond brick house, trimmed with brownstone, has a typically Greek Revival style low hipped roof, projecting cornice, and classical portico (enriched with later 19th-c. ornament). The brick frieze is punctuated with cast-iron grilles similar to those in Wilmington. A side yard is surrounded by a ca. 1900 classical iron fence. Stanly's 2-story brick office stands to the rear.

CV 17 The Blue Gable

Ca. 1932; 501 Pollock St.

The trademark steep gables and English cottage styling of the little Pure Oil service station recall the corporation's design of a domestic character intended to fit into residential neighborhoods. The bright blue roof earned the building its nickname.

CV 18 Patrick Gordon House

Ca. 1771; 213 Hancock St.

The gambrel-roofed frame house, built for attorney Patrick Gordon, is the most intact example of a type common in 18th-c. New Bern. Notable features include flush exterior sheathing and walls filled with brick nogging—unusual in eastern N.C. At the gable end facing the street rises a massive, Flemish-bond chimney with an unusual sloped weathering on its face. Also atypical is the full basement of brick and ballast stone, which contains a large cooking fireplace and brick and ballast stone floor paving. The plan is an expanded version of the hall-parlor plan, with three unheated rear rooms (the central one containing the stair) within the gambrel form.

CV 19 Charles Bates House

Ca. 1805; 210 Hancock St.

The 2½-story, early Federal style townhouse, built of brick in Flemish bond with a side-passage plan, has an unusual arrangement. It stands on a raised basement like other Trent River waterfront buildings, with a street entrance—which contained the kitchen—but the main entrance is on the south side, reached by a flight of brownstone steps on the gable end.

CV 20 Bryan House and Office

1803–5 (Martin Stevenson, carpenter), 1820, 1828; 603–5 Pollock St.; private, not open to public

The stylish, side-hall-plan brick townhouse was built for merchant James Bryan. The elegant, open-arched portico features slender paired colonnettes and a modillion and dentil cornice. The Federal interior finish is documented as the work of Martin Stevenson Sr., a respected local carpenter-builder. Adjoining is the 1-story, gable-fronted frame office, built during the 1820s for his son John Herritage Bryan, a lawyer and U.S. congressman. While Stevenson was remodeling the drawing room in Greek Revival style in 1828, Bryan advised his wife from Washington, D.C., "You know that the chair boards as they are called are out of fashion."

CV 21 Tryon Palace

1767–70 (John Hawks, architect), reconstructed 1952–59 (William Graves Perry, architect); Pollock and George Sts.; open regular hours

Present-day Tryon Palace is a reconstruction of N.C.'s colonial capitol and governor's residence, built 1767–70 and destroyed by fire in 1798. The newly appointed Gov. William Tryon insisted on construction of a handsome and substantial public building. Despite resistance from Regulators, the piedmont farmers who objected to the taxes for the project, he oversaw its successful completion. To design and execute the building, Tryon brought to New Bern an English architect, John Hawks, and probably employed artisans from Philadelphia and elsewhere.

After developing several designs, Hawks and Tryon settled on a Georgian edifice in the Palladian manner. Hawks probably drew inspiration from English architectural books by Isaac Ware, James Gibbs, and Abraham Swan, as well as standing buildings in England. As shown in Hawks's drawings and as reconstructed, the symmetrical, 2½-story main block centers on a pedimented pavilion with entrances on both the land and water sides. (See Introduction, Fig. 24.) The plan, three rooms deep, is organized around a central, skylit stair hall. The largest of several formal, richly ornamented rooms is the council chamber at the southeastern corner. Service rooms occupy the basement, which opens onto a service terrace on the land front. Creating a forecourt on the land front, curving colonnades lead to 2-story wings: a kitchen on the east, a stable on the west. Gardens extend on all sides. Upon its completion, the palace was regarded as one of the finest buildings in the colonies. One world traveler praised it as being "in the pure English taste; all the ornamentation ex-

CV 21 *Tryon Palace*

tremely simple and placed with considerable taste and intelligence."

The palace served as N.C.'s first permanent capitol and governor's residence. Tryon soon left to become governor of New York, and the palace was subsequently occupied until the eve of the Revolution by Gov. Josiah Martin. It was made obsolete when the state's capital was moved to Raleigh in 1792–94. In disrepair and only occasionally used, in 1798 the palace burned by accident but the west wing (the stable) survived.

Pride in the palace persisted over the years. In the 1890s N.C. planned to build a rendition of it as the state's building at the World's Columbian Exposition in Chicago, but funds were insufficient. In the 1920s and 1930s, interest mounted in research toward rebuilding the palace. In the 1940s, Mrs. Maude Moore Latham, a New Bernian residing in Greensboro, established trust funds for the reconstruction, stipulating that the state also provide financial assistance.

The 1952–59 reconstruction, overseen by the Tryon Palace Commission, was aided by the remarkable survival of Hawks's original plans and elevations. Gertrude Carraway, local historical leader, located Hawks's drawings in New York, and this was complemented by discovery of other Hawks drawings in London, as well as by archaeological investigations and historical research. The palace was rebuilt on its original foundations under the supervision of restoration architect William Graves Perry of Perry, Shaw, Hepburn, Kehoe, and Dean of Boston. In 1991, discovery of a description written by Hawks in 1783 and a drawing of the grounds, probably by surveyor C. J. Sauthier, enhanced understanding of the rooms' uses, specifics of finish and detail, and the formal layout of the grounds.

CV 22 Tryon Palace Complex

Around the reconstructed *Tryon Palace several other restored houses open to the public illustrate New Bern's architectural development from the 1780s to the 1880s, including representative side-passage townhouses. The **Dixon-Stevenson House** (1826–33; 609 Pollock St.; open regular hours),

built for tailor and merchant George Dixon, is a frame townhouse with a typical New Bern stair passage where an arch frames the dogleg stair. Federal style finish combines with occasional Greek Revival touches, and the platform between the chimneys, locally called "captain's walks," is a feature variously attributed to fire prevention and river views. Next door, the **Daves House** (ca. 1813; 613 Pollock St.; open regular hours) is another frame, side-passage-plan townhouse with very simple finish and exposed face chimneys.

Around the corner on Eden St., the **Jones House** (ca. 1808; 231 Eden St.) shows the combination of side-passage-plan townhouse with engaged two-tier porch. In typical New Bern fashion, at one time the ends were enclosed. The **Robert Hay House** (ca. 1804, 1816; 227 Eden St.; open regular hours) is a remarkably intact version of the frame, side-passage-plan townhouse built for New Bern's artisans. Carpenter Benjamin Good built the first section with a side-passage plan and only one chamber per floor, and Robert Hay, a highly respected Scots-born chairmaker, expanded it to the rear with additional chambers and a double porch. Recently restored, it is interpreted to Hay's period from a detailed inventory illustrating the domestic life of a prominent artisan.

CV 23 John Wright Stanly House

1779–83; 307 George St.; open regular hours

The conservative, academic exterior and elaborate late Georgian interiors of the Stanly House rank it as the finest dwelling of its style and period in the state. Long-stand-

cv 23 *John Wright Stanly House*

ing tradition and circumstantial evidence suggest that it was designed by John Hawks, architect of *Tryon Palace who remained in New Bern, but no documentation has been found. The opulent residence was built for merchant John Wright Stanly, a Virginian who traded in Jamaica and Philadelphia, moved to New Bern, and flourished as a blockade-runner during the Revolution. The exterior flush-boarded sheathing forms a sleek background for heavy quoins, a modillion cornice enriched with fretwork, a pedimented entrance, and pediments above the windows at the first-floor level. The double-pile, center-passage plan has four rooms of differing sizes, with the front rooms larger and more ornate than the rear ones. The center passage is divided by a transverse arch that frames a large stair passage; there is also a service stair. Sophisticated late Georgian woodwork in the spirit of Abraham Swan's books resembles Hawks's drawings for the palace. Mantels, doorways, and windows feature crossetted surrounds, pediments, and swelling friezes. Cornices are enriched with dentils and modillions, and chair boards and wash boards are intricately carved. The magnificent main stair, which rises in three flights, has elaborate carved mahogany brackets—the finest in the state—and a ramped railing echoed on the opposite wall of the staircase. The house was moved from its Middle St. site in 1966 and restored as a house museum as part of the Tryon Palace Complex. Furnished according to the detailed inventory of Stanly's possessions at his death from yellow fever in 1789, it illustrates a fashionable and luxurious way of life rare in 18th-c. N.C.

CV 24 800 Block, Pollock St.

West of the *Tryon Palace Complex, in an area that was once part of the *Long Wharf area along the Trent River, the 800 block of Pollock St. presents a remarkable urban streetscape of 18th- and 19th-c. frame dwellings, which include the state's principal survival of small-scale urban housing of the late 18th and early 19th centuries. Although large houses of these eras survive in good numbers in N.C., the once-numerous little houses of N.C.'s early urban life have almost all van-

cv 24 *Nathan Tisdale House*

ished. Several small early houses, which display a full range of traditional forms, plans, and finishes, stand among later 19th-c. frame houses of compatible scale. A number of these properties were owned by leading local artisans.

The **Nathan Tisdale House** (ca. 1810; 803 Pollock St.) exemplifies the center-chimney, gable-roofed house form that was especially popular for the relatively small frame dwellings built for the town's artisans. This 2-story version has a gable-fronted orientation and abuts the sidewalk—an arrangement common in 17th- and 18th-c. English and colonial cities. In this compact plan, a tight stair rises alongside the chimney. Finish is of neat Federal style. The house was built for silversmith Nathan Tisdale on a lot he inherited from his father, William, also a silversmith. An early 19th-c. smokehouse has been moved here and attached to the house. **All Saints Episcopal Chapel** (1895; 809 Pollock St.) is a Carpenter Gothic style frame chapel erected as a mission by Christ Church to serve the southwestern portion of the city, a predominantly working-people's area called Long Wharf. The dark, rich color scheme emphasizes the picturesque details, while a scissors truss motif recurs in the exterior stick style detail and the interior ceiling. The **Pendleton House** (ca. 1815; 815 Pollock

St.) shows the continuation of the gambrel-roofed form, common in New Bern during the 18th c., in small dwellings into the early 19th c. The little frame house with a side passage and one main room has a shed porch, shed dormers, and exposed face chimney characteristic of the era. The house was probably built for sea captain Sylvester Pendleton or his son Simeon. The **John H. Jones House** (ca. 1810; 819 Pollock St.) repeats the 2-story, 2-room, center-chimney form of the *Nathan Tisdale House, but with a side-gabled orientation. It was built for Jones on land he bought from Tisdale in 1803 and sold to leading house carpenter Martin Stevenson in 1815. The **Alston-Charlotte House** (mid-18th c.; 823 Pollock St.), a small, hall-parlor-plan house with gambrel roof, likewise abuts the street and stands on a high foundation. One of the oldest small houses in town, it was owned—but not necessarily occupied—by silversmiths William Tisdale and Nathan Tisdale, and after 1815 by house painter William Charlotte, in whose family it remained until 1879. The **Silas Statham House** (ca. 1800–1810; 816 Pollock St.), a tiny cottage that probably had a hall-parlor plan originally, despite alterations over the years retains its simple shed dormers and a shed porch.

CV 25 Trent Court

1940–41; A. Mitchell Wooten and John J. Rowland (Kinston), architects; Fowler-Jones Construction Company; Fleet St. and Walt Bellamy Dr. (formerly New South Front St.)

Located in the old *Long Wharf area, the substantial and well-designed public housing complex retains its high quality of planning and construction in a tree-shaded setting. Architects Wooten and Rowland designed similar schemes for two New Bern public housing projects, Trent Court for whites and *Craven Terrace for blacks. Exemplifying prototype designs seen elsewhere in the South, the 2-story brick buildings are executed in a Flemish-bond brickwork variation with cast concrete trim, cantilevered concrete porch roofs, and large bas-relief panels depicting children playing with toys and musical instruments.

Johnson St.–E. Front St. Neighborhood:
Since the 18th c., the compact, tree-shaded neighborhood reaching north of Broad St. to the Neuse River and extending westward from E. Front St. to Metcalf St. has been regarded as New Bern's finest residential section. Some of the town's earliest colonial houses and finest residences from the Federal era stand here. Several houses along the river maintain their orientation to the water from back or side yards. The western edge of the neighborhood is defined by the tree-shaded Academy Green, with its two brick school buildings. The architecturally rich area boasts exceptional examples of nearly every style—usually of frame construction—and covers a range from the mid-18th to the 20th centuries. Many houses show a series of construction phases.

The area remained fashionable during the industrial boom era, with some of the principal houses of that period built here. Development pressures resulted in the subdivision of the large yards surrounding the early houses to create building sites for smaller variations on the late Queen Anne, Colonial Revival, and foursquare forms. New Bern's preference for the side-passage plan continued in a large number of 2-story, gable-fronted houses—a prevalent early 20th-c. house form in tidewater towns. The residential quality of the neighborhood is enhanced by important houses of

CV 25 *Trent Court*

worship, clustered around the intersection of New and Middle Sts.

CV 26 Eli Smallwood House and Jones-Jarvis House

Ca. 1810–12; Asa King, carpenter; 524–28 E. Front St.

In contrast to the row houses seen in some cities, New Bern merchants preferred freestanding, side-passage-plan residences set on relatively spacious lots. These two brick townhouses show the form at its finest, with entrance porticoes stepping up directly from the sidewalk and large side and rear lots opening toward the river, where once stood associated outbuildings, warehouses, and wharves. Originally a second entrance led to Smallwood's business office in the front room of his house. The two nearly identical townhouses epitomize Federal period New Bern's high level of craftsmanship. The beautiful Palladian form porticoes have slender turned columns and arched ceilings. Intricate modillion cornices include a delicate rope or cable molding, a frequent feature of New Bern's finest work. The excellent workmanship continues in the Flemish-bond brickwork and elaborate interiors. In each

house the side passage contains an arch framing a delicate stair that leads to a large, second-floor drawing room. The more elaborate of the two was built ca. 1811–12 for Eli Smallwood, a merchant and shipowner engaged in trade with the West Indies and the major ports of the Middle Atlantic and New England states. Local house carpenter Asa King executed the interior finish, which resembles the work at *St. John's Masonic Lodge.

CV 27 Charles Slover House and Dependency

1848–49; Hardy B. Lane, attributed builder; 201 Johnson St.

The massive, 3-story brick house is New Bern's prime example of the Greek Revival style and one of the finest in the state. The symmetrical house with 5-bay facade is executed in Flemish-bond brickwork and accentuated by a modillion cornice and in-antis Doric-order doorway. The design, especially the diminution of the windows from the full-height first story to the small, 3/3 windows in the third story, recalls New England townhouses in Salem and other cities. Behind the house stands its original

cv 26 *Jones-Jarvis House and Eli Smallwood House*

cv 27 *Charles Slover House and Dependency*

2-story brick kitchen and slave quarters and a brick smokehouse—rare examples of such urban outbuildings. Built for Slover, a leading merchant trading with the West Indies, and his wife, Elizabeth, who came from Massachusetts, the house was the headquarters of Gen. Ambrose E. Burnside during Union occupation of New Bern and was later owned by Caleb D. Bradham, inventor of Pepsi-Cola.

CV 28 The Louisiana House
Ca. 1800–1810; 529 E. Front St.

The double porch with enclosed ends shows a form long prevalent in New Bern. Philadelphia visitor William Attmore commented in 1787 on the many "Balconies or Piazzas" in front and back of houses, "convenient on account of the great Summer Heats here. . . . Often two Stories high, sometimes one or both ends of it are boarded up, and made into a Room." The frame house of traditional gable-roofed, 4-bay form was probably built for Levi Dawson, a member of the N.C. House of Commons. The double porches with the enclosed ends at the second-floor level are a slightly later Federal period addition, as are the 2-story rear shed rooms. In the late 19th c. this was the home of Mary Bayard Devereaux Clarke, a writer and poet who named it the Louisiana House. It was later home of Bayard Wootten, an important early 20th-c. photographer.

CV 29 Larry I. Moore House
1908; Herbert W. Simpson, architect; 511 E. Front St.

The big, symmetrical frame house, with tall Corinthian portico overlapping a 1-story wraparound porch, presents one of the town's finest surviving examples of the Southern Colonial style popular among the city's leading merchants, industrialists, and professionals. Moore was a local attorney.

CV 30 Coor-Bishop House
Ca. 1770s, 1904; Herbert W. Simpson, architect; 501 E. Front St.

A time capsule like many others in the neighborhood, the house began as a Georgian style residence akin to the *Coor-Gaston and *John Wright Stanly houses. During the lumber boom the house was reoriented and transformed for Edward K. Bishop, commission merchant and wholesale lumber and grocery dealer, into an ebullient example of Simpson's Southern Colonial style, with clusters of Corinthian columns adorning a 1-story porch that carries around the large, 2-story house with projecting pavilions, bays, and dormers.

CV 31 Jerkins-Richardson House
1848–49; 520 Craven St.

cv 31 *Jerkins-Richardson House*

A late version of the side-gabled, side-passage plan, the house at a prominent corner is dramatized by its height on a tall basement and paired chimneys linked by a captain's walk.

CV 32 Smith-Whitford House
Ca. 1780, late 19th c.; 506 Craven St.

Like many in town, the house combines various eras of construction. The interior retains essentially its original Georgian finish, while the exterior displays 19th-c. embellishments, including a fanciful sawnwork porch.

CV 33 John D. Flanner House
1855; 305 Johnson St.

The Italianate house, one of the first in New Bern, exhibits the characteristic bracketed cornice and low hipped roof of the style but carries forward the familiar side-passage plan. Timbers are inscribed with the date Oct. 17, 1855, "John D. Flanners House," and the names "Marshall" and "Willis," probably the carpenters, perhaps slaves. Flanner, a merchant, had recently married Nancy Jerkins, whose father gave her the lot.

CV 34 William B. Blades House
1903; Herbert W. Simpson, architect;
602 Middle St.

CV 34 *William B. Blades House*

The magnificent house is among the state's prime renditions of the energetic synthesis of Queen Anne style massing and early Colonial Revival detail. It was built for lumber magnate William B. Blades, who with his brother James came from Bishopville, Md., and by the 1880s had established the large sawmill and logging operation that developed into the Blades Lumber Company, with William as president and his three younger brothers as officers. Blades is said to have selected and saved choice woods for the

project. This was the first of several family commissions for architect Simpson, who created a flamboyant design that expressed the stature of the family and their business. Planned to take maximum advantage of the corner site, the big house presents two exuberantly different facades featuring towers, gables, bays, tall chimney stacks, and broad porches, enriched with opulent classical detailing. The irregular plan, with a large corner entrance hall, is treated with equally lavish Colonial Revival and late Victorian finish.

CV 35 Foy-Munger House
Ca. 1881; 516 Middle St.

The eclectic Victorian house is representative of the many large, elaborate houses built in the neighborhood during the city's late 19th-c. lumber boom, with an asymmetrical form and bold brackets and shingles. It was built for merchant Claudius E. Foy.

CV 36 St. Paul's Catholic Church
1841; Hardy B. Lane, builder; 504 Middle St.

The Greek Revival church was erected by local house carpenter Lane as a simple, temple-form structure and gained its front tower in 1896. New Bern lawyer William Gaston, a prominent Catholic layman, had obtained from New York architect A. J. Davis an elaborate Gothic Revival design, but when lack of money precluded its construction, this simpler church was built.

CV 37 Centenary Methodist Church
1904; Charles Granville Jones (New York),
and Herbert W. Simpson, architects;
SE corner Middle and New Sts.

Combining Romanesque Revival and chateauesque features, the big brick church boldly expresses its auditorium plan and emphasizes its diagonal placement on its corner site. It was designed by Jones in collaboration with local architect Simpson. Two powerful and unequal towers with spires and bartizans flank a semicircular, arcaded entrance porch. These accentuate the polygo-

cv 37 *Centenary Methodist Church*

nal volume of the sanctuary, a large auditorium with radiating pews beneath an open truss ceiling. The interior was updated in 1965. This is among the finest of the state's many large Methodist churches built with auditorium plans in Romanesque Revival style. Methodism in New Bern dates from George Whitfield's preaching in 1739, and the first church, St. Andrew's Chapel, was built in 1802 on Hancock St.

CV 38 Coor-Gaston House
Ca. 1785–87; 421 Craven St.; open regular hours

cv 38 *Coor-Gaston House*

The unusual, 2½-story frame house displays an urban gable-end orientation, with 2-tier piazzas with Chinese trellis railings inset into the side of the house. Other notable details include the marl (local shell-rock) and English-bond brick foundations and the Diocletian windows in the gable ends. Arranged to accommodate the inset porch, the principal rooms have sophisticated Georgian finish, including crossetted mantels and door and window frames akin to those at *Tryon Palace, the *John Wright Stanly House, and *Bellair. Long thought to date from ca. 1770, the house has principal timbers evidently cut after the growing season of 1785. Built for James Coor, a leading political figure, from 1818 to 1844 it was the home of William Gaston, lawyer, member of Congress, and judge of the state supreme court.

CV 39 First Church of Christ, Scientist
1907; Herbert W. Simpson, architect; 406 Middle St.

Local architect Simpson designed two nearly identical, temple-form structures for small congregations, this one for the Christian Science congregation established in 1894. The 1-story, gable-fronted building gains monumentality from its Ionic portico, front Venetian window flanked by doorways, and arched windows along the sides. Mary Baker Eddy, founder of Christian Science, contributed $3,000 and gave the cornerstone.

CV 40 Craven County Courthouse
1883; Sloan and Balderston (Philadelphia), architects; John B. Lane, builder; William Hay, painter; 300 Broad St.; open business hours

Designed by the Philadelphia firm of Samuel Sloan, which took several important commissions in N.C. after the Civil War, the courthouse is among the state's prime examples of the Second Empire style. After the early 19th-c. courthouse burned in 1861, hard times following the Civil War delayed construction of a replacement. Built by leading local contractor John B. Lane, son of antebellum builder Hardy B. Lane, the courthouse features a tall, peaked, 3½-story tower and mansard roof adorned with cresting. A rich polychrome program sets off the dark red brick: colorful patterned slate roof, cast-iron lintels and sills with Eastlake style ornament, and dark horizontal brick banding. (See Introduction, Fig. 49.)

CV 41 Federal Building

1932–34; Robert F. Smallwood (New York), architect; 415 Middle St.

In an early reference to the local architectural identity, the massive red brick edifice was described at its dedication as "of Colonial design, planned by the architect, Robert F. Smallwood, of this city to blend with the Colonial homes in New Bern." Smallwood, a New Bern native, had established an architectural practice in New York City by 1915. The scale and quality of the 3-story building, with its recessed portico with tobacco-leaf columns, Georgian Revival detail, and tall cupola, owed more to the influence of New Bern's congressmen than to the size of the city. The courtroom contains a mural depicting local history scenes. (See Introduction, Fig. 65.)

CV 42 Temple Chester B'nai Sholem

1908; Herbert W. Simpson, architect; 505 Middle St.

Architect Simpson repeated the format of the Christian Science church in the small temple but varied it by using the Corinthian order and a central entrance flanked by windows. Although Jews had resided in New Bern since at least the early 19th c., this was the first synagogue built, for a congregation organized in 1894.

CV 43 Thomas McLin House

Ca. 1810–15; 507 Middle St.

The center-chimney plan and inset front porch of the 1½-story frame house make it a Federal style coastal cottage unique in town: five bays wide with a flush-sheathed facade centering on a double door with a delicate fanlight. The house was probably built for McLin, a merchant and coppersmith.

CV 44 John Carruthers Stanly House

Ca. 1810, ca. 1843, ca. 1891; 405 Johnson St.

The frame house, which began as a 2½-story Federal period dwelling with a center-chimney plan and its gable front to the street, was enlarged over the years. It was built for Stanly and his wife, Kitty Green Stanly. Born a slave and evidently a son of merchant John Wright Stanly, John C. Stanly prospered as a barber, gained his freedom, and became one of the wealthiest free blacks in the antebellum South, owning several town lots, rural property, and more slaves than any other free black in the South. Kitty Green Stanly was a founding member of the *First Presbyterian Church, and the couple owned pews there.

CV 45 John R. Green House (Presbyterian Manse)

Ca. 1820; 411 Johnson St.

The 2½-story, frame side-hall-plan house was built for Green, a free black tailor who employed several journeymen and apprentices in his tailoring shop. He lived in the house until 1842, when it was purchased by the First Presbyterian Church. Early 20th-c. additions have somewhat obscured the original form and 3-bay width of the house. The fine Federal style interior finish reflects the prosperity achieved by free black artisans in early 19th-c. New Bern.

CV 46 St. John's Masonic Lodge and Theater

1801–9; John Dewey, builder; 514 Hancock St.

The unique Federal period edifice was built as the first permanent home for St. John's Masonic Lodge, which was formed in 1772. The 7-bay facade displays the sophisticated use of the popular Federal style motif, the colossal arch, elliptical in form and set into a broad pedimented pavilion in a reinterpretation of the Palladian format established by the palace. The temptation is strong to look for the hand of William Nichols, for whom such creative handling of classical motifs would have been familiar from his youth in Bath, England, but only the role of builder John Dewey, member of the lodge, appears in lodge records. The first floor originally housed a theater that has remained in nearly continuous use since 1805. The exterior and the theater have been altered, but the splendid second-floor lodge room retains superb

Federal finish plus trompe l'oeil wall paintings dating from 1860. (See Introduction, Fig. 25.)

CV 47 First Presbyterian Church

1819–22; Uriah Sandy, Martin Stevenson Sr., John Dewey, builders; 412 New St.

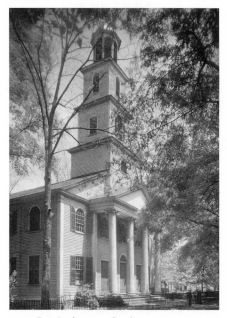

cv 47 *First Presbyterian Church*

The graceful frame edifice is the finest Federal style church in the state. Its skillfully proportioned form and elegant detail complement the sophisticated geometry of the interior spaces. No architect has been identified, though again it is tempting to look to William Nichols as designer. The Wren-Gibbs format evokes New England precedents, but Uriah Sandy, the contractor, was New Bern bred. It is possible that Asher Benjamin's patternbooks influenced its design. The large, gable-fronted building is dominated by a 4-stage belltower and the city's earliest heroic portico. The interior is extraordinarily fine. At either end of the transverse-entrance vestibule, arches frame semicircular stairs, and from the vestibule two doorways open into the large, light sanctuary with its elliptical vaulted ceiling and airy galleries on three sides. Unexpect-

edly, the pulpit (a restoration of the original) stands on a podium between the two front entrances, an arrangement seen in New England meetinghouses of about 1800 and in a few mid-19th-c. Presbyterian churches in N.C. The congregation was established in 1817 and almost immediately began construction of this, their first and only church.

CV 48 New Bern Academy

1806–10; 514 New St.; open regular hours

cv 48 *New Bern Academy*

Standing amid its tree-shaded green, the handsome, Flemish-bond brick school was built to replace the town's first academy, built on the same site in 1766 and destroyed by fire in the 1790s. Evoking the persistent influence of the palace, the 5-bay facade has a central pavilion with an oculus in the pediment. The octagonal cupola, like the semicircular portico, is a well-documented reconstruction of the original. Certain exterior details, including the paired modillions of the cornice, the semicircular portico, and the elliptical fanlight, suggest the hand of William Nichols, who employed similar motifs at *Hayes near Edenton.

On the grounds stands the **Bell Building** (1884; Samuel Sloan, architect; 517 Hancock St.), designed by the Philadelphia architect to supplement classroom space in the old academy. The 7-bay, hip-roofed brick building restates the familiar Palladian format in simplified Italianate style, with three round-headed windows in the pedimented pavilion, capped by a belfry.

cv 49 *New Bern Fire Department*

CV 49 New Bern Fire Department
1927–28; 420 Broad St.

A playful Mediterranean style enlivens the 2-story brick fire station, which features a curved, arcaded loggia at the second-level firefighters' quarters, flanked by windows with iron balconies—a romantic contrast to the fire truck bays below. It was built to house the city's two firefighting companies, the Atlantic Company (est. 1845) and the Button Company (organized by Union soldiers in 1865 as the New Bern Steam Fire Engine Company but renamed for a new "Button steam fire engine" in 1884). The copper bear projecting from the central parapet was originally on the city hall but was moved here in 1935. A firefighting history museum is located in the rear.

CV 50 Ulysses S. Mace House
Ca. 1884; 518 Broad St.

New Bern's most elaborate Italianate residence was built for the town's leading pharmacist when Broad St. was a fashionable avenue. Intricate sawnwork brackets and spandrels ornament its bays, porches, and cornices.

CV 51 Hawks House
Ca. 1760s, 1810s, 1975 (moved from Metcalf St.); 517 New St.

Exemplifying the relatively modest, 1½-story gambrel form common among merchants' houses in 18th-c. New Bern, the oldest portion of this house—the western three bays—was probably built for merchant John Green before 1769. Francis Hawks, son of architect John Hawks, bought the house in 1807 and enlarged it to its present width, with a center-passage plan and shed porch.

CV 52 Palmer-Tisdale House
Ca. 1767, ca. 1800, ca. 1830; 520 New St.

The Georgian style frame house, enlarged by Federal style additions, was owned by a number of men prominent in early New Bern and N.C. The original 5-bay front section with its massive, Flemish-bond end chimneys was built ca. 1767 for Robert Palmer, a justice of the colonial supreme court. Subsequently it was owned by Martin Howard, chief justice of the colony; William Tisdale, a politician and silversmith who engraved the Great Seal of the state; and John Louis Taylor, the first chief justice of the state's supreme court. The center-passage plan interior retains Georgian and later finish. The ca. 1767 full basement contains two large cooking fireplaces, one with an original bake-oven.

CV 53 George H. White House
Late 18th c., ca. 1890; 519 Johnson St.

Located on the back property of the *Palmer-Tisdale House, within the conservative, 2-story frame house with restrained sawnwork porch lies a smaller 18th-c. dwelling with heavy timber frame, probably the house left in 1840 by merchant Asa Jones to the use of "my woman Esther . . . during her natural life." In 1888 the property was purchased by George H. White, who expanded the house to its present form. Born a slave in Bladen Co., White graduated from Howard University and served in the N.C. legislature and then in the U.S. Congress (1897–1901), where he was the last black congressman until 1928. In the yard is a frame **Office** (ca. 1800–1810) believed to have been the law office of John L. Taylor, first chief justice of the N.C. Supreme Court, who resided at the *Palmer-Tisdale House.

cv 54 *St. Cyprian's Episcopal Church*

CV 54 St. Cyprian's Episcopal Church
1910−12; Herbert W. Simpson, architect;
604 Johnson St. at Queen St.

Established formally in 1866, though it had been temporarily organized as early as the 1830s, the black Episcopal congregation used the old Baptist church on this site from 1866 until 1910. In 1910 the congregation laid the cornerstone for this brick church designed by architect Simpson, who had planned all of New Bern's new turn-of-the-century churches. Named for an early Christian bishop of Carthage, the large church in Gothic Revival style is dominated by a corner tower with crenellated roofline, from which extend gabled facades. The interior has a scissors truss ceiling and Gothic Revival detailing.

CV 55 St. Peter's A.M.E. Zion Church
1923−40; 617 Queen St.

The massive brick church with broad gabled facade and truncated twin towers is the home of a Methodist congregation that traces its origins to St. Andrew's Chapel, built on Hancock St. in 1802. In 1863 the African Methodist Episcopal Zion missionary (later bishop) James Walker Hood came south to New Bern and Beaufort, both of which were under Union control and had considerable numbers of black Methodists. Under his leadership St. Andrew's Chapel and *Purvis Chapel in Beaufort affiliated by 1864 with the African Methodist Episcopal Zion Church, thus becoming the first in the state to join the organization begun in the North in 1796. St. Peter's is described as "The Mother Church of Zion Methodism in the South." In 1879 the congregation became St. Peter's and built a frame church on this location. After the church burned in 1922, rebuilding took many years, slowed by the Great Depression, but was completed in the 1940s.

CV 56 Cedar Grove Cemetery
Est. 1800; Queen St., N side of 600 block

The large, picturesquely landscaped burial ground was established by Christ Church after the yellow fever epidemic of 1798 filled the old churchyard to capacity. The triple-arched gateway and walls, built of local shell-rock known as marl, were erected in 1854 when the city assumed ownership of the cemetery. The cemetery contains exceptional tombstones and markers of all periods, as well as much ornamental ironwork. Early family vaults and mausoleums include simple brick ones from the Federal period and others in the eclectic tastes of the mid-19th c. One of the finest markers is the Greek sarcophagus-shaped marble monument to William Gaston, designed by New York architect A. J. Davis, friend of Gaston's son-in-law Robert Donaldson.

CV 57 Union Station
1910; 416 Queen St.

In 1906, New Bern's passenger traffic gained a boost with completion of the Norfolk and Southern Railroad tracks linking New Bern northward to Elizabeth City and Norfolk, which complemented the Atlantic Coast Line link south to Wilmington (1893) and the old Atlantic and N.C. Railroad east-west line. As a hub serving three lines, New Bern soon gained Union Station, a dignified, 2-

story building of pressed brick with raised brickwork.

CV 58 Long Wharf Neighborhood

From the 18th c. onward the Long Wharf area west of *Tryon Palace along Lawson's Creek and the Trent River served a mix of manufacturing and residential uses typical of city fringes. Laid out as an extension of the original street grid in 1779, by the early 19th c. the lots, owned by free black and white investors, most of whom lived elsewhere, were occupied by both black and white families. This pattern continued until the mid-20th c. Such riverside industries as a brick manufacturer and a steam mill drew workers to live nearby. After the Civil War, Long Wharf grew as a center of black life, with several key institutions located here.

In the section of Long Wharf bounded by Pollock, Liberty, and First Sts. and the waterfront, most of the 19th-c. structures have been destroyed, but several examples of popular local house forms survive from the late 19th and early 20th centuries. Many are modest, side-gabled, 1½-story cottages, including some built for freedmen soon after the Civil War. Frame I-houses were erected for prospering homeowners in the ca. 1880–1910 era, such as the **Charles Harris House** (ca. 1885; 1020 Church St.), one of several with an exposed face chimney of familiar New Bern type. One- and 2-story gable-fronted houses, often with side-passage plans, were built in rows for rental by both black and white investors. Others were built as owners' residences, such as the **George A. Moore House** (ca. 1925; 305 Jones St.), built for a grocer who was treasurer of the New Bern Negro Business League in 1926. Craftsman style houses, including bungalows and foursquare 2-story houses, of brick as well as frame, were constructed for professionals and tradesmen in the 1920s. **St. John Missionary Baptist Church** (1926; 1130 Walt Bellamy Dr. [New South Front St.]), a big brick church featuring round-arched windows and a front entrance tower, displays the polychrome brickwork that was a speciality of the town's black brickmasons. The cornerstone notes that the congregation was established in Long Wharf in 1856.

CV 59 Greater Duffyfield

CV 59 *500 Block, First Ave., Greater Duffyfield*

The large area north of Queen St. developed as a series of predominantly black neighborhoods during the first years of freedom following the Civil War. In the late 19th and early 20th centuries, many black businessmen and professionals resided here, and black businesses and institutions relocated from downtown as Jim Crow practices took effect in the early 20th c. Now known as the Duffyfield neighborhood named for a local landowner, the area developed as several discrete neighborhoods. The first was **Dryborough**, laid out in 1806 between Queen, West, Bern, and Cedar Sts. and soon occupied by black and white residents. The last was **West End** (The Avenues), platted in 1911 on First, Second, and Third Aves. north of Broad St. and drawing black and white buyers amid the local lumber boom.

Although a fire in 1922 leveled some 1,000 houses, and there have been substantial losses over the years, those that remain represent a range of popular house types. These include scattered 1½-story cottages and I-houses of the late 19th c. Houses of the early 20th c. include many gable-fronted houses—the 100 **Block of First Ave.**, for example—and a few large, owner-occupied residences, such as the **J. T. Barber House** (ca. 1925; 621 West St.), a brick foursquare house built for the longtime principal of the West St. School.

Several institutions are important landmarks. **First Baptist Church** (1908; Cypress

St.) is a Gothic Revival, brick building with corner tower. Opposite the church, **Greenwood Cemetery** (bounded by Cypress, Bern, F, and A Sts.), begun before 1872 and with records as a city cemetery from 1882, contains a distinguished collection of stones for African Americans, including a rare grouping of antebellum markers probably moved from other locations. **Rue Chapel A.M.E. Church** (1873, 1941; Joseph F. Lewis, Willie Becton, builders; NW corner Oak and Elm Sts.) is a Gothic Revival brick church with a pair of towers flanking the front gable. **Craven Terrace** (1940–41; A. Mitchell Wooten and John J. Rowland, Kinston, architects; Fowler-Jones Construction Company; Oak St.), a public housing development erected for black residents contemporary with *Trent Court, comprises 2-story brick buildings with plaques of children playing with balls and drums. A notable survivor from the black business district that once flourished along Queen St. is the **Dr. Hunter Fisher Office** (ca. 1908; 830 Queen St.), a small, well-kept, false-fronted frame building with front porch, which served for many years as a doctor's office.

CV 60 Riverside

1100–1500 blocks of National Ave., N. Pasteur St., N. Craven St., and side streets N of downtown

New Bern's first suburb, developed between 1894 and 1912 on old farmland, lies along National Ave. between the Atlantic and N.C. Railroad and the Neuse River. Riverside shared key elements with other early N.C. suburbs, which continued previous urban patterns: repetition of the town grid; a mix of residential, commercial, and industrial uses, especially along the river; a spectrum from small rental dwellings to speculative houses to custom-built residences; a range of working- and middle-class residents; and standard covenants that restricted occupancy to whites, required a setback of 20 feet from the street, and set a minimum house cost of $1,000. National Ave. has some of the largest and most stylish dwellings, such as the **William Dunn House**

(1912; Herbert W. Simpson, architect; 1404 National Ave.), a big brick and shingled Prairie style house. Local builders erected simple versions of popular American house styles, often continuing the local side-passage plan—as in the narrow, gable-fronted dwellings in simplified Queen Anne style in the **1200 Block, National Ave.** Several Foursquare houses with Craftsman or classically detailed porches stand in the **1300 Block, National Ave.** Some of many small gable-fronted bungalows line the **1500 Block, N. Craven St.** The former **Riverside Graded School** (1922; James F. Gause Jr. and Leslie N. Boney, Wilmington, architects; 1211 N. Pasteur St.) is a red brick school building in a vivid Mediterranean spirit with tile pent roof on tall brackets. **Riverside Methodist Church** (1919–20; 405 Avenue A) combines an unusual form and octagonal clerestory with Gothic Revival detailing.

CV 60 *William Dunn House*

CV 61 Ghent

1400–1800 blocks of Rhem, Spencer, and Park Aves., S side Trent Blvd., W of downtown

New Bern's second suburb and its only streetcar suburb, Ghent shows the transition to mainstream 20th-c. suburban patterns. Laid out in 1906 on old farmland beside the Trent River, its development intensified in 1912 when the Ghent Land Company bought the property and ran a streetcar line out to it. In contrast to *Riverside, the development was strictly residential and solidly middle class, with a $2,000 minimum house cost. The old preference for the side-passage plan vanished in favor of standard national types. Especially popular were the Colonial

Revival, the foursquare, and the bungalow. Some houses follow models seen in Sears, Roebuck, and Company catalogs and may have been built from prefab kits. Several houses feature exaggerated Craftsman motifs and startlingly overscale porch pillars, most notably the **Frank Godfroy House** (ca. 1913; 1602 Spencer Ave.), a Sears design where the bungalow takes on a Mount Vernon scale. A **Lustron House** (ca. 1950; 1415 Rhem Ave.) exemplifies the post–World War II experiment in prefab housing with tan, porcelain-enamel steel panels and a picture window.

CV 62 Bellair

Ca. 1790–93; NE side NC 43, 2.0 mi. NW of NC 55, New Bern vic.; private, visible from road; open limited hours

cv 62 *Bellair*

Unique in the state as a plantation house rendered in the Palladian manner of *Tryon Palace, Bellair is also one of the few 18th-c. brick plantation houses in N.C. The broad 7-bay facade, central pedimented pavilion with oculus, hip roof, and fine, Flemish-bond brickwork link it with the palace and other Georgian edifices, while the shallow, 1-room depth of the center-passage-plan house gives a curious stage-set appearance. The interior has academic Georgian finish nearly identical to work seen in New Bern's *John Wright Stanly and *Coor-Gaston houses; any connection with architect John Hawks (d. 1790) remains undocumented. The house is also notable in having a full raised basement, with the brick walls set on a foundation of cut marl, a local shell-rock. The 18th-c. brick smokehouse displays glazed header diapering in a lozenge pattern,

a rare feature in eastern N.C. Located on a plantation formerly owned by the politically prominent Speight family, Bellair was built for planter Wilson Blount, for its timbers were evidently cut in 1790–92. Since 1838 the property has descended in the Richardson family, who have recently restored the house.

CV 63 Chapman's Chapel

The crossroads community along the old Greenville highway near the Pitt Co. line was named for a nearby chapel founded in the late 19th c. by members of the Chapman family. Two of the county's principal late Federal plantation houses, built for brothers, stand within a quarter-mile of each other. Slightly different in style and period, they both typify the persistent Carolina I-house form. The oldest, the **Church Chapman House** (ca. 1830; NE side NC 43, 0.2 mi. SE of SR 1476), is a 3-bay, 2-story frame house with rear shed rooms and a front shed porch. It is covered with beaded weatherboarding and is flanked by two end chimneys, one displaying Flemish-bond brickwork and the other common-bond brickwork. The **Alfred Chapman House** (1839–41; NE side NC 43, 0.15 mi. NW of SR 1476) has single, stepped-shoulder, common-bond chimneys dated 1839 and 1841 and simplified Federal–Greek Revival woodwork. A number of important outbuildings remain on the property, including the county's only surviving plank structure.

CV 64 James City

S side Trent River and W side Neuse River, off US 70

The small community on the Trent River south of New Bern is heir to a unique history as a freedmen's settlement established during the Civil War. After New Bern was occupied by federal forces in 1862, the city quickly became a haven for thousands of slaves from throughout the region. If they came behind Union lines, they were considered free by the U.S. government, even before the Emancipation Proclamation was issued early in 1863. "When the Yankees took

New Bern," recalled a former slave from Onslow Co., "all who could swim the river and get to the Yankees were free. Some of the men swum the river and got to Jones County then to New Bern and freedom."

In 1863, the Rev. Horace James, a Massachusetts army chaplain, was appointed superintendent of Negro affairs in N.C. He established several refugee camps for the multitudes of slaves who had escaped to Union-held territory in eastern N.C. The largest was built south of New Bern at the confluence of the Trent and Neuse rivers, on land taken by Union forces when they captured the city. Here streets were laid out, 50-by-60-ft. lots assigned, and some 800 small wooden houses built. Initially called the Trent River camp, toward the end of the war it was renamed James City after the man who had established it.

After the war, aided for a time by the Freedmen's Bureau, as many as 1,700 residents continued to live in James City, establishing churches, running a school, improving the houses, participating in local politics, and working as farm laborers and in various trades. In 1867 the U.S. government restored the land to its former owners, who refused requests to sell the property to the occupants but continued to rent tracts to them. In the 1890s, after long and bitter litigation with a new landowner, who likewise refused to sell the land, the people of James City were able to purchase land just south of the old settlement; here a "new" James City gradually came into existence, though some families continued to live on rented land in "old" James City for many years. By the 1960s, "old" James City had virtually vanished.

In "new" James City, some 20 unpretentious 1- and 2-story houses stand from the ca. 1890–1930 period of development, along with many more recent structures. The principal landmarks are two brick churches, **Jones Chapel A.M.E. Zion Church** (ca. 1915; Elder St., w of US 70) and **Mount Shiloh Missionary Baptist Church** (ca. 1924; John St., w of US 70). The latter, whose gabled front and corner tower are easily visible from US 70, was built for a congregation that began in 1866 in "old" James City and moved to "new" James City to find a permanent home. *See* Joe A. Mobley, *James City: A Black Community in North Carolina, 1863–1900* (1981).

CV 65 Tom Haywood Store
Ca. 1880–90; SW side US 70, 0.3 mi. NW of SR 1100, Croatan

The late 19th-c. frame general store includes an original section that retains much of its character, plus a ca. 1940 gas-pump canopy. The store is famous for the "self-kicking machine" created in 1937 by the store's proprietor, Tom Haywood. Featured on a Universal News Reel in 1937, the machine consists of a hand-operated crank connected to an adjacent rotary "kicker" bearing four well-worn shoes. To be kicked, the user leans over in front of the kicker and turns the crank. The original machine is now at the N.C. Museum of History in Raleigh, but a replica remains at the original site.

CV 66 Croatan Presbyterian Church
1884; NW corner US 70 and SR 1100, Croatan

The Carpenter Gothic church displays the finest sawnwork found in rural Craven Co., with a bracketed cornice and sawn circle-and-arrow motifs applied to the frieze. Built in 1884 as a simple rectangular frame meetinghouse, in the 20th c. it gained the portico, belltower, and rear extension. The interior retains its original Gothic-influenced woodwork and pews.

Jones County (JN)

JN 1 Trenton

Established when Jones Co. was formed from Craven Co. in 1779, Trenton was named after the Trent River, which traverses the county and is navigable to this point. Later highway and railroad builders bypassed Trenton, limiting its growth but protecting its charm. On the southern edge of the town is a large, dark millpond, now known as Brock's, which is embowered by cypress trees draped with Spanish moss. Gristmills have operated at the site for over two centuries, with the present **Brocks Mill**, a frame building, dating from the 1940s. The small town is the seat of a sparsely settled county, where swamps and forests occupy much of the land.

Early 19th-c. architecture in the town and county shows a strong influence from New Bern at the mouth of the Trent River, though Trenton's oldest buildings were largely overbuilt in later periods. Simple mid-19th-c. Greek Revival and Italianate houses and later 19th-c. Italianate, Gothic Revival, and Queen Anne buildings create a varied but integrated architectural fabric. Jones St. (NC 58) leading into town from the west is the principal residential corridor, with several fine frame houses. Dominating the small brick commercial district is the centrally located **Jones County Courthouse** (1939; SW corner Market and Jones Sts.), a WPA Colonial Revival building of Flemish-bond brick veneer with a broad entrance pavilion and polygonal cupola. To its rear stands the former **Jones County Jail**, a small, 19th-c. brick jail with corbeled brickwork marking the pedimented gable ends and arched windows.

Grace Episcopal Church (1885; NW corner Lake View Dr. and Weber St.) is the Carpenter Gothic Episcopal church at its best, beautifully detailed and perfectly preserved, with its picturesqueness intensified by its mossy canopy. The battens of the board-and-batten walls form an arcaded cor-

JN 1 *Grace Episcopal Church*

nice, complemented by the scalloped bargeboards and scalloped, triangular heads of windows and entrance.

Trenton Methodist Church (late 19th c.; E side Market St., N of Jones St.), an otherwise simple Gothic Revival frame church, boasts a fanciful entrance tower where bartizans sprout from the four corners of the spire, each topped with a turned finial for a lively medieval effect. **Trenton Pentecostal Holiness Church** (late 19th c.; W side Market St., S of Jones St.) features triangular window openings and triangular ventilators on the 3-stage corner tower capped by a slim spire.

JN 2 E. M. Foscue House
3rd quarter 19th c.; N side SR 1002, 2.8 mi. E of NC 41, Trenton vic.; private, visible from road

The 2-story farmhouse represents a post–Civil War resurgence of agricultural prosperity in the county, with a 2-tier gabled porch and bracketed eaves with gable end returns typical of the era. A contingent of outbuildings includes some contemporary with the house.

JN 3 *Foscue Plantation*

JN 3 Foscue Plantation

Early 19th c.; E side US 17, 1.5 mi. S of
SR 1002, Pollocksville vic.; private, open by
appointment

A key example of New Bern influence on
Jones County's early 19th-c. architecture, the
2-story brick house with side-passage plan
stands out in the flat coastal farmland. Flemish-bond brickwork on the front contrasts
with common bond on the sides, where corbeled brickwork outlines the pedimented
gables. Federal style interior finish also indicates New Bern influence. Built for Simon
Foscue, who received the land from his father at his marriage in 1801, the property is
maintained by a Foscue family trust.

JN 4 Lavender-Barrus House

Ca. 1825; E side US 17 (Main St.), 0.15 mi. S
of Trent River Bridge, Pollocksville; private,
visible from road

The small, highly visible house displays the
engaged double porch common in the region. In one of several variations of an exterior stair arrangement, the northern bay of
the porch is enclosed to protect the stair,
which offers the only access to the second
story. Apparently built for Bryan Lavender
about 1825, the house was occupied from
1835 to 1870 by Roscoe Barrus, a merchant
who operated a store and warehouse at the
nearby Trent River bridge.

JN 5 Bryan-Bell Farm

Ca. 1845, 1919 portico; S side NC 58, 1.8 mi.
W of US 17, Pollocksville vic.; private, visible
from road

The plantation house approached by a long
allée of trees features a monumental Corinthian portico, part of a transformation executed in 1919 by Hiram Bell for his son, returning World War I veteran E. E. Bell, to
make the family's traditional frame house
into a Neoclassical country seat. Outbuildings of various periods include a large, hip-
roofed barn. The vast expanse of surrounding fields and woodlands reflects land use
patterns little changed since the mid-19th c.

JN 6 Sanderson House

Ca. 1800; E side SR 1115, 0.5 mi. N of SR 1114,
Pollocksville vic.; private, visible from road

JN 6 *Sanderson House*

The unusual pair of chimneys on the western side, joined in an arch over a doorway,
distinguish this 1½ story frame house, which
is finished in a simplified New Bern Federal
style.

JN 7 Cypress Creek Methodist Church

Mid-19th c.; SE side NC 41, 0.25 mi. N of
SR 1134, Comfort vic.

The frame, Greek Revival church shows the
arrangement favored by rural congregations
of the mid-19th c.: a rectangular form with
a pedimented gable front and large, 24/24
sash windows emphasized by wide, plain
cornerposts, frieze, and base molding.

JN 8 Shine House

Early 19th c.; E side SR 1003, 0.2 mi. S of SR 1134, Comfort vic.; private, visible from road

The 2-story, frame, double-porch coastal house has the ends of the porch enclosed on the second level to create a three-sided room, a pattern also seen at the *Louisiana House, New Bern. Built with Flemish-bond end chimneys and Federal finish, the house was constructed for Col. James Shine, planter and state senator. Here in 1819 Shine hosted President James Madison and Secretary of War John C. Calhoun, who were on a coastal inspection tour. Previously, George Washington recorded during his southern tour in 1791 that he had "lodged at one Shine's," apparently an older house in the vicinity.

Carteret County (CR)

See Tony P. Wrenn, Beaufort, North Carolina *(1970).*

Beaufort (CR 1–16)

Beaufort's uniquely captivating and intensely regional townscape expresses its long history as a small fishing and shipbuilding town, where life focused on the sea and was relatively isolated from the rest of the state until recent years. Its unassuming architectural character and quiet ambience give it a simpler charm than the wealthier and more fashion-conscious ports of Edenton, New Bern, and Wilmington. Its site, too, distinguishes it from other N.C. coastal towns, for it lies opposite the strategic Beaufort (Old Topsail) Inlet, which provides direct access to the open sea and a view of the Atlantic Ocean unique among N.C. ports.

One of the four oldest towns in N.C., Beaufort (pronounced Bow-fort, not Bew-fort as in South Carolina) was settled early in the 18th c. on the site of an Indian village—Wareiock, meaning "Fish or Fishing Town"—and was first known as Fishtown.

Located opposite Beaufort Inlet (Old Topsail Inlet), which links Bogue Sound with the Atlantic Ocean, it had a good harbor for fishermen and shipbuilders, but without a river leading deep into the hinterlands, it did not develop into a major port. The town was named after Henry Somerset, duke of Beaufort and a lord proprietor. By 1713 a grid plan was laid out, with streets named Queen, Anne, and Orange as well as Moore, Pollock, and Turner. In 1722 Beaufort was made a port of entry and county seat of newly formed Carteret Co., and it was incorporated in 1723. By 1765, however, there still were only a dozen houses.

After the American Revolution the town grew as a shipbuilding and fishing community. In 1810 Jacob Henry, a Beaufort resident and state legislator, reported that it had 585 people, 74 dwellings, 10 stores, 8 artisan shops, and a church. The town had "a very considerable reputation" for building "some of the swiftest sailors and best built vessels in

CR 1–16 *Beaufort, 1971*

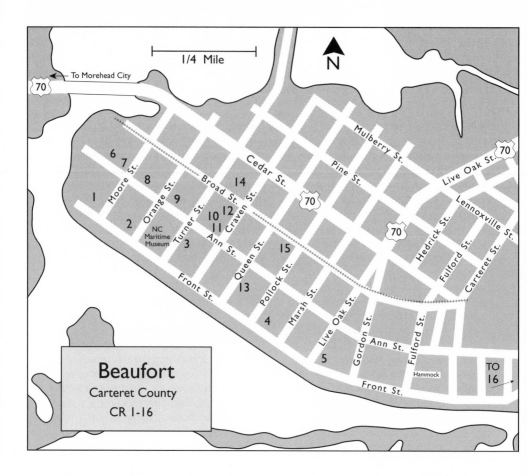

Beaufort
Carteret County
CR 1-16

the United States." The "chief dependence of the People, however, is on the fisheries," including whale, porpoise, and especially mullet. His description of Beaufort's attractions remains apt. The town enjoyed a "boundless view of the ocean, continually enlivened with vessels sailing in all directions." The "sea breeze . . . with refreshing coolings throughout the day" attracted summer visitors, and "much benefit is experienced by those [who] make occasional excursions hither to obviate the debility induced by the heat, in the vicinity of the sluggish rivers and extensive Swamps of the low country." "It is strictly a marine Village, and those who are fond of the amusement connected with the water may here receive full gratification; whilst bathing in the Surf and walking on the beach are likely to recover the Valetudinarian."

Beaufort's position on the inlet made it a port for privateer operations during the War of 1812—Capt. Otway Burns was a local hero—and soon after the war, planning began on *Fort Macon nearby to replace previous forts to defend the inlet. The antebellum era brought new prosperity, and as the Atlantic and N.C. Railroad was built eastward, some envisioned Beaufort as the "future great seaport of North Carolina." A visitor in 1853 admired the "very neat residences" and lots "tastefully laid out and ornamented with evergreens and flower shrubs."

Union forces occupied Beaufort in Mar. 1862 and remained for the duration of the war. Left shabby after the war, the town recovered gradually, then blossomed as a seaside resort, with boardinghouses and a boardwalk along the waterfront. Fishing continued as the mainstay of the economy, and by 1880 the town developed as a center for marine biology research, begun with the Johns Hopkins Seaside Laboratory. In the 20th c. the U.S. Bureau of Fisheries established laboratories at Beaufort, as did the Duke University Marine Laboratory. The 20th c. also brought a railroad link and eventually a highway bridge tying Beaufort to Morehead City. Development of the Intracoastal Waterway as a popular route for leisure as well as commercial vessels has brought new activity to the maritime community, where menhaden fishing boats and shrimp trawlers coexist with luxurious yachts and sailboats from distant ports. Long-standing local interest in preservation is complemented by the North Carolina Maritime Museum.

Although the waterfront has been transformed in the late 20th c. from the warehouses and docks of the old fishing town into a retail center catering to the growing tourist and boating crowd, behind its changing waterfront, the little grid-plan town retains its undisturbed scale and distinctive coastal architecture. Shaded by old, windswept live oaks and bordered by white picket fences, the regular streets are lined by a remarkable collection of frame houses with endless porches.

Beaufort's architecture spans the years from the 18th through the 20th centuries and ranges from tiny cottages to imposing Queen Anne residences as well as a series of stylish churches. Because the town was settled early and economy dictated conservation of building materials, there are many cases where small dwellings of the 18th or early 19th c. are concealed within larger 19th- and early 20th-c. houses. (Many of the local date plaques refer to the first building on a site.) A few floor plans dominate, mainly the hall-parlor, side-passage, and center-passage plans. There are many small houses, including some "story-and-a-jump" dwellings where the half-story has the roof plate several feet above the floor level, giving a bit more height to the upper chambers.

With similar forms built year after year, Beaufort's houses show the subtle variations

possible within a long-lasting vernacular building tradition. In particular Beaufort contains the state's prime concentration of multisloped roofs and engaged piazzas that characterize N.C. coastal architecture, with gable roofs extending to shelter a full-width porch. In some cases the porch and rear shed rooms are set within a single, uninterrupted broad gable. More often the gable roof takes a dramatic multisloped form: a steep pitch begins at the ridge, then breaks to a gentler slope—or slopes—to shelter the porch in front and, in many cases, a porch or shed rooms in the rear. Beaufort's porches come in all shapes and sizes: engaged in this traditional coastal fashion or attached in various ways to suit changing styles; tall or short, one tier or two; and plain, classical, or decorated with late 19th-c. sawn and turned work. Several porches have open ceilings with windows or vents that allow air into the attic of the house. Upper porches provide a view of the harbor and catch the sea breeze even on the hottest days. Beaufort offers the state's richest "porchscape," where the sunlit whole is vastly more than the sum of the seemingly simple parts.

CR 1 100 Block, Front St.

The row of waterfront houses on the western end of Front St. presents a scene long beloved by visitors and photographers. Built from the late 18th c. into the early 20th c., mostly as private residences, these houses with their harbor views were well placed for use as boardinghouses in the late 19th- and early 20th-c. heyday of the town as a seaside resort, and many owners built long double piazzas swept by sea breezes. The **Duncan House** (107 Front St.), at the very end, has a 2-tier porch extending six bays along a house that developed in the 19th c. in two sections, perhaps beginning as early as ca. 1790. Engaged under the double-slope roof, the porch has locally typical, turned, "milk-bottle" columns that probably date from the late 19th c. The house at **115 Front St.**, with its porches sweeping around it, was built ca. 1890 on the site of the old Beaufort Custom House. The **Manson House** (117 Front St.), with its divided, 2-tier porch, was built ca. 1880 and was a popular boardinghouse. The champion in porch span is the **Davis House Hotel** (123–25 Front St.), where a 2-tier piazza with turned columns stretches thirteen bays to unify three houses of different ages. Part of the oldest, no. 125, may date from as early as 1769, and others date from the 19th c. During the late 19th c. Miss Sara Davis operated a popular boardinghouse here, which she expanded over the years, acquiring additional houses and extending the porches accordingly. A memoir of Beaufort in the 1890s recalled that "the Davis House porches were always filled with happy boarders enjoying the south wind that always seemed a little more delightful in Beaufort." The **Davis House** (127 Front St.) is an asymmetrical, 4-bay house with a portico and 2-tier porch. The 200 block continues with a diverse sequence, ranging from the simplicity of the **Nelson House** (1790 onward; 205 Front St.), a classic Beaufort type, with asymmetrical plan and engaged roof sheltering the 2-tier front piazza, to the imposing Queen Anne–Colonial Revival hybrid style **Boone-Pate House** (ca. 1916; 207 Front St.), with its interaction of broad porch, polygonal bays, and pediments with fanlights.

CR 2 Jacob Henry House

1794–1802; 229 Front St.

The multisloped roofline sheltering a 2-tier engaged porch and rear shed rooms epitomizes Beaufort architecture. The foundation shows the local use of ballast stone. The most ambitious Federal era house in Beaufort, it was built for Henry, a Jew prominent in state political circles and in early struggles over constitutional rights. (See Introduction, Fig. 16.)

CR 3 Historic Beaufort Restoration

Turner St. between Ann and Front Sts.; open regular hours

The cluster of historic buildings permits visitation to several local building types—and a chance to catch the breeze from a second-story porch or two. Some of the buildings are original to the site. The **David Bell House** (early 19th c.; 123 Turner St.) is a classic example of the Beaufort townhouse, little altered and open to the public. The Bell family was prominent in Beaufort from its early days, and this house stands on land purchased in 1766 by Joseph Bell, sheriff and town leader. His grandson David, who inherited the property, probably built the house. The 2½-story frame house displays the local use of the side-passage plan, fronted by a typical 2-tier piazza with simple posts and railings. Likewise characteristic of Beaufort is the simple but well-crafted Federal style finish throughout the house: a graceful, open-string stair; delicate moldings outlining flat panels on doors and wainscoting; and mantels that illustrate a distinctive local type. Paneled pilasters carry a frieze where the end blocks atop the pilasters curve inward in a sinuous ramp. In secondary mantels the design is reduced to a molded fireplace frame and a plain ramped frieze beneath the shelf. The **Josiah Bell House** (early 19th c.; 138 Turner St.) is another characteristic Beaufort house with 2-tier engaged piazza, which has been expanded over the years.

CR 3 *David Bell House*

Other properties were rescued and moved here, including the tiny **Apothecary Shop** (mid-19th c.) with its elaborate false front, and the former **Carteret County Courthouse** (early 19th c.), a simple frame building said originally to have been one large room. The little **Leffers House** (mid-19th c.), an excellent example of the small coastal cottage, has a hall-parlor plan with only the hall heated; the stair rises from the rear shed room. The finish is characteristically plain and neat, with 2-panel and batten doors and simple sheathing.

The **Old Jail** (1828–29; Elijah Whitehurst, builder; E side 100 block Turner St.), moved here in 1977 from its original site on the courthouse square, is a stoutly built jail, 2 stories tall with a center doorway, an intriguing survivor of the domestic scale of such facilities in the mid-19th c. Its stuccoed brick walls are some 2 feet deep, assuring security, with iron-barred windows. As was customary, the jailer also made his residence here. Local tradition claims it was built by brickmasons also employed at *Fort Macon.

CR 4 U.S. Post Office

1937; Louis A. Simon, supervising architect of the Treasury; 800 block Front St.

The red brick, Colonial Revival post office features simple, classical details and an arched entry with Doric columns. The intact interior features murals (1940) by Simka Simkhovitch depicting Cape Lookout Lighthouse, the local wild island horses, a lifesaving scene, and other local images representative of the federal art program.

CR 5 Gibbs House

Ca. 1851; 903 Front St.

In a notable exception to Beaufort's preference for traditional house forms, the waterfront house has mainstream Greek Revival proportions and detail in its boxy form, shallow hip roof, wide eaves, and heavy paneled posts of its 2-tier porch. Used in the late 19th c. by the Johns Hopkins marine scientists, it played a role in the early history of marine biology in the United States.

CR 6 Jessie Piver House

Ca. 1790; 125 Ann St.

The essence of the local vernacular, the modest 1½-story house has a double-slope roof sheltering the piazza. The porch has no ceiling, and upper windows shaded by the porch provide ventilation into the upper chambers. The asymmetry of the facade

CR 6 *Jessie Piver House*

reflects the hall-parlor plan, with only the hall having a chimney.

CR 7 Peter Piver House

Ca. 1790; 131 Ann St.

Another characteristic small house type, again with a hall-parlor plan and single chimney, this dwelling shows the tall half-story locally called a story-and-a-jump, plus a small attached porch and rear chambers.

CR 8 St. Paul's Episcopal Church

1857; 209 Ann St.

The small but forcefully designed Gothic Revival church expresses the picturesque

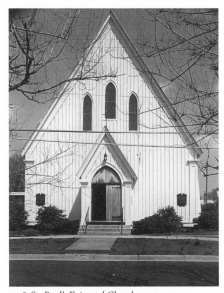

CR 8 *St. Paul's Episcopal Church*

quality of Richard Upjohn's board-and-batten parish churches in straightforward fashion, accentuated by paneled corner pilasters of Greek Revival character. A trio of lancet windows fills the gable front above the steep-gabled vestibule, and small lancets continue along the buttressed sides. The interior has a dark-stained, scissors truss roof contrasting with light walls. This is the first and only church of St. Paul's, organized in 1855 as successor to St. John's Church (est. 1724).

CR 9 Leecraft Houses
Ca. 1850s; 301, 305, 307 Ann St.

The trio of residences built for members of the Leecraft family show local carpenters' robust renditions of Greek Revival motifs from Asher Benjamin's *Practical House Carpenter* (1830) and other works. First built is the symmetrical house at no. 301, with a center-passage plan accentuated by a 2-tier, pedimented entrance portico. A striking pair of nearly identical twins are the second and third Leecraft Houses at nos. 305 and 307, boldly detailed, side-passage-plan houses whose broad rectilinear forms are emphasized by wide corner pilasters—akin to those at St. Paul's nearby—and friezes beneath a wide hip roof, plus entrance porches with paneled pillars and Greek key pilasters.

CR 10 Old Burying Ground
Est. 1724; block between Ann, Craven, and Broad Sts.

A visitor in 1853 found "the choicest beauty spot of Beaufort" to be this burying ground, where the "pillars of white stone and marble

CR 10 *Old Burying Ground*

amid the beautiful evergreens of live oak and yeopon and variety of flowers, render this . . . the most beautiful place of the kind I ever saw." One of the state's oldest and loveliest cemeteries, it is shaded by ancient trees and filled with lichen-encrusted markers. There are a few plain cypress markers, but most are of stone. Several graves are covered in brick, and there are notable ironwork fences. Stones include table-stones, obelisks, and military markers. The best known is Capt. Otway Burns's tomb, surmounted by a cannon from his War of 1812 privateer. Marked stones include those made in Boston, Charleston, Brooklyn, and Baltimore, reflecting the lack of local stone coupled with the town's seaward orientation. The stuccoed wall with its rhythmic ball-topped pillars unites the burial ground with nearby churches.

CR 11 Ann St. Methodist Church
1854, 1896–98; 419 Ann St.

CR 11 *Ann St. Methodist Church*

The handsome frame church exemplifies the auditorium-plan churches promoted by Methodist publications in the late 19th c. Its two corner entrance towers flank a broad shingled gable, where a large, stained-glass window lights the auditorium-plan sanctuary with adjoining Sunday school. When Methodists organized in Beaufort in 1778, they used the old Anglican church. A great revival in 1810–11 increased their numbers, and in 1820 they erected a simple frame church, *Purvis Chapel. After a second church was built in 1854, Purvis Chapel was given to the black members. When more space was needed in the 1890s, the 1854 building was transformed into "a new and magnificent church."

CR 12 Purvis Chapel
1820, ca. 1900; 217 Craven St.

CR 12 *Purvis Chapel*

The frame Methodist chapel built in 1820 and named after Methodist revivalist James Purvis was given to the black members when a new church was built in 1854. During the Civil War, when Beaufort was under Union occupation, missionary James Walker Hood visited the community and persuaded Purvis Chapel to join the African Methodist Episcopal Zion Church—with St. Andrew's (later *St. Peter's) in New Bern one of the first in the state to do so. Probably around 1900, perhaps about the time *Ann St. Church was rebuilt (1896–98), the congregation remodeled the facade of old church. Fronting the simple, weatherboarded Gothic Revival sanctuary, a pair of contrasting towers—one short, the other taller with a cross-gable belfry—are linked by a projecting portico with two square pillars. Accented by the wall of the *Old Burying Ground, the whole creates a composition of great presence.

CR 13 Burnside's Headquarters
Early 19th c., 1850s; 120 Queen St.

The 2-story, gable-fronted house with side-passage plan is a common form in Beaufort, but here the 2-tier porch features unusual Gothic Revival style trim in the form of bargeboard-like friezes with pointed drops. A smaller, older house exists within. Tradition claims that Gen. Ambrose E. Burnside occupied this house during the Civil War.

CR 14 Carteret County Courthouse
1907; Herbert W. Simpson (New Bern), architect; Corner Broad and Craven Sts.

The dark red brick walls of the New Bern architect's Neoclassical Revival courthouse serve as a foil for white wood and granite trim. Corinthian porticoes shelter the western and southern entrances, and a domed octagonal cupola crowns the roof.

CR 14 *Carteret County Courthouse*

CR 15 Beaufort Railroad Depot
1905; 620 Broad St.

The unusually handsome little stuccoed station is dominated by a tall, bellcast hip roof of red tile, which rests on deep, curved brackets. Although the Atlantic and N.C. Railroad reached Morehead City in the 1850s, rail service was slow in making a connection to Beaufort. Not until 1905 was a railroad bridge built across the Newport River and the station erected, as Beaufort became part of the Norfolk and Southern system. After passenger service ceased, the depot served as a library and civic office.

CR 16 Beaufort Fisheries
Ca. 1934; E extension of Front St.

The complex of functional, wood-and-tin-clad gabled buildings exemplifies the many fisheries that have flourished along the coast.

Though not considered an edible fish, menhaden was once the state's most valuable commercial fish for its yields of oil used in a variety of products and for its meal, once used in fertilizers but later primarily in livestock and poultry feed. Menhaden has declined in commercial importance, and this is the state's last operating menhaden plant. The fish move in enormous schools, pursued and collected in nets by highly specialized boats. Based on a catch of 80 to 150 million fish, this facility annually produces an estimated 10,000 tons of meal and up to 450,000 gallons of oil. Fish are cooked in the large central building with a large metal smokestack, with the other buildings connected by pipes and conduits.

CR 17 Morehead City

Morehead City was the latecomer among the state's port towns. Though nearby Beaufort had long enjoyed one of the state's best inlets and harbors, its growth was restricted for want of river connections into the interior. In 1853 John Motley Morehead, governor of N.C. from 1841 to 1845 and an avid proponent of railroads and internal improvements, purchased a strip of land by Bogue Sound at the mouth of the Newport River, opposite Beaufort, in anticipation of its becoming the eastern terminus of the Atlantic and N.C. Railroad (later named the Atlantic and East Carolina), which linked Beaufort Inlet to the state's major east-west and north-south railroads at Goldsboro. Morehead's vision of a major Atlantic port for N.C. was only partially realized, and then only in the mid-20th c. The town's development was interrupted by the Civil War, and subsequent growth came slowly, though the rail connections eventually boosted the new town beyond its older neighbor in population and commercial activity. Today Morehead City is the state's only deepwater port north of Wilmington, with a sprawling, state-owned port facility developed in the mid-20th c. at its eastern edge on the Newport River. As a place of predominantly simple 20th-c. architecture, it presents a different personality from Beaufort, but it is a pleasant town with an interesting mix of maritime commercial and summer resort elements.

The town's grid plan extends along a narrow strip of land bisected by the railroad. Long rows of plain, 1- and 2-story brick commercial buildings face one another across the tracks along Arendel St., the broad main street. The **Morehead City Passenger Depot and Freight Depot** (early 20th c.; sw corner Arendel and S. 6th Sts.) are typical wood frame depots of their era, now preserved as shops. The busy waterfront on Bogue Sound is lined with long-popular seafood eateries such as the Sanitary Fish Market and Captain Bill's, set amid the docks of a large, sport-fishing fleet.

The most distinctive downtown landmark is the former **Morehead City Municipal Building** (1926; Jones Bros. [Wilson], builders; R. D. Gladding, consulting engineer; 202 S. 8th St.), now the police station, a rare N.C. example of the Florentine Renaissance Revival style (cf. *U.S. Post Office, Greenville). The design source has not been identified. Quoins frame the 2-story stuccoed edifice with a low-pitched hip roof that shelters a shallow, 3-bay, recessed portico with Ionic columns. Lavish classical detailing enriches the building, including contrasting quoins and entrances with broken scroll pediments.

CR 17 *Morehead City Municipal Building*

Residential blocks of frame houses flank Arendel St., chiefly early 20th-c. frame bungalows, foursquares, and gable-fronted houses. A recurring local house form is the pyramidal-roofed cottage with a wraparound porch that curves at the corner. A handsome group of spacious, comfortable summer houses of the 1920s to 1950s, interspersed with more recent development, faces Bogue Sound on either side of the Atlantic Beach bridge. Southwest of the downtown area along the sound is a section known as "The Promised Land," an early 20th-c. collection of small frame houses, many owned by former residents of a whaling community on Shackleford Banks called Diamond City, which was abandoned by the early 20th c. after a series of devastating storms. Older residents still point out certain story-and-a-jump houses said to have been placed on rafts and floated across the sound to Morehead City.

CR 18 Fort Macon

1821 (Gen. Simon Bernard, designer; Capt. William Tell Poussin, drawing), 1826–34 (construction directed by Lt. William A. Eliason); Bogue Point on Fort Macon Rd., E end of NC 58; open regular hours

CR 18 *Fort Macon*

A prime attraction on the coast, N.C.'s greatest 19th-c. fortification is a work of both military and aesthetic power. Its form is based on a concentric series of sunken, irregular pentagons invisible from the inlet and barely visible from land beyond its perimeter. At the center is an open yard, or parade, enclosed by a labyrinth of rooms within a raised terreplein, which is encircled in turn by a moat and a gently sloping outer embankment, called the **Glacis**. Every detail is handled with precision. The brickwork is exceptionally fine, with rubbed brick used on the arches. Connecticut freestone is used lavishly in ramps, sills, lintels, stairs, and stringcourses. Ironwork trim is delicately wrought, and woodwork is carefully executed in the Greek Revival manner.

Macon, the third fort to guard Beaufort Inlet (replacing Fort Hampton of ca. 1808, which was covered by the expanding inlet) was named for Nathaniel Macon, congressman from Warren Co., N.C. It was part of the French-influenced "third system" of defenses along the coast—successor to two previous and more informal phases of defense building. After the War of 1812 the United States began this unified system of coastal defense, much of which was designed by Gen. Simon Bernard, formerly Napoleon's military engineer. Assisted by another French émigré officer, Capt. William Tell Poussin, Bernard visited coastal sites and planned forts in the advanced French tradition. Poussin's survey of the harbor at Beaufort and his 1821 plan for the sunken, pentagonal fort were the basis for Fort Macon. Construction was supervised by three separate officers between 1826 and 1834, when the fort was finally garrisoned. In the 1840s Capt. Robert E. Lee directed construction of stone jetties to stabilize the site. In Apr. 1861 Confederate troops seized the fort, but it fell to Union land and sea forces a year later and remained in Federal hands for the duration of the war. The fort was garrisoned again during the Spanish-American War and World War II. It is now a state park.

CR 19 Octagon House

Ca. 1855; N side NC 24, 1.0 mi. W of NC 58, Cape Carteret vic.; private, visible from road

Built for planter Edward Hill at his Cedar Point plantation on the White Oak River, this is the larger of the two antebellum octagon houses standing in N.C. (cf. *The Octagon House, Hyde County), a form promoted by New York phrenologist Orson S. Fowler in his book *A Home for All* (1848). The 2-story, bracketed frame house has two bays to a side and is topped by a cupola centered among four interior chimneys. The plan has three rooms on either side of a center hall. Several early farm outbuildings including a smokehouse also survive.

CR 20 Hadnot's Creek Primitive Baptist Church

Early–mid 19th c.; E side SR 1104, 1.5 mi. N of NC 58, Peletier vic.

The austere, weatherboarded church possesses an extraordinary presence that derives from its utter simplicity. Epitomizing the "barn-like" quality that once informed many 18th- and 19th-c. churches, it is a rectangular, 2-story building with the entrance in the gable end and large, 2/2 windows in both stories. Planed sheathing finishes the sanctuary, where benchlike pews and a gallery focus on the pulpit at the northern end opposite the entrance. Unpainted and unchanged, it is carefully tended by a small congregation. A small, sandy cemetery lies nearby. As early as 1815 the Neuse Baptist Association met at Hadnot's Creek.

CR 21 Newport River Primitive Baptist Church

Ca. 1885; 901 Church St., Newport

The straightforward, 1-story, weatherboarded church shows the Primitive Baptists' continuing preference for simplicity in the midst of an eclectic era. The gable front has two entrances flanking a window, and such modest flourishes as corner pilasters, gable returns, and a triangular-headed vent in the gable. The interior is neatly sheathed with narrow boards and features plain pews focused on the pulpit, which stands in front of a small, recessed chancel. The congregation traces its history back to 1780, and records recall that an earlier church burned during the Civil War when it was in use as a hospital for Union troops.

CR 22 Harlowe Community

Although Carteret Co.'s economy is primarily oriented to the sea and much of the county is covered with wetlands, the adequately drained sections have supported productive agriculture since the 18th c. The Harlowe community, a prosperous farming section, grew up along the **Clubfoot and Harlowe Creek Canal** (planned 1797, completed 1828, Hamilton Fulton and others, engineers; parallel to and on E side NC 101), a narrow, 19th-c. waterway connecting Clubfoot Creek on the Neuse River in Craven Co. and Harlowe Creek on the Newport River in Carteret Co. The canal was designed to give New Bern access to the Atlantic via the Newport River and Beaufort Inlet, avoiding the longer and more dangerous route via Pamlico Sound and Ocracoke Inlet. The canal fell into disuse as New Bern's status as a port declined, but local residents recall that shallow-draft boats used the canal for shipping produce and fertilizer until better roads and trucks made water travel obsolete in the 1920s and 1930s.

Local landowners took advantage of the market access afforded by the canal, and a few farmhouses of the era survive, several associated with the Bell family. In an evocative setting of shade trees, a fenced yard, and surrounding outbuildings amid broad fields, the **Rufus Bell House** (mid-19th c.; W side NC 101, 0.6 mi. N of SR 1155; private) is a compact frame house of the regional story-and-a-jump form, with the gable roof reaching down over rear shed rooms. A full-width, hip-roof porch rises at the central bay to shelter a second-floor balcony. A breezeway links the house to a rear kitchen and dining room. The outbuildings include a brick smokehouse. Just to the south, the **Benjamin Borden House** (mid-19th c.; N side NC 101 opp. SR 1155; private) is a prominent, 2½-story, 5-bay, frame house with simple Greek Revival details, also set in a grove along with an early brick smokehouse.

CR 23 "Down East" Villages

A string of small coastal communities on Core Sound lies along US 70 and connecting secondary roads that wind among the marshes and forests east of Beaufort: Otway, Straits, Harkers Island, Gloucester, Marshallberg, Smyrna, Williston, Davis, Sea Level, and Atlantic. Few individual buildings stand out as architectural landmarks, but the consistent character of the vernacular building fabric and the waterside settings convey a strong sense of lifeways long bound to the sea. Fishing and boat building have been the traditional means of livelihood. Marshallberg and Atlantic in particular retain groups of late 19th- and early 20th- c. frame houses, many of a compact, I-house form and some with decorated porches, informally set at odd angles on narrow roads amid groves of oak, pines, and myrtle. Although some inlanders refer to much of eastern N.C. as "Down East," for purists the term applies only to this small section.

CR 24 Cape Lookout Lighthouse

1857–59; S end of Core Banks; exterior access only

The first of the big lighthouses along the N.C. coast, this is the second lighthouse erected at Cape Lookout, midway between the beacons at Cape Fear and Cape Hatteras. It is one of three antebellum lighthouses surviving in N.C.—along with *Bald Head Lighthouse and *Ocracoke Lighthouse— and served as a prototype for the major lighthouses subsequently erected on the Outer Banks. The masonry structure, 169

feet high, went into operation on Nov. 1, 1859, with a first-order Fresnel lens; the light now has a DCB 24 optic. In 1873 the shaft was painted in black-and-white diagonal checkers to identify it to passing ships, and a keeper's dwelling was built. The lighthouse is still in active use with an automated light, but like the *Cape Hatteras Lighthouse it is threatened by erosion. Part of Cape Lookout National Seashore, the site is accessible by ferry services from Beaufort or Harkers Island.

CR 25 Portsmouth Village

N end of Portsmouth Island, Cape Lookout National Seashore

A ghost town today, Portsmouth was once the second largest town on the Outer Banks, after *Ocracoke. The settlement was authorized by the colonial assembly in 1753. Located on the southern side of Ocracoke Inlet, the village served as a transshipment point for seagoing vessels approaching the inlet into Pamlico Sound. Because of the

CR 24 *Cape Lookout Lighthouse*

CR 25 *Portsmouth Village*

hazards of the inlet, the ships were "lightered"—relieved of their cargoes, which were then either reloaded after ships made safe passage over the Ocracoke Bar or transferred to smaller vessels for shipment to New Bern and other ports. Portsmouth grew from about two dozen families in 1800 to a peak in 1860 of 685 inhabitants, of whom about 100 were black. Villagers fled in advance of the town's capture by Union forces in 1861, and the community never regained its vitality after the Civil War. Fishing replaced shipping as the primary occupation, and a lifesaving station was established on the island in 1894. The population dwindled gradually so that by the mid-1960s there were only three permanent residents. The site was transferred to the National Park Service in 1976 as part of the Cape Lookout National Seashore.

Sand has buried the oldest buildings here, but a poignant cluster of simple vernacular buildings still stands from the late 19th and early 20th centuries, making the place a memorable spot worth the boat ride and the battle with notorious mosquitoes. These structures include the **Methodist Church**, a simple, weatherboarded church with Gothic Revival windows and a front entrance tower with belfry—the bell still works; the **Post Office and General Store**, a gabled, frame building where the old safe and mail clerk's office remain; a former **Schoolhouse**, a hip-roof, frame building with a nearby cistern; the shingled **Lifesaving Station Complex**; and simple frame dwellings in various states of repair and decay—all with an incredible sense of a life interrupted but still remembered despite the onslaughts of wind, sea, and sand. Part of Cape Lookout National Seashore, the island may be reached by private passenger ferry service (no vehicles) from *Ocracoke from late spring to early fall and at other times on demand and weather permitting.

Onslow County (ON)

ON 1 Jacksonville

Ever since the Marine Corps carved Camp Lejeune out of the forests of Onslow Co. during World War II, the small county seat on the New River has experienced both the benefits and the challenges of being the principal town near a major military base. In the downtown two notable brick buildings survive across from the remodeled 1904 courthouse on Old Bridge St.: the sturdy Beaux Arts classical **Bank of Onslow** (1916; Henry E. Bonitz [Wilmington], attributed architect; 214 Old Bridge St.) and the surprisingly fanciful Tudor Revival **Masonic Temple** (1919; Henry E. Bonitz [Wilmington], architect; 216 Old Bridge St.), built for Lafayette Lodge No. 83, established in Jacksonville in 1825.

ON 1 *Pelletier House*

The town's oldest building is the **Pelletier House** (ca. 1856; N side Old Bridge St. on the E bank of the New River), a tiny, Greek Revival building restored by the county historical society. The front entrance on the narrow end is sheltered by a porch that is an extension of the hip roof, a local treatment seen in other 19th-c. houses in the county. Tradition suggests that the 2-room structure was built as a shop and bachelor quarters for merchant Rufus Pelletier. The public park between house and river includes **Wantland Spring**, which influenced the selection of the site as county seat in 1753. Southwest of the downtown, the **Mill Ave. Neighborhood** retains a collection of late Victorian style

houses of merchants and professional families amid workers' housing and bungalows.

ON 2 Southwest Primitive Baptist Church

Early to mid-19th c., early 20th c.; N side NC 53, 2.25 mi. W of US 258/NC 24, Jacksonville vic.

The white frame building is among the oldest of the Primitive Baptist churches numerous in eastern N.C., sharing a tradition of plain churches in keeping with the tenets of the faith. The large frame building with beaded weatherboarding and a beaded board-and-batten interior probably had a side-entry, meetinghouse plan originally. Later an extra bay was added, and the church was given a typical longitudinal plan with two front entrances. Unusual is the shallow pent roof on the front and sides that throws water away from the foundations. Nearby stand several houses associated with the local Walton family and **Southwest School**, all dating from the early 20th c.

ON 3 Catherine Lake

In the mid-19th c. a village developed on the shores of this picturesque, 45-acre natural lake along with a complex of turpentine distilleries. A few houses associated with the community's merchant families survive. The lake also attracted summer residents who believed that the "balsamic properties" of the

ON 3 *John A. Avirett House*

pine trees and the turpentine distilleries prevented malaria.

The most prominent house is the 2-story frame **John A. Avirett House** (ca. 1855; s side NC 111, 0.1 mi. E of SR 1211; private). It was erected as the summer home of Onslow Co.'s leading mid-19th-c. turpentine mogul, who came here to escape malaria and built the most sophisticated antebellum house in the county. The eclectic Greek Revival-Italianate residence is built on a T-plan that maximizes the breeze. A center passage runs between two front rooms and leads to a rear dining room ell; a 1-story porch surrounds the main block and connects to either side of the rear ell, and full-height windows open onto the porch. Antebellum life at both Catherine Lake and the 25,000-acre Avirett plantation—which lies beyond public view in the Richlands area—are described by James Battle Avirett, son of John A. Avirett, in *The Old Plantation: How We Lived in Great House and Cabin before the War* (1901).

ON 4 Futral Family House
Ca. 1885, ca. 1904; private, no public access

The 1-story house is a well-preserved example of a once-abundant regional house type—the log house of the tidewater and coastal plain—which has virtually disap-

peared from the landscape. The original hall-parlor-plan section is a 1-story, saddle-notched log house. This type of construction, with logs left round and joined with saddle notches, was common among eastern N.C. log houses, in contrast to the squared logs with V-notches and half-dovetail notches more usual in the Piedmont. The dwelling rests on piers of lightwood blocks traditional in the area. The house was built for farmer David Futral and his wife, Rachel, who owned the small farm where they raised food crops and livestock and extracted tar and turpentine stores from their woodlands. About 1904 their son Amos added a garret, rear shed rooms, and a side kitchen and dining room wing and built a porch along the front, giving the house a coastal cottage form.

ON 5 Venters Farm
Late 19th and early 20th c.; both sides US 258, S of jct. w/SR 1229, 2 mi. S of Richlands; private, visible from road

Located in an area so fertile that the community was called Richlands, this is one of the largest farms in Onslow Co., with an extensive collection of tenant dwellings and agricultural buildings evidencing the tenant system that developed after the Civil War.

ON 4 *Futral Family House*

The farm of some 700 acres was established in the 1890s by Wayne and Julia Stephens Venters, who put together tracts from their parents' adjoining farms. Typical of the era, the land was farmed by tenants who received half the crop in exchange for their labor, while the owners provided house, fertilizer, seed, and equipment. Tenants included both black and white farmers. Several of these farming families, who included the Stephens, Humphrey, Waley, Brinson, and other families, worked Venters lands for two or three generations. Initially cotton and corn were the principal crops of the farm, with a shift from cotton to tobacco cultivation in the 20th c. The farm continues as a working farm in Venters family ownership.

The centerpiece of the farm is the **Venters House** (1896; Mr. Rouse, carpenter; w side US 258), a large, 2-story Italianate frame house two rooms deep with bracketed eaves and a 2-story front porch. What makes the farm especially remarkable is the survival of several of the **Tenant Houses** built from the 1890s into the 1940s, which face one another across US 258. They include 1-story coastal cottages of the 1890s and symmetrical hip-roofed dwellings of the early 20th c. as well as smaller, gable-sided dwellings. The many outbuildings include a smokehouse and carriage house near the big house, as well as tobacco barns, animal barns, and equipment and storage structures from many years of agricultural change.

ON 6 Richlands

Cotton and tobacco provided the foundation for the late 19th- and early 20th-c. development of the antebellum village of Richlands. Today it is a pleasant town of shady residential neighborhoods with simple, late Victorian style frame houses and a business district of 1- and 2-story brick commercial buildings. W. Foy St. is particularly notable.

ON 7 Adams School

Late 19th c.; W side SR 1302, 2.6 mi. N of US 258, Richlands vic.

The little white frame building is a classic example of the 1-room country school with a gable-fronted entry and small belfry. It is preserved as a community meeting hall.

ON 8 Palo Alto

Ca. 1840; NE side SR 1434, 6.2 mi. S of US 17, Belgrade vic.; private, visible from road

The large, 2-story, 5-bay frame plantation house was the center of an agricultural and turpentine operation of some 9,500 acres, developed by David W. Sanders, one of the state's largest antebellum planters. Unusual features are the crenellated interior end chimneys, small center cupola, and Palladian windows in the gable ends. The full-width, 2-story engaged porch originally had two tiers. Sanders's grandson, Daniel L. Russell, governor of N.C. from 1897 to 1901, was born and spent his early childhood here.

ON 9 Isaac Newton Henderson House

Ca. 1900; attributed to carpenters Lawrence Smith and Linnie Parker; W side SR 1428, 0.2 mi. S of SR 1744, 0.15 mi. N of NC 24, Hubert; private, visible from road

Two-story, side-passage-plan houses with gable or hip roofs oriented to the front recur across Onslow Co. This well-preserved, gabled version with a decorated, 2-story porch was built for a prosperous turpentine producer and Methodist preacher.

ON 10 Swansboro

Laid out in 1770, the little town at the mouth of the White Oak River near Bogue Inlet thrived on naval stores, shipbuilding, and fishing through the mid-19th c. Later it was home to a series of lumber mills. Today the town is experiencing a resurgence as a vacation and boating community. Vernacular domestic and commercial buildings span Swansboro's history, and though some key buildings received 20th-c. alterations, overall the waterfront village retains much of the ambience of a small working port.

Two houses date from the early decades of the town's founding. The 2-story **Peter Ringware House** (ca. 1778; 219 Main St.), built for a ship's captain, displays the region's hallmark 2-tier, full-width engaged porches

ON 10 *Swansboro, waterfront view*

on both front and rear, and much of its original late Georgian finish survives. Around the corner the dormered, 1½-story **Jonathan Green House** (late 18th c.; 114 Elm St.) also exhibits an engaged porch, with a double-shouldered chimney of Flemish-bond brick at the eastern gable end. The cluster of commercial buildings along Front St. includes the 2-story **William Pugh Ferrand Store** (1839; 122 Front St.), much altered but notable as a rare early commercial building of brick on a ballast stone foundation. Several late 19th- and early 20th-c. frame stores face the street with gable or parapet fronts.

A few simple antebellum houses survive in town, but most of the housing dates to the turn-of-the-century heyday of the Swansboro Land and Lumber Company and is characterized by the familiar I-house form and locally produced sawn and turned detailing in gables and porches. An intact group of 2-story houses of the lumber boom era, many with 2-story porches, lines **Walnut St.** Of particular interest from this period is the **William Edward Mattocks House** (early 20th c., Robert Lee Smith, carpenter; 109 Front St.), a board-and-batten house built in the regional vernacular and styled by its owner to resemble an older family homestead. A deep, engaged, 2-story porch faces the waterfront and the main approach to town over the White Oak River bridge.

Pender County (PD)

PD 1 Burgaw

Named for a nearby creek and plantation, the community that developed here along the Wilmington and Weldon Railroad in the mid-19th c. became county seat a few years after Pender Co. was made from New Hanover in 1875. The town is laid out around the courthouse square, with modest brick commercial rows bounding two sides of the square and frame dwellings of the late 19th and early 20th centuries beyond. The **Pender County Courthouse** (1936; William Dietrick [Raleigh], architect; Courthouse Square) is a conservative Colonial Revival building on an H-plan with Flemish-bond brickwork, contrasting classical trim, and a 2-stage wooden cupola surmounting the central hip-roofed block. The parklike square contains several historical monuments and is generously planted with live oaks, magnolias, and azaleas. The bracketed, board-and-batten central portion of the nearby **Burgaw Depot** (1850, 1898, 1917; 102 E. Fremont) is believed to be the last antebellum depot on the route of the Wilmington and Weldon Railroad, one of the state's first two railroads, completed in 1840. The passenger waiting room section on the south was added in 1898.

PD 2 St. Helena Russian Orthodox Church

1932; E side SR 1412, 1.2 mi. NW of US 117, St. Helena

In the early 20th c., Wilmington entrepreneur Hugh MacRae developed agricultural colonies in New Hanover and Pender counties to which he recruited groups of European immigrants. The largest and most successful were at Castle Hayne in northern New Hanover Co., occupied principally by Dutch flower bulb producers, and St. Helena in Pender Co., populated over time by Italians, Poles, Hungarians, Austrians, Belgians, Danes, and others, including Russians who had previously immigrated to Austria. Few buildings survive from the earliest de-

PD 2 *St. Helena Russian Orthodox Church*

velopment of these colonies that reflect the ethnic traditions of the immigrants. The chief architectural landmark is this brick Russian Orthodox church, complete with an onion dome and a cornerstone written in Russian, which translates "Russian Orthodox Cathedral Church Dedicated to the Saints and Apostles Peter and Paul 1932." The active congregation still celebrates Old Christmas on Jan. 7.

PD 3 Moore's Creek National Battlefield

NC 210 at SR 1100, W of Currie; open regular hours

At the wooded, creekside site of one of the opening engagements of the American Revolution, a collection of commemorative monuments flavors the place with a spirit of long veneration. On Feb. 27, 1776, a group of 1,000 patriots defeated a loyalist force of about 1,600 at the bridge over Moore's Creek, foiling a loyalist rendezvous with British regulars at Wilmington and averting conquest of the colony by royal governor Josiah Martin. A reconstructed bridge crosses the creek and traces of the patriot earthworks and the old colonial stage road remain. The site has been commemorated since the mid-19th c. It became a state park in 1897 and was transferred to the federal government in 1926. The Patriot or **Grady Monument** (1857; William Struthers [Philadelphia]), an 18-foot brownstone obelisk, is one of the earliest patriotic commemorative monuments in N.C. Early 20th-c. monuments include the Heroic Women or **Slocumb Monument** (1907), a 6-foot marble likeness of a woman on a 10-foot granite pedestal honoring the contributions of the women of the Lower Cape Fear to the patriot cause. A trail and exhibit on the early naval stores industry of the region, including boxed pines and a tar kiln, is one of the few places that celebrate the source of the state's "Tar Heel" nickname.

PD 4 Hopewell Presbyterian Church and Cemetery

Ca. 1870; E side US 117, 1.1 mi. S of SR 1318, Watha vic.

Standing alone against a broad backdrop of cultivated fields, isolated churches across the region reveal the presence of long-established but dispersed rural communities whose existence may not otherwise be obvious to the traveler. The congregation here was founded about 1800, and the present frame building—a simple, gable-fronted church with porch recessed under the gable—was built about 1870. The cemetery includes the grave of Hinton James, the first student to matriculate at the University of North Carolina in 1795, who went on to become an engineer, mayor of Wilmington, and state legislator.

PD 5 Carolina Industrial School at Shelter Neck

Early 20th c.; E side SR 1318, 3.2 mi. E of US 117, between US 117 and NC 53, Watha vic.; private, visible from road

The picturesque campus of well-kept white frame buildings includes a small chapel, a schoolhouse, and a 2-story dormitory in an exceptionally complete example of an early 20th-c. rural educational facility. One of three schools built by the Unitarian Church

in southeastern N.C. by the early 20th c., it provided basic education and training in domestic and agricultural arts for local children. After expansion of the public school system in the 1920s, the facility was converted to a camp and conference center for the now merged Unitarian-Universalist denomination.

PD 6 Poplar Grove

Ca. 1850; SE side US 17, 0.25 mi. N of New Hanover Co. line, Scotts Hill; private, open regular hours

PD 6 *Poplar Grove*

Planter Joseph N. Foy built the tall, symmetrical plantation house in the 1850s to replace an earlier house which is said to have burned in 1849. He had inherited the plantation purchased by his father in 1795, which was then "commonly known by the name of Poplar Grove." By 1860 Poplar Grove was worked by sixty-four slaves who lived in twelve houses and raised peas, corn, beans, and swine. A strong Unionist though a slaveholder, Foy declared his motto, "Union Forever." Beginning in the 1870s Joseph's son Joseph T. Foy, a political leader in newly formed Pender Co., further developed the plantation and adapted to a new day by successfully raising peanuts—then a novelty—in large quantities.

Raised on a full brick basement, the large, 2-story house features a center-hall plan, straightforward Greek Revival interior finish, and double-tiered rear porch linked by an exterior stair. The high basement and rear porch configuration are designed to deal with the hot, humid coastal climate. The basement opens beneath the rear porch into a brick-paved service area akin to examples in Wilmington, giving access to a back terrace surrounded by the domestic outbuildings. Notable outbuildings include a large brick smokehouse, a smaller brick building described as a kitchen, a frame carriage house, frame tenant house, sheds, and other structures. The house and outbuildings are restored, and the site is open to the public, providing a rare glimpse of coastal plantation architecture of the 19th c.

PD 7 Sloop Point

Ca. 1726; 1760; private, no public visibility or access

Sloop Point is among the most important early coastal houses in the state. Dendrochronology dating indicates that the original house was built in 1726, evidently as a 1- or 1½-story dwelling. In the mid-18th c. the house was expanded dramatically, with the addition of rear shed rooms, the deep front porch, and a higher and broader pitched roof covering the full 50-foot length of the house from front to back in a single great gable. An ingenious system of vents and chutes improved airflow. The house has a 3-room plan, with a big, English-bond chimney serving the large room on the north. Especially striking is the massive double chimney of Flemish-bond brick that serves the two smaller rooms on the south. A doorway in an arch between the two bases leads from a small porch into a small vestibule, which then opens into the two adjacent rooms. The interior is simply finished in Georgian style of at least two eras.

One of the few pre-Revolutionary buildings in the Lower Cape Fear region, the house is a rare survivor from a now sparsely

PD 7 *Sloop Point*

represented era of settlement. The original section may be the oldest building standing in the state. The house is located on Sloop Point projecting into Topsail Bay, a spot marked on Moseley's 1733 map as owned by "J. Ashe"—John Baptista Ashe, who had settled in the Lower Cape Fear area in the 1720s and became a political figure and progenitor of a large and influential family. His son John was a leader in the Revolutionary cause. Sold by Samuel Ashe in 1795, after a series of owners in the early 19th c. Sloop Point was owned by the MacMillan family for more than a century and has been renovated by new owners.

PD 8 Operation Bumblebee Naval Ordnance Test Facility Structures

1946–48; U.S. Navy; Kellex Corp., George and Lynch, contractors; various locations along NC 50, Topsail Beach

PD 8 *Operation Bumblebee Naval Ordnance Test Facility*

A short, exciting, and long-secret saga in post–World War II defense history left a unique series of structures in the quiet beach resort community. Only recently has the story of the pioneer missile facility been recovered from formerly classified documents. At the end of World War II the Navy selected what then was an undeveloped and isolated Topsail Island as the location for Operation Bumblebee, a top-secret, experimental project to develop and test ramjet missiles, which heralded the nation's jet aircraft and missile programs. The operation was named for the bumblebee, which although aerodynamically unable to fly, does not know this and flies anyway. The program was developed jointly by the Navy and the applied physics laboratory at Johns Hopkins University. The island had been used during World War II as a weapons testing site for Camp Davis at nearby Holly Ridge and was still under government lease.

Some 500 men arrived in mid-1946, and within months the necessary buildings were erected on the sandy island from specifications by the Kellex Corp. The **Assembly Building** is a 77-by-82-foot structure of explosion-proof concrete construction where the missiles were assembled; these ranged in size from 3 to 13 feet long, some of the earliest being called "flying stovepipes." The missiles were transported the short distance across the island—overland or through a tunnel—to the 60-by-72-foot **Launching Pad** at the oceanside, where observers watched from a bombproof bunker as the missiles were fired. Nine reinforced concrete towers were constructed at precisely calibrated intervals up and down the beach—each 16 feet square in plan, 3 or 4 stories tall, and set on 30-foot concrete slabs on 20-foot pilings, to assure perfect stability. One was the **Control Tower** (Flake St. at S. Anderson Blvd.) midway between the Assembly Building and the Launching Pad. The other eight towers were **Observation Towers**, each fitted with measuring and photographic equipment to record the missile flights. Over 200 missiles were tested during a period of 18 months, some flying at supersonic speeds up to 1,500 miles per hour and demonstrating the viability of ramjet technology. Although the Topsail facility was intended to be permanent, after only 18 months Operation Bumblebee required a longer range and more reliable weather, and the site was abandoned in 1948. The equipment was moved to other research sites at White Sands, N.M.; Inyokern, Calif.; and Cape Canaveral, Fla. But the experiments conducted at Topsail in ramjet design formed the basis for all modern jet aircraft engines, especially supersonic jets, as well as for long-range missiles.

In 1948 the U.S. government returned the island to local ownership, and gradually a beach resort community developed. Today the sturdy, reinforced concrete structures still stand. The Assembly Building is a community center with a small local museum on "Missiles and More." All but two of the towers survive—two adapted as cottages, another linked to a fishing pier—as distinctive sentinels along the island. And at the Jolly Roger Motel at the site of the rocket launches, the bombproof **Observation Bunker** is used for storage, while the 4-inch-thick concrete Launching Pad is still evident as the motel's patio.

New Hanover County (NH)

See Tony P. Wrenn, Wilmington, North Carolina: An Architectural and Historical Portrait *(1984); S. Carol Gunter,* Carolina Heights, Wilmington *(1982); Davyd Foard Hood, Christopher Martin, and Edward F. Turberg,* Historic Architecture of New Hanover County, North Carolina *(1986).*

Wilmington (NH 1–95)

The port city rising above the Cape Fear River contains the state's richest collection of 19th-c. urban architecture. From 1840 to 1910 Wilmington was the state's largest city. Because of relatively modest subsequent growth coupled with sustained preservation efforts, the community has retained more of its 19th- and early 20th-c. character than the state's other principal cities.

Wilmington is dramatically sited on a bluff on the eastern bank of the river, presenting a splendid prospect when viewed from the us 17 highway bridge and the boats that ply the river from the waterfront. It lies some 30 miles upstream from the mouth of the Cape Fear, the state's only major river that opens directly into the Atlantic Ocean. Here the two main branches of the river come together, one draining the old plantation region to the northeast, the other

coming from the vast backcountry beyond Fayetteville. The town, variously called New Carthage, New Liverpool, Newton, and finally Wilmington after the English patron of the colonial governor Gabriel Johnston, was laid out in 1733 and chartered in 1739–40. As the backcountry developed, Wilmington soon supplanted *Brunswick Town as the principal port on the Cape Fear, an important outlet for naval stores, lumber, and rice, and the focus of wealth, culture, and political power in the Lower Cape Fear region. Commission merchants, who bought and sold merchandise as it arrived at the docks, played a key role in the city's life. Growing to 1,000 inhabitants by 1790, Wilmington drew people from many locales, particularly South Carolina, Barbados, New England, and the mid-Atlantic colonies as well as England, Scotland, Germany, and Africa.

Town growth accelerated in the antebellum years. Wilmington leaders promoted

NH 1–95 *Wilmington*

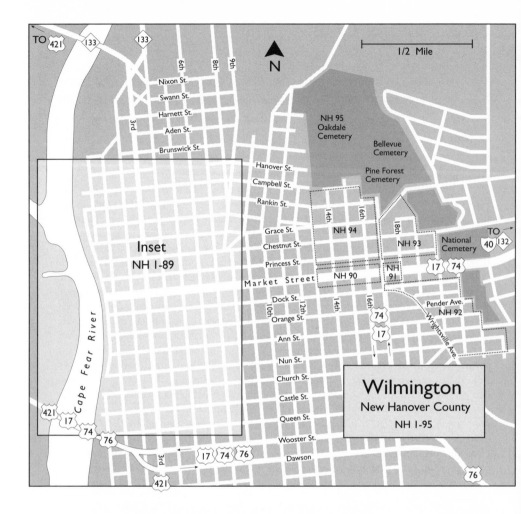

6th
8th
9th

Nixon St.

Swann St.

Harnett St.

3rd

Aden St.

Brunswick St.

NH 95
Oakdale
Cemetery

Bellevue
Cemetery

Hanover St.

Pine Forest
Cemetery

Campbell St.

Rankin St.

14th

16th

Grace St.

NH 94

18th

Chestnut St.

NH 93

National
Cemetery

TO
40 132

Princess St.

NH
91

17 74

Inset

NH 1-89

Market Street

NH 90

Dock St.

10th

12th

14th

16th

74

Pender Ave.
NH 92

Orange St.

Cape Fear River

Ann St.

17

Wrightsville Ave.

Nun St.

Church St.

Castle St.

421

17

Queen St.

Wilmington

New Hanover County

NH 1-95

74 76

Wooster St.

3rd

17 74 76

Dawson

421

76

construction of one of the state's first two railroads, the Wilmington and Weldon (originally the Wilmington and Raleigh). When completed in 1840, the 161-mile line was the longest railroad in the world. In the 1840s and 1850s that north-south route became part of a growing fan of connections from Wilmington: rail lines to South Carolina and toward Charlotte, plank and dirt roads, and an improved river channel plied by steamships. In 1820 the town of 2,600 people had ranked fourth in the state, but it grew to 4,744 by 1840 and to over 7,000 by 1850, surpassing New Bern, Fayetteville, and Raleigh to become the state's largest city. With nearly 10,000 people in 1860 Wilmington was, however small compared to major Atlantic Coast cities, a metropolis for the

rural state. The population was evenly divided between blacks and whites. Black Wilmingtonians included many free and enslaved artisans, particularly in the building trades. At midcentury, white Wilmingtonians included members of the Lower Cape Fear plantation gentry as well as immigrants from northern states and Europe. Over half the merchants in 1860 had been born outside N.C., and many of the leading builders and architects came from northern cities.

During the Civil War, Wilmington, guarded by the guns of *Fort Fisher, remained open longer than any other major southern port, keeping the Wilmington and Weldon Railroad the "lifeline of the Confederacy." Trade flourished and fortunes grew as 1,700 blockade-runners spirited car-

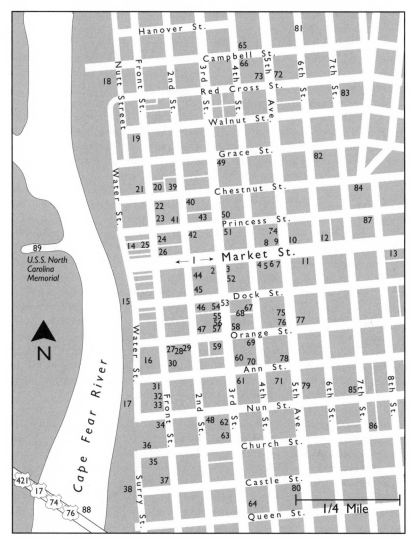

Downtown Wilmington Inset NH I-89

goes through the Union blockade before Fort Fisher fell on Jan. 15, 1865. The city was occupied by Union troops on Feb. 22.

After the war Wilmington recovered as a shipping and manufacturing hub and became an important center for lumber, fertilizer, and iron industries as well as truck farm wholesaling. With the population growing to 17,000 by 1880 and 20,000 by 1890, Wilmington maintained its status as the state's largest city. Central to its growth was the headquarters and repair shops of the Wilmington and Weldon Railroad and the Atlantic Coast Line, which in the 1890s absorbed the Wilmington and Weldon and several other lines. Rail connections with South Carolina and Georgia helped make Wilmington an important cotton compressing and exporting center.

As people flocked to work in these enterprises, the city expanded beyond its old boundaries to encompass black and white working- and middle-class neighborhoods on the north, south, and east. This was a period of intense political turbulence entwined with social and economic change. Tension between Republican and Democratic and black and white political forces burst into violence in 1898, when whites burned the black newspaper office and took control of local government.

Growth continued after 1900, expanding the city eastward into new suburbs, creating more residential separation among races and classes, and supporting many handsome new commercial and institutional buildings. But N.C.'s booming piedmont industrial cities quickly outstripped Wilmington. In 1910 Wilmington's population of 26,000 was second to Charlotte's 34,000, and by 1930 the port city of 32,000 ranked 8th in size among N.C. cities. A World War II military boom was followed by a postwar slump. The departure of the Atlantic Coast Line headquarters to Florida in 1960 dealt the city a severe blow.

Late 20th-c. Wilmington is experiencing another boom that has pushed its population past the 60,000 mark. Interstate 40, in part paralleling the old Wilmington and Weldon route, gives new access to the rest of the state and nation: "Barstow, Calif., 2,554 miles," says the sign. Beach and retirement development has mushroomed; the state port is busy with national and international shipping; the University of North Carolina at Wilmington is growing; and new industries include a major movie and television production business. An early leader in local preservation efforts, the city actively promotes tourism and its historic character as part of its revitalization.

Wilmington's architecture of every period possesses a boldness and directness evoking the forceful and resilient spirit of the city's merchants, shippers, and politicians as well as its architects and craftsmen. Frequent fires in the 18th and 19th centuries—a predictable consequence of the naval stores industry and the cotton trade—repeatedly leveled business blocks and destroyed most of the early buildings (which 18th-c. accounts describe as frame and brick structures, many with piazzas). Thus the city's architecture dates principally from ca. 1840 onward. Proudly "city-like," it combines indigenous coastal building forms with sophisticated urban designs that reflect the ambitions and far-flung connections of its mercantile leaders. Especially notable is Wilmington's devotion to the bracketed, vented, Italianate idiom from about 1850 through the 1880s.

Each generation commissioned work by nationally prominent architects—Thomas U. Walter, Samuel Sloan, Kenneth Murchison Jr., Carrere and Hastings, Hobart Upjohn, Henry Bacon (who spent his childhood in Wilmington)—but the city also supported native and immigrant architects and builders. Prominent among these in the mid-19th c. were carpenter-architect James F. Post from New Jersey and brick contractors John C. and Robert B. Wood from Nantucket; Post continued in the late 19th c., as did several long-established black builders, including Alfred Howe and other members of his family. By the early 20th c. a new generation of architects, including Charles McMillen, Henry E. Bonitz, Burett Stephens, Joseph Leitner, Lynch and Foard, James F. Gause, and Leslie Boney had settled in Wilmington and created a resident architectural community.

Wilmington's unique ambience derives from more than its architecture alone. Its position on the riverside bluff gives special emphasis to its riverfront, and the whole city possesses a subtropical verdancy bestowed by live oaks, Spanish moss, azaleas, oleanders, and the occasional palm tree. The texture of the city is enriched by 19th- and early 20th-c. brick paving, ironwork, street furniture, and civic monuments. Vestiges of the old gritty vitality still emanate from the waterfront, where recreational and retail development has not entirely supplanted the working riverscape.

There are several outstanding concentrations of architecture. Market St., the broad thoroughfare extending inland (eastward) from the waterfront, presents a striking sequence of buildings from every era. The state's best grouping of 19th-c. maritime commercial architecture overlooks the waterfront from the business district. Imposing civic and religious buildings punctuate the blocks. A large, intact, 19th-c. residential section, encompassing the old town borders, frames the business district. Block after block of principally 19th-c. dwellings, from workers' cottages to merchants' mansions, fill the shaded grid of streets. The streetscape is especially consistent from Market St. south to Castle St. and from the waterfront to 5th Ave. (the old eastern edge), and there are important buildings as well in the blocks from Market north to Red Cross St. The Northside area beyond the old railroad yards and tracks, and the Southside section encompass large areas of 19th- and early 20th-c. housing and several notable churches, as do the streets just east of 5th Ave. Early 20th-c. suburbs continue eastward, from the band of modest housing that begins about 8th St., to the more expensive suburbs farther east. Even more than in most cities in this guide, the following list is but a small sampling of important architecture.

Market St.:

Market St. is a remarkable boulevard with architecture from every period. A cast-iron, open-air Market House (1847–48) once stood at the foot of Market St. where the first blocks—the old commercial center—are flanked by consistent, well-detailed brick commercial buildings typical of the late 19th and early 20th centuries. The street is punctuated by fragments of the plaza that once ran down its center. Proceeding eastward from 3rd St., Market St. is lined by imposing residential architecture interspersed with churches.

NH 1 Market St. Statuary and Street Furniture

Wilmington's early 20th-c. public statuary is among the finest in the state, and much of it appears in Market St. At Water St. stands the remarkable **Anti-Germ Individual Cup Fountain** (1915), which has a horse fountain on top (with a horse in bas-relief), and below, two individual cup fountains, reminders of the Progressive era's emphasis on sanitation and public health. Also here are

two of several stone markers erected by the New Hanover Co. Historical Commission to designate historic sites during the early 20th-c. fervor for patriotic commemoration.

At Market and 3rd Sts. the **George Davis Statue** (1909–11; Francis Packer [New York], sculptor) is a realistic figure on a tall base, erected by the United Daughters of the Confederacy to commemorate the Wilmingtonian who served as attorney general of the Confederacy. Near the intersection with 4th St. rises the **Harnett Obelisk** (1906; M. G. Delahunty [Philadelphia], designer), erected by the N.C. Society of the Colonial Dames in honor of the "colonial heroes of the Lower Cape Fear," including Cornelius Harnett. At the center of Market St. and 5th Ave. is the **Kenan Memorial Fountain** (1921; Carrere & Hastings [New York]), given by scientist and philanthropist William Rand Kenan Jr. in memory of his parents; Kenan would have known the New York architectural firm through their work for his brother-in-law Henry Flagler, the Standard Oil magnate.

NH 2 Burgwin-Wright House
Ca. 1770, ca. 1845; 224 Market St. (SW corner 3rd St.); open regular hours

The late Georgian townhouse combines a regional form and elegant Georgian style finish. The 2-story frame house stands high on a cellar that includes elements from an early jail. The double-slope gable roof breaks below the ridge to incorporate 2-tier piazzas

NH 2 *St. James Church, Burgwin-Wright House*

front and rear. The rear wing was added ca. 1845. A Venetian motif entrance opens into a center passage with a fine late Georgian stair, flanked by a pair of rooms to the east and a single large room on the west. Some interior work has been reconstructed, but the stair hall and second story are original, including arched niches in the large upper room. British immigrant Burgwin came from Charleston and established himself among Wilmington's mercantile elite. In 1799 he sold the house to Joshua G. Wright, a judge and member of an important Wilmington family that owned the house until 1869 and expanded it over the years. The house and grounds have been restored as state headquarters of the National Society of the Colonial Dames in N.C., early leaders in historic preservation who acquired the property in 1937.

NH 3 St. James Episcopal Church

1839–40; Thomas U. Walter (Philadelphia), architect; John Norris (New York), supervising architect; C. H. Dahl (New York), principal carpenter; John C. Wood, principal mason; 1871 (roof and ceiling); 1885 enlargement, Henry Dudley (New York), architect; 1923– 24 great hall, Hobart Upjohn (New York), architect; 1 S. 3rd St. (at Market St.)

The state's first full-blown essay in the Gothic Revival style was the first of Wilmington's many buildings designed by nationally prominent architects. The large and wealthy parish established in 1729, dissatisfied with its "barn-like" colonial church, obtained a design for a new church from Philadelphia architect Thomas U. Walter. The symmetrical, stuccoed brick building with central entrance tower is enriched with pinnacles, battlements, modest buttresses, and molded labels over the lancet windows. Its design reflected the influence of Bishop John Henry Hopkins's *Essay on Gothic Architecture* (1836). At the laying of the cornerstone in 1839 rector R. B. Drane commended the vestry's choice of the Gothic style as most likely to "fill men with awe and reverence, to repress the tumult of unreflecting gaiety, and to render the mind sedate and solemn." On its completion the church

was cited by N.C. bishop Levi Silliman Ives as "a model of Church Architecture" and helped promote the Gothic Revival in the state. The parish employed New Yorker John Norris as supervising architect. This job inaugurated Norris's brief but prolific career in Wilmington, which included a handsome customhouse (now lost) before he went on to design key buildings in Savannah. Later additions enriched and continued the Gothic character of the church, including the handsome truss roof of 1871 and the chancel and transept of 1885, both designed by Gothic Revival specialist Henry Dudley of New York.

NH 4 Temple of Israel

1875–76; Alex Strausz and James Walker, architects; Abbott (Cape Fear) Building Company, builders; 1 S. 4th St.

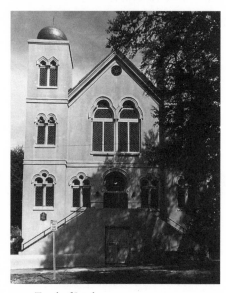

NH 4 *Temple of Israel*

This is the oldest (1872) Jewish congregation organized in the state. Jews had numbered among Wilmington's community's leaders from the 18th c., beginning with David David's arrival in 1738. In 1852 a Jewish burial society was formed, and by 1855 the Hebrew Cemetery had opened in Oakdale Cemetery. In 1876 the new temple was praised in the *American Israelite*: "For simple elegance this temple is unsurpassed in the United States." Trefoils and Saracenic arches filled with geometric stained glass, together with the twin, onion-domed towers, make the edifice unique in the city; these exotic themes were regarded as more suitable for a temple than classical or Gothic motifs. The Abbott Building Company was established by Joseph C. Abbott, a Union general who became a prominent local manufacturer, developer, and political figure immediately after the war.

NH 5 Mary Jane Langdon House

1870; E. W. Brown, architect; Alfred Howe, contractor; 408 Market St.

The symmetrical, 2-story, Italianate house five bays wide with arched entrance porch exemplifies postwar continuity in building. Built for the widow Langdon by Howe, a leading black contractor, the residence is notable for the survival of detailed construction specifications, including the porch "of neat and handsome appearance, with proper shaped roof . . . supported by four tasteful & ornamental pillars or columns in front, and half antae in the rear."

NH 6 Martin-Huggins House

1870; James F. Post, architect-builder; 412 Market St.

The best preserved of the city's Second Empire houses was built for Alfred Martin, commission merchant and turpentine manufacturer. Contractor Post combined a mansard roof with the familiar composition of corner pilasters, bracket cornice, and canopy porch.

NH 7 Carolina Apartments

1906–7; Robert L. Shape, L. K. Motz (New York), architects; Henry E. Bonitz, supervising architect; Central Carolina Construction Company, contractor; 420 Market St.

The imposing apartment house exemplifies the city leaders' connections. It was designed by a New York architect and built by a Greensboro construction firm for Wilmington investors. The 6-story apartment house,

NH 7 *Carolina Apartments*

executed in a Mediterranean or Renaissance Revival style in dark, Flemish-bond brick, features handsome stone and iron detail, including iron balconies.

NH 8 John A. Taylor House

Ca. 1846; Benjamin Gardner, attributed builder; 411 Market St.; open business hours

The extraordinary residence of almost brutally geometricized classical forms is built of pressed brick and fronted in stunning white marble. Within the entrance bay recessed between pilaster-framed bays, the robust doorway is framed by pilasters and an entablature. A marble belvedere tops the low hip roof. Taylor was a New York businessman

NH 8 *John A. Taylor House*

with steamboat and railroad investments. The house was advertised in 1891 as "that truly superb and costly Residence in Marble and Pressed Philadelphia brick." Originally the severity of the design was softened by a walled formal garden, and there were brick outbuildings. The cannons on the roof recall its use (1892–1951) as armory of the Wilmington Light Infantry; the WLI also housed the museum established by the Daughters of the Confederacy, which developed into the present Cape Fear Museum.

NH 9 First Baptist Church

1859–70; Samuel Sloan (Philadelphia), architect; 421 Market St.

The big brick church in "Early English Gothic" style was the first N.C. project of prolific Philadelphia architect Samuel Sloan, a specialist in Baptist churches. He was commissioned after members of the congregation went north to recruit an architect. Towers of unequal height flank the gabled facade and rise to broach spires—the one on the east soars 197 feet above the street. Builder John Hanby is said to have come to Wilmington to execute the attenuated spires. Originally the exterior was more ornate, with corbels (recently restored), pinnacles, and finials as well as patterned slate. In July 1861 the unfinished church was boarded up, and completion was delayed until 1870.

NH 10 Bellamy Mansion

1859–60; James F. Post, architect-contractor; Rufus Bunnell, draftsman-architect; Elvin Artis, carpenter; 503 Market St.; open regular hours

NH 10 *Bellamy Mansion*

The spectacular, columned mansion epitomizes the opulent and ebullient classicism of the eve of the Civil War. It was built for Dr. John D. Bellamy, physician, planter, and a director of the Bank of the Cape Fear and the Wilmington and Weldon Railroad. Leading local builder-architect Post employed the young architect Rufus Bunnell of Connecticut to assist with drawings and specifications, while family tradition credits the idea for the design to Dr. Bellamy's daughter Mary. Wilmington free black carpenter Elvin Artis and other black artisans employed by Post constructed the vast frame house. The 25-foot columns, the louvered blinds, and other millwork were manufac-

NH 9 *First Baptist Church*

tured in New York. With war clouds looming, architect Bunnell returned north shortly before the house was completed. In 1865 the residence served as officers' quarters during Union occupation, before returning to Bellamy family use. The big house blends the locally favored center-passage plan, deep porches, and Italianate motifs with ornate classical elements. Executed on a scale seldom rivaled in the state's domestic architecture, the mass of the house is expanded by the colossal Corinthian-order porches along three sides. The broad center passage is flanked by four large rooms per floor, with high ceilings, heavy moldings, and shady blinds at the many large windows. The basement holds the kitchen, dining room, and other service rooms, and the attic contains children's rooms and a stair to the cupola with its capital view of the city. The **Bellamy Slave Quarters** forming the wall at the rear property line—a rare survival of an important antebellum urban building type—is a substantial, 2-story brick structure with multiseat privies and what was probably a laundry on the first floor and storage and sleeping chambers above. The mansion has been restored as a museum of history and design arts.

NH 10 *Bellamy Slave Quarters*

NH 11 William J. Price House
Ca. 1855; 514 Market St.; open business hours

The brick Italianate structure has a side-passage plan and boasts a later, Stick-style porch.

NH 12 St. Paul's Evangelical Lutheran Church
1859–69; James F. Post, supervising architect; 1907 addition, Henry E. Bonitz, architect; 603 Market St.

Construction of the brick, Gothic Revival style church with central tower and spire was begun before the Civil War, interrupted, and finally completed for a bilingual congregation important in a town with many German residents. An 1869 account of its dedication in the *Lutheran Visitor* praised its Gothic style as "the only legitimate style for German churches" and its interior as "the most elegant . . . we have seen this side of the ocean." The walls were stuccoed and scored to resemble stone in 1874.

NH 13 National Guard Armory (Cape Fear Museum)
1935–37; H. Colvin Linthicum (Raleigh), architect; 1990 addition, Jefferies and Faris, architects; 814 Market St.

A typically militaristic version of the late Gothic mode widely used in armories, the locally important example of WPA-sponsored construction has served since 1970 as a regional history museum. Architect H. Colvin Linthicum was the son and former associate of Hill C. Linthicum of Durham.

The waterfront (along Water and Nutt Sts.) and the commercial district, which encompass N. and S. Front and 2nd Sts., Princess, Market, and Dock Sts., offer an outstanding collection of late 19th- and early 20th-c. masonry commercial and public buildings. The predominant architecture is of 2- and 3-story brick construction.

Water St.

NH 14 U.S. Customhouse (Alton Lennon Federal Building)
1916–19; James A. Wetmore, supervising architect of the Treasury; N. Water St. between Market and Princess Sts.

The imposing, Beaux Arts classical building, 3 stories high and twenty-five bays long, presides over the waterfront. Temple-fronted wings advance at either end to flank a central courtyard. Their pedimented facades with Tower of the Winds pilasters and delicate iron balconies quote from John Norris's temple-form customhouse (1840s), which was razed for this facility.

NH 15 J. W. Brooks Building
1920; 10–18 S. Water St.

NH 15 *J. W. Brooks Building*

A strong element in the waterfront, the 3-story brick building combines offices and warehouse. It extends a half-block along Water St. and stands partially over the river on a stone and concrete base. The office entry has the dates of the firm's founding (1899) and the construction of the building (1920). Brooks was a wholesale grocer and commission merchant.

NH 16 Wilmington Iron Works
Late 19th–early 20th c.; 201–3 S. Water St. (at Orange St.)

Recalling the long-standing integration of industrial, mercantile, and residential uses in pre-20th-c. cities, the complex of brick, frame, and metal buildings reaching from Water St. to Front St. maintains an important presence in the streetscape and city life. A wall of ballast stone and cobblestone may be 18th c. Utilitarian brick structures erected in the late 19th and early 20th centuries were expanded for the iron works, which was founded in 1838 and occupied various locations before this one.

NH 17 Chandler's Wharf
19th c., 1970s; Water St. at Ann St.

The assemblage of waterfront structures, developed as shops and waterside dining, combines houses, boats, brick and Belgian block paving, docks, and other features. Two warehouses and most of the paving are original to the site, while other elements were moved in or built new.

Nutt St.

NH 18 Wilmington and Weldon and Atlantic Coast Line Buildings
Late 19th–early 20th c.; 507–19 Nutt St.; open business hours

A few big brick buildings survive from the huge rail complex central to the city's economy until 1960. First the Wilmington and Weldon (chartered 1834) and then the Atlantic Coast Line (a conglomerate formed by 1900) had their headquarters in Wilmington. The oldest structures here are the pair of the long, 1-story brick freight **Warehouses** with arched openings framed by pilaster strips. The northern warehouse was built before 1880; the southern, ca. 1882. At the eastern end of the 1882 warehouse stands the 3-story **Atlantic Coast Line Office Building** (1900). The office building is now the Wilmington Railroad Museum, and the warehouses hold a convention center and shops. Two blocks north other railroad-related warehouses continue in use, the most striking being the **Hall and Pearsall Warehouse** (ca. 1907; Joseph Schad, builder; 711 Nutt St.), a big, brick structure with tall parapet and Flemish-bond brickwork.

N. Front St. and adjacent sites

NH 19 The Cotton Exchange
1880s–1930s; 307–21 Front St.; 308–16 Nutt St.; open business hours

The block of brick warehouse and commercial buildings, convenient to docks and tracks, served businesses in cotton and other agricultural products. Endangered in 1972, the block was rescued and renovated for shops and offices. The **Alexander Sprunt and Son Building** (1919–20; Henry E. Bonitz, architect; 321 N. Front St.) is an elegant building "of classic structure," red brick trimmed with stone pilasters, cornice, and pedimented entrance. It was built as offices of the cotton exporting firm founded by James Sprunt in 1866, which grew into a major international business. The other buildings are substantial, utilitarian brick structures. Those at **311, 313, and 315 Front St.** served as a wholesale grocer, a printing company and a furniture store, and a Chinese laundry and a seed store, respectively. The structures facing Nutt St. include 2-story warehouses of ca. 1900, the **Dahnhardt Building** (1880s; 310 Nutt St.), which began as a mariner's saloon and boardinghouse and later housed a grocer and a peanut cleaning operation, and the 4-story **Boney-Harper Milling Company** (1886; 314–16 Nutt St.), which produced hominy, grits, and cornmeal and is among the city's finest industrial buildings with its pilaster strips framing arched windows and rising to a gabled parapet.

NH 20 Murchison National Bank Building

1902; Charles McMillen, architect; John H. Brunjes, builder; 200 N. Front St.

The corner building of blond brick makes emphatic use of quoins, voussoirs, and coursed brickwork. The bank, organized in 1899 and named for K. M. Murchison, a New York and Wilmington businessman, had grown rapidly. Architect McMillen had arrived from Minnesota to design the *Masonic Temple.

NH 21 Murchison Building–First Union Building

1913; Kenneth M. Murchison Jr. (New York), architect; 201–3 N. Front St.

The 10-story skyscraper in Neoclassical Revival style incorporates the classic tripartite scheme, with a stone base of columns and keystoned arches, a brick shaft adorned with decorated panels, and a 2-story stone cap with pilasters and copper palmette cresting. The architect, son of businessman K. M. Murchison, was a New York architect who enjoyed continued Wilmington patronage.

NH 22 U.S. Post Office

1936–37; R. Stanley Brown, architect; 152 N. Front St.

The quietly handsome post office was described on completion as "of southern colonial style, built of brick with limestone trimming, 114 by 182 feet." The symmetrical building centers on a recessed portico fronted by tobacco-leaf columns and is capped by a lantern. The lobby mural by William F. Pfol of Winston-Salem, *Wilmington in the 1840s*, depicts a waterfront where captains of local commerce stand in front of John Norris's customhouse, which is said to have inspired the architect's design of this post office.

NH 23 George R. French and Sons Building

1873; 116 N. Front St.

Cited in 1884 as "the first full iron front in the city," this is the older of two surviving examples. Arcades of Corinthian colonnettes mark the upper stories of the 4-bay, 4-story facade, which is capped by an acanthus bracketed cornice. Massachusetts merchant French established his business in Wilmington in 1822, and his sons' continued operation fostered the claim in 1912 that it was the oldest business in the state. When French opened this store, it was one of the first businesses built beyond the old retail center on Market St.

NH 24 MacRae-Otterbourg Building

1878; 25 N. Front St.

The second of the surviving cast-iron facades in Wilmington, the 3-story facade is neatly ordered by engaged colonnettes and a bracket cornice. Erected by merchant Donald MacRae, the building later housed Louis Otterbourg's retail clothing business.

NH 25 Masonic Temple

1898–99; Charles McMillen, architect;
B. F. Miles, stonecarver; 17–21 N. Front St.

The massive, 4-story, Romanesque Revival edifice has the lower 2 stories of rock-faced brownstone, the upper 2 of pressed brick. The first 2 floors were rented for stores and offices, and the third and fourth held Masonic halls and a ballroom. Single and paired windows in arched surrounds are separated by pilasters of increasing order. The finely carved stonework—Masonic symbols above the windows and the foliated corner entrance—was executed by Miles, who is probably the Fred Miles who carved stonework at Biltmore and the Drhumor Building in Asheville. Although local architect James F. Post had submitted a design, the Masons selected Minnesota architect McMillen, a specialist in Masonic temples, who moved to Wilmington and established a successful practice.

NH 26 Atlantic Trust and Banking Company

1910–12; Joseph F. Leitner, architect; Joseph Schad, builder; 2–4 N. Front St.

The first of Wilmington's skyscrapers, the classically detailed, 9-story tower spikes the city skyline. It was designed by Atlantic Coast Line architect Leitner. (See Introduction, Fig. 58.)

S. Front St. and adjacent sites

NH 27 Mitchell-Smith-Anderson House and Office

Ca. 1740, office ca. 1840; 102–4 Orange St.

Recalling 18th-c. accounts of brick houses with piazzas, the Flemish-bond brick townhouse is believed to be the city's oldest structure—one of very few 18th-c. buildings to survive Wilmington's many fires. Probably built for Edward Mitchell, a planter from Charleston, S.C., and sold in 1744 to Bladen Co. planter John Smith, the 2½-story dwelling has an unusual plan—a center passage flanked by two rooms on the east and a room and inset porch (later enclosed) on the west overlooking the river. Elongated, triple-hung windows in the second story opened onto balconies, now lost. Ballast stones appear in the base of the wall. The adjacent board-and-batten office was built for Dr. Edwin A. Anderson.

NH 28 Hogg-Anderson House

Ca. 1825; Solomon Nash, attributed builder;
110 Orange St.; open business hours

The side-passage-plan townhouse combines a simple entrance portico facing the street with a double piazza at the rear. A local memoir attributes construction to Solomon Nash, prominent free black builder.

NH 26 *Front Street, showing Atlantic Trust and Banking Co.*

NH 29 St. John's Lodge

1803–5; Joseph and Benjamin Jacobs, builders; 114 Orange St.; open business hours

Built as a Masonic lodge, the Flemish-bond brick structure of late Georgian style retains a Masonic mural in the original lodge room that is probably the work of one Mr. Bellanger, "Profile-taker, Painter, and Lodge's Decorator," ca. 1808. Built when the street ran at a much lower level, the 2-story building appears almost as a 1-story building on a raised basement. It became a residence in 1825 and is now part of St. John's Museum of Art.

NH 30 Salvation Army Building

1923; James B. Lynch, architect; 215 S. Front St.; B&B

Local architect Lynch produced an eclectic blend of Dutch colonial gables and Italianate brackets in his robust design for the Salvation Army quarters.

NH 31 Wells-Brown-Lord House

Ca. 1773, ca. 1857; 300 S. Front St.

Sited high above the waterfront, the house was probably built for ship's carpenter Robert Wells. It was remodeled and given its Carpenter Gothic trim shortly before the Civil War.

NH 32 Fishblate House

1878; John H. Hanby, builder; 318 S. Front St.

The Italianate house with side-passage plan and wraparound porch continues the use of the popular vented, bracketed frieze. In 1878 the local paper reported that materials were being hauled to Sunset Hill—a popular picnicking site—for "a fine residence on the beautiful spot" for Mayor Solomon Fishblate. Hanby was a prominent contractor in the postwar era. Across the street stand other examples of the local bracketed idiom, dating from various eras.

NH 33 Honnet House

1881, 1915; 322 S. Front St.

Jeweler George Honnet erected a side-passage-plan, Italianate house akin to Mayor Fishblate's and called the house "Sunset Hill" after its picturesque site. His son and successor in his jewelry business added the Colonial Revival Ionic portico, a complement to the portico that then graced the neighboring *Dudley-Sprunt House.

NH 34 Dudley-Sprunt House

1820s, 1840s, 1895, ca. 1930; 400 S. Front St.

Standing on a property known as "Brow of the Hill," the brick house was built by 1825 for Edward B. Dudley, governor (1837–40) and president of the Wilmington and Weldon Railroad. The house was expanded in 1895 and given a towering Ionic portico by James Sprunt, cotton merchant, British vice-consul, and local historian, and his wife, Luola Murchison Sprunt, state Colonial Dames president and leader in cultural and historical activities. Their son, J. Laurence Sprunt, removed the portico and replaced it with a simple entrance portico. A massive stone retaining wall encloses the grounds overlooking the river.

NH 35 Hooper House

Ca. 1820–21; 6 Church St.

This rare Wilmington example of a small, early, frame house escaped the fires that destroyed its contemporaries nearer the center of town. Originally oriented to the south, the 1½-story dwelling with deep porch stands on a raised basement and retains its late Georgian finish. The unusual plan has a center passage flanked by large front rooms and very small rear chambers. Timber dating indicates that it was built ca. 1821, when Archibald Maclaine Hooper received the land after the division of his father's estate. Hooper was a lawyer and editor of the local *Cape Fear Recorder.*

NH 36 Cassidey-Harper House

Ca. 1828, 1910; 1 Church St.

The picturesque frame house built for ship carpenter James Cassidey features the only early gambrel roof in the city. The double porch on the west side overlooks the river.

NH 37 Wessell-Harper House

Ca. 1846; 508 S. Front St.; open business hours

One of the city's purest examples of the Greek Revival style, the house has a symmetrical 5-bay facade defined by Ionic pilasters and a broad entablature. Jacob Wessell was one of many German-born businessmen prominent in 19th-c. Wilmington.

NH 38 Cameron-Hollman-Newkirk House

Ca. 1800, late 19th c.; 510 Surry St., moved 1973 from across street

Highly visible above the river, the tripartite Federal style house—unique in Wilmington—overlooks ruins of the Broadfoot Ironworks and dock. Built for Capt. George Cameron, it received its elaborate millwork trim later in the century.

N. 2nd St. and adjacent sites

NH 39 Hotel Cape Fear

1923–25; G. Lloyd Preacher & Company (Atlanta and Raleigh), architect; 115–25 Chestnut St. at N. 2nd St.

Designed by a prolific hotel architect, the 9-story brick building is the only survivor of the city's several pre–World War II hotels. It combines fireproof concrete construction with conservative Neoclassical detail.

NH 40 Cape Fear Club

1912–13; C. H. P. Gilbert (New York), architect; Joseph F. Leitner, supervising architect; Kenneth M. Murchison Jr. (New York), consulting architect; Wallace and Osterman, builders; 124 N. 2nd St.

The Colonial Revival edifice was erected for a men's club founded in 1852, reorganized in 1866 by former Confederate officers, and is still a bastion of Wilmington society. Taking the form of a red brick mansion trimmed in white marble, it was "patterned closely after the Colonial style of architecture," reported the local newspaper, with "long commodious verandas, with large white columns" evoking antebellum glories.

NH 41 Messenger and Southern Bell Telephone and Telegraph Building

1899–1906; Charles McMillen, architect; 121–27 Princess St.

Architect McMillen, "the capable architect for the magnificent Masonic Temple soon to be under construction," designed the "handsome structure of pretty architectural design." Built of Philadelphia pressed brick and trimmed in brownstone, it was to be "the best equipped newspaper and publishing establishment in North Carolina." This is one of many fine masonry commercial buildings in this area. The emphatic, direct design with arcaded second-story windows beneath a corbeled cornice continues in a series of five buildings, which began at the corner and extended west.

NH 42 Mugge Building

1892–93; 200 Princess St.

NH 42 *Mugge Building*

The eclectic Romanesque and chateauesque brick building has a jaunty corner tower (once capped by a conical roof) and an angled entrance with cast-iron column. It was built to house Carl Mugge's saloon and cafe, plus his residence above.

NH 43 Bonitz Building

1906; Henry E. Bonitz, architect; 215 Princess St.

Prolific local and regional architect Bonitz built the narrow, classically detailed business building for his own office. He emblazoned its facade with "Henry E. Bonitz/Architect" in the frieze and architectural instruments and the dates 1894 and 1906 in wreaths beneath the arched window.

S. 2nd St. and adjacent sites

NH 44 Destrac House
Ca. 1842; 19 S. 2nd St.

Accommodating the steep topography, the Greek Revival, side-passage-plan townhouse stands on a high basement that was used for commercial purposes, with a 2-tier porch serving domestic chambers above. It was built for baker William Destrac.

NH 45 DeRosset House
1841; C. H. Dahl, carpenter; 23 S. 2nd St.

NH 45 *DeRosset House*

The grandest of Wilmington's vented, bracketed, Italianate style houses occupies an imperial setting overlooking the river. It was built for Armand J. and Eliza Lord DeRosset. He was a physician and later commission merchant, part of a large and prominent local family of French origins. Constructed by carpenter Dahl, who had come to work on *St. James Episcopal Church, the house began as a 2-story dwelling with Greek Revival features including the fine Doric porch. In 1854 the family invested in a 2-story rear addition and interior redecoration, and in 1874 they elevated the roof, added the bracket cornice and cupola, and put on a solarium. In 1912 further expansions occurred to the rear. The basement now contains the offices of the Historic Wilmington Foundation.

NH 46 St. Thomas Catholic Church Building
1845–47; Robert B. Wood, attributed architect; 208 Dock St.

The design of the Gothic Revival stuccoed church with crenellated roofline was inspired by nearby *St. James Episcopal Church, which the Wood brothers had built a few years earlier. Deconsecrated after a fire in 1966, it is now a performing arts center.

NH 47 Ballard-Potter-Bellamy House
Ca. 1846; 121 S. 2nd St.

Combining Greek Revival and Italianate features—from one or two building campaigns—the symmetrical frame house has Doric porch columns and paneled pilasters with a bracketed and vented cornice under the broad hip roof. Built for merchant Jethro Ballard, the house was sold to Samuel Potter in 1851, who insured it as "nearly new" in that year.

NH 48 Benjamin W. Beery House
Ca. 1853; 202 Nun St.

The massive, frame, Italianate house stands 3 stories above a raised basement. Its roof monitor may actually have been used by a captain, for the house was erected for Capt. Benjamin W. Beery, shipbuilder and Civil War privateer, who owned the Eagles Island shipyard and built Confederate vessels, including the ironclad *North Carolina.*

N. 3rd St. and adjacent sites

NH 49 Lazarus House
Ca. 1816, ca. 1854; 314 Grace St.

The stuccoed townhouse began as a Federal period dwelling set on a grounds occupying a full block. It was erected for Aaron Lazarus, who came from Charleston and established a mercantile empire and became a founder and director of the Wilmington and Weldon Railroad. Without a synagogue in Wilmington, Lazarus worshiped at *St. James Episcopal Church. Dr. F. J. Hill, also associated with the railroad, expanded the house in Greek Revival style and added Italianate touches.

NH 50 City Hall–Thalian Hall
1855–58; John M. Trimble (New York), architect; portico, Robert B. Wood (Wilmington), architect; James F. Post, superintendent of construction; G. W. Rose and Robert B. Wood, builders; 102 N. 3rd St. (City Hall), 310 Chestnut St. (Thalian Hall); open business hours

NH 50 *City Hall–Thalian Hall*

At the zenith of antebellum prosperity, Wilmington civic leaders commissioned leading theater specialist John Trimble of New York to design their combination city hall and theater, a grand and eclectic Italianate building with municipal chambers in front and a theater to the rear. But instead of Trimble's intended front portico akin to that at the north side, the building committee commissioned local architect-builder Robert B. Wood to design the towering Corinthian portico, to add "elevation and dignity to the principal front." In the main (second) story of the stuccoed brick building, Doric-order pilasters separate arched windows and carry a heavy entablature with acanthus modillions. The superbly appointed theater interior, with its garlanded cast-iron columns carrying the balconies, has been restored and is one of the few surviving theaters of the many Trimble designed. Seating 1,000 when built in a city of 10,000, over the years it hosted a series of luminaries—Tom Thumb, Oscar Wilde, Lillian Russell, and Marion Anderson, among many others—as well as many political meetings.

NH 51 *New Hanover County Courthouse*

NH 51 New Hanover County Courthouse
1892; A. S. Eichberg (Savannah), architect; James F. Post, supervising architect; SE corner N. 3rd and Princess Sts.; open business hours

The splendid, towered courthouse is a grand survivor of the state's assertively eclectic civic buildings of the late 19th c., most of which were destroyed in this century. Rich in corbeled brickwork and terra-cotta detail, the red brick building combines Queen Anne massing with Romanesque Revival elements, and emphatically vertical towers with horizontal bands of stone. A contrasting style appears in the symmetrical, stone-faced Neoclassicism of the **New Hanover County Courthouse Annex** (1924–25; Leslie Boney, architect) at the rear.

S. 3rd St. and adjacent sites

NH 52 Donald MacRae House
1901; Henry Bacon, architect; 25 S. 3rd St.

Architect Bacon, who had spent his childhood years in Wilmington, designed a few residences for old friends in the city, notable among which is Wilmington's prime example of the Shingle style. It is one of several MacRae family commissions, which also included work in the mountain resort community of Linville, N.C. Donald MacRae

NH 52 *Donald MacRae House*

was a prominent businessman and developer. Bacon supervised construction as well as providing the plans. The beautifully detailed house, asymmetrically massed with a corner tower and bands of shingles above brick, displays fine Craftsman style joinery with work in natural woods by the Beautelle Manufacturing Company. Now the parish house for *St. James Episcopal Church.

NH 53 Confederate Memorial

1924; Henry Bacon, architect; Francis Packer, sculptor; S. 3rd St. at Dock St.

The evocative memorial of unusually high artistic quality embodies the Beaux Arts collaboration of sculpture and architecture, with sculptor Packer's vibrant bronze figures representing courage and self-sacrifice against Bacon's classical base and shaft. Other notable 3rd St. furniture includes a **Horse Watering Trough** (ca. 1880; J. L. Mott Iron Works; plaza between Orange and Ann Sts.).

NH 54 Bridgers House

1905; Charles McMillen, architect; Joseph Schad, builder; 100 S. 3rd St.; B&B

Architect McMillen, who came to Wilmington to build the *Masonic Temple, designed for Elizabeth Eagles Haywood Bridgers, recent widow of the son of Wilmington and Weldon Railroad leader R. R. Bridgers, a massive stone house in an opulent rendition of the Neoclassical Revival. The house, fronted by a tall, semicircular Ionic portico, is built of limestone quarried in Indiana and cut by the Columbia (S.C.) Stone Company. Stonecutter foreman J. H. Niggel came to Wilmington for this project and

stayed to found the Carolina Cut Stone Company.

NH 55 Savage-Bacon House

Ca. 1850, ca. 1909 (alterations); 114 S. 3rd St.

The Italianate frame house, simplified in the early 20th c., is notable as the boyhood home (1880s) of Henry Bacon Jr., best known as architect of the Lincoln Memorial in Washington, D.C. His father, Henry Bacon Sr., was an engineer sent to the city to superintend construction of the *New Inlet Dam. The younger Bacon maintained connections with Wilmington friends that resulted in several N.C. commissions.

NH 56 Savage House

1851; John C. and Robert B. Wood, builders; James F. Post, carpenter; 120 S. 3rd St.

NH 56 *Savage House*

A quintessential patternbook house with fine ironwork, the 2-story, stuccoed brick dwelling emulates the "Cubical Cottage in the Tuscan Style" in A. J. Downing's *Architecture of Country Houses* (1850). It is one of several Wilmington houses with a low, bracketed roof and a canopy porch with cast-iron trellises; the iron porch cresting is a rare survival. Masonry was done by the Woods and woodwork by Post—an arrangement that Post's ledgers show was common in the city's mid-19th-c. construction jobs. The house was built for Edward Savage and sold to his brother Henry in 1863.

NH 57 Zebulon Latimer House

1852; John C. and Robert B. Wood, builders; James F. Post, carpenter; 126 S. 3rd St.; open regular hours

The 2-story, stuccoed brick dwelling, the most elaborate of the city's masonry houses in the Italianate style, is well documented as the work of the Wood Brothers and James Post for Connecticut native Latimer, a banker and merchant. The walls enriched with quoins, ornate window caps (added later) and bracketed and vented cornice contrast with the classical porch with Tower of the Winds columns. Fine ironwork canopies the side porch and cordons the yard. One of the city's few surviving slave quarters stands to the rear. The house has been restored and furnished in full-blown Victorian fashion, interpreting life among wealthy Wilmingtonians in the flush years before the Civil War. (See Introduction, Fig. 31.)

NH 58 First Presbyterian Church

1926–28; Hobart Upjohn, architect; J. L. Crouse, contractor; Roach and Rowe, stone contractors; S. 3rd St. at Orange St.

At the summit of the bluff, the great Gothic Revival church emerges from the trees to preside over the cityscape. Wilmington Presbyterians had organized a church by 1785, and First Presbyterian Church was accepted in the Fayetteville Presbytery by 1817. A church completed in 1821 burned and was replaced by a Gothic Revival brick church (1859–61; Samuel Sloan, architect); in that church served the Reverend Joseph R. Wilson (1874–85), father of Woodrow Wilson. After that church burned in 1925, the congregation employed Hobart Upjohn—"said to be one of the nation's greatest church architects"—to design a church that, according to the local newspaper, was "expected to be one of the finest in the entire south." The massive structure of rough-cut stone displays Upjohn's fluent Gothic Revival style, domi-

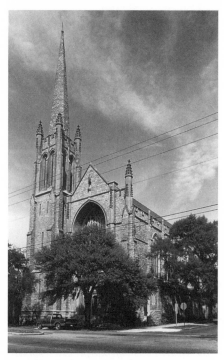

NH 58 *First Presbyterian Church*

nated by a corner tower with a needle spire. (The rooster weathervane was cast by the *Wilmington Iron Works.) For the parish hall and other facilities, Upjohn shifted to a Tudor Revival mode.

NH 59 Henry and Edward Latimer Houses

1882–83; 202, 208 S. 3rd St.

The two similar brick houses, with ornate window heads and bracket cornices, were built for the two sons of Zebulon Latimer. The local newspaper reported on June 11, 1882, that "the Messrs. Latimer" were tearing down old houses and preparing to build new ones to be "an ornament and improvement to that locality." Carriage houses and servants' quarters survive as important parts of these urban establishments. By 1893 Henry's house at no. 202 had gained a mansard roof. Later it was the home of Mary Lily Kenan Flagler Bingham, a Wilmingtonian who had married multimillionaire Henry M. Flagler in 1912 and, after Flagler's death, Robert

Worth Bingham. Her funeral was held here in 1917.

NH 60 John C. Bailey House
Ca. 1864; 219 S. 3rd St.

Built during the Civil War for Bailey, a Swedish-born patternmaker and partner in an iron foundry that evolved into the *Wilmington Iron Works, the asymmetrical Italianate house features a fine ironwork fence and gate, of a type seen also at the *Bellamy Mansion and elsewhere, probably made by Bailey's firm.

NH 61 Murchison House
Ca. 1876 (James Walker, architect), ca. 1910, 1915; 305 S. 3rd St.

The handsome brick house with carriage house and stable stands amid a large, iron-fenced lot. It began as a towered Second Empire style house built for Lucy and David Murchison. He was a banker and merchant. Along with other local residences, it was remodeled in Colonial Revival taste in the early 20th c. for Lucy Murchison or her daughter Lucille Marvin.

NH 62 McKoy House
1887; James F. Post, architect; Alfred Howe, builder; 402 S. 3rd St.

This vivid example of Queen Anne style combines energetic massing with grids, fans, brackets, and bosses ornamenting its multiple gables and inset balconies. The design, published in *Carpentry & Building* in 1886, was adapted by architect-builder Post—his plans for the house survive—and was constructed by prominent black contractor Howe. The house was built for attorney William B. McKoy and his wife, Katherine Bacon, sister of architect Henry Bacon. (Bacon had sent sketches of another design, but they chose a published plan instead.)

NH 63 C. W. Worth House
1893, ca. 1910; D. Getaz (Knoxville, Tenn.), architect; 412 S. 3rd St.

Wholesale grocer and commission merchant Worth erected a full-blown Queen Anne

style house and remodeled it with Neoclassical elements about fifteen years later, creating a lively ensemble with billowing tower and porches.

NH 64 Alfred Howe House
Ca. 1870; Alfred Howe, builder; 301 Queen St. (NE corner Queen and S. 3rd Sts.)

The 1½-story, mansard-roofed house, built in the Second Empire style popular briefly after the Civil War, was the home of a leading black contractor, member of a family prominent in civic and church affairs.

N. 4th St. and adjacent sites

NH 65 Fire Department and Market, #3
1907–8; Henry E. Bonitz, architect; R. R. Brady, contractor; 602–6 N. 4th St.

In this municipal complex of fire station and city market, architect Bonitz combined a rusticated base and crenellated upper stories to create a castle-like image.

NH 66 St. Andrews Presbyterian Church (Holy Trinity)
1888–89; Adolphus Gustavus Bauer, architect; 520 N. 4th St.

The Gothic Revival church is the chief Wilmington work by architect Bauer, associate of Philadelphia architect Samuel Sloan, who after Sloan's death completed his major works in the state, including the Executive Mansion in Raleigh and the School for the Deaf in Morganton. This ambitious brick church displays Bauer's fearlessly eclectic combination of towers, gablets, arches, rose windows, and ornamental brickwork.

S. 4th St.

NH 67 Wilkinson-Belden House
Ca. 1810, ca. 1885, ca. 1900; 116 S. 4th St.

Porches are important throughout the city's residential architecture. Here the broad, bracketed porch wraps around a spacious, 1½-story, bracketed and vented dwelling, one of several local examples of a smaller

Italianate house. The quiet street has old brick paving and a variety of house types and eras beneath great trees.

NH 68 Cottage Lane

Cottage Lane, as it was known by 1850, extends into the 100 block between S. 3rd and 4th Sts., one of several such lanes and alleys in the city; many of the buildings that once lined them have been lost. Here two important examples of such modest urban buildings still survive. The **Wiley-Williams Cottage** (ca. 1845; 311 Cottage Lane), described by owner Elizabeth Wiley as five or six years old when she insured it in 1851, is a 1½-story frame dwelling with end chimney—probably typical of many that once housed Wilmingtonians. It is especially important as the home of artist Elizabeth A. Chant, who came to Wilmington in 1922. She was not only an important painter in her own right but teacher of Wilmington artists Claude Howell, Henry J. MacMillan, and others. The nearby **Hart Carriage House** (1852; James F. Post, builder; 309 Cottage Lane) is a 2-story brick building with parapet gables. Carriages and equipment occupied the first story, while the upper story served as domestic space, initially probably as slave quarters.

NH 69 Rankin-Orrell House
Ca. 1897; 318 Orange St.

The full-blown, well-preserved Queen Anne style house exemplifies the mode's complex massing, with its insets and projections, including a corner turret, porch, and balcony, complemented by varied textures and abundant turned and sawn decoration.

NH 70 Sutton-Hedrick House
Ca. 1820; 222 S. 4th St.

One of the most intact survivors from early 19th-c. Wilmington and probably typical of what once existed, the simply finished structure is akin to houses in other coastal towns. The 2-story frame dwelling, covered with beaded siding, has exterior end chimneys and a double-slope gable roof that shelters the full-width porch. When insured in 1849, it was noted as "frame, with two piazzas, two chimneys, and 'old.'"

NH 71 Tileston School
1871–72 (John A. Fox [Boston], architect; James Walker, supervising architect; Strausz and Rice, builders), 1910 (Joseph F. Leitner, architect), 1919 (Henry E. Bonitz, architect), 1937 (Leslie N. Boney, architect); 400 Ann St., between S. 4th St. and S. 5th Ave.

The original Italianate section with corbeled brickwork, located at the south of the complex, recalls an important chapter in post–Civil War history, the efforts of northern reformers to assist education in the South. Amy Bradley of Maine arrived in Wilmington in 1866 to offer free education to poor white children. Money for a building came from Mary Tileston Hemenway of Boston, and the architectural design from a prominent Boston architect. Deeded in 1910 to the city, it was expanded as a public school, with additional structures typical of various eras.

N. 5th Ave.

NH 72 St. Stephen A.M.E. Church and Annex
1880–88; Lewis Hollingsworth, architect-builder; 502 N. 5th Ave.

The congregation's history began when Methodist evangelist William Meredith preached in Wilmington in 1798; by 1803 Francis Asbury preached to a fellowship of 878 Africans and a few whites, who founded Front St. Methodist Church. When Wilmington was occupied by Union troops in Feb. 1865, the black members sought to affiliate the church with the national A.M.E. denomination, but this effort failed. In May, 642 black members, most of them newly emancipated, withdrew and established an A.M.E. congregation that met in a wooden church. In 1880 St. Stephen's began construction of a large brick church. Church trustee Lewis Hollingsworth drew the plans, trustee Daniel Lee supplied bricks, and many church members contributed their labor. The late Gothic Revival structure features a tall, spired corner tower and an imposing and severe gabled facade. The magnificent sanctuary, with woodwork executed by church members, features columned balconies with quatrefoil lancet arches and an exposed truss ceiling. The **Annex** built in 1913 in complementary Gothic Revival style provided an important community service facility with medical offices and a swimming pool as well as Sunday school rooms.

NH 73 *Mahn-Holly House*

a bay window projecting from the front gable end, and porches recessed on either side. In 1900 it was the home of May Mahn, widow of a turpentine distiller; later it was the residence of engineer Frank Holly.

NH 74 Von Glahn House and Conoley House

1859, 1852; James F. Post, architect-builder; 19, 15 N. 5th Ave.

These two side-passage-plan houses, built as a pair, exemplify the scale and finish of residences built for the antebellum middle class. Both display the local Greco-Italianate style in stuccoed brick, with classical porches featuring the locally popular Tower of the Winds order, pilasters dividing the three bays, and bracketed, vented cornices beneath broad eaves. No. 19 was built ca. 1859 for Henry Von Glahn, German-born merchant, and now holds city offices. No. 15 was built in 1852 for John J. Conoley, a clerk.

S. 5th Ave. and adjacent sites

NH 72 *St. Stephen A.M.E. Church and Annex*

NH 73 Mahn-Holly House

Ca. 1895; 413 Red Cross St.

The ornate little house presents an unusual melding of narrow form and plan—a doubled shotgun plan—with the ornament and lively massing of the Queen Anne style,

NH 75 Wessell-Hathaway House

1854; James F. Post, builder; 120 S. 5th Ave.

Built for German-born merchant Jacob Wessell by leading local builder James F. Post and soon sold to another merchant,

James Hathaway, this is a solid, frame, 5-bay house in the local Italianate idiom. Construction records include bills for materials and shipping charges for the columns featuring the locally popular Tower of the Winds order. The iron fence is of the same era.

NH 76 H. B. Eilers House
1852; 124 S. 5th Ave.

The brick Italianate house, built for an attorney and merchant in partnership with Jacob Wessell, boasts the city's most spectacular collection of ornate ironwork, including frieze vents, steps, porch, fence, and gate marked with Eilers's name and the year 1852. The contemporary carriage house and slave quarters stand to the rear on Orange St.

NH 77 Richard Price House
1840; 125 S. 5th Ave.

Typical of the city's plainly finished houses of the early and mid-19th c., the 2-story dwelling with center passage was built for Richard and Catherine Price. He was a ship carpenter and later a merchant and harbormaster.

NH 78 The St. Mary Catholic Church
1908–11; Rafael Guastavino, father and son, architects; 220 S. 5th Ave.

NH 78 *The St. Mary Catholic Church*

Built in the Spanish Baroque style by Spanish architect Rafael Guastavino and his son of the same name, the powerfully composed, Greek-cross-plan church displays the firm's famous self-supporting masonry dome of "cohesive construction," made of tile and roofed in ribbed copper. No steel or wood beams or nails were used in construction. The sanctuary sheltered by the great dome is finished with brick walls and ceiling of dazzling geometric-patterned tile. Twin towers, topped with tiled domes, flank the baroque gabled entrance bay. The church is akin to Guastavino's Church of St. Lawrence (1907) in Asheville, where he had come to work at Biltmore. Guastavino's unique self-supporting tile vaulting technique was employed in many of the nation's principal public buildings of the period, but the two N.C. churches are unusual examples of Guastavino designs for entire buildings.

NH 79 Fifth Avenue Methodist Church
1889–90; B. D. Price (Philadelphia), architect; Porter & Godwin (Goldsboro), builders; 409 S. 5th Ave.

The big, brick church, featuring unequal towers recessed on either side of a broad, gabled facade, was designed for the congregation by B. D. Price of Philadelphia, a prolific designer and publisher of Methodist church plans and a leading proponent of the auditorium sanctuary with its curved seating focused on the pulpit. Here, in typical fashion, he combined it with an adjoining Sunday school section; doors between open to create a larger worship space. The fine stained glass was made by local artist E. V. Richards. The church was organized in 1847 by Front St. Methodist Church to accommodate growth on the south side. (See Introduction, Fig. 52.)

NH 80 Fire Station No. 2
1915; James F. Gause Jr., architect; L. H. Vollers, builder; 600 S. 5th Ave.

The robustly eclectic brick fire station is among the most distinctive in town, combining a Dutch or Flemish curved facade gable with heavy Italianate brackets and a campanile side tower. Now an office.

The area east of 5th Ave. developed after the Civil War and is filled with housing from large to small, built for both white and black residents, ranging from workers' cottages to ornate Queen Anne style residences.

N. 6th St. and adjacent sites

NH 81 Sixth St. Truss Bridge
1910–11; DesMoines Bridge and Iron Company; N. 6th St. over railroad tracks

Of several truss bridges that once spanned cuts in and around the city, this is the sole survivor, an excellent example of a Pratt truss.

NH 82 St. Mark's Episcopal Church
1871; Emerson and Fehmer (Boston), architects; Alfred Howe, attributed supervising architect and builder; 220 N. 6th St.

NH 82 *St. Mark's Episcopal Church*

An important southern project by a noted Boston firm, on its dedication in 1875 the Gothic Revival church was described in a national Episcopal journal as "the first Church consecrated in the Diocese for colored people . . . of brick and church-like in style. The designs were furnished by Emerson and Fehmer, of Boston, Mass. The roof is sharp, the chancel recessed, the windows pointed Gothic." Contributions had come from Wilmington and from New York, Boston, and Washington. The Episcopal

Church, unlike other Protestant denominations, reunited its northern and southern dioceses soon after the war. In N.C. the church soon established missions for black members, many of which developed into parishes. St. Mark's was the first of these to erect a church. Donations—and designs—from northern benefactors were common, but this is the only known example by the distinguished Boston firm of William Ralph Emerson and Carl Fehmer. Alfred Howe, senior warden of the first vestry, probably took a leading role in construction.

N. 7th St. and adjacent sites

NH 83 Whiteman House
1899; W. H. Willis, builder; 404 N. 7th St.

The late Queen Anne style house, combining Stick-style and Italianate motifs, a polygonal bay, and an ornate porch, was built for John H. Whiteman, African American businessman, owner of a lumber and coal business, and organizer of the United Charity Association. Whiteman family members became prominent educators here and in South Carolina.

NH 84 Chestnut St. Presbyterian Church
1858; Mr. Moody, builder; 718 Chestnut St.

The small, board-and-batten church combines patternbook Carpenter Gothic and local Italianate motifs. Originally it was painted and sanded to imitate brownstone. It was built by First Presbyterian Church as a mission chapel after a local religious revival and soon became Second Presbyterian Church. In 1867 the church was purchased by the newly formed black congregation, Chestnut St. Presbyterian.

S. 7th St. and adjacent sites

NH 85 Gregory Congregational Church
1880; S. B. Weston, builder; 609 Nun St.

The Gothic Revival brick church, with a gabled facade and tall corner tower, was built as part of the Gregory Normal Institute. It was sponsored by the American Missionary Association, a Congregational group from New England, which in Apr. 1865 sent teachers to establish schools for blacks in Wilmington. Philanthropist James J. Gregory of Marblehead, Mass., aided in construction of new buildings in 1880–81, including a schoolhouse and teacher's home—both lost—and this church.

NH 86 St. Luke A.M.E. Church

1944; Leslie N. Boney, architect; 419 S. 7th St.

In 1944 fire destroyed the twin-towered brick church built in 1878 for a congregation formed in 1861. It was immediately rebuilt along the old lines, with designs supplied by Wilmington architect Boney.

N. 8th St. and adjacent sites

NH 87 Giblem Lodge

1871–73; 720 Princess St. (at 8th St.)

The austere, 3-story masonry building, executed in late Greek Revival style, was built by and for the members of Giblem Lodge No. 2, founded in 1856 as the city's first black Masonic lodge. The lodge hall served as a cultural center, site of the state's first black Agricultural and Mechanical Fair in 1875, the city's first library for blacks, and a city market. Five lodges still meet here.

NH 88 Vertical Lift Bridge

1969; N.C. Department of Transportation; Bridge No. 13 on US 17, Cape Fear River, via Wooster and Dawson Sts.

The big bridge over the Cape Fear River provides a landmark and a fine view of the waterfront. With a vertical clearance of 65 feet above the river, the bridge is 3,033 feet long and has a truss lift span with a reinforced concrete deck on steel girders and prestressed concrete girders. In contrast to the typical drawbridges that break in the middle, here the entire center section of the bridge ascends between the two great towers to allow occasional tall ships to pass.

NH 89 USS *North Carolina* Battleship Memorial

Commissioned Apr. 9, 1941; moored in the Cape Fear, opp. Market St.; National Historic Landmark; open regular hours

In its time the ship was the greatest sea weapon ever built by the United States, the first of the modern battleships and possessor of a venerable record, earning twelve battle stars in all. Sentenced to salvage for scrap in 1960, the battleship was rescued with help from the contributions of N.C. schoolchildren. The battleship memorial is now a popular attraction with a great view of the city, accessible by road or via a short boat ride from the foot of Market St.

Eastern Suburbs:

The eastern suburbs of Carolina Heights, Carolina Place, and Winoca Terrace extend from 14th to 23rd Sts. flanking Market St. They date from ca. 1906 into the 1920s. As in other cities, early 20th-c. entrepreneurs combined several factors—real estate acumen, access to modern sanitation and conveniences, the proximity of trolley lines, residential patterns increasingly segregated by race and class, and popular Colonial and other revival styles of architecture—in creating these new middle- and upper-class suburbs. Wilmington's first suburbs, begun between 1906 and 1911 east of the city, were well established by World War I and essentially completed by the Great Depression. They were laid out in grid plans and served by the trolley line. The outermost came first, then the blocks between them and the old city. In the wake of this first generation of suburbs, subsequent development has continued in similar direction and style to the present.

NH 90 Market St., 1300–1600 Blocks

Along the broad thoroughfare, civic leaders erected some of the grandest houses and institutional buildings. The 1300–1600 blocks reflect the prosperity of the 1920s. Local pride of that era is evident in the massive **New Hanover Co. High School** (1919–25, Leslie N. Boney for W. J. Wilkins, architect; 1307 Market St.), a sand-colored brick facility with lavish glazed tile blending abstract and classical motifs. Similar materials appear in the nearby temple-form, Corinthian porticoed **Trinity United Methodist Church** (1920–21; Leslie N. Boney for W. J. Wilkins, architect; 1403 Market St.); it was built for a congregation that began as a Sunday school in 1889 and met for a time in the *Giblem Lodge building. Some commissions went to out-of-town architects, such as the Georgian Revival style **Hargrove Bellamy House** (1925–27; Northup and O'Brien [Winston-Salem], architects; 1417 Market St.). But local architects still predominated, as seen in the Gothic Revival churches: **St. Andrews-Covenant Presbyterian Church** (1917, 1921; Kenneth M. Murchison Jr. [New York] and James F. Gause Jr., architects; 1416 Market St.); and **St. Paul's Episcopal Church** (1956–58; James B. Lynch and Osborne G. Foard, architects; 1601 Market St.).

NH 91 Market St., 1700 Block

This deeply shaded block of Market St. is lined by an ensemble of Colonial Revival mansions built for the city's newly suburban elite and set in large, landscaped lots. Some were part of the initial building campaign of *Carolina Heights, when Chicago-born architect Burett Stephens designed several residences for developer Mary Bridgers. The brick, Georgian Revival style **Bluethenthal House** (1917; James F. Gause Jr. and James B. Lynch; 1704 Market St.) was built for Herbert and Janet Weil Bluethenthal, of a leading merchant family. The grandly porticoed, brick **Bridgers-Emerson-Kenan House** (1908, Burett H. Stephens; 1909, Joseph F. Leitner; 1923, Carrere & Hastings [N.Y.]; 1931, Leonard Shultze [N.Y.]; 1705 Market St.), begun for Mary Bridgers, neighborhood developer, was later home of Thomas Emerson, president of the Atlantic Coast Line, and of heiress and philanthro-

NH 91 *Bridgers-Emerson-Kenan House, 1700 Block, Market St.*

pist Sarah Graham Kenan, sister of Mary Lily Kenan Flagler and William Rand Kenan Jr. Sarah Kenan had N.Y. architect Thomas Hastings renovate the house when she acquired it, and Leonard Schultze planned the elaborate rebuilding of the interior after a 1931 fire. It is now the residence of the president of the University of North Carolina at Wilmington. The frame, Neoclassical **Bridgers-Brooks House** (1910–11; Burett H. Stephens; 1710 Market St.) was built for Mary Bridgers and then owned by J. W. Brooks, Wilmington wholesale grocer. The columned, frame **Holt-Wise House** (1908–9; Burett H. Stephens; 1713 Market St.), described when new as "of the semi-Colonial style," was built for Edwin C. and Delores Holt. A member of the Alamance Co. textile family, he had come to Wilmington as president of the Delgado Cotton Mills. In 1916 the Holts sold the house to Jessie Kenan Wise, sister of Sarah, Mary Lily, and William Rand Kenan Jr.

NH 92 Carolina Place

Developed from 1906 into the 1920s on the southern side of Market St. and extending from 17th to 23rd Sts., this was the city's first suburban development. Initiated by the American Suburban Corporation of Norfolk, Va., Carolina Place aimed at working- and middle-class residents who would take the trolley to work. As was typical, deed restrictions set a minimum house cost ($1,500), required adherence to the street plan, and prohibited liquor sales or selling of lots to blacks. The densely filled blocks combine a grid with a few curving streets.

NH 92 *Carolina Place*

Houses are typically frame, 1- and 2-story, with boxy forms and various renditions of the Queen Anne with classical detail, the foursquare, and especially the bungalow in every permutation.

NH 93 Carolina Heights

Located on the northern side of Market St. from 17th to 20th Sts. and developed from 1907 into the 1920s, Carolina Heights was planned as a luxurious suburb by Wilmingtonian Mary Bridgers, daughter of Wilmington and Weldon Railroad executive Rufus Bridgers. After beginning her own house on Market St. she bought several blocks to develop as "a delightful and roomy suburb" where minimum dwelling costs went to $4,500 and setbacks were at least 30 feet. Under the hand of Burett H. Stephens and other architects, spacious lots were filled with large Colonial Revival, foursquare, and bungalow houses for leading business and professional families. Prominent among those facing Market St. are the shingled **James O. Carr House** (1908; Burett H. Stephens; 1910 Market St.) and the "Elizabethan" style **Joseph H. Hinton House**

(1912; Joseph F. Leitner; 1919 Market St.) of brick with curvilinear gables.

NH 94 Winoca Terrace

Developed from 1911 into the 1920s, the area north of Market St. between 14th and 17th Sts. filled back toward town. Named by a schoolgirl's patriotic suggestion, WI-NO-CA was developed by the Wright family in a wooded terrain made attractive by the trolley line. Predominantly Colonial Revival houses designed by architects for a fashionable clientele include the **A. S. Williams House** (1915; John Russell Pope [New York], architect; 102 N. 15th St.); the **Thomas H. Wright House** (1927; James F. Gause Jr., architect; 110 N. 15th St.); and the picturesque "Anne Hathaway" style dwelling copied from *House and Garden* for the **Glasgow Hicks House** (1928; William D. Brinkloe [Easton, Md.], architect; 410 N. 15th St.). After the suburbs were established, a number of substantial houses were built in areas between the developments, such as the **Alexander Sprunt House** (1929–30, Arthur C. Nash [Chapel Hill], architect; 1615 Chestnut St.), a massive, brick, Colonial Revival mansion by the architect who worked in similar style at the University of North Carolina in Chapel Hill, a Sprunt family philanthropy.

NH 95 Oakdale Cemetery

1852–present; N end N. 15th St.

Founded by Wilmington businessmen in 1852, Oakdale is the state's first and finest picturesque cemetery, with a rolling landscape, curving pathways, and varied plantings among its clusters of graves. A late 19th-c. observer found it "one of the most beautiful of all the attractive spots which modern taste and sentiment have prepared for the repose of the dead." Originally 65 acres, now 128, the parklike cemetery is dotted with markers that range from simple slabs to imposing mausoleums, many of them imported from urban makers. Highlights include the Confederate monument (1872), Henry Bacon's classical marker (1924), and fine 19th-c. iron furniture, fences, and arches, notably the delicate arched gate to the Hebrew Cemetery (1855).

From the 18th c. onward, Wilmingtonians developed a series of summer communities along the nearby sounds, Wrightsville, Greenville, and Masonboro. Many of their summer cottages still stand, including some with quite lavish grounds. Most are set back behind thick vegetation, visible only from the sounds they were built to enjoy.

NH 96 St. Andrew's on the Sound Episcopal Church

1924; Leslie N. Boney, architect; NE corner US 76 and SR 1411, Wrightsville vic.

The Spanish Colonial style of the stuccoed church with its curved gables provides an exotic accent in the subtropical forested landscape. Successor to *Mount Lebanon Chapel, it was built to serve residents of the Wrightsville, Greenville, and Masonboro soundside communities, long-standing summer retreats for Wilmingtonians.

NH 97 Airlie Gardens

S side SR 1411, 0.5 mi. E of US 76, Airlie Gardens; open regular hours

The gardens, with azaleas, camellias, and dogwoods among lakes and old oaks, were part of an estate owned by Pembroke Jones, a Wilmingtonian rice magnate who with his wife, Sarah, became part of New York and Newport high society of the Gilded Age. (Elsewhere on the Jones's estate, at Pembroke Park, their son-in-law, the architect John Russell Pope, designed a small **Temple of Love** for their garden; it is now a feature of the Landfall development that occupies Pembroke Park.) This section, once the property of Thomas Wright, was bought in 1948 by W. A. Corbett, who called the place Airlie Gardens and opened it to the public.

At the entrance to the gardens stands the tiny, frame **Gatehouse** (1948) built by Corbett. From 1948 to 1974 the gatekeeper was the artist Minnie Evans. Inspired by visions in her dreams, here she made many of the paintings and drawings that eventually gained her a national and international reputation. Many of her works are at St. John's Museum of Art in Wilmington. A focal point in the gardens is **Mount Lebanon Chapel** (1835), which Thomas H. Wright built as a summer chapel for soundside communities, a small, pedimented, frame church with lancet windows.

NH 98 Masonboro Sound

Beginning in the colonial period, Wilmingtonians repaired to Masonboro Sound to escape the summer heat and enjoy solitude or socializing. Their cottages ranged from simple affairs to elaborate mansions, all with broad porches. Fires and storms have taken the oldest cottages, but several stand from the 1870s onward, most of them only faintly glimpsed from the Masonboro Sound Rd. The most distinguished is **Live Oaks** (1912–13; Henry Bacon, architect), a highly original composition by architect Bacon for Walter and Agnes MacRae Parsley. Built of coquina, it is a 2-story, octagonal villa encircled by porches, with a cross-hall plan open to the central cupola.

NH 99 Wrightsville Beach

Wrightsville Beach has a unique history that began as a streetcar commuter beach for Wilmington residents. Wilmingtonians had enjoyed the barrier island's beaches for years and built the Carolina Yacht Club in 1853, but systematic development began in the 1880s when the Wilmington Sea Coast Railway Company built a line from Wilmington and platted 55-foot lots on the island. Cottages were built close together and near the streets in a neighborly grid. Prominent city families typically moved with their servants for extended stays in their cottages. Each morning the businessmen boarded the early train—after a dip in the ocean—to arrive at their city offices by 8:30 for a day's work, "cheered all through the hot day in town by the thought of the cool breezes and breakers awaiting them on their return in the afternoon." Visitors also came out from the city to spend a day at the beach.

In 1902 the steam locomotive railroad was replaced by electric streetcars by the Consolidated Railway, Light, and Power Company, the same firm that in 1904 erected Lumina—a grand dance pavilion still fondly remembered—at the southern end of the streetcar line. Though the tracks are long gone, locations are still given in terms of the line, from Station 1 to Station 7 at Lumina. As development expanded north and south during the early 20th c., life at Wrightsville Beach was changed by a major fire in 1934, a highway bridge in 1935, and removal of the streetcar tracks in 1939. Subsequent development has continued to expand the resort's size and density, with the pace and scale of new construction intensifying in the late 20th c.

Vestiges survive of old Wrightsville Beach. Along the first few blocks of S. Lumina Ave. stand several early frame cottages, 1½ or 2 stories, typically covered with wood shingles, trimmed in white or green, and expanded by porches. A few date from the 1880s and 1890s, and others from the early 20th c. Northward from Stone St. to Salisbury St., where short, narrow streets flank N. Lumina Ave., a number of the original modest, frame, 1- and 2-story cottages with deep porches are tucked among big new houses.

NH 100 Carolina Beach

Settled in the 1880s and incorporated in 1925, the beach resort community possesses an unpretentious vitality. At the town center stand several mid-20th-c. motels, stores, and other buildings of simplified Moderne style: the former **Carolina Beach Town Hall** (1942; sw corner Carolina Ave. and Carl Winner St.), built by the WPA, a 1-story, stuccoed masonry building with stepped entrance pavilion, and the **Ocean Plaza Cafe** (ca. 1944; NE corner Carolina and Harper Aves.). Best of all is the 2-story **Joy Lee Apartments** (1943–45; 317 Carolina Ave. N), a vivid improvisation on Moderne and Art Deco themes built during and shortly after the war by its owners, Mr. and Mrs. Grover L. Lewis, from concrete block they made themselves, and decorated with Mr. Lewis's hand-molded concrete circular motifs composing balustrades, spiral stairs, and fence around the swimming pool.

NH 101 Fort Fisher

1861–65; E side US 421, at SR 1542, Federal Point; National Historic Landmark; state historic site; open regular hours

Built near the southern tip of the peninsula between the Cape Fear River and the Atlantic Ocean, Fort Fisher was the largest earthwork fortification in the Confederacy. Construction began in 1861, and by 1864 the earthen fort extended half a mile across the peninsula and a mile down the beach. Its purpose was to protect the New Inlet access to the Cape Fear River from the blockading Union fleet and thus to keep the port of Wilmington open to Confederate blockade-runners. With the fall of Mobile in Aug. 1864, Fort Fisher became the last important coastal fortification under Confederate control and Wilmington the chief port, supplying Lee's armies in Virginia via the Wilmington and Weldon Railroad, the "lifeline of the Confederacy." On Jan. 15, 1865—after two days of the heaviest naval bombardment of land fortifications known to that date—

Fort Fisher fell. With the Confederacy virtually isolated from the outside world, Lee's surrender at Appomattox came three months later. Long abandoned, the site was used as a military post during World War II and in 1960 was purchased by the state for preservation and interpretation. Although erosion has taken its toll, important elements remain. The parapet is well preserved, and the transverses and gun emplacements still stand. (See Introduction, Fig. 32.)

Brunswick County (BW)

*Of the important cultural and economic centers of 18th- and 19th-c. N.C., ironically it is one of the most powerful—the rice plantations of the Lower Cape Fear—that has most completely vanished from the architectural landscape. The closest rivals to the great plantations of Virginia and South Carolina lay here along the lower reaches of the Cape Fear River, where families of Barbadian and South Carolina background established vast estates and a political power base—and built imposing houses and plantation complexes. With large slave workforces their plantations yielded abundant rice and some indigo in addition to tar, pitch, and timber from the longleaf pine forests. Rice growing along the Lower Cape Fear was renewed after the Civil War, then diminished precipitously in the face of competition from Louisiana and other areas better suited to mechanized production. By the late 19th c. nearly all of the Lower Cape Fear plantation complexes had disappeared. Of the many plantation houses that once lined the river, only *Orton has survived, while the ruins of *Brunswick Town recall the port established by the early colonists.*

Today Brunswick Co. is best known to North Carolinians for its beach communities—Yaupon, Long, Holden, Ocean Isle, Sunset, and most recently Bald Head—which have been built up mostly since 1954, when Hurricane Hazel laid waste to earlier beach housing. Southport, until recently the county seat, and other sites are related to maritime transportation and military history where the Cape Fear opens into the Atlantic.

BW 1 Southport

See Carl R. Lounsbury, The Architecture of Southport *(1979).*

Southport is a pleasant maritime community where canopies of ancient live oaks shelter unpretentious, 19th-c. frame houses. Settled by the late 1740s when Fort Johnston was built at the strategic site near the mouth of the Cape Fear River, it was home to river

BW 1 *Southport*

pilots who guided ships through the Cape Fear's dangerous channels. Platted in 1792 as Smithville, it was made county seat in 1808. In the antebellum period it developed into a summer retreat for Wilmingtonians who came downriver to enjoy healthful ocean breezes. After the Army Corps of Engineers built the *New Inlet Dam (1881) to improve the channel, the town was renamed Southport in anticipation of its becoming a major seaport, and subsequent growth produced its late 19th- and early 20th-c. commercial area and neighborhoods. But rail connections were slow to come, and Southport remained small. It lost county seat status in 1978 when a centrally located courthouse and county government complex was created at Bolivia.

Streets extend in a broken grid along the riverfront, and the first four blocks off the river offer a good collection of regional vernacular building forms spanning over a century.

A few buildings survive from the antebellum era, with changes over the years. Overlooking the river, the **Fort Johnston Officers Quarters** (1805–9; E. Bay St.) is the oldest surviving component of a military installation that dates from 1748. The brick building with a 2-story, hip-roofed central block and 1-story wings has a 1950s portico that replaced a 2-story porch. The antebellum **Brunswick County Courthouse** (ca. 1854; attributed to W. D. Morrell, builder; E. Moore St.) is a plain, brick, gable-fronted building with a 1920s porch and 1960s wings. Next door, the antebellum main block of **St. Philips Episcopal Church** (ca. 1860, 1894–96; E. Moore St.) retains Greek Revival features in its pedimented gable and wide corner boards; in 1894 it gained a bracketed belltower with steeple, and a Gothic window replaced the original central entrance.

Several notable houses line Bay St. overlooking the river. The oldest is the **Walker-Pyke House** (ca. 1800–1820; 239 E. Bay St.), a 2½-story frame dwelling built as a Wilmingtonian's summer home; it features a clipped gable roof, dormer windows, and a later, 2-story porch. Across the street, the **Brunswick Inn** (1859; 301 E. Bay St.) comprises two frame houses of traditional 2-story form joined in an H-plan, with a full-width, 1-story porch and simple Italianate details suggesting Wilmington influences; it takes its name from its late 19th-c. tenure as a fashionable hotel, though it has resumed its original use as a private residence. Especially prominent is the **Thomas M. Thompson House** (ca. 1868; 216 W. Bay St.), built shortly after the Civil War for the owner and captain of a blockade-runner—one of few such adventurers who made it through the war without losing his ship or his life. The large, cubical frame house continues Italianate motifs popular in the Lower Cape Fear in the antebellum period, with bracketed eaves, a 2-story porch, and a cupola atop the shallow hip roof.

Most of the building stock in the town's historic core dates from the late 19th- and early 20th-c. building boom. Local builders continued familiar 1- and 2-story house forms with occasional flourishes of sawn and turned ornament. Among the most distinctive small houses of this period are the **Samuel Swain House** (1889; 106 W. Moore St.), a bracketed, gable-fronted, frame house with a matching gabled and bracketed porch, described when new as a "tasty cottage"; the **James Pearce House** (1877, 1893; 406 Brunswick St.), a vernacular tri-gable form with fish-scale shingles and lancet windows in the gables; the **Richard Dosher Sr. House** (1889; 112 N. Lord St.), a square-plan cottage built for a river pilot, with a low, bracketed, pyramidal roof in a form that recurs frequently across town.

Several larger, 2-story houses show Queen Anne and Colonial Revival influences. The rambling, 2-story **Adkins-Ruark House** (1890; 119 N. Lord St.) has steep, shingled front and side gables that flare out over deep cornices, and bay windows and bracketed porches echo motifs in the gables. The house was built for E. H. Adkins, a river pilot whose grandson, journalist and author Robert Ruark, spent much of his childhood here. The **A. E. Stevens House** (1894; A. E. Stevens, builder; 319 Atlantic Ave.) is a house of idiosyncratic form, with a steep roofline rising two full stories over a recessed porch and a second-story gabled projection overhanging the sidewalk, all embellished with turned and sawnwork ornament.

Major institutional buildings of the turn of the century include the **Masonic Lodge** (late 19th and early 20th c.; 203 E. Nash St.), a large, frame, temple-form structure with a pedimented portico; **Trinity Methodist Church** (1890; Henry Daniel, builder; 211 E. Nash St.), the town's finest Carpenter Gothic building, graced by a pair of towers with belfries and spires; and the former **Brunswick County Jail** (1904; E. Nash St.), a 2-story, brick building with iron bars in the segmental-arched windows. The jail is owned by the local historical society and open by appointment.

The early 20th-c. commercial district of 1- and 2-story brick storefronts extends along Moore and Howe Sts. The 2-story, 6-bay **Smith Building** (ca. 1925; 107–9 E. Moore St.), with its applied stone pilasters, is the largest and most elaborately ornamented commercial building. The former **Amuzu Theater** (1918; 111 N. Howe St.), a landmark known to generations of vacationers at nearby beaches coming to town for evening entertainment, takes the prize for the best-named movie house in the state.

BW 2 Oak Island Lighthouse and Coast Guard Station

Near end of NC 133, both sides of road, Southport vic.; lifesaving station (1889), private; lighthouse (1958), no public access

The U.S. Lifesaving Service established a station here near the mouth of the Cape Fear River in the late 1880s toward the end of the first phase of lifesaving station construction along the N.C. coast. When the U.S. Coast Guard, successor to the Lifesaving Service, erected a new station in 1932, the original 1½-story building was sold and moved to the south side of the road to serve as a private beach cottage. It shares elements found in the first group of stations erected in the picturesque cottage mode, with board and batten sheathing the upper half, kingpost ornament in the steep gables, and a small observation tower. The Coast Guard station on the north side of NC 133 remains an active lifesaving facility; in 1992 a modern building replaced the 1932 station.

Navigation lights were introduced to Oak Island by the late 1840s to supplement the lighthouse on *Bald Head Island across the mouth of the Cape Fear River. Rising behind the Coast Guard station, the present **Oak Island Lighthouse** (1958) is the principal beacon at the mouth of the Cape Fear River. It is the newest lighthouse in the United States and was the second most powerful light in the world when completed. The straight-sided, cylindrical form of the 169-foot reinforced concrete tower is in marked contrast to the tapered profiles of the 19th-c. brick lighthouses up the coast. The concrete was tinted during construction to create the three wide horizontal bands of gray, white, and black.

BW 3 Fort Caswell (N.C. Baptist Assembly)

1827–1940s; end of NC 133, Southport vic.; private, limited public access (see note)

Now serving as a religious retreat, the complex of fortifications and other buildings reflects developments in military architecture from the early 19th c. to World War II. Of particular interest is the impressive grouping of Colonial-Revival-influenced housing and other support buildings erected in the first decade of the 20th c., one of the last major collections of this class of standardized military design in the country.

The eastern end of Oak Island was of strategic military importance because it overlooks the primary channel into the Cape Fear River. In the early 19th c. the federal government selected the site as part of a network of permanent, state-of-the-art defenses on the Atlantic coast that also included *Fort Macon. Fort Caswell was begun in 1827 and named for Richard Caswell, the first governor of the state of N.C. (1776–80). Initial construction was supervised by Maj. George Blaney of the U.S. Army Corps of Engineers. After his death in 1836, work resumed under Lt. Alexander J. Swift and was completed in 1838.

The original brick and stone fort, of which only sections survive, was roughly pentagonal in shape and protected by a moat. The cross-shaped inner citadel contained living quarters and storerooms. At the beginning of the Civil War the fort was seized by the Confederates, who held it until Jan. 1865, when Union forces captured *Fort Fisher at the other inlet into the Cape Fear (cf. *New Inlet Dam). With the fall of Fort Caswell imminent, the Confederates blew up the powder magazines in their retreat, leaving the fort heavily damaged.

The fort stood ungarrisoned until a rebuilding program began in 1895 and was hastened by the Spanish-American War in 1898. Several new batteries of reinforced concrete were constructed at points along the beach, including one at the site of the old fort, which was further destroyed by the new emplacement. Beginning in 1898 a complex of some two dozen large frame buildings was erected in a broad sweep across the grounds for housing and other support functions. Based on standard plans issued by the Quartermaster General's Office, most buildings are 2 stories tall, with 1- or 2-story porches often wrapping two or more sides. Plans vary, frequently with pro-

BW 3 *Fort Caswell*

jecting bays and complex rooflines reflecting late Queen Anne influences, while details are generally Colonial Revival, with repeated use of Palladian windows and simple classical details.

Fort Caswell served as an artillery training center during World War I and a submarine tracking station in World War II. In the late 1940s the installation was declared surplus and sold to the Baptist State Convention of N.C., which converted the property to a summer religious retreat. While the original fort and the later batteries are ruins, most of the early 20th-c. buildings have been maintained for new uses. Note: Public access is limited to the off-season, when the facility is not in use by Baptist groups.

BW 4 Bald Head Island/Smith Island

At mouth of Cape Fear River; accessible by passenger ferry from Southport (no automobiles)

For generations this wooded island at the mouth of the Cape Fear River was inhabited only by wildlife and the keepers of the lighthouses that have stood here. Known for most of its history as Smith Island after Thomas Smith, who acquired it in the early 18th c., it is now commonly called Bald Head, a name originally applied only to the round, sandy expanse of its southwestern edge. The southernmost tip of the island is Cape Fear, beyond which lie Frying Pan Shoals, a treacherous shelf that stretches 20 miles into the sea and inspired mariners' fears that gave the cape its name.

The island's strategic location among the shoals at the river's mouth has made it a site for lighthouses since 1794. The present **Bald Head Lighthouse** (1817; Daniel S. Way, builder), is the oldest in the state, a 110-foot octagonal tower of brick faced with stucco and trimmed with brownstone. Its walls ta-

per from about 5 feet thick at the base to about 3 feet at the top. Their weathered texture enhances the lighthouse's image of strength prevailing through countless storms. The light originally had fifteen lamps and reflectors, but these have been removed, and the lighthouse is no longer operational.

In 1903 the Light House Board replaced the old lighthouse with a 159-foot steel tower, called the Cape Fear Lighthouse. Although that lighthouse was destroyed when a new lighthouse was built across the channel on Oak Island in the 1950s, three cottages with simple, Stick-style detail remain of the **Cape Fear Lighthouse Complex** (1903). Lighthouse keeper "Cap'n Charlie" Swan and his two assistants occupied the buildings as the only inhabitants of the island for three decades. Long abandoned, the

BW 4 *Bald Head Lighthouse*

cottages have been restored as part of the recent resort development.

Initiated in 1970, low-density resort development on the island has been regulated by architectural and environmental guidelines intended to ensure harmony with the setting and protect natural features and wildlife. Some 10,000 acres of wetlands are preserved as natural areas. Automobiles are prohibited, and transportation is by electric vehicles. The golf course (1970s; George Cobb, landscape architect) integrated within the overall development is considered by many to be one of the most beautiful in the country.

BW 5 New Inlet Dam and Swash Defense Dam (The Rocks)

1875–81, 1883–89; Henry Bacon Sr., chief engineer; accessible from the northern end at Fort Fisher (New Hanover Co.)

The two massive seawalls of rock, totaling over 3 miles in length, number among the state's greatest 19th-c. engineering achievements. New Inlet opened during a storm in 1761, creating a dangerous second inlet to the Cape Fear River and the port of Wilmington. During the Civil War, Confederate blockade-runners protected by the guns of *Fort Fisher darted through the inlet. After the war, the Army Corps of Engineers proposed a seawall to close off New Inlet and force the river's full flow through the old channel between Smith Island and Oak Island, thus deepening the channel and allowing portage of larger ships at Wilmington. Construction began in 1875 under the supervision of Henry Bacon Sr., a Massachusetts native who had spent most of his life building railroads in New England and the Midwest. (His son, architect Henry Bacon Jr., spent his boyhood years in Wilmington during the project and later designed the Lincoln Memorial as well as several works in N.C.)

The first completed section, called the New Inlet Dam, is almost a mile long, as much as 120 feet wide at the base, up to 37 feet high, and contains over 180,000 cubic yards of stone. Workmen laid the foundation by extending rafts of logs and brush,

BW 5 *New Inlet Dam and Swash Defense Dam*

called mattresses, in sections across the water and sinking them with stone. Shell rock was added until the barrier was high enough to be finished and capped with large pieces of granite. The second dam, called the Swash Defense Dam, connects Zeke's Island and Smith Island and was constructed afterward to avert the possible opening of yet another inlet south of the first dam. It is over 2 miles in length but less massive than the New Inlet Dam. The dams have withstood the elements with only minor repairs and still serve their original purpose.

Note: There is pedestrian access to the New Inlet Dam from Battery Buchanan at *Fort Fisher. Visitors may walk along the dam at low tide but are advised that they could become trapped offshore at high tide.

BW 6 Brunswick Town and Fort Anderson

Founded 1725, abandoned by 1830, fort constructed 1862; SR 1333, S of Orton Plantation; state historic site; open regular hours

The 18th-c. town of Brunswick thrived as a colonial port and the residence of royal governors, but it was largely abandoned at the beginning of the Revolution and lay in ruins by 1830. Stabilized as a state historic site, its remains evoke a distant time: the walls of the colonial church and the exposed foundations of other buildings within a riverside forest dense with Spanish moss.

Brunswick was laid out about 1725 by Maurice Moore of South Carolina, who with his brother Roger of *Orton established great plantations on the Lower Cape Fear River. Leaders in the colony resided in the port town. Gov. Gabriel Johnston took office here in 1734, and in 1758 Gov. Arthur Dobbs occupied a house called Russellborough. After Dobbs's death in 1765, Gov. William Tryon resided at Russellborough until he completed construction of *Tryon Palace in New Bern. In 1765 a group of local colonists surrounded Russellborough to protest the Stamp Act, placed Tryon under house arrest, and successfully thwarted local implementation of the Stamp Act.

By the late colonial period, Wilmington, located 15 miles upstream, had eclipsed Brunswick, which was plagued by hurricanes, humidity, and mosquitoes, so that there were few residents when the British burned the town in 1776. Some families returned after the Revolution, but the site was deserted and in ruins by 1830, and in 1842 Brunswick was sold to the owner of *Orton plantation. Toward the end of the 19th c., however, as patriotic veneration of colonial sites mounted, Brunswick gained attention as a colonial town and the site of the Stamp Act resistance, and political and cultural leaders initiated pilgrimages and commemoration of the site. In 1952 the Sprunt family, owners of *Orton, donated the Brunswick property to the state for preservation as a historic site.

Archaeological investigations and contemporary descriptions indicate that the 1- and 2-story houses of Brunswick had some of the state's earliest known uses of the broad, full-width porch or piazza, a distinctive feature that became characteristic of coastal architecture. The form is believed to have developed from European, Indian, and African influences in the West Indies. The **Maurice Moore, James Espy**, and **Hepburn Reanolds House Ruins** showed evidence of such porches. **Russellborough**, which Governor Tryon described in detail in 1765, stood 2 stories above a raised basement and measured 45 by 35 feet, with four rooms per floor, plus "a Piaza Runs Round the House both Stories of ten feet Wide with a Ballustrade of four feet high, which is a great Security for my little girl."

The great ruin of **St. Philip's Church** (1754–68, burned 1776) symbolizes Brunswick's former prominence. (See Introduction, Fig. 23.) The most ambitious colonial church in N.C., it was burned by the British and never rebuilt. Its 22-foot-tall, uncovered brick walls indicate its grand scale. Gov. Arthur Dobbs may have had a hand in planning the building. As an engineer and surveyor-general of Ireland he had supervised construction of the Parliament House in Dublin and other public buildings. The church is rectangular in plan, 76 feet long and 56 feet wide, with arched windows and entrances at the western end and sides. The brickwork is Flemish bond above an English-bond water table, with fine rubbed, gauged brick in the arches. A Venetian chancel window in the eastern end, 15 feet high, dominates the church.

During the Civil War the Confederates built an earthen defensive work called **Fort Anderson** (1862) over part of the town site. The fort was abandoned under heavy bombardment by the U.S. Navy after the fall of *Fort Fisher and *Fort Caswell in 1865. Well-preserved mounds offer vantage points from which to view the remains of the old town.

BW 7 Orton

Ca. 1730, ca. 1840, 1910; Kenneth M. Murchison Jr., architect; Robert Swann Sturtevant, landscape architect; entrance E side SR 1529, opp. SR 1530, 0.5 mi. S of NC 133; 0.8 mi. drive to office on private road; grounds open to public; house is private

BW 7 *Orton*

Epitomizing the romanticized ideal of the grand southern mansion, Orton is the lone survivor of the great plantations that once flourished along the Lower Cape Fear River. Initially the planters produced mainly naval stores from the pine forests, then turned to large-scale rice cultivation. Maurice and Roger Moore, sons of Gov. James Moore of South Carolina, established vast estates (9,210 and 12,780 acres patented, respec-

tively) on the Lower Cape Fear in the 1720s. In 1734 a traveler to the locality described his visit to the home of Roger Moore, "the chief gentleman in all Cape Fear," whose brick house half a mile from the river enjoyed a fine view of Brunswick. Moore's brick house is believed to constitute the core of the present house. The plantation is said to be named for the town of Orton in the English Lake Country. When "King" Roger Moore died in 1750, his estate included 250 slaves, an extraordinary number in colonial N.C. Orton was owned in the early 19th c. by Benjamin Smith, governor of N.C., until financial reverses forced him to sell the place, "one of the most valuable rice plantations in the country."

Dr. Frederick Jones Hill, who purchased the plantation in 1826, later enlarged it to its present Greek Revival temple form with monumental Doric portico, a rare instance of this type in N.C. domestic architecture. By the eve of the Civil War, Orton plantation contained 9,000 acres and produced a half-million pounds of rice annually. Neglected after the war, the house was adapted as a hunting retreat by Kenneth M. Murchison, a Fayetteville native and New York businessman. After Murchison's death, his daughter, Luola Murchison Sprunt, and her husband, Wilmington civic leader and historian James Sprunt, renovated the house with the assistance of her brother, New York architect Kenneth M. Murchison Jr., and added flanking Colonial Revival wings. The romantic classical composition gained widespread fame as an icon of Old South architecture. The Sprunt family also transformed the rice fields into a bird refuge—using some of the old ditches and drains to flood the fields for the autumn migrations—and created magnificent gardens designed in part by Robert Swann Sturtevant of Massachusetts.

Hertford County (HF)

HF 1 Winton

Established as county seat in 1766 and named for landowner Benjamin Wynns, Winton was burned by a Union force on Feb. 20, 1862—the first total destruction of a town in the Civil War. Although the town resumed its role as county seat after the war, it never regained its former prosperity. The oldest buildings date from the turn of the century.

At the southern end of Main St. is the **Calvin Scott Brown School**, a public elementary school complex established by Calvin Brown as Chowan Academy in 1886. A recent graduate of Shaw University in Raleigh, Brown came to the county as minister at *Pleasant Plains Baptist Church and saw a need for a school for local black students. In 1923 the school was incorporated into the county system as the sole black high school in the county. It was renamed in 1943 for Brown, its founder and longtime principal, who distinguished himself as an educator and clergyman, serving as president of both the State Teachers Association and the State Baptist Convention. The chief early building is **Brown Hall** (1926), a small, handsome Colonial Revival auditorium building with portico and simple classical detailing.

HF 1 *Brown Hall*

The most prominent residence in town is **Gray Gables** (1899; N. Main St.), a big Queen Anne style house with a corner tower, shingled gables and bays, and wraparound porch with elaborate millwork—fabricated by Winborne and Rea, Edenton "Manufacturers of Building Material," and brought here by boat. It was built for James S. Mitch-

ell II, son of Ahoskie area planter William W. Mitchell. After service in the Confederacy, James, like many of his generation, moved to town, where he established a grocery that provided supplies and credit to farmers.

HF 2 Parker's Ferry
SR 1306 and SR 1175 across Meherrin River

One of only three small river ferries in the state, Parker's Ferry has been operated across the Meherrin River since the early 20th c. Crossing the river by ferry evokes bygone eras of waterborne travel.

HF 3 Harrellsville

The crossroads community, originally a landing on the Wiccacon River, contains a variety of white frame houses and other buildings from its turn-of-the-century heyday, when it had seven general stores, two fisheries, and two gristmills. At the crossroads of NC 45 and SR 1002 stands the 2-story, frame **Mason and Son Store** (1905), a well-preserved country store with decorative shingling emphasizing the tall gable front, a shed porch sheltering the recessed entrance, and, inside, traditional shelves stocked with a multiplicity of goods. In the outlying countryside beside the Chowan River, on NC 45 and on secondary roads including SR 1441, SR 1438, and SR 1437, there are a number of 2-story frame farmhouses, particularly I-houses, usually with shed porches and rear shed rooms, which along with their clusters of frame outbuildings recall the neighborhood's 19th-c. agricultural prosperity.

HF 4 Bethlehem Baptist Church
1902; Willis Hofler (Gates Co.), builder; SW corner NC 561 and SR 1427, Harrellsville vic.

In this distinctive gable-fronted church the boldly sculpted tower features three gables, one atop the other, amplifying the geometry of the triangular-headed doors and windows and lozenge decorations. The congregation was formed in 1835 from Ahoskie Baptist Church. For this, the congregation's third church on the site, the builder's contract specified a "nice, handsome, workmanlike building" to cost $375. Across the road is the **Adkins House** (mid-19th c.; private), a Greek Revival frame house with a 2-story central portico.

HF 5 Ahoskie

The town began in the 1880s with the arrival of the Norfolk and Carolina Railroad and the logging boom in southern Hertford Co. The sawmill village that sprang up near the old Ahoskie Baptist Church and the Mitchell family's farm was incorporated by 1893 and given an old Indian place name. While the old plantation culture in the northern section declined, the railroad invigorated the forested, swampy southern section. Boosted by the 1899 establishment of a big sawmill by the Branning Manufacturing Company, which also had mills in Edenton and Columbia, Ahoskie eclipsed *Murfreesboro as the county's business center. Black and white families moved from depressed farming areas to find work. "These people came here with the idea of making money," recalled one oldtimer. "They were not bound by tradition nor awed by aristocracy. The place had no vested interests to defend the status quo, and no status quo to defend."

Ahoskie's commercial, institutional, and residential architecture of the early 20th-c. boom era focuses on the cluster of ambitious commercial architecture at **Main St. and Railroad St.**, facing the railroad tracks. At the corner is the Beaux Arts classical **Bank of Ahoskie** (1926; N. Railroad at Main St.), faced in limestone with its entrance inset beneath an arch. Wrapping around it, the 3-story, brick **Garrett Hotel** (1923–26; 201 W. Main St.) presents facades on both Railroad and Main Sts.; it was erected by leading local builder J. R. Garrett. Across Main St. the **Farmers-Atlantic Bank** (1918; 119 W. Main St.) is a boldly rendered Beaux Arts classical bank in red brick and limestone with Doric

columns in antis. The 3-story **Mitchell Hotel** (1910; 131–35 W. Main St.) is one of the largest of several Italianate commercial buildings. The former **U.S. Post Office** (1940; Louis A. Simon, supervising architect of the Treasury; 201 W. Main St.), now the town hall, typifies the modest, red brick, Colonial Revival architecture of public works post offices.

HF 5 *Bank of Ahoskie and Garrett Hotel*

The residential streets north and south of Main St. include simplified Queen Anne and Colonial Revival style residences, period cottages and Craftsman foursquares, and especially robust Craftsman bungalows in brick and frame. The boom years also produced many blocks of simply finished I-houses and gable-sided cottages as well as the 2-story, gable-fronted, side-passage-plan houses, such as those built by a single developer in the 400 block of **N. McGlohon St. N. Maple** and **N. Catherine Sts.** and **N. Catherine Creek Rd.** are among the principal concentrations of houses built for black families in this era—cottages, bungalows, and shotgun houses as well as larger residences in popular styles.

On the south side of town stands the **McGlohon-Mitchell House** (ca. 1830s; Drew Holloman, attributed builder; 233 W. South St.), the farmhouse of Dr. Jesse H. Mitchell, who sold much of the land for the town of Ahoskie and became its first mayor. The 2-story frame house has simple Federal and Greek Revival detail akin to the *William W. Mitchell House and others in the area attributed to a free black carpenter named Drew Holloman; frame outbuildings include a dairy and a smokehouse.

HF 6 William W. Mitchell House

Ca. 1832; Drew Holloman, attributed builder; N side NC 42, 0.2 mi. E of NC 11, Ahoskie vic.; private, visible from road

HF 6 *William W. Mitchell House*

Once the center of a 1,500-acre plantation, the prominent I-house, five bays wide with a center-passage plan, displays transitional Federal to Greek Revival detail. Tradition and stylistic evidence credit its construction to free black carpenter Drew Holloman. The many outbuildings include an office and a schoolhouse. A strong Baptist and supporter of education, William W. Mitchell was a founder of the Chowan Baptist Female Institute (1848) in *Murfreesboro and helped keep it afloat after the Civil War.

HF 7 James Newsome House (Wynnewood)

Ca. 1830; Drew Holloman, attributed builder; W side NC 11 opp. NC 42, Ahoskie vic.; private, visible from road

The 2-story, hall-parlor-plan plantation house with simple Federal style detail related to the nearby *William W. Mitchell House is likewise attributed to free black carpenter Drew Holloman. Outbuildings include a former slave house, a smokehouse, a barn, and other structures. The dwelling was the center of a plantation of some 1,100 acres, with from 150 to 300 acres under cultivation for corn, sweet potatoes, grains, peas, and by 1860, five bales of cotton; swine and cattle ranged the woods.

HF 8 Union

Site of a tavern as early as 1770, the crossroads had a post office named Union by

HF 8 *Union*

1833. Of architectural interest is the cluster of late 19th-c. houses of locally distinctive character near the junction of NC 461 and SR 1108. Like several other houses built in *Murfreesboro, *Woodland (Northampton Co.), and elsewhere, these frame houses combine conservative forms with exuberant millwork including bracketed cornerposts, sawnwork porches, bracketed eaves, spiral-curled bargeboards, and openwork gable decorations. Probably derived from *Bicknell's Village Builder* (1870), their idiosyncratic execution shows kinship with the late work of Jacob Holt, a prolific builder in antebellum Warrenton, N.C., and postwar Chase City, Va., whose protégés may have remained in the region.

HF 9 Pleasant Plains Baptist Church and Pleasant Plains Rosenwald School

Early, mid-20th c.; E and W sides US 13 at SR 1132, 1.3 mi. S of NC 461, Pleasant Plains

The center of a venerable rural black community, Pleasant Plains is described as having had a free black Baptist church as early

HF 9 *Pleasant Plains Rosenwald School*

as 1845. After the mid-19th-c. frame church burned, the present **Pleasant Plains Baptist Church** was erected in 1949—a substantial, brick church in Gothic Revival style, with its pair of unequal towers rising to crenellated caps and flanking a gable with two Tudor-arched entrances.

The frame **Pleasant Plains Rosenwald School** was one of the first Rosenwald schools built in the county. Grants from the foundation established by philanthropist Julius Rosenwald, president of Sears, Roebuck, and Co., in cooperation with educator Booker T. Washington of Tuskegee, aided construction of over 800 public schools for blacks in N.C. between 1917 and 1948—more than in any other state in the South. The neatly detailed frame building takes a form seen in a few other schoolhouses of the era, with a gable-fronted center section topped by a belfry and larger rear section with classrooms on either side. In 1963 the building was renovated as a community center.

HF 10 The Cedars

Ca. 1830; NW side SR 1167, 0.4 mi. SE of NC 11, Murfreesboro vic.; private, visible from road

Like houses in *Murfreesboro, the hip-roofed, frame plantation house displays unusually stylish Federal elements, including a modillion cornice, transoms with fan tracery, and central portico. An off-center passage is flanked by two large rooms heated by exterior end chimneys. Mid-19th-c. outbuildings include a large plank smokehouse dated 1842. Its early history is uncertain, but since 1860 the farm has descended through the Browne family.

Murfreesboro (HF 11–13)

Established in 1787 at William Murfree's plantation landing and ferry site on the Meherrin River near its opening into the Chowan River, Murfreesboro was developed by William's son, Revolutionary War officer Hardy Murfree. The town on its high, healthful river bluff, prophesied a visitor in

1786, was "destined to become a commercial emporium, as large quantities of tobacco & other produce finds its way to the Landg from Virginia & this state." Like many Federal period entrepreneurs, Hardy Murfree envisioned ambitious internal improvements to transform trade routes and promote commerce—in this case a long canal to siphon trade from above the rapids of the Roanoke River, across Northampton Co. to his wharves on the Meherrin and thence to seaport markets. Although Murfree's vision was never realized, in the 1790s Murfreesboro prospered. Designated as an official port of entry in 1790, it profited from triangular commerce among N.C., the West Indies, and New England. Entrepreneurs from New England, especially Boston, were drawn here, including merchant and shipbuilder William Rea, members of the Wheeler family, and others. Taking an interest in educational as well as commercial aspirations, the New Englanders joined with native residents to establish the first of several local academies in Murfreesboro.

Murfreesboro weathered economic ups and downs tied to regional and national currents. In 1807, his dream of a mercantile city thwarted, Hardy Murfree left for Tennessee, where a new town of Murfreesboro—briefly the capital of the state—was named for him. His son, William Hardy Murfree, stayed in N.C. and was elected to the U.S. Congress. For a time Murfreesboro enjoyed trade that crowded the streets with wagons bearing produce from as far as the Blue Ridge and brought so many ships to its wharves that "one could cross the river on the decks of vessels lying in the stream." In 1810, a visitor found the town of about 500 people "a very flourishing place," with ten stores and two taverns and merchants doing "a great deal of business." Several stylish brick houses were under construction as well as "a very large and elegant Brick Academy." After the War of 1812, however, Murfreesboro's fortunes sagged, its energies sapped by illness and westward migration: in 1823 even William Murfree left to join his family in Tennessee.

The town revived briefly amid the general agricultural prosperity of the late antebellum era. Local education blossomed with the building of two denominational schools in the early 1850s, the Wesleyan Female College and the Chowan Baptist Female Institute (predecessor of present-day Chowan College). Their massive buildings were among the biggest construction projects in the state at the time. The contractor, Albert Gamaliel Jones of Warren Co., also built local residences in his sturdy Greek Revival style.

After the Civil War, the "quiet and moral village" of "cultured and refined people" hung on as a small port and academy town but saw its fortunes wane while towns along the new rail lines burgeoned. The Wesleyan Female Institute burned in 1893 and Chowan College closed in 1943. In the 1960s and 1970s, efforts began to reopen the college and attract new businesses, and in reaction to losses of its historic buildings, especially in the downtown, the town became an early focus of state preservation attention. Several 19th-c. buildings have been restored, and some are open to the public. In the late 20th c. various old houses have been moved to new sites in Murfreesboro from the outlying countryside and from other sites in town.

HF 11 Roberts-Vaughan House

Early 19th c., mid-19th c.; 130 E. Main St.; open regular hours as visitors' center

The big, richly detailed late Federal and early Greek Revival house epitomizes the mercantile panache of antebellum Murfreesboro. Merchant Benjamin Roberts probably built the 2-story eastern portion in the first decade of the 19th c.; its original configuration is uncertain. About 1835 merchant Uriah Vaughan expanded the house to a double-pile plan with center passage and portico. The tall Doric portico and elaborate cornice of pierced dentils, guilloche molding, and modillions present a virtuoso display of antebellum carpentry. The interior is equally rich in its show of woodgraining and marbling. Illustrating the domestic complexes common in early 19th-c. towns are several outbuildings, including an office, a carriage house, a kitchen, and especially notable, a

two-cell outbuilding, which incorporates a dairy with sawn vented cornice.

HF 12 The Columns

1851–52; Albert Gamaliel Jones; Chowan College Campus

HF 12 *The Columns*

The centerpiece of Chowan College, the massive, 3-story building of stuccoed brick was one of the largest of several big Greek Revival edifices erected during a statewide boom in denominational schools and academies. It was built for the Chowan Baptist Female Institute (est. 1848) by Warren Co. builder Jones, who also erected main buildings at Wesleyan Female College (main building destroyed) and present-day Louisburg College in Louisburg, N.C. Here the mass of the building is emphasized by a full-width portico of eight fluted Doric columns, and a big octagonal cupola caps the low hip roof.

HF 13 Broad St. Historic District

Murfreesboro's oldest buildings, recalling its Federal era mercantile heyday, are scattered along Broad St. and nearby streets in a small district extending along the Meherrin River parallel to Main St. Some have been restored, furnished, and opened as house museums. In a region long dominated by frame construction, this is one of the few concentrations of early 19th-c. brick architecture outside New Bern. High-quality, Flemish-bond brickwork characterized the buildings of ca. 1810, while 1:3 common or American bond appeared by the late Federal era, ca. 1815–1820.

The **John Wheeler House** (ca. 1810; 403 E. Broad St.; open to public) is a 2-story Federal style house of Flemish-bond brick, embellished with a cornice of pierced dentils and a fanlight over the front entrance; the 2-story porch dates from the mid-19th c. When the house was constructed ca. 1810 for William Hardy Murfree and his business partner George Gordon, it included a store, but after Wheeler bought the place in 1814, he rearranged partitions to form the present center-passage plan for entirely domestic use. Wheeler married three times and had nineteen children. Several children and grandchildren attained prominence, including his son John Hill Wheeler, a political figure and historian, and his grandson, historian and novelist John Wheeler Moore. Nearby is a freestanding brick dependency (ca. 1820), built in 1:3 bond brickwork; interpreted as a dining room, it was one of several dependencies that once stood here, including a kitchen. Also in the yard is a dovetailed plank outbuilding moved from the countryside—an accessible example of this important regional construction method.

HF 13 *John Wheeler House*

The **Morgan-Myrick House** (ca. 1820; 402 Broad St.) is a sturdy, 2-story, brick dwelling in 1:3 bond, set on a high basement and featuring a corbeled cornice beneath its hip roof. It was built for merchant James Morgan, who left in 1830 for Texas—and, some say, owned the beautiful slave Emily Morgan, who inspired the song, "The Yellow Rose of Texas." The **Worrell House** (1877; 401 E. Broad St.) across the street is a delectable frame cottage built by a lumberman for his daughter and known locally as the "Gingerbread House" for its vivid sawnwork. Most remarkable are the flat porch

HF 13 *Worrell (Gingerbread) House*

posts cut out to depict standing figures. The neighboring 2-story, brick **Southall House** (ca. 1815–20) is among the earliest houses in town with 1:3 bond brickwork. It was later owned by lumberman E. W. Worrell.

Several early brick buildings stand on nearby Williams St. The **Rea Store** (ca. 1800; E. Williams St.; open to public) is one of the oldest commercial buildings in N.C., a 2-story, Flemish-bond brick structure under a hip roof, with flush-paneled doors and other features that display the neat, plain workmanship typical of the purpose. The store was built for William Rea, a Boston merchant engaged in Murfreesboro–New England trade who with his brothers outfitted several ships at Murfreesboro. To the rear stands the **Winborne Law Office** (1872; 4th St.), a gable-fronted, board-and-batten commercial building moved here from Main St. The 1-story, Flemish-bond **Peter Williams House** (ca. 1810; private) exemplifies the smaller houses of the Federal era. The small, brick **Murfree-Smith Law Office** (early 19th c.; Williams St.; open to public), also neatly finished with Flemish-bond brickwork and dentil cornice, was built for the Murfree family and has been a law office, post office, school, and jail.

HF 13 *Rea Store*

Farther up Broad St., the **Hertford Academy** (1810; 200 E. Broad St.; open to public) is a 2-story, Flemish-bond brick building that housed a local academy chartered in 1809. Here in 1848 began the Chowan Baptist Female Institute, which in 1852 moved to *The Columns. **Melrose** (ca. 1810, mid-19th c. and later additions; 100 E. Broad St.) was originally the smaller, 2-story brick home of businessman and politician William Hardy Murfree; after he left for Tennessee, the house was enlarged and eventually received its Ionic portico.

Two notable Greek Revival houses stand nearby on Wynn St. The **Pipkin-Harrell-Chitty House** (1820s, 1850s; attributed to Albert Gamaliel Jones; 207 N. Wynn St.) is a symmetrical, 2-story, frame house expanded from an earlier dwelling. Its large-scale Greek Revival detail and "spool" corner-posts typify the work of builder Jones, contractor for *The Columns. The **Camp House** (early, mid-19th c.; w side N. Wynn St., 1 block N of Broad St.), a big, Greek Revival house with broad portico, was moved here from Broad St.

Several early houses stand north of Broad St. toward the river, including some that were moved from various sites and extensively restored. The **Cowper-Thompson House** (ca. 1790; 405 North St.), on its original location, presents a house form seen more often in Virginia, 1½ stories with five dormers across the gable roof and a center-passage plan one room deep. The **"Overseers House"** (1840s; NE corner North and 4th Sts.) shows the Greek Revival style in a 1-story, hip-roofed version. Other local clusters of 19th-c. architecture moved to new sites include a subdivision along Jay Trail southwest of the town center.

HF 14 Como

The chief landmark of the farming community is the **Buckhorn Baptist Church** (1913; SW corner US 258 and SR 1316), one of the most striking of the region's highly individualized Gothic Revival country churches. The

HF 14 *Buckhorn Baptist Church*

well-kept church possesses great architectural presence that derives from its unusually grand scale, dramatized by an enormous pinnacled tower. Located on a site associated with an 18th-c. Anglican chapel, it was built for a congregation established in 1835 from the old Meherrin Baptist Church during a period of evangelism.

The adjoining village of Como possesses an appealing cluster of late 19th-c. houses, many quite small but ornately finished in Italianate and Queen Anne styles, and complemented by plantings, fences, and outbuildings. An academy operated near the church ca. 1840–1915, serving the surrounding rural community and giving the village a certain luster.

Nearby, a stand of magnolias, a long avenue of pecan trees, and a white picket fence create an ideal setting for the **Vernon Place** (late 1820s, early 20th c.; NW side US 258, 0.2 mi. NE of SR 1316; private, visible from road), still the center of a large farming enterprise. Built for Richard Green Cowper, politician and cotton planter, the T-plan house is finished in simple Federal–Greek Revival style, while its Colonial Revival porch and most of the outbuildings are early 20th c.

Around the Como community, the area bounded by the Meherrin and Chowan rivers and the Virginia line encompasses an old rural neighborhood with plantation houses spanning the 19th c. A scenic byway runs through this agricultural landscape, and several farms and farmhouses of interest line the loop of roads formed by SR 1320, SR 1315, and SR 1310 west of US 258.

Bertie County (BR)

BR 1 Windsor

The small town on the Cashie River was settled by 1722, when Bertie Co. was formed from Chowan Co. Located on the Gray family plantation and known first as Gray's Landing, the community was made county seat in 1774 and named for the English castle. It was seat of a long-settled rural county, which included some of N.C.'s largest plantations, most notably those along the Roanoke, Chowan, and Cashie rivers. Today Windsor is a quiet community with architecture dating principally from the 19th and early 20th centuries. Brick commercial buildings of the early 20th c. are concentrated in the 100 block of S. King St. In the grid of shaded streets flanking King St., predominantly frame residential architecture ranges from Federal and Greek Revival dwellings to Queen Anne and Colonial Revival houses and bungalows.

Anchoring the commercial district is the **Bertie County Courthouse** (1887, 1906, 1939; NW corner King and Dundee Sts.), built as a brick, Italianate structure described at its cornerstone laying as a "magnificent temple of justice . . . commensurate with the demands of this age of progress"; it gained a portico and wings in 1906 and 1939, respec-

tively. South of the courthouse stands the **Confederate Monument** (1896), erected by local veterans and featuring a soldier atop a tapered pillar.

The **Freeman Hotel** (ca. 1840–50; E side York St. at Granville St., moved 1981 from Granville St. at Queen St.) is a rare survival of an antebellum frame commercial building, a 2-story structure with Greek Revival details, pedimented gable ends with fanlights, and a 2-tier porch. **St. Thomas Episcopal Church** (1839; 207 W. Gray St. at Queen St.) began as a small, frame, Greek Revival church and later gained lancet windows and other Gothic Revival features. **Cashie Baptist Church** (1910), on the opposite corner, is a large, twin-towered brick church in Romanesque Revival style, built on the site of its 1854 frame predecessor.

Among the varied residential streetscapes, one of the strongest concentrations lies along S. King St. In the 200 block, for example, a sequence of early 20th-c. houses includes the **Matthews House** (ca. 1920; 204 S. King St.), a Southern Colonial mansion with Corinthian portico, which contrasts with two bungalows and a Queen Anne style dwelling built for members of the Madre family at 206, 208, and 210. The **Gray-Gillam House** (ca. 1790; 305 S. King St.) and the **J. B.**

BR 1 *Matthews House and S. King St.*

Gillam House (ca. 1790; 401 S. King St.) are both 2-story frame houses with double-shouldered, Flemish-bond chimneys. Typical of early town life, both stand flush with the sidewalk.

BR 2 Rosefield

1786–91; Gilbert Leigh, builder; 1855 additions; N side US 17, S edge of Windsor; private, visible at a distance from road

BR 2 *Rosefield*

Rosefield, a plantation house at the southern edge of town, is still owned by descendants of John Gray, who acquired the land in 1729. The town of *Windsor was established on part of the plantation. The frame house is one of the few 18th-c. houses in the region whose builder is documented. Like many planters' dwellings it began small: the 3-bay section to the east, 2 stories with a single room and a passage on each floor, finished in simple Georgian style, was built by Gilbert Leigh, who in 1786 contracted with Stevens Gray to build the 28-by-18-foot house, "to be done in a good workmanlike manner what belongs to a carpenter & Joiner." Leigh, a master builder active in Edenton and the Albemarle area, may also have executed the 2-story, 2-bay addition a few years later. The house has grown with subsequent generations of the Gray family. The front porch and a 2-story rear ell were added in 1855. A family cemetery and outbuildings remain.

BR 3 Windsor Castle

Ca. 1858, ca. 1908; 209 W. Watson St., 1 block E of NC 308, Windsor; private, visible from road

The antebellum plantation house built by one generation was aggrandized by the next

with an early 20th-c. classical portico evoking the glories of the Old South. Patrick Henry Winston, who came to Bertie Co. as a schoolteacher and became a successful lawyer, bought part of the old Gray family plantation in 1858, retained its nickname "Windsor Castle," and soon built the 2-story frame house in Greek Revival-Italianate style. Here he and his wife, Martha Byrd, raised four accomplished sons: George T. Winston, president of present N.C. State University, the University of Texas, and the University of North Carolina; Robert W. Winston, judge and author; Patrick H. Winston Jr., newspaper publisher and attorney general of Washington; and Francis D. Winston, leader in the Democratic party campaigns of 1898 and 1900, judge, and lieutenant governor. Francis D. Winston continued to reside at Windsor Castle and ca. 1908 added the Colonial Revival portico with full-height Ionic columns.

BR 4 Liberty Hall

1850s; S side SR 1108, 0.1 mi. W of SR 1100, Grabtown; private, visible from road

The massive, frame house epitomizes the growing architectural ambitions and plantation wealth of the antebellum period. The 2-story, double-pile house stands high on a raised basement and is treated in sturdy Greek Revival style with paired windows and hefty corner pilasters and porch pillars. The plantation house was erected for Lewis Bond, who soon moved to Tennessee. In 1868 it became the home of Lucy Rascoe Outlaw and her husband, David Outlaw, a planter, lawyer, politician, and U.S. congressman. It remains in the family.

BR 5 Thomas Bond House

Early 19th c.; N side NC 308, 0.4 mi. NW of US 13 BYP, Windsor vic.; private, visible from road

This prominent example of the tall, neatly detailed, Federal period I-house features handsome double-shouldered, Flemish-bond brick chimneys. The unusual enclosed entrance porch was an early addition.

BR 6 Elmwood

Mid-19th c.; W side SR 1101, 0.5 mi. S of NC 308, Windsor vic.; private, visible from road

In contrast to the verticality of the nearby Bond house, Elmwood presents the broad proportions of the Greek Revival style, and features a pedimented porch and gables. The original side-passage-plan dwelling was expanded to form a center-passage plan two rooms deep. An antebellum kitchen and dairy stand to the rear. The house was first the home of the Watson family, later the Madre family, in which it remains.

BR 7 Hope Plantation

1796–1803; end of SR 1114, SW side NC 308, 4.0 mi. NW of Windsor; open regular hours

BR 7 *Hope Plantation*

An outstanding site, both for the spectacular plantation house itself and for its meticulous restoration, Hope was built for David Stone as the seat of the 1,000-acre plantation he received from his father on his 1793 marriage to Hannah Turner. The couple had eleven children, five of whom died in infancy. David Stone, educated at the College of New Jersey (now Princeton University), served as governor of N.C. (1808–10) and U.S. senator (1812–14). He owned more than 8,000 acres here and in Wake Co. and as many as 139 slaves who cultivated wheat, corn, and other crops.

Displaying Stone's exceptional wealth and sophistication, the 2-story, frame structure stands on a high brick basement with a deck-on-hip roof and porticoes on both front and rear. Chinese lattice railings enclose the deck and porticoes. The overall form with 2-tier

main entrance portico follows a Palladian-influenced scheme, somewhat akin to the earlier Miles Brewton House in Charleston. David Stone owned builders' guides by both Abraham Swan and William Pain, copies of which are in his library, and certain details of the house indicate inspiration from these.

The unusual plan is adapted from plate XLI in Abraham Swan's *British Architect* (1758ff.), which Swan noted as having been adapted from Palladio. As employed by Stone, the layout creates a strong sense of procession from the yard to the porch to the passage, and thence up to the principal rooms. On the first floor, front and rear entrances open into a broad central passage between asymmetrically disposed flanking rooms—a parlor and a dining room on the east and two chambers on the west—heated by exterior end chimneys. A wide but surprisingly simple enclosed stair rises from the passage to the second story, which contains a large ballroom—opening onto the upper portico—and a smaller library lined with original glazed bookcases for Stone's more than 1,400 books. One of the oldest surviving service stairs in the state—along with that in the *John Wright Stanly House in New Bern—provides discreet access between floors and the kitchen and storage areas in the raised basement.

By the mid-20th c. the house had fallen into decay. Its dramatic restoration has been the work of the Historic Hope Foundation. Furnishings include a superb collection of early regional pieces, arranged to conform with Stone's estate inventory. Outbuildings are being reconstructed or acquired, including an early frame smokehouse and a dovetailed plank outbuilding. Moved to the site from northern Bertie Co. is the **Samuel Cox House** (ca. 1800), a typical small, hall-parlor-plan farmhouse adapted as a caretaker's house.

BR 8 King-Bazemore House

1763 (date brick); on grounds of Hope Plantation; open regular hours

This fine early house, with the hall-parlor plan prevalent in the region from the early 18th to the mid-19th centuries, is one of

BR 8 *King-Bazemore House*

N.C.'s best examples of a modest-sized, colonial house open to the public. The gambrel roof, hall-parlor plan, and full shed porch and rear shed rooms are characteristic of substantial mid-18th-c. dwellings in northeastern N.C. and the Chesapeake. The house is one of only two gambrel-roofed houses in N.C. with brick end walls (cf. *Myers-White House, Perquimans Co.). The end walls, laid in Flemish bond, contain interior chimneys with T-shaped stacks—a feature seen more often in Virginia than in N.C. Chimney bricks are inscribed with the building date and the initials of William and Elizabeth King, members of the county's rising planter class.

The dwelling is finished in restrained Georgian style and displays the highest quality carpentry of its time and place. The main room or hall features paneled wainscoting and a fully paneled end wall with built-in, glazed cupboards flanking the mantel. The parlor also features a paneled end wall, but here the fireplace is flanked by closets. The upper chambers are more plainly finished. The arrangement of regional period furniture, based on an estate inventory, depicts the original use of the plan, with the multi-function hall entered directly from the front and rear porches. From the hall one may enter the more private parlor used as sitting room and bedchamber, or mount the enclosed stair to chambers above. In 1974 the long-vacant house was given by the Bazemore family to the Historic Hope Foundation and moved 5 miles to *Hope Plantation for restoration. Outbuildings moved and restored here include an early frame smokehouse.

BR 9 Republican Baptist Church
Early 20th c.; NE side SR 1225, opp. SR 1247, Republican

A double-towered, frame country church, one of a number of large, dramatically composed churches in the northern coastal plain, features a tall spire countering the symmetry of the facade.

BR 10 King-Freeman-Speight House
Early 19th c. and later; SW side NC 308, 1.9 mi. SE of SR 1247, Republican vic.; private, visible from road

This farmstead is best known as the birthplace of the landscape painter Francis Speight, who returned to eastern N.C. late in his career and painted many Bertie Co. scenes, including this place. The unusual dwelling consists of two separate houses. The earlier one, ca. 1800, evolved in phases from a 1-story, hall-parlor dwelling, a form to which it has been returned recently. The second house, ca. 1830, set at right angles to the first, is a 2-story, Federal style structure with a parlor and side-passage plan. The house retains such early 19th-c. details as tapered porch posts and original paint and woodgraining. A smokehouse, a kitchen, and a 2-room schoolhouse or office survive.

BR 11 Woodville

Woodville was one of several plantation neighborhoods in the Roanoke Valley where interconnected families of planters and slaves formed a rural community. Several 19th-c. plantation houses running south to north along NC 11/42 illustrate facets of Federal and Greek Revival rural architecture. All are private, and those cited are visible from the road. Probably the oldest is the **Bazemore House** (ca. 1800; NW corner NC 11/42 and SR 1128), a small coastal cottage with engaged porch and double-shouldered chimneys. More elaborate is the **Pugh-Urquhart House** (1801; W side NC 11/42, opp. SR 1128), a tripartite Federal style house with 1-story wings flanking a 2-story, pedimented central block. It was built for Whitmel Hill Pugh, one of several local planters who subsequently moved to the sugar cane lands of Louisiana.

This plantation was called Woodville and gave its name to the larger community. The **Yellow House** (early 19th c.; E side NC 11/42, 0.1 mi. S of SR 1120), 2 stories tall and five bays wide with a locally prevalent L-plan and rear service stair, was built for William Alston Pugh and remained in the family until 1945. **Grace Episcopal Church** (mid-19th c.; SE corner NC 11/42 at SR 1120) is a small, frame church with belltower and Gothic Revival windows, set in an extensive churchyard. The **Averitte-Pugh House** (mid-19th c.; NE corner NC 11/42 and SR 1109) repeats the broad proportions and hip roof typical of the antebellum era, enriched by paired windows with Italianate hood moldings.

BR 12 St. Frances Methodist Church

1845; Thomas Bragg, attributed builder; N side NC 308, 0.4 mi. W of NC 11/42, Lewiston

The frame church, moved from Woodville to Lewiston in 1896, is one of the few surviving works attributed to regional builder Thomas Bragg, a native of the New Bern area who worked for a time in Warrenton, then moved to Northampton Co. His sons became a governor, a general, and an architect. The simple Greek Revival church has a fine interior with fluted Doric columns carrying a curved gallery; the bracketed entrance tower is slightly later. The old cemetery is still maintained in Woodville. There are plans to move the church again, to *Hope Plantation.

BR 13 Pineview

1838; Joshua Brown, builder; E side SR 1205, 0.3 mi. N of NC 308, Roxobel vic.; private, visible from road

Constructed by its owner, carpenter-farmer Joshua Brown, after his return from a stint in construction in Mississippi, this L-shaped house typifies the middling range of antebellum plantation houses, with its 3-bay, 2-story form, hall-parlor plan, and rear ell finished with conservative Federal details. The complex including a dairy, smokehouse, kitchen, and office continues in the family as the center of a working farm.

BR 14 Oaklana

Ca. 1827; Mr. Bazemore, carpenter; NW side SR 1249, 1.2 mi. NE of SR 1208, Roxobel vic.; private, visible from road

The 2-story, central-passage house with rear ell takes a form typical of the region. Planter Perry Cotten Tyler built the house soon after he purchased the property in 1825, replacing a house erected in the mid-18th c. on land granted to William Whitfield in 1722. Named for the trees in the yard, Oaklana has descended in the Tyler family. A large smokehouse of dovetailed planks and a small dairy survive.

BR 15 Aulander

The little railroad town retains its rows of 1- and 2-story brick commercial buildings, some with corbeled cornices and pilasters. Notable among the modest frame houses is the **Jenkins House** (late 19th c.; 105 Harmon St.), a symmetrical, picturesque cottage in the spirit of A. J. Downing, with a tall, steep, front roof gable accentuated by a lancet window, a decorated porch, and side bay windows. The town (inc. 1885) grew up around a sawmill on the Norfolk and Carolina Railroad during the late 19th c. logging boom. The story goes that it was named Orlando but was spelled phonetically to distinguish it from the Florida town.

BR 16 Askew-Felton-Harrell House

1819 (date brick); E side NC 45, 0.1 mi. S of SR 1332, Colerain vic.; private, visible from road

This is a dated example of an important regional form, a 2-story, 3-bay house with hall-parlor plan, shed porch, and rear shed rooms. The surviving double-shouldered end chimney contains a brick carved with the date 1819.

BR 17 Ashland

Ca. 1830s; E side NC 45, 0.25 mi. N of SR 1360, Ashland; private, visible from road

The big, 2-story frame house near the highway features stylish Greek Revival detail including a broad porch with Doric columns.

Like several local plantation houses, the 5-bay, L-plan dwelling contains a secondary service stair in the 2-story rear ell. The house was built for Augustus Holley, who named his 1,100-acre plantation on the Chowan River in honor of Henry Clay's home in Lexington, Ky.

BR 18 Capehart's Baptist Church
1918; SE side SR 1364, 0.1 mi. SW of NC 45, Taylors Store vic.

One of several local country churches with unusually dramatic facade and tower treatments, Capehart's Baptist Church expresses the early 20th-c. prosperity of a congregation begun in 1824. Despite new siding, the building maintains a strong architectural presence, with twin towers framing a porch recessed beneath a trio of arches with drop pendants.

BR 19 Holy Innocents Episcopal Chapel
Ca. 1880; N side SR 1502 at dead end, Merry Hill vic.

The tiny Gothic Revival structure was erected as a family chapel by Mary Capehart of Avoca plantation shortly after her husband died, leaving her a widow with seven small children—hence the name of the chapel. There being no Episcopal church in the immediate community, this served as a chapel of ease, with occasional services held by ministers from Windsor or Edenton. The Capehart house at the huge soundside Avoca plantation has been taken down, but the chapel has been maintained by the family. It captures the picturesque quality of the Gothic Revival in diminutive form, with slender lancet windows and sharply pointed roofs accentuating the three units of vestibule, nave, and chancel.

BR 20 Scotch Hall
Ca. 1838; SE side SR 1511, 3.3 mi. E of NC 45, Merry Hill vic.; private, visible from road

The seat of the largest antebellum plantation (8,000 acres) in Bertie Co., the 2-story, frame house overlooks the mouth of the Roanoke River where it opens into the Albemarle Sound. Scotch Hall was the setting of the 1851 novel *Bertie*, by George Throop, a tutor of the Capehart children, which gives a vivid account of antebellum plantation life. The house, built for George Washington Capehart, is a substantial but unpretentious late Federal style house with center-passage plan. The land facade has a small, pedimented porch, while the river front has a full-width shed porch. The plantation, known as Scots Hall by 1726, was bought in 1811 by George's father, Cullen Capehart. The Capeharts' vast riverside plantations produced corn, cotton, livestock, and beans, and the family also operated a fishery. Scotch Hall remained in the family until the late 20th c.

BR 21 Sans Souci Ferry
SR 1500 across Cashie River, 1.8 mi. S of NC 308

Known after an old plantation with an enticingly carefree name, the cable-drawn free ferry operates at an old and picturesque ferry location. The ferry is especially well known because of the series of views painted in different seasons by the artist Francis Speight, a Bertie Co. native.

BR 22 Charlton-Jordan House
Ca. 1738; private, no public visibility or access

Exemplifying the first durable buildings erected in N.C., this important, early brick house on the northern bank of the Roanoke River is similar in form to the *Newbold-White House in Perquimans Co. (1730) and Virginia examples. Its compact form and resplendent brickwork are characteristic of

BR 22 *Charlton-Jordan House*

N.C.'s finest buildings of the early and mid-18th c., an era from which nearly all the other structures have vanished. Notable features include the Flemish-bond brick walls with all glazed headers, segmental-arched openings, a high English-bond foundation, and interior end chimneys with T-shaped stacks. The dwelling follows a 3-room plan; its interiors were lost in a fire. The dwelling is thought to have been built about 1738, the year William Charlton sold to Joseph Jordan the 300-acre tract "on which I now liveth," along with "the plank and brick that was got or procured for the use and furnishing of the Dwelling house." Jordan owned the property until his death in 1776.

BR 21 *Sans Souci Ferry*

Martin County (MT)

*The rural county offers diverse country routes that lead through a varied landscape of farmland and small towns. Along the Roanoke River, in the northern and western part of the county, an antebellum plantation economy flourished, with kinship and architectural ties with neighboring Halifax and Bertie counties, which was followed after the Civil War by extensive reliance on the tenant system. The southern section, with different soils and settlement patterns, tended toward smaller farmsteads, best seen in the *Farm Life community. In contrast with some northern coastal plain counties where many farming areas have become depopulated, Martin Co.'s rural landscape is still occupied with working farmsteads.*

MT 1 Williamston

The trading center and county seat on the Roanoke River was incorporated in 1779 on a plantation called "Skewarkey" and named for William Williams, an officer in the American Revolution. Williamston is a thriving, middle-sized town, which retains typical 19th- and early 20th-c. architecture, concentrated in the grid-plan center. The former **Martin County Courthouse** (1885–87; E. Main St.) is the principal 19th-c. landmark, a symmetrical, brick building with front entry tower and bold corbeling, rendered in an Italianate style unique among the state's surviving courthouses. The **Main St. Commercial District** offers a solid row of early 20th-c. brick buildings, accentuated by the little **Bagley Building** (1830; 117 E. Main St.), a rare survival of a pedimented, frame, 1-story store in Greek Revival style. The **City Hall** (1960; Charles C. Benton [Wilson]; 106 E. Main St.), one of the last works of an architect best known for his Colonial Revival designs, presents a crisply

geometric example of small-town modernism, with its facade dramatized by an off-center clock tower and aluminum trim. The **U.S. Post Office** (1938; Louis A. Simon; 121 E. Main Street), a red brick WPA building in Colonial Revival Style, features a mural depicting the Wright Brothers' first flight (1940).

Late 19th- and early 20th-c. residential areas include Main and Church Sts. Williamston's oldest house is the **Asa Biggs House** (1835–65; 100 E. Church St.; open limited hours). The frame house of Federal and Greek Revival styles was built as a 2-story, side-hall plan dwelling for Asa Biggs and his wife, Martha Elizabeth Andrews; they enlarged it over the years to accommodate their family of ten children. Biggs was a lawyer, congressman, U.S. senator, and judge. One of the county's best examples of Greek Revival domestic architecture is the **Cushing Biggs Hassell House** (1847; Albert Gamaliel Jones, builder; 138 Church St.; private). Jones, a prolific Warren Co. builder who also worked in Williamston and in *Murfreesboro, displayed his distinctive style in the 2-story, hip-roofed house with Doric cornice and large, bull's-eye cornerblocks.

MT 2 Sunny Side Oyster Bar

1930, 1935; 1102 Washington St., at US 17/64/13 BYP, Williamston

A venerable and lively part of eastern N.C.'s tradition of local oyster bars, the little gable-fronted frame structure was built in 1935 on the southern side of C. T. Roberson's grocery store to increase business. Named for its

MT I *Martin County Courthouse*

sunny exposure, the oyster bar maintains its trademark simplicity and singleness of purpose. The back room is the oyster bar itself, with zinc counters, sawdust on the floors, and gleaming tongue-and-groove sheathed walls and ceilings. Open only during oyster season; everyone comes, do not expect elegance.

MT 3 Skewarkey Primitive Baptist Church
1853; SW of jct. US 17 and US 17/64/13 BYP, Williamston

The congregation, organized ca. 1780, is mother church to many in the region, where the Primitive Baptist faith thrived in the 19th c. Now surrounded by commercial development, the gable-fronted, frame building maintains the simplicity typical of Primitive Baptist meetinghouses, including plain pews and a gallery.

MT 4 Jamesville

The small town beside the Roanoke River began in the 18th c., but its oldest buildings are the frame dwellings and brick stores from the late 19th and early 20th centuries, when the Jamesville and Washington Railroad, locally known as the "Jiggle and Wiggle," and later rail connections boosted trade. The **Jamesville Primitive Baptist Church** (1865–70; E side NC 171, 0.2 mi. S of US 264) was built by the minister, Clayton Moore, a local landowner whose house was burned during the Civil War and who moved into the previous church with the promise of building a new one. The simple, gable-fronted, frame building is now used by the Jamesville Woman's Club. A famous local institution is the **Cypress Grill** (1936, 1948; S side Roanoke River, 0.1 mi. N of Water St.), a small, frame building overlooking the river. Here in about 1936 William R. Roberson built with his friends a 1-room riverside party house, where they held fish fries from the river's seasonal bounty of herring, rockfish, and sturgeon. Soon popular demand led to its becoming a restaurant, which burned in 1946 and was rebuilt by Roberson's son Red, who still owns the place. Open only when the fish run in early spring and attracting everyone for miles around to eat fried fish and hushpuppies, the grill is a tasty bite of social and eating history.

MT 5 Lilley Family Industries and Farms
Late 19th–early 20th c.; jct. SR 1516 and SR 1521, and SR 1114 just W of SR 1516, Williamston vic.; private, visible from road

At the crossroads where two generations of the Lilley family operated rural industries, a cluster of buildings evokes an aspect of the rural economy now seldom surviving. By 1880, at the **Kader Lilley Farm**, Kader Lilley had established a cotton gin and a steam-powered lumber and gristmill, and by 1884 he had added a general store. Early in the 20th c. his sons opened a woodworking shop and a lumbering business as well as a second general store, built in brick. Although some of the frame industrial buildings have deteriorated, the handsome, 2-story, brick store remains one of the county's prime examples of its type, along with the substantial, four-square, Lilley residence with wraparound porch. Other Lilley family farms and farmhouses extend out from the crossroads. Just south at SR 1114 lies the **Sylvester Lilley Farm**, established by one of Kader Lilley's sons ca. 1910; along with a 1½-story frame house is an outstanding complex of frame tobacco barns, a grading house, a mule barn, packhouses, and other outbuildings the family built as part of their tobacco farming enterprise.

MT 6 Farm Life District
Early 20th c.; both sides NC 171, and W along SR 1530, Roberson Store vic.

The large, rural neighborhood in the southeastern part of the county is located in an area that was dominated by subsistence farming until the late 19th c., when the introduction of tobacco growing brought new profits and supported construction of new farm buildings. In contrast to the plantation section along the Roanoke River, here farmers had small holdings averaging 50 to 75 acres. Families raised tobacco as the chief cash crop but also continued to produce food crops for

MT 6 *Roberson Farm*

their own sustenance. The Farm Life area possesses a distinctive quality defined by the unusual compactness of its farmsteads and the orderliness of its farm landscape. Frame barns and other outbuildings are gathered in tight courtyards around unpretentious, well-kept, frame farmhouses or aligned in rows extending from the house to the road. One of the finest examples is the **Roberson Farm** (NE corner NC 171 and SR 1540), where a tidy quadrangle of frame barns leads to a symmetrical, frame I-house, and more barns reach out to the rear. An early center of community life was **Smithwick's Creek Primitive Baptist Church** (1897; N side SR 1106 at SR 1516), an austerely plain, frame meetinghouse; a small, frame **Baptismal House** stands beside the creek nearby. The educational centerpiece was the **Asa Manning Farm Life School** (1922; E side NC 171, 0.4 mi. S of SR 1530), a sturdy brick structure with a big belvedere. (See also Introduction, Fig. 35.)

MT 7 Smithwick-Green Farm

Early 19th c.; W side US 17, 1.3 mi. N of SR 1106, Corey's Crossroads vic.; private, visible from road

One of many 19th-c. I-houses lining US 17 south of *Williamston, this is a prominent and well-preserved example of the county's Federal period plantation houses. The house is believed to have been built for the Smithwick family and was acquired in the late 19th c. by John and Araminta Green, in whose family it has remained. The tall, frame I-house has a center-passage plan heated by double-shouldered end chimneys, plus a shed

porch and rear shed rooms. The Greens added the long kitchen-dining ell to the rear early in the 20th c. as well as building the cluster of agricultural buildings behind the house.

MT 8 Bear Grass Primitive Baptist Church

Early–mid 19th c.; N side SR 1001 E of SR 1106, Bear Grass

The pristine Primitive Baptist Church has paired front entrances in the gable end and generous windows along the sides lighting the simply furnished interior. Bench pews in three ranks are separated by two aisles, and additional pews flank the pulpit. Men and women traditionally sat separately. The congregation was formed in 1828 from *Skewarkey Church near Williamston.

MT 8 *Bear Grass Primitive Baptist Church*

The community of Bear Grass (named after a spiky local plant) comprises a pleasant grouping of frame houses and general stores. The centerpiece is the early 20th-c. brick **Bear Grass School**. Local pride is accentuated by the late 20th-c. figurative sculptures by local artist Henry C. Cowin, including a life-sized, upright bear in front of the school; a figure of George Washington across the street; and a military monument elsewhere in town—all part of the county's lively tradition of artistic expression.

MT 9 Everetts

Following US 64 brings the traveler through this cluster of handsomely detailed, brick commercial buildings beside the Atlantic Coast Line Railroad (now part of CSX Trans-

MT 9 *Barnhill's Store*

portation System). **Barnhill's Store** (1905; NE corner N. Broad St. and US 64), continuously owned by the Barnhill family, is the largest of these structures, rich with corbeled brickwork trim and retaining its wooden ceiling and old shelves. The **Simon Everett Store** (ca. 1880s) beside the railroad is another neatly finished general store. A line of small, frame houses faces the railroad. Everetts evokes the crucial role of such small railroad crossings in the increasingly market-oriented farm economy of the late 19th and early 20th centuries. The village had at its zenith two banks, a dry goods store, a general merchandise store, and a soda shop. Standing along the roads near Everetts are many tenant houses owned by the Barnhill family, who painted them all "Barnhill yellow."

MT 10 Robersonville

The pleasant market town was incorporated in 1870 and about 1880 became a station on the Atlantic Coast Line Railroad (now the CSX System). Robersonville focuses on the classic scene of turn-of-the-century frame houses overlooking the tracks that bisect the community. These range from Italianate to Queen Anne to Colonial Revival and bungalow modes, but all share broad porches, a fine vantage from which to watch the trains go by. A village of 300 people before the county's first tobacco market opened here in 1900, by 1920 Robersonville had grown to a town of nearly 1,200.

Tobacco prosperity supported construction of the **Main St. Commercial District**, where solid blocks of brick commercial buildings are punctuated by two banks indicative of the town's early 20th-c. prominence: the former **Farmers Banking & Trust Company** (1921; now the town hall), a dignified, classical vault bank with Ionic columns in antis, and the former **Bank of Robersonville** (ca. 1910), a 3-story, brick building—"skyscraper number 1" in its day—with a columned corner entrance and pilasters rising to a broad entablature. The simple, Romanesque Revival style **First Christian Church** (1913; Main St.) is a red brick building with corner tower opening into an auditorium plan with Akron-plan Sunday school. The oldest building in town is **Stonewall Lodge No. 296** (1871; Main St.), a simplified Greek Revival style frame building with a belltower atop the hip roof; it has served as a multipurpose community building as well as a lodge over the years.

MT 10 *Robersonville, view along Railroad St.*

The **Robersonville Primitive Baptist Church** (1910; sw corner Outerbridge and Academy [US 64] Sts.; open limited hours) typifies small-town versions of the denomination's architecture, with its central entrance tower providing a bit more flourish than the plain rural meetinghouses; it now holds a regional museum of folk art. From the same era are several big, columned, Southern Colonial houses typical of the early 20th c., with an especially prominent pair facing each other at the junction of N. Main and Academy Sts.: the **W. J. Little House** on the southwest and the **Roberson House** on the southeast.

MT 11 Hassell Area Rural Neighborhood
Early–late 19th c.; NC 142, E and W of Hassell

Highway 142 is one of the most interesting of several routes in the county where farmhouses of many eras line the road, standing alone or among clusters of outbuildings. Some of these are vacant and decaying; others are well maintained. The typical forms are symmetrical, center-passage-plan I-houses and 2-story, side-passage-plan dwellings; many have restrained Federal or Greek Revival detail, end chimneys of brick, and shed porches. The **Sherrod-Ethridge Farm** (ca. 1810–20; N side NC 142, 0.8 mi. E of NC 11) is an especially good example, a 3-bay I-house with neat Federal detail, accompanied by an early smokehouse and a schoolhouse. The **Sherrod-Best-Ethridge**

House (ca. 1810–20; s side NC 142, 1 mi. E of SR 1002) presents a similar form with a 20th-c. rear ell; its cadre of outbuildings includes a flower house, a washhouse, a corn barn, and a smokehouse from the late 19th and early 20th centuries.

The neighborhood also offers several examples of the hall-parlor or center-passage house of 1½ stories with engaged porch and shed rooms, the regional coastal cottage form. Many 1-story, frame, tenant houses still stand from the early 20th c., usually of two-room, center-chimney type, some taking an L-plan, others repeating the linear plan of the simplified bungalow. Outbuildings include symmetrical, single-bay, frame barns, corncribs, and, most numerous though fast dwindling, log and frame tobacco barns of the early 20th c.

The **Ballard-Salsbury-Eubanks Plantation** (early and late 19th c.; N side NC 142, 0.3 mi. W of SR 1002) is one of the county's most complete farm complexes, centering on a 1½-story, frame, Federal style house with side-passage plan, which was transformed into a Gothic Revival cottage in the late 19th c. with dormers, bargeboards, and a sawnwork porch. Notable among the many outbuildings are two plank structures— a kitchen and a smokehouse—and frame buildings including a tenant house, a carriage house, a schoolhouse, a corn barn, and tobacco barns. The house was probably built ca. 1810 for Joseph and Elizabeth Ballard, and in 1842 the place was sold to James Salsbury, in whose family it remained for many years.

MT 11 *Ballard-Salsbury-Eubanks Plantation*

MT 12 Roanoke River–Oak City Rural Neighborhood

Somewhat more remote than the other rural drives in the county, a loop into northwestern Martin Co. traverses an evocative landscape of plantations and tenant farms—sweeping up NC 903 northwest of *Hamilton, and thence back by way of SR 1332 and NC 125, with a side trip on secondary roads southwest of NC 125. There is a strong sense of continuity from the antebellum plantation economy—whose large, conservative, frame houses still stand in various conditions of repair—and the tenant system that developed as successor after the Civil War, reflected in an unusually complete survival of tenant farmsteads, with their small, frame dwellings and a few outbuildings.

MT 13 Hamilton

The 19th-c. architecture of the small Roanoke River port presents popular mid- and late 19th-c. styles in unusually bold, even exaggerated renditions. Although no carpenter or shop has been named, this distinctive quality—shared with several houses on outlying farms—suggests a common builder. Hamilton, originally called Milton, was incorporated in 1804 and renamed, probably for Alexander Hamilton, to avoid confusion with the town of Milton in Caswell Co. The community thrived modestly as a river port, trading in the county's farm products. Mid-19th-c. prosperity produced several of the buildings clustered along Front St. (NC 903/125). The most striking is the **Darden Hotel** (1843–55; Front St.), a gable-fronted, side-passage-plan building with a memorable, double-tier portico supported by columns that distill the Ionic order to its essentials—with squared pillars and exaggerated volutes. **St. Martin's Episcopal Church** (1880; P. C. Hull [Norfolk, Va.]; David L. Martin, builder) is a fully realized, Gothic Revival style rural church, with buttressed tower, lancet windows, and truss ceiling. Many of Hamilton's buildings feature cheerfully overscaled forms and details, such as the tall, steep front gables of the Gothic-cottage-inspired **Bryant House** (1885) and **Everett**

MT 13 *Darden Hotel*

House (1882), facing each other across N. Front St. Overscale Greek Revival detail likewise accentuates the pediment front, frame **Conoho Masonic Lodge** (1850s; Liberty St., moved). From the later 19th c. there are several L- and T-shaped Italianate and Queen Anne style houses, many with neatly fenced yards.

MT 14 Hickory Hill

Ca. 1840; W side NC 903 just N of Hamilton; private, visible from road

MT 14 *Hickory Hill*

The 2-story, 3-bay, hip-roofed house features the area's characteristic verve in its application of bold Greek Revival detail that contrasts with the airy sawnwork porch. Built for planter Simon Turner Price, it was later owned by John M. Sherrod and the Salsbury and Everett families.

MT 15 Sherrod House

Ca. 1825; ca. 1850; W side NC 125/903, opp. SR 1416, Hamilton vic.; private, visible from road

The most notable feature of the conservative, 2-story, frame house is the pedimented entrance porch with the same exuberantly vernacular Ionic pillars as the *Darden Hotel. The house was remodeled for John J. Sherrod, one of the county's largest farmers, who bought the place in 1843. The collection of outbuildings includes several early 20th-c. frame barns.

MT 16 Fort Branch

1862–63; N side SR 1416, 1.1 mi. E of NC 125, Hamilton vic.; private, open to public

One of N.C.'s best-preserved Civil War earthwork fortifications, the fort is a popular local attraction. Built to protect vital railroad bridges up the Roanoke River at Weldon, it escaped attack and has survived remarkably intact.

MT 17 Spring Green Primitive Baptist Church

1878; NE corner SR 1315 and NC 903, SW of NC 125, Spring Green

The landmark church repeats the austerity and symmetry of many Primitive Baptist churches, with a pair of doors and upper windows in the gable front, the latter lighting the gallery. Tall, shuttered windows occur along the sides. Home of a congregation established in 1811, the church lies at the center of a rural community of well-kept farmsteads.

MT 18 Jesse Fuller Jones House

Early 19th c.; NE side SR 1409, 1.0 mi. SE of NC 903, Spring Green vic.; private, visible from road

The prominent, 2-story, frame, plantation house exemplifies the persistent simplicity of the county's architecture. An asymmetrical, 4-bay facade reflects an off-center passage with two flanking rooms, plus rear shed and a simple shed porch. Outbuildings range from a 19th-c. smokehouse to several early 20th-c. frame structures. Jones was a planter and physician whose office, dispensary, and sickroom are reported to have stood here.

MT 19 Mac Taylor Farm

1883, early 20th c.; S side NC 125, 0.6 mi. E of NC 903, Hamilton vic.; private, visible from road

Enclosed by picket and rail fences and shaded by pecan trees, the well-kept farmstead of red and white farm buildings is among the county's finest from the late 19th and early 20th centuries. McGilbrey "Mac" Taylor built the simple, 2-story, frame house, and he and later his son Luther erected the barns and other outbuildings. Considered a model of good husbandry, the farm produced the family's food crops, livestock, fruit, and cash crops of tobacco, peanuts, and corn.

Northampton County (NP)

NP 1 Jackson

Center of a county that supported a plantation society by the mid-18th c., the community known as Potecase Bridge became Northampton Court House when the county was formed in 1741. In 1826 it was renamed Jackson, probably for Andrew Jackson. As the Roanoke Valley plantation culture blossomed in the antebellum era, Jackson and the surrounding county thrived. Leading citizens took prominent roles in state affairs. Today Jackson is the seat of a sparsely populated county with a compact downtown where a spacious courthouse green with an imposing courthouse and clerk's offices is surrounded by houses from the 19th and early 20th centuries.

The **Northampton County Courthouse** (1858, A. J. Riggs [Goldsboro], builder; 1939, A. Mitchell Wooten [Kinston], architect) is one of the state's finest antebellum Greek Revival "temples of justice," here with the courtroom set high on a raised basement, dignified by an Ionic portico. Detailed, unsigned specifications survive. The design is attributed locally to Henry K. Burgwyn, a prominent local planter who had studied engineering at West Point. Architect Wooten's WPA-funded addition to the rear forms a T-plan and repeats the scale and finish of the original.

NP 1 *Northampton County Courthouse*

The **Northampton County Clerk's Office** (1831; Thomas Bragg, Abraham Spencer), a small, boldly designed brick building, has Flemish-bond brickwork, coved plastered cornices, and stepped gables with fini-als—a revival or continuation of mid-18th-c. masonry techniques. It was one of the first such buildings erected to be "in all respects . . . fire proof," with brick walls, plastered walls, and zinc-covered roof and shutters. Three doors served three original rooms in line. Thomas Bragg, who consulted in the design, was a prolific 19th-c. builder in Warrenton, then Jackson. Contractor for the clerk's office was bricklayer Abraham Spencer of Oxford, who also built the similar *Halifax County Clerk's Office (1833). Between the two 19th-c. buildings stands the second **Clerk's Office** (1900; B. F. Smith Fireproof Construction Company [Washington, D.C.]), a brick structure of domestic bungalow character. Simple 20th-c. office buildings occupy the rear of the square.

The **Commercial District** along Jefferson St. (US 158) contains typical early 20th-c. brick stores. The most prominent is the (former) **Peoples Bank and Trust Company** (ca. 1904; 100 W. Jefferson St.) east of the courthouse, a simplified Italianate structure with corbeled brickwork and inset corner entrance; it now holds municipal offices. Several 19th-c. houses overlook the courthouse green. The **Bowers House** (late 1860s, Thomas Bragg St.), a picturesque cottage with Gothic Revival lancet windows, is said to have been built from a plate in *Godey's Lady's Book* by a black contractor who was elected to the state legislature before he finished the house—probably John Thomas Reynolds (legislator 1868–70). The **Thomas Bragg Jr. House** (ca. 1835, Thomas Bragg Sr., builder; Thomas Bragg St.) is a typical

NP 1 *Bowers House*

NP 3 *Occoneechee Trapper's Lodge*

2-story, 5-bay, frame house with simplified Greek Revival detail, built for Thomas Bragg Jr. (governor of N.C. 1855–59, U.S. senator 1859–61) probably by his father, the prominent builder. The rambling Queen Anne style **Peebles House** (19th c.; 101 W. Calhoun St.) began as a traditional, 2-story, gable-roofed house and was expanded twice in the 19th c., including a tower and wraparound porch added in the 1890s by Judge Robert Peebles for his daughter's marriage. The **Church of the Saviour** (1904; Church St.) is a simple example in stone of the Gothic Revival favored by Episcopalians.

NP 2 Mowfield

Early 19th c.; N side US 158, 4.0 mi. W of Jackson, Jackson vic.; private, visible at a distance from road

The massive, frame plantation house takes a unique and memorable form with a full, 2-tier piazza integrated beneath a broad hip roof. Its romantic power was captured in a painting by American realist Edward Hopper. The L-shaped house developed in stages during the early 19th c. and displays Georgian and Federal stylistic elements. The Mowfield plantation of 1,364 acres was the seat of the colorful Amis family, beginning with William Amis, who probably built the initial section of the house. He and his son John were horse breeders of national reputation and owners of the great thoroughbred sire Sir Archie. The Amis family sold the place when they left for Mississippi. Later in the 19th c. the plantation was purchased by Confederate officer and political leader Matt Ransom of nearby Verona plantation. Ransom's villa at Verona, once a showplace, is one of several important local plantation houses that lie beyond public view or in decay.

NP 3 Occoneechee Trapper's Lodge

Ca. 1955–present; Q. J. Stephenson; S side SR 1310, 0.5 mi. W of US 158, Garysburg; private, visible from road

The marvelous little concrete building and its surroundings represent the lifetime work of artist Quinton Judson Stephenson. As a construction dragline operator, Stephenson began collecting local specimens of petrified wood, Indian artifacts, rocks, and fossils about 1950. He began his Earth Museum about 1955 to display the prehistoric richness of the region to the public in a safe, permanent form. Much of his work dates from the late 1970s onward. Typical of many visionary artists, Stephenson densely studded the structure with sparkling objects, animal forms made from natural materials, prehistoric artifacts, and inspirational and explanatory inscriptions.

NP 4 Garysburg United Methodist Church

1853, late 19th c.; S side SR 1207, 0.1 mi. W of US 301

The simple, symmetrical, frame church began as a pediment-front Greek Revival building and later received Gothic Revival style lancet windows as well as an entrance vestibule garnished with the ornate sawnwork of a style popular in the county in the 1870s and 1880s. The congregation originated as Moore's Chapel a few years before itinerant Methodist minister Francis Asbury wrote in 1788, "Preached at Moore's in Northampton—once a poor, dead people, but now revived." In the mid-19th c. the members sold the old chapel and moved to the new railroad village of Garysburg, where in 1849 local leader Roderick Gary donated a tract for the new church.

NP 5 Lee-Grant Farm

Ca. 1830; NE side NC 46, 1.7 mi. NW of I-95, Gaston vic.; private, visible from road

The well-detailed I-house, five bays wide with a center-passage plan, features especially fine Federal–Greek Revival detail in the reeded pilasters, pinwheel rosette cornerblocks, and interior finish. It is part of a farm complex with outbuildings of many eras.

NP 6 Concord Methodist Church

Late 18th c., late 19th c.; N side SR 1300, 1.5 mi. W of SR 1324, Seaboard vic.

The essence of the country church: a 1-room, gable-fronted, wooden building with plain finish. The congregation began in 1793, as Methodism blossomed in the Roanoke Valley. The frame may be quite early, but the present character reflects a late 19th-c. rebuilding. A tiny congregation maintains the building and its cemetery.

NP 7 Bellevue

Mid- to late 18th c.; N side SR 1311, 0.2 mi. E of NC 305, Jackson vic.; private, visible from road

A striking example of a traditional house form, the gambrel-roofed house stands high on a basement and is flanked by sturdy brick chimneys of Flemish bond; a front shed porch and rear shed rooms expand the living space. This house type was prevalent in the region and in nearby Virginia during the mid- and late 18th c. (see *King-Bazemore House, Bertie Co.). Planters Joseph and Lawrence Smith are associated with its early history. Since the mid-19th c. the plantation has been in the Ramsay family.

NP 8 Mount Carmel Baptist Church

1847; N side SR 1311, 2.0 mi. W of US 158, Jackson vic.

In this well-preserved, pediment-front, country church with simple Greek Revival detail,

NP 8 *Mount Carmel Baptist Church*

two front entrances flank a tall, broad, central window.

NP 9 Parker House

Late 18th c.; N side US 158, 1.0 mi. W of US 258, Murfreesboro vic.; private, visible from road

The gambrel-roofed house, which originally stood about 4 miles south in Hertford Co., was rescued from decay and moved here by a descendant of the original owner, Francis Parker, a Quaker and a small planter. The house follows the typical hall-parlor plan plus rear shed rooms and a full-width, front shed porch. The reconstructed, T-stack chimneys are based on a local model.

NP 10 Milwaukee

The chief claim to fame of this railroad village, settled ca. 1889 and named for the Wisconsin city, is its remarkable **U.S. Post Office Sign** above the entrance to the small, frame post office. Depending on the viewer's angle, the wooden sign reads alternately "Milwaukee," "Post Office," and "North Carolina," with the letters painted on vertical baffles. The first sign was created about 1925 by longtime postmaster Alfred J. Panton, after a sign he had seen in St. Louis. Replacements were made in about 1960 and in 1985 by Panton's son Charlie.

NP 11 Woodland

The village settled ca. 1835 was named for the Wood family, early Quaker settlers. Quakers were present in Northampton Co. as early as the 1680s, and by 1750 a goodly number had settled in the area around Rich Square and Woodland. The tradition persists, as indicated by the **Cedar Grove Quaker Meetinghouse** (1868, 1965; N side NC 258, 0.15 E of W town limit), a plain, 1-room, frame building with mid-20th-c. wings, home of a meeting organized a few miles south of town in 1760. The Roanoke and Tar River Railroad, later part of the Seaboard Air Line System, arrived in the late 1880s. Woodland contains several late 19th-c. frame houses that share distinctive

NP 11 *House on Main St., Woodland*

millwork ornament attributed to local builder and millwork manufacturer William Jessup, whose shop was in nearby George. Repeated themes include bracketed corner pilasters and porch posts, porch friezes of spindles and trefoil-like curlicues, leafy bargeboards and gable ornaments featuring circular windows, and sawnwork lunettes, waves, trefoils, and pendants. Examples concentrate on Main St.: **112 W. Main**; the **Frank Griffin House** (ca. 1890), 121 W. Main; the **John Griffin House**, 203 W. Main; and the **Burgwyn House**, 207 E. Main. Another example appears in the **Harrell-Benthall-Whisnant House** (early and late 19th c.; NC 35, just W of NC 258) at the edge of town. Related houses appear in nearby **Rich Square** and **Potecasi** as well as in *Union in Hertford Co. There are some similarities with the late work of builder Jacob Holt of Warrenton, N.C., and Chase City, Va., and his protégés.

NP 12 Duke-Lawrence House

Mid- and late 18th c.; S side NC 305/561, 2.0 mi. E of US 258, Rich Square vic.; private, visible at a distance from road

NP 12 *Duke-Lawrence House*

The complex and unusual T-plan house reflects two 18th-c. construction phases. The western section—the stem of the T—was a frame, 1½-story, gable-roofed house with a Flemish-bond brick gable end that incorporates an interior end chimney. This section was built for Virginia native John Duke, perhaps shortly after he acquired the property in 1747. Some years later Duke added the crosspiece of the T, built of brick also laid in Flemish bond with glazed headers. The addition takes a curious form, with its western elevation 1 story tall adjoining the earlier section and the eastern elevation rising 2 full stories to light the upper rooms. This section also has a high basement with cooking fireplace. The fine interior paneling was removed to Richmond, Va., in the 1930s.

Halifax County (HX)

Halifax (HX 1–4)

Strategically located on the Roanoke River below the great falls and at the intersection of two major colonial roads, Halifax was established in 1758 as the seat of the new county and soon developed into an important inland trade center. Town and county were named for the earl of Halifax, a promoter of trade and agriculture in the American colonies. As a focus of the plantation economy of the Roanoke Valley, as well as a county seat and borough town, the community was home to several of the state's political leaders of the late 18th and early 19th centuries, including Federalist William R. Davie and Anti-Federalist Willie Jones.

In 1776 Halifax hosted meetings of the N.C. Provincial Congress and the Council of Safety, which made the town the site of events celebrated in state history. On Apr. 12, 1776, the Fourth Provincial Congress adopted a resolution empowering N.C.'s delegates in the Continental Congress to vote for independence should the matter arise. The Halifax Resolves, as the action was later called, made N.C. the first colony to take official action toward independence. On Aug. 1 the president of the Council of Safety gave the first public reading of the Declaration of Independence in the state. And on Dec. 18 the Fifth Provincial Congress adopted the state's first constitution.

In the mid-19th c., Halifax saw its status reduced to a quiet country town. The Wilmington and Weldon Railroad, built in the late 1830s, made Weldon a rail and river trade center that siphoned business and population away from Halifax. The county's dispersed urban development of the 19th c. generated a series of small, competing towns rather than a single urban focus. In the early 20th c. a statewide surge of historical activities brought the old town new attention, as Halifax's role in the Revolutionary era led the local chapter of the DAR to rescue the "Constitution House" in 1916. Local preservation efforts mounted in the 1940s, and a state historic site was developed in the 1960s.

There are today two Halifaxes: the state historic site that encompasses much of "old Halifax," the colonial town that reached from Prussia St. to the Roanoke River, and the "new town of Halifax," begun in the 1840s when the center of town, including the site of the courthouse, shifted southwest toward the railroad tracks that ran west of town.

HX 1 Historic Halifax State Historic Site

The state historic site area extends along King and Dobbs Sts. from St. David St. to the Roanoke River. Within the grounds are several restored 18th- and 19th-c. buildings, which offer public access to important regional building types. Two early 19th-c. civic buildings are of special interest. The **Halifax County Jail** (1838, Abraham Spencer, builder; King St.) typifies jail construction in the late 18th and early 19th centuries: the 2-story gabled building of brick laid in 1:3 common bond follows an essentially domestic form, with plain, sturdy workmanship throughout. The **Halifax County Clerk's Office** (1833; Abraham Spencer, builder; King St.) is a small public building of fireproof construction and strong architectural pres-

HX 1 *Halifax County Jail*

ence, with Flemish-bond brick walls, stepped gable parapets, and plastered, coved cornice. In 1831 Spencer had built the similar *Northampton County Clerk's Office in Jackson, and the Halifax commissioners copied that example in time-honored fashion.

The **Owens House** (late 18th c.; St. David's St. w of Dobbs St.) exemplifies the small, gambrel-roofed house prevalent in northeastern N.C. in the late 18th c., with a side-passage plan and simple Georgian finish. The **Tap Room** (late 18th and early 19th c.; King and St. David's Sts.), another small, gambrel-roofed house, served as part of a tavern complex. The **Eagle Tavern** (early 19th c.; King and St. David Sts.) began as a tripartite house but had its wings raised to two stories. The **Burgess "Constitution" House** (sw of King St. near amphitheater) is a small, 1-story, frame house with a gable roof, containing a side passage and a single main room plus shed and attic chambers; of uncertain date, the restored house traditionally described as the "Constitution House" is now interpreted to reflect its early 19th-c. usage. An imaginative reconstruction depicts a long-lost townhouse in the **Joseph Montfort House Interpretive Structure** (1984; Richard Newlon and Assoc. [Washington, D.C.], architects; Terry Harper, archaeologist). Somewhat in the spirit of Robert Venturi's steel-frame sketch of Benjamin Franklin's home in Philadelphia, the abstracted, weatherboarded building indicates the general form of Montfort's 2-story, 18th-c. residence and shelters its archaeological remains.

The **Sally-Billy House** (ca. 1810, Fishing Club Rd., 0.5 mi. E of King St.) presents the only accessible example of the Roanoke River Valley's T-plan, tripartite plantation villas. This compact version has a front stair lobby with Chinese lattice stair, a single rear parlor in the main block, and small wing rooms. The compression of the central 2-story, pedimented section to a single bay width emphasizes the richness of its detail, including the dentil and modillion cornice and the entrance portico with tapered posts and Chinese lattice balustrade. Before being moved here, the house stood on a plantation near Scotland Neck. It was built for planter Lewis

HX 1 *Sally-Billy House*

Bond but takes its unusual name from later resident Sarah Norfleet Smith, widow of William R. Smith; in a common practice she was called "Sally Billy" to distinguish her from other Sally Smiths in the neighborhood.

HX 2 St. David's St. Area

Adjoining the state historic site and surviving from early days in Halifax is the **Royal White Hart Masonic Lodge No. 2** (1820s; St. David's St.), one of the oldest lodge buildings in the state—a tall, dignified, plain building of weatherboarded frame, still used by the lodge established in 1764. **First Baptist Church** (1880s; N side St. David's St., E of Norman St.) is a simple, frame church with entrance tower, built for one of the county's oldest black congregations (est. 1865). The **William R. Davie House** (late 18th c.; sw corner Norman and St. David's Sts.), a side-passage townhouse with late

HX 2 *Royal White Hart Masonic Lodge No. 2*

Georgian–early Federal detail, was built for the Federalist leader who served as governor, envoy to France, and "the father of the University of North Carolina."

HX 3 Downtown Halifax

The centerpiece of the town that developed toward the railroad is the **Halifax County Courthouse** (1909, Wheeler and Stern [Charlotte], architects; Courthouse Square on King St.), an imposing brick courthouse with Corinthian portico and domed cupola. A replacement for an antebellum temple-form edifice, this is one of several courthouses designed in the popular Neoclassical mode of Charlotte architect Oliver Wheeler and various associates. Its neighbor, the second **Halifax County Clerk's Office** (1880s), is a small, Romanesque Revival building of dark red brick with a front entrance tower.

HX 3 *Halifax County Courthouse*

The commercial blocks along King St. consist chiefly of 1- and 2-story brick buildings with corbeled trim. A contrast appears in the **Bank of Halifax** (1923; SE corner King and Pittsylvania Sts.), with its emphatic classical details including Ionic columns in antis and a fanciful metal finial dated 1923; founded in 1906 by Fletcher Gregory and others, the bank weathered the Great Depression and later merged with Branch Banking and Trust of Wilson. Around the corner stands the **Walter Clark Law Office** (ca. 1872; S side Pittsylvania St., just W of King St.), a little, 2-room, brick structure typical of county seat law offices, once graced with a fancy sawnwork porch; it was built for Halifax Co. native Walter Clark early in his distinguished career as attorney, justice and

chief justice of the state supreme court, progressive reformer, and historian.

HX 4 S. King St. Residential District

South of the business district and outside the original town limits, S. King St., along with neighboring blocks of Dobbs and Prussia Sts., presents a range of Federal, Greek Revival, Queen Anne, and Colonial Revival residential architecture, punctuated by two Gothic Revival churches. Many houses embody several eras of construction, such as the **Daniel-Hervey-Hill House** (ca. 1826; late 19th c.; NW of corner King and Church Sts.), which was built for congressman John Daniel as a tripartite country residence with pedimented center section and 1-story wings, and expanded during the late 19th-c. ownership of attorney Thomas N. Hill.

A spirited rendition of the Gothic Revival appears in the **Church of the Immaculate Conception** (1889; Edwin Durang [Philadelphia], architect; E side King St., just N of Church St.), where two unequal towers, one with an open belfry, flank the central gable, which features a gabled vestibule and rose window. Hibernia and Harriett, daughters of local Roman Catholic

HX 4 *Church of the Immaculate Conception*

leader Michael Ferrall, donated funds to build the church on family land. At the dedication in 1889 a local newspaper reported that the "frame structure of Gothic architecture . . . is after plans drawn by the celebrated architect, Durang, of Philadelphia. Though small, it is very pretty."

Across the street, **St. Mark's Episcopal Church** (1854–55; sw corner King and Church Sts.) epitomizes the board-and-batten Gothic Revival churches built by Episcopal parishes under the influence of Richard Upjohn's *Rural Architecture* (1852ff.). Tradition reports that rector Frederick Fitzgerald drew the plans, but he may have had Upjohn's book at hand. The steep gable roof is topped by a small belfry, and the vertical emphasis recurs in narrow lancet windows and an entrance porch with sawnwork gable ornament.

The **Fletcher Gregory House** (1923; SE corner King and Church Sts.) was built for a local banker and political figure who, like many of his generation, favored the Southern Colonial style, with a towering portico and decorated pediment. **Glen Ivy** (1850s; w side King St., just NE of Bradley Dr.) is a raised cottage of Greek Revival style, with a low hip roof and unusually large windows. It was moved here from its original location as the country home of Edward Conigland, an Irish-born attorney who was one of several important Catholic laymen in 19th-c. Halifax.

HX 5 Halifax County Home and Tubercular Hospital

1923; Benton & Benton (Wilson), architects; N side NC 903, 1.5 mi. W of NC 125, Halifax vic.; operates as 4-H center

Amidst the statewide effort to improve care for the poor in the early 20th c., the county employed the prolific Wilson architectural firm of Benton & Benton to plan a new county home in accord with modern standards. The architects designed a facility in their favored red brick, Colonial Revival style, which paradoxically reiterated the Roanoke plantation houses' tripartite villa format, with central 2-story pavilion and portico flanked by 1-story wings. Built not far from the county's original poorhouse (ca. 1845), it was considered one of the best facilities of its kind in the state. On the outlying farm, residents raised some of their own food.

HX 6 The Hermitage, Glen Burnie

Early 19th c.; private, not visible from road

Of the T-plan, tripartite villas that once adorned the plantation society of the Roanoke Valley, this graceful example is among the few survivors. The 2-story, pedimented central block and flanking wings are finished in late Georgian style. (The plan of the house resembles The Grove, late 18th-c. home of political leader Willie Jones, which stood near Halifax and was the earliest of the T-plan villas of the area.) The house was evidently built about 1810 for Rebecca Norfleet and Thomas Blount Hill, who called the place The Hermitage. Their son sold the property to John Tillery, a leading local planter, and since the antebellum period the plantation has remained in the Tillery family, who call it Glen Burnie. Carefully restored in the late 20th c., the plantation includes a mid-19th-c. board-and-batten kitchen, smokehouse, and dairy.

HX 7 Scotland Neck

Scotland Neck began as a rural neighborhood named for the group of 1722 Scots settlers who soon left to join their kin along the Cape Fear. In the antebellum period it developed into a prosperous area of interconnected plantations, which included the villages of Clarksville and Greenwood. After the Civil War, energy focused on boosting town growth, drawing people from the nearby countryside as well as immigrants from other states and countries. Local entrepreneur John Hyman bought land for a new town between Clarksville and Greenwood and, with grand vision, laid out the present town of Scotland Neck with its broad main street. The town incorporated in 1867 and grew quickly after the 1882 arrival of a branch of the Wilmington and Weldon Railroad.

Main St. has several handsome, early 20th-c., brick commercial buildings. The

HX 7 *Main St., Scotland Neck*

Scotland Neck Bank (1914; Peyton Keel and R. J. Mauney, builders; SE corner Main and 10th Sts.) features a diagonal, columned corner entrance bay and free classical detail against pressed-brick walls; the bank was organized in 1891 by local businessmen. The **Biggs Building** (1903; 1000 Main St.), which once housed the largest general mercantile store in the county, is a 3-story brick building, with arched windows and a metal, bracketed cornice with nameplate. In back is an unusual survival of rear living quarters with an outside stair. In the **Josey Building** (1904; 1014 Main St.) red and tan brickwork accentuates the arcade of windows and corbeled cornice beneath the metal name and date parapet.

The residential area west of downtown includes houses from the late Italianate and Queen Anne styles to the bungalow and Colonial Revival. The **Napoleon Bonaparte Josey House** (1882; 1104 Church St.), built for a prominent merchant whose father had sold the land for Scotland Neck to Hyman, displays the Italianate style, T-shaped with ornate porch, bracket cornice, and decorated gables. Particularly striking is the **Max Hoffman House** (1889; H. G. Jones, builder; 1103 Church St.), with a peak-roofed entrance tower, lavish Eastlake style millwork on the tower and porch, and a floral-patterned slate roof enlivened by ornate dormers. It was built for Hoffman, a German immigrant who became one of Scotland Neck's "first and best merchants," proprietor of a general

store, and town commissioner. Contractor H. G. Jones, who evidently built several local houses, advertised in 1891 the availability of "Brackets of all styles, Fancy Scroll work of all descriptions."

East Scotland Neck developed as the center of railroad activity, warehouses, and working people's houses. Although the tracks have been pulled up and the fine brick freight depot razed, the frame **Scotland Neck Depot** (ca. 1890; 1005 Greenwood St., E of Main St.) survives as a farm supply business. The former **Scotland Neck Cotton Mills** (1889–90; H. G. Jones, builder; S side E. 9th St. at Greenwood St.) is a typical, 2-story, brick facility whose once-proud, 6-story tower is now truncated to 3 stories. Organized by local businessmen, it is claimed as the oldest continuously operating hosiery mill in the country. In the 1880s and 1890s several

HX 7 *Max Hoffman House*

owner-built residences and "cottages" were constructed. In 1901 local investors began building houses in the "thriving suburb" for rent and sale to working families. Still standing along E. 9th and adjacent streets, these are typically 1-story, frame houses, many with modestly decorated front porches, shaded by deciduous trees planted by the developers.

North Main St. is a premier residential avenue, which includes part of old Clarksville. Trinity Episcopal Church (1925; NE corner Main and E. 13th Sts.), a picturesque, late Gothic Revival church with corner entrance tower, was built to replace an 1886 church that burned; that sanctuary had been built when parishioners of the rural *Old Trinity Episcopal Church (damaged by fire in 1884) decided to build a new church in town, though they continued to maintain Old Trinity and use its burial ground. The Gerson Hoffman House (1911; 1403 Main St.), a massive, Southern Colonial Revival house with full-width Corinthian portico, was built for merchant Max Hoffman's younger brother and business partner, who became "one of Scotland Neck's wealthiest and most influential citizens." The Gilliam-Pritchard House (late 19th c.; 1508 N. Main St.) is a multigabled, late Italianate dwelling with delicate floral millwork akin to H. G. Jones's work at the *Max Hoffman House. In the Claude Kitchin House (1840s; ca. 1902; 1723 N. Main St.) an antebellum house was transformed into the massive, Southern Colonial home of Claude Kitchin; son of Congressman W. H. Kitchin, he assisted in planning the successful Democratic state election campaign of 1898 and soon became an influential congressman (1901–23) and majority leader (1916–19). The Samuel Kitchin House (ca. 1895; 1735 N. Main St.), built for another member of the prominent political family, shows the complex massing and ornate decoration of the Queen Anne style.

Scotland Neck Plantation Area:

The plantation neighborhood, dominated by a few interconnected families, was an important social and architectural unit of the landscape during the zenith of the Roanoke Valley planter culture. The Scotland Neck neighborhood, where the Smith and Evans families were prominent and the Episcopal Church was a focal point, enjoyed a taste for new ideas in architecture and landscape design. Much has been lost or lies beyond public view, but a few landmarks still stand.

HX 8 Old Trinity Episcopal Church
1854–55; Frank Wills (New York), architect; E side US 258, 0.4 mi. S of SR 1118

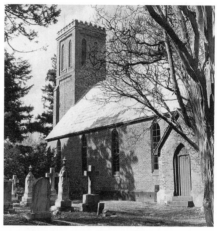

HX 8 *Old Trinity Episcopal Church*

Joseph Blount Cheshire, Episcopal priest, took an avid interest in the architectural and horticultural trends of his era and promoted new ideas and plantings among his parishioners here and at *Calvary Episcopal Church, Tarboro. For Trinity Parish (est. 1831) he obtained a simple, Gothic Revival design from Frank Wills of New York, a leading proponent of the Ecclesiological movement. The symmetrical but picturesque brick building, constructed by slave workmen owned by the Smith family, is dominated by a central, crenellated entrance tower and lit by lancet windows. After an 1884 fire destroyed an elaborate interior paint scheme, a new church was built in Scotland Neck, and Old Trinity was restored for occasional use. The picturesque churchyard contains old crepe myrtles, hollies, and magnolias.

HX 9 Magnolia

1840s; E side US 258, 0.5 mi. N of SR 1118, Scotland Neck vic.; private, visible from road

Built for Adelaide Evans and her husband, James N. Smith (son of Sarah and William Smith of the *Sally-Billy House), Magnolia is a spacious, double-pile, frame house with Greek Revival details inspired by Asher Benjamin's *Practical House Carpenter* (1830ff.). The wide center passage features a curved "wishbone" stair. The house stands amid a formal garden of firs, hollies, laurels, crepe myrtles, ginkgos, and other plantings remaining from Adelaide Smith's more elaborate garden of the 19th c. Her marked copy of A. J. Downing's *Treatise on Landscape Gardening* (1841) also survives. Family tradition recalls that rector Joseph Blount Cheshire helped Mrs. Smith lay out the grounds. Once the center of a plantation of more than 3,000 acres, the house and grounds are still part of a large working farm.

HX 10 Kehukee Primitive Baptist Church

1872; NE corner NC 125 and SR 1810, Scotland Neck vic.

The simplicity of the frame country church is in keeping with the beliefs of the Primitive Baptists. The congregation traces its origins to the 1742 establishment of Kehukee Church, which stood east of Scotland Neck

HX 10 *Kehukee Primitive Baptist Church*

and was mother church of the large Kehukee Baptist Association. The 1827 association meeting at Kehukee was the scene of the lasting schism between Missionary and Primitive Baptists. The present church was erected in 1872 on a new site south of Scotland Neck. The central entrance tower with spire was added in 1901 with the aid of local sawmill operator John Coughenour, whose residence stands across the road. The **John Coughenour House** (ca. 1890; SW corner NC 125 and SR 1810; private) is a big, 2-story, frame house rendered picturesque by its multitude of steep gables—three each on the front and east and western sides—adorned with shingles and ornate gable decorations. Its ornate porch was replaced in the 20th c.

HX 11 Whitehead-Douglass Farm

Ca. 1880, early 20th c.; S side SR 1100, 2.1 mi. W of US 258, Scotland Neck vic.; private, visible from road

Presiding over a broad valley from a hilltop, the farmstead recalls the post–Civil War renewal of agricultural prosperity and subsequent shifts in agriculture over the years. The 2-story, frame house (ca. 1880) features the typical front roof gable and a rear kitchen ell. Across the road stands a huge, 110-foot, frame mule barn with gambrel roof (1930s). It is the most imposing of some two dozen substantial outbuildings from the mid-19th through the mid-20th centuries, including a 19th-c. brick smokehouse and frame corncrib, tobacco barns, several frame barns and a frame silo, peanut drying structures, and ten tenant houses. Under W. T. and Clifford Whitehead and, after 1929, R. B. Douglass, this has been a large farm producing a wide range of crops.

Dawson Crossroads–Enfield Plantations: Along SR 1003 east of Enfield lies an especially evocative survival of a 19th-c. antebellum plantation neighborhood. Several interrelated houses share 2-story frame construction and either hall-parlor or center-passage plans, with conservative detailing ranging from late Georgian to Federal to Greek Revival. Many frame sheds and barns survive, a few from the ante-bellum period, more from the late 19th and early 20th centuries. A large but dwindling collection of tobacco barns and tenant houses—typically 1-story dwellings of two rooms with a center chimney, often with two front doors—recalls the transformation of social and economic patterns in the late 19th c. With the late 20th-c. revolution of agricultural labor by mechanization, these are rapidly disappearing.

HX 12 Dawson-Deberry House
Early 19th c.; SE corner SR 1003 and SR 1103; private, visible from road

The boldly detailed, Federal period house has a 2-room plan and an unusual, full-height portico sheltering paired doors that open into both rooms in both stories.

HX 13 David Barrow House
Early 19th c.; S side SR 1003, 1.8 mi. W of SR 1103; private, visible from road

The tall, severe, 6-bay-wide house probably embodies several building phases. In 1836 its owner, Barrow, moved to Louisiana, where he amassed a fortune and built Afton Villa, an important Gothic plantation house.

HX 14 Montgomery Whitaker House
Mid-19th c.; SE side SR 1003, 1.2 mi. E of SR 1100; private, visible from road

The mainstream, Greek Revival plantation house of typical broad form beneath a low hip roof features a heavy, Asher Benjamin-influenced entrance with Greek key pilasters.

HX 15 Whitaker's Chapel
Early and mid-19th c.; S side SR 1003, 0.4 mi. E of SR 1100; National Historic Shrine, United Methodist Church

A long-revered church in a fine rural setting. Whitaker's Chapel was organized ca. 1740 as an Anglican congregation and embraced Methodism ca. 1776. In 1828, after a division in the Methodist movement, Whitaker's

Chapel hosted the first annual conference of the Methodist Protestant church. The core of the present frame church is a simple, rectangular block with Federal era finish and molded weatherboards. It may have been standing when the conference was held here. The narthex and interior finish date from ca. 1850 and later. A cemetery adjoins the church.

HX 16 Myrtle Lawn
Early 19th c., mid-19th c.; N side SR 1003, 0.3 mi. E of SR 1100; private, visible from road

HX 16 *Myrtle Lawn*

The house combines the traditional, vertical form and Federal style detail of its ca. 1816 portion with a decorative Italianate porch built when the house was expanded in the mid-19th c. An outstanding group of outbuildings includes a temple-form plantation office, a carriage house, a dairy, a log vegetable storage building, and other structures, some set on wood block foundations. The plantation was home of the locally prominent and prolific Whitaker family from the 18th through the mid-20th centuries. Other Whitaker family plantations in the area include Shell Castle and Strawberry Hill, which are not visible from the road.

HX 17 John A. Lawrence House
Mid-19th c.; SW corner SR 1003 and SR 1100; private, visible from road

The broad proportions of the house and simplified Greek Revival detail typify its antebellum construction date, but it, like many of its era, encompasses elements of a smaller dwelling of the Federal period. There is a large group of substantial outbuildings.

HX 18 Enfield

The county's oldest town, originally called Huckleberry Swamp, was settled by the 1730s and later named for Methodist leader John Wesley's hometown of Enfield, Middlesex, England, reflecting the strength of Methodism in the area. It served as seat of Edgecombe Co. until the county was divided into Halifax and Edgecombe counties in 1758. The original town lay west of the present town center.

The principal landmark surviving from "Old Enfield" is **The Cellars** (ca. 1800; 404 Whitfield St.), a big, 2-story, frame house once the center of a plantation. Unusually large with its center-passage plan two rooms deep, it boasts fine workmanship in its four tall chimneys of Flemish-bond brickwork, robust molded door and window frames, modillion cornice, and double-molded weatherboards. The house was probably built by 1806 for John Branch, whose son Joseph, tradition claims, played host here to the Marquis de Lafayette during his American tour in 1825.

In the 19th c., Enfield was transformed into a market town oriented to the Wilmington and Weldon Railroad. Repeating Halifax's example, the town center moved east from "Old Enfield" to create "New Enfield" along the tracks. The principal commercial buildings—1- and 2-story brick stores, with occasional facades in stone with Romanesque Revival or classical themes—stand along **Railroad St.**, **Whitaker St.**, and **Whitfield St.** The **Atlantic Coast Line Passenger Station** (1920s; E side track, at N end S.E. Railroad St.) is a handsome little brick depot with deep eaves carried on bold brackets. Across the tracks is a 2-story, concrete signal tower with tile roof. The dominant downtown building is the **Masonic Temple** (1924–25; Benton & Benton [Wilson], architects; S.E. Railroad St. at Market St.), a 3½-story edifice of blond brick with classical pilasters and cornices, plus Masonic symbols in terra-cotta.

In a classic railroad town arrangement, rows of mid- to late 19th-c. frame houses line the tracks along **Railroad St.** This and other residential streets feature Italianate, Queen Anne, Colonial Revival, and bungalow houses, punctuated by churches. At the **Enfield Baptist Church** (1916; NW corner S. Dennis and W. Burnette Sts.) a classical portico fronts a domed, polygonal, red brick church enclosing an auditorium-plan sanctuary with curved pews slanting down to a corner pulpit. The **Romulus Bragg Parker House** (1887; 315 W. Franklin St.) exemplifies the popular I-house form with facade roof gable, Italianate windows, and a wraparound porch; it was the birthplace of state supreme court chief justice R. Hunt Parker. An unexpected note appears in a rare example of a **Lustron House** (early 1950s; 122 N. Dennis St.), a sleek little 1-story house with picture windows, the product of a short-lived, post–World War II experiment in factory-made housing. Manufactured in Columbus, Ohio, Lustron houses had steel frames covered with porcelain-enameled steel panels in gray (as here), tan, yellow, or blue and were shipped complete with heating and plumbing fixtures and kitchen appliances.

HX 19 Branch Grove

1840s; S side NC 481, 0.9 mi. E of US 301, Enfield vic.; private, visible from road

This unusually late tripartite plantation house is executed with transitional Federal–Greek Revival details. An earlier, 1-story dwelling stands to the rear. The house was built for Samuel Branch, whose son Alpheus founded Branch Banking and Trust, an important regional bank. This area of the county contains a wealth of frame tenant houses and turn-of-the-century tobacco barns.

HX 18 *Atlantic Coast Line Passenger Station*

HX 20 Jones-Anderson House

Mid-19th c.; N side SR 1214, 0.8 mi. E of NC 48, Ringwood vic.; private, visible from road

The 1-story, double-pile house with hip roof exemplifies a popular antebellum form, enriched with a fashionable bracketed frieze, bracketed entrance, and airy sawnwork porch posts, similar to motifs seen in Edgecombe Co. and probably inspired by popular mid-19th-c. patternbooks. A matching office stands in the yard.

HX 21 Ita Store

Ca. 1880s; S corner SR 1327 and SR 1339, Ita

The frame general store was built for the Garrett family, who also established the Medoc Vineyards in the area. As a crossroads trade center in a sparsely populated rural area, it has met different needs through changing times, containing a post office from 1891 to 1905, serving as commissary for a lumber company in the early 20th c., and selling gasoline as well as groceries and dry goods. The 2-story, gable-fronted store has flanking shed extensions and wood-sheathed interior lined with shelves and heated by a stove with a suspended chimney.

HX 22 Ivy Hill

Ca. 1800, ca. 1847; S side SR 1002, 3.4 mi. E of NC 561, Hollister vic.; private, visible from road

Two houses stand at right angles, exemplifying successive generations of the region's domestic architecture. The older of the two is a well-finished, late Georgian dwelling with hall-parlor plan. Linked to it by a passage, a side-passage-plan addition displays large-scale, Greek Revival work akin to nearby Warren Co. houses attributed to builder Albert Gamaliel Jones. The first house was probably built for planter Isham Matthews, the second for his son Thomas.

HX 23 Bethesda Church

Ca. 1852; James Boseman, attributed builder; N side NC 561, 1.0 mi E of NC 48, Brinkleyville vic.

The well-kept, frame country church has a simple, pedimented gable end and little

bracketed hoods over the twin entrances. The congregation was established ca. 1852 by local Methodists led by William H. Wills, who later served as president of the denomination's General Conference.

HX 24 Oakland

1820s; NE corner NC 4 and SR 1310, Airlie; private, visible from road

HX 24 *Oakland*

The plantation society of Warren and western Halifax counties produced a group of elaborately detailed, late Federal style plantation houses of which Montmorenci in Warren Co. and Prospect Hill in Halifax Co.— both lost—were the grandest. Like Elgin in Warren Co., Oakland combines the distinctive Federal detail of the Montmorenci school with the pediment-front house form with transverse front hall and paired rear parlors. Probably built for Elizabeth Alston Williams, niece of William Williams of Montmorenci, Oakland has been in the Thorne family since 1856. The complex includes a line of 19th-c. outbuildings.

HX 25 Samuel T. Thorne House

Ca. 1912; E. L. Pike (Enfield), builder; W side NC 4, 0.4 mi. N of SR 1310, Airlie vic.; private, visible from road

A rural rendition of the "Southern Colonial" house popular in the early 20th c., the symmetrical, frame house is dominated by a portico of Corinthian columns. It was built for Samuel T. Thorne, a farmer and owner of a cotton gin, gristmill, and store. The farmstead includes a stone dairy and a smoke-house as well as several barns.

HX 26 Clark-Patterson House

Ca. 1890; W side NC 4, 0.8 mi. N of SR 1310, Airlie vic.; private, visible from road

Built for Henry Clark, known as an eccentric bachelor, the hexagonal-plan house with projecting ells stands out as unique in the county's generally conservative architecture. The central hexagonal room rises to a cupola. Ornate woodwork, shingling, etched glass, and metalwork accentuate its ebullient individuality.

HX 27 Littleton

The railroad town on the old Raleigh and Gaston route has a typical late 19th- and early 20th-c. commercial district facing the place where the tracks once ran. The settlement was named for Little Manor, the plantation of William Person Little; he was the nephew and adopted son of Thomas Person, planter and Anti-Federalist political leader who had previously owned the plantation. The spectacular Federal style plantation house, Little Manor, or Mosby Hall, which stood at the edge of town, is now a ruin. Littleton's oldest landmark is **Person's Ordinary** (late 18th, early 19th c.; s side Warren St., just E of Mosby Ave.; open by appointment), a restored, 1½-story house with a 3-room plan, believed to have been the tavern owned by Person and later Little. The main residential avenue is **Mosby Ave.**, lined by Colonial Revival houses and especially substantial and well-detailed bungalows, plus a series of brick churches of various denominations of the late 19th and early 20th centuries. Littleton also retains several very small, 19th-c. workers' houses, 1 story tall and one bay wide, some of which stand on Ferguson St., just west of Person's Ordinary.

HX 28 Roanoke Rapids

The riverside textile town has eastern N.C.'s principal concentration of textile mill architecture, particularly its many blocks of mill houses. (See Introduction, Fig. 45.) In the early 20th c. the power site at the great falls of the Roanoke River developed quickly into the largest town in the county and one of eastern N.C.'s leading manufacturing centers. Roanoke Rapids grew up as several individual mill villages, and as a result there are two separate commercial districts on Roanoke Ave., the main street, which is also NC 48. The most intact concentrations of mill housing lie at the northern end of town, flanking Roanoke Ave. between 1st and 9th Sts., on Hamilton, Washington, Madison, Monroe, Jackson, and other presidentially named streets.

HX 28 *Mill village, Roanoke Rapids*

The story of the town's development is somewhat complicated. In the early 1890s, Weldon merchant and Confederate veteran Maj. Thomas Emry—frustrated in attempts to develop factories along the old canal in Weldon—shifted his efforts upstream. He engaged out-of-state investors in a project to create an industrial city, "Great Falls," to harness the waterpower of the Roanoke River.

One investor, the wealthy eccentric John Armstrong Chanler (Chaloner) of New York, took special interest in the endeavor, suggesting the name Roanoke Rapids and commissioning his friend, distinguished New York architect Stanford White of McKim Mead & White, to design a knitting mill, church, hotel, and some fifty houses. Church and hotel are gone, and only vestiges of the brick mill survive within the huge paper mill beside the river. The original "Old Town" mill village (a) stood on present-day Washington, Jefferson, and Hamilton Sts. between 1st and 4th Sts., east of Roanoke Ave. Most if not all of the first mill houses are ev-

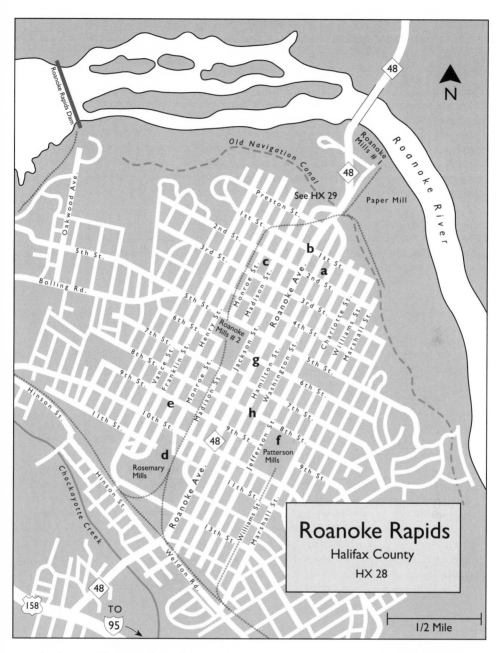

Roanoke Rapids

Halifax County

HX 28

1/2 Mile

idently gone. Tradition claims that the small, gambrel-roofed dwellings, locally known as **Turtleback Houses**, on corner sites in Old Town are remnants of White's mill housing (the best preserved is at Hamilton and E. 1st Sts.), but this remains undocumented.

In 1897 Emry and others opened a second factory, Roanoke Mills, also beside the river, and soon employed Samuel F. Patter-son, son of a prominent piedmont textile family, as manager. A commercial district developed on Roanoke Ave. near the river (**b**). Beginning in 1896 the Roanoke Mills Company began building workers' housing in the section called "New Town" west of Roanoke Ave. (**c**). With more than 100 houses, 6 brick stores, 3 churches, and thriving industries, in 1897 Roanoke Rapids was incorporated to include both Old Town and New Town, with Emry as mayor. The *Manufacturers' Record* exulted that "the work which has been done in two years makes the development one of the most remarkable in the whole country for that period."

The houses built in New Town set a lasting pattern that continued for several years. Standing on alternating lots, these were typically 2-story, frame dwellings of two principal types: narrow, hip-roofed, single-family houses of five rooms, or gable-roofed duplexes four bays wide, with three rooms per side, normally with a center chimney. Both had front porches and neat, plain detail. **Monroe** and **Madison Sts.** between 1st and 4th Sts. comprise especially well-preserved blocks of the New Town houses. There are rows of identical houses as well as alternating hip- and gable-roofed forms. Their 2-story height contrasts with the more common 1-story mill houses in the state, of which there are also examples here. These same house types continued to be built by the hundreds after 1900 as the community expanded to encompass five mill villages.

In 1900 Samuel F. Patterson and other investors formed the Rosemary Manufacturing Company, which built a mill designed by Boston engineer Fred S. Hinds to produce cotton damask. Powered by electricity, it could be built a distance south of the river. **Rosemary Mills** (1901 and later; bounded by Jackson, W. 10th, W. 13th, Henry, and Vance Sts.) (**d**) expanded over the years, with three facilities by 1915 and others added in 1929 and later. The original section seen from Madison and 10th Sts. is a 2-story, functional, Romanesque Revival, brick structure with tower. Near the new village of Rosemary—for a time a town separate from Roanoke Rapids proper—expanded settlement southward away from the river. Rosemary workers' housing, built along Madison, Monroe, Henry, and Franklin Sts. (**e**), continued patterns familiar from New Town, but there were larger duplexes as well. More substantial and stylish residences were built for supervisory personnel. In addition, Rosemary had its own Roanoke Ave. commercial section.

In 1910 Samuel Patterson, his brother John, and others opened **Patterson Mills** (1910 and later; E side Jefferson St. at 8th and 9th Sts.) (**f**), which continued the functional brick architecture of its predecessors. It was located in the eastern section of Rosemary, and again housing repeated established types. Houses built for mill executives included the **President's House** (1910; 502 Washington St.), a frame residence of Queen Anne–Colonial Revival style, originally occupied by Patterson, then by his successor, J. A. Moore. With new paper mills along the river adding to growth, the total population of Roanoke Rapids and Rosemary in 1910 was 2,580, a figure that doubled by 1920. Especially after he moved to the community in 1911, Samuel F. Patterson developed a forceful, generally progressive model of industrial paternalism. In 1919 he took on ownership as well as management. Although conditions would change radically after his death in 1926, during his management Roanoke Rapids and Rosemary gained fame for modernity and a progressive, paternalistic concern for education, health care, cultural opportunities, and community pride as well as profits.

In the late 1910s and early 1920s, as the mills continued to expand, new workers' housing was built, some houses on lots between older houses, others in newly opened sections west of the old villages. Many of these were mail-order houses from the Aladdin Homes Company, which manufactured prefabricated suburban and industrial housing. Popular models included "The Edison" bungalow, often built to fill lots among older houses, and "The Gretna" a side-gabled, 1-story cottage typically erected in new sections.

Various Aladdin models were also built for privately owned residences, including "The Rochester," a 1919 foursquare at Jackson and W. 8th Sts., and 1920s bungalows on Jackson St., such as "The Marsden" at 417, "The Plaza" at 419, and "The Pomona" at 512. More elaborate Aladdin houses include "The Villa, a Bit of Old Italy" at 537 Roanoke Ave. and the "Brentwood" in stucco at Roanoke Ave. and 8th St.

HX 28 *419 Jackson St. ("The Plaza," by Aladdin Homes)*

Along Roanoke Ave. imposing new buildings gradually filled in between the two older commercial districts (**g**). Of several houses built in the 1920s and in a variety of popular styles, the most striking is the **Councill-Coburn House** (1920s; 521 Roanoke Ave.), built for a local banker as a massive, rustic, log residence with bays projecting to either side of a big stone chimney, complemented by a matching log garage–servants' quarter and former stable. Local leaders also commissioned key institutional buildings to define the community's tone. In 1917, encouraged by Patterson, the Episcopalians employed New York architect Hobart Upjohn, grandson of Richard Upjohn, to design their new church. His engagingly simple design for **All Saints Episcopal Church** (SE corner Roanoke Ave. and E. 7th St.)

produced a picturesque little wood-shingled church set in a heavily shaded lot.

Upjohn's principal work here showcased Patterson's grand vision for the community. The **Roanoke Rapids Junior-Senior High School** (1920, Hobart Upjohn, architect; Hamilton St.) (**h**) is a magnificent, Tudor Revival secondary school built of brick with terra-cotta and stone trim and crenellated towers in a "classic Elizabethan style" that invoked "the venerable buildings in the great centers of learning in Oxford and Cambridge." It boasted every modern educational amenity and facility, including science labs, a gymnasium, an indoor swimming pool, and an auditorium to seat 2,000. Costing some $500,000 to build, the school was one of the most ambitious public school buildings erected during the statewide campaign for better schoolhouses.

In 1929 the Simmons Company of New York purchased three of the textile firms, beginning the end of local paternalism. In 1950 Simmons sold the mill houses to private owners, and in 1956 J. P. Stevens Company bought the textile factories. Unionization struggles, which had begun in the 1930s, intensified in the 1970s, as dramatized in the movie *Norma Rae*. In 1988 the mills were sold to the Bibb Company; the paper

HX 28 *Roanoke Rapids Junior-Senior High School*

factories are owned by Champion Paper Company.

HX 29 Roanoke Canal and Chockoyotte Aqueduct
1819–23 (Hamilton Fulton, engineer), 1890s–1904; Roanoke Rapids to Weldon; portions accessible as part of local park

HX 29 *Chockoyotte Aqueduct*

One of the nation's best examples of early 19th-c. canal construction is the 7-mile canal built to bypass the rapids and handle the 44-foot drop at the Great Falls of the Roanoke River—a stream the Indians had called "the river of death." (The river was dammed in the 20th c. to create lakes and reduce flooding.) The canal and its locks were part of the ambitious—though never fully realized—Roanoke Navigation System intended to connect the Blue Ridge Mountains and the Atlantic Ocean. Much of the construction was planned and supervised by Hamilton Fulton, an English civil engineer trained under John Rennie and Thomas Telford in Britain, who had come to N.C. in 1819 to plan and direct the state's internal improvements. At the falls of the Roanoke he entered a project already begun, but it was he who designed the aqueduct and other key elements. After Fulton left N.C. in 1826, additional stages of the navigation system were completed. Traffic through the canal and along the river thrived for a time, but like many early 19th-c. canals, success was cut short by competition from railroads within a few years. Late in the 19th c. a project was begun to rebuild the old canal as a power source for local factories (including the

*Weldon Corn Mill), but this endeavor soon dwindled in the face of competition from Roanoke Rapids.

Important remains of the Roanoke Canal exist along the route from above Roanoke Rapids downstream to Weldon. At Roanoke Rapids are the cut-stone **Locks** (w side NC 48, just s of Roanoke River, Roanoke Rapids), the first of a series of double locks, each of which had a lift of 9 feet. The structure of fitted, coursed stone includes stone ducts for filling and emptying the locks. The two brick **Power Houses** (1901) here were built as part of the Roanoke Navigation and Water Power Company's effort to use the canal as an energy source. Several deep cuts and other features also survive along the canal route. (See Roanoke Rapids map.)

The most spectacular structure is the fine, dressed stone **Chockoyotte Aqueduct** just west of Weldon (1821–23; N side US 158, trailhead at end of SR 1704/1705 access road, A. Edwin Akers Park), which carried the canal across Chockoyotte Creek. The aqueduct, which Fulton designed and supervised, was described in an 1831 report: "[Of] excellent workmanship and beautiful[,] it is formed of hewn stone, very neatly dressed, and of the most durable quality, resting on a rock foundation. It is 110 feet long, its greatest height 35 feet, and has a clear width of waterway of 18 feet; the arch has a span of 30 feet, is 29 feet wide, and is elevated 22 feet above the surface of the creek at common height." The tight masonry joints between the cut stones are only about ⅛ inch wide; skillfully laid voussoirs form the arch over the stream. Except for minor repairs the aqueduct stands as built.

HX 30 Weldon

The river and railroad town (inc. 1843) was a terminus of the Wilmington and Weldon Railroad, which joined northern lines there. From the 1840s onward it was an important trade center, a role that intensified during the Civil War when the Wilmington and Weldon was the "lifeline of the Confederacy" between the blockade-runners at Wilmington and Lee's armies in Virginia. Although the railroad bridge over the Roanoke

HX 30 *Bank of Weldon*

was burned near the end of the war, a new bridge was built in 1867, and local merchants labored to resuscitate business. In the 1880s and 1890s efforts concentrated on improving the Roanoke Navigation Canal to use it as a power source for industrial plants, including a cotton mill that promised "Weldon has a brilliant future before it." Although the envisioned industrial city did not materialize here—it was outstripped by the new manufacturing town of *Roanoke Rapids in the 1890s—nevertheless the era from ca. 1880 to 1930 did bring growth and new construction, and the principal architecture dates mainly from this era.

Railroad and commercial architecture clusters at the junction of Washington Ave. (the main street), E. 1st St., and the railroad track; the main line arrives in town on a high trestle. The oldest is the brick **Weldon Freight Depot** (ca. 1840, ca. 1859; N side 1st St. at Washington Ave.), one of the few antebellum buildings of the Wilmington

and Weldon line. It began as a 1-story, brick warehouse and was raised to the present 2-story office building with hip roof and bracket cornice, perhaps as early as 1859. The **Weldon Union Station** (ca. 1915; open to public as a library) is a characteristic early 20th-c. brick facility with deep eaves. (See Introduction, Fig. 42.)

From this intersection several handsome brick commercial buildings extend south along Washington Ave., beginning at the flatiron-shaped northern corner. The architectural gem of the commercial district is the former **Bank of Weldon** (ca. 1895; 121 Washington Ave.), a tiny, gutsy rendition of the Richardsonian Romanesque style, 1 story tall and 11½ feet wide, with a gabled facade of rough-hewn stone framed by pilasters with leafy capitals, which distills the usually monumental style into miniature. The **Pierce-Whitehead Hardware Co.** and neighboring **Weldon Furniture Co.** (1902, ca. 1905; 212–16 Washington Ave.) are 2-story, bracketed brick blocks with G. L. Mesker Company metal trim.

The **Washington Ave. Neighborhood** south of the commercial district has the chief concentration of residential architecture of the late 19th and early 20th centuries, including frame, Queen Anne and Colonial Revival houses, several bungalows, and masonry churches in popular revival styles. Prominent among the transitional Queen Anne–Colonial Revival residences is the **Smith-Dickens House** (1901–2; T. W. Russell, architect-builder; 400 Washington Ave.), a 2½-story house with high hip roof, wraparound porch with corner pavilion, and free classical details, built for William R. Smith, a Confederate veteran from Virginia, railroad agent and organizer of the Bank of

HX 30 *DeLeon F. Green House*

HX 30 *Benjamin M. Mills Jr. House*

Weldon. The **Weldon Methodist Church** (1910–11; Wheeler and Stern [Charlotte]; NE corner Washington Ave. and 5th St.) is a Gothic Revival, brick church with crenellated towers, designed by the Charlotte firm who planned the *Halifax County Courthouse. The Gothic Revival style **Grace Episcopal Church** (1870s; NW corner Washington Ave. and 5th St.) began as a more ornate brick church with pinnacles but was stuccoed in the 1880s and simplified in the early 20th c. The Southern Colonial style appears in several houses, including the **Lee Johnson House** (1903; 511 Washington Ave.) with its tall Ionic portico and high hip roof. The **Weldon Baptist Church** (1915; R. T. Daniel [Weldon], architect-builder; NE corner Washington Ave. and E. 7th St.) employs a classical vocabulary with Ionic portico and cruciform plan in the spirit of Charlotte architect J. M. McMichael.

Two blocks east of Washington Ave. is the most imposing residence in town, the Georgian Revival style at its finest, rendered with the high-quality materials and workmanship readily available to a few fortunate clients during the depression. The **DeLeon F. Green House** (1934; William Lawrence Bottomley, architect; 401 Cedar St.) is a red brick mansion, 2½ stories tall with flanking 1½-story wings and a porch with Doric columns. New York and Richmond architect Bottomley, a leading proponent of the Virginia-influenced Georgian Revival, had several projects in N.C., the best known of which is Tatton Hall in Raleigh.

The former **Weldon Corn Mill** (1890s; E side US 301, just N of US 158, near 1st St.) recalls late 19th-c. efforts to exploit the waterpower of the canal. A stark, brick, industrial building of 2 and 3 stories with gable roof, corbeled brickwork, and arched windows, the mill was part of a complex that included a grain elevator, cottonseed oil mill, and cotton gin.

An architectural surprise appears on the western edge of town. The **Benjamin M. Mills Jr. House** (1947; S side US 158 at Holmes Dr.) is one of a few N.C. examples of modest but innovative houses built in a crisply geometric rendition of the International style. Built just after World War II for Benjamin and Laura Mills, leaders in the black community, the house of flat-roofed, intersecting blocks is constructed of concrete-covered concrete blocks and features ribbon windows at the corners and a rounded glass block wall at the entrance. The Millses' design source is as yet unidentified, but the owner-builder of a similar house in Durham recalls using a design from a magazine.

Edgecombe County (ED)

(Edgecombe Co. entries for Rocky Mount and Whitakers appear in the Nash Co. section.)

Tarboro (ED 1–28)

Tarboro is one of the most architecturally distinguished small towns in eastern N.C. Stylish antebellum buildings and handsomely planted green spaces—including a colonial town common and one of the state's most beautiful churchyards—combine with a lively variety of late 19th- and early 20th-c. buildings.

From Tarboro's colonial origins as a minor port (est. 1760) at the head of navigation on the Tar River, the grid plan, the old street names, and the *Town Common survive. In the antebellum era, as the area's cotton trade burgeoned, Tarboro developed unusual panache for a small courthouse town. One fashion-conscious antebellum lady refused an invitation to spend Christmas with her brother in Tarboro, for "to tell the truth, I have enough clothes to wear in Raleigh or in Rocky Mount, but not enough to wear in Tarboro." Town and county leaders prided themselves on their progressive farming interests, and here as elsewhere, outward-looking planters and merchants incorporated new ideas in architecture along with agricultural innovations. The steamboat- and cotton-based prosperity of the 1850s supported construction of fully realized Gothic Revival and Italian villa modes and the employment of English-born architects Edmund G. Lind of Baltimore and William Percival of Raleigh and Richmond. Other houses, many of which feature picturesque lattice and curvilinear sawnwork porches, reflect inspiration from 19th-c. patternbooks such as those of A. J. Downing, Calvert Vaux, and Samuel Sloan. On the eve of the Civil War, Tarboro was thriving, with a branch of the Wilmington and Weldon Railroad newly completed and several major buildings new or under construction.

After the Civil War, civic leaders pressed for industrial development and rail connections. "Property here cannot advance," insisted the *Tarboro Southerner* in 1883, "unless interests other than selling goods to the farmer are developed. . . . We want factories." Textile mills, fertilizer manufacturing, and beginning about 1890, tobacco sales bolstered modest growth. Establishment of Carolina Telephone & Telegraph as well as local banks further boosted the town's economy.

New attention to beautification and sanitation accompanied rebuilding of the commercial district and expansion of the town limits. Residential development extended north along Main St. past the Common toward the railroad. Industrial plants were built along the riverfront (these were razed in the late 20th c.). Eastward along the river, **Panola Heights** developed after the Civil War as a predominantly black neighborhood, where a number of early 20th-c. houses still stand among many newer residences. To the west and northwest, industrialists built small **Mill Villages** with grids of streets lined by 1- and 2-story mill houses. The corporate patterns of hierarchy and uniformity are still clear despite superficial changes by private owners. Tarboro's most intact historic architecture concentrates in the town center and the residential areas immediately flanking Main St.

ED 1 Central Business District

Several blocks of 1- to 4-story, commercial brick architecture typical of the late 19th and early 20th centuries line Main St. from the Tar River to the Common. Although the 19th-c. courthouse was replaced in 1964 by a massive, Neocolonial facility, much of the early 20th-c. downtown survives and thrives. Among the prominent landmarks are the **Masonic Building** (1908–10; Herbert W. Simpson [New Bern], architect; 301 Main St.), a 3-story, corner building of pressed brick with bracket cornice and free classical detail, and the **Henry Clark Bridgers Build-**

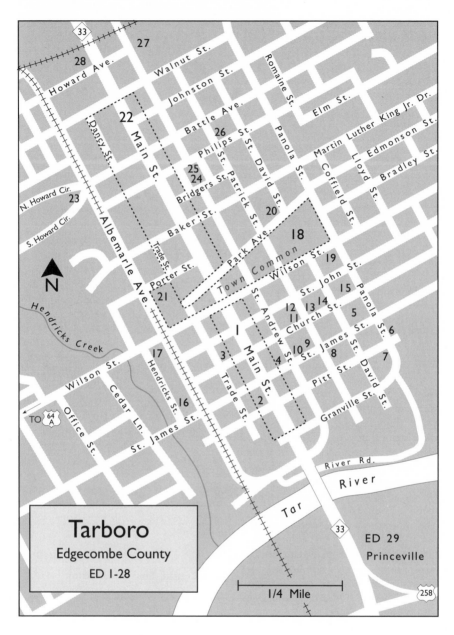

Tarboro

Edgecombe County

ED 1-28

TO 64 A

N

33

ED 29
Princeville

Tar River

River Rd.

1/4 Mile

258

ing (1907; 431–35 Main St.), another large, brick building dominating a prominent corner and featuring eclectic classical motifs. The **U.S. Post Office** (1914; Oscar Wenderoth, supervising architect of the Treasury; 525 Main St.), of pale stone with a dignified Doric portico, exemplifies the restrained Beaux Arts classicism promulgated from Wenderoth's office. Classicism continues in the **First Baptist Church** (1926–28; 605 Main St.), a symmetrical composition with portico and steeple.

ED 2 Redmond-Shackleford House
1885; 300 Main St.

Sheltered by a walled garden, the flamboyant, Second Empire style residence of stuccoed masonry is dramatized by a vivid polychrome paint scheme. The rich interior decorative painting is attributed to Edward Zoeller, a Bavarian fresco painter who settled in Tarboro in the 1850s. A detached brick kitchen stands to the rear. The house was built for Claudia and Kate Redmond, daughters of a wealthy merchant. Kate married local industrialist Jonathan Shackleford.

ED 3 Dozier House

Ca. 1860; Edmund G. Lind (Baltimore), attributed architect; 112 W. Church St.

The 2-story, brick townhouse of Italianate style is probably the work of architect Lind, who designed for several local clients concurrently with his work at the plantation house *Coolmore. A central, arch-headed entrance pavilion dominates the facade; paired windows feature heavy lintels; and a bracket cornice carries around the house.

ED 4 Carolina Telephone & Telegraph Company Building

1912; Rose & Company (Rocky Mount), attributed architects; 120 E. St. James St.

Built as headquarters of the company that was founded in Tarboro by George Holderness, William Powell, and others and developed into a major regional corporation, the 3-story, brick building features pilasters, paired windows, and bold classical details.

The original town limits lay south of the Common, and here the residential grid of streets east of Main St. is lined by old trees and a rewarding variety of well-kept buildings, from simple Federal style dwellings through the Queen Anne and Colonial Revival styles. A few landmarks are especially outstanding.

ED 5 Calvary Episcopal Church and Churchyard

1859–68 (William Percival, architect; Thomas H. Coats, builder); parish house and cloister, 1922–23, 1926 (Hobart Upjohn, architect); 411 E. Church St.

One of the finest antebellum Gothic Revival churches in the state stands within a memo-

ED 5 *Calvary Episcopal Church and Churchyard*

rably beautiful churchyard epitomizing the 19th-c. spirit of picturesque landscape. The planting of exotic specimens was begun by the Reverend Joseph Blount Cheshire, who became rector in 1842 and graced his churchyard—and parishioners' gardens—with his avocation. He studied A. J. Downing and other authorities on landscape gardening and obtained plants from distant sources. The story is told that one day an elderly resident passed by the churchyard while Cheshire was gardening and chided him for making the place so beautiful he was "enticing folks to die."

Calvary Church was organized in 1833, successor to earlier parish churches that came and went between ca. 1749 and 1822. A small, frame church was erected in 1840. Under Cheshire's leadership, in 1859 the parish of 33 communicants set out to build a church to accommodate 500. The church was designed by architect Percival, who had come from England to Raleigh by way of Virginia and worked in the late 1850s in Tarboro, Raleigh, Yanceyville, and Chapel Hill. (See Introduction, Fig. 30.) The brick walls, the unequal towers with spires, and the roof were in place when the Civil War halted construction. Parishioners' profitable cotton crop of 1867 financed completion, and the church was dedicated in 1868. The brick walls never received the intended stucco cover; their natural patina is now part of the church's charm. Typical of the Early English Gothic style, surface ornament is minimal, and the interior is dominated by an exposed truss ceiling. The **Parish House and Cloister** evidence the tact that endeared architect Hobart Upjohn to many Episcopal parishes in the early 20th c.

ED 6 St. Luke's Episcopal Church
1892–94; NE corner Panola and Pitt Sts.

The simplified Gothic Revival church with corner tower was built for a congregation established in 1872 for black members of *Calvary Episcopal Church. The austere exterior contrasts with the richly finished Gothic Revival interior.

ED 7 John C. Jones House
1870s; Jerry Rutledge, attributed carpenter; 411 Pitt St.

One of several decorated cottages of the postwar era, the 1-story, L-shaped, frame house features the sawn and latticework front porch popular in mid-19th-c. Tarboro. It is said to have been built by carpenter Jerry Rutledge for Prof. John C. Jones, a prominent late 19th-c. educator and second principal of the black public school. Later it was owned by Dr. Alexander McMillan, physician, and Viola Gray McMillan, teacher, missionary, and founder of Union Baptist Church.

ED 8 Howard Memorial Presbyterian Church
1908–9; SE corner St. Patrick St. at St. James St.

The church is a confident blend of Neoclassical and Romanesque Revival styles in rich red brick, with a double ranges of windows, a robust tower, and vigorous classical entry all emphasized by bold brickwork. Its composition suggests an influence from the colonial Christ Church, Philadelphia, but the free use of classical motifs is pure turn of the century. In 1909 the *Tarboro Southerner* de-

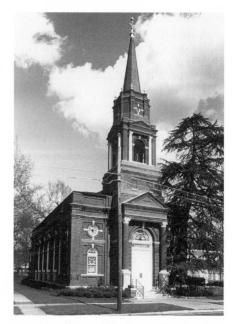

ED 8 *Howard Memorial Presbyterian Church*

scribed it as "Grecian, except the small, short steeple." The architect is unknown.

ED 9 Baker-Howard House
Ca. 1800; 210 E. St. James St.

Although its history is uncertain, the well-detailed, 2-story, frame house with Flemish-bond chimneys is among the oldest in town. For many years it has served as law offices.

ED 10 Williamson House
1850s; 204 E. St. James St.; private

The little, 1-story, gable-roofed, frame house displays the local use of a picturesque lattice porch on even a tiny dwelling, here two main rooms with a center chimney.

ED 11 Cotten-Engelhard-Howard House
1820s, 1860 (Edmund G. Lind [Baltimore], architect), ca. 1900; 210 E. Church St.

In 1860 J. A. and Margaret Cotten Engelhard employed E. G. Lind to update the house built for Tarboro merchant Spencer Cotten. Lind employed his customary Italianate style for additions, complemented by elaborate interior painting. In the late 19th c. it was the home of business and political leader George Howard.

ED 12 Howard-Holderness House
1890s; William P. Rose (Raleigh), architect; 508 St. Patrick St.

The dramatically massed, frame house epitomizes the liveliness of the late Queen Anne style with its pediments, turrets, and rich surface ornament, here combined with a classically detailed porch. Designed by prolific architect Rose and published in his promotional booklet, *That House* (1900), the residence was built by George Howard for his daughter Harriet and her husband, George Holderness, a founder of Carolina Telephone & Telegraph.

ED 13 Parker-Cheshire House
Ca. 1810; 302 E. Church St.

Typical of the simple, conservative dwellings built for Tarboro's leading citizens before the mid-19th c., the 2-story, frame house has a 2-room plan, restrained early Federal details, and a later latticed porch. It was built for merchant-planter Theophilus Parker. His daughter Elizabeth married Episcopal priest Joseph Blount Cheshire, who came to Tarboro in 1842, and the couple lived here over half a century.

ED 14 Cheshire-Nash House
Ca. 1869; 310 E. Church St.

The brick, Gothic cottage was erected for Annie Gray Cheshire by her father, Joseph Blount Cheshire, the rector of *Calvary Episcopal Church, supposedly when she was ten. At nineteen she married businessman

ED 14 *Cheshire-Nash House*

S. S. Nash. The cottage continues the taste for the picturesque that informs the church and churchyard.

ED 15 Matthewson House
Late 19th c.; 414 E. Church St.

ED 15 *Matthewson House*

The decorated cottage with millwork intact and a vivid paint scheme suggests the original richness of many small houses now stripped of their ornament. It was built as his own home by George Matthewson, a black builder prominent in 19th-c. Tarboro. The ornate lattice porch shares features with antebellum and later 19th-c. houses in Tarboro and environs and may indicate Matthewson's role in their construction.

ED 16 Tobacco Warehouses
Early 20th c.; W of Albemarle Ave. from St. James St. to Wilson St.

West of downtown along the rail spur stands a group of big, brick tobacco warehouses—survivors of many built in the early 20th c. when sale of the region's bright-leaf tobacco was a mainstay of the economy. Pilasters alternate with segmental-arched windows, and corbeled brickwork accentuates the facades. Skylights and big, unimpeded spaces permitted the display and inspection of each farmer's golden crop by tobacco company buyers.

ED 17 Tarboro Water Plant
1934–35; William C. Olsen (Raleigh), engineer; Albemarle Ave. at Wilson St.

The wpa public works building is recalled locally as one of the first construction projects begun after building activity stopped in the Great Depression. It is one of several water plants designed by Olsen in the region, including those in *Elizabeth City and *Rocky Mount. The handsome and quietly monumental red brick building is enriched with Neoclassical detail, including a Palladian motif entrance, and large, arched windows light the interior.

ED 18 Town Common
1760; bounded by Albemarle Ave., Wilson St., Park Ave., and Panola St.

ED 18 *Town Common*

Dividing the original town grid from subsequent development to the north is the Town Common, one of the state's finest urban spaces. When Tarboro was established in 1760, 50 acres were set aside as "Commons for the use of the said Town." Although the eastern and western sections were whittled away as Tarboro grew, the northern portion survives as a revered park dotted with memorials: a Confederate monument (1904); an obelisk dedicated to Louis D. Wilson, local political leader; a stone bearing a metal marker cast from the *Maine*, honoring the Spanish-American War dead; and a cast-iron fountain memorializing Edgecombe Co. soldier Henry S. Wyatt, who was killed at Bethel Church in 1861—the first Confederate death in battle and inspiration for the state's "First at Bethel" motto. The only known example of a colonial common left in the state, the shaded, 16-acre green serves as a public gathering place and is flanked by residences with deep porches, displaying a full range of eras and styles. In recent years parts of the riverside south common have been reopened as a park.

ED 19 Weddell-Pender House
1860s; 411 E. Wilson St.

The board-and-batten, Carpenter Gothic cottage has delicate bargeboards accentuating its steep gables. Set into the angle of the L-plan is a decorative lattice porch akin to those seen on houses of various forms throughout the town.

ED 20 L. D. Pender House
Ca. 1912; 306 E. Park Ave.; private

One of the earliest and most striking of Tarboro's many bungalows, with exaggerated pillars and Oriental brackets, it is thought to have been constructed by local builder Charlie Pulley for Lorenzo D. Pender, who ran a hardware store.

ED 21 Norfleet Cotton Press
Ca. 1840; W end of Town Common at Albemarle Ave.

ED 21 *Norfleet Cotton Press*

Isaac Norfleet constructed this press in the mid-19th c. on his plantation southwest of Tarboro. Originally used to press fruit for cider and wine, it was converted to process cotton about 1860. The structure of mortised and tenoned heart pine timbers stands 22 feet high and contains a central vertical shaft. A large wooden screw, 19 inches in diameter, was powered by mules hitched to the sweeps—long beams attached to the top of the shaft. The screw drove down a wooden packing block to compress 300 to 350 lbs. of cotton into bales. Moved to the

Common ca. 1938, the press was restored in 1976 by the Edgecombe Co. Historical Society. Such structures were once a frequent sight in cotton-growing areas, but most have vanished.

ED 22 North Main St.

Great trees and period street lamps enhance the series of 19th- and early 20th-c. houses along one of the region's prime residential thoroughfares. The well-kept houses lining the broad street range from antebellum Greek Revival and Italianate dwellings to later 19th-c. Italianate and Queen Anne styles and early 20th-c. Colonial Revival houses and bungalows. A sampling includes the **Pender House** (ca. 1860; 807 Main St.), a Greek Revival house with the locally popular, picturesque latticed porch, and the **Morris-Powell House** (ca. 1890; 912 N. Main St.), a dramatically asymmetrical and eclectic 2-story, frame house in an Italianate–Queen Anne blend, associated with Arthur Morris, founder of the local Morris Plan Bank, and William Powell, first president of Carolina Telephone & Telegraph.

Farther north are the **Pippen House** (1870s; 1003 Main St.), a richly detailed, L-shaped Italianate residence on a spacious lot; the **Hart House** (1909; 1109 Main St.), a locally unusual rendition of the Southern

Colonial residence with Corinthian portico; a series of L-shaped Queen Anne cottages (ca. 1900; 1301–15 Main St.); and the **M. S. Brown House** (ca. 1925; 1402 Main St.), a spacious bungalow with side gables and a front dormer, built for Brown soon after he opened his Coca-Cola bottling plant next door in 1925.

An important series of antebellum villas stands at intervals on the western side of N. Main St. They once faced Main St. across deep lawns, but now they are screened by newer houses. These, in company with the nearby *Barracks, constitute a unique survival of antebellum suburban development in the state. The **Hyman-Philips House** (1840s; 106 W. Philips St.) is a 2-story, double-pile-plan, frame house with Greek Revival porch and Italianate bracket cornice. Essentially in original condition is the **Pender-Lanier House** (ca. 1840s; 1004 Main St.), a spacious, simply finished, Greek Revival house with a center-passage plan two rooms deep, a broad porch, and a polygonal cupola. **Norfleet** (1858, 20th c.; Norfleet Court, 1100 Main St.) began as a 1-story, frame, Gothic Revival house and has been remade in various forms over the years.

The residential areas flanking N. Main St.
continue the grid plan and a variety of late

19th- and early 20th-c. houses, which grew up around earlier residences built north of town.

ED 23 The Barracks

1858–61; William Percival, architect; 1100 Albemarle Ave.

ED 23 *The Barracks*

One of Percival's two surviving suburban villas of the 1850s, the eclectic brick residence is similar in some respects to his Montford Hall in Raleigh. A complex plan circulates around a central, skylit rotunda. The architect freely combined Italianate and classical motifs: the portico features fluted columns taking their order from the Tower of the Winds, the Athenian temple widely emulated by 19th-c. American classicists, while the complex roofline and cupola, bracketed eaves, and arched windows give a picturesque flavor. Named for a former military encampment on the site, The Barracks was built in 1858 for William S. Battle, son of an old planter family and a major investor in *Rocky Mount Mills.

ED 24 Blount-Bridgers House (The Grove)

Ca. 1808; 130 Bridgers St.; open regular hours

The grandest early 19th-c. house in Tarboro, it was built for politician Thomas Blount on a 296-acre tract north of town and singled out in 1810 as "a very good house, the best that is in the county." The large frame dwelling typifies the scale and quality of the largest planters' houses of its era, standing 2 stories plus attic atop a high basement. Four tall Flemish-bond chimneys and attic lunettes emphasize its mass. Distinctive fea-

ED 24 *Blount-Bridgers House*

tures include the individualized Georgian-Federal interior woodwork and the asymmetrical double-pile plan: large front rooms flank the front passage; the rear passage, wider to accommodate the stair, is flanked by smaller rear rooms. The airy lattice porch around all four sides was added in the mid-19th c. It is now an arts center featuring works by painter Hobson Pittman.

ED 25 Pender Museum (Everett House)

Ca. 1810; 1018 St. Andrews St.; open by appointment for research only

The beautifully detailed little house epitomizes the scale, plan, and form of many traditional dwellings of its era. The double-sloped gable roof extends to cover a shed porch in front and shed rooms flanking an open porch in back. The high-quality craftsmanship, including intricate cornice molding and tapered porch posts, recalls that many well-built houses of the late 18th and early 19th centuries were quite small. Double-shouldered end chimneys and brick pier foundations were rebuilt when the

ED 25 *Pender Museum*

house was moved here from its rural site in 1969. The hall-parlor plan has an enclosed stair from the hall to the attic chambers.

ED 26 MacNair House

Late 1890s; William P. Rose, Raleigh; 1103 St. Patrick St.

Designed by Raleigh architect Rose and published in his booklet, *That House* (1900), the large, frame house typifies the late Queen Anne style, with its high hip roof breaking into gables and dormers and its wraparound porch adorned with spindlework and a corner pavilion.

ED 27 Coats-Walston House

Early 1860s; Thomas H. Coats, builder; 1503 St. Andrews St.

ED 27 *Coats-Walston House*

Advertised for sale in 1865 as "a new brick 'English Cottage,'" the picturesque house was evidently drawn from Minard Lafever's *Architectural Instructor* (1856). Built as Coats's own residence and an advertisement of his modern taste and skill, the house presents many innovative features: the hip roof interrupted by a front central gable and a cupola, the "Italian" blocks accenting the windows, the rafter brackets of the eaves, the diminution of the second-story windows, and an elaborate ventilation and insulation system. A detached brick kitchen and board-and-batten smokehouse complete the ensemble. Coats, a Virginia-born contractor, built several buildings designed by architect William Percival.

ED 28 Atlantic Coast Line Railroad Depot and Freight House

Freight House, 1884; Depot, ca. 1910; NW corner N. Main and Howard Sts.

Long neglected, the railyard buildings still recall the importance of the railroad to Tarboro's development. A rare survivor of late 19th-c. railroad architecture is the **Freight House** beside Howard St., a long, rectangular structure with expressive brickwork defining large, arched doorways and flanking pilasters. The **Depot**, with a 2-story center pavilion and 1-story wings, features free classical detail in vivid red brick with white trim.

ED 29 Princeville

Settled in 1865 by newly freed blacks, the community just across the Tar River from Tarboro was originally called Freedom Hill and was one of the state's earliest communities established by and for freedmen. It was incorporated in 1885 and renamed for leading citizen Turner Prince. The most prominent architectural landmark is the **Mount Zion Primitive Baptist Church** (1890s; w side Church St., s of US 258), a simple, weatherboarded, gable-end church erected for a congregation established in 1871. In front of the church stands a powerfully realized stone bust, erected in 1896 by churchman John Bell to memorialize the Reverend Abraham Wooten, minister and community reformer.

ED 30 Coolmore

1859–61; Edmund G. Lind (Baltimore), architect; S side US 64A, 0.5 mi. E of SR 1207, Tarboro vic.; National Historic Landmark; private, visible from road

Set behind a grove of large magnolias and deciduous trees on a 12-acre lawn, the plantation villa and its matching outbuildings form an extraordinary ensemble of late antebellum taste. Coolmore was built for Dr. Joseph J. W. Powell, a prominent planter and physician, at the zenith of the area's cotton prosperity. Architect Lind of Baltimore not only designed the mansion but also recruited workmen and assisted in selecting materials, furnishings, and decorations—all from Baltimore. The 2-story, frame house

ED 30 *Coolmore*

with 1-story wings features a cupola and ornate bracketed cornice. The interior, with a central stair spiraling to the cupola, features ornamental plaster and a splendid ensemble of trompe l'oeil painting executed by Ernst Dreyer of Baltimore, an immigrant painter from St. Petersburg, Russia. Outbuildings continue the Italianate villa theme, including a smokehouse, a carriage house, servants' quarters, and a gas house to the rear as well as the kitchen, which has been moved to the northern side of the road. A few hundred yards to the east stand an earlier farmhouse and several later tenant houses.

ED 31 Hart House

Ca. 1890; S side US 64A, 0.05 mi. W of SR 1217, Hartsease; private, visible from road

The prominent, Queen Anne style farmhouse displays a form far more common in town than in the countryside. Ells and bays break up the 2-story, gable-roofed block, and a wraparound porch with turned posts carries around the front and side. It was part of a rural community called Hartsease after Richard Hart, a farmer and merchant who operated a store and post office nearby. A series of small, frame tenant houses extends east across the open fields.

ED 32 Old Town Plantation House

1785; N side SR 97, 0.7 mi. W of SR 1406, Rocky Mount vic.; private, visible at a distance from road

Among the oldest houses in the inner coastal plain, this is one of the few surviving examples of the small, carefully finished frame

dwellings built for planters in the 18th c. The gambrel roof, English-bond foundation, double-shouldered Flemish-bond chimneys, full-width shed porch, and hall-parlor plan with enclosed stair are all hallmarks of an architectural tradition that developed by the mid-18th c. and changed little for several decades. The enclosed porch rooms are reconstructed from physical evidence; the rear ell is new.

ED 32 *Old Town Plantation House*

The house was built in 1785 for Jacob Battle, a wealthy and industrious farmer, in the year of his marriage to Penelope Edwards. Jacob extended the landholdings he received from his father, Elisha, who had come from Virginia to Edgecombe Co. in 1747 or 1748, established a plantation, and become a political leader and progenitor of the large and prominent Battle family. At the time of his death in 1814, Jacob was the owner of extensive acreage and more than 100 slaves. Old Town Plantation continued in the hands of descendants until the early 20th c. Endangered at its original location 2 miles east, the house was moved and restored in 1980.

ED 33 Cool Spring

1890; NE corner NC 97 and SR 1406, Rocky Mount vic.; private, visible from road

This unusual house in its grove of trees evokes an archetypal southern image, created by the low hip roof reaching out to shelter a deep porch on all four sides. The dwelling within the porch has an asymmetrical plan, with the front door opening into a sitting room. This is the third dwelling on a site long occupied by the Battle family, part of much larger holdings. The first house, built in the 18th c. for Elisha Battle, burned, as did the subsequent house built in the 1850s. A latticed breezeway connects to a 2-room kitchen said to survive from the 1850s.

ED 34 St. John's Episcopal Church
1891; S side 200 block E. Main St. at Cemetery St., Battleboro

The village church is an especially fine example of the board-and-batten, Gothic Revival mode favored by Episcopalians who continued to be inspired by Richard Upjohn's *Rural Architecture* (1852ff.) as they erected mission churches in the late 19th c. The corner entrance tower rises to a crenellated roofline and tall spire, complementing the board-and-batten walls and lancet windows. On its completion it was praised by Bishop Theodore Lyman as "so tasteful and well-ordered a Church Building."

ED 35 Stewart House
Late 18th–early 19th c.; W side SR 1415, 1 mi. N of SR 1407, Phillips Crossroads vic.; private, visible from road

The 1½-story, frame plantation house, five bays wide with three gabled dormers, has characteristic craftsmanship includes Flemish-bond, double-shouldered chimneys and simple, late Georgian details. Little is known of its early history.

SR 1409 and nearby roads traverse a long-settled agricultural area with many notable houses and broad fields dotted with farm buildings and 1-story, frame tenant houses, which typically follow 2-room plans with center chimneys or L-plans.

ED 36 Williams Primitive Baptist Church
Mid-19th c.; N side SR 1428, 0.5 mi. E of SR 1409, Wrendale vic.

Incorporating more of the spirit of the Greek Revival than most rural Primitive Baptist churches, the small, weatherboarded church has a pedimented front and long, 12/12 windows along the sides. It was built for a congregation founded in the late 18th c.

ED 37 Speight's Chapel Methodist Church
1877; NE corner SR 1409 and SR 1428, Wrendale vic.

The simple, picturesque, Gothic Revival frame church features a corner tower with vestibule. It was built for a congregation established in the mid-19th c. by the Reverend John Francis Speight of *The Cedars.

ED 38 The Cedars (Speight House)
1860; William Ruffin, attributed builder; W side SR 1409, 0.4 mi. N of SR 1428, Wrendale vic.; private, visible from road

ED 38 *The Cedars*

The 2-story, T-plan, frame house displays the local Italianate idiom at its liveliest, with bracket cornice, molded window hoods, bull's-eye windows in the second story, and a fanciful version of the lattice porch. It was built for Methodist minister John Francis Speight and his wife, Emma Lewis Speight; he died soon after it was finished. Their son, Dr. Richard Harrison Speight, occupied it until 1919, and his medical office remains at the site. Outbuildings include tobacco barns, a mule barn, a packhouse, a smokehouse, and animal sheds.

ED 39 Josiah Cutchin House
1830s; E side SR 1409, 2 mi. N of SR 1428, Wrendale vic.; private, visible from road

The 5-bay I-house, with center-passage plan plus rear shed rooms, combines late Federal and early Greek Revival details. Two enclosed stairs—in the passage and south parlor—reportedly gave boys and girls separate access to unconnected, second-floor rooms. A smokehouse, a mule barn, and a pack-house survive.

ED 40 J. M. Cutchin House

Mid-19th c.; W side SR 1409, 2.4 mi. N of SR 1428, Wrendale vic.; private, visible from road

Standing in a grove of trees surrounded by open fields, the little house exemplifies a prevalent rural house type of the 19th c.: the 1-story, Greek Revival cottage with hip roof, 3-bay facade, and center-passage plan—here with a rear shed and rear ell. The full-width, hip-roofed porch has simple lattice and sawnwork akin to several in Tarboro and the county. Several barns and tenant houses survive.

ED 41 Brick School

1895; W side US 301, Bricks

One of many southern black schools aided by northern donors, the Joseph K. Brick Agricultural, Industrial and Normal School began in 1895 on land donated by Julia Brewster Brick of Brooklyn, N.Y., to the American Missionary Association and named in memory of her husband. With her continued support the school developed from an elementary and farm life school into a high school and junior college that served the black youths of the rural region, as well as local farmers, until it closed in 1933. Since 1953 the campus has operated as the Franklinton Center of the United Church of Christ. The oldest buildings date from the early 20th c. and include the old **Brick High School**, a 1-story frame structure with hip roof and banks of windows, and three frame **Faculty Houses** of foursquare and bungalow types, such as the gable-fronted residence of principal T. S. Inborden. More recent buildings are of brick in late Colonial Revival style.

ED 42 Pittman-Cobb House

Early 19th c.; N side SR 1423, 1.6 mi. E of NC 33, Red Hill vic.; private, visible from road

The 2-story plantation house follows a locally unusual side-passage plan and has especially fine, late Federal detailing, a dentil cornice, molded weatherboards, and Flemish-bond chimneys. The late 19th- and early 20th-c. outbuildings include a smokehouse, an office, tobacco barns, and livestock barns. Several saddlebag-plan, frame tenant houses stand across the road.

ED 43 Cedar Lane

1848; E side NC 33, 0.35 mi. S of NC 97, Leggett; private, visible from road

The simply detailed, 2-story, Greek Revival house with contemporary outbuildings was the seat of a medium-sized plantation before and after the Civil War. Built for James D. Savage, it was later home of the prominent Fountain family.

ED 44 Wilkinson-Hurdle House

Ca. 1885; N side NC 97, 1.3 mi. E of NC 33, Leggett vic.; private, visible from road

The decorated rural cottage continues a picturesque tradition begun in Tarboro and Edgecombe Co. in the 1850s: a relatively modest frame house, 1 story tall and one room deep plus a rear ell, which presents a fashionable face to the road, with bracketed eaves, sinuous bargeboards, and an ornate, sawnwork porch.

ED 45 Grace Episcopal Church

1894; E side US 258, 0.2 mi. N of NC 97, Lawrence

The late Gothic Revival, frame church features an unusual side-entrance vestibule—perhaps recalling English parish churches—beneath steep, shingled gables. Chancel furnishings were carved by Kate Cheshire, sister of Bishop Joseph Blount Cheshire. The mission was one of several rural churches founded from *Calvary Episcopal Church, Tarboro.

ED 46 Speed

The former railroad village, its tracks long gone but with Railroad St. still the principal thoroughfare, retains key buildings from a livelier era. A most remarkable pair consists of the tiny, stone-fronted **U.S. Post Office**

ED 46 *Speed Fire Dept. and U.S. Post Office*

(formerly Farmers Banking and Trust Co., 1920), the essence of banker's Beaux Arts classicism in miniature, which stands alongside the **Speed Fire Dept.** The board-and-batten **Speed Depot** (1923) stands at the western end of Railroad St., and along the adjoining grid of streets are frame houses from modest, saddlebag dwellings to late Queen Anne residences. Across NC 122 on SR 1508 is **St. Mary's Episcopal Church**, another of the county's mission churches in Carpenter Gothic style.

ED 47 Cullen Pippen Houses

Late 18th and early 19th c.; S side NC 111, 0.4 mi. E of SR 1524, Tarboro vic.; private, visible from road

Its visibility down a long stretch of NC 111 gives special prominence to the 2-story, gable-roofed, Federal style house. The tall mass of the narrow, 3-bay house; the verticality of the double-concave-shouldered, Flemish-bond chimneys; and the hall-parlor plan characterize Federal period domestic architecture of the region. The older house on the property, a 1-story, hall-parlor Georgian cottage, has been moved up alongside the larger house, and both have been restored.

ED 48 Wilkinson-Dozier House

Ca. 1825; E side SR 1526, 1.7 mi. SE of SR 1524, Tarboro vic.; private, visible from road

The 2-story, frame plantation house is distinguished by a 2-tier portico, where slender, turned columns, linked by a lattice balustrade, carry a pediment with enriched cornice. This is one of several local houses with individualized Federal detailing, including lavish reeding. The house was probably built for Silas and Sally Wilkinson shortly after they married in 1822; he accumulated holdings of over 1,500 acres. Recently moved here from other sites are a 1½-story, hall-parlor-plan farmhouse of ca. 1825 and a ca. 1830 kitchen and barn. (See Introduction, Fig. 27.)

ED 49 Danielhurst

Ca. 1825, ca. 1850; NW side SR 1523, 0.1 mi. NE of US 64; private, visible from road

Two houses are joined in distinctive fashion. The Federal period, hall-parlor-plan cottage was built for John H. Daniel, a Primitive Baptist minister. He subsequently enlarged it with a perpendicular, 2-story addition in robust, vernacular Greek Revival style, with a 2-tier porch and pedimented ends.

ED 50 Cotton Valley

Ca. 1844; E side US 258, 0.6 mi. N of SR 1601; private, visible from road

The plantation house features robust Greek Revival details adapted from the pattern-books of Asher Benjamin. Built for planter Baker Staton, the 2-story, 5-bay house has pairs of chimneys at each pedimented gable end, indicating the double-pile, center-passage plan. The wraparound porch with lattice posts reflects the locally picturesque style of the 1850s and later. Several outbuildings remain.

ED 51 Old Sparta
Jct. NC 42 and SR 1601

This archetypal country crossroads began by 1830 when the post office and plantation center was known simply as Sparta. It was probably renamed to avoid confusion when the Alleghany Co. seat was established as Sparta in 1859. **Edmondson's Store** (ca. 1875; sw corner NC 42 and SR 1601) epitomizes the country stores essential to the late 19th- and early 20th-c. rural economy and social life. The 2-story, weatherboarded building presents a pedimented gable end to the highway; the original central entrance was later shifted to the corner, and pent roofs were added to suit changing needs. The countertop post-office unit and other store fittings remain. The **Old Sparta Primitive Baptist Church** (1856; N side NC 42, 0.2 mi. w of SR 1601) shows the denomination's preference for simplicity in gable-end, weatherboarded churches; a polygonal pulpit bay was added later. The nearby **Old Sparta School** (1880s) is a plain little weatherboarded building typical of rural schools before the great early 20th-c. schoolhouse campaigns. **St. Ignatius Church** (1918), now Old Sparta Advent Church, is a simple, rectangular frame chapel clad in wood shingles, built for one of several rural missions established by *Calvary Episcopal Church in the late 19th and early 20th centuries. The **Conetoe Depot** (N side NC 42, 0.2 mi. w of SR 1601), moved here from the village of Conetoe, is one of the few survivors of the many board-and-batten depots that once stood in the county.

ED 52 Bracebridge Hall
Ca. 1826, ca. 1840, later expansions; W side SR 1601, 0.6 mi. NE of NC 43, Old Sparta vic.; private, visible from road

A fine, Doric porch and other Greek Revival details derived from the patternbooks of Asher Benjamin distinguish the 2-story, 5-bay house. Planter Jonas Carr erected a 1-story dwelling here, to which he added the Greek Revival front block before his death

in 1843. His son, Elias, who inherited the property and made further expansions, was an agrarian reformer in the post–Civil War era and governor of the state. Grounds include formal gardens with large oaks, crepe myrtles, camellias, azaleas, English boxwoods, and towering magnolias. A large barn, ca. 1860, is among the several outbuildings. (See Introduction, Fig. 29.)

ED 53 Vinedale
Ca. 1855; S side NC 42/43, 0.3 mi. W of US 258, Pinetops vic.; private, visible from road

A country version of the Italianate villas being built in Tarboro in the 1850s, with cupola and bracketed eaves, the house was built for John A. Vines on a 1,600-acre plantation that produced cotton, corn, grains, and livestock.

ED 54 St. Lewis
NC 42 W of SR 1109

The village, named after the locally prominent Lewis family, flourished as a 19th-c. agricultural center but declined when the East Carolina Railway (1901) drew trade to the new railroad towns of Pinetops and Macclesfield. It maintains a sense of community presence, with tall trees lining the road and several 19th- and early 20th-c. houses. Set back on the northern side of NC 42 is the **Pitt House**, which combines an ornate, late 19th-c. front section with a simpler, early 19th-c. house to the rear and is surrounded by many frame outbuildings.

ED 55 Griffin Farm
1905, 1922; N side NC 42, 0.6 mi. E of NC 124, St. Lewis vic.; private, visible from road

An evocative and complete early 20th-c. farm complex. When Charlie and Hattie Griffin moved here, there was a typical, 1-story, hip-roofed house on the site. As their family grew to include eleven children, they expanded it into a 2-story residence, fronted with a simplified version of the popular Southern Colonial portico. The pecan grove exemplifies a widespread practice in the early 20th c., and outbuildings including tobacco barns recall the importance of tobacco cultivation.

ED 56 Atkinson-Barnes House

1813–20, late 19th c.; S side NC 42, just E of Wilson Co. line, St. Lewis vic.; private, visible from road

ED 56 *Atkinson-Barnes House*

This landmark house along a well-traveled road began as a 1-room-plan dwelling, 2 stories tall plus a rear shed, finished in simple Federal style. Built for farmer Aaron Atkinson, the house descended through several generations of daughters. William Barnes probably lengthened the house in the late 19th c. by building the 1-story east wing to the side and stretching a porch across the whole facade.

ED 57 Garrett-Wiggins House (Adelphia)

1854; W side NC 111/122, 0.6 mi. N of SR 1003, Wiggins Crossroads; private, visible from road

This picturesque, hip-roofed cottage was built for Joseph John Garrett, planter and physician. Lavish Italianate detail, especially the (recently reconstructed) lattice porch with quatrefoil motifs, points to local use of

ED 57 *Garrett-Wiggins House*

William Ranlett's popular book, *The Architect* (1847). The doctor's office reiterates the design, and several other outbuildings complete the complex. Owned for many years by the Wiggins family, the farmstead has been restored recently.

ED 58 Few in Number Primitive Baptist Church

Ca. 1890; N side SR 1003 0.4 E of NC 111/122, Wiggins Crossroads

ED 58 *Few in Number Primitive Baptist Church*

The weatherboarded church has a strictly symmetrical gable end with shuttered windows flanking the entrance and simple gable returns; lancet windows along the sides add a Gothic Revival touch. Built on property transferred by the Webb family to the trustees of the congregation in 1889, this is one of several churches built in the coastal plain for black Primitive Baptist congregations. Its full name, the Primitive Baptist Church of God's Holy Chosen Few in Number, expresses the denomination's predestinarian theology.

ED 59 Daughtridge Farm

Late 19th–early 20th c.; E side SR 1002, 0.7 mi. N of SR 1006, Rocky Mount vic.; private, visible from road

The large and picturesque turn-of-the-century tobacco farm complex centers on a frame house beneath great trees and illustrates a full range of outbuildings. About 1900 the Daughtridge family expanded the 1-story house of the 1880s by adding the 2-story front addition with late Victorian and Colonial Revival trim. At least twenty outbuildings, most painted white, range behind the house, including a carbide gas house, a commissary, a cook house, and various sheds. Frame and log tobacco barns, packhouses, grading houses, and barns stand in the fields beyond. John C. Daughtridge also operated a Rocky Mount livery stable, ran a sawmill on his farm, and worked as a contractor. Nearby are farms and businesses operated by other family members. (See Introduction, Fig. 6.)

Nash County (NS)

See Richard L. Mattson, The History and Architecture of Nash County, North Carolina *(1987), and Kate Mearns,* Central City Historic Buildings Inventory: Rocky Mount, North Carolina *(1979).*

Nash County, lying just west of the fall line that creates the falls of the Tar River at Rocky Mount, marks a transition from the coastal plain to the gently rolling terrain of the piedmont landscape. The northern part of the county, alongside Fishing Creek and the plantation cultures of Halifax and Warren counties, has a number of early plantation houses as well as many tenant farmhouses. The southern portion has smaller farms with buildings mainly from the late 19th c. onward. The county's varied rural landscape is dotted with many small trading towns and densely occupied by inhabited farmsteads, where tobacco barns and tenant houses recall the redefinition of the landscape in the late 19th and early 20th centuries.

NS 1 Nashville

The county seat offers an especially clear example of small-town development patterns: distinct urban sectors are well defined as the main business thoroughfare of W. Washington St. opens into the shaded residential boulevard of E. Washington St. Although Nashville began as county seat in 1778, railroad-based prosperity from the 1880s into the 1920s transformed the community. Its predominantly late 19th- and early 20th-c. architecture covers a classic range of forms and styles.

At the heart of town, the conservative, red brick **Nash County Courthouse** (1921; John C. Stout [Rocky Mount], architect; W. Washington St.) proclaims its purpose with its graceful full-height portico. Tall, arched windows at the second level light the spacious, Colonial Revival courtroom.

W. Washington St. has simple brick stores

NS 1 *S. Boddie St., Nashville*

from the turn of the century, plus such surprises as the sleek, Moderne curves of the stuccoed **Nashville Fire Department** (mid-1930s), which began life as George Wheeless's Chevrolet dealership. Following a frequent pattern, the transition from commercial to residential sectors is marked by a corner church: the **First Baptist Church** (1914; John C. Stout [Rocky Mount], architect; E. Washington St. at S. Alston St.), a Romanesque Revival building with lively, Flemish-bond brickwork and a corner tower; now the Nash Co. Cultural Center.

Amid the many handsome residences shaded by the tall maples and other trees along E. Washington St., two of the most imposing were erected by local businessman and civic leader George Bissette. First he built an ornate, Queen Anne style residence, the **Bissette-Braswell House** (1898; 205 E. Washington St.), which boasted the town's first ceramic bathtub and the telephone number "1." Soon Bissette adopted the newly popular Southern Colonial style and built a symmetrical, columned house at the eastern end of Washington St., the **Bissette-Cooley House** (1911; John C. Stout, attributed architect; N. 1st St. at E. Washington St.). It was later home of longtime congressman Harold Cooley. E. Washington St. offers many other renditions of popular styles from Italianate to bungalow. The **William B. Boddie House** (1880s; 201 E. Washington St.) is a double-pile, hip-roofed cottage with a lacy millwork porch. The broad, symmetrical **Nick Ross House** (1918; 112 E. Washington St.) was the bungalow home of a dairy farmer and Nashville mayor. Nearby 1st, Alston, Boddie, and Church Sts. repeat these architectural themes.

Rising north of the courthouse along N. Boddie St., the **Cobb Hill** neighborhood (bounded by Cedar, Elm, Alston, and Vale Sts.) developed as an African American community during Nashville's early 20th-c. growth. A variety of house forms was built for owners and renters. The oldest, the small, saddlebag-plan houses along N. Boddie St., accommodate the slope of the terrain. Hip-roofed cottages, gable-fronted bungalows, and side-gabled dwellings also stand along the neighborhood's tree-lined streets. An especially well preserved bungalow is the **Boddie-Cooper House** (1915–25; Fess Cooper, builder; N. Richardson St. at Cedar St.), with characteristic exposed rafters, shingled gables, and tapered posts. It was built by Cooper, a prominent local carpenter, for Carleton Boddie, a barber, and Cooper later resided here.

NS 2 Van Buren-Batchelor House

Ca. 1880s; NE side NC 58, 0.2 mi. N of US 64, Nashville vic.; private, visible from road

The late Italianate farmhouse is one of the county's finest post–Civil War era houses. In a variation on the I-house form, a gabled entrance pavilion breaks out from the symmetrical, 2-story facade. Robust chamfered and bracketed posts enrich the porch. The farm has several period outbuildings and tenant houses.

NS 3 Boddie's Mill

Mid-19th c.; W side SR 1300 at Peachtree and Stoney creeks, 1.2 mi. SW of NC 58, Nashville vic.

NS 3 *Boddie's Mill*

Beginning with Nathan Boddie's gristmill sited just east of here in 1778, the Boddie family operated a mill at this location until 1928. They built the present tall and austere 2-story frame mill with its heavy timber frame in the mid-19th c. Overlooking a tree-rimmed millpond, this is among the last of the dozens of mills that once ground grain along the county's streams.

NS 4 Mitchell-Matthews House

Ca. 1860; Jacob Holt school; NW corner
NC 58 and SR 1310, Matthews Crossroads;
private, visible from road

The symmetrical, 2-story, frame house displays the rectilinear, hip-roofed form and eclectic Greek Revival-Italianate detail of Warrenton builder Jacob Holt's work, including bracketed porch and eaves. The large front windows slide into the wall.

NS 5 Castalia

Settled ca. 1850, the town was named by the local schoolmaster after a sacred spring near Mount Parnassus. Main St. has a variety of frame stores and houses from the late 19th and early 20th centuries, including the **S. J. Bartholomew Houses I and II** built for a merchant and cotton gin owner. In the 1890s Bartholomew occupied a 2-story, Italianate house with a bracketed, 2-tier porch, and in 1918 he joined the trend to the Colonial Revival by building a house with full-width portico under a hip roof, designed by architect John C. Stout of Rocky Mount. Two landmarks stand at the center of a small, African American community at the western edge of town: the **Castalia Baptist Church** (early 20th c.; N side SR 1321, 0.7 mi. w of NC 58), a slightly asymmetrical frame church with its pair of towers exemplifying a strong tradition among African American churches, and across the road, the frame **Castalia School** (1920s), one of more than two dozen Rosenwald schools built in the county, which followed standard models to provide well-arranged and well-lit classrooms.

NS 6 Taylor's Store

Jct. SR 1004 and SR 1310

The cluster of early to mid-20th-c. buildings forms the quintessential eastern N.C. crossroads trading center. From its perch on the hill, Mr. Taylor's country style, Neoclassical Revival house (an ambitious ca. 1915 remodeling of an older dwelling) oversees the frame store and cotton gin complex—still in operation. Cottages and bungalows gather around the crossroads.

NS 7 Perry-Vick-Battle House

Ca. 1795; SE side SR 1310, 0.3 mi. W of
SR 1004, Taylor's Store vic.

Facing the old Raleigh-to-Halifax stage road, the small, Georgian, frame dwelling has beaded weatherboards and double-shouldered, Flemish-bond chimneys that characterize high-quality 18th-c. craftsmanship. Its hall-parlor plan and 1-story height recall the modest scale of all but the most ambitious planters' houses. Among the 19th-c. farm outbuildings are an office, a smokehouse, and a playhouse. Built for Ephraim Perry, it was later home of John Perry, who began a cotton gin here.

Hilliardston–Fishing Creek Area:
The plantation community of Hilliardston
developed in the late 18th c. along the Raleigh-
Halifax stage road and was named after a
local family. Linked to the plantation culture
of nearby Halifax Co. (just across Fishing
Creek), northern Nash Co. was home to some
of the county's largest planters. The area has
some of the county's earliest houses, which dis-
play conservative forms and well-executed, late
Georgian and Federal workmanship.

NS 8 Burt-Woodruff-Cooper House

Ca. 1825; N side SR 1310, 0.3 mi. E of SR 1403,
Hilliardston vic.; private, visible from road

A landmark of the Hilliardston plantation community, the 2-story, frame house was built for physician-planter William Burt. At five bays wide, with a center-passage plan two rooms deep, it is one of the county's largest Federal period houses.

NS 9 Battle-Cooper-Hicks House

Ca. 1780; E side SR 1403, 2.5 mi. N of SR 1310,
Hilliardston vic.; private, visible at a distance
from road

Beautifully sited in rolling farmland, the modest house exemplifies important early forms. It began as a 1½-story, gambrel-roofed dwelling with a shed porch across the front and rear shed rooms. The 1-story, gable-roofed side addition, known as the weaving room, is attached by an enclosed breezeway. A family cemetery and several 19th-c. farm outbuildings remain. The house was built for William Battle, part of a large regional family, and remains in the family.

NS 10 York Chapel

1885; E side SR 1421, 0.1 mi. S of SR 1310, Hilliardston vic.

The Methodist country church on the old stage road was named for preacher William York, who pursued its construction. The modest, gable-end frame church features a little gabled porch and a latticed belfry atop the roof.

NS 11 Blackjack

Ca. 1800; E side SR 1510, 0.5 mi. SE of SR 1500, Hilliardston vic.; private, visible from road

Probably built for John Hilliard, the plantation house exhibits the simplicity and verticality of the area's late 18th- and early 19th-c. dwellings. The 2-story house follows a hall-parlor plan and is finished with beaded weatherboards and late Georgian woodwork. The porch and additions date from the 20th c. A tree-lined lane and outbuildings of various eras complete the ensemble.

NS 12 Elm Lane

Mid-, late 19th c.; N side SR 1510, 1.5 mi. W of NC 48/4, Gold Rock vic.; private, visible from road

Behind the picturesque sawnwork porch the farmhouse is a traditional 1-story dwelling, five bays wide with a center passage between two main rooms, plus rear shed rooms. The multitude of outbuildings includes an office and farm belltower, a 19th-c. schoolhouse, and tenant houses, including one signed in 1909 by builder J. C. Christmas. Corncribs and stables stand across the road. The farm was established by Benjamin D. Mann and operated by his son W. R. Mann in the late 19th and early 20th centuries.

NS 13 The Meadows

Early 19th c.; SE side SR 1510, 1.7 mi. NE of NC 48/4, Gold Rock vic.; private, visible from road

On a 1,300-acre tract he bought in 1806, planter Robert Carter Hilliard built one of the largest houses in the neighborhood, 2 stories tall and five bays wide, with a center-passage plan two rooms deep. Fine workmanship includes a modillion cornice, molded weatherboards, and double-shouldered chimneys of Flemish-bond brick. The 1-story entrance porch is said to repeat the original.

NS 14 Whitakers

The railroad community centers on the tracks that still carry freight and passenger trains through town. Begun as Whitaker's Turnout on the Wilmington and Weldon, the village grew after the Civil War, especially in the early 20th c. Brick and frame stores cluster at the center, and frame houses overlook the tracks along Railroad St. to the north and south. Extending from the junction of White St. (US 301) and Pippen St. are several Queen Anne and Colonial Revival frame houses. The tiny, frame, gable-fronted former **Whitakers Town Hall** (ca. 1900; 106 W. Pippen St.) now serves as the library. The **Whitakers School/Enfield Academy** (1922;

NS 13 *The Meadows*

W. Pippen St.) is an unusually ambitious public school building, with bays advancing on either side of the entrance, and lavishly decorated with molded terra-cotta featuring classical motifs and scholarly endeavors.

NS 15 Oak Forest (Bellamy and Philips Houses)

1820s, 1905; D. J. Rose, builder; N side NC 4, 1.4 mi. W of US 301, Battleboro vic.; private, visible from road

Two 2-story, frame houses exemplify continuity and contrasts between two eras. The earlier dwelling, built for the Reverend William Bellamy, is a symmetrical, 2-story, frame house with a hall-parlor plan plus rear shed rooms. Traditional craftsmanship appears in the beaded weatherboards, dentil cornice, and restrained, Federal style classical details. Symmetry and conservative classicism also inform the early 20th-c. house built nearby by Rocky Mount contractor D. J. Rose for Joseph Battle Philips, a proponent of progressive farming in the area. It features a high hip roof, deep porch with Ionic columns, and a center-passage plan. Several agricultural buildings reflect the long use of the farm.

NS 16 Hidden Path (Dr. Franklin Hart Farm)

Ca. 1780, ca. 1845, 1912; E side SR 1525, 1.5 mi. S of NC 4, Rocky Mount vic.; private, visible from road

A long chronology of agriculture and architecture is evident on the plantation owned by the Hart family from the mid-18th to the mid-20th c. Dominating the 2-story, Greek Revival house, an idiosyncratic portico with two tall, banded columns of solid wood shelters an inner, 2-tier entrance porch. The 1½-story rear wing is an older Hart family house. Domestic dependencies include an antebellum stone and frame smokehouse and a board-and-batten kitchen. Representing the 20th-c. shift to tobacco cultivation are several unusual concrete tobacco barns, a big frame packhouse, and a number of small frame tenant houses with saddlebag and shotgun plans.

NS 17 *Bellemonte*

NS 17 Bellemonte

Ca. 1817; 3400 N. Wesleyan Blvd. (W side US 301, 3.5 mi. N of NC 43), campus of N.C. Wesleyan College, Rocky Mount vic.; open business hours

The fine Federal period plantation house now serves as college offices. Built for planter and physician John F. Bellamy, Bellemonte repeats the symmetrical, 5-bay facade and center-passage plan executed with such fine workmanship as Flemish-bond brick chimneys, a modillion cornice, and double-molded weatherboards seen on several of the finest houses in Nash and Halifax counties. The unusual, 2-tier entrance portico features sturdy columns and lattice balustrades. The ell was added a few years later. The interior, finished with Federal style reeded mantels and paneled wainscoting, has an unusual plan variation, with two rooms west of the passage and a single room to the east, plus an enclosed stair against the rear wall. After a period of vacancy, the house was moved to its present site in 1988 and restored.

NS 18 Dortch House

Early 19th c.; SW corner NC 43 and SR 1544, Dortches; private, visible from road

The 2-story, Federal plantation house possesses unusually fine detail, most notably the beautiful Venetian and triple windows enriched with Ionic pilasters. The porch with delicate millwork dates from the late 19th c. The house was built by planter William Dortch, whose son, William T. Dortch, was a prominent lawyer and political figure. A rear wing dates from the late 18th c.

NS 19 Coley House

1880s, ca. 1910; E side SR 1608, 0.5 mi. S of SR 1607, Dortches vic.; private, visible from road

This especially handsome rendition of the popular tri-gabled farmhouse of the late 19th and early 20th centuries stands in a shaded farmyard with several outbuildings, early 20th-c. tobacco barns, and packhouses. Farmer John Thomas Coley began the 2-story, center-passage-plan house as a front addition to his earlier 1880s dwelling, and after his death his widow, Ellen Baker Coley, finished the project, including the decorated, 1-story porch across the symmetrical facade. (See Introduction, Fig. 36.)

NS 20 Benvenue

Ca. 1830, ca. 1844, 1889; 330 Southern Blvd. (N side SR 1615, 0.2 mi. N of SR 1544), Rocky Mount vic.

The Second Empire or "French" style with mansard roof and ornate millwork was still fashionable in the 1880s, when businessman and Democratic politician Benjamin Bunn expanded his antebellum family residence into an ambitious, T-plan house with bay windows and a mansard roof covered in floral patterned slate. Elected mayor of newly incorporated Rocky Mount in 1867, by 1889 Bunn was a congressman whose residence was a local political and social center as well as home to his large family.

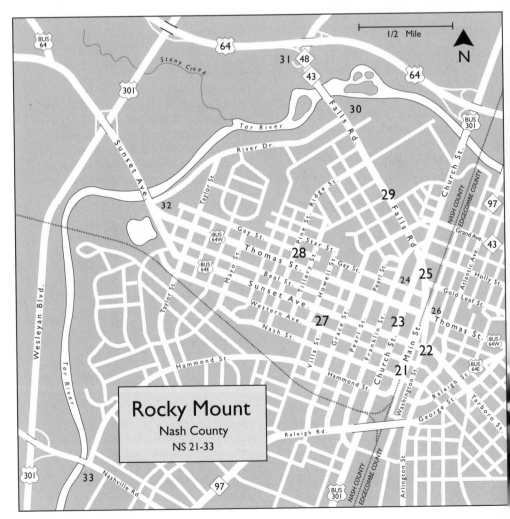

Rocky Mount
Nash County
NS 21-33

Rocky Mount (NS 21–33)

The broad sweep of Main St., where the railroad runs straight down the center of a wide commercial avenue, gives Rocky Mount a memorable urban image unrivaled in the state. From either side of the 134-foot-wide thoroughfare, the center city offers a long, panoramic view of classic Main St. architecture from its early 20th-c. heyday. This great railroad boulevard represents many aspects of the city's history: the centrality of the railroad, its position as a regional trade center, and the division of the city by the Nash-Edgecombe county line running down the center of the railroad.

Named after a mound at the falls of the Tar River, Rocky Mount gained a post office in 1816 and in 1818 became the site of an early textile mill powered by the falls, but the town was not incorporated until 1867. The Wilmington and Weldon Railroad came through in 1840, drawing development east toward the depot and inaugurating a long era of railroad growth. Most of the city's architecture dates from a burst of construction from the 1890s into the 1920s, generated by the establishment of the Rocky Mount Tobacco Market and the Atlantic Coast Line's repair shops. "Come to Rocky Mount, go into business and get wealth," urged a promoter in 1892. The population rose from 650 in 1890 to 12,000 in 1920 and over 20,000 in 1930. As fast as entrepreneurs built banks and stores and warehouses downtown, developers erected blocks of houses for black and white workers and filled suburbs with fashionable residences. Leading builders included contractors D. J. Rose and S. S. Toler as well as architect John C. Stout, specialist in Colonial Revival work.

NS 21 Main St.

Anchoring downtown from the south, the **Atlantic Coast Line Railroad Passenger Station** (1903, 1911–12, 1916; D. J. Rose, builder) stands as one of eastern N.C.'s last big depots, a massive, 3-story edifice of deep, rosy red brick, with arched windows of simplified Romanesque Revival style. It was built in stages, first a 2-story central portion, then flanking wings, and finally the third story.

Predominantly 2-story masonry commercial buildings define both sides of Main St., with storefronts featuring classical, Italianate, and Romanesque Revival motifs, ornate brickwork, and occasional pressed metal

NS 21 *100 Block S.E. Main St., Rocky Mount (Rocky Mount National Bank at center)*

from the 1890s through the 1920s. Banks repeat familiar vault and temple themes, notably the **Rocky Mount Savings Bank** (1926; Milburn & Heister [Washington, D.C.], architects; 142 S.W. Main St.), with pilasters and entablature framing a big, plate-glass opening. Exotic touches appear in the arcaded loggia at **125 N.E. Main St.** and the Art Deco motifs at **147 N.E. Main St.** Breaks in scale include some tiny (1-story, 1-bay) stores with stylish fronts—**186 N.W. Main St.** and **122 and 114 N.W. Main St.**— and a few massive blocks rising three stories tall, such as **163 S.E. Main St.** with its dominant cornice and broad windows. Two big banks anchor the principal intersection at Sunset and Tarboro Sts.: the rusticated, brick and stone **Planter's Bank** (1906; Herbert W. Simpson [New Bern], architect; 100 S.W. Main St.) and the **Rocky Mount National Bank** (ca. 1918; Milburn & Heister [Washington, D.C.], architects; D. J. Rose, builder; 101 S.E. Main St.), a fine, small skyscraper with a 2-story stone base and exuberantly ornate brickwork rising 4 more stories to an arcade topped by a tile roof.

NS 22 Washington St.

Located in Edgecombe Co., Washington St. parallels Main St. on the east. The 100 block of S. Washington St. boasts handsome commercial buildings ca. 1900–1920, many featuring intact storefronts with ornate corbeled brickwork. Filling a trapezoidal corner point, the eclectic **May and Gorham Drugstore** (1904, 1906; D. J. Rose, builder; 101 N. Washington St.) with its heavy, bracketed cornice and arched windows is a local institution, a classic, early 20th-c. drugstore complete with soda fountain and shelving.

NS 23 Church St.

The street paralleling Main on the west was once a prime residential avenue, but routing of US 301 along it transformed it into a commercial automobile thoroughfare. It retains several landmarks from the early 20th-c. boom era. Two early automobile-oriented structures feature 2-story designs focused on first-story automotive access, with the auto

area inset within the building, thus keeping the streetscape intact. The original **Marks Brothers, Inc., Building** (1928; S. S. Toler [Rocky Mount], contractor; 400 S. Church) has a stepped parapet roofline above an open first story framed by pilasters. The neighboring **Fire Engine Company No. 2 Building** (1924; Benton & Benton [Wilson], architects; D. J. Rose, builder; 404 S. Church St.) features stone-framed fire engine doors, a bank of windows in the second story, and a deep tile roof in a Mediterranean spirit. **First Baptist Church** (1907–12; James M. McMichael [Charlotte], architect; 200 S. Church St.) repeats its Charlotte architect's favored classical themes in red "velvet" brick and granite, with a portico of Ionic columns and a robust cornice extending around the T-plan building.

Among the city's most striking edifices is the **Masonic Temple** (1927; H. Robert Diehl, architect; S. S. Toler & Son, builders; 122 N. Church St.), a spectacular rendition of the Masons' favored Egyptian Revival architecture. The 3- and 4-story brick structure is fronted by a limestone facade of great presence and mystery, with subtly tapering forms rising to a sweeping winged cornice with Masonic symbols above a blind loggia with stout, lotus-order columns.

NS 23 *Masonic Temple*

NS 24 *Hardee's No. 1, Rocky Mount*

NS 24 Hardee's No. 1, Rocky Mount
1961; 329 N. Church St.

A regional popular-culture landmark. In 1961 Rocky Mount businessmen Leonard Rawls and Jim Gardner opened their first self-service, charcoal-grilled hamburger restaurant in this clean-lined little box of red and white tile, aluminum, and glass. In 1960 Wilber Hardee had begun cooking hamburgers on charcoal in his Greenville restaurant, and soon thereafter he went into business with Rawls and Gardner, who magnified Hardee's into a major regional, then national, chain. (Hardee's original building in Greenville is now a medical office.)

NS 25 Tobacco Industrial District

Clustering around the railroad tracks at the northern end of downtown are several of the many big tobacco factories and warehouses central to the city's early 20th-c. growth. These concentrate on Goldleaf, MacDonald, and Pearl Sts. and Falls Rd. Especially prominent is **Fenner's Warehouse** (ca. 1903, 1910; D. J. Rose; 298 Falls Rd.), a large, 2-story brick building with pilasters and high curved rooflines. One of the oldest is **222 E. Goldleaf St.** (1892–1907), which began with a frame structure and gained a brick engine room, warehouse, and other components. The **Imperial Tobacco Company Factory** (1903; 200 MacDonald St.) is a massive brick building with tall smokestack and water tower, built for the British competitor of the American Tobacco Company. The **China American Tobacco Company Factory** (1919–20; 436 N. Pearl St.) was the last big downtown tobacco factory built, with a capacity of 70,000 pounds of tobacco per day. Pilaster strips emphasize the mass of the large, 3-story building.

NS 26 Manhattan Theater and Savoy/Booker T. Theater
Ca. 1925, ca. 1926; 122, 130 E. Thomas St.

The centerpieces of a small, brick commercial district are these two boldly designed brick theaters, both built to serve black audiences in the early 20th c. Theaters for black audiences were vital elements in southern cities, typically located in the black business districts, but few still stand. The Manhattan's streamlined Art Deco facade evoked a sense of modernity and urbanity suitable to a theater. The Savoy, renamed the Booker T. by 1936, features a classical facade with arched windows and a classical figure in relief. Both now house churches.

NS 27 Western Suburbs

Suburban growth expanded Rocky Mount as it did every other growing N.C. city in the early 20th c., with the most prestigious development reaching mainly westward. An architecturally interesting street, illustrating a full range of popular types of the early 20th c., **Sunset Ave.** is the principal west-to-east (one-way) residential thoroughfare, which extends for many blocks from the western edge of town into the center. The long street is lined by foursquares and bungalows as well as examples of Spanish Colonial and Colonial Revival styles, and even a prefabricated Lustron House. **Pearl St.**, just west of downtown, is one of several central-city streets recalling the ca. 1890s–1910s spurt of residential growth, with houses from late Queen Anne to early bungalows and foursquares. **Villa Place** (bounded by Nash, Villa, Park, and Hammond Sts.) continues the story of early 20th-c. suburban growth in substantial houses for railroad executives and the simpler frame bungalows of bookkeepers, ticket agents, and salesmen. The architectural showplace of this near western residential area is **Machaven** (1907–8; Harry P. S. Keller [Raleigh], architect; 306 S. Grace St.), a spectacular Colonial Revival mansion built of brick and stone for J. W. Hines, a developer and industrialist known as "the 'ice king' of the state" for the ice plants he established in railroad towns from Rocky Mount to Salisbury.

NS 28 Happy Hill

Ca. 1900–1930; NW of Main St. on Thomas, Pine, Beal, Star, Tillery, and nearby streets

Among the most intact of the city's traditionally black, early 20th-c. neighborhoods, Happy Hill grew quickly to accommodate people moving into town to work in tobacco manufacturing, railroad, and other jobs. In 1907 a few houses stood here, and by 1920 a large and dense neighborhood had developed. Various investors built groups of primarily rental houses, including shotgun houses, gable-fronted bungalows, and hip-roofed cottages.

NS 29 Falls Rd.

Linking downtown with the mills, Falls Rd. developed as a prestigious residential avenue running northwest of town. A grand edition of Rocky Mount architect John C. Stout's favored Southern Colonial style appears in the **Frank S. Spruill House** (ca. 1910; 462 Falls Rd.), built for the attorney for the Atlantic Coast Line Railroad. The **Dr. J. P. Whitehead House** (1922; D. J. Rose, builder; 517 Falls Rd.) exemplifies the brick Georgian Revival mode. Other houses play variations on popular Queen Anne and Colonial Revival themes.

NS 30 Rocky Mount Mills

Early 19th–early 20th c.; both sides NC 43/48 (Falls Rd.) on S side Tar River; Rocky Mount Mill is best viewed from Battle Park on N side of Tar River

The falls of the Tar River here powered one of N.C.'s first textile mills. In 1818 investors Joel Battle, Peter Evans, and Henry Donaldson began manufacturing cotton in a 4-story stone building. This was the second cotton mill established in the state. In 1847 Edgecombe Co. planter James B. Battle and his son William S. Battle (who built *The Barracks in Tarboro) acquired the mill. They operated the mill with slave and free black workers until 1852, when they began to employ white workers. After Federal troops destroyed the mill in 1863, a new one was built in 1865, only to burn to the ground in 1869.

It was replaced by the oldest mill building here, the utilitarian brick **Mill No. 1**, built in 1870 and enlarged in 1871. The company was reorganized in the 1880s. Expansion in the late 19th and early 20th centuries produced a series of brick buildings forming a large complex. From the river side of the mill the stone foundation of the antebellum mill can be seen as well as the race, dam, and shaft opening—vestiges of the waterpower system. The company is one of the oldest—if not the oldest—cotton spinning mills still in operation in the country. (See Introduction, Fig. 44.)

The mill is part of a larger ensemble including several houses. The **Benjamin Battle House** (1835; Falls Rd.), a handsome, late Federal, frame residence with a center-passage plan two rooms deep, was built for the son of mill founder Joel Battle and now houses offices for the company. Also believed to date from the antebellum mill era is the small, Greek Revival style **Superintendent's Cottage** (1830s; 1107 Falls Rd.). The large bungalow south of the Battle House began as a community center and later served as supervisor's house, then commissary. Other housing reflects mainly late 19th- and early 20th-c. construction, principally 1-story dwellings following saddlebag and L-plans. Many have two front doors, permitting either single-family or duplex use. In the 1940s the company employed Wilson architect Thomas Herman to update the houses with latticework porches and other improvements.

NS 31 Stonewall

Ca. 1830; S side SR 1544, just W of NC 43/48 and US 64, Rocky Mount vic.; open limited hours

Overlooking the Tar River, Stonewall was built for Bennett Bunn, one of the region's richest planters and businessmen, who owned as many as 100 slaves. Extraordinary in a region where even the wealthiest residents built frame houses, Bunn's massive brick house proclaimed his position. Standing 2 stories above a raised basement, the house of Flemish-bond brick is finished in late Federal style, with flat arches over the

NS 31 *Stonewall*

windows and a fanlit entrance. The central passage focuses on a perilously steep wishbone stair at the center. Elaborate woodwork here and in the four flanking rooms repeats a distinctive local version of Neoclassical motifs, with mantels and doorways featuring various renditions of the Ionic order. About 1916 the Ionic portico was added and the house was rehabilitated upon its purchase by Rocky Mount Mills. It has been restored as a local house museum.

NS 32 Rocky Mount Waterworks

1935; William C. Olsen (Raleigh), engineer; NE corner Sunset Ave. and River Dr.

NS 32 *Rocky Mount Waterworks*

The splendidly sited waterworks, a project of the Federal Emergency Administration of Public Works, exemplifies the blend of stripped classicism and Art Deco favored for many WPA projects. The brick office building, pumping facility, and low concrete tanks remain essentially unchanged. Olsen's firm designed water plants in many N.C. towns in the mid-20th c.

NS 33 Atlantic Coast Line Pump Station

1920s, 1963–73; Nashville and Hammond Sts.; open regular hours

In an early adaptive-use project lauded as a preservation model, the abandoned pump station was rescued by the Rocky Mount Arts and Crafts Center. Built beside the Tar River to service the repair shops of the Atlantic Coast Line Railroad, the pumping station was converted to an art studio and classrooms, and the cylindrical water tank accommodated an art gallery, classrooms, offices, and arena theater.

NS 34 West Mount

Jct. of SR 1717 and SR 1544

During the 1950s writer Jack Kerouac frequently visited his sister Caroline, first at her home in Rocky Mount and later in her small house in this typical rural crossroads village (then called Big Easonburg Woods). He spent many hours at the **Country Store** at the crossroads. In rumpled jeans and scruffy beard he became a familiar if exotic character to local residents as he worked on the books that later brought him worldwide fame, including *On the Road* and *The Dharma Bums.*

NS 35 Garland Duke Ricks House

Ca. 1850, ca. 1870, ca. 1890s; N side NC 97, 1.5 mi. E of Stanhope; private, visible from road

The little house in its pecan grove recalls the local evolution of small house forms. The first Ricks to build here erected a 1-story, hall-parlor-plan dwelling. After the Civil War, Garland Ricks made the old house into the rear wing of the present 1-story, frame house with center passage plan, and later in the century his son extended the rear wing and built a front porch garnished with millwork.

NS 36 Stanhope

The crossroads village on the old stage road (the route of NC 97), which began in the mid-19th c. around an early academy and churches, retains a sampling of late 19th- and early 20th-c. architecture. The essence of the small-town church appears in the **Stanhope Baptist Church** (1898; s side NC 97, 0.2 mi. w of SR 1950), where the entrance, a louvered window, and a little tower line up along the axis of the gable front. Sweetest of the town's several small frame houses is the **Harper House** (1887; N side NC 97, w corner SR 1950), built for a schoolteacher, a simple, gable-sided cottage with center passage and rear ell, its front porch bedecked with delicate scrollwork from the balustrade to the swaglike brackets.

NS 37 Crenshaw-Bissette House

1840s; SE corner NC 97 and SR 1137, Stanhope vic.; private, visible from road

Built as the seat of a plantation formed by Daniel Crenshaw, who operated a stagecoach inn here on the Raleigh-Tarboro road, this is one of the oldest houses in the neighborhood. It also served as a post office. The 2-story house features an unusual treatment of the engaged porch: the end bays at the second story are enclosed as sleeping rooms, and the open area between them is cordoned by a delicate sheaf-of-wheat balustrade. Several early outbuildings survive.

NS 38 A. R. Beard House

Ca. 1885; W side SR 1961, 1.1 mi. S of SR 1109, Bailey vic.; private, visible from road

When he built one of the county's many neatly finished 1-story frame houses with a characteristic front roof gable, farmer and local builder Beard added a touch of cheery individuality by gracing the scrollwork of the front porch with little birds—always painted blue. Several other 1-story frame houses, clusters of tobacco barns, and the occasional family cemetery surrounded by cultivated fields may also be seen along SR 1961, offering an excellent sampling of the southern Nash Co. tobacco landscape.

NS 39 Bailey

The small retail center on the Norfolk and Southern Railroad has a cluster of brick stores regarding the railroad. The little **U.S. Post Office** (early 20th c.; E end Main St. commercial district, N side) gains verve from its construction of locally made, floral-patterned concrete blocks. The shady residential streets have a pleasant array of hip-roofed cottages and bungalows. The chief attraction is the **Country Doctor Museum** (Vance St., w off Oak St. [NC 581], s of RR tracks; open limited hours), a small, L-shaped building adorned with a simple turned and bracketed porch. It features a composite restoration of the offices of two local physicians, Dr. Howard Franklin Freeman (1857) and Dr. Cornelius Henry Brantley (1890), fitted out with period furnishings and equipment.

NS 40 Murray's Mill

1810–1960s; W side NC 231 on Turkey Creek, 0.3 mi. N of NC 97, Samaria vic.

Located on an old road called the Green Path, this mill site has served since the early 19th c. The mill (enclosed and weatherboarded in the 1960s) and the nearby miller's house are said to contain elements of the original buildings.

NS 41 Spring Hope

A remarkably complete and compact small railroad town, Spring Hope presents a full assemblage of architecture from its turn-of-the-century heyday. The optimistically named community was incorporated in 1889 on a new spur line built by the Wilmington and Weldon Railroad from Rocky Mount. By the 1910s Spring Hope flourished as a cotton shipping station, with 1,500 citizens and five contractors and builders.

Main St. has a small commercial district of 1- and 2-story brick buildings facing the tracks and the board-and-batten **Spring Hope Depot** (ca. 1890; Main at Ash Sts.; open regular hours), which was built for the Wilmington and Weldon Railroad.

Churches mark transitional corners from downtown to the main residential thoroughfares. **First Baptist Church** (1909–10; Henry E. Bonitz [Wilmington], architect; H. S. Poole [Rocky Mount], contractor; E. Nash

NS 41 *Spring Hope Depot and Commercial District*

St.), a twin-towered, brick edifice of simplified Romanesque Revival style, defines the northeastern end of the business district. To the southeast stands the eclectic, Gothic Revival **Gibson Memorial Methodist Church** (1910; B. D. and Max C. Price [Atlantic Heights, N.J.], architects; E. Branch and S. Walnut Sts.) with its dramatic corner entrance tower and auditorium plan typifying work by the popular Philadelphia-area Methodist church designers.

South and east of the business district, well-preserved frame houses present a familiar spectrum from gabled cottages and Queen Anne dwellings to Colonial Revival houses and bungalows. A stylistic shift appears in two neighboring houses built for a local physician: the asymmetrical, Queen Anne style **Dr. Hassell Brantley House I** (1893–94; 225 E. Branch St.) and the **Dr. Hassell Brantley House II** (1912; John C. Stout, attributed architect; 301 E. Branch St.), a big, Southern Colonial residence with central Ionic portico and flanking, 1-story, wraparound porch. The predominant architecture is more modest. The prevalent house type is the symmetrical, gable-roofed cottage with picturesque front roof gable and decorative porch, such as the **Griffin-Batchelor House** (ca. 1895; 206 S. Pine St.), built for a downtown merchant. Almost as numerous are the decorated L-shaped cottages and Queen Anne houses such as the **Spivey House** (ca. 1900; 110 N. Walnut St.), a Queen Anne cottage built for a storekeeper. (See also Introduction, Fig. 56.)

Wilson County (WL)

See Kate Ohno and Robert Bainbridge, Wilson, North Carolina, Historic Buildings Inventory *(1980), and Kate Ohno,* Wilson County's Architectural Heritage *(1981).*

Wilson (WL 1–5)

The county seat and tobacco market town is one of the principal commercial centers of the central coastal plain, with handsome and diverse architecture from the 1890s onward. In 1849 Tosnot Depot on the Wilmington and Weldon Railroad and the old farming village of Hickory Grove were joined and named for local Mexican War hero Louis D. Wilson. The community was designated county seat when Wilson Co. was established in 1855. After the Civil War, business recovered quickly as rail connections made Wilson an agricultural center and cotton market. Growth was further boosted by a branch of the Wilmington and Weldon from Wilson to Fayetteville in the 1880s and by the 1908 arrival of the Norfolk and Southern Railroad.

The greatest boom began in the 1890s as Wilson developed into a nationally important tobacco market. With cotton prices dropping, eastern N.C. farmers shifted to tobacco cultivation. Tobacconists from the "Old Belt" region of the northern Piedmont came east to open a new area to tobacco sales and manufacturing. By 1900 more than a dozen tobacco warehouses and redrying plants joined the cotton mill and cotton gins along the tracks. Between 1900 and 1920 the town's population grew from 1,500 to 16,000. In 1919 Wilson's tobacco sales soared to over 42 million pounds, and by the 1920s it was the nation's top tobacco marketing center, selling 65 million pounds of tobacco annually and becoming one of the country's wealthiest towns of its size.

New banks, stores, and hotels were built along Nash St. East of the railroad, a large African American business section and residential area developed along E. Nash and E. Green Sts. East Wilson remains one of the state's most intact early 20th-c. black neighborhoods. West of the central business district, a series of predominantly white neighborhoods emerged along W. Nash and nearby streets. Wilson's residential architecture encompasses a range from Italianate and Queen Anne style houses to the Colonial Revival style but is especially noteworthy for its fine collection of bungalows. Early 20th-c. Wilson supported a remarkable number of architects and builders for its size, including Charles C. "Colonial" Benton and Frank Benton (Benton & Benton), Thomas Herman, Solon B. Moore, Oliver Nestus Freeman, the Jones Brothers, and Wilkins & Wilkins. Their work is interlaced with that of practitioners from Rocky Mount, Wilmington, Raleigh, Greensboro, and more distant cities.

WL 1 Central Business District

The compact downtown, centering on the railroad tracks and Nash St. and Goldsboro St., comprises several blocks of handsomely detailed, masonry commercial and institutional buildings. The commercial architecture ranges from 2-story, Italianate stores of the 1870s to the simpler storefronts and a few small skyscrapers of the 1920s. Classical motifs dominate among institutional buildings. The **Wilson County Courthouse** (1924; Fred A. Bishop, architect; 125 E. Nash St.,

WL 1 *Wilson County Courthouse*

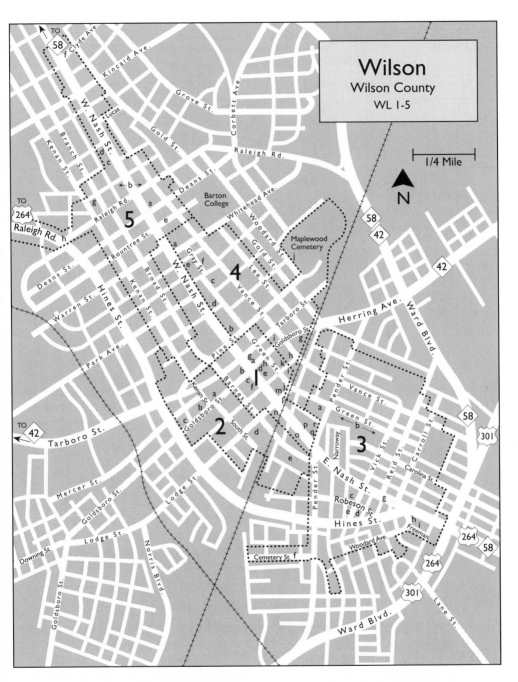

NW corner) (**a**) occupies a prime corner, a handsome, Neoclassical Revival building with giant-order Corinthian columns forming the recessed portico facing Nash St. and a secondary portico on Goldsboro St.

Across the street, now used as an arts center, the **Branch Banking and Trust Company Building** (1903; 124 E. Nash St., sw corner) (**b**) combines classical details and striated buff brick in a Renaissance Revival composition dramatizing its corner site. Founded in the 19th c. by Wilson's "mer-

WL 1 *200 Block, E. Nash St.*

chant prince" Alpheus Branch, son of an old Halifax Co. planter family, the firm developed into BB&T, one of the state's leading financial institutions. The **Davis Building** (1916; Solon B. Moore, architect; 200 E. Nash St., SE corner) (c) is a large, 4-story commercial building with free classical details. At the northeast corner stands the **Planter's Bank** (1920; 201 E. Nash St., NE corner) (d) with monumental Ionic columns carrying a full entablature. The 200 block of E. Nash St. displays a concentration of notable commercial buildings, the oldest of which is the **Winstead-Hardy Building** (1865, ca. 1900; 205–7 E. Nash St.) (e), a 2-story, brick structure of Italianate style, with elaborate corbeling and a metal cornice. The 4-story, stone veneered **U.S. Post Office and Courthouse** (1927; James Wetmore, supervising architect of the Treasury; 224 E. Nash St.) (f) offers an elegant example of federally sponsored Beaux Arts architecture, now a science museum.

Beside the county courthouse rises the former **First National Bank of Wilson Building** (1926–27; Charles C. Hartmann [Greensboro], architect; 113 E. Nash St.) (g), an 8-story skyscraper that was until 1966 the tallest building in town. Of reinforced steel and concrete, the structure is sheathed in granite and buff brick and is treated in a stylized classical mode, with the usual tripartite arrangement of base, shaft, and crown.

North on Goldsboro St., the **Wilson Municipal Building** (1938; Frank W. Benton, architect; Jones Bros., builders; 112 N. Goldsboro St.) (h) presents a streamlined, symmetrical facade with Art Deco detail; WPA funds assisted in construction. On nearby Green St. the **Wilson Bus Station** (1938; Jones Bros., builders; 307 E. Green St.) (i) shows the streamlined Moderne style favored for bus stations, with rounded corners and an off-center Art Deco entrance pavilion. The **Boykin and Anderson Oil Company** (1922; 312 E. Green St.) (j) was built as a Standard Oil filling station at a time when many gas stations emulated residential forms to suit residential areas, but this one is extraordinary in taking a bungalow form with its "porch" as the canopy over the gas pumps. **Fire Station No. 1** (1926; Solon B. Moore, architect; 209 N. Douglas St.) (k) shows the locally popular Mission style in a domestic-scale, brick building with broad eaves resting on large brackets.

An important ensemble focuses on the

railroad crossing. The **Atlantic Coast Line Railroad Passenger Station and Freight Depot** (1923–24; A. M. Griffin [Wilmington], architect; 401 E. Nash St.) (**l**), still a passenger stop, is a handsome, tile-roofed, brick building in modified Mission style, with curvilinear gables and a long, umbrella canopy along the track. Three former railroad hotels stand within sight. The **Cherry Hotel** (1919–23; Charles C. Hartmann [Greensboro], architect; Joe W. Stout & Company [Sanford], contractor; 333 E. Nash St.) (**m**) epitomizes the 1920s railroad hotel, a 6-story building with Beaux Arts details designed by Greensboro architect Hartmann, protégé of New York hotel specialist William L. Stoddart. The **Terminal Inn** (ca. 1920; Solon B. Moore, architect; 406 E. Nash St.) (**n**) is an eclectic, 2-story brick building with curvilinear gables.

East of the railroad tracks stands Wilson's oldest hotel building, the **Orange Hotel** (1906; 526 E. Nash St.) (**o**), a 2-story frame structure with a 2-tier porch. It was built by black businessman and community leader Samuel H. Vick as the first hotel for blacks in Wilson at a time when Jim Crow laws made travel difficult for blacks.

This 500 block of **E. Nash St.** became the city's black main street in the late 19th and early 20th centuries. Both black and white entrepreneurs led in its development. The predominant architecture is of 1- and 2-story frame and brick blocks, several with vigorous brickwork detail. The **Oddfellows Hall** (1894; 549–51 E. Nash St.) (**p**) is one of downtown's oldest and best-preserved commercial buildings, a 3-story brick building six bays wide, with ornate corbeled brickwork. It was built as Hannibal Lodge No. 1552 by Samuel H. Vick, who promoted black fraternal organizations statewide. At the eastern corner of the block rises the **First Baptist Church** (Jackson Chapel First Missionary Baptist Church) (1913; 571 E. Nash St.) (**q**), a Romanesque Revival, brick edifice, with a 3-story belltower dominating the corner. The sanctuary follows an auditorium plan with sloping floor, curved pews, balcony, and vaulted ceiling. Just north stands **St. John A.M.E. Zion Church** (1915; Charles C. Benton [Wilson], attributed architect; John Barnes, builder; 119 N. Pender St.) (**r**), a large, brick church in Gothic Revival style, with stone trim, lancet arches, and crenellated corner towers, one topped with octagonal minaret. The richly finished sanctuary is planned around a central recessed dome.

WL 1 *First Baptist Church, 500 Block, E. Nash St.*

WL 2 Tobacco Warehouse and Manufacturing District

The industrial sector to the south, southeast, and southwest of the commercial district once flourished as a regional center of tobacco sales and manufacturing, which employed hundreds of workers and drew thousands of farmers and buyers during tobacco sales season. (See Introduction, Figs. 46 and 47.)

The auction sales warehouses concentrate around the junction of E. Kenan and S. Goldsboro Sts. southwest of the central business district. These brick warehouses are large, 1-story blocks with sweeping roofs punctuated by raised, rectangular skylights. In their cavernous spaces bright with natural light, farmers displayed their tobacco for sale, and tobacco buyers purchased the leaf at fast-paced auctions. Parapets emphasize their impressive street facades. The **Hi-Dollar (Watson Centre Brick) Warehouse** (1900 and later; 232 S. Goldsboro St.) (**a**) boasts elaborate brickwork in the parapeted facade, with pilasters and panels and arched doors and windows. The **Farmer's Warehouse** (1903, 1912, 1920s; 310 S. Goldsboro St.) (**b**) comprises several stages of expansion, with its Kenan St. front enlivened by touches of Art Deco. One of the last of the great warehouses to be built is among the finest and largest, the **Smith Warehouse** (1927–28; Solon B. Moore, attributed architect; Jones Bros., contractors; 410 S. Goldsboro St.) (**c**) repeats the stepped parapets, pilasters, and corbeled brickwork on a facade that fronts a warehouse covering a full city block.

Tobacco manufacturing focused in the area southwest of S. Lodge and E. Barnes Sts. straddling the railroad. The manufacturing district included prize houses, redrying plants, stemmeries, and other buildings, primarily utilitarian brick structures enlarged over the years. The largest complex is the **Imperial Tobacco Company Factory** (1903, 1910, 1919–20; C. C. Davis and Otis K. Asbury [Richmond], architects; S. Lodge St. at South St.) (**d**), with distinctive towers, erected by a British competitor of the American Tobacco Company. It is the only big tobacco factory of its era still standing

WL 2 *Smith Warehouse*

in eastern N.C. The **Farmers Cotton Oil Company** (1902–1940s; 500 E. Barnes St.) (**e**) comprises various structures for processing cottonseed into oil, making fertilizer, and other purposes. Looming high is the **Fertilizer Plant**, a tall, frame structure 75 by 100 feet with a clerestory mixing tower that runs the length of the building.

WL 3 East Wilson

During Wilson's tobacco growth boom, many rural blacks moved to town to work in the tobacco factories and in other occupations and professions. In the 19th c. blacks had lived throughout the community, but in the 20th c. patterns of residential segregation solidified, and the area east of the railroad tracks developed into a large African American neighborhood. Although the majority of black residents worked in tobacco factories and service occupations, an influential black middle class formed, which included teachers, preachers, morticians, barbers, building craftsmen and contractors, and other businesspeople.

Rather than moving into areas that were originally white or mixed, in East Wilson black citizens lived in a newly developed area, where black and white investors built houses for purchase and for rent. Black business leader Samuel H. Vick bought 40 acres of farmland in 1902 and laid out large lots along E. Green St. where he and his friends built homes. He developed other sections, including "Vicksburg Manor," with 25-foot lots for workers' small houses. In contrast to many N.C. cities, where mid- and late 20th-c. urban renewal programs leveled many early 20th-c. African American neighborhoods, East Wilson has survived remarkably intact.

WL 3 *600 Block, E. Green St.*

The most prestigious avenue in the early 20th c. was E. Green St. The chief landmark is **Mercy Hospital** (Wilson Hospital and Tubercular Home) (ca. 1913; Benton & Moore, architects; 504 E. Green St.) (a), a brick building with powerful Doric portico. Dr. F. S. Hargrave and other investors built it as successor to his earlier hospital (1905) for blacks, employing a leading local white architect to design it. It is slated for restoration as a community center. The **600 and 700 Blocks of E. Green St.** (b) comprise residences built for prominent African American citizens in the Queen Anne, late Italianate, American foursquare, and bungalow styles. Oak trees planted by Samuel H. Vick once stood on each side and along the central median. His own residence, the **Samuel H. Vick House** (1904; Charles C. Benton, architect; 622 E. Green St.; stone veneer, ca. 1980) is an expansive, 2-story house with corner tower dramatizing the high hip roof. Vick, a native of Nash Co., became principal of the Wilson Graded School, postmaster, and a Presbyterian Sunday school missionary, and he led in establishing the Orange Hotel, the Commercial Bank, the Lincoln Benefit Society, and Mercy Hospital. Next door is the Colonial Revival style residence of a physician and founder of the hospital, the **Dr. Frank S. Hargrave House** (ca. 1920; 624 E. Green St.). The street also features

Queen Anne residences, such as the 2-story **Hardy Johnson House** (ca. 1901; 705 E. Green St.), with its porch extending into a polygonal corner pavilion, and the 1½-story **Halley B. Taylor House** (ca. 1913; 721 E. Green St.), a blend of Queen Anne and Colonial Revival motifs, built for a Presbyterian minister.

Although middle-class houses of similar type and form appear on Pender and E. Nash Sts., most of the neighborhood consists of smaller dwellings, some built for their owners, others built as rental housing (82 percent of some 1,000 houses were rental in 1928). Black and white investors built rental houses in units of two or three or an entire block or more. Many house types line the streets. Especially numerous are side-gabled cottages, often with the center gable rising in front and a plain or decorated porch. Four-room-plan cottages with recessed corner porches, somewhat more spacious, went by the local name of "square-built" houses, seen for example in the **800 Block of Robeson St.** (c).

The very narrow house form—known locally as an "endway," but more widely termed a shotgun house—was built in great numbers. The shotgun house was built for working people in towns throughout the early 20th-c. South, and they were especially numerous in African American neighborhoods. These narrow dwellings have a gable

WL 3 *1000 Block, Robeson St.*

front, usually with a door and one or two windows; the plan has a single file of rooms running front to back, typically three but sometimes four rooms deep. Such houses suited developers' 25-foot lots. Many shotgun houses are interspersed among other house forms, while others stand in rows reflecting a developer's unit. Details varied with the times, from turned porch posts and decorative vents of ca. 1900 to touches of bungalow-influenced millwork in the 1920s. An especially intact group of shotgun houses, ca. 1900, stands in the **1000 Block of Robeson St. (d)**. Other clusters appear in the 100 block of S. Reid St. and along Narroway St. A row erected in the 1920s for S. H. Vick along **Vick St. (e)** features simplified, bungalow-inspired detail. Shortly before World War II the N.C. Mutual Insurance Company, the large, black-owned and -operated firm headquartered in Durham, built a row of simply finished shotgun houses on **Cemetery St. (f)**.

WL 3 *Round House*

The bungalow was built in myriad forms—as seen, for example, on **E. Nash St.**: gable-fronted bungalows with inset corner porches; symmetrical gable-fronted bungalows, some of which were designed as duplexes; and side-gabled bungalows with front dormers. One unusual bungalow, the **Oliver Nestus Freeman House** (ca. 1910, 1920s; Oliver Nestus Freeman, builder; 1300 E. Nash St.) **(g)** was the home of the town's preeminent stonemason. A native of the county, Freeman studied at Tuskegee Normal School and taught there before returning to Wilson, where he continued to teach as well as to execute distinctive masonry work throughout town. He built this residence as a brick cottage ca. 1910, then transformed it into a stone bungalow. Over the years he added a series of stone garden sculptures, including a 7-foot dinosaur. Around the corner, Freeman built an unusual rental house, the **Round House** (1940s; Oliver Nestus Freeman, builder; 307 Freeman St., SW) **(h)**, made of rough stone on a circular plan with wedge-shaped rooms.

WL 4 Old Wilson

Wilson's principal examples of 19th-c. domestic architecture concentrate in the neighborhoods west of the commercial district along W. Nash—which retains a few of the 19th-c. mansions from its early days as the premier residential avenue—W. Vance, and

W. Green Sts. The area, which developed as a patchwork of small subdivisions, has been called "Old Wilson" in recent years.

The town's prime vestiges of the picturesque architecture of the mid-19th c. stand here. These include works attributed to Oswald Lipscomb, a Virginia-born builder who came here in 1849, the year he married Penelope Rountree of Wilson, and established a regional building practice. After the Civil War Lipscomb and his partner J. T. Barnes built a sash-and-blind factory and a planing mill. Lipscomb displayed the Italianate style in the **Davis-Whitehead House** (ca. 1858, 1872; 600 W. Nash St.) (**a**), a 2-story house with central entrance pavilion and bracketed cornice, built for James Davis and his wife, Adeline Rountree, Lipscomb's sister-in-law. The Queen Anne style appears in such big houses as the **James Rountree House** (ca. 1888; 206 W. Nash St.) (**b**) and in exuberantly decorated cottages of the late 19th and early 20th centuries, with their broad, wraparound porches.

WL 4 *Davis-Whitehead House*

Amidst the cluster of such small houses in the 200 and 300 blocks of W. Green St., the **John Y. Moore House** (ca. 1882; 314 W. Green St.) (**c**) captures the fancy with a lighthearted bird motif in the porch trim. There are also examples of the region's widely built, 2-story, gable-fronted houses with side-passage plans, as in the **200 Block of W. Green St.** and elsewhere. A landmark institution is the **Wilson Primitive Baptist Church** (1920; Solon B. Moore, architect; Jones Bros., builders; 301 W. Green St.) (**d**), a

Gothic Revival, brick church built for the county's oldest congregation (est. 1750s as Tosnot, later Toisnot, Church); its elaborate architecture contrasts with the prevailing plainness of rural examples.

The early 20th-c. transition from the Queen Anne style to the Colonial Revival figures prominently. The **Henry Groves Connor House** (1907; 109 Gray St.) (**e**), blending irregular massing and classical detail, was built for Connor, Democratic leader, N.C. Supreme Court justice, and U.S. district judge as well as father of R. D. W. Connor, historian and first archivist of the United States. The area also has some of Wilson's many fine bungalows, such as the **Robert S. Wilkins House** (1920s; 106 Gray St.) (**f**), a symmetrical bungalow with clipped gables, erected for a principal in the prolific building firm of Wilkins & Wilkins.

Here as elsewhere in town are some fine, small-scale apartment houses. The **Colonial Apartments** (1918; H. T. Crittenden, builder; 300 N. Goldsboro St.) (**g**) was among the first and finest of several moderate-sized, handsomely detailed apartments—a 3-story, H-shaped, brick structure with central courtyard and inset porches at the corners. The **Varita Court Apartments** (1923–25; Thomas B. Herman, architect; 205 N. Goldsboro St.) (**h**) is a 3-story, U-shaped, red brick building in Tudor Revival style with crenellated roof parapet, polygonal bay windows, and an Art Nouveau, stained-glass entrance canopy at the head of the recessed courtyard. Another face of the medieval revivals appears in **St. Timothy's Episcopal Church** (1906; 202 N. Goldsboro St.) (**i**), an asymmetrical, Gothic Revival, brick church with tower.

Bordering the residential section, the **Maplewood Cemetery Gates** (1922; Solon B. Moore, architect; Woodard St. at Maple-

WL 4 *Maplewood Cemetery Gates*

wood St.) (j) open into the municipal cemetery established in 1876. Architect Moore employed a conventional tripartite composition, with a vehicular arch flanked by towers and arched pedestrian entrances, but in contrast to the usual classical or medieval somberness, the Mission style in blond brick with green tile roofs offers an unexpectedly cheering prospect. In the cemetery, one especially memorable gravestone evokes the era when traveling carnivals punctuated small-town life: the marker erected by the J. J. Jones Carnival to Prof. Antoine Szegadi Danton, the Hungarian high diver who, after drawing crowds in Wilson, "leaped from life into eternity at Goldsboro, N.C. the night of May 13, 1904."

WL 5 West Wilson Suburbs

Wilson's western suburban development of the 1910s and 1920s comprises one of the state's finest assemblages of this era of residential architecture. A series of small, grid-plan developments created a continuous residential sector reaching north and west of the town center. Clients employed local builders and local and out-of-town revivalist architects to produce a spectrum of houses from robust bungalows to Georgian Revival and Tudor Revival mansions. The homes of Wilson's business leaders exemplify the quality of materials, proportion, and detail that made this a golden age for residential architecture.

In the 1910s and 1920s, as tobacco brought Wilson unprecedented wealth, W. Nash St. extended westward as the premier residential avenue, with a reputation as one of the state's finest streets. Interweaving family and business ties and displaying continuity from antebellum plantation to New South business center, leading entrepreneurs lined the street with handsome houses. The prime example of the locally favored, Virginia-influenced, Georgian Revival style is the W. W. Graves House (ca. 1922; Harry Barton [Greensboro], architect; Joe W. Stout & Company [Sanford], contractors; 800 W. Nash St.) (a), built for a member of a local planter family who became a real estate developer. Greensboro architect Barton, specialist in Beaux Arts courthouses, designed

WL 5 *W. W. Graves House*

a richly finished, symmetrically composed house. The main block is seven bays wide, with a trio of dormers on the tile roof. The red brick walls are sparked by robust classical details in pale stone, which focus attention on the central entrance bay.

The 900 block of W. Nash St. (b) is especially impressive and diverse. The **Williams-Cozart House** (ca. 1903; 900 W. Nash St.), built for a planter, exemplifies the white-columned, Southern Colonial Revival style once prevalent in Wilson. Built for Jesse and Mattie Branch Williams, daughter of leading local banker Alpheus Branch, the house set the tone for development. In 1912 it became the home of U. H. Cozart, a Granville Co. "Old Belt" tobacconist who came to Wilson early in the 1890s to open up eastern N.C.'s tobacco boom. The neighboring **Norborne M. Schaum House** (ca. 1925; James Raleigh Hughes, Greensboro, architect; Wilkins & Wilkins, builders; 904 W. Nash St.) shows the red brick, Georgian Revival style at its best. Schaum was a tobacconist who came from Henderson and married Cozart's daughter Doris. Across the street, the **Selby Anderson House** (ca. 1917; Solon B. Moore, architect; 901 W. Nash St.) shows the work of a prolific local architect in a large bungalow with a deep porch and Tudor Revival, half-timbering detail. It was built for another pioneer tobacconist and banker and his wife, Ellen Branch, daughter of banker Alpheus. Next door, the **Thomas M. Washington House** (ca. 1925; 903 W. Nash St.) is a Dutch Colonial, brick house of similar scale, with tile-covered gambrel roof, home of another pioneer tobacconist from Granville Co. and partner of U. H. Cozart.

Bungalows are especially numerous in the 1000 and 1100 blocks. Among Wilson's

WL 5 *Selby Anderson House and Thomas M. Washington House*

prime examples is the **E. F. Nadal House** (1916–17; B. J. Boyles, builder; 1007 W. Nash St.) **(c)**, an expansive composition of elegantly rustic California character, combining rough stonework and dark-stained stickwork in the gables and porch. The stylistic versatility of architect Solon B. Moore appears in the eclectic, Georgian Revival style **Harry Abbitt House** (1926; Solon B. Moore, architect; Wilkins & Wilkins, builders; 1105 W. Nash) **(d)**. These architects and builders continued the same themes in successive blocks westward.

WL 5 *E. F. Nadal House*

During the boom years from the 1890s to the depression, small-scale real estate developments filled in the grids of streets flanking W. Nash St.—from Park Ave., Broad St., and Kenan St. south and east of Raleigh Rd., to N. Kincaid St., North Ave., N. Lucas Ave., and others north and west. Standing beneath large deciduous trees is one of the state's prime collections of early 20th-c. popular domestic architecture, with large and small houses from the Queen Anne and Colonial Revival to the Dutch Colonial, Tudor Revival, foursquare, and Georgian Revival styles plus a few Mission or Spanish Revival motifs.

This section of Wilson is best known for its fine bungalows from the 1910s and 1920s. These 1- and 1½-story dwellings range from simple versions—such as those built on N. Kincaid and N. Lucas—to full-blown California and Oriental bungalows and English cottage and Colonial Revival versions. (See Introduction, Fig. 60.) Wilson's bungalows emphasize the capacity of the bungalow, with its integration of form, plan, and detail, to create a small and economical dwelling that is also a fully realized, stylish house. Rough stonework, much of it credited to Wilson stonemason Oliver Nestus Freeman, gives texture and substance to a variety of types. On Rountree St. **(e)**, the **W. T. Barkley House** (1917–20; 114 N. Rountree St.) is a robustly western style bungalow with stone porch posts and hefty stickwork accenting the flared Oriental gables. By contrast, the neighboring **Allie Fleming House** (ca. 1920; 112 N. Rountree St.) interprets the bungalow in picturesque, English-cottage fashion with rough stone chimneys and porch posts, half-timbered gables, and a rolling, thatch-form roof with eyelid dormers. The **Gordon B. Jones House** (ca. 1925; Jones Bros., builders; 207 Clyde Ave.) **(f)** offers a confident Colonial Revival version built as the home of a leading builder.

A notable vestige of early Wilson now stands within this later development. In the

Moses Rountree House (1869–70; Oswald Lipscomb, builder; 107 N. Rountree St., moved from W. Nash St.) **(e)** Lipscomb built for his brother-in-law, a leading merchant, a 1½-story Gothic cottage with a trio of steep wall dormers accentuating lancet windows.

Colonial Revival houses large and small appear regularly among the bungalows, plus a few more exotic accents. The **Arthur A. Ruffin House** (ca. 1920; Jones Bros., builders; 911 Branch St.) **(g)** is a tropical-flavored, stuccoed house with tile roof, reportedly inspired by a house in Coral Gables, Fla. Ruffin, agent for the Gulf Oil Co. and an organizer of the Washington-Florida Short Route Association to promote US 301, bought the plans from the Florida owner and had a local firm build it as a permanent evocation of sunny Florida.

In the 1920s **Raleigh Rd. (h)** emerged as another elite avenue, with big, Georgian Revival residences shaded by towering trees behind deep lawns. The occasional Tudor Revival accents include the especially fine **W. T. Lamm House** (ca. 1924; Thomas B. Herman, architect; Jones Bros., builders; 410 Raleigh Rd.), an asymmetrical composition of half-timbered gables with a slate roof and intricate stained and leaded glass. A surprise appears in the **Sarvis Bass House** (1946; 927 Raleigh Rd.), a gleaming, white-stuccoed residence with the streamlined forms, flat roof, and ribbon windows of the rarely seen domestic Moderne style, built for the progressive owner of a local ironworks, who insisted on a modern house.

WL 6 London's Church
1895; W side SR 1327 (London Church Rd.), 0.1 mi. N of NC 42, Wilson

The gable-fronted frame church with paired entrances is the first church in the county erected for an African American congregation. It was named for its founder, London Woodard. He was born a slave in 1792 and owned by the Woodard family until 1854, when his wife, a free woman, bought his freedom. In 1866 Woodard, a longtime Primitive Baptist, became a preacher and initiated plans for a congregation independent of Toisnot (later *Wilson) Primitive Baptist

Church. The congregation thrived and in 1895 erected this church. In 1992 it was moved here when the highway was widened. (See Introduction, Fig. 39.)

WL 7 Joshua Barnes House
Ca. 1844; W side SR 1327 (London Church Rd.), 2 mi. N of NC 42, at jct. w/SR 1326 and SR 1329; private, visible from road

WL 7 *Joshua Barnes House*

The 2-story frame house typifies the region's Greek Revival plantation houses in its broad proportions, low hip roof, symmetrical 3-bay facade, and 1-story porch with sturdy, Doric-inspired pillars. The center-passage plan two rooms deep incorporates an earlier 19th-c. dwelling. This was home of Gen. Joshua Barnes, planter and politician who led in the establishment of Wilson Co., and later of his daughter Nanny and son-in-law Alpheus Branch, an industrialist who founded the business that became Branch Banking & Trust (BB&T).

WL 8 Elm City

As businessmen strove to revitalize trade after the Civil War, George Howard of Tarboro bought a tract on the Wilmington and Weldon Railroad, persuaded the company to relocate the depot there, and in 1873 initiated development of the town of Toisnot— the old Indian name for a nearby swamp. In the 1890s the town was rechristened Elm City. Still shaded by its namesake trees, it retains a cluster of brick stores on **Main St.** (SR 1003), focusing on the **Elm City Depot** (ca. 1909; N side Main St.), a brick building with a slate-covered hip roof with overhangs carried on curving brackets. Several late 19th-c.

houses feature a locally distinctive wrap-around porch form, with pedimented pavilions at the corners and accenting the front entrance. The most exuberant is the **Deans-Doles House** (ca. 1895; John B. Deans, builder; 200 E. Main St.), a 1½-story dwelling with porch and pavilions enriched with shingles, a fanlight, and turned and sawn millwork. Residences in Southern Colonial style include the **R. S. Wells House** (1910; Charles C. Benton [Wilson], architect; 301 E. Main St.), with its Corinthian portico, and the **G. A. Barnes House** (1892–1902; 201 Nash St.), with its portico of clustered Ionic columns, home of a founder of the Toisnot Banking Company.

WL 9 Jonathan Thomas House

Early 19th c.; N side NC 42, 1.6 mi. E of US 301, Wilson vic.; private, visible from road

Standing beside a well-traveled highway, the hall-parlor-plan farmhouse presents an early example of the coastal cottage, with its double-sloped roof sheltering the front porch and rear shed rooms. A front porch chamber reflects the tradition of "preacher's rooms."

WL 10 Moore's Primitive Baptist Church

1874; N side NC 42, opp. SR 1507, Holdens Crossroads vic.

The prominently sited, frame church retains its gable-fronted form and austerely simple character. The front entrance is flanked by plain, 6/6 sash windows, and along the sides are three windows and secondary entrances. Simplicity continues with match-boarded walls and ceiling and pine pews facing the pulpit. The church was named for its founder and builder, Elder Andrew Jackson Moore.

WL 11 Felton-Lamm Farm

Early 20th c.; NW corner US 264 and NC 91, Saratoga vic.; private, visible from road

A grove of big shade trees, a white frame farmhouse and a cluster of sheds, and a long train of tobacco barns—over twenty at last count—form the archetypal image of coastal plain agricultural life. Located near a well-traveled intersection and visible at a distance across the level farmland, the complex illustrates a long-familiar rural scene now rapidly vanishing as farmers abandon traditional tobacco barns for modern, bulk curing systems or turn from tobacco to other crops. The symmetrical, 1-story farmhouse takes a common regional form, square in plan with a low hip roof, a broad front porch, and a long ell containing the kitchen reaching to the rear.

WL 12 White Oak Primitive Baptist Church

Late 19th c.; NW side NC 222, 0.2 mi. NE of NC 91, Saratoga

A well-kept example of the plain country church prevalent in the county, the 1-room, gable-fronted building has two front entrances and large, 6/6 windows along the sides. A side entrance with batten door suggests the interior may originally have followed the meetinghouse plan, with pews facing a pulpit on the opposite side. Established in 1830, the church became the focus of a community known by 1864 as Saratoga.

WL 13 James Scarborough House

Ca. 1821; Jack Windham, attributed builder; S side NC 222, 0.25 mi. W of US 264, Saratoga vic.; private, visible from road

Among the finest early 19th-c. houses in the county, the tall, 2-story plantation house takes a classic I-house form, with a center-passage plan and rear shed rooms. Double-shouldered chimneys of Flemish-bond brick complement the Federal detail. This has been the home of the Scarborough family since its construction for Maj. James Scarborough, a planter and a long-lived veteran of the American Revolution. Family tradition puts its construction two years before his fourth marriage, to Martha Eason in 1823.

WL 14 Barnes-Eagles House

Ca. 1845, 1914 porch; SW corner NC 58 and SR 1626, Evansdale vic.; private, visible from road

Built for planter William Barnes, brother of politician Joshua Barnes, the double-pile, Greek Revival dwelling was remodeled with a Southern Colonial style portico for Joseph C. Eagles, 20th-c. tobacconist and legislator.

WL 15 W. H. Applewhite Farm

1840s, 1870s; W side US 58, 1.0 mi. W of NC 222, Stantonsburg vic.; private, visible from road

Like many of his neighbors, farmer Henry Applewhite built a 2-story frame house in simplified Greek Revival style with a hall-parlor plan. After the Civil War his son, veteran William H. Applewhite, expanded the house, adding a double-tier front porch, breezeway, and back kitchen. He also built the outbuildings that still define the farmstead, including a tenant house, stables, sheds, and a packhouse and tobacco barns. The farm remains in the family.

WL 16 Daniel Whitley House

Mid-19th c.; W side US 58, 0.4 mi. N of NC 222, Stantonsburg vic.; private, visible from road

The pyramidal-roofed cottage features an unusual plan, with two front doors and four rooms of equal size with corner fireplaces served by a single central chimney. Except for the reworked porch, the house is executed in a stylish, Greek Revival-Italianate mode. A pyramidal-roofed kitchen is linked to the rear by a breezeway.

WL 17 Applewhite-Yelverton-Aycock House

Mid-19th, early 20th c.; E side SR 1628 (Shelton Ave.), 0.2 mi. N of NC 222 (S. Main St.), Stantonsburg; private, visible from road

About 1914 farmer John L. Yelverton hired John Wilson, Wilson contractor, to remodel the 2-story Applewhite family house by removing the double piazza and adding a Southern Colonial portico and wraparound porch. The farmstead retains many domestic and agricultural outbuildings and a ca. 1900 cotton gin across the road.

WL 18 Dr. Edwin Barnes House

Ca. 1840; W side SR 1602, opp. SR 1626, Evansdale vic.; private, visible from road

Built for a country doctor, this is one of several local houses with a distinctive blend of traditional and stylish elements. An I-house with two adjacent front doors serving a hall-parlor plan features such simplified Greek Revival elements as pedimented gable ends,

WL 15 *W. H. Applewhite Farm*

symmetrical moldings with cornerblocks, and a shed porch with tapered, fluted pillars.

WL 19 J. T. and Louisa Graves House
1860s or 1870s; E side SR 1602, 0.2 mi. S of SR 1542, Evansdale vic.

The persistence of simple Greek Revival elements defines the spacious, 1-story house, which has a low hip roof, big windows and sidelighted central entrance, and a broad porch with sturdy pillars. It was built for Dr. Barnes's daughter Louisa and her husband, Dr. James Thomas Graves, who married in 1860.

WL 20 Wiley Simms House
Ca. 1840; W side SR 1602, 0.1 mi. N of SR 1542, Evansdale vic.; private, visible from road

The frame house repeats a local pattern: an I-house with hall-parlor plan and two adjacent front doors, with simple Greek Revival detail in the pedimented gables, and shed porch with reeded pillars and Greek key ornament. A typical expansion is the rear ell with kitchen and dining room. Tradition claims the house was built for James or Benjamin Simms and, after 1862, was the home of Wiley and Sarah Simms.

WL 21 Lucama

Named for three sisters, Lulie, Carrie, and Mary Borden, the small town retains vestiges of its railroading heyday. Incorporated in 1889 around a depot on the Wilson and Fayetteville line, Lucama grew with local brick and lumber industries along with farming and had some 500 people by 1910. Passenger and freight trains still pass through the business district, with its cluster of frame and brick stores. Late Queen Anne cottages and bungalows stand along Main St. and Blalock Rd. beneath tall oaks. Especially lively in form is the **Lucas-Bass House** (ca. 1900; 201 Blalock Rd.), a rambling, Queen Anne cottage with five gables marching across the roofline. The **Lucama Depot** (1904–5; E side US 301, 0.1 mi. W of Main St.), moved and renovated for offices, has typical board-and-

WL 22 *Bullock-Dew House*

batten siding, diagonally boarded doors, and a roof overhang on brackets.

WL 22 Bullock-Dew House
Ca. 1902; N side NC 1136, 0.3 mi. W of NC 581, Bailey vic.; private, visible from road

The Queen Anne style residence presents an unusual full-blown rural rendition of the style. Family tradition recalls that farmer Washington P. Bullock was determined to build "the best house in Wilson County." Said to have been constructed by a contractor from Wilson, where several such residences were under way, the big frame house with its asymmetrical massing and high hip roof features the period's variety of forms and materials, including the inset upper porch and projecting gables, gable ornaments and crockets, windows outlined by tiny panes of stained glass, and a wraparound porch with spindlework framing circular openings. Owned from 1916 to 1979 by William Dew and his descendants, the house was carefully renovated in the 1980s.

WL 23 Lamm's School
Ca. 1922; N side US 264, 0.3 mi. W of I-95, Lamm

During the statewide campaign for consolidation of rural schools, Wilson Co. built a number of schoolhouses, including three stuccoed, Mission style schools—Lamm's, Bullock's and Sims's—that contrasted with the more usual Colonial Revival, red brick facilities. The original polychrome paint scheme accented the arched parapet over the central entrance and the parapeted gable of the auditorium rising behind it.

Pitt County (PT)

See Michael Cotter, Kate M. Ohno, and Mary Hollis Barnes, The Architectural Heritage of Greenville, North Carolina *(1988), and Scott Power,* The Historic Architecture of Pitt County, North Carolina *(1991).*

Greenville (PT 1–15)

Despite the depredations of urban renewal in the mid- and late 20th c., the county seat and university town retains notable examples of the architecture of its late 19th- and early 20th-c. ascendancy as a regional tobacco manufacturing and educational center. Established as Martinborough in 1774 and renamed in 1787 for Gen. Nathanael Greene, the trading center on the Tar River grew slowly for a century and by 1890 had some 1,900 residents. In the 1890s, with the arrival of a branch of the Wilmington and Weldon Railroad and the introduction of tobacco growing as an alternative to the tyrant "King Cotton," Greenville burgeoned as a tobacco market and processing center. A further boost to the town's status and economy came when East Carolina Teachers Training School opened in Greenville in 1909. By 1911 the town of 5,000 people "grows day and night and seems to work overtime. No town in the state has grown more in the past ten years." The teachers' college has subsequently expanded into East Carolina University, and Greenville has become a city of 50,000, second only to Wilmington in the region.

Downtown landmarks from the late 19th and early 20th centuries express Greenville's ambitions in a prime era of city building. Many illustrate the crisscrossing patterns of architectural practice across the region, with works by George F. Barber of Knoxville, Tenn., Herbert Woodley Simpson of New Bern, Charles C. and Frank Benton (Benton & Benton) of Wilson, and Milburn & Heister of Washington, D.C. Beyond the city center, the college campus and early suburban developments likewise recall the early 20th-c. growth era.

Central Business District

PT 1 Pitt County Courthouse
1910–11; Milburn & Heister (Washington, D.C.), architects; Central Carolina Construction Company (Greensboro), contractors; NW corner Evans and W. 3rd Sts.

PT I *Pitt County Courthouse*

Using formulas that accommodated local budgets as well as the renewed taste for symmetry and classicism, Milburn & Heister gained many commissions during the state-wide courthouse building boom of the early 20th c. In this buff brick courthouse, the firm's characteristic composition of hip roof, tall cupola, and prominent porticoes is tailored to its site, with Ionic porticoes sheltering entrances on the eastern and southern sides. The Confederate memorial dates from 1914.

PT 2 U.S. Post Office (Federal Building)
1913–14; Oscar Wenderoth, supervising architect of the Treasury; 215 S. Evans St.

The most elegant building in the city, the Renaissance Revival post office has a graceful Florentine spirit evoked by its palazzo-like form, stuccoed walls, red tile roof, and arcaded loggia sheltering the entrance. Tall,

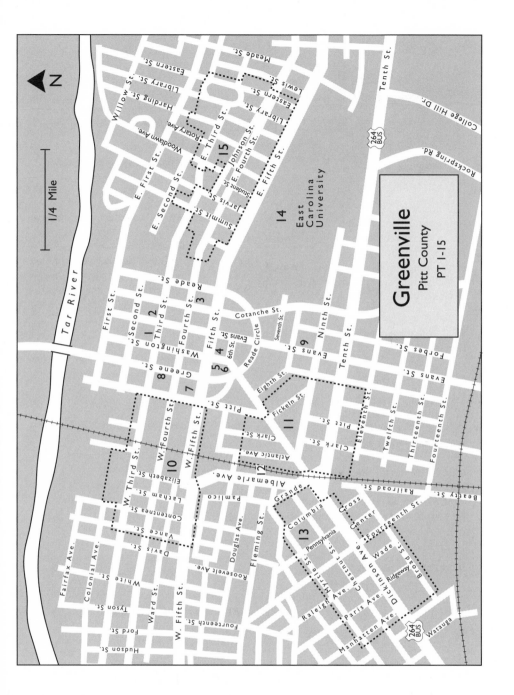

N

1/4 Mile

Tar River

Greenville
Pitt County
PT 1-15

U. S. Post Office, Greenville, N. C.

PT 2 *U.S. Post Office*

Italianate windows carried on consoles light the first story, and smaller, simpler ones occur in the attic beneath the broad eaves. In keeping with the Beaux Arts post office program during Wenderoth's tenure, the quality of the building reflected the growing stature of Greenville in its tobacco boom years.

PT 3 William H. and Jennie M. Long House

1917–18; Benton & Benton (Wilson), architects; 200 E. 4th St.; open business hours

Lawyer and politician William H. Long and his wife, Jennie, employed the prolific firm of Benton & Benton to design a brick mansion dominated by a massive portico with a Tower of the Winds order. Luxurious details include the ornate brickwork, a tile roof, leaded glass, and a variety of Colonial Revival mantels in the high-ceilinged rooms. Once part of a fashionable residential section, the house now serves as law offices.

PT 4 Robert Lee Humber House

1895, 1911–16, 1940s–1950s; 117 W. 5th St.; open business hours

Product of a series of building campaigns, the frame house was the birthplace and home of Robert Lee Humber Jr., an international lawyer, promoter of world peace, and the moving force in establishing the N.C. Museum of Art. After studying at Oxford and the University of Paris, Humber lived in Paris from the 1920s until the invasion of France in 1940. He then returned to Greenville with his wife, Lucie Berthier, whom he had met in Paris. The couple moved into the

house built for his father in 1895 as a gable-fronted, late Italianate dwelling and remodeled in 1911–16 in Colonial Revival style. The Humbers enriched the interior with imported mantels and a walnut-paneled sitting room. The house is the Eastern Office of the N.C. Division of Archives and History.

PT 5 Greenville Municipal Building

1939; Frank W. Benton (Wilson), architect; SW corner 5th and Washington Sts.

Stripped-down classical forms and simplified Art Deco details combined in many government buildings of the 1930s, presenting a balance of dignity, modernity, and economy suited to straitened times. Benton's design for the Greenville facility followed immediately upon a similar design for the *Wilson Municipal Building.

PT 6 Jarvis Memorial Methodist Church

1904–7; Herbert W. Simpson (New Bern), architect; R. J. Cobb and C. V. York, contractors; 510 S. Washington St.

Like *Centenary Methodist Church in New Bern, Simpson's imposing, blond, brick church exemplifies the popularity of the auditorium plan and Romanesque Revival style among Protestant congregations at the turn of the century. Bold entrance towers accented by bartizans flank a broad gable with stained-glass windows. The sanctuary (enlarged in the 1960s) has a slanting floor focusing on the pulpit. The church complex has expanded to cover much of a city block.

PT 7 Greenville Bus Station

1941–42; Frank W. Benton (Wilson), architect; 310 W. 5th St.

A modest but thoroughgoing example of the Moderne style popular in the 1930s and 1940s, the little bus station is one of an endangered breed of mid-20th-c. architecture. Architect Benton used simple forms, rounded corners, and broad overhangs to create a streamlined effect associated with fast, modern transportation.

PT 8 *James L. Fleming House*

PT 8 James L. Fleming House

1901–2; George F. Barber (Barber & Kluttz)
(Knoxville), architect; C. B. West, builder;
302 S. Greene St.; open business hours

The large, frame Queen Anne style house
typifies the work of the prolific Tennessee
mail-order architect, whose plans for the residence survive. Barber's favored pairing of
corner turret and front gable enliven the
roofline, and their decorative shingles set off
the patterned slate roof. Ornate ironwork
appears in the porch posts, balustrade, and
fence. Fleming, an attorney, mayor, and state
legislator, took a key role in establishing East
Carolina Teachers Training School in Greenville. The house has been renovated for the
Pitt-Greenville Chamber of Commerce.

PT 9 Jones-Lee House

1890–95; Charles T. Munford, developer and
contractor; 805 S. Evans St.

Such exuberant surface ornament—patterned shingles, lattice, sawnwork, and Stick-
style decoration with a half-timber effect—
on a relatively modest dwelling epitomizes
the late 19th-c. penchant for the "tasty" and
"artistic." The narrow, 2-story house is the
sole survivor of a row of five in a once-dense
residential area.

Adjoining areas

PT 10 Skinnerville

In the 1880s businessman Harry Skinner began selling lots for the city's first suburb (also
known as West Greenville) on a tract west of
the city limits and north of 5th St. Develop-

ment continued through the 1910s and
1920s, as Queen Anne and Colonial Revival
houses were complemented by varied bungalows. The neighborhood's fashionable heyday was followed by pressures from the
growing university. The **J. R. Moye House**
(1902–3; Herbert W. Simpson; 408 W. 5th
St.) exemplifies New Bern architect Simpson's confident blend of Queen Anne massing and Colonial Revival details. College
life has altered a number of the principal
residences, such as the **Edward B. Ficklen
House** (1902; 508 W. 5th St.), a big, towered,
Queen Anne style house, the prime survivor
of many such houses. It was built for a tobacconist who came from Danville, Va.,
market center of the Old Bright Leaf Tobacco Belt, to participate in the expansion
of the tobacco economy in eastern N.C.
Among the best of several Colonial Revival
and Georgian Revival houses is the **Judson
H. Blount House** (1933; 500 Elizabeth St.),
a symmetrical, 2½-story, red brick residence with 2-story wings, built for a fertilizer manufacturer.

PT 11 Tobacco Warehouse District

S of downtown, between Evans St. and
Dickinson Ave.

Clustered near the tracks are several large,
brick tobacco sales, manufacturing, and
storage buildings of the early 20th c., along
with standard commercial structures of the
same era. The functional brick complexes
have expanded steadily over the years. The
E. B. Ficklen Tobacco Company (1897–
1920s; Ficklen and 9th Sts.) includes a
3-story factory with arched windows and

PT 11 *E. B. Ficklen Tobacco Co.*

pilasters, built in 1897 as a stemmery and prizery, plus other 1- and 2-story buildings. Spacious, 1-story brick buildings constitute the **Liggett & Myers Tobacco Company** (ca. 1910–1920s; 10th St. at tracks). The **Imperial Tobacco Company** (1902–29; H. J. Blauwelt [Richmond], architect; Charles H. East, contractor; Atlantic Ave.), a competitor to the American Tobacco Company, comprised a series of massive brick buildings until a fire destroyed part of the complex in 1991. Notable among the survivors is the **Office** (1916), with its ornate corbeling.

PT 12 Roxy Theater

1948; 629 Albemarle Ave.

Greenville was an important center for black cultural life in eastern N.C. throughout the Jim Crow era. The Roxy Theater, built by local investors soon after World War II, is one of the most intact of many theaters that served black audiences. In 1951 it was leased to the Booker T. Theater Corporation of Rocky Mount. The streamlined Moderne architecture, characteristic of mid-20th-c. theaters, extends to the marquee and ticket booth.

PT 13 Higgs Neighborhood

SW of downtown, NW of Dickinson Ave.

As the tobacco economy expanded, accompanied by other enterprises such as a lumber mill, a textile mill, and a slaughterhouse, the Higgs brothers developed several residential streets to meet the growing demand for housing. The **J. W. Higgs House**, the developer's own Queen Anne–Colonial Revival residence at 1112 Dickinson Ave., is among the largest houses, but the area also includes notable bungalows and cottages on Broad, Chestnut, Dickinson, Ridgeway, Wade, and other streets, exemplary of the small-scale housing that made up much of eastern N.C.'s early 20th-c. urbanization. The **Agnes Fullilove School** (1924; Wilson, Berryman, & Kennedy [Raleigh and Columbia], architects; C. B. West, contractor; NW corner Chestnut St. and Manhattan Ave.) is a polychromed building of red brick with limestone accenting the arcaded entrance pavilion. Limestone medallions depicting an open book and a wise owl inspire scholarship. Originally West Greenville Grammar School, it is one of many projects by a leading public school specialist.

PT 14 East Carolina University

E of downtown, S of E. 5th St.

In 1907, after eastern N.C. leaders won their campaign in the legislature for a state-supported normal school in their region, Greenville and Pitt Co. outbid seven other towns competing for the institution by raising $100,000 for financial assistance through local bond issues. When East Carolina Teachers Training School was established on old farmland at the eastern edge of Greenville, architects C. C. Hook of Charlotte and Herbert Woodley Simpson of New Bern designed the first campus buildings—typified by present **Jarvis Hall** (1909)—in the functional, free classical, red brick architecture of the time. Former governor Thomas Jarvis of Greenville, a member of the building committee, encouraged the use of "handsome and most durable" tile instead of slate for the roofs, a choice that lent a Spanish Mission flavor. Similar designs continued in the architecture of the 1920s, with H. A. Underwood of Raleigh as architect. **McGinnis Auditorium** (1951) introduces a late Art Deco note in the stylized motifs and lettering of its clean stone facade. In the late 20th c. the campus has expanded rapidly, and several of the earliest buildings have had their distinctive red tile roofs replaced.

PT 15 College View

1909–1940s; E of downtown, N of E. 5th St., S of E. 1st St.

An especially intact early 20th-c. suburb, the grid-plan neighborhood developed in tandem with the college across 5th St. Bungalows of all sizes and types dominate—as seen in, for example, the 400 blocks of **S. Jarvis St.** and **Student St.** An unusual number of Spanish Revival houses suggests an influence from the college buildings, such as two built for leading tobacconists, the **W. H. Dail Jr. House** (1920s; 605 E. 5th St.),

PT 15 *College View*

a large, symmetrical residence of tan brick with a tile roof and opulent classical detail, and the **Dr. Paul Fitzgerald House** (1920s; 1203 E. 5th St.), a stuccoed cottage-bungalow. An unusual rendition of the Spanish motif appears in the picturesque, towered **R. H. Gaskins House** (1928; 309 S. Library St.). The **Dr. L. C. Skinner House** (1920s; 805 E. 5th St.) is an especially fine Georgian Revival house in red brick. The **Dr. Karl B. Pace House** (1920s; 404 S. Summit St.) introduces a Prairie style element with its asymmetrical massing, dark brown shingled walls, and deep eaves.

PT 16 Wedigan Mathias Moore II House

2d quarter 19th c.; S side SR 1529, 0.25 mi. W of SR 1538, Pactolus vic.; private, visible from road

One of Pitt Co.'s many farmhouses that take the I-house form, this 5-bay frame house is larger than most in the county. It is handsomely finished with such Federal and Greek Revival details as pedimented gable ends and window surrounds with cornerblocks accentuating the flush-sheathed facade beneath the shed porch. The house and farm have long been associated with the Moore family.

PT 17 Thomas Sheppard House

Ca. 1850; S side SR 1550 opp. SR 1552, Stokes vic.; private, visible from road

Located beside an 18th-c. millpond, the house was built for planter and mill owner Sheppard in a conservative, Federal–Greek Revival style characteristic of the county, distinguished by the county's only Greek Revival entrance portico. The unusual plan of the 2-story house has two rooms flanking a center stair on the first floor and three rooms above. A late 18th-c., hall-parlor-plan dwelling in the rear yard may have served as kitchen.

PT 18 Pactolus

Situated adjacent to US 264, Pactolus— named for a classical city in Asia Minor— exemplifies the antebellum country village encircled by productive farmland. Growing up around trade with a Tar River landing, the community prospered prior to the Civil War with numerous plantations and the Midway Male and Female Academy. Among several antebellum plantation houses is the **William Lawrence Perkins House** (1840s; s side SR 1560, 0.2 mi. E of SR 1561), a big, 2-story dwelling with simplified Greek Revival details. One of the county's prime expressions of the post–Civil War efforts to regain prosperity appears in the **James Rubin Davenport House** (ca. 1870; s side SR 1560, opp. SR 1561), a 2-story, L-shaped, frame house with ornate sawnwork porches on two sides, a bracket cornice, and 2-story bay window; it was built for Davenport, an entrepreneur who came to Pactolus soon after the war and operated a store, a saloon, a cotton gin, and a fertilizer factory. Davenport's late 19th-c. **Store** with a parapet false front stands nearby, as do several outbuildings.

PT 19 Grimesland

Ca. 1790s, ca. 1850; N side SR 1569, 0.25 mi. E of NC 33, Grimesland vic.; private, visible at a distance from road

The plantation house set among broad fields is the seat of a family long prominent in local, state, and national political arenas. Built

PT 19 *Grimesland*

for planter and state legislator William Grimes and his wife, Ann Bryan Grimes, it was later the home of their grandson Bryan Grimes, a Confederate general, and his son, J. Bryan Grimes, N.C. secretary of state. The traditional 5-bay, 2-story house has a symmetrical facade accentuated by a fanlit entrance. Flanking 1-story wings are mid-19th-c. Greek Revival additions. The plantation retains important 19th-c. outbuildings, including a brick cistern, a stone meathouse or dairy, servants' quarters, and others.

PT 20 Daniels-Tucker Farm
Mid-19th c.; W side SR 1759, 0.3 mi. S of SR 1700, Simpson vic.

PT 20 *Daniels-Tucker Farm*

Centering on a coastal cottage with engaged porch and shed rooms, the farmstead presents an unusually complete 19th-c. ensemble exemplary of the medium-sized farms numerous in the county. Among the antebellum outbuildings are a 2-room detached kitchen, a log smokehouse, and a large frame barn. From later years of farming are a stable, a corncrib, and a 2-story tobacco packhouse. Across the road is the Tucker family cemetery, one of many small family burying grounds that dot the county. J. A. K. Tucker, farmer and county sheriff, bought the farm from John and Benjamin Daniels in 1872.

PT 21 Red Banks Primitive Baptist Church
1893; NE corner SR 1704 and SR 1725, Greenville vic.

Although development surrounds its once-pastoral site, the small church recalls the quiet simplicity and unswerving conservatism of rural Primitive Baptist churches. The weatherboarded frame building repeats the gable-fronted, rectangular form and paired front entrances long familiar when it was built in 1893. One of the oldest Baptist congregations in the county, Red Banks was established in 1758.

PT 22 St. John's Episcopal Church
1893–95; Stephen Gus Barrington, attributed local builder; SE corner SR 1917 and SR 1753, St. John's

The gable-fronted frame church, with Gothic Revival touches in its pointed-arched openings, vestibule, and chancel, stands at the center of a quiet agricultural village that flourished modestly after the Civil War. The congregation descends from Grace Chapel, founded in 1821, which shared a chapel with Free Will Baptists and Disciples of Christ.

PT 23 St. Jude's Catholic Church
1933; SW corner Queen and Highland Sts., Grifton

In contrast to the plain frame churches that predominate in the county, this Catholic church in the railroad village of Grifton presents a striking composition in a Spanish Mission Revival style. Stuccoed walls emphasize the bold form. The curvilinear gable front opens into a 2-story, arched recess, which frames a large rose window; the entrance is screened by an arcade with spiral columns. Reportedly constructed with donations from a widow in New York State, the church on its hilltop site is now home to the Hillside Free Will Baptist Church.

PT 24 Abram Cox House
1790s, ca. 1850, ca. 1870; E side SR 1723, 0.25 mi. S of NC 102, Ayden vic.; private, visible from road

The ebullient sawnwork of the double porch and the ornate bracketed gables and cornice veil the 18th-c. origins of the 2-story farmhouse. Double-shouldered end chimneys of Flemish-bond brick indicate the quality of

PT 24 *Abram Cox House*

the late Georgian house. Probably built for planter Abram Cox, the house was inherited by his grandson Abram Cox III, who returned from the Civil War and prospered sufficiently to update his house in stylish fashion.

PT 25 Ayden

Ayden possesses unusual architectural distinction for a small railroad town, in both its compact commercial district and its early 20th-c. residential areas. Like several other Pitt Co. towns, Ayden was a child of the railroad. The Scotland-Neck-to-Kinston branch of the Wilmington and Weldon Railroad arrived in 1890, and Ayden was incorporated in 1891. Local landowner W. H. Harris, who persuaded the railroad company to run the line through his land, promptly platted lots and offered them for sale. The town soon attracted two new schools, Carolina Christian College in 1893 (a Disciples of Christ school, which later relocated to Wilson and became Atlantic Christian College, now Barton College), and a Free Will Baptist theological seminary in 1896, predecessor of Eureka Bible College (1926). Profiting from lumber, milling, finishing plants, banks, and mercantile stores, Ayden grew steadily during the early 20th c. By 1930, when growth was halted by the Great Depression, it was the second largest town in the county.

The **Central Business District** has an excellent collection of early 20th-c. commercial buildings, focused on East and West Aves. flanking the railroad tracks, and the nearby intersections of Lee and 2nd and 3rd Sts. The **Ayden Town Hall** (1915; West Ave.) presents an unexpectedly bold gesture in its small-town setting, a 2-story, brick building with a powerfully composed central tower, executed in a stylized Lombard mode, with deep, arcaded cornices and energetic forms evoking the spirit of Philadelphia architect Frank Furness. More typical commercial edifices appear throughout the central business section. Anchoring opposing prime corners are 2- and 3-story, red brick bank buildings with classical entrances angled toward the intersection: **First National Bank of Ayden** (ca. 1910–12; 203 South Lee St.), which features a tobacco-leaf motif at the pedimented entrance, and its onetime competitor, **Farmers and Merchants National Bank** (1915; 105–7 2nd St.).

Tree-lined neighborhoods extending from 2nd and 3rd Sts. contain a range of traditional vernacular houses and fashionable residences from the 1890s to World War II— Italianate, Queen Anne, Colonial Revival, and especially bungalows and foursquare houses. Ayden is best known for its collection of Craftsman bungalows. Many stand along W. 3rd St. and nearby streets, the

PT 25 *Ayden Town Hall*

PT 25 *Lloyd and Lillian Turnage House*

prime early 20th-c. neighborhood known as Westhaven. The **Lloyd and Lillian Turnage House** (ca. 1923; Benton & Benton [Wilson], architects; Grover McLawhorn, contractor; 811 W. 3rd St.), built for a leading mercantile family from plans by Wilson's principal architects, is an especially striking bungalow, with robust Craftsman stickwork, a sweeping gable roof, and a deep porch extending to shelter a porte-cochere. The **C. R. Tyndall House** (1923; 709 W. 3rd St.), built for another local merchant, is a classic small bungalow with neat Craftsman details.

South of the business district, a cohesive African American neighborhood developed as rural residents were drawn to factory jobs and other opportunities in the growing town. Concentrated along **S. East Ave., S. West Ave., S. Lee St., Planter's St., Seminary (6th) St.**, and nearby streets are blocks filled with houses from the 1910s and 1920s: rows of frame, shotgun dwellings (300 block E. 6th St.) and cast-stone cottages (100 block W. 6th St.) and bungalows (Planters St.) and scattered I-houses.

Ayden's eastern side developed first around Carolina Christian College, which stood just east of the railroad. E. 2nd and E. 3rd Sts. have some of the town's oldest houses, such as the 2-story, bracketed **R. C. Cannon House** (ca. 1895; 411 E. 2nd St.) and the ornate, rambling, 1-story **Robert and Cora Smith House** (ca. 1900; 309–11 E. 2nd St.), built for a merchant and civic leader. The restrained Georgian Revival style **Thelbert Worthington House** (1930; Leila Ross Wilburn [Atlanta], architect; 215 E. 3rd St.) was designed by one of the most prominent woman architects of the early 20th c. Worthington bought the plans from a pattern-

book of Wilburn's designs, then had a local contractor build the 2-story, red brick house.

PT 26 Winterville

The village began in the 1880s with the pioneering efforts of Amos Graves Cox, son of a farmer and woodshop owner, to manufacture and sell cotton planters. After the Scotland-Neck-to-Kinston branch of the Wilmington and Weldon Railroad ran through Cox's land in 1890, trade and growth blossomed. Typical of early 20th-c. railroad towns, Winterville has a compact row of 1-story, corbeled, brick commercial buildings focused at the corner of Depot and W. Railroad Sts. The 1922 construction of the 2-story brick **A. W. Ange and Company Store** at the corner of W. Main and Mill Sts. marked a shift from the railroad toward the highway and the automobile. Workers' cottages built during the 1890s make up the bulk of the town's earliest dwellings, along Main St. between NC 11 and Mill St., many of which continue forms used for small houses for over a century. Especially numerous are 1-story, side-gabled houses with center entrances sheltered by porches, with ells at the rear. Businessmen and professionals built larger residences during the early 20th c. along Church, Cooper, and Blount Sts. The former **St. Luke's Episcopal Church** (1903; NW corner S. Church and Sylvania Sts.) is a diminutive, Gothic Revival frame structure now used as the Winterville Historical and Arts Museum.

PT 27 Charles and Maggie McLawhorn House

1910; NW side NC 903, 2.4 mi. W of NC 11, Winterville vic.; private, visible from road

The big, frame, Colonial Revival farmhouse and its ensemble of frame outbuildings epitomize the progressive farmsteads of the early 20th c. As recalled by family stories, when Charles and Maggie Barnhill McLawhorn's family of eight children outgrew the small, 1-story farmhouse—still standing nearby— where they had lived since their marriage in 1889, Charles had his brother Lorenzo cut timber from the family farm to build a new house adjacent to their old one. By 1910 the foursquare, hip-roofed, double-pile house with its wraparound porch with Doric columns was ready for the family. A full complement of early 20th-c. outbuildings is aligned to the rear and side of the house: smokehouse, stilted dairy, storage shed, carbide pit, playhouse, washhouse, three-portal garage, commissary, and two-stall wagon shed.

PT 28 Bethany Free Will Baptist Church

1922–25; W side NC 903, 2.5 mi. N of NC 102, Ayden vic.

Unusual among the county's generally plain country churches, this brick structure embraces the nationally popular Romanesque and Gothic Revival styles. The central entrance tower rising from the broad, gabled facade features stepped buttresses and a crenellated parapet. The church replaced one built in 1881 for the newly formed congregation.

PT 29 Plank Road Toll Keeper's House

1850s; SE corner US 264A and US 13, Lang's Crossroads

Local tradition reports that the little frame house was built for the toll keeper on the old Raleigh-Greenville plank road constructed in the 1850s, making the dwelling a rare survivor from an important chapter in transportation history. The 1-story house has a pair of doors opening into two main rooms, plus a rear shed and kitchen.

PT 30 Farmville

Pitt Co.'s tobacco culture is clearly depicted in the railroad town of Farmville, which lies at the center of some of the most productive acreage in the county. Established in the mid-19th c. around the Antioch Disciples of Christ Church (1854) and the Pitt County Female Institute (1857), Farmville was incorporated in 1872. The community blossomed as a market center when the region turned to tobacco cultivation and marketing at the end of the 19th c. and the East Carolina Railway arrived in 1900. Large brick

and metal-clad tobacco warehouses located throughout the community signal its role as western Pitt Co.'s only tobacco market. Prominent among these is the **Monk Tobacco Warehouse** (1913; W. Wilson St.), a long, low, brick building with skylit roof and parapeted fronts with large, arched entrances to admit wagons full of tobacco.

The tobacco boom supported construction of the substantial brick commercial buildings along Main St. Key banks represent the range of styles. The (former) **Bank of Farmville/R. L. Davis Store Building** (1904; 121–23 S. Main St.), one of several brick Italianate stores, displays ornate corbeled brickwork featuring arcades, diamonds, and pilasters, and a curved parapet marked "1904/BANK." Beaux Arts classical dignity defines a prominent corner in the **Bank of Farmville** (1921; Benton & Benton [Wilson], architects; 129 S. Main St.), a 3-story stone building with Doric columns in antis flanking the entrance and pilasters carrying a Doric cornice.

PT 30 *Bank of Farmville*

Residential architecture on Main, Church, and nearby streets includes a spectrum of modest, vernacular forms of the 19th c. and nationally popular styles of the early 20th c. The **Dr. Paul Erastus Jones House** (ca. 1920; 502 N. Main St.), the most striking of several robust bungalows, features a boldly angled porch and strong Craftsman detail. The **James W. May House** (ca. 1860; 213 S. Main St.), a simply detailed, frame, Greek Revival cottage on a raised foundation, was home of a town founder and now contains a local museum. The Southern Colonial style appears in a pair of nearly identical red brick houses with monumental porticoes that face each other across Church St.: the **Joseph Warren Parker House** (ca. 1915; 201 W. Church St.), home of a leading merchant and civic leader, and the **Harris House** (ca. 1920; 200 Church St.), which Parker built for his daughter Mary Vivian and her husband, John Thomas Harris. The **William Leslie Smith House** (1920–23; 307 W. Church St.) presents the county's prime example of the Spanish Mission Revival style, a romantic composition with corner tower, tile roof, and deep, arcaded porch. The **Mary Finetti May Lewis House** (ca. 1905; 401 W. Church St.) is a traditional I-house enriched with a projecting entrance pavilion and bracketed porch.

PT 31 Benjamin May-Lewis House

1830s, 1850s; N side NC 121, 0.3 mi. E of US 264A, Farmville vic.; private, visible from road

The well-preserved, prominently sited plantation house, long associated with the locally influential May and Lewis families, typifies the conservative character of the area's antebellum architecture. The 2-story frame dwelling began as a late Federal house with a hall-parlor plan and was expanded in the mid-19th c. to a 2-room depth with pairs of end chimneys and simple Greek Revival style finish. Outbuildings include an antebellum frame smokehouse as well as later tobacco barns, a packhouse, a tenant house, and sheds. Constructed probably by planter Benjamin May III, the house descended in the family and was home of Benjamin May Lewis Jr., agriculturalist and county commissioner.

PT 32 Samuel Vines House

1813 (date brick); N side SR 1247, 1.1 mi. W of SR 1245, Kings Crossroads vic.; private, visible from road

Constructed for Samuel Vines, a captain in the War of 1812, the simple, late Georgian dwelling follows a traditional hall-parlor plan and displays fine craftsmanship in its paneled doors, beaded weatherboards, and

heavy, simple moldings. A late 19th-c. detached kitchen is linked to the side of the main house by a wraparound porch. Outbuildings include an early 19th-c. smokehouse and plantation office, plus sheds and a commissary from later years, when the farm was owned by the Smith family.

PT 33 Falkland

Originally known as "Faulkner House," named after George Faulkner, who established an ordinary here in the 1780s, the old Tar River trading village retains several well-maintained, Greek Revival and Victorian dwellings that line the old routes, NC 43 and SR 1247. At the heart of town stands one of the county's principal antebellum plantation houses: the **Dr. Peyton Mayo House** (ca. 1859; jct. of NC 43 and NC 222), a squarely built, 2-story house with bracket cornice and delicate sawnwork porch that blends Greek Revival and Italianate elements.

PT 34 Green Wreath (Foreman House)

Ca. 1780, ca. 1791, early 19th c.; SW side NC 43, 0.3 mi. NW of NC 121, Falkland vic.; private, visible from road

Among the oldest houses in the county, Green Wreath illustrates the early 19th-c. transitions from modest to ambitious plantation houses and from the late Georgian to the Federal style. It was the seat of one of the county's largest plantations, which was established by John Foreman, who accumu-

PT 34 *Green Wreath*

lated over 6,000 acres here. As was typical in the late 18th c., he built a relatively simple, 1½-story, gambrel-roofed dwelling. His son Ivey, who added another 4,000 acres, transformed the house in the early 19th c. with the front addition of the elaborate Federal style residence 2 stories tall with a center passage plan. Double-shouldered brick chimneys are laid in Flemish bond, and a (reconstructed) 2-story entrance portico dominates the symmetrical facade. Numerous early 19th-c. outbuildings include a brick springhouse, a frame barn, and a plantation office.

Greene County (GR)

GR 1 Snow Hill

Bypassed by interstates and barely touched by four-lane highways, Greene is one of the least-developed counties in the coastal plain and one of the most pleasant to visit. Plantation houses of traditional form and unusually rich detail recall an era of prosperity in the early and mid-19th c. Snow Hill, the county seat, has been spared thus far the strip development of its larger neighbors and retains a quiet air of eastern N.C. small-town gentility that has eroded elsewhere. The county seat was authorized in 1811 and incorporated in 1828, taking the name of a nearby plantation known for a hill of white sand. It became seat of a county formed as Glasgow in 1791 but renamed in 1799 for Gen. Nathanael Greene, the Revolutionary War leader for whom Greenville and Greensboro were also named.

At the heart of Snow Hill, a small commercial district of 2-story brick storefronts flanks the **Greene County Courthouse** (1934–35; Thomas B. Herman [Wilson], architect, T. A. Loving [Goldsboro], contractor; N. Greene St. at S.E. Second St.), a simple, WPA-era, red brick Colonial Revival building—the county's fourth courthouse—that fulfills its symbolic role from its perch above Contentnea Creek. **Greene St.** southwest of the downtown is the principal residential avenue, with great trees shading large frame houses. A few houses survive in altered form from the mid-19th c., but the main attractions are the several fine variations on the Queen Anne and Colonial Revival styles.

The town's best-known architectural landmark is **St. Barnabas Episcopal Church** (1887; W. T. Faircloth, Porter & Godwin, builders; SE corner S.E. Fourth St. and St. Barnabas Rd.), a picturesquely sited and carefully preserved church in the Carpenter Gothic style, reflecting the influence of Richard Upjohn's *Rural Architecture* (1852ff.) on Episcopal church design for a half-century. It shares with *Grace Episcopal Church in Jones Co. the use of an arcaded

GR 1 *St. Barnabas Episcopal Church*

cornice linking the battens of the board-and-batten walls, a subtle technique that makes each wall surface a stylized arcade. A scissors truss kingpost adorns the front gable, and the motif continues as the exposed roof truss in the simply finished interior.

GR 2 Haywood Best House

Early 19th c.; N side SR 1149, 0.2 mi. NW of NC 903, Snow Hill vic.; private, visible from road

The big, 2-story house incorporates the county's typical blend of conservative form with well-crafted, late Georgian and early Federal detail. The broad, asymmetrical, 5-bay facade probably reflects two construction phases. A full-width shed porch retains fine original work including chamfered posts, heavy molded rails, and delicate square balusters. There are several outbuildings, including an early meathouse. This is one of three surviving plantation houses built by the Best family, one of the county's wealthiest in the antebellum period. Although the county retains a good number of early and mid-19th-c. plantation houses, many of them lie beyond public view.

GR 3 Best Lodge

Late 18th c., 19th c.; NW side SR 1143, 0.1 mi. S of SR 1149, Shines Crossroads; private, visible from road

One of the oldest houses in the county, with notable Georgian interiors, the plantation house repeats the symmetrical, 5-bay form with end chimneys and a broad, 2-tier front porch. It is thought to have been built for Henry or Benjamin Best, of a family who came from Virginia.

GR 4 Titus Carr House

Ca. 1870; N side SR 1244, 0.1 mi. W of NC 91, Castoria; private, visible from road

GR 4 *Titus Carr House*

The 2-story frame house repeats the symmetrical, hip-roofed form, center-passage plan, wide pilasters, and bracket cornice seen in other local examples, such as the *Speight-Bynum House, but its lacy porch of scroll-sawn curvilinear members lends it a jauntily picturesque air. It may have been built for Carr a few years after his 1866 marriage to Ada Little of Beaufort Co., when he was establishing himself as one of the county's leading farmers and operator of two general stores. Several frame outbuildings appear to be contemporary with the house. By one account the community name Castoria is derived from "Carr's-store-i-a."

GR 5 Tabernacle Methodist Church

1880s, mid-20th c.; W side SR 1229, 0.3 mi. S of SR 1232, Walstonburg vic.

The small, well-tended, frame country church combines the simple, front-gabled form prevalent from the early 19th c. onward with a simple, Doric-columned portico from the 20th c. Across the road is the **Dr. John R. Deering House** (early 19th c.; private), one of the county's many traditional, 2-story plantation houses, here with an unusual, asymmetrical 4-bay front that may reflect an original side-passage-plan house later expanded.

GR 6 Ruffin-Dawson House

Late 1850s; N side SR 1234, .25 mi. SW of NC 58, Walstonburg vic.; private, visible from road

With its trio of sharp gables enlivening the facade, this picturesque cottage shares the Carpenter Gothic spirit seen in works attributed to Oswald Lipscomb, a builder active in Wilson and Edgecombe counties. Lancet windows with tracery fill the gables, complemented by board-and-batten walls. The porch with simple posts is more recent. Thought to have been built for Etheldridge and Elisabeth Ruffin, this is one of several Greene Co. houses built for planter families with a taste for the Downingesque mode.

GR 7 Speight-Bynum House

Ca. 1850; W side SR 1231, 0.4 mi. N of SR 1232, Walstonburg vic.; private, visible from road

The eclectic, Greek Revival-Italianate style house belongs to a group of mid-19th-c. plantation houses in the county whose details point to a single, as yet unidentified carpenter. The house displays the characteristic double-pile, center-passage plan under a low hip roof. Wide pilasters with arched panels mark the corners, matching posts support the porch, and brackets enliven the eaves—details shared with the *Titus Carr House and others. The outbuildings range from an antebellum smokehouse to mid-20th-c. agricultural buildings. The house was built for James Pell Speight, planter and politician, on a 400-acre tract given him by his father, Methodist minister Seth Speight. With about 160 acres of improved land and nineteen slaves in 1850, the plantation produced corn, grains, livestock, and, by 1860, cotton. Since the late 19th c. the farm has been the home of the Bynum family.

GR 8 Meadow Primitive Baptist Church

Mid-19th c.; E side SR 1303, 0.5 mi. S of NC 91, Walstonburg vic.

The simple, weatherboarded church embodies the prevailing conservatism of a denomination important in this and nearby counties. It has the characteristic paired entrances in the gable front, three plain, 9/9 sash windows along each side, and secondary entrances at the sides and rear.

GR 9 Maury

GR 9 *Maury Depot*

Although the tracks of the old East Carolina Railway were pulled up years ago, the little community retains vestiges of its early 20th-c. heyday as a railroad village. The **Maury Depot**, a small, bracketed, board-and-batten building, survives as a privately owned warehouse, complete with its neatly painted sign, while a row of frame stores with false fronts faces the railroad bed.

GR 10 Hookerton

Known in the 18th c. as Caswell's Landing, the community on Contentnea Creek was incorporated as Hookerton in 1817 and was the home of several early 19th-c. academies. Today its chief point of interest is **Hookerton Christian Church** (mid-19th c.; NE corner Church and 5th Sts.), one of the oldest Disciples of Christ church buildings in N.C. An unusual detached belltower with tapering walls and a shallow, pyramidal cover stands to the left of the Greek Revival, temple-form sanctuary. The exterior was brick veneered in this century, but the interior retains its original gallery on three sides.

Lenoir County (LR)

Kinston (LR 1–7)

The Neuse River trading center and county seat was incorporated in 1762 as Kingston in honor of George III; the *g* was dropped after the Revolution. The community remained tiny until the 1858 arrival of the Atlantic and N.C. Railroad, then gained economic energy in the 1890s when a branch of the Wilmington and Weldon Railroad boosted textile manufacturing and tobacco market-

ing. In 1895 the local paper predicted, "A new era for Kinston! This is what the opening of a tobacco market here last week meant. . . . Our business men are united and enthusiastic for making Kinston a great tobacco town." The community grew from 1,700 in 1890 to 4,100 in 1900 to 9,700 in 1920. Fires in the 1890s destroyed much of the town, so that the historic architecture dates chiefly from the rebuilding, industrial growth, and rapid expansion of the early

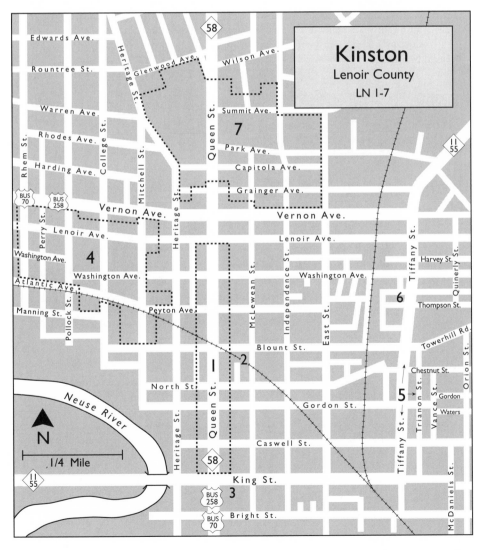

20th c. and illustrates the region's urban patterns of that era both in architectural types and town layout.

LR 1 Queen St. Commercial District

Running several blocks north from the Neuse River, Queen St. was one of eastern N.C.'s early 20th-c. retail showplaces, and it remains one of the region's grandest main streets. Displaying the town's rising stature in the tobacco boom era, the long, broad commercial avenue boasts unusually diverse and ambitious commercial and public buildings, which punctuate long blocks of 2- and 3-story brick storefronts with Italianate and classical treatments. (See Introduction, Fig. 55.) In recent years many of the facades long covered by mid-20th-c. materials have been rejuvenated.

LR 1 *Lenoir County Courthouse*

The **Lenoir County Courthouse and Annex** (1939; A. Mitchell Wooten and John J. Rowland, architects; Annex, 1981, Burnstudio [Raleigh], architects; E corner Queen and King Sts.) models 1930s stripped classicism, its clean-lined, symmetrical composition and geometricized details rendered with a sleekness that anticipates the modernism of the post–World War II era. The 1981 rear annex deftly complements the original building.

Defining the important corner two blocks north of the courthouse at Queen and Gordon Sts., a trio of banks displays variations of Beaux Arts classical formulae. The big, 2-story **Branch Banking and Trust** (originally the National Bank of Kinston; 1908, Herbert W. Simpson [New Bern]; remodeled 1925; 136 N. Queen St.) has a heavy entablature carried by four full-height Corinthian columns. The **Farmers and Merchants Bank** (1924; Benton & Benton [Wilson]; 200 N. Queen St.), a narrow, 5-story building designed as a small skyscraper, features classically detailed base, shaft, and cap. The **Citizens Savings Bank** (1903; 201 N. Queen St.) stands 3 stories tall with a domed tower commanding the intersection. On the fourth corner, the **Canady Building** (1899; 131–35 N. Queen St.) is a corbeled, 3-section, brick commercial building in Romanesque Revival style, built to house the hardware and agricultural implement business of B. W. Canady, "a pioneer in the development of Kinston's industrial life" in tobacco and textile manufacturing.

A short distance north, the former **U.S. Post Office** (1914; Oscar Wenderoth, supervising architect of the Treasury; 300 block Queen St.) displays a dignified, tripartite composition, faced in stone, with a tall portico dominating the central block—typical of the Beaux Arts work of Wenderoth's office. The **Queen St. Methodist Church** (1911; 500 block N. Queen St.) enlivens the street with two domed towers and an array of Romanesque and Eastlake ornament.

LR 1 *Queen St. Methodist Church*

Towering over downtown is the 11-story stepped height of the former **Hotel Kinston** (1928; Herbert B. Hunter [High Point], architect; 501 N. Queen St.), a remarkable blend of Moorish motifs and Art Deco spirit, with an arcade at street level and polychromed diaperwork in a blind arcade in the upper story. Local investors developed the project to provide Kinston with the first-class hotel needed to attract businessmen. The **B. F. Canady House** (ca. 1883; 600 N.

Queen St.), the 2-story, frame, Italianate residence of the merchant and industrial pioneer, is the last of the late 19th-c. houses that once lined the northern end of the street.

LR 2 Atlantic and East Carolina Freight Depot

1900; SW side Blount St. between N. Queen and N. McLewean Sts.

The handsome brick depot, with an unusual monitor roof and segmental-arched openings along its 11-bay sides, stands along the diagonal route of the railroad tracks. It was built to accommodate growing freight traffic generated by tobacco sales and manufacturing at the turn of the century.

LR 3 Peebles House (Harmony Hall)

Ca. 1775, early–mid-19th c., early 20th c.; 109 E. King St.; open limited hours

A vestige of early Kinston, the 2-story, frame house with 2-story porch, longtime home of the Peebles family, is thought to encompass an 18th-c. dwelling used by James Glasgow, N.C. secretary of state, during the American

Revolution. The house was expanded during the 19th and early 20th centuries. It is now a house museum commemorating the life of Kinston resident Richard Caswell, the first governor of N.C. after independence.

Kinston's oldest residential neighborhoods flank Queen St. for several blocks to the east and west and contain a variety of house types as well as substantial brick churches, primarily from the early 20th c.

LR 4 Mitchell Town

The neighborhood west of Queen St. covers several blocks between Atlantic and Vernon Aves. Businessman Adolphus Mitchell bought the land in 1882 and farmed it for about ten years before selling lots during the tobacco boom years. Development proceeded sporadically through the 1910s and into the 1920s, attracting middle-class residents and producing houses that range from late Queen Anne to Colonial Revival houses and bungalows, including some manufactured by the Aladdin Company.

LR 5 East Kinston

A large residential section east of Queen St., particularly the grid of streets around Tiffany St., contains clusters of late 19th- and early 20th-c. houses. Here, as west of Queen, farmland was developed to meet the growing demand for housing. James A. McDaniel and other family members developed a small area known as **Trianon**, with Queen Anne and Colonial Revival residences, bungalows, and cottages aimed at middle-class occupants, arranged around his own residence on Gordon St. Most of the area was developed with modest houses meant for Kinston's growing number of working families; many of these were built for African American residents. There are several clusters of early 20th-c. shotgun houses, with an especially well-preserved grouping of more than twenty shotgun-plan dwellings standing along **Harvey St.**, which have been reno-

LR 5 *Trianon*

vated recently for continued use. (See Introduction, Fig. 61.)

LR 6 White Rock Presbyterian Church (former First Baptist Church)
1858; NW corner Thompson and N. Tiffany Sts.

Praised at its 1858 dedication as "neat and elegant," "well and tastily arranged," the small, temple-form frame church is boldly treated with Doric pillars and antae defining the recessed porch, and matching pilasters accenting the corners and the square belfry. Built for the antebellum Baptist con-

LR 6 *White Rock Presbyterian Church*

gregation and located near the center of town, it was sold to the black Presbyterian congregation in 1900 and moved to its present site.

LR 7 The Hill

Kinston's most exclusive early 20th-c. neighborhood is located on N. Queen St., Park Ave., and nearby streets. Businessman Jesse W. Grainger bought land north of the town, where he farmed for a time, then began to sell off lots. The area attracted business and professional families who gradually built an impressive collection of Colonial and Tudor Revival residences. For his own daughter, Capitola, and her husband, Dr. T. D. Edwards, Grainger built **Sarahurst** (1902–4; Herbert W. Simpson [New Bern], architect; 1201 N. Queen St.), a house in architect Simpson's favored Southern Colonial style. The most imposing residences are the **H. C. Hines House** (1929; Mr. Shackelford, architect; 1118 N. Queen St.), a massive, Tudor Revival brick mansion set behind a brick wall, and **Vernon Hall** (1913–14; 145 W. Capitola Ave.), a grand Georgian Revival house in red brick with a monumental Ionic portico. Post-1920 Colonial Revival residential architecture continues north and westward along Rountree St. and Perry Park. A neighborhood landmark is the large, red brick **Grainger High School** (1926; Leslie N. Boney [Wilmington], architect; 300 Park Ave.), with handsome Neoclassical details and monumental Corinthian porticoes.

LR 8 Parrott-Askew-Moseley House

Late 18th–early 19th c.; E side NC 58, 0.3 mi. S of SR 1703, Kinston vic.; private, visible from road

The dignified, 2-story house, a very compact dwelling with a Flemish-bond chimney, was built as an addition to a smaller, 18th-c. house that now serves as the east wing. Because of the loss of county records to fire, the history of this and many other rural buildings is sketchy.

LR 9 Dunn-Canady House

Early 19th c.; N side SR 1722, 0.1 mi. E of SR 1720, Graingers vic.; private, visible from road

LR 9 *Dunn-Canady House*

The unusual house presents a variation on the region's coastal cottage form. The tall, broad gable roof that covers the center-passage-plan dwelling also shelters an inset front porch flanked by porch chambers and a row of narrow rooms across the rear. The structure stands on massive piers of stone and coquina, a local shell-rock conglomerate. Only traces of the Federal finish survived the years of neglect that preceded its recent renovation. The history of the plantation is uncertain before its ca. 1820 occupation by the Reverend John Patrick Dunn, an early leader in the Disciples of Christ movement in eastern N.C.

LR 10 Cobb-King-Humphrey House

Early 19th c.; N side US 70 opp. SR 1903, Kinston vic.; private, visible from road

The frame I-house of simple Federal style stands close to the highway, an old east-west route. It served as Union headquarters and then as a hospital during the nearby Battle of Wyse Fork (Mar. 8–10, 1865), the second largest land battle fought in N.C. during the Civil War. One Union soldier recalled that on Mar. 10, "Most of the wounded were gathered in and about Dr. Cobb's house. The piazza was covered with men who had been placed there when it began to rain."

LR 11 Wooten-Whaley House

Mid-19th c.; W side SR 1904, 0.8 mi. S of SR 1903, Loftins Crossroads vic.; private, visible from road

Sited on a rise among broad fields, the temple-form plantation is unique in the county. Although the national Greek Revival style favored pediment-fronted temples of domesticity, this notion found little use in N.C., where builders adapted the style to familiar forms and plans. The gable-fronted house follows a side-passage plan and is dominated by a full-height, pedimented portico with plain, squared pillars. Interior chimneys rise at the gable ridgeline. The simple, robust Greek Revival woodwork is akin to other houses in the county.

LR 12 Jesse Jackson House

Early 19th c.; NW side NC 11/55, 0.1 mi. NE of jct. of NC 11 and NC 55, Kinston vic.; private, visible at a distance from road in winter

Standing on a bluff overlooking the broad bottomlands along the Neuse River, this conservative frame house was the center of one of the county's largest plantations. It exemplifies the classic I-house form, five bays wide with exterior end chimneys and a center-passage plan, finished in simple Federal style.

LR 13 *Croom Meetinghouse*

LR 15 *Dempsey Wood House*

LR 13 Croom Meetinghouse

Early 19th c.; N side NC 55, Sandy Bottom

The stark simplicity of the weatherboarded meetinghouse evokes the character of many 18th- and early 19th-c. churches. The traditional meetinghouse arrangement has doors on the long sides as well as in the gable front. Originally the plain pews focused on a centrally placed pulpit, but now they face the pulpit at the rear gable end. The congregation began as Sandy Bottom Baptist Church in 1803 and met in "the Brother Croom Meeting House," which tradition identifies as the present building.

LR 14 Wiley Joel Rouse House (The Sycamores)

Ca. 1840; NW corner NC 55 and SR 1152, Strabane; private, visible from road

Longtime home of the Rouse family, the 1½-story house with detached kitchen repeats the region's coastal cottage form with engaged porch, extended by a detached kitchen placed to the side in a local usage. The kitchen has one of several local examples of the exposed face chimney characteristic of the New Bern sphere of influence.

LR 15 Dempsey Wood House

Ca. 1860; N side SR 1324, 3.5 mi. SW of US 70, Kinston vic.; private, visible from road; B&B

The big 2-story plantation house repeats a typical Greek Revival form with a double-pile, center-passage plan beneath a broad hip roof but displays freewheeling eclecticism in its carpentry, including an Italianate bracketed cornice, Gothic-inspired panels in the tall pillars and pilasters, and eccentric frames and panels emphasizing the windows.

LR 16 Cedar Dell (Kennedy Memorial Home)

Ca. 1820, late 19th c.; SR 1338, 0.4 mi. E of SR 1324, Kinston vic.; private, visible from road

Built for the long-established Herring family, the side-passage-plan, Federal style, brick plantation house was enlarged in the 1880s by planter William Lafayette Kennedy, who transformed it into a fashionable center-passage-plan residence with ornate dormers and bay windows, bracketed porch, floral-patterned slate roof, and correspondingly rich interiors. He later gave the plantation to the Thomasville Baptist Orphanage, which opened the Kennedy Memorial Home here in 1914.

LR 17 Parrott-Coleman Farm

Early 20th c.; N side US 70, 0.2 mi. W of SR 1324, Kinston vic.; private, visible from road

All the elements of a prosperous eastern N.C. farm of the early 20th c. are preserved in this highly visible farmstead, a favorite sight for

LR 17 *Parrott-Coleman Farm*

travelers along US 70. Shaded by its oak grove, the spacious 1½-story, white frame house takes a modified bungalow form with its wide-dormered tin roof painted a rich green. Behind extends a retinue of agricultural buildings, including a mule barn with belfry, a dairy, sheds, and tobacco barns bordering the broad, flat fields.

LR 18 LaGrange

LaGrange is an archetypal little railroad town just off US 70, where late 19th- and early 20th-c. houses line the tracks for several blocks, still watching the trains go through. Formerly called Moseley Hall for a nearby plantation, the community began to grow with the 1857 arrival of the Atlantic and N.C. Railroad. It was incorporated in 1869 and named for Lafayette's estate near Paris. Brick commercial buildings cluster at the crossing, most notably the **Kinsey Feed Store** (early 20th c.), with its original storefront and metal cornice.

LR 18 *Shade Wooten House*

School, a military school that flourished in LaGrange in the 1880s. The **LaGrange Presbyterian Church** (SE corner S. Caswell and W. Washington Sts.) and the **LaGrange Free Will Baptist Church** (SE corner N. Caswell and E. James Sts.) are both frame, Gothic Revival churches of the 1890s.

LR 19 Langhorne Hardy House (Westbrook House)

Ca. 1808; S side SR 1535, 0.2 mi. E of SR 1001, Institute vic.; private, visible from road

Traditional, Federal era craftsmanship informs the tall, 2-story, frame plantation house, including beaded weatherboarding and double-shouldered chimneys of Flemish-bond brick. It stands upon a raised basement, unusual in the county. Across the road, as throughout this section of the county, stand many frame tobacco barns recalling the growth of tobacco cultivation in the early 20th c.

LR 18 *Kinsey Feed Store*

From the crossing extend blocks of 1- and 2-story frame houses of cross-gable or simple Queen Anne form, many with turned or sawn ornament and most painted white, chiefly along Caswell, Washington, and Railroad Sts. The surprising little **Shade Wooten House** (mid-19th c.; 204 W. Railroad St.) is a vividly picturesque Gothic cottage, with board-and-batten walls and zigzag bargeboards, built immediately before or after the Civil War as one of the first houses in town. The **Col. Adam C. Davis House** (131 E. Railroad St.), the most ambitious of several Queen Anne style residences, was the home of the founder and principal of the Davis

LR 20 Institute

The community takes its name from the Lenoir Collegiate Institute founded here in 1853 by Methodist minister W. H. Cunningham. The frame dormitories and classroom buildings—simple Greek Revival structures of domestic form—were erected between 1853 and 1858 for the coeducational academy. After the school closed in 1878, its facilities became private residences and were altered accordingly. Typical of the Institute buildings is the hip-roofed, double-pile **Gibbons-Hardy House** (NE corner SR 1532 and SR 1539; private), originally the dormitory and dining hall.

Wayne County (WY)

Goldsboro (WY 1–13)

See Barbara Hammond, An Architectural Inventory of Goldsboro, North Carolina *(1987).*

Goldsboro blossomed as a commercial hub at the junction of the state's first major north-south and east-west railroads. In 1838 landowner Arnold Borden built a hotel where the new Wilmington and Weldon Railroad crossed the old New Bern–Raleigh road. At this stopover point a new town sprang up, called Goldsborough's Junction after railroad construction engineer Matthew T. Goldsborough. In 1850 it supplanted nearby *Waynesborough as county seat. In 1856 the N.C. Railroad was completed from Goldsboro westward to Charlotte. This was followed by an eastward extension, the Atlantic and N.C. Railroad, completed from Goldsboro through New Bern to the new port at Morehead City in 1858. Rail connections to all points of the compass forecast Goldsboro's growth as a shipping town for the region's corn, naval stores, and cotton. Rebounding quickly after the Civil War, by the 1880s Goldsboro had grown to seventh largest town in the state.

Around the turn of the century, trade shifted from cotton to tobacco and truck crops. A diverse industrial economy developed producing cottonseed oil, textiles, lumber, and brick and tile. Between 1900 and 1910 the population doubled from 5,800 to nearly 12,000. The town expanded its civic amenities as well as its size—paving the streets, opening a park, and establishing a streetcar system by 1911. In 1902, Goldsboro acquired an exuberantly classical city hall and, in 1914, its first skyscraper. In 1924, civic pride and a City Beautiful mood led to the removal of train traffic from down the middle of Center St. to the west side of town. During this era Goldsboro clients commissioned designs by architects from

New Bern, Wilmington, Raleigh, Charlotte, Washington, D.C., and New York City, as well as from Goldsboro builder Milton Harding. In 1923 the first skyscraper was surpassed by the 10-story *Wayne National Bank, designed by New York architect Alfred C. Bossom. Goldsboro's central business district has several blocks of late 19th- and early 20th-c. commercial and public buildings punctuated by an unusually diverse series of houses of worship. Beyond lie residential sections of the late 19th- and, especially, the early 20th-c. boom era.

WY 1 Wayne County Courthouse
1913; Milburn & Heister (Washington, D.C.), architects; 224 E. Walnut St.

Occupying a square east of the commercial district, the courthouse typifies Frank Milburn's conservative Neoclassical Revival work: a buff brick building with Ionic porticoes on three sides. On its completion, county commissioners proclaimed, "We have a magnificent building, admired and praised by one and all." On the northwestern corner of the square, the **Isaac F. Dortch Law Office** (ca. 1884; 218 E. Walnut St.) recalls the small law offices that were once a fixture in courthouse towns, here with intricate brick corbeling and Italianate arched windows. Dortch was a prominent lawyer and politician.

WY 2 Central Business District

Along Center St., long blocks of late 19th- and early 20th-c. brick commercial buildings face the broad street, where a median replaced the old railroad tracks. (See Introduction, Fig. 50.) The big, ornate **Paramount Theater** (1882; 139 S. Center St.), with 3-story, Italianate storefront with metal quoins, was built by the Weil family as the Armory Building, where the "Home Guard" drilled on the third floor. From 1883 to 1886 Temple Oheb Sholom leased worship space

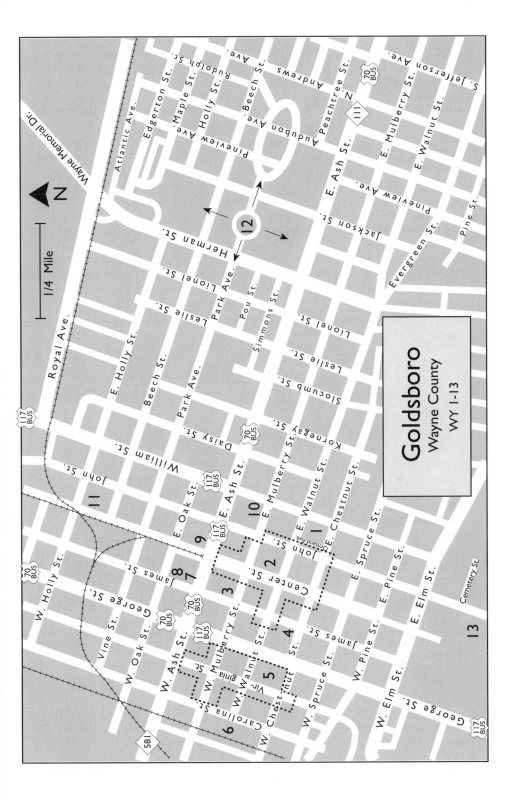

Goldsboro
Wayne County
WY 1-13

on the second floor; retail businesses occupied the first floor. It has been a theater since 1908. Next door, the 2-story **L. D. Giddens and Sons Building** (1868; 135 S. Center St.), with an ornate metal front with bay window at the second story, built for a jewelry firm established in 1859, is accented by the **Giddens Clock**, erected in 1877 and electrified in 1924. The **Serotta's (Castex) Building** (ca. 1886; 107 S. Center St.) features an elaborate metal cornice with a raised central pediment. Built on the site of Arnold Borden's 1838 railroad hotel, the 8-story **Goldsboro Hotel** (1924–26; William L. Stoddart [New York], architect; 100–104 S. Center St.) dominates the downtown, a brick hotel with classical cast-stone detail typical of prolific hotel designer Stoddart.

WY 2 *Paramount Theater, L. D. Giddens Building*

North of Walnut St., the **Goldsboro Drug Company Building** (1870; 101 N. Center St.) is a 2-story, Italianate store distinguished by the iron mortar and pestle with RX logo on the roof above the corner entrance. Goldsboro's first telephone office occupied the second floor. The **George Waters Building** (1877; 142 N. Center St.), long the Palace Drug Store, retains its pressed-metal front.

The street's boldest architectural statement appears in the **Goldsboro City Hall** (1902; Herbert W. Simpson [New Bern], architect; 214 N. Center St.), a wonderfully eccentric, Neoclassical Revival building of yellow brick with a portico and a tall, domed cupola. Memorably monumental statues of Blind Justice and Liberty surmount the pavilions flanking the portico. (See Introduction, Fig. 57.)

The commercial district continues along

the parallel John and James Sts. and Walnut St., the principal cross street. The **Borden Building** (1914; 100 S. James St.), rising 6 stories in Flemish-bond brick veneer with simple classical ornament, was the first skyscraper in town, which Al Smith, visiting from New York in 1915, compared to "a baby's first tooth." It was exceeded by the former **Wayne National Bank** (1923; Alfred C. Bossom [New York], architect; NE corner Walnut and James Sts.), 10 stories high, with an arcaded, stone-faced base and modillion cornice accentuating a simply detailed brick shaft—still the tallest building in town. The English-born architect Bossom, who had an important national practice based in New York City, designed banks in Durham, Charlotte, and Goldsboro, of which only this one survives intact.

WY 2 *Wayne National Bank*

On John St., several vigorously eclectic, brick buildings of the early 20th c. include the **Oddfellows Building** (1906; Henry E. Bonitz [Wilmington], architect; Porter & Godwin, contractors; 111–15 N. John St.), a blend of Italianate and Romanesque motifs, with foliated columns at the arched corner entrance. South on John St., two substantial brick churches occupy prominent corners, both rendered in Gothic Revival style with unequal, crenellated towers flanking broad gables: **First Baptist Church** (1912; James M. McMichael [Charlotte], architect; 125 S. John St.) and **St. Paul's Methodist Church** (1883–85; Milton Harding [Goldsboro], architect; 200 S. John St.).

WY 3 St. Stephen's Episcopal Church
1856–57 (John W. Priest [New York], architect; Charles Palmer [Raleigh], builder), 1885 (Milton Harding, builder); 200 N. James St.

According to the church history, priest Frederick Fitzgerald "secured the plan of an Early English Gothic church . . . perfected by John W. Priest," an Ecclesiologist architect from New York. The gable-fronted, red brick building has the steeply pitched roof and lancet arch windows favored by antebellum Episcopalians. The crenellated corner bell-tower was erected in 1885 by local contractor Milton Harding, who refaced the front of the church to match.

WY 4 Weil Houses
1875; G. S. H. Appleget, attributed architect; 200 and 204 W. Chestnut St.

Remnants of a fashionable 19th-c. neighborhood immediately west of Center St., these twin Italianate residences were built by brothers Henry and Solomon Weil. The L-shaped, 2-story frame residences epitomize the postwar Italianate style in their asymmetry, tall arched windows with hood molds, bracketed eaves, projecting bays, and ornate porches. Family letters allude to an unnamed Raleigh architect—possibly G. S. H. Appleget, who advertised that he had designed "all the best buildings, with only a few exceptions in Raleigh, Goldsboro, and Greensboro." The Weil brothers, German Jews who came to Goldsboro in midcentury by way of Baltimore, helped rebuild the town's mercantile economy, and their family served as leaders in business and civic affairs for several decades. Henry and Mina Weil's daughter, Gertrude Weil, a state leader in

woman suffrage, race relations, and health reform, lived in her parents' house until her death in 1971. Following a long preservation campaign in the 1980s, the houses have been restored for new uses. (See Introduction, Fig. 53.)

WY 5 Western Residential District

The grid-plan neighborhood west of downtown, once the leading residential section, includes Italianate, Queen Anne, Colonial Revival, and bungalow residences. The district runs west of George St. along Walnut, Mulberry, Virginia, and other streets. Part of the area was Borden family farmland, and family members' houses here include the **Frank K. Borden House** (1883; 103 S. George St.), a Queen Anne style frame house, and the **Murray Borden House** (1927; 201 N. George St.), a Georgian Revival residence. The **Harry Fitzhugh Lee House** (1920–22; John Guillette, architect; J. A. Jones, contractor; 310 W. Walnut St.), a Dutch Colonial house in brick with a roof of Ludovici tile, was built for a member of the Lee family of Virginia who married Julia Borden, daughter of Frank Borden.

WY 6 Goldsboro Union Station
1907–9; Leitner & Wilkins (Wilmington), architects; W side Carolina St. at end of W. Walnut St.

Now a warehouse, the big, brick depot retains glimmers of its old grandeur from Goldsboro's railroad years. It was built on the Borden farm west of downtown early in the town's efforts to shift railroad traffic away from Center St. As a union station it served the Atlantic Coast Line, the Southern, and the Norfolk and Southern. The eclectic, 2-story, red brick structure, seven bays wide with flanking wings, features curvilinear gables on three sides. A tower once overlooked the tracks.

WY 7 First Presbyterian Church
Ca. 1856; 111 W. Ash St.

Recalling Goldsboro's antebellum ambitions, the sophisticated, Greek Revival church of stuccoed brick is one of the state's

WY 7 *First Presbyterian Church*

few examples and its most academic version of a nationally popular design—a temple-form structure with a distyle portico in antis. A square belfry repeats the pilasters of the facade. Now a meeting hall for a local preservation organization.

WY 8 Temple Oheb Sholom
1886; Milton Harding, builder; 314 N. James St.

WY 8 *Temple Oheb Sholom*

Goldsboro's Jewish citizens have played a prominent role in business and civic affairs since the town's incorporation. This vigorously composed, brick temple, built for one of the state's oldest and most distinguished Jewish congregations, combines Romanesque and Gothic elements, with pilasters of the gable front rising through the crenellated cornice.

WY 9 Goldsboro Fire Department
1939; 109 E. Ash St.

Built as a WPA project, the red brick firehouse presents a striking white stuccoed fa-

cade, with pilasters carrying a broad frieze with "Goldsboro Fire Department" in Art Deco low relief beneath a jagged tile cornice.

WY 10 St. Mary's Roman Catholic Church
1889; 201 N. William St.

A rarity in an overwhelmingly Protestant region, the Catholic church displays the eclecticism typical of the late 19th c., with a rose window in the facade and an ornate belfry atop a polygonal corner entrance tower.

WY 11 Million-Gallon Water Tower
1938; SE corner Holly and Center Sts., N of downtown

Rising from a railroad warehouse district, the water tower has a curvaceous "million-gallon" tank 87 feet across, built of steel with iron-ribbed details and topped by a pinnacle. With a water level of 100 to 125 feet, it stands on tall legs with a stair spiraling around the central standpipe. This is one of a number of similar water towers in eastern N.C. towns.

WY 12 Herman Park Area

After 1900 Goldsboro's residential development moved eastward. One attraction was **Herman Park** (1890; 900–1000 Park Ave.), an 18-acre park Henry and Solomon Weil deeded to the city in 1890 as a "public park and pleasure grounds" named in honor of their brother Herman. The picturesque, hip-roofed pavilion was built in 1902 by German immigrant Augustus A. Kleinert.

A grid of streets around the park contains the town's prime collection of early 20th-c. residential architecture, shaded by a canopy of giant oaks. The first blocks of **Park Ave.** and **Beech St.** just west of the park feature Colonial Revival houses and vigorously exe-

WY 12 *Herman Park Pavilion*

cuted bungalows as well as a few English cottage accents. The most striking early Colonial Revival residence—one of the first houses built after the Weil property opened up for development along Park Ave.—is the **Oettinger-Spicer House** (ca. 1898; Charles W. Barrett [Raleigh], architect; 619 Park Ave.), in which vestiges of Queen Anne massing energize the symmetrical composition. A pedimented entrance pavilion emerges from the foursquare form with high hip roof, and a 1-story porch with Doric columns and a roof balustrade bows out at the entrance and reaches west to a porte cochere. Published in architect Barrett's *Colonial Southern Homes* (1903), the house was built for Adolph Oettinger and his wife, Edna Weil, daughter of Solomon Weil.

WY 12 *Oettinger-Spicer House*

Among the most robust Craftsman bungalows is **706 E. Beech St.** (1929), with stone piers, a porte cochere, and a wooden grille filling the broad front porch gable. The **Goldsboro High School** (1927; Starrett and Van Vleck [New York], architects; Beech St. N of Herman Park), designed by a prolific New York firm, shows Goldsboro's stature during the great era of schoolhouse building—a grand, Georgian Revival school in Flemish-bond brick with an elaborate, porticoed entry pavilion.

WY 13 Wilmington and Weldon Freight Station

Ca. 1880; W side S. John St. opp. Cemetery St.

With the loss in the late 20th c. of many of the handsome brick freight stations that once stood along the old Wilmington and Weldon route, this long, brick building re-mains as one of the best surviving examples. Typical features include the broad, segmental-arched openings flanked by pilasters, which carry a corbeled cornice beneath a broad hipped roof.

WY 14 Waynesborough State Park

W side US 13/117 BYP, 1.1 mi. S of NC 581 (Ashe St.), Goldsboro vic.

Waynesborough on the Neuse River was established in 1787 as the first seat of Wayne Co. With the coming of the Wilmington and Weldon Railroad through the county in 1840, the nearby station town of Goldsboro overshadowed the older village, and Waynesborough had totally vanished by the end of the Civil War. In recent years five frame buildings have been moved in from various locations around the county to commemorate the site in a public park: the 1-room **Wiggins House** (mid-19th c.); the **Dr. Bryan Kennedy Office** (ca. 1870), a small country doctor's office; the **Faircloth Law Office** (1868), a little temple-form lawyer's office originally located in downtown Goldsboro; **Park Hill School** (1911), a representative 1-room rural school; and **Bethany Meetinghouse** (1878), a gable-front Quaker meetinghouse.

WY 15 Sasser House

Mid-19th c.; S side SR 1007, 0.05 mi. W of NC 581, Goldsboro vic.; private, visible from road

The small farmhouse illustrates the mid-19th-c. blend of the classical and the picturesque in a popular house form: the symmetrical, hip-roofed cottage, with double-pile, center-passage plan, Greek Revival details, and lacy, sawnwork porch.

WY 16 William Francis Atkinson House

Ca. 1850; NW corner SR 1007 and SR 1226; private, visible from road

The form of the eclectic, Greek Revival-Italianate plantation house—2 stories high with hip roof and double-pile, center-hall plan—typifies cotton planters' big houses of the time, but the full-width, 2-tier porch with big square pillars is an unusually grand ges-

WY 16 *William Francis Atkinson House*

ture, even for the flush 1850s. The Atkinsons were a prominent Neuse River planter family in Wayne and nearby Johnston counties. Of several big family houses along the old River Rd. (now Brogden Rd.), only this and the *Atkinson-Smith House, built for William's brother in Johnston Co., still stand.

WY 17 Ebenezer Methodist Church

1880; Milton Harding (Goldsboro), builder; SE corner US 70 and SR 1234, Goldsboro vic.

Described upon its completion in 1880 as "a little beauty," the Carpenter Gothic country church presents the full complement of picturesque components: board-and-batten siding, bracketed eaves, lancet arch windows, and scissors truss roof. It was built for a congregation established in the 1840s in an area where Methodism was especially strong in the 19th c.

WY 18 Raymond Stafford House

Late 19th c.; E side SR 1318, 1.2 mi. N of SR 1317; private, visible from road

A surprise in the rural landscape, the Italianate brick I-house features unusually rich details: segmental-arched windows with hood molds, a bracketed cornice, and sawnwork shed porch. Chimneys rise at the rear, a contrast to the usual gable-end placement.

WY 19 Gov. Charles Brantley Aycock Birthplace

Ca. 1840 and later; SR 1542, 0.6 mi. E of US 117, Fremont vic.; state historic site; open regular hours

Located on the farm where Charles Brantley Aycock, the state's "education governor,"

was born in 1859, the house and farm buildings were moved here from a nearby site on the Aycock farm and restored for interpretive purposes. The complex communicates a sense of the unpretentious, utilitarian character of typical 19th-c. farmsteads, even those of middling farmers and small planters. The farmstead centers on a modest, 1-story, hall-parlor-plan frame dwelling built by Aycock's father about 1840. It is simply finished and convincingly furnished, including the chamber on the engaged porch. Outbuildings, some original, others reconstructed, include a small frame kitchen, a smokehouse, a corncrib, a stable, and others. A 1-room frame schoolhouse (ca. 1880), originally the Oak Plain School that stood at nearby *Fremont, was moved to the site to

WY 19 *Gov. Charles Brantley Aycock Birthplace*

commemorate Aycock's leadership in public education. Elected governor in 1900, he led the Democratic party ticket in the white supremacy campaign that put the party in control for more than half a century. Meeting campaign promises to reform education, Governor Aycock canvassed the state in support of public education. During his tenure hundreds of rural and small-town public schools were built, and major advances were made in curriculum and teacher training.

WY 20 Fremont

First called Nahunta, after an Indian name for a nearby swamp recorded as early as 1711, the little town grew up around a depot on the Wilmington and Weldon Railroad and was renamed in 1869 after the line's chief engineer. The compact grid of streets flanking the railroad presents a handsome ensemble of late 19th- and early 20th-c. small-town architecture. The turn-of-the-century commercial row of 1- and 2-story brick stores along E. Main St. includes several fine Italianate facades, such as **127 E. Main St.**, which retains its storefront. Characteristically, a prime corner is marked by the former **Branch Banking and Trust Company Building** (125 E. Main St. at Sycamore St.), a columned temple form typifying early 20th-c. bankers' use of classicism to project an image of stability. Lining E. and W. Main St. and nearby blocks, houses beneath big trees sample the Italianate, Queen Anne, Colonial Revival, and bungalow modes, with an especially fine Craftsman bungalow at 304 E. Main St.

WY 21 John A. Barnes House
Late 19th c.; N side SR 1343, 0.2 mi. E of NC 581; private, visible from road

A rare example of 19th-c. brick farmhouse construction in eastern N.C., the symmetrical, 2-story house boasts elaborate brickwork such as mouse-tooth cornices, corbeled string courses, and hood molds. The 1-story porch, slate roof, and brick rear ell are original. Built for Civil War veteran Barnes, it was restored in the 1970s by his grandson. A full contingent of outbuildings survives.

WY 22 Dred Yelverton House
1910–15; Barber & Kluttz; N side NC 222, 0.3 mi. W of NC 111, Eureka vic.; private, visible from road

In a good country rendition of the Colonial Revival style, the foursquare mass of the farmhouse is broken by dormers, projecting gables and bays, and a full-width, 2-tier porch with a pedimented central bay.

WY 23 Eureka

Clustered at the crossroads are several 1-story, turn-of-the-century, frame commercial buildings, some with square parapets and intact storefronts. North along Church St. (SR 1520), **Eureka Methodist Church** (1884) is a frame country church with touches of the Gothic Revival style in its triangular-headed openings.

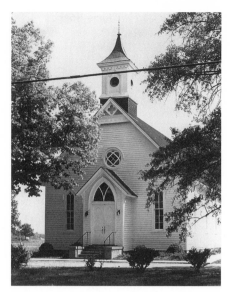

WY 23 *Eureka Methodist Church*

WY 24 Whitfield-Isler Farm
Mid-19th c.; N side US 70, 0.2 mi. E of SR 1719, Goldsboro vic.; private, visible from road

A landmark beside a busy road, the small farmhouse represents a popular mid-19th c. form: the 1-story, hip-roofed, center-hall-plan, Greek Revival house with wide corner pilasters and a bracket cornice that adds an Italianate flavor. The porch has been replaced. The farmstead includes a double-pen kitchen and a packhouse.

WY 25 Seven Springs

The community incorporated as Whitehall in 1855 was renamed in 1951 for the fashionable mineral springs resort, the Seven Springs Spa, which operated here from 1881 to 1945. One of several such places in the coastal plain now largely lost and forgotten, the resort has closed and lies off the beaten path, though "Seven Springs Water" is still bottled and sold to faithful customers who swear by its healthful properties. On a rise at the head of the small main street lined by 1-story stores stands the **Church on the Hill** (1874; s side NC 55, opp. SR 1731), a frame church with spire that has served both Presbyterian and Methodist congregations.

WY 26 Mac Carr Williams House

Ca. 1850; NE corner SR 1745 and SR 1915, 1.7 mi. NE of NC 55, Mount Olive vic.; private, visible from road

Built during the prosperous 1850s, the plantation house has a bold, simple, Greek Revival character akin to buildings in nearby *Kenansville, Duplin Co. Typical of the regional school of work, the 2-story, double-pile house with hip roof has broad corner pilasters, heavy Greek Revival details, and a 2-tier entrance portico with stout, square pillars. After long neglect, the house was moved about 2 miles and restored.

WY 27 Mount Olive

The produce marketing center is best known for the cucumber pickles processed here. Incorporated with its present biblical name in 1870, it encompassed the old Wilmington and Weldon depot village of Enterprise. The community traded in naval stores, then shifted to truck farming, and in 1924 the Mount Olive Pickle Company opened. The layout and architectural fabric create a textbook eastern N.C. railroad town. Long rows of simple, brick storefronts face the tracks dividing **Center St.**; industrial buildings flank the railroad north and south of the central business district; white frame houses fill the grid of side streets; and sturdy, red brick, Gothic and Romanesque Revival churches anchor key corners.

Especially striking is the **First Methodist Church** (1911–13; Henry E. Bonitz [Wilmington], architect; 120 E. James St.), which epitomizes the Romanesque Revival style, auditorium plan, and corner location favored by Methodists of the era. Vivid brickwork and contrasting stone accentuate the corner entrance tower and round arched openings, typical of the architectural gusto of Henry Bonitz, whose work appears in towns along the railroads radiating from Wilmington. The congregation was organized in 1870, the same year Mount Olive was chartered.

A WPA Georgian Revival style **U.S. Post Office** (1931–33; James A. Wetmore, acting supervising architect of the Treasury; 124 W. James St.) stands one block off Center St. The town's white frame houses span the years and styles, such as the Greek Revival style **Sutherland House** (mid-19th c.; 108 W. Main St.), the Queen Anne style **Farrior-Wooten House** (1890s; 107 N. Chestnut St.), and the Southern Colonial style **Perry-Cherry House** (ca. 1904; 308 W. Main St.) with its curving portico of Ionic columns. The town has saved the **Mount Olive Passenger Depot** (early 20th c.), a frame station with hip roof and broad eaves, which has been moved from the tracks to behind the *Sutherland House on W. Main St. to serve as a community center.

Johnston County (JT)

JT 1 Smithfield

See Mary M. Shoemaker, An Inventory of Historical Architecture in the Town of Smithfield *(1977).*

Founded in the 1770s as a tobacco inspection point on the Neuse River land of John Smith, Smithfield remained a small county seat and trading center until the 1886 arrival of the Wilmington and Weldon (later Atlantic Coast Line) Railroad. Growth mounted when the town became a regional tobacco marketing center amid the early 20th-c. expansion of tobacco cultivation that followed cotton's dominance in the coastal plain.

JT 1 *Johnston County Courthouse*

The central landmark is the **Johnston County Courthouse** (1921; Harry Barton [Greensboro]; 212 E. Market St.), one of the state's finest Beaux Arts classical courthouses and one of several by Greensboro architect Barton. The stone-veneered building features two monumental tetrastyle porticoes—recessed in antis on the Market St. facade and projecting with a pediment on the 2nd St. side—and classical detailing inside and out. Across S. 2nd St., the red brick **Centenary Methodist Church** (1911–14; 140 E. Market St.) presents a different blend of classical motifs with a central dome and two Ionic-order porticoes facing intersecting streets.

The business district along E. Market and 3rd Sts. has substantial brick commercial architecture from the early 20th-c. to-

bacco boom years. The vividly handsome **Hood Brothers Building** (1923; D. J. Rose [Rocky Mount], builder; 100–104 S. 3rd St.) is a 3-story, red and cream brick building with classical ornament. The 3-story, parapeted **Austin Building** (1921; 127–31 S. 3rd St.) was once heralded as the largest department store in eastern N.C. The **First Citizens Bank Building** (1913; Joe W. Stout & Company [Sanford], builders; 241 Market St.), first headquarters of what is now one of the state's largest banking firms, is a compact, classically detailed building of blond brick. Farther east, the 1-story, red brick, Federal Revival style (former) **U.S. Post Office** (1935; Louis A. Simon, supervising architect of the Treasury; 405 E. Market St.) shows the attention to regional revival styles typical of WPA public buildings; it now holds law offices.

West of the business district, beside the river stands the **Pou-Parrish American Legion Hall** (1938; 104 S. Front St.), an Adirondack style recreation building of round logs erected on the old town common as a WPA project. Also near the river is the **Primitive Baptist Church** (1875; 204 S. Front St.), which repeats the simple, gable-fronted form, paired entrances, and austere interior typical of the denomination. Moved next door is one of Smithfield's few antebellum buildings, the **Hastings House** (ca. 1853; 202 S. Front St.), a symmetrical, 2-story frame house with center-passage plan and simple, pedimented, 2-story porch. The other principal antebellum building is the temple-form, Greek Revival and Italianate **Masonic Hall** (ca. 1852; 115 N. 2nd St.).

The town's prime 19th- and early 20th-c. residential sections are concentrated along 2nd and 3rd Sts., Hancock St., and the 200–400 blocks of S. 4th St. Exemplifying the picturesque forms and lavish ornament of late 19th-c. Smithfield are two big, bracketed, Italianate residences with millwork typical of the Wilson & Waddell factory in *Wilson's Mills: the **Massey-Wilson House** (ca. 1885; 105 Bridge St.) and the **Hood-**

JT 1 *William R. Long House*

Strickland House (1889; C. S. Byrd, builder; 415 S. 4th St.). There are many Queen Anne cottages with high hip roofs and elaborate millwork. Reflecting 20th-c. prosperity, Smithfield has a multitude of Colonial Revival houses and some especially fine bungalows. The **William R. Long House** (1921; John C. Stout [Rocky Mount]; 216 N. 2nd St.) is a small but monumental Colonial Revival residence expertly rendered by a leading practitioner. The **Wellons-McGowan House** (ca. 1905; 307 N. 2nd St.) presents the Southern Colonial style in a larger residence. Among the varied bungalows are the **Sheppard House** (ca. 1922; 401 N. 2nd St.), with its geometric motifs, and the **Southerland House** (ca. 1920; 230 N. 3rd St.), low slung and covered in wood shingles. The **Sanders House** (ca. 1920; 412 N. 3rd St.), with its peaked gable and half-timbered effect, provides a picturesque, English cottage accent.

JT 2 Yelvington-Lee House (Johnston Co. Visitors' Center)

1880s; W side Industrial Park Dr., 0.9 mi. N of US 70 BUS, W of I-95 (exit 95, Smithfield); open regular hours

The 2-story frame house combines simple Italianate and Queen Anne details, with a wraparound porch rising to 2 stories at the center bay. Threatened on its site in central Smithfield, the house was moved here in 1988 by the Chamber of Commerce to serve as offices and a visitors' center. The well-preserved interior with turned and molded wood-

work provides a glimpse into a small-town, middle-class residence of the late 19th c.

JT 3 Selma

See Thomas A. Greco, Historical Architecture of Selma, N.C. *(1980).*

Located near the old Mitchener's Station on the N.C. Railroad, Selma was incorporated in 1873 and named for the Alabama city. The town blossomed after 1886, when a new branch of the Wilmington and Weldon Railroad crossed the old N.C. Railroad at Selma, creating a major regional rail junction. These lines were subsequently absorbed in the Atlantic Coast Line and Southern Railway companies. At the eastern end of downtown, the chief landmark is the **Selma Union Station** (1924; A. M. Griffin [Wilmington], architect; E. Railroad St.), now a passenger stop for Amtrak. As designed by ACL architect Griffin, the V-shaped plan of the eclectic, red brick building reflects its purpose as a joint venture of the ACL and the Southern Railway. The central control tower with stepped parapet gables is flanked by 1-story wings from which covered waiting areas extend along both tracks. North beside the track stands **Mitchener's Station** (3rd quarter 19th c.), a board-and-batten depot believed to date from the early days of the N.C. Railroad.

JT 3 *Selma Union Station*

Railroad trade also created Selma's late 19th- and early 20th-c. commercial and residential architecture. The commercial district centers on N. Raiford St. Especially striking is the **Person-Vick Building** (1916; 101 S. Raiford St.), with its overhanging roof on big brackets, polychrome brickwork, and arcaded loggia emphasizing its corner position. It was built as the medical offices of Dr. James Person and Dr. George Vick. (The latter was the son of Dr. Joshua Vick, brother-in-law of former Selma pharmacist Lunsford Richardson, who named his pharmaceutical company Vick Family Remedies and his best-selling salve Vick's VapoRub in honor of the elder Dr. Vick.) At the next corner is the Neoclassical Revival style **People's Bank** (1922; 100 N. Raiford St.), now the Municipal Building, with recessed front portico and pilasters along the side street. The 1-story **J. A. Mitchener Building** (1925; 202–8 N. Raiford St.) features opulent terra-cotta facades, where pilasters frame broad storefront bays and carry an enriched entablature topped by urns.

Typically, some of the town's finest houses proudly faced the railroad tracks, though most of these are now lost. The chief survivor is the **William E. Smith House** (1912; 309 W. Railroad St.), a Southern Colonial style house with Ionic portico, home of a leading merchant and banker. Other early 20th-c. residences concentrate along W. Anderson St. and the side streets north of the railroad, among them the **Nowell-Mayerburg-Oliver House** (1912; Albert S. Atkinson [Washington, D.C.]; 312 W. Anderson St.), a late Queen Anne style house with corner tower designed by Atkinson, a Johnston Co. native who later designed the house at *Brook Hill Farm.

Prominent among several substantial early 20th-c. public school buildings still in use in the county is the **Selma Graded School** (1922; Benton & Benton [Wilson], architects; Joe W. Stout & Company [Sanford], contractor; W. Richardson St.), an especially fine, 3-story brick building in Collegiate Tudor style with patterned brickwork and stone quoins and balustrade. (See Introduction, Fig. 62.)

JT 4 Waddell-Oliver House

1892; attributed to Wilson & Waddell, builders; N side SR 1003, 0.25 mi. E of I-95 (exit 98), Selma vic.; private, visible from road

The richly decorated, Italianate cottage features the popular central-gable roof form of

JT 4 *Waddell-Oliver House*

the era, garnished with brackets that also adorn the porch, gabled side wings, and quarter-round side porches. The house was built for Charles B. Waddell, son of John A. Waddell, cofounder of the Wilson & Waddell lumber mills and contracting firm at *Wilson's Mills. Later it was the home of merchant James Oliver and his descendants.

JT 5 Boyette Plank House

First half 19th c.; E side SR 2110, 0.3 mi. S of NC 222, Kenly vic.; private, visible from road

This important, dovetailed plank dwelling retains one of a handful of surviving stick-and-mud chimneys in the state, an almost extinct chimney form that once numbered in the thousands. Especially in sections lacking good building stone, chimneys were often fashioned from logs or sticks and daubed with clay. The method was common in N.C. during the colonial period and continued in use through the 19th c. This 1-room slave house was on the farm of George Boyette, whose early 19th-c. house (enlarged ca. 1860 and ca. 1900) stands across the road. (See Introduction, Fig. 11.)

JT 6 Kenly

Kenly is one of several Johnston Co. railroad towns—along with Princeton, Micro, *Selma, *Four Oaks, and *Clayton—that developed with the construction of the N.C. Railroad in the 1850s and a branch of the Wilmington and Weldon in the 1880s. All retain commercial districts focused on the railroad, with adjoining residential sections. In Kenly, **E. Bailey St.** off S. 2nd St. (NC 222) is the finest residential street, with a

JT 7 Iredell Brown House and Kitchen

well-tended grouping of Queen Anne and Colonial Revival houses under great shade trees.

JT 7 Tobacco Farm Life Museum

NW side US 301, 1.1 mi. N of I-95 (exit 107), Kenly, just S of Wilson Co. line; open regular hours

The private museum commemorates early 20th-c. lifeways of tobacco farm families across eastern N.C. The **Iredell Brown House** (1909–10), a small, early 20th-c., eastern N.C. farmhouse, represents thousands of such houses across the region, with a central gable and hip roof porch. It is furnished to illustrate the 1920s–1930s era. Along with its detached kitchen and smokehouse, the house was relocated from rural Johnston Co., and a tobacco barn was brought in from another farm. A newer building houses exhibits on life in rural eastern N.C. in the period.

JT 8 Watson-Sanders House

Early 19th c.; SW side SR 1007, 2.2 mi. SE of I-95, Smithfield vic.; private, visible from road

Although 1-story houses with engaged porches abound across the county, this 2-story frame house is one of the region's westernmost examples of the engaged 2-story porch, a form concentrated in the coastal areas. The house was the center of one of the large Neuse River plantations in eastern Johnston Co.

JT 9 Old Union Primitive Baptist Church

Mid- to late 19th c.; NE side SR 1007, 0.3 mi. SE of SR 2523, Brogden vic.

The sparely finished, wooden building is one of the best preserved of several similar

Primitive Baptist churches in the county. The simplicity and severity of these modest buildings, with paired, gable-end doors for the separation of the sexes, reflect the beliefs of the denomination. The congregation was formed ca. 1806 and in 1826 was one of the Johnston Co. Baptist churches that separated from the evangelical Raleigh Baptist Association.

JT 10 Atkinson-Smith House

Ca. 1850; Brogden vic.; private, no public visibility or access

The opulent, eccentrically detailed house recalls the lifestyle of the county's very wealthiest planters in the flush 1850s. The seat of Elijah Atkinson's 5,000-acre plantation, this was one of four grand Atkinson family houses along the River Rd. (now Brogden Rd.), of which the other survivor is the *William Francis Atkinson House (ca. 1852) across the Wayne Co. line. The 2-story, double-pile house features a superimposed portico with Doric beneath Ionic columns, and ornate Greek Revival and Italianate details. The plan has a broad central hall with stair set into a niche. William A. Smith, who acquired the place when he married Atkinson's widow, was a Unionist and later Republican who served as U.S. congressman and president of the N.C. Railroad and the Western N.C. Railroad.

JT 11 Harper House, Bentonville Battleground State Historic Site

1850s, 1865; N side SR 1008, 3.0 mi. E of US 701, Newton Grove vic.; open regular hours

Bentonville was the site of the largest and bloodiest battle ever fought in N.C., and the last major battle of the Civil War. Here on Mar. 19–21, 1865, 20,000 Confederate soldiers under Gen. Joseph E. Johnston struggled one last time to halt the march of Gen. William Tecumseh Sherman's army of 60,000 men. The typically plain, 2-story, double-pile plantation house, erected during the 1850s for John Harper, is interpreted to recall its use as a hospital by both armies during and after the battle. Several period outbuildings moved to the site suggest its wartime appearance.

JT 12 Carowood (Marshall Lee House)
1885; S side NC 55, 0.2 mi. E of NC 242, McKoy; private, visible from road

The prominent I-house shows the Italianate brackets, paired segmental-arched windows, and decorated porch typical of the Wilson & Waddell manufacturing and construction firm of *Wilson's Mills. Several contemporary outbuildings remain in the farmyard. Across NC 55 is **Calvary Baptist Church** (ca. 1900), a small frame church built on land donated by farmer Marshall Lee in 1895 and displaying the same segmental-arched windows as the house. This stretch of NC 55 running through Johnston and Sampson counties has a series of notable farmsteads indicative of local agricultural prosperity of the late 19th and early 20th centuries.

JT 13 Benson

Chartered in 1887 on the new branch of the Wilmington and Weldon Railroad between Wilson and Fayetteville, Benson quickly became a transportation and trade center for one of the state's most productive agricultural areas. The main commercial and residential avenues reflect the prosperity of early 20th-c. merchants, planters, and cotton buyers. Main St. is lined by a strong series of mostly brick commercial buildings. Prominently stationed beside the railroad, the chief commercial landmark is the splendid, Neoclassical Revival **Farmers Commercial Bank** (1921; 100 W. Main St.), its cut-stone surfaces enriched with fluted pilasters, egg-

JT 13 *Farmers Commercial Bank*

and-dart moldings, and garlands. Two large, red brick, Gothic Revival churches punctuate Church St.: the **Benson Methodist Church** (1917; 205 E. Church St.), with its buttressed, 3-tier tower, and the **Benson Baptist Church** (1915; 200 W. Church St.). The former **Benson High School** (ca. 1915; 300 block of E. Church St.), a 3-story, brick school with segmental-arched windows, has been adapted as the town's municipal building, one of the state's successful historic school building conversions. The finest of several Southern Colonial style residences is the **C. T. Johnson House** (1912; 109 N.W. Railroad St.; B&B), home of a cotton buyer.

JT 14 Hannah's Creek Primitive Baptist Church
Mid-19th c. (ca. 1834 or ca. 1866); NW side US 301, 0.3 mi. SW of SR 1330, Benson vic.

JT 14 *Hannah's Creek Primitive Baptist Church*

The plain, weatherboarded building is one of the oldest Primitive Baptist church buildings in the state and a rare example of the traditional meetinghouse plan. The main entrance (with a modern vestibule) is still centered on the long side. Inside, the pews are arranged in a *U* shape around the pulpit opposite the entrance. The women's entrance is in the western gable end; the men's is on the east. Many early meetinghouses that originally had such a plan were later modified to locate the main entrance in the gabled front and a long aisle leading to the pulpit opposite. The adjacent sandy cemetery contains marked graves dating from the late 19th c. From the mid-18th c., Baptists were strong in Johnston Co., and several of the county's congregations—including Hannah's Creek, formed in 1817—were among those that in 1826 broke away from the evangelical Raleigh Baptist Association to emphasize "primitive Christianity."

JT 15 Josephus Johnson House

1870s; W side SR 1330, 3.0 mi. N of US 301; private, visible from road

The Italianate style, frame farmhouse follows an unusual Greek cross plan, with chimneys at all four gable ends. Windows have segmental-arched heads, and porches with chamfered posts shelter three of the four corners. Outbuildings include mule and hog barns and a smokehouse.

JT 16 Four Oaks

The intact, small railroad community has a commercial district along tracks and residential sections along Baker, Church, Main and Railroad Sts. The **Dr. John H. Stanley House** (ca. 1913; 502 N. Main St.; private), one of the county's best examples of the Southern Colonial style, is surrounded by an ornate 19th-c. iron fence from the old Cameron family house that stood on Hillsborough St. in Raleigh.

JT 17 Crantock Farm

Ca. 1840; W side SR 1504, 1.2 mi. N of NC 210, Smithfield vic.; private, visible from road

The 2-story, T-plan, Greek Revival plantation house features the style's typical low-pitched hip roof, wide corner pilasters, symmetrically molded window and door frames with cornerblocks, and heavy, paneled porch posts. It was built for planter John Washington Avera. There are several frame barns and other outbuildings.

JT 18 Elizabeth Methodist Church

1853; S side SR 1010, 1.6 mi. W of SR 1504, Smithfield vic.; private, visible from road

The austere, Greek Revival, temple-form church is the county's most ambitious antebellum church. Built to replace an 1842 structure that burned, the church was named for Elizabeth Peters Sanders, second wife of John Sanders, who owned a farm nearby.

JT 19 Sanders House

Ca. 1793, 1850s; N side SR 1010, 0.4 mi. E of SR 1330, Smithfield vic.; private, visible from road

Several 19th-c. houses associated with the Sanders family, prominent in the county's affairs since the 18th c., stand along SR 1010 and adjacent roads. The southeastern section of this complex house was a compact, 2-story dwelling with exterior end chimneys built in the late 18th c. for Col. John Sanders. His son Willis enlarged the house in the 1850s with a 2-story addition oriented to the present roadway, and later generations of the family made further alterations and embellishments.

JT 20 Tanglewood Farm

1835, 1875, 1915; S side SR 1010, 0.6 mi. W of SR 1330, Smithfield vic.; private, visible from road

JT 20 *Tanglewood Farm*

The county's most intact 19th-c. farmstead illustrates agricultural practices from 1835 to the 1940s. The seat of the Tomlinson family for five generations, the original 1835 Greek Revival dwelling built for Bernice Harris Tomlinson has been enlarged twice. The many outbuildings include an 1835 smokehouse, a farm bell, and the only large mule barn (ca. 1910) surviving in the county.

JT 21 Walter Moore House

Ca. 1832; E side SR 1330 N of SR 1510, Polenta community; private, visible from road

The large, 2-story, T-plan plantation house with 2-tier porch and pedimented gable ends is embellished with intricate Federal style woodwork, including a cornice of pierced dentils, guilloche molding, and shaped modillions akin to work at the *Roberts-Vaughan House in Murfreesboro. The house is a focus of a prosperous agricultural community formerly known as Polenta—named for unknown reasons for the Italian cornmush. Several other later 19th- and early 20th-c. houses associated with the community stand along SR 1330 and connecting roads. New subdivisions on old agricultural lands are ushering in a new era for this and other rural sections within commuting distance of Raleigh.

JT 22 White Oak (Sanders-Hairr House)

Late 18th c.; W side SR 1525, 0.2 mi. S of NC 42, Clayton vic.; private, visible from road

JT 22 *White Oak*

The 2½-story, frame plantation house of exceptional craftsmanship and elaborate, late Georgian detail was built for planter Reubin Sanders, one of the wealthiest men in the county. Double-shouldered, Flemish-bond brick chimneys stand at the pedimented gable ends, flanked by bull's-eye windows. The full-width, 1-story porch is one of the best of its period in the state, with a coved ceiling, intricate cornice, tapered posts, and delicate balustrade. The interior follows an unusual variation of the 3-room plan.

JT 23 Clayton

Settled by 1845 as Gulley's Store and incorporated as Clayton in 1869, the community owes its growth to the N.C. Railroad, which was built through the county in the early 1850s. By the early 1900s, cotton-based pros-

JT 23 *B. M. Robertson Mule Co.*

perity made Clayton one of the wealthiest towns of its size in the nation. The long, commercial district along Main St. retains several early 20th-c., 2-story, brick stores with ornamental corbeling. Though many of the best turn-of-the-century houses have been lost or altered, residential sections north and south of Main St. retain a strong collection of early 20th-c. dwellings, most notably along S. Fayetteville St. and Horne St., and an interesting group of frame houses is tucked between the commercial district and the tracks along 1st St. north of Main. The **Durham-Ellington-Compton House** (ca. 1850; 613 E. Main St.), the town's oldest, is a Greek Revival dwelling facing the railroad. The **B. M. Robertson Mule Company** (1914; 112 S. Lombard St., s of Main St.), with mule heads cheerfully painted on its brick wall, is a reminder of farmers' reliance on the mule prior to World War II. The Colonial Revival style **Horne Memorial Methodist Church** (1912–16; E. Second St.) has brilliant stained-glass windows said to be from the Tiffany studios.

JT 24 Ellington-Ellis Farm

Ca. 1835, mid-1850s; N side SR 1004, 0.2 mi. W of SR 1553, W of Clayton; private, visible from road

One of the most complete of the county's antebellum farm complexes. The 2-story, T-plan, Greek Revival dwelling, erected ca. 1835 for planter John T. Ellington, was remodeled in the 1850s to face the new N.C. Railroad to the southwest. The farm has a remarkable collection of antebellum outbuildings, including a smokehouse, a 4-seat ladies' privy, and a playhouse. Dominating the complex is a unique 20-foot-tall bell-tower that rises from the smokehouse. Several more structures were added in the early 20th c. by Charles Penny Ellis. (See Introduction, Fig. 37.)

JT 25 Wilson's Mills

The community grew up around the lumber mill of John Marshall Wilson and John A. Waddell, who came here from Warren Co. in 1866 and set up operations as Wilson & Waddell in the timberlands beside the N.C. Railroad. Along with their sons, the men manufactured building materials and contracted for buildings in eastern and central N.C., especially in booming towns such as Raleigh and Durham along the route of the N.C. Railroad. The firm built in many styles but most often favored an Italianate style with heavy brackets and lavish millwork from their factory. The business closed in the 1920s. Although only one brick wall remains of the mill and factory, several of the firm's houses survive in the community, and the *William G. Wilson House, home of a son of the town's founder, has been moved to a new location outside the town. Other houses associated with the operation include the **Anthony Thomas Uzzle House** (ca. 1870; E side SR 1908, 0.2 mi. N of RR tracks; private), an ornate, Italianate cottage; the **Parker-Wilson-Corbett House** (1875; S side of RR tracks, 0.2 mi. E of SR 1908; private), a 2-story Italianate style house; the 2-story, frame **Charles Ruffin Tomlinson House** (ca. 1879; NE corner SR 1910 and SR 1908; private); and the Gothic Revival style **Wilson's Mills Christian Church** (1888; SR 1908 at SR 1901).

JT 26 William G. Wilson House

Ca. 1866, ca. 1900; S side SR 1915, 0.3 mi. S of US 70; private, visible from road

The 2-story frame house, a ca. 1900 remodeling by W.G. Wilson of the 1-story house of his father, John, is the largest and most elaborate of the surviving houses associated with the Wilson family of *Wilson's Mills, featuring a full-width, 2-story, hip-roofed porch with spindle frieze, bracketed posts, and Chippendale-inspired balustrade. The house was moved in recent years from Wilson's Mills.

JT 27 Brook Hill Farms

1935; Albert S. Atkinson (Washington, D.C.), architect; S side NC 42, 1.2 mi. W of NC 96; private, visible from road

Occupying a knoll overlooking the rolling landscape of northern Johnston Co., the distinguished Tudor Revival residence of brick and stucco was built for Dr. Raymond Elmore Earp. Architect Atkinson was a native of the county. Formal gardens center on latticed gazebos, and farm buildings cluster to the southeast.

Harnett County (HT)

HT 1 Lillington

The county seat, named for Revolutionary hero Alexander Lillington, was incorporated in 1859, four years after Harnett Co. was carved out of Cumberland Co., but few buildings date from before the 20th c. Typical 1- and 2-story, brick commercial buildings cluster around the 1898 courthouse, which was stripped of its belltower and encased in brick in 1959. Behind it the former **Harnett County Jail** (1906; W. L. Landrum [Atlanta], contractor) suggests the earlier character of the courthouse with its parapet gable dormer and square cupola on a high hip roof. A small group of late Queen Anne and Colonial Revival style houses faces Front St. west of the commercial district. **Lillington Middle School** (ca. 1920; S. 11th and James Sts.) is a 2-story brick school with a broad, 4-column portico and white brick trim.

HT 2 Summerville (Tirzah) Presbyterian Church

Ca. 1848, ca. 1870; S side SR 1291, 2.1 mi. W of US 421, W of Lillington

HT 2 *Summerville Presbyterian Church*

This picturesque little church, the county's oldest, began as a simple, Greek Revival building and was updated with the Gothic Revival steeple and lancet windows after the Civil War. The Scots congregation was es-tablished in 1811 as Tirzah Church, the center of Summerville, county seat in the 1850s. The cemetery's 19th-c. gravestones include several by Scots stonecutter George Lauder of Fayetteville.

HT 3 Chalybeate Springs

Once a health resort, the community was named for the salts of iron found in its spring water. Prominent among the frame houses from its early 20th-c. prime is the **David Senter House** (ca. 1910; N side SR 1429, 0.1 mi. W of US 401) in simplified Southern Colonial Revival style, with a 2-story portico and a 1-story wraparound porch.

HT 4 Angier

The railroad community began in 1898 when the Duke family of Durham built the short Cape Fear and Northern Railway from Apex into Harnett Co. to aid lumberman John C. Angier—brother-in-law of Benjamin Duke and president of the Cary Lumber Company—in extracting the county's timber. Angier was incorporated in 1901 and grew with the railroad, which the Dukes extended to *Erwin, *Dunn, and eventually Durham to serve their textile and tobacco factories, and reorganized as the Durham and Southern in 1906. A row of simple, 1- and 2-story, brick commercial buildings lines the now-abandoned railroad bed. The frame, hip-roofed **Angier Depot** (ca. 1905; Depot St. at Broad St.) stands at its original location, adapted as chamber of commerce offices and community center. East of the commercial district on NC 210 (Depot St.) is **Yesteryear Square**, a collection of buildings moved from outlying areas to commemorate local history. Among them is **Williams Grove School** (1892), a typical frame, 1-room, 1-teacher country schoolhouse that served the area until 1925. The interior contains the original blackboards and reproductions of period desks and other furnishings.

HT 5 *James Archibald Campbell House*

HT 5 James Archibald Campbell House
1891 and later; N side US 421/NC 27, just W of Buies Creek

The epitome of the word *rambling*, the 1-story frame house with its multiple gables and porches was built in several stages during the occupancy of James Archibald Campbell, Baptist minister, educator, and founder of nearby Buies Creek Academy (later Campbell University). It has been restored by the Harnett Co. Historical Association as a community center. Also at the site are the **J. A. Campbell Birthplace**, a mid-19th-c. 1-story frame farmhouse moved from its original location near Angier, and **Poe's Post Office**, a small, frame building with overhanging front gable that served the village of Buie's Creek until 1899.

HT 6 Kivett Hall
1901–3; Z. V. Kivett, builder; Campbell University, Buies Creek

The towered, Italianate, brick structure was erected by Kivett as the multipurpose main building for Campbell College, a Baptist institution established in 1887. It now houses the law school. Made of brick manufactured on campus, it shares the arched openings and corbeled brickwork of industrial and college architecture of the era. The campus that evolved around a central green beside Kivett Hall consists primarily of red brick buildings in simplified Colonial Revival style typical of the early to mid-20th c.

HT 7 Erwin

The railroad and textile mill community began with the 1902 founding of Erwin Cotton Mills, managed by William A. Erwin as an extension of the Duke family textile mills in Durham. Given a choice between naming the town for himself or for the owners, Erwin named it Duke. But in 1925, after Trinity College in Durham was transformed with Duke family support into Duke University, the school's president requested a change in the name of the textile village to avoid confusion, and the town then became Erwin.

The modernized denim mill (on Denim St.) remains in operation at the center of one of the best-preserved one-industry communities in the state. Neatly ordered with numbered and lettered streets—A, B, C, etc.—the community presents all the typical components and interrelationships of the early 20th-c. mill village with unusual clarity. Most of the workers' houses have been individualized since the mill divested ownership, but the hierarchy of forms remains. The most common type is a 1-story, T-plan house, but some rows have 2-story versions of the same plan. A group of Queen Anne style houses with wraparound porches built for managers stands on H St. on the southern side of the tracks. The central business district of brick commercial buildings focuses on Denim St., and there are churches of various denominations.

HT 8 Dunn

Harnett Co.'s principal town was incorporated in 1887 and named for a construction engineer of the Atlantic Coast Line Railroad. It boomed as a rail, lumber, and manufacturing center in the early 20th c. The small business district centered on Broad St. retains several turn-of-the-century brick commercial buildings with Italianate storefronts. The town has an especially fine collection of Southern Colonial style residences south of Cumberland St. (US 421). A prime example is the **Kenneth L. Howard House** (Dunn Woman's Club) (1908–9; 402 S. Layton Ave.), an Ionic-columned residence built as a free copy of the North Carolina Building at the Jamestown Ter-Centennial Exposition of 1907, which was designed by Joseph S. Ledbetter and Charles Lester of Winston-

HT 8 *Kenneth L. Howard House*

Salem. Although the exposition building surely inspired many similar residences across the state, this is one with a specific family tradition. Another version of the style is the **Wilson-Kozma House** (ca. 1912; 303 Pearsall St.) with Corinthian portico.

The **Gen. William C. Lee House** (ca. 1915; 209 W. Divine St.; open to public) is a big, brick house with a full-width portico, built for businessman Jefferson Davis Barnes and later home of Major General Lee, a celebrated pioneer army paratrooper. It contains the chamber of commerce and a museum memorial to Lee. The **Tilghman-Pope House** (1916–18; Sam Pittman, contractor; 208 Pearsall St.) is a rustic, shingled Craftsman bungalow with a wide dormer and engaged porch, built for lumberman and banker Granville M. Tilghman, a Maryland native. He came to Dunn when his lumberman father posted his four sons in ACL railroad communities from Maryland to South Carolina to attend to the family business.

Recalling the frame buildings that once housed many local industries, the **John A. McKay Manufacturing Company Complex** (ca. 1895–1910; Divine St. at Seaboard Coast Line tracks) is a picturesque cluster

HT 8 *John A. McKay Manufacturing Co.*

of weathered, board-and-batten industrial buildings. McKay began manufacturing turpentine distillery equipment in 1889, then shifted to production of farm implements as the turpentine industry moved farther south. The **John A. McKay House** (1910), the owner's Southern Colonial style residence, stands at the northern end of the complex. Among the products of McKay's foundry is an iron post-and-chain fence.

A venturesome architectural statement appears at the **Charles Parrish Memorial Nursing Home** (ca. 1938; W side N. Ellis Ave. between Harnett and Edgerton Sts.), an Art Moderne building with rounded corners, horizontal bands of string courses, and a stylized entrance pavilion. The former **Magnolia Ave. School** (1918; Charles C. Wilson, architect; W side Magnolia Ave.) is a handsome, 2-story, red brick school in Collegiate Tudor style, renovated by the county as a business development center.

HT 9 Lebanon

Mid- and late 19th c.; E side NC 82, 0.6 mi. N of Cumberland County line, Dunn vic.; private, visible from road

The beautifully sited plantation house has the simple, symmetrical, hip-roofed form, center-passage plan, and restrained Greek Revival detail typical of the mid-19th c., combined with a decorated, 2-tier entrance porch of the later 19th c. Planter Farquhard Smith built the house on land his grandfather settled in the mid-18th c., and it has continued in the family. The plantation was named for the great cedars in the yard, destroyed in 1954 by Hurricane Hazel. During and after the nearby Battle of Averasboro in Mar. 1865, the house was used as a Confederate hospital.

HT 10 Ivy Burne

1872–1910; E side NC 217, 0.4 mi. S of SR 2027, Linden vic.; private, visible from road

This is one of several notable farms in the prosperous agricultural section around *Linden. Within a great grove of oaks, the house was developed in stages from 1872 to 1910 by farmer and civic leader John Murchison Hodges. He built a small, 1-story, frame dwelling when he married Sallie McNeill, and as the family grew he enlarged the dwelling to create a spacious, rambling house with a 2-story, shingled front bay, broad porch, rear ells, and a kitchen wing. Frame and log outbuildings include a kitchen, a smokehouse, a corncrib, and tobacco barns.

HT 11 Woodside

Mid-19th c., enlarged ca. 1889; S side SR 2027, 0.2 mi. W of NC 217, Linden vic.; private, visible from road

The substantial frame house on a raised foundation attained its present form when planter John Williams enlarged a 1-story, Greek Revival house to 2 stories. The house retains the hip roof and symmetrical form of its predecessor, while the decorated, 2-story porch (similar to *Lebanon's) reflects the later 19th-c. work.

HT 12 J. C. Byrd House

Ca. 1923; NE corner US 401 and SR 2026, 2.3 mi. N of Cumberland Co. line, Bunnlevel vic.; private, visible from road

Seat of a prominent farm on the Raleigh-Fayetteville highway, the late example of the Southern Colonial style features an Ionic portico and 1-story, wraparound porch. Its owner ran a sawmill and a gristmill across the road, but after the dam broke during World War II, millpond and mills disappeared. During the 1930s the house served as the Lakeside Tourist Home, accommodating travelers on the highway.

HT 13 Hattadare Indian Village

Ca. 1976; W side US 401, 1.7 mi. N of Bunnlevel

This roadside display memorializes the legend that the region's Lumbee Indians descended from survivors of the Lost Colony who joined the Hatteras Indians of the Outer Banks and moved inland. James Lowry (Dr. Chief Little Beaver) coined the name Hattadare—for the Hatteras Indians and the family of Virginia Dare, the first English child born in the New World. Over the years he created this complex, using Surewall, a fiberglass construction material, to fashion life-sized figures associated with the Lost Colony and regional history.

HT 14 Thorbiskope

1820s, 1840s; S side SR 2050, 0.9 mi. W of SR 2045, Linden vic.; private, visible from road

The plantation house, one of several along the Little River, illustrates two generations of regional architecture. In the front is a symmetrical, 2-story, 5-bay, Greek Revival plantation house with pedimented, 2-tier portico and a center-passage plan; to the rear is a 1½-story, Federal period dwelling with 2-room plan and engaged porch. Both sections were built for John Elliot, son of George Elliot of nearby *Ellerslie in Cumberland Co. and one of the area's largest planters, with 8,000 acres in 1850. Long known as "The Bluff" for its location above the river, the plantation received its Scots-derived name in the early 20th c. The house and two outbuildings are under restoration by a descendant.

Cumberland County (CD)

Fayetteville (CD 1–23)

Located at the head of navigation of the Cape Fear River, the Fayetteville area was settled as early as 1739 when 350 Scots Highlanders arrived at what became known as Cross Creek. In 1778 Cross Creek and nearby Campbellton consolidated as Upper and Lower Campbellton. During the ensuing migration of Scots from their native land into the Cape Fear region, the river port became their principal economic and cultural center. Celebrated among the Scots settlers was Flora McDonald, who aided the escape of Bonnie Prince Charlie (Charles Stuart) to France after the Battle of Culloden. She came to N.C. with her husband, Allan, and from 1774 to 1779 lived on a plantation in the area.

Renamed Fayetteville in 1783 to honor the French general who assisted the American Revolutionary cause, the town hosted Lafayette on his 1825 American tour. Federal period Fayetteville prospered as a trading center for the vast backcountry drained by the Cape Fear and lands westward. Vying with New Bern as the largest town in the state, the river port's merchants and politicians strove to improve its prospects on many fronts. In

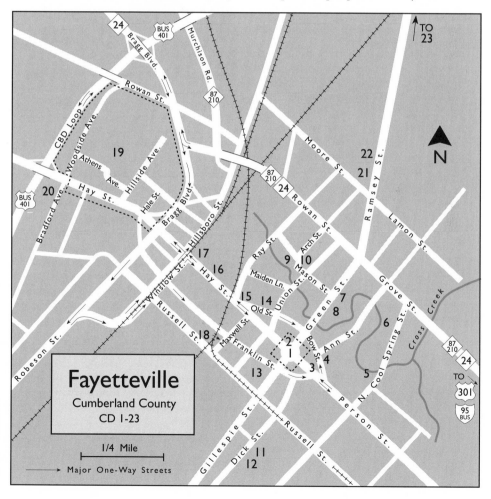

Fayetteville
Cumberland County
CD 1-23

1/4 Mile

Major One-Way Streets

the 1790s Fayetteville contended for designation as capital of the new state, and in the early 19th c. investors strove to boost commerce with schemes for canals and railroads, but without success. The energetic town attracted many entrepreneurs, including New Haven architect and engineer Ithiel Town, who in 1819 erected a famous truss bridge across the river, called the Clarendon Bridge after an old name for the river. Slightly before this, English-born architect and engineer William Nichols, recently of Edenton, moved to Fayetteville and built a waterworks, two banks, and probably other projects as well as serving as state architect in Raleigh.

A major blow to Fayetteville's fortunes came in 1831 when a devastating fire destroyed some 600 buildings. Phoenix-like, the city rebuilt and thrived with Cape Fear steamboat trade from Wilmington to the backcountry; the establishment of cotton mills, including Phoenix and Rockfish in the 1830s; and the construction of plank roads, including "the Appian Way of North Carolina" built in 1848 northwest to Bethania near Salem. (Fragments of the plank road have been located beneath the city's streets.) In 1838 a U.S. arsenal was established on Haymount overlooking the city. Its construction continued into the 1850s. During the Civil War Fayetteville remained an important open river port until 1865, when Sherman's troops burned the Confederate-held arsenal, four cotton mills, and several other structures, leaving the town to rebuild once again. Rail lines were finally carried to Fayetteville in the late 19th c., and mergers brought it into the Atlantic Coast Line Railroad system, creating important links north and south and boosting the city's commercial growth in the new century.

The early 20th c. also brought Fayetteville to a turning point with the 1918 founding of Camp Bragg as a World War I training camp just outside the city. Today known as Fort Bragg, it has become a major military complex. Fayetteville has experienced both the positive and the negative effects of such an installation: dramatic population increase and economic growth generally taking the form of expansive suburban and commercial strip development. Bragg Blvd. epitomizes the mid-20th-c. strip. Despite the ravages of fire and late 20th-c. destruction, many elements of an earlier Fayetteville still dot the city, several the objects of local preservation efforts.

CD 1 Market House

1832; Market Square; National Historic Landmark

CD 1 *Market House*

Standing at the juncture of four principal streets at the hub of downtown, the Market House is Fayetteville's civic landmark and logo. Its form and function descend from medieval English precedents, with its arcaded open market for regulated sale of foodstuffs at street level and the town hall above. The building was directly influenced by its predecessor, the 18th-c. arcaded market and townhouse destroyed in the 1831 fire. The city rebuilt promptly on the old foundations, but in a new and assertively eclectic fashion combining classical and Gothic Revival motifs. Round and pointed arches frame the open market at street level. The municipal hall above has Ionic pilasters between round-arched windows. Thin Ionic colonnettes and spiky obelisks accentuate the cupola with clock and belltower. In 1906 the building was rescued from destruction in an early preservation victory.

CD 2 Market Square

Framing the central square are masonry commercial buildings in diverse sizes and styles from the late 19th and early 20th centuries. Rising 10 stories above the northwestern corner is the elegant **National Bank of Fayetteville** (1923–26; Charles C. Hartmann [Greensboro], architect; 100 Hay St.), the city's first skyscraper, built of fireproof masonry and steel construction and sheathed in pale gray granite, with restrained, classical facades reiterating the Ionic order of the *Market House it faces. Brick commercial buildings of ca. 1880–1915 stand opposite at 101–7 **Hay St.**, while the Romanesque Revival brick **Knights of Pythias Building** (208 E. Russell St.), though shorn of its original tower, emphatically anchors the southwestern corner. Defining the southeastern corner are the 4-story, Second Empire style **Sedberry-McKethan Drugstore** (ca. 1884; 102 Person St.) and the **Stein-Lawyers Building** (1916; 101 Gillespie St.), a colorful, 5-story, Mediterranean Revival style office building with a clipped corner addressing the square.

CD 3 Liberty Row
Early–late 19th c.; N side, 100 block of Person St.

Liberty Row consists of fourteen adjoining brick buildings reaching east from the *Market House to the triangular end of the block known as Liberty Point. Despite changes over the years, this is one of the state's best examples of a 19th-c. commercial row. The Point is cherished locally as the site of the June 20, 1775, Liberty Point Resolves declaring support for the patriot cause. (The present **Liberty Point Store**—the 2-story, parapet-gabled building at the eastern end— may predate the 1831 fire; it was standing by 1833 and known as the "Liberty Point Store" by 1842.) Other buildings date from a rebuilding after an 1846 fire—with brick construction and fire walls. During the 19th c. the row housed the tradesmen vital to Fayetteville. In the 20th c. the area declined as the town's commercial center shifted, but in recent years many of the buildings have been renovated. From the angle of Bow St., the back side of the row reveals a variety of 19th-c. construction techniques.

CD 4 First Presbyterian Church
1816, 1832 (A. J. Davis [New York], architect), 1922 (Hobart Upjohn [New York], architect); SE corner Bow and Ann Sts.; open by appointment

After their 1816 church burned in the 1831 fire, the city's oldest congregation set about to rebuild. Robert Donaldson, a Fayetteville native who had become a wealthy New York businessman, persuaded architect A. J. Davis to provide plans. Davis's drawing for the church roof structure used the "Town Truss" principle developed by his partner Ithiel Town; the truss still survives in the attic. The church, which also incorporates parts of

CD 3 *Liberty Row, with Market House and National Bank of Fayetteville at left*

the 1816 brick walls, has a portico and steeple designed in 1922 by popular revivalist architect Hobart Upjohn, as well as mid-20th-c. interiors.

CD 5 Cool Spring Place
1788–89; 119 N. Cool Spring St.; open by appointment

Innkeeper Dolphin Davis advertised in the *Fayetteville Gazette* of Sept. 14, 1789, "Cool Spring Tavern. The Subscriber begs leave to inform the public, that he has opened a Public House, in Fayetteville, near the Cool Spring." Customers soon came to Fayetteville to attend the state's constitutional convention, at which ratification of the U.S. Constitution (defeated in Hillsborough in 1788) passed on Nov. 21, 1789. This tavern is believed to be the only surviving building linked with that convention. Now a law office, Cool Spring Place is evidently the oldest structure in Fayetteville, with the inn at the core of an early 19th-c. expansion, which features an engaged double piazza, fanlit entrance, Flemish-bond brick chimneys, and Federal style interior woodwork.

CD 6 Evans Metropolitan A.M.E. Zion Church
1893–94; James Williams, carpenter; Joseph Steward, bricklayer; 301 N. Cool Spring St.

A landmark in Methodist history, Evans Metropolitan A.M.E. Zion Church traces its origins to the founding on this site of the first Methodist church in Fayetteville. About 1780 Henry Evans, a free black Virginia shoemaker and licensed Methodist minister,

arrived in Fayetteville en route to Charleston. He decided to remain and preach to the slave population. After a period of persecution by local authorities, he was permitted to preach in town, where his congregation grew to include both blacks and whites. By 1800 Evans had built a frame church on this site, which Bishop Francis Asbury visited several times and referred to as the "African Meeting House" in 1803. The establishment of a church by a free black that served both black and white members was a rarity in early 19th-c. N.C. Becoming a focus of the black community after emancipation, in the 1890s Evans Church undertook construction of the present sanctuary, its fourth building. The brick edifice with its elaborate corbeling and unequal towers flanking a central gable exemplifies a form prevalent among African American churches of its era. Across the street is **Cross Creek Cemetery**, an old graveyard with many fine stones. (See Introduction, Fig. 51.)

CD 7 St. John's Episcopal Church
1817–18, 1832; William Drummond, architect; 302 Green St.

Upon its founding in 1817 St. John's promptly began construction of a brick church, evidently an early Gothic Revival edifice. Whether William Nichols or Ithiel

Town, both in Fayetteville in the late 1810s, took a hand in its design is unknown. When the 1831 fire burned the church, the parish quickly rebuilt on the old walls. The local *Carolina Observer* noted on July 3, 1832, "St. John's Church . . . introduces into our Southern Country a style of architecture to which, we have been hitherto unaccustomed. The taste, observable throughout, is of the ancient Gothic, and the execution reflects great credit on the skill of the Architect, Mr. Drummond." The rectangular nave of the stuccoed brick church with lancet windows may survive from the first building, while the crenellated front gable and corner towers with startling clusters of spires evidently display later Gothic work. Architect William Drummond, who came from Washington, D.C., subsequently worked on the State Capitol in Raleigh.

CD 8 Kyle House
Ca. 1855; 234 Green St.

Scots merchant James Kyle bought the former Fayetteville Academy lot on fashionable Green St. and built a fine brick house, which is now a lone survivor used as town offices. The eclectic residence combines a Doric porch and bracketed cornices. Cast-iron balustrades enrich the porch and roof.

CD 9 Phoenix Lodge No. 8
Ca. 1855; 221 Mason St.

Still serving its original purpose, the Greek Revival style frame lodge features a hip roof and a porch with octagonal columns. It is home of one of the state's oldest Masonic lodges. Established as the Union Lodge by the Grand Lodge of Scotland in the mid-18th c., in 1793 the group was chartered as the Phoenix Lodge by the newly established Grand Lodge of N.C. and erected their first meeting hall on this site.

CD 10 Mansard Roof House
Ca. 1883; 214 Mason St.

This diminutive example of the Second Empire style features fanciful ornament in proportion to its small scale, including ornate

woodwork and a mansard roof of patterned tin topped with delicate iron cresting.

CD 11 Fayetteville Woman's Club and Oval Ballroom
Ca. 1820; William Nichols, attributed architect; 225 Dick St.; open limited hours

One of the city's few buildings predating the 1831 fire, the frame house was built as the central office of the Bank of the United States. It is thought to have been the work of William Nichols, who had recently moved to Fayetteville from Edenton. The bank had its vault in the basement, offices on the first floor, and cashier's domestic quarters on the second floor. After the bank charter expired in 1836, the property became a private residence and was a childhood home of artist Elliot Daingerfield. In the 1940s the house was acquired by the Woman's Club. The Federal form and detail of the house, distinguished by a graceful, superimposed portico, are enriched by an overlay of late Victorian decoration.

The small, freestanding, frame **Oval Ballroom** (ca. 1818) in the yard contains a room of sumptuous Adamesque style unique in the state. Slim Ionic pilasters and classical moldings define an oval chamber that Thomas Waterman praised as "an outstanding example of a Regency room of fine detail worthy of New York or Philadelphia craftsmen." The ballroom, possibly also by Nichols, was built as an addition to the local Halliday residence. When that house was razed, the little ballroom was moved here. (See Introduction, Fig. 26.)

CD 12 Nimocks House
Ca. 1804; 225 Dick St.; open limited hours

A fine, accessible adaptation of the coastal cottage form, the Nimocks House has a small, front entrance portico and a full-width, engaged porch in back. The unusual plan circulates around a massive central chimney—a feature common in New England but rare in N.C. A front entrance lobby opens into a parlor on either side, while behind the chimney a rear lobby contains a curious, partially enclosed barrel stair. The finish throughout is of inventive Adamesque style.

CD 13 Cumberland County Courthouse

1926; Harry Barton (Greensboro), architect; Franklin and Gillespie Sts.

CD 13 *Cumberland County Courthouse*

Harry Barton, a Greensboro architect who specialized in public buildings, displayed his command of Beaux Arts classicism in the imposing 3-story edifice of pale, stone-gray terra-cotta, and in good Beaux Arts fashion repeated the Ionic order established in the *Market House and Charles Hartmann's *National Bank of Fayetteville.

CD 14 First Baptist Church

1905–10; S. W. Foulk & Son (Greensboro), architect; 200 Old St. at Anderson St.

The large, brick church in Romanesque Revival style has the corner towers and auditorium plan popular in its era. It was designed by a leading Greensboro firm for a congregation established in 1837.

CD 15 Hay St. Methodist Church

1907–8; Wheeler, Runge, & Dickey (Charlotte), architects; J. H. Harbin (Lexington) contractor; 1924 (Sunday school); 1953 (education building); intersection of Hay, Old, and Ray Sts.

The imposing, late Gothic Revival church of pressed brick occupies the same site as the original Hay St. Methodist Church established in the 1830s. Three towers flank broad gables filled with stained glass and tracery, and the dominant entrance tower at the western corner opens into a semicircular, auditorium-plan sanctuary with curved seating focusing on the pulpit. Pull-down

CD 15 *Hay St. Methodist Church*

doors partitioned off the Akron-plan Sunday school before a separate Sunday school was added in 1924.

CD 16 Prince Charles Hotel

1924–25; 430 Hay St.

CD 16 *Prince Charles Hotel*

Built by local investors to attract Florida-bound rail and highway travelers, the 7-story hotel near the depot was erected of fireproof construction in concrete, steel, and brick, enriched with classical details. The name celebrates the Bonnie Prince, Scots hero of Flora McDonald's saga. After years of active service, it experienced a period of decline but has been revitalized as a downtown hotel.

CD 17 Atlantic Coast Line Railroad Station

1911; Joseph F. Leitner (Wilmington), architect; corner Hay and Hillsboro Sts.

The brick station, built for the newly established (1908) Atlantic Coast Line Railroad that consolidated many rail lines into a major national system, exhibits a lively, Dutch Colonial Revival style unusual in the city. In continuous use at the heart of the city, it was restored in the late 1980s as the Amtrak station.

CD 18 Cape Fear and Yadkin Valley Railway Passenger Depot

Ca. 1890; A. B. Williams and T. A. Klutz, contractors; 148 Maxwell St.

Characterized by arcaded facades designed to ease passenger and baggage flow, the Romanesque Revival, brick depot served the other major rail line that fed the city's economy. The CF&YV merged with the Atlantic Coast Line in 1900.

CD 19 Haymount

Ca. 1817–ca. 1950; Hay St., Hale St., Hillside Ave., Athens Ave. and environs

On a high vantage above downtown, Haymount is Fayetteville's most intact early residential section. Begun in the early 19th c. as Hay Mount or "the Hill," the neighborhood became a fashionable suburb. Its buildings represent trends from a long span. Among the earliest are the **Robert Strange Town House** (ca. 1817; 114 Hale St.), a simply detailed, 2-story, frame dwelling built for the distinguished judge and novelist and his wife Jane Kirkland; the **Smith-Lauder House** (ca. 1853; 118 Hillside Ave.), a frame, Greek Revival house with side-hall plan and pedimented roof and portico, built for Scots stonecutter John Smith and later home of the famed Scots stonecutter and tombstone maker George Lauder; and the **E. J. Hale House** (ca. 1847; 630 Hay St.), a combination of Greek Revival and Italianate styles built for longtime local editor Hale. More numerous are houses from the early 20th c., such as the **Monaghan House** (ca. 1900; 119 Hillside Ave.), a Queen Anne style cottage with pyramidal roof, wraparound porch, and sawnwork; the **Charles G. Rose House** (1911; 215 Hillside Ave.), one of many fine Colonial Revival residences; and a full array of bungalows.

CD 20 Museum of the Cape Fear Historical Complex

W side Bradford Ave. at Arsenal Ave., S of Hay St.; open regular hours

Occupying a former nurses' dormitory built in the 1940s for nearby Highsmith Hospital, the state-owned **Museum of the Cape Fear** offers exhibits and programs on the history and culture of southeastern N.C. Next door, under restoration by the museum is the **E. A. Poe House** (1897; Ruffin Vaughn [Fayetteville], builder; 206 Bradford Ave.), a 2-story frame house of symmetrical Colonial Revival design with ornate wraparound porch, erected by a leading local builder for the family of a brick manufacturer. Across a pedestrian bridge spanning the CBD Loop behind the museum is **Arsenal Park**, a 4.5-acre greenspace commemorating the North Carolina Arsenal, which was established by the federal government in 1838, expanded by the Confederates during the Civil War, and destroyed by Sherman's army in Mar. 1865. Archaeological studies were conducted before the CBD Loop bisected the arsenal site in 1991. A steel frame "**Ghost Tower**" (1992) marks the location of the original northwest tower of the facility. The **Arsenal House** (1862; 822 Arsenal Ave.), a 1-story board-and-batten house, the only surviving structure from the arsenal, will serve as a park interpretive center after restoration.

CD 21 St. Joseph's Episcopal Church

1896, 1916; Ramsey and Moore Sts.

The picturesque ecclesiastical complex comprises a church, parish hall, and parsonage linked by arcades and unified by dark green, shingled walls and organic forms in a quietly

CD 21 *St. Joseph's Episcopal Church*

sophisticated blend of the Shingle style and the Gothic Revival. The congregation of black Episcopalians grew out of *St. John's after the Civil War. Benefactor Eva Cochran of Yonkers, N.Y., gave funds and may have suggested an architect (as yet unidentified). At the dedication in 1897 the local newspaper asserted that "with the exception of Mr. Vanderbilt's church at Biltmore, there is no church interior in the State so beautiful as that of St. Joseph's." After a 1916 fire destroyed all but the church, the complex was quickly rebuilt.

CD 22 Belden-Horne House and Barges Tavern
Early 19th c.; 519 Ramsey St.; open business hours

When Simeon Belden rebuilt his house on Green St. soon after the 1831 fire, his residence continued the Federal style—the side-hall plan, the delicate fanlight—and added touches of the new Greek Revival. The double porches and decorative ceiling painting in the front parlor are particularly noteworthy. Endangered by commercial development, the house was moved a few blocks north to serve as the Fayetteville Convention and Visitors' Bureau. Next door is **Barges Tavern**, originally located near the old courthouse downtown. A remnant of the small, frame houses once prevalent in Fayetteville, it is thought to have served as a tavern.

CD 23 Veterans Administration Hospital
1939; 2300 Ramsey St. (US 401 N)

A memorable, 2-story replica of the Fayetteville *Market House crowns the central en-

CD 23 *Veterans Administration Hospital*

trance pavilion of the massive, 6½-story, red brick, Georgian Revival main building. This wonderfully specific local reference epitomizes national VA policy of customizing standard hospital designs to reflect local architecture—during the 1930s era of Federal projects that created regional Colonial Revival public buildings across the country. Other campus buildings repeat the Georgian Revival theme. Confederate breastworks also survive on the grounds.

CD 24 Camp Ground Methodist Church
Ca. 1860, Christopher and Ruffin Vaughn, builders; S side SR 1413 (Campground Rd.), 0.25 mi. W of US 401 BYP

Named for the camp-meeting revivals held here before the church was built, this carefully detailed, frame church has a pedimented front with paired entrances flanking and surmounted by plain sash windows, which are repeated in both stories along the sides. This is among the few Greek Revival country churches whose builder is known: local carpenters Ruffin and Christopher Vaughn, the latter a church member. Located behind the mid-20th-c. brick sanctuary, the old church serves as a chapel.

CD 25 Fort Bragg Military Reservation
Access limited to military personnel and residents; special permission required to visit

CD 25 *Post Chapel, Fort Bragg*

Established in 1918 as Camp Bragg, a field artillery unit named for N.C. Confederate general Braxton Bragg, in 1922 the base was designated Fort Bragg, a permanent army post. During the interwar period, the post building program stressed beautification and produced a unified group of handsome architecture arranged in a formal, Beaux Arts layout. In 1940 a massive construction campaign readied Fort Bragg for World War II, making it into the world's largest military installation at the time. Within a few months a workforce sometimes of more than 20,000 erected some 2,500 buildings costing $32 million. The base became the training facility for all five Airborne Divisions.

The architectural centerpiece is the predominantly interwar-era collection of substantial revival style architecture unified by stuccoed walls and tile roofs. The **Post Headquarters**, **Theater**, and **Officers Club** feature a variety of classical motifs, as does the handsome **Post Chapel**, with its staged, Wren-Gibbs type tower and rusticated, round-arched windows. In the "Normandy" area, streets of officers' residences around the parade ground follow a generally Spanish Revival style. Essentially identical within each rank, they range from 2-story residences for generals and colonels to 1-story houses for majors and bungalows for NCOs.

CD 26 Ellerslie
Ca. 1790; 1840s; no public visibility or access

Built for Scots planter George Elliot, the original section of the T-shaped house is one of the few late 18th-c. plantation houses along the Upper Cape Fear River—a 1½-story dwelling with a 3-room plan and porches that originally extended around all four sides. Like several of their family in the area, the Elliots added a 2-story, Greek Revival style house in front and made the old house into a rear ell.

CD 27 Linden

The little railroad town near US 401 straddles the Cumberland-Harnett Co. line and contains several frame houses sheltered by great moss-hung trees. **Sardis Presbyterian Church** (1916; s side NC 217, 0.1 mi. w of SR 1700) is a modest brick church with classical portico and belfry, built as successor to an antebellum frame sanctuary. One of the most appealing late 19th-c. country churches in the region is **Parker's Grove Methodist**

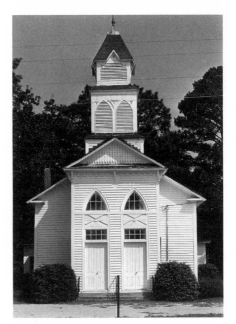
CD 27 *Parker's Grove Methodist Church*

Church (1876 and later; N side NC 217, 0.7 w of SR 1700), built on land given by a member of Sardis Church. The simple, gable-fronted sanctuary was completed in 1876 and some years later received its jaunty front entrance tower. Above the paired doors the carpenter combined pairs of sawnwork panels and Gothic openings, gables, brackets, and Eastlake cutwork to create a crisply eclectic ensemble.

CD 28 William Smith House
Early 19th c.; S side SR 1801, 0.1 mi. E of NC 82, Godwin vic.; private, visible from road

One of several plantation houses associated with the local Smith family, the 2-story, frame house features a double portico sheltering paired front entrances, bounded by a delicate sheaf-of-wheat balustrade.

CD 29 Old Bluff Presbyterian Church
1850s; end of SR 1709, 0.4 mi. from SR 1802, Wade vic.

Old Bluff, organized in 1758 after visits by evangelist Hugh McAden, is home to the oldest Presbyterian congregation in Cum-

CD 29 *Old Bluff Presbyterian Church*

berland Co. and one of the three mother churches in the Highland Scots settlement area of the Upper Cape Fear. The revered landmark is among the finest of several Greek Revival frame churches of the area. Its pedimented front has a 1-story inset entrance porch flanked by entrances to the gallery stairs. Intricate pierced and sawn detail suggests classical moldings. The graveyard includes a mid-19th-c. commemorative marker by Scots carver George Lauder of Fayetteville.

CD 30 Falcon Tabernacle

1898; Julius Culbreth, builder; E side West St., just N of Culbreth St., Falcon

This unusual, octagonal structure was the birthplace of the Pentecostal Holiness Church formed in the 1911 consolidation of the Fire Baptized Holiness Association and the Holiness Church. The local builder is said to have modeled the small, board-and-batten "Octagon Tabernacle" after the tents that housed revival meetings. In 1952 the

CD 30 *Falcon Tabernacle*

tabernacle was incorporated into the apse of a new brick church, but in 1974 a restoration extracted it from the church and set it not far from its original site.

CD 31 Cape Fear Baptist Church

1859; E side SR 2233, 2.5 mi. NE of NC 87, Grays Creek vic.

Built for one of the county's oldest Baptist congregations (est. ca. 1790), the big, Greek Revival country church features a massive portico with banded, square pillars. It is one of a small number of churches in the region—most of them Presbyterian—in which the pulpit stands against the front wall, between the two main entrances.

CD 32 Big Rockfish Presbyterian Church

1855; John McDonald, builder; E side SR 2274, 0.75 mi. N of NC 59, Hope Mills vic. (visible from I-95 and US 301)

The straightforward, Greek Revival church repeats the region's temple form and pedimented front with double doors and restrained carpentry detail. The congregation was organized in 1844 as the Presbyterian Church of Rockfish Factory, the mill community now known as *Hope Mills, which had a strong tradition of revivals and Sunday schools from the 1830s onward. After meeting for several years in a building shared with other congregations, the members built their own church, with construction supervised by carpenter and church elder John McDonald.

CD 33 Hope Mills

The village on Little Rockfish Creek retains a cluster of industrial buildings and dwellings from its long history as a cotton manufacturing town. It began as Rockfish, the second of two cotton mills established by local landowner Charles Peter Mallett in the Fayetteville area during the state's 1830s boom in cotton mill construction. Opened in 1839, by the 1840s Rockfish was the largest cotton mill in the state. Twice the size of any other industry in Cumberland Co., the factory had 4,400 spindles and 148 workers (100 of them women) producing over a million yards of cotton sheeting a year. A vital supplier of the Confederate army, in 1865 the mill was burned by General Sherman's troops. Postwar recovery came slowly. In the 1880s Philadelphia banker William C. Houston rebuilt and expanded the operation as Hope Mills Manufacturing Company. New mills and more than 100 new operatives' houses were erected. During the 20th c. the mills changed hands several times, then ceased operation.

Clusters of mill-related buildings flank Main St. near Rockfish Creek. On **E. Patterson St.**, overlooking the creekside site of the 1830s Rockfish mill burned by Sherman's men, stand two early 19th-c. houses probably built for supervisory personnel—rare survivors of their era: **210 E. Patterson St.** is a coastal cottage with central doorway and late Federal trim, and **218 E. Patterson St.** is a 1-story, Greek Revival style house with full-width porch, jib windows, and stone end chimneys. On Main St. and west stand factories, housing, and stores from the Hope Mills postwar era. The former **Hope Mills Bank** (ca. 1905; sw corner Main and Trade Sts.) is a 2-story brick structure, now the town hall. **Trade St.** contains a compact, small-scale commercial district of brick stores, accented by the **Alice L. Gilbert Store** (ca. 1915; 205 Trade St.), a tiny structure covered in rusticated pressed metal, with cornice embossed "Alice L. Gilbert." The **Hope Mills Manufacturing Company Factory** (1904 and later; w side Atlantic Coast Line tracks, opp. W. Patterson St.), a multipart, brick building in typical functional Italianate style, retains a landmark water tower near the street. Around the mill are several blocks of 1-story, frame mill houses built by the Hope Mills Manufacturing Company. The uniform rows on **Railroad, Middle, and Ellison Sts.** (ca. 1919) consist of T-shaped duplexes with center-facade gables, porches, and scalloped sawnwork, four rooms on each side. Another cluster on **Trade St.** (pre-1914) includes smaller, typically 3- and 4-room, single-family dwellings and duplexes with side-gabled roofs and shed porches. Moved to **44 Trade St.** is a 19th-c. mill house of a type once common in town—a wide, 1-story, gable-fronted house with board-and-batten walls and decorative windows.

Sampson County (SP)

See Thomas R. Butchko, An Inventory of Historic Architecture: Sampson County, North Carolina *(1981).*

SP 1 Clinton

When Sampson, the largest county in the state, was created in 1784 and named for local planter and politician John Sampson, a courthouse was erected here. In 1822 the county seat was established as Clinton, named for landowner and political figure Richard Clinton, an heir of Sampson. The town flourished as an educational, trade, and political center, energized by an influx of Connecticut merchants in the 1830s. After the Civil War and destruction of the commercial district by an 1877 fire, Clinton rebounded as an agriculture and timber market, aided by the 1886 completion of a branch of the Wilmington and Weldon Railroad. In 1889 Populist leader and local newspaper publisher Marion Butler reported "remarkable improvements" in town. The community, with continued gradual growth in the 20th c., remains the trade and political center of a vast agricultural county.

Downtown centers on the square dominated by the **Sampson County Courthouse** (1937–40; R. R. Markley, architect), a red brick, Colonial Revival style building erected by the WPA around the 1904 Romanesque Revival courthouse, from which the central cupola with blind Justice weathervane survives. Enclosing the square are 1- and 2-story, brick commercial buildings from the turn of the century. Some feature pressed-metal facades, such as the **Bethune Building** and the **Powell Building** (1902; 120 and 118 E. Main St.), built after a fire destroyed their predecessors. South of the courthouse stands the chief reminder of railroad days, the long, brick **Clinton Depot and Freight Station** (ca. 1920; W. Elizabeth St.).

Clinton's residential architecture encompasses a continuum from Greek Revival to bungalow, with several especially stylish Greek Revival houses illustrating the antebellum influence of northern newcomers. The **W. Main St.–N. Chesnutt St.** neighborhood just west of the courthouse offers the principal collection. The **Dr. William G. Micks House** (ca. 1851; 212 W. Main St.) was built for a physician from Norfolk who is said to have copied the unusual tripartite form and bold Greek Revival details from the Elmira, N.Y., home of his wife, Cornelia Rathbone. The town's oldest residence is the **Richard Clinton Holmes House** (ca. 1826, 1835; 302 W. Main St.), a 2-story, side-passage-plan house expanded to a symmetrical, center-passage plan in Greek Revival style. The **Allmond Holmes House** (1856, 1912; 311 W. Main St.) combines a Greek Revival main block with the colossal portico and wraparound porches of the next era of Neoclassicism in the early 20th c. The **Amma F. Johnson House** (1868 and later; 320 W. Main St.), built for the son of a Yankee businessman, displays the asymmetrical form and ornate millwork of the late 19th c.

Antebellum Chesnutt St. was known as "Yankee Row" for the northern origins of the first residents. The **Alfred Johnson House** (1830s; 109 N. Chesnutt St.) is one of three local Greek Revival dwellings built as temple-form houses with side-passage plans, a type unusual in N.C. and attributed to the Middletown, Conn., origins of merchant Johnson and others. The **Amma Chesnutt House** (ca. 1847; 201 N. Chesnutt St.), built for Johnson's partner, is a symmetrical, Greek Revival house that shares with the Johnson house such distinctive details as peaked, crossetted door and window frames and heavy corner pilasters; the portico came in 1910.

The **College St.** area east of the courthouse developed around the Clinton Academy (est. 1826), on whose site now stands the **College St. Elementary School** (1911; 606 College St.), a red brick school with Ionic portico. The street is dominated by the massive **Graves-Stuart House** (1840s; 600 College St.), a temple-form residence built for L. C. Graves, Philadelphia native and president of the Clinton Female Academy; it was renovated as a bank in 1982. The **Col. John Ashford House** (ca. 1839, 1869; 615 College St.) presents another version of the Greek Revival with the square, Doric-type pillars characteristic of Sampson and nearby Duplin Co. Next door stands the **Henry L. Stewart House** (1926; 617 College St.), planned by its owner as a foursquare house of specially designed cement blocks manufactured in Kinston. Across the street, the **Clyde Carroll House** (ca. 1920; 616 College St.), with its deep porch and wood-shingled walls, is one of Clinton's many fine bungalows.

Early 20th-c. residential architecture is diverse and widely distributed around town. The **F. L. Turlington House** (1919; Leila Ross Wilburn [Atlanta], architect; Hardy Royal, builder; 234 Beaman St.) is an asymmetrically massed, boldly detailed bungalow that lumberman Turlington had built from a house-plan book by Atlanta architect Wilburn, one of the most prolific woman architects in the South in the early 20th c. The **Robert Herring House** (1916; 216 Sampson St., B&B) is a massive, Southern Colonial Revival style house with dominant portico, built for a lumberman.

SP 1 *Graves-Stuart House*

SP 2 *James S. Simmons House*

SP 2 James S. Simmons House

Ca. 1904; W side US 421, 0.2 mi. S of SR 1809, Beamans Crossroads vic.; private, visible from road

Farmers in northern Sampson Co. built a series of cottage-style houses ornamented with a verve equal to the larger houses of the late 19th and early 20th centuries. This prominent, well-kept example typifies the form: a 1-story house with tri-gabled roof and a full display of vivid local millwork, including turned and sawn porch trim and a shingled, star-studded front gable. The form and plan are also typical of the region: a center-passage plan with two main front rooms and smaller, unheated back rooms, creating an asymmetrical gable end that suggests a development from the older type with rear shed rooms.

SP 3 Sampson Weeks House

Ca. 1880; W side SR 1809, 1.7 mi. N of US 421, Beamans Crossroads vic.; private, visible from road

In this small farmhouse, as in the nearby *James S. Simmons House and others, exuberant millwork gives panache to a 1-story dwelling with front center gable. Brackets and sawnwork adorn the eaves and gables, and the wraparound porch drips with sawn and turned ornament.

SP 4 John E. Wilson House

Ca. 1878; E side SR 1631, 0.6 mi. S of NC 55, Spivey's Corner vic.; private, visible from road

Another familiar form—the 2-story house, one room deep, plus a long rear ell—displays local farmers' relish for stylish adornments: a 2-tier porch of sawn and turned work, brackets outlining the gables, and

SP 4 *John E. Wilson House*

arched doors and windows. Besides his farm, Wilson operated cotton gins, sawmills, and a shuttle factory in nearby Dunn.

SP 5 Thirteen Oaks (Lovett Warren Farm)

1902; N side US 13 at SR 1647, W of Newton Grove; private, visible from road

The well-kept farmstead centers on the Lovett Warren House, a prominent example of the 2-story, traditional farmhouses that late 19th- and early 20th-c. farmers continued to build, enriched with decorative millwork and a front roof gable.

SP 6 Newton Grove

An old trading center, Newton Grove was begun in the 1810s near the intersection of the Wilmington-Raleigh and Tarboro-Fayetteville stage lines. The principal landmark is the **Our Lady of Guadalupe Catholic Church and Rectory** (1873, 1935; Irvin Dr.; visible from US 701), a late Greek Revival church with Gothic Revival touches (and a 20th-c. steeple), built for one of eastern N.C.'s few rural Catholic parishes, originally St. Mark's. The rectory nearby is a brick, Colonial Revival style residence with arcaded, cloister-like porches.

South of the town center the **Archibald Monk House** (ca. 1824; Weeks Park, w side US 701, 0.3 mi. s of US 13; open limited hours) is an early example of the regional variation of the coastal cottage form. The rear secondary rooms are under the main gable roof rather than in a rear shed, and the

SP 6 *Archibald Monk House*

end chimneys, located in front of the roof ridge, heat the front rooms only. The house and several small log and frame outbuildings were moved here in 1979 and restored by the Newton Grove Historical Society.

SP 7 Isaac Williams House

Ca. 1868; S side NC 55 opp. NC 50, Newton Grove vic.; private, visible from road

The highly visible farmhouse, built soon after the Civil War, illustrates the local transition from an antebellum, front cross-gable house type to the tri-gabled form of the picturesque cottage that grew popular in the later 19th c.

SP 8 Lischer Williams House

Ca. 1910; S side NC 55, 0.4 mi. W of NC 50, Newton Grove vic.

With its lively roofline and ornate porch, the 1½-story, frame farmhouse is one of the county's numerous small Queen Anne houses indicative of the agricultural prosperity around the turn of the century. Here two projecting gabled bays flank the front entrance to create a symmetrical profile, and a turned porch bends out to emphasize the swelling form. Farmer Williams built the house with help from his brothers.

SP 9 Lovett Lee House

Ca. 1880; W side SR 1725, 1.0 mi. S of NC 50, Suttontown vic.; private, visible from road

Showing the exuberant local embellishment of traditional forms, the frame I-house boasts a 2-tier porch with intricate sawn balustrade and lace-like frieze. There are several early 20th-c. barns and outbuildings.

SP 10 Francis Pugh House

Ca. 1850; N side NC 403, 0.6 mi. E of US 701 BUS, Clinton vic.; private, visible from road

A distinctive mid-19th-c. house type in the county features a broad cross gable projecting as a front porch from a symmetrical, 1-story house. Many, like this example, are finished with bold, simple Greek Revival details, including square Doric pillars and cornerposts.

SP 11 Cherrydale

1832, ca. 1850; N side SR 1919, 0.4 mi. W of SR 1909, Turkey vic.; private, visible from road

The tall, unadorned, late Federal style I-house follows the familiar hall-parlor plan, expanded by a rear shed addition that was raised to 2 stories ca. 1850. Built for Lewis Moore, of the area's pioneering Moore family, it has remained in family ownership.

SP 12 Marcheston Killett House

Ca. 1865; W side SR 1222, 1.8 mi. NW of US 701, Clinton vic.; private, visible from road

This neatly finished, 1½-story house shows the locally popular cross-gable form, where the large cross gable projects as the front porch. Here Italianate brackets and ornate chimneys combine with Greek Revival features. Farmer Killett oversaw construction of his house. The rear ell incorporates a log kitchen, and there are several outbuildings, including a tobacco barn, a packhouse, and others.

SP 13 Oak Plain Presbyterian Church

1859–60; John Fred Taylor and William Chesnutt, builders; S side SR 1943, 0.7 mi. S of SR 1945, Waycross vic.

The fine little Greek Revival frame church is one of many temple-form churches built for rural Presbyterian congregations of the Cape Fear region. Beautifully sited with its lawn and cemetery shaded by oaks and magnolias, the church has tall, triple-hung sash windows that rise nearly the full height of the

SP 13 *Oak Plain Presbyterian Church*

walls and light a gallery with a delicate sheaf-of-wheat railing. Built for a congregation formed in 1859, the church is attributed to church members and carpenters Taylor and Chesnutt. The steeple was added in 1976.

SP 14 Lewis Highsmith House

Ca. 1840; W side US 421, 1.5 mi. S of NC 41, Harrells vic.; private, visible from road

The prominently sited, 2-story frame house has the only full-width, 2-tier, engaged porch in the county. A porch stair runs between levels. The hall-parlor plan is augmented by a 2-story rear shed—a conservative usage, like the simple, Federal style finish that continued locally into the 1840s. The house was built for planter Highsmith, owner of some 1,000 acres. Among the outbuildings is a plank smokehouse.

SP 15 Harrells Masonic Lodge

Ca. 1841; S side NC 41, Harrells

The 2-story, pediment-front, Greek Revival frame building is a rare example of the antebellum Masonic lodges that once stood in many eastern N.C. communities. Like others, it had a schoolroom below and meeting room above.

SP 16 Dr. Jeremiah Seavey House

1841; Isaac B. Kelly, attributed builder; E side SR 1100, 0.3 mi. S of SR 1007, Harrells vic.; private, visible from road

The county's most imposing antebellum plantation house features a pedimented, 2-story entrance portico framed by moss-hung oaks and large magnolias. The plan has a center passage between two main rooms, plus a long rear ell. The square, Doric-type pillars of the portico, like the carpentry throughout, exemplify the simple, forceful Greek Revival work of Sampson and Duplin counties, here credited to local builder Kelly.

SP 17 Ivanhoe
SR 1100, southern tip of county

Located among moss-hung trees on the banks of the Black River, the crossroads of Ivanhoe developed after a branch of the Cape Fear and Yadkin Valley Railroad arrived ca. 1888. The railroad consolidated a large rural neighborhood established by Scots families in the 1730s. Near the center of the community are the **W. M. Corbett Store** (ca. 1893; w side SR 1100), a 2-story, frame country store with a meeting room on the second story, and the small, decorated **Dr. Hollingsworth Office** (ca. 1908; private).

Ivanhoe's two churches stand beneath great moss-draped oaks amid sandy graveyards on SR 1102, just west of SR 1100, 0.2 mi. south of Ivanhoe. The pristinely beautiful **Black River Presbyterian Church** (1859) is among the finest of the Greek Revival, temple-form rural churches built for descendants of Scots pioneers. This is the fourth building of a congregation organized in 1740—the first recorded Presbyterian congregation established in N.C. Its pedimented portico has simple, Doric pillars of local type, and the central entrance leads to a simply finished sanctuary, with galleries supported by pillars. The cemetery contains many early graves, notable 19th-c. gravestones, and two cypress grave fences. Across the road is the **Ivanhoe Baptist Church** (1893), a white frame church that blends simplified Greek Revival and Gothic Revival elements.

The **Beatty-Corbett House** (ca. 1850, ca. 1900; w side SR 1100, 1.5 mi. s of Ivanhoe at Black River Bridge; private) is an expansive riverside residence comprising a spacious Greek Revival house and a large Neoclassical Revival addition with monumental portico, all surrounded by endless porches overlooking the Black River. This location was featured in the movie *Rambling Rose.*

SP 18 Clear Run
NC 411 at Black River

The most intact of many rural crossroads in the county, Clear Run is unique in that it grew up dependent on boat trade on the Black River, named for its tannin-dark water. Here Amos J. Johnson established a mercantile center in the late 19th c. and operated steamboats between Clear Run, the northern limit of navigation on the Black River, and the port of Wilmington. The ruins of the steamer *A. J. Johnson* are still visible at low water where it sank in 1914. The most prominent building is the **Marvin Johnson House** (ca. 1898; James L. Cooper, builder), a foursquare, frame house with 2-tier entrance porch, built for A. J.'s son. The county's sole surviving 19th-c. cotton gin, the original general store (ca. 1870s), and the ca. 1900 furniture store are among more than a dozen agricultural and mercantile structures beside the dark and placid stream.

Duplin County (DP)

DP 1 Kenansville

Noted for its high and healthful location, the community was settled in the mid-18th c. largely by Presbyterian Scots-Irish families who called it Golden Grove. After the county seat was located here in 1784, it was known as Duplin Courthouse, and when the town was laid out in 1818, it was named Kenansville after a family who had settled in the area in the 1730s. Construction of the Wilmington and Raleigh Railroad (later the Wilmington and Weldon) through the county in the late 1830s boosted prosperity from forest and agricultural products. With its courthouse, a Masonic hall, several churches, and academies, antebellum Kenansville enjoyed a reputation as "one of the most flourishing and dashing little towns in North Carolina."

Kenansville's fortunes diminished after the Civil War but improved in the early 20th c. The community has continued to grow as a center for a large agricultural county with a developing agribusiness economy. The county still possesses many small farmsteads and tenant houses, mainly coastal cottages, gable-sided, 1-story dwellings, and gable-fronted bungalows, as well as frame and occasionally log tobacco barns and other farm buildings.

More than a dozen buildings from antebellum Kenansville are interspersed among modern development. The distinctive local Greek Revival architecture probably reflects a single shop; local tradition cites Thomas Sheppard and Isaac Kelly as builders of some. Stout, square-in-section pillars with Doric-type capitals define nearly every porch; broad pilasters rise as cornerposts; and heavy, squared-off moldings contrast with delicate balustrades. Variations on center-passage plans integrate indoor-outdoor spaces: porches inset within the main block of the house, or folding doors and full-length windows that make porches into outdoor rooms and interior passages into extensions of porches.

At the town center, the **Duplin County Courthouse** (1911–12; Wheeler and Stern [Charlotte], architects) is a tan, brick structure built on an H-plan, with a central portico, dome, and free classical detail that blends with the earlier buildings. To replace the antebellum courthouse, county officials followed an age-old pattern and inspected courthouses in Halifax and Sampson counties to "decide upon the kind of courthouse they should build in Duplin," then hired a popular Charlotte firm well acquainted with counties' budgets, needs, and preferences.

Northwest of the courthouse, the **Dr. David Gillespie House** (ca. 1858; 210 Seminary St.) is a prime example of the local Greek Revival style. The symmetrical, 2-story house has a double portico of heavy, squared pillars, fluted pilasters breaking out from the broad cornerposts, and pedimented gable ends. Its peaked, crossetted window and door frames are a local hallmark.

DP 1 *Dr. David Gillespie House*

Main St. (NC 24/NC 11) has the principal concentration of antebellum buildings. The gable-fronted **Kenansville Baptist Church** (1850s; s side Main St. at Routledge St.) displays the local Greek Revival style in its slightly peaked window surrounds and heavy corner pilasters. The **Kelly-Farrior House** (**Cowan Museum**) (1850s; 411 S. Main St.; open regular hours), a 2-story, Greek Revival house with a conservatory lit by continuous sash windows, is attributed to local cabinet-maker and builder Thomas Sheppard. He is also credited with constructing the similar **Isaac Kelly House** (1850s; 211 S. Main St.) for his son-in-law, a prominent local merchant also cited as a builder of several Greek Revival houses in the region. Especially striking is the **Graham House** (406 S. Main St.), which combines the local Greek Revival style with Italianate brackets and Gothic Revival panels and has an inset, full-height porch that fills the eastern 2 bays of the 3-bay facade. **Grove Presbyterian Church** (1855; s side Main St., opp. Stokes St.), akin to the Baptist church, has a pedimented front and simple, square-in-section belfry outlined with paneled pilasters, plus triangular-headed windows that add a Gothic Revival touch. The congregation, one of the state's two oldest Presbyterian congregations, with Black River, was formed by Scots-Irish immigrants who settled here ca. 1736.

DP 1 *Grove Presbyterian Church*

Liberty Hall (mid-19th c.; 409 S. Main St.; open regular hours) is a simply detailed, Greek Revival house that was the longtime home of the large and prominent Kenan family. Planter Thomas Kenan, grandson of the Thomas Kenan who immigrated from Ireland in the 1730s, established a plantation here. When he moved to Selma, Ala., in 1833, his son Owen Rand Kenan remained. An attorney and planter who served in the Confederate House of Representatives, Owen rebuilt the house after a fire and expanded it over the years. He and his wife,

Sarah Graham, had a large family. Among their grandchildren were Mary Lily Kenan, who married Henry Flagler, cofounder of the Standard Oil Company, at a grand wedding in the parlor at Liberty Hall; William Rand Kenan Jr., a scientist who led in developing the Union Carbide Company; and Sarah Graham Kenan. William and Sarah, heirs of their sister Mary Lily's immense Flagler fortune, became important philanthropists. In the 1960s the property was restored by Kenan family members as a house museum.

DP 2 Dr. Needham Herring House
1853; S side NC 24/50, 1 mi. W of NC 11/903, W of Kenansville; private, visible from road; B&B

Distinguishing the hip-roofed, Greek Revival house is a richly eclectic, 2-tier portico, with lancet panels on the Doric pillars and a balustrade with a sheaf-of-wheat motif atop tiny Ionic colonnettes. The complex also includes a frame carriage house, a 3-pen smokehouse, and a large barn contemporary with the house. The farmstead was built for Herring, a planter and physician.

DP 3 Waterloo
Early 19th c.; E side NC 111/903, 2.2 mi. N of NC 11, Albertson vic.; private, visible from road

Originally the 2-story main block of this unusual house contained only one main room on the first floor and two on the second, heated by a single chimney on the east gable end. Originally there were a shed room on the east and a gabled porch on the west; expansions have been made in the 20th c. Finish typifies good craftsmanship of the late 18th and early 19th centuries, with beaded weatherboards and chamfered porch posts. The early history of Waterloo is uncertain. It may have been built by 1809 when David Carter, a free black landowner, sold the property to planter Henry Grady. In 1831 Grady deeded the 400-acre farm known as "Waterloo" to Daniel Simmons, husband of his daughter Eliza Ann Grady, and the couple made their home here.

DP 4 Hebron Presbyterian Church

1890; W side SR 1551, 0.2 mi. NE of SR 1554, Pink Hill vic.

DP 4 *Hebron Presbyterian Church*

This pristine and utterly simple country church epitomizes the long use of the classic, gable-fronted form with a single entrance and large, plain sash windows along the sides and rear. The congregation was founded at the Sutton Branch Schoolhouse in 1886,during an upsurge in evangelism by the Wilmington Presbytery's Home Missions movement. A well-kept, sandy cemetery adjoins.

DP 5 William S. Boney House

1878–90; N side NC 41, 0.6 mi. W of NC 11, Wallace vic.; private, visible from road

In 1878 Boney, a farmer and owner of nearby Boney's Mill, began construction of one of the county's most unusual dwellings, a project said to have taken twelve years. The 2-story house with its full-width, 2-tier engaged porch follows a unique plan: the sym-

DP 5 *William S. Boney House*

metrical facade bends gently inward from the gable ends, and the gable roof and decorated porch follow suit. The rooms radiate from a central foyer. Descendants believe that Boney devised the layout to accommodate a curving stair. Boney had the timbers for the house cut at his water-powered sawmill.

DP 6 Wallace

Punctuating the line of the Wilmington and Weldon Railroad are several small railroad towns of various eras. The railroad began in Wilmington in 1836 as the Wilmington and Raleigh, running northwest to link with the capital. When Raleigh investment fell short, the route shifted northeast (at Faison) toward Weldon and was completed in 1840, but not until 1855 was the line renamed the Wilmington and Weldon. In 1900 the Wilmington and Weldon became part of the Atlantic Coast Line Railroad, which had headquarters in Wilmington.

Wallace is the southernmost of the Duplin Co. towns along the route and a major business center. Here, as in *Teachey, *Rose Hill, *Magnolia, *Warsaw, *Faison, and Calypso up the line, rows of handsome, brick commercial buildings and frame houses with broad porches face the railroad that bisects the town. Grid-plan neighborhoods with frame houses and brick churches flank the railroad. The town of Wallace is believed to have been named for Stephen Wallace, a president of the Wilmington and Weldon Railroad. The central landmark is the **Wallace Railroad Depot** (ca. 1920; between N. and S. Railroad Sts. at E. Boney St.), still beside the tracks, a distinctive frame depot with dormers rising from its broad, bellcast hip roof.

DP 7 Teachey

This quiet railroad village gathers at the rail crossing the essential community components: a frame, Gothic Revival style **Presbyterian Church** (ca. 1900; 116 N.E. Ave.); a gable-fronted, frame **Lodge** (ca. 1870); a small frame store and some larger brick ones; and several decorated frame houses, including the **MacMillan House** (1908; 107 N.W. Ave.), with a tower and double porch presiding over the intersection.

DP 8 W. G. Fussell Farm

Early 20th c.; W side SR 1146, 0.1 mi. N of SR 1133, Rose Hill vic.; private, visible from road

Set in a pecan grove, the frame farmhouse combines the clean, American foursquare form with Craftsman details. A shingled packhouse and myriad other outbuildings recall the importance of tobacco to the area's early 20th-c. prosperity.

DP 9 David Fussell House

Mid- to late 19th c.; N side SR 1133, 0.6 mi. W of SR 1146, Rose Hill vic.

DP 9 *David Fussell House*

The frame house beside the road is among the county's best-kept examples of the coastal cottage form as built from the late 18th c. through the early 20th c. Here the porch is inset beneath the broad gable roof and has the local Doric-type pillars; the kitchen attached to the side—another local form—has a similar porch.

DP 10 Rose Hill

The community began as a naval stores depot with turpentine distilleries, and later industries included a cotton gin and a coffin factory, which operated from 1907 to 1992. A cluster of modest brick stores addresses the railroad, and along the tree-shaded streets stand representative examples of late Queen

Anne, bungalow, and Colonial Revival style domestic architecture. Rose Hill boasts the **World's Largest Frying Pan** (1963; Town Square), a 2-ton frying pan 15 feet in diameter, built to recognize the area's poultry producers and capable of cooking 365 chickens at a time.

DP 11 Concord Missionary Baptist Church

Mid-19th c.; W side SR 1101 at NC 903, Concord

The country church, built for an early 19th-c. Baptist congregation, combines the traditional gable-end form with crossetted Greek Revival door and window frames. The portico is a later addition. Nearby stands the **Stallings-Newkirk House** (early, mid-19th c.; E side SR 1101, 0.1 mi. S of Concord; private), a simply finished, 2-story, plantation house that began with a hall-parlor plan and was expanded with rooms to the right, plus a shed porch and rear shed. The depression in the yard survives from the old Wilmington to Raleigh stage road, of which only a few sections remain.

DP 12 Dickson Farm

Early and mid-19th c.; E side SR 1917, 0.2 mi. N of SR 1915, Magnolia vic.

An excellent example of the coastal plain cottage form prevalent in the county. The broad, deep gable roof shelters an inset porch in front and shed rooms to the rear. The house began as a smaller dwelling with one main room and two small rear rooms. It was enlarged ca. 1850 with an additional room, and the porch was rebuilt with sturdy, Greek Revival pillars. Another porch on the right side links the house to the separate kitchen. The home of Robert and Mary Dickson, part of a family that came to the county by the mid-18th c., the farmhouse remained in the Dickson family and has recently been restored.

DP 13 Magnolia

Named for its trees in 1857, the town was once the largest in the county and center of a bulb-producing industry. Despite the loss of its brick depot, it retains rows of 19th- and early 20th-c. frame houses that line Railroad St. and nearby blocks, including Greek Revival-Italianate cottages and Queen Anne and Colonial Revival residences. The library occupies a late 19th- or early 20th-c. **Frame Store** (104 W. Main St.) with bracketed false front, once a common commercial building type. The **Magnolia Academy** (1858; 120 S. Railroad St.) is a big, frame, Italianate edifice with bracket cornice, ornate windows, and central belltower atop the entrance pavilion.

DP 14 Warsaw

According to local tradition, the railroad town incorporated in 1855 was named after resident Thaddeus Love, who was locally associated with a popular novel entitled *Thaddeus of Warsaw* (1803). Now a principal business center, Warsaw has a good collection of brick commercial buildings facing the railroad, and blocks of frame and brick houses. The prime early 20th-c. residential avenue is E. Hill St., with examples of late Queen Anne, Colonial Revival, and bungalow styles, most notably the ornate Queen Anne style **Lucius P. Best House** (1894; 110 E. Hill St.), built for a merchant and cotton gin owner.

DP 15 *Buckner Hill House*

DP 15 Buckner Hill House

Ca. 1850s; NE side SR 1354, 2.8 mi. SE of NC 50, Faison vic.; private, visible from road

In this unusually massive, Greek Revival-Italianate style house a unique expansion of the center-passage plan has two 12-foot-wide axial passages that intersect at the center, separating four large rooms in the corners. When the broad doorways on all four sides are opened, the passages serve as interior porches. The house was built for Dr. Buckner Hill and his wife, Anna Maria Ward, on a 3,000-acre plantation that produced corn, rice, cotton, sweet potatoes, and grapes. The nearby Wilmington and Weldon Railroad, of which Dr. Hill was a stockholder, provided easy access to markets.

DP 14 *Warsaw Commercial District*

DP 16 William Wright Faison House

1830s; SW side SR 1304, 0.25 mi. S of SR 1354, Faison vic.; private, visible from road

Located on a plantation established in the 18th c., the house repeats the mid-19th-c. form with four rooms opening into a broad center passage, rendered in simple Greek Revival style. The tall pillars replaced a 2-tier porch in the 20th c.

DP 17 Faison

First known as Wrightsville Post Office, the town was established in the 1830s as Faison's Depot on the Wilmington and Raleigh (later Wilmington and Weldon) Railroad on land owned by Henry Faison, member of a local planter family of French Huguenot origins. With rail connections north and south, it prospered as a shipping point for forest and farm products. In the 20th c. it became a truck farming center, one of the largest fruit and vegetable exchanges in the nation, and since the 1929 establishment of the Cates pickle factory, a focus of cucumber sales and pickling.

In the antebellum period, planter families established homes here and made Faison the "Acropolis of Society" in Duplin Co. Several of their handsome residences survive, particularly along Main St. (NC 50). Best known is the **Faison-Williams House** (1853; Mr. Hines, builder; 701 W. Main St.; B&B), built for Isham Faison, a planter, postmaster, railroad agent, and civic leader known as "the patriarch of Faison." The center-passage-plan frame house has a broad, 2-tier porch with decorative sawnwork, plus flanking 1-story wings with

DP 17 *Faison-Williams House*

arched windows. Family tradition recalls a Mr. Hines as builder, probably William Hines or Enoch Hines, listed as Duplin Co. carpenters in the 1850 census. This was later the home of Faison's niece, Mary Lyde Hicks Williams, an artist known for her depictions of late 19th-c. plantation life.

After the Civil War, merchants and professionals built frame residences that continued familiar blends of Greek Revival and Italianate styles. The **J. B. King House** (ca. 1874; 206 W. Main St.) displays the transitional Greek Revival-Italianate style with double porch and decorative bargeboards. The **Thomas Perrett House** (1870s; 305 W. Main St.) is 2-story, side-passage-plan house with hip roof, where sawnwork lattice posts and brackets enrich 1-story porches. The **Walter L. Hicks House** (1886; 304 W. Main St. at N. Faison Ave.), a symmetrical, 2-story house, combines Greek Revival and Italianate motifs behind a 2-tier bracketed porch. At the **Dr. John M. Faison House** (1880s; 302 S.E. Center St.) a rectilinear, 2-story block with hip roof is enlivened by gables, 2-tier porches, and bay windows. By contrast, the **B. B. Witherington House** (ca. 1890; 407 W. Main St.) is an asymmetrical, Queen Anne style, frame house of intersecting ells, garnished with millwork from the bracketed porch and bay window to the gable ornaments. The board-and-batten **Faison Depot** (1888; 106 Park Cir.) has been moved from trackside to serve as a community facility.

The commercial district is compact and diverse. A notable survival of antebellum commercial life is the **Moore Lee Thornton Store** (ca. 1850–70; 205 Main St.), a 1-story, frame store with tall false front and double door. It was built for a relative of the present owner, Dr. William Thornton, the Duplin Co. native and astronaut. Facing the railroad are several late 19th- and early 20th-c. commercial buildings, including the brick **Southern Produce Distributors Building** (ca. 1900; 118 N.W. Center St.), with its tripartite false front and clerestory roof, which housed an early produce sales business. The former **C. F. Hines General Merchandise Store** (ca. 1900; 111 S.W. Center St.), more recently a fire station, features an original pressed-metal front at the upper level. Produce sheds from the early 20th c. stand near the tracks, as does the big **Charles F. Cates and Sons Pickle Plant** (1931; W. Center St.), which includes its original building and old wooden pickle tanks.

DP 18 Calypso Methodist Church
Ca. 1910; SW side SR 1317, Calypso

The energetic massing and corbeled brickwork of the small, Romanesque Revival church with its corner tower make it one of the most architecturally striking churches in the county.

DP 19 Bryan Whitfield Herring House
Ca. 1855; N side SR 1311, 0.6 mi. W of SR 1006, Calypso vic.; private, visible from road

The frame plantation house combines the 5-bay, 2-story, gable-roofed form and pairs of exterior end chimneys typical of the Federal era, with Greek Revival and Italianate motifs on the 2-tier entrance porch. In 1984 the house survived a tornado that destroyed its barn, outbuildings, and old trees.

DP 20 George W. Albritton Farm
Ca. 1910–30s; E side US 117 ALT, 0.8 mi. N of SR 1317, Calypso vic.; private, visible from road

The farmhouse blending Queen Anne and Craftsman features was home to a local pioneer in strawberry cultivation, who patented the Albritton strawberry. Across the fields, at the edge of the town of Calypso—once a thriving strawberry market center—stand the small houses built for workers on the strawberry farms, with an especially intact row of frame, gable-fronted **Strawberry Workers' Houses** on Parker St., including shotgun-plan houses and bungalows.

DP 21 J. L. Albritton Farm
1870s–80s; S side SR 1317, 1.0 mi. NW of NC 403, Calypso vic.; private, visible from road

The farmstead centers on a small 1½-story house of characteristic local form, with two front rooms flanking a passage, heated by end chimneys standing in front of the roof ridge; two smaller unheated rooms are to the rear. The dwelling is garnished in the picturesque spirit of the times with a front center gable and decorative porch. Outbuildings include tobacco barns and early 20th-c. hog houses, sheds, and garages.

DP 22 Dudley-Hicks House
Early 19th c., ca. 1847; N side NC 403, 0.4 mi. NE of SR 1317, Calypso vic.; private, visible from road

Amid the antebellum cotton prosperity, an early 19th-c. frame house was expanded into a massive, Greek Revival, temple form with broad pediment. Stout porch pillars and other details repeat the local Greek Revival carpentry. The house served as a summer home for the family of Gov. Edward B. Dudley of Wilmington and later as a dormitory for the nearby Franklin Military Institute, a Civil War training school for the local "Confederate Greys."

Bladen County (BL)

BL 1 Trinity Methodist Church

Ca. 1848; Alexander Carter, attributed carpenter; NW corner Broad and Lower Sts., Elizabethtown

BL 1 *Trinity Methodist Church*

The principal historic landmark of the county seat, the tall frame church occupies a commanding site on the main street near the Cape Fear River. Although Elizabethtown was founded with Bladen Co. in 1773 and received repeated visits from itinerant Methodist evangelist Francis Asbury, town and Methodism grew slowly. In 1834 the Elizabethtown Methodist Church was founded and a meetinghouse was erected. About 1848, amid prosperity based on the local naval stores industry, the congregation erected the present church. The severely plain building exemplifies the houses of worship constructed by most mid-19th-c. evangelical congregations, who emphasized functional spaces designed for maximum seating and hearing of the word. A single entrance with double-leaf door opens from the unadorned gable front into the sanctuary, which features a gallery on three sides and is brightly lit by 12/12 windows.

BL 2 Bladen Lakes State Forest Naval Stores Exhibit

SR 1511, 0.5 mi. E of NC 242, Bladen Lakes State Forest, Elizabethtown vic.; open Mar.–Nov.

Until the late 19th c. the vast stands of resinous, longleaf pine across N.C.'s coastal plain were the world's most productive source of naval stores—the tar, pitch, and turpentine used for waterproofing and preserving the wooden ships and hemp ropes of 18th- and 19th-c. naval and merchant fleets—and the industry was the source of the state's nickname, "Tar Heel State." The depletion of the region's longleaf pine forests and the close of the era of wooden ships ended the industry in the early 20th c. Naval stores production was by its nature ephemeral, and there are few physical remains to suggest its importance. The staff at Bladen Lakes State Forest has created an exhibit on the industry within a longleaf pine plantation that includes a reconstructed "tarkel" (tar kiln), boxed pine trees, and a turpentine distillery with a copper kettle that was used in a local distillery at the turn of the century.

BL 3 Stewart-Cromartie-Liles House

Late 18th c.; mid-19th c.; NE side NC 210, 1.1 mi. SE of US 701; private, visible from road

The rambling, handsomely sited frame house probably began with the Stewart family's small dwelling in the 18th c. During the 19th c. it was expanded into a long, I-house form with shed porch and rear shed and ell for the Cromartie family, leaders at nearby *South River Presbyterian Church.

BL 4 South River Presbyterian Church

Ca. 1850; NE side NC 210, 2.1 mi. SE of US 701

The little frame church is a fine example of the area's pediment-front, Greek Revival country churches, with corner pilasters carrying a wide frieze, and large, simply framed 12/12 windows. It was erected to serve a rural community dominated by Scots families, including the Cromarties.

BL 5 Mount Horeb Presbyterian Church

1845 (George Cromartie, contractor), 1932; NW corner NC 87 and SR 1712

A landmark on the old Elizabethtown-Wilmington road, the small frame church is the first and only building of a congregation established in 1845, when Presbyterians were expanding their numbers in the region. The 1-room, gable-fronted, frame sanctuary received a harmonizing portico in 1932, followed by the Sunday school wing.

BL 6 Carvers Creek Methodist Church

1859; Alexander Carter, attributed carpenter; W side NC 87, 0.3 mi. S of SR 1730, Carvers

The frame church of quiet Greek Revival simplicity stands amid an old Quaker settlement area where in the late 18th c. the indefatigable minister Francis Asbury first organized the Methodist movement in the county. Paired entrances, sheltered by a pedimented portico with octagonal columns, open into a sanctuary with galleries reaching across the tall, broad windows. Across the highway at the end of a lane, the related **Carvers Creek A.M.E. Zion Church** (late 19th or early 20th c.), formed after the Civil War by black members, raises twin towers above a brick veneered sanctuary.

BL 7 Oakland Plantation

Late 18th c.; N side SR 1730, 1 mi. NE of NC 87, Carvers vic.; private, visible at a distance from road

BL 7 *Oakland Plantation*

Standing on a bluff overlooking the Cape Fear and approached by a long allée of red cedars and moss-hung oaks, Oakland is a rare survivor of the great plantations that once flourished along the river. The long, 2-story house is of brick laid in Flemish bond, with double piazzas across both land and river fronts. The unusual plan, one main room deep, has an off-center passage plus a lateral passage along the land front. The house is believed to have been built for Gen. Thomas Brown shortly after the Revo-

lution, on land inherited by his wife, Sarah Bartram, who died in 1779. She was cousin to the famous naturalist William Bartram, who had explored her father's Cape Fear lands and described them in his *Travels*.

BL 8 Elwell's Ferry

SR 1730 at Cape Fear River, Carvers vic.

At a crossing where a ferry has operated since the turn of the century, a 2-car ferry still plies the river, providing travelers with a unique view of the Cape Fear and recalling the importance of ferries to the region's transportation until recent times.

BL 9 Clarkton

Established as Brown Marsh Station with the arrival of the Wilmington, Charlotte, and Rutherford Railroad by 1860, the town was renamed for merchant, farmer, and turpentine distiller John Hector Clark in 1874 and in the 20th c. developed into a tobacco warehouse center. Local landmarks include the **Clarkton Depot** (1915; NE corner Elm and Hester Sts.), a small, frame structure built for the Seaboard Air Line Railway and moved to a nearby site to serve as town hall in 1975, and the **John Hector Clark House** (ca. 1863; SE corner S. Grove St. and E. Green St. [NC 211]), an unusual, board-and-batten example of the coastal cottage with its porch inset under the deep gable roof.

BL 10 Brown Marsh Presbyterian Church

1828; Thomas Sheridan, carpenter; SE side SR 1700, 0.2 mi. S of SR 1712, Clarkton vic.

The oldest church in the county, Brown Marsh beautifully epitomizes the plain,

BL 10 *Brown Marsh Presbyterian Church*

straightforward meetinghouses built for the Scots Presbyterians of the Upper Cape Fear region. Settlers typically erected log meetinghouses, then replaced them with modest frame structures such as this one, only to replace nearly all of those with larger, Greek Revival churches in the 1840s and 1850s. This predominantly Scots congregation, which existed at least as early as 1795 and has roots going back to 1765, built two meetinghouses before erecting the present frame building. A chalk inscription on the ceiling, "Thos Sheridan 1828 [or 1818?]," suggests the construction date and the builder, a prominent local free black carpenter. The meetinghouse arrangement has an entrance centered in the long side as well as one in the gable end. Plain benches and a simple gallery focus on the pulpit, now located at the gable end.

BL 11 Bridger Company Building
1911; NE corner Railroad St. and NC 410/242, Bladenboro

The centerpiece of the village was built by the Bridger family, founders of the Bladenboro Cotton Mill that was the town's economic basis. The big, 2-story, brick commercial building, rendered in robust, free classical style, overlooks the railroad tracks from a prominent corner.

BL 12 Purdie Methodist Church
Ca. 1845; SW side NC 87, 2.8 mi. SE of NC 131, Tar Heel vic.

About 1845 Anna Maria Purdie, widow of planter James B. Purdie, built this small, Greek Revival chapel near her plantation as the successor to the old "Purdy's Chapel" built by her father-in-law, James S. Purdie, ca. 1800, where the Methodist evangelist Francis Asbury preached on at least three visits.

BL 13 Purdie Place
Early 19th c.; private, no public visibility or access

Like *Oakland, this 2-story, brick, Federal style plantation house overlooking the Cape Fear has engaged double porches front and rear. It features an exterior stair on the rear

porch and a (possibly later) stair in the off-center passage. Revolutionary veteran James S. Purdie, who lived until at least 1808 on the opposite side of the river, established the plantation, and after his death in 1818 it was the home of his son James B. and his son's wife, Anna Maria Purdie.

BL 14 Walnut Grove
1850s; N side NC 87, 0.5 mi. E of NC 131, Tar Heel vic.; private, visible from road

BL 14 *Walnut Grove House*

The remarkably complete antebellum plantation complex was built for James Robeson, descendant of Thomas Robeson, who was granted this land in 1735. The centerpiece of the complex is the symmetrical, 2-story, frame plantation house of restrained Greek Revival style. In a composite of current style and regional custom, the double-pile house has a 2-tier portico in front and a double piazza in back. The 19th-c. outbuildings include a dairy, a kitchen, a smokehouse, and a log barn. During the Civil War, James's widow, Eliza Robeson, managed the 5,000-acre plantation while her sons served in the Confederate army. Adjoining the plantation to the south on NC 87 is **Beth Car Chapel**, a Gothic Revival style Presbyterian chapel dating from the early 20th c., surrounded by a graveyard and live oaks laden with Spanish moss.

BL 15 Truss Bridge
Early 20th c.; SR 1316 over Cape Fear River, Tar Heel vic.

One of a fast-dwindling number of steel truss bridges, this through-truss bridge has survived while its larger companion, the McGirt Bridge that crossed the river at Elizabethtown, was replaced in the 1980s.

BL 16 Harmony Hall

Late 18th c.; end of SR 1351, S side SR 1318, 1.6 mi. W of NC 53, Tar Heel vic.; open limited hours

This small, frame, plantation house on the northeastern side of the Cape Fear presents a striking example of a regional form, with engaged double porches on land and water facades and a partially enclosed exterior stair rising between the landside porches. Here, in a rare survival, the exterior stair provides the only connection between first and second stories. The interior is simply finished and has a hall-parlor plan, later partitioned to create a center passage. According to local tradition, Harmony Hall was built before the American Revolution for James Richardson, a shipper to the West Indies who settled in Bladen Co. Restored as a local historic

BL 16 *Harmony Hall*

site after years of neglect, the house stands on a tract that extends down to the river. Recently acquired secondary buildings include the **Shaw-MacMillan Kitchen** moved from Columbus Co., a good example of the region's round-log, saddle-notched construction covered with board and batten; it rests on lightwood piers.

Columbus County (CB)

CB 1 Whiteville

The county seat, named for a local land-owner, was established in 1808 along with Columbus Co. (named for Christopher) and grew slowly as a political and trading center. The town plan focuses on the courthouse square at the junction of Madison St. (US 701) and Jefferson St. (US 74/76). The **Columbus County Courthouse** (1914–15; Joseph F. Leitner [Wilmington], architect) is the county's third, succeeding a wooden courthouse of 1809 and a brick one of 1852. In 1913 county commissioners employed Leitner, architect for the Atlantic Coast Line, to design a courthouse of fireproof construction. The straightforward design with its bold, simplified Doric portico reflects Leitner's scheme as amended to reduce the construction cost from $100,000 to $50,000—eliminating a proposed dome, limiting fireproof construction to the vaults, and replacing iron with terra-cotta trim. Several turn-of-the-century brick stores frame the courthouse circle.

CB 1 *Columbus County Courthouse*

A second community focus came with the Wilmington and Manchester Railroad in 1853. After the depot was established at Vineland, a mile south of the courthouse, to avoid disruption to the older community, a second commercial district developed by the tracks. The **Whiteville Atlantic Coast Line Depot** (ca. 1900; E. Main and Railroad Sts.) is a long, brick building with the deep eaves and shaped brackets typical of the era.

Several residential areas have predomi-nantly late 19th- and early 20th-c. architecture. These include **Madison St.** south of the courthouse, where an unexpected note appears in the **Smith House** (mid-19th c.; 214 N. Madison St.), a fully realized Gothic cottage with board-and-batten walls and acute side and central gables flounced with curved bargeboards, plus a matching out-building; another is **Pinckney St.** to the north, where the richly shingled **Coleman-Burns House** (ca. 1900; 206 Pinckney St.) presents a lively Queen Anne composition with projecting gables and bays and a peaked entrance tower in the elbow of the facade.

CB 2 Pentecostal Fire Baptized Holiness Campground

Mid-20th c.; E side US 701, 3.6 mi. S of NC 130, Whiteville vic.

A mid-20th-c. version of an important 19th-c. religious form, this complex has a large, frame arbor with a deep, encompassing hip roof, with a row of adjoining concrete block cottages—exemplifying the continued vitality of the camp-meeting tradition that began in the 18th c. among evangelical Presbyterians, Baptists, and Methodists.

CB 3 Chadbourn

The town on the Wilmington and Manchester Railroad began around the sawmill established by the Chadbourn family of Wilmington; it was incorporated in 1883. The lumber business gradually fell off, but by the early 20th c. citizens exploited Chad-

CB 3 *Chadbourn Atlantic Coast Line Depot*

bourn's rail connections to make it a tobacco market, truck farming center, and "strawberry capital." Local strawberry culture began in the 1890s, when local businessman Joseph Brown experimented with planting the berry, then in 1895 persuaded a Chicago newspaper publisher to sponsor a railroad trip and real estate venture, the Chadbourn Excursion of the Sunny South Colony, to entice impoverished midwesterners to move to Columbus Co. and take up strawberry farming on the cutover timberlands; some 160 families did so, and with the Sunny South Colony local strawberry production blossomed—from 600 crates shipped north on rail cars in 1896 to 350,000 crates in 1905—and made Chadbourn for 10 years the biggest strawberry market in the world. Although production diminished after an incursion of strawberry weevils and the strawberry market closed in 1973, berries are still raised locally, Chadbourn continues its annual Strawberry Festival begun in 1926, and the strawberry civic logo brightens street signs and other spots. The **Chadbourn Atlantic Coast Line Depot** (1910; Colony St.; open regular hours), recalling the centrality of railroading to the community, is an especially fine example of the frame depots of the period, with a jaunty roofline, patterned siding, and brackets; it has been restored as a local museum.

The business district on E. Railroad Ave. and N. Brown St. retains modest brick commercial buildings from the early 20th c. Houses from the growth era of the early 20th c. include bungalows and Colonial Revival residences, most prominently the **Robert E. Lee Brown House** (1910; Joseph F. Leitner [Wilmington], architect; 108 N. Howard St.), designed by the prolific Wilmington architect as a "colonial style residence" with an Old South aura suited to its client.

CB 4 Fair Bluff

Fair Bluff overlooks the dark waters of the Lumber River beneath moss-hung trees. Two buildings date from its early years as a river trading center. The **Powell House** or Trading Post (early 19th c.; E side Main St. at Orange St.) is a small, frame, coastal cottage with later expansions. It is said to have been built by John Wooten as a river trading outpost that preceded the town. Reflecting antebellum and later turn-of-the-century prosperity, the **Smith House** (mid-19th, early 20th c.; 213 Main St.) combines the traditional 2-story, 5-bay form with later porch and trim.

CB 5 Snowden Singletary House

Early 19th c.; SW side SR 1700, 0.3 mi. SE of US 701 BUS, Clarkton vic.; private, visible from road

One of the oldest houses in the county, the well-sited farmhouse typifies the I-house form with end chimneys, a slightly asymmetrical facade, and a shed porch balanced by rear shed rooms. The Singletary family, prominent farmers, settled in the area in the early 18th c., and the house has remained in the family. A family story recounts that in the 1850s Snowden Singletary's sister-in-law, Margaret Ann Currie, climbed through an upstairs window to elope with John Hector Clark, later founder of *Clarkton in Bladen Co.

CB 6 Lake Waccamaw

The arrival of the railroad along the northern shore of this large natural lake in the 1860s stimulated turpentine and lumber operations and encouraged tourism at the lake. The **Lake Waccamaw Atlantic Coast Line Depot** (ca. 1900; E side NC 214, S of US 74/76) was designed and erected by Herbert Smith, an employee of the Atlantic Coast Line who is said to have directed construction of several ACL depots in the Carolinas. The combination freight and passenger station exhibits typical board-and-batten siding, projecting signal bay, brackets, and kingpost gable ornaments. Nearby is the **Francis Beers Gault House** or Flemington Hall (1925; James B. Lynch [Wilmington], architect; W side NC 214, S of US 74/76), a large, frame, Colonial Revival house built for one of the region's leading lumbermen. It is now the administration building of Lake Waccamaw Boys Home.

CB 7 *Weyman Methodist Church*

CB 7 Weyman Methodist Church and Cemetery

1886; G. M. Summerell, builder; NE side NC 87, 0.2 mi. SE of NC 11

The little frame church, standing off the road at the end of an allée of trees, offers a refreshing break in a rather desolate section of highway. The present T-shaped building with a simple portico is an 1886 rebuilding of a church erected soon after the congregation's founding in 1840 and appears to incorporate elements of the original building. The cemetery retains late 19th-c. gravestones and wrought-iron fencing.

Robeson County (RB)

See Robert M. Leary and Associates, An Architectural and Historical Survey of Central Lumberton, N.C. *(1979); and Philip S. Letsinger,* An Inventory of Historic Architecture of Maxton, N.C. *(1982).*

RB 1 Lumberton

Named for the Lumber River, Lumberton has been the county seat and trading center of Robeson Co. since its founding in 1788. Its history is tied to the county's tripartite heritage of Native Americans (known as the Lumbee Indians), Scots, and African Americans. Nineteenth-century Lumberton, a rough-and-ready turpentine manufacturing center, was destroyed by fire in 1897. The architectural character of Lumberton reflects its proud rebuilding in the early 20th c., when local businessmen replaced the declining turpentine industry with cotton manufacturing, tobacco marketing, and banking.

Although the town centerpiece of the period—architect Frank Milburn's columned, brick Robeson County Courthouse (1908) in its parklike square—was razed in 1974 to make way for a formidable new brick courthouse, the surrounding blocks, especially **N. Elm St.** and **N. Chestnut St.**, are filled with early 20th-c. commercial architecture in various Italianate and classical styles. The **National Bank of Lumberton** (1914; 213 N. Elm St.) is a splendid little Beaux Arts bank with a creamy terra-cotta facade of paired Corinthian columns carrying a deep entablature. The town's oldest building is the small, brick **Proctor Law Office** (1830s; 517 N. Elm St.), a survivor of 19th-c. fires. The **U.S. Post Office** (1931; 606 N. Elm St.) repeats the predominant classical theme in a Georgian Revival building with inset portico. Other renditions of classicism appear in the **Planters Bank** (ca. 1925; 312 N. Chestnut St.), a dignified composition with rusticated stone base and three red brick stories above, and the more flamboyant **Carolina Theater** (1927–28; S. S. Dixon [Fayetteville], architect; U. A. Underwood Company [Wilmington], contractor; 319 N.

RB 1 *Carolina Theater*

Chestnut St.), a big, 3-story, brick building with molded stone trim and urn-topped roof balustrade.

North of the business district along Caldwell and adjoining streets lies the main late 19th- and early 20th-c. neighborhood. The **Luther Henry Caldwell House** (1903–4; T. M. Burney, builder; 209 W. 8th at Caldwell St.), built for a leading merchant, is the town's finest Queen Anne style house, with ornamental gables and a 2-tier porch reaching into an octagonal pavilion, touted as "the most modern, up-to-date residence in this section" by the local newspaper. On **N. Elm St.** north of 11th St., broad lawns and tall trees define a neighborhood of popular early 20th-c. styles, especially the

RB 1 *Luther Henry Caldwell House*

Colonial Revival in many forms and occasional ventures in Mediterranean Revivals.

RB 2 Humphrey-Williams House

1846; E side NC 211, 4.8 mi. NW of I-95, Lumberton vic.; open by appointment with Lumberton Visitors Center

One of the few antebellum plantation complexes in Robeson County centers on the house built for planter Richard Humphries, whose grandfather first acquired land here in the 18th c. The 2-story frame house, finished with simple, Greek Revival work, displays unusual emphasis on the porch living space, with the porch wall wainscoted and doors opening into both front rooms as well as into the center passage. The porch posts have capitals resembling coils of rope and stand on bases that are set forward of the porch floor, a feature seen more often across the South Carolina line, probably a strategy to slow decay. Outbuildings include an earlier house converted to a barn, a carriage house, a smokehouse, a servant's house, tobacco barns, and a mid-19th-c. store that served as the Raft Swamp Post Office (est. 1856). The farm won a 1991 Farm Heritage Award from the National Trust for Historic Preservation.

RB 3 Old Main, Pembroke State University

1923; NC 711, Pembroke

Pembroke State College for Indians was the nation's only 4-year, degree-granting institution exclusively for Indians from 1940 to 1954, when the Supreme Court decision ended racial segregation in schools. It began as the State Normal School for Indians in 1887, serving the county's large Lumbee Indian population. Old Main (1923), the oldest building on the campus, is a large, red brick structure with modest classical details. Following a 1973 fire, it has been restored as the Native American Resource Center.

RB 4 Maxton

The small railroad town boasts especially handsome buildings from its early 20th-c.

heyday. Centered on an 1862 depot on the Wilmington, Charlotte, and Rutherford Railroad, the village of Shoe Heel developed as the naval stores and lumber industries exploited nearby pine forests. The community expanded after the 1884 arrival of the Cape Fear and Yadkin Valley (CF&YV) Railroad. In 1887 the name was changed to Mack's Town for the many local Scots whose names began with *Mc* and *Mac*, and soon it was shortened to Maxton. After Maxton's rail lines were absorbed by the Seaboard Air Line and Atlantic Coast Line, the companies built a union station to serve both lines. In addition to its turpentine distillery, sawmill, and sash-and-blind factory, early 20th-c. Maxton flourished as a mercantile center for cotton farmers and the emerging truck farming business and boasted banks, schools, churches, fine houses, and Carolina Methodist College. The imposing Main Building (1912; Clint Parrish [Rockingham], architect) of the college burned in 1973.

Standing at the town center alongside the railroad, the **Maxton Union Station** (ca. 1915; 127 W. Central St.) is a brick building featuring a deep, bellcast roof covered with tile, handsome brickwork, and such Georgian Revival motifs as the Palladian dormer and flat arches over the windows. Nearby is the old **CF&YV Freight House and Cotton Platform** (ca. 1884; 121 Railroad St.), a utilitarian, frame building from Maxton's early days. Facing the railroad from the north is Maxton's most distinctive landmark, the **Patterson Building** (1911; Clint Parrish [Rockingham], attributed architect; Patterson and McCaskill Sts.), a classically detailed, flatiron building with a rounded corner dramatized by the cylindrical, domed clock tower added at local demand soon after construction. It was erected from designs by the architect of Carolina College to house the newly organized Bank of Robeson.

The town's late 19th- and early 20th-c. churches feature pairs of towers flanking broad central gables: **First Presbyterian Church** (1906; 302 N. Patterson St.), a Gothic Revival church of buff brick with crenellated detail; **St. George Methodist Church** (1885; 1950; E. Sanders St. at 5th St.), a late 19th-c. church transformed in

RB 4 *Patterson Building*

1950 with a concrete block veneer and red brick quoins; **St. Matthews A.M.E. Church** (1923; S. Patterson St.), a Gothic Revival building with corbeled brickwork; and **St. Paul's Methodist Episcopal Church** (1905–6; Henry E. Bonitz [Wilmington], architect; W. Sanders St. and Florence St.), a vigorous composition of locally made concrete block simulating rusticated and smooth stone, described in 1905 as "cement stone."

Maxton also offers a full range of late 19th- and early 20th-c. houses. **McCaskill**

RB 4 *St. Paul's Methodist Episcopal Church*

Ave. has an especially diverse grouping including the **W. J. Currie House** (ca. 1876; 350 McCaskill Ave.), a gabled Italianate cottage; the **Bailey Phillips House** (ca. 1913; 405 McCaskill Ave.), with its typical Southern Colonial portico in Ionic order; and the **Lathrop-Carter House** (1890; 459 McCaskill Ave.), another Italianate residence. Notable small house types appear in Queen Anne cottages; symmetrical, 1-story houses with tall pyramidal roofs and big porches; and bungalows, including the **John P. Stansel House** (1920; W. K. Moser, builder; 613 McCaskill Ave.), reportedly an Aladdin prefabricated house. **Patterson St.** north and south of the railroad also runs the gamut from bungalows and cottages to Southern Colonial mansions. The **Angus Currie House** (ca. 1896; Joe Hooper, builder; W side S. Patterson St.), a symmetrical cottage with steep facade gables flanking a tower, is one of several local houses credited to Hooper, a well-known black carpenter. The **McKinnon House** (1903; 369 N. Patterson St.), which combines Queen Anne massing with Colonial Revival detail, was built by lumberman Daniel McKinnon for his mother and sisters.

RB 5 Centre Presbyterian Church

1850; E side SR 1312, 0.2 mi. N of NC 71, Maxton vic.

RB 5 *Centre Presbyterian Church*

The big, frame church shares with other rural Presbyterian churches in the area the pedimented front, simple Greek Revival details, and windows at two levels lighting a spacious sanctuary with gallery. Its history is unusual. The congregation was organized by 1797, and in its earlier church the Presbytery of Fayetteville was established in 1813. In 1841

Floral College was established on an adjoining campus. The church served as school chapel, and the first president of the school was its pastor. The association continued until the school closed in 1878. Moved to the church grounds (1966) and restored as the education building is the 2-story, hip-roofed, frame building that was **Steward's Hall** of Floral College.

RB 6 Red Springs

"The Athens and the Saratoga of Robeson County" (1905) and "The Town of Handsome Homes" (1911) were the proud mottoes of this small railroad town when merchants and lumbermen commissioned a remarkable group of late Queen Anne and early Colonial Revival residences and institutional buildings—some by Charlotte and Wilmington architects—that still give Red Springs its architectural distinction. Named for the iron-oxide-tinged water of local mineral springs, the town was incorporated in 1896. Located on the Cape Fear and Yadkin Valley Railroad, it blossomed as a lumber manufacturing center graced by a hotel, churches, and a Presbyterian women's college. In 1911 the *Red Springs Citizen Trade and Industrial Edition* promoted its healthful climate, good fellowship and hospitality, and residences "surrounded by generous lawns and protecting shade trees and by educational and religious opportunities which surround the family with invaluable privileges and safeguards." Asserting that "no town of its size in the entire South can boast of as many handsome dwelling houses as Red Springs," the paper lauded the town's "Splendid Spirit of Co-operation to Improve and Build Up." In 1984, after a tornado ravaged much of the town, that splendid spirit returned as citizens rebuilt their community.

The chief downtown landmark is the **First Presbyterian Church** (1904–8; C. Walter Smith [Atlanta], architect; N. Vance St. at W. Third Ave.), a small but monumental Romanesque Revival brick church with a corner tower rising from a rusticated stone base. Hard hit by the 1984 tornado, the

RB 6 *First Presbyterian Church*

church has been painstakingly rebuilt, including its fine stained-glass windows.

South Main St. offers one of two principal concentrations of "handsome houses." The town's prime example of the Southern Colonial Revival style is the **A. P. Pearsall House** (1909; James M. McMichael [Charlotte]; 308 S. Main St.), built for a leading lumberman as a full-blown rendition of "classic Colonial style," with massive Corinthian portico and opulent detail. Other houses of lumbermen and merchants present a spectrum of late Queen Anne and early Colonial Revival styles: the **William P. Kay House** (ca. 1910; 409 S. Main St.), a symmetrical cottage with pyramidal roof and expansive porch; the **John J. Thrower House** (ca. 1910; 502 S. Main St.), a late Queen Anne cottage with steep gables and classical detail; the **Edward Hamilton House** (ca. 1905; 511 S. Main St.), blending Queen Anne massing with Colonial Revival symmetry and a Palladian motif center dormer; and the **William Gibson House** (1912; James M. McMichael [Charlotte], architect; 517 S.

RB 6 *A. P. Pearsall House*

Main St.), another big, Southern Colonial Revival house.

Variations on the Craftsman style of the 1910s and 1920s include the **McRae House** (518 S. Main St.) and the **Huggins House** (603 S. Main St.), another bungalow said to be manufactured by the Aladdin Company. The southern end of the street is anchored by the **Archie Buie House** (ca. 1902; 722 S. Main St.), a Queen Anne style house with swelling corner towers, variegated millwork, and wraparound porch.

E. Third Ave. and other streets just east of the business district constitute the other focus of "handsome homes," accented by the Gothic Revival style **Trinity Methodist Church** (1911; 204 E. 3rd Ave.). The **Dr. J. L. McMillan House** (ca. 1900; 215 E. 3rd Ave.) and the **W. J. Johnson House** (ca. 1895; 222 E. 3rd Ave.) blend Queen Anne and Colonial Revival elements in their massing and eclectic classical motifs; the latter features a crenellated, octagonal corner tower. An important early essay in the Colonial Revival style by its leading Charlotte proponent appears in the **Martin McKinnon House** (1898; C. C. Hook [Charlotte], architect; 225 E. 3rd Ave.), asymmetrically composed with free classical details.

Northeast of the business district stands the former **Flora MacDonald College** (1900–1910; C. C. Hook/Hook & Sawyer [Charlotte], architects; bounded by College St., 2nd Ave., and Peachtree St.). Founded by the Fayetteville Presbytery as Red Springs Seminary in 1896, the school was renamed in 1915 for the Scots heroine who had lived in southeastern N.C. in the 1770s. The school was led by President Charles G. Vardell, who also established its well-known gardens. The **Main Building** is a big, brick, Neoclassical Revival complex built in stages. Vardell, operating as contractor and superintendent, probably adjusted Hook's elaborate, Beaux Arts master plan to the tight budget. The centerpiece (1906) combines grand gesture and utilitarian simplicity, with a towering portico and dome dignifying a plain, 4-story, brick building. The central rotunda is an extraordinary turn-of-the-century room, aswirl with encircling balustrades and eccentric woodwork. The college closed in 1961 when the Presbyterians founded St. Andrew's College in Laurinburg. The campus is now the Flora McDonald Academy.

RB 7 William James Johnson House

1913; Okel and Cooper (Montgomery, Ala.), architects; SE side SR 1780 (Shannon Rd.), 0.2 mi. SW of NC 71, Red Springs vic.

Lumberman Johnson commissioned this Mediterranean villa style residence and,

RB 6 *Main Building, Flora McDonald College*

ironically enough, built it of fireproof concrete, brick, tile, and stucco, with every modern convenience. The landscaped estate with curving drives and fountains was built on a model farm of over 1,200 acres.

RB 8 Philadelphus Presbyterian Church

1860–63; Gilbert P. Higley, attributed builder; NE side SR 1318, 0.2 mi. NW of NC 72, Philadelphus

Built for a congregation organized before 1795, this is the most academic of the temple-form frame churches built for rural Scots Presbyterians in the region. Tradition cites Higley, a carpenter from Hartford, Conn., as builder. His New England origins may have influenced his use of Greek Revival themes, particularly the Doric portico set in antis beneath a broad pediment. In contrast to urban examples, the church retains a meetinghouse simplicity and more vertical proportions than the academic model. (See Introduction, Fig. 28.)

RB 9 Williams-Powell Farm

Ca. 1830; W side SR 2256, 1.0 mi. S of SR 2255, Orrum vic.; private, visible from road

The 2-story house presents a distinctive regional porch treatment also seen in nearby South Carolina: the full-height pillars of the 2-tier entrance portico stand forward of the porch floor, a feature to retard decay. The house employs a regional variation of the hall-parlor plan, with the stair rising from the central open porch in the rear shed. One of the county's oldest houses, it is described by family tradition as built by a local black carpenter for Giles Williams as the seat of his 1,500-acre plantation. The place remains in family ownership.

RB 10 Ashpole Presbyterian Church

1860; N side SR 1138, 0.2 mi. W of NC 130, Rowland vic.

The large, frame, temple-form church shares the directness and simplicity of Greek Revival country churches throughout the Presbyterian congregations of the area. Its unusual, tall belfry rises from amid its grove of trees. Except for the 1929 replacement of twin entrances by a single doorway, the building remains unaltered, including the gallery carried on Doric columns. The church descends from a nearby late 18th-c. union meetinghouse for Presbyterians and Methodists; in 1796 the Presbyterians established their own church here.

Hoke County (HK)

HK 1 Raeford

A 19th-c. turpentine distilling center on the Aberdeen and Rockfish Railroad, Raeford became the seat of Hoke Co. when it was formed in 1911 from portions of Cumberland and Robeson counties. Located in a section settled mainly by Scots families, the railroad town grew with its cotton mill, forest industries, and cotton and tobacco trade. Despite a late 20th-c. downtown fire, the town retains much of its early 20th-c. character. At the center stands the **Hoke County Courthouse** (1912; Milburn & Heister [Washington, D.C., and Columbia, S.C.], architects; J. A. Jones [Charlotte], builder; N. Main St.), a compact, tan brick building in the prolific architectural firm's conservative Neoclassical Revival idiom. South of the courthouse, the brick commercial district lining the broad (85-foot-wide) Main St. is punctuated by two substantial, 3-story buildings with free classical cornices: the former **Bank of Raeford** (ca. 1925) and the **Raeford (Bluemont) Hotel** (1927). The commercial section terminates at the **Aberdeen and Rockfish Railroad Depot** (ca. 1910), a small, brick station with a bellcast hip roof. In the residential blocks on three sides, prime examples of predominant styles include the turreted Queen Anne style house at **813 N. Main St.** and the **J. W. McLauchlin House** (ca. 1905; Marcus Dew, contractor; 111 S. Highland St.), a Southern Colonial style residence with Corinthian portico.

HK 2 Sandy Grove Methodist Church

Early 20th c.; W corner SR 1003 and SR 1105

The frame country church of great architectural presence follows an L-plan composed of two broad, gabled ells. From the elbow rises a dramatic tower with open belfry and tall spire.

HK 2 *Sandy Grove Methodist Church*

HK 3 Antioch Presbyterian Church

1882 (Nathan Hall, builder), portico and steeple 1957; SE corner NC 211 and SR 1105, Antioch

The most recent of the area's fine collection of rural Greek Revival churches built for Scots Presbyterians, the large, frame church differs little from its antebellum counterparts. Its plain, gable-fronted form was augmented in 1957 with a harmonious portico and steeple. The congregation was established in 1833 as a continuation of the Raft Swamp Church (1789).

HK 4 Mill Prong

Late 18th or early 19th c.; S side SR 1120, 0.3 mi. W of SR 1124, Edinburgh vic.; under museum development

The handsome plantation house repeats a regionally prevalent plan: a hall-parlor arrangement plus two rear shed rooms flanking an open porch from which the stair rises. In the 1830s the shed was raised to 2 stories, and later a back kitchen wing was added. Unusually fine craftsmanship of Federal character begins with the 2-tier entrance portico, featuring chamfered and tapered posts on squared bases arched at the bottom to prevent decay. Exuberant Federal mantels

HK 4 *Mill Prong*

HK 6 *Longstreet Presbyterian Church*

with fans and reeding have been returned to the house. Mill Prong is believed to have been built for John Gilchrist, a leader among the local Scots settlers. After 1834 it was the home of the McEachern family. The family cemetery contains several fine markers, including work by George Lauder of Fayetteville.

HK 5 Bethel Presbyterian Church

1855–56; Peter Monroe, builder; N side SR 1139, 0.2 mi. E of US 401

When local carpenter Peter Monroe erected the austerely simple, Greek Revival church for this old Scots Presbyterian congregation (est. 1776), he placed the pulpit against the front wall of the gable-fronted building—an arrangement seen in a few other area churches, including *Longstreet Presbyterian. In the early 20th c. the pulpit was moved to the opposite end, and a portico and domed belfry were added.

HK 6 Longstreet Presbyterian Church

1845–48; N side Longstreet Rd., Fort Bragg Military Reservation, 7 mi. W of Reilly St., from Cumberland Co.; special permission required (see note)

The isolated rural church is among the most interesting and best preserved of the area's

important collection of country Greek Revival churches built for Scots Presbyterians. It is the third building of a pioneer congregation organized in 1758 (along with *Old Bluff Presbyterian Church in Cumberland Co. and Barbecue Church in Harnett Co.) after a visit by evangelist Hugh McAden. The cemetery contains stones from the late 18th c. The building presents a striking contrast between the plain, meetinghouse character of the body of the church and the ambitious treatment of the facade, with a full-height portico with attenuated columns sheltering a stylized Palladian window and paired entrances. Here, as in a few other Presbyterian churches in the state, the pulpit stands against the front wall, beneath the Palladian window, and galleries carry around the simply finished sanctuary.

Note: The site is part of a large U.S. Army training ground and weapons range. The church is maintained and hosts an annual reunion. Approach to the church is from the Cumberland Co. side through Fort Bragg, and special permission is required.

Scotland County (SC)

SC 1 Laurinburg

The town was a minor trading post before the Wilmington, Charlotte, and Rutherford Railroad arrived about 1860. Selected as county seat after Scotland Co. was created in 1899 (and named in honor of the area's Scots heritage), Laurinburg prospered with the agricultural county's cotton boom from the late 19th c. until the end of World War I. The brick business district along S. Main St. includes the **McDougald Building** (1901; Henry E. Bonitz [Wilmington], architect; 101 S. Main St.), a 3-story hotel and furniture store featuring architect Bonitz's characteristically bold brickwork.

Early 20th-c. residential architecture concentrates on W. Church St. (US 74)—especially the 300–600 blocks—and Cronly St., S. Main St., and the neighborhood around the **Central School** (1906) on McRae St. The chief landmark of Church St. is the brick, Gothic Revival style **Laurinburg Presbyterian Church** (1907; 600 W. Church St.). Residences of leading merchants include the eclectic, tile-roofed, Colonial Revival style **Z. V. Pate House** (1924; 315 W. Church St.) and the **John F. McNair House** (1899, 1912, 1926; 502 W. Church St.), which has undergone repeated transformations from Queen Anne style to Neoclassical Revival to Tudor Revival. The **Thomas J. Gill House** (1904; 203 Cronly St.) is an unusual 2½-story house with Craftsman influences, built for a local merchant and later home of his son Edwin Gill, longtime state treasurer.

SC 2 Laurel Hill Presbyterian Church

1856; Peter Monroe, attributed builder; E side SR 1321, 0.75 mi. SW of US 15/501, Laurinburg vic.

The county's oldest church is an austere, Greek Revival building with pedimented gable front and simple, double-hung sash windows along the sides. The interior has a gallery carried on octagonal columns.

Founded here in 1797 by Scots families, Laurel Hill is mother church to several congregations.

SC 3 William Washington Bullard House

1882; N side SR 1411, 0.2 mi. E of SR 1415, Wagram vic.; private, visible from road

Among the finest of the county's abundantly decorated Victorian farmhouses of the late 19th c. cotton boom, this big, L-shaped house features a 2-tier sawnwork porch, elaborate brackets and other millwork, and a kitchen-dining wing to the rear.

SC 4 Richmond Temperance and Literary Society Hall

1860; NE side SR 1411, 0.1 mi. N of SR 1405, Wagram vic. (follow signs to John Charles McNeill House from US 401); open limited hours

SC 4 *Richmond Temperance and Literary Society Hall*

Known locally as the Temperance Hall, the small, hexagonal, brick building, 16 feet on a side, is a variant of the octagonal mode of the mid-19th c. This unique landmark housed a society active in the area (then Richmond Co.) for a half-century, its purpose symbolized by the wooden finial composed of an overturned wine glass on a Bible. Part of the broader American temperance society movement, this group was begun in 1855 by local young men who, concerned over the intemperance of elder Scots-men in the area, organized the society with local women and soon erected this Temp-erance Hall. At one time the ceiling was painted blue and had a star for each mem-ber—initially red, repainted black if a mem-ber broke the temperance vow, and white when the member died. It was restored as a museum in 1959. The frame cottage nearby is a portion of the birthplace of N.C. poet John Charles McNeill, moved and restored in 1967.

SC 5 Stewart-Hawley-Malloy House

Ca. 1800; N side SR 1609, 0.2 mi. W of SR 1610, Laurinburg vic.; private, visible from road

The oldest house in the county, this early I-house takes a classic regional form, with balancing front shed porch and rear shed rooms. It has a center-passage plan and re-strained, late Georgian finish. The dwelling was built for Scots immigrant James Stewart, farmer, postmaster, and storekeeper in the former village of Stewartsville, of which the house is the only reminder. This was also the birthplace in 1826 of Joseph R. Hawley, later Union general, governor and senator from Connecticut, and president of the U.S. Centennial Commission.

SC 6 McRae-McQueen House

Early 19th c.; 1870s; SW corner SR 1621 and US 501, Johns vic.; private, visible from road

Prominently sited beside a major highway, the farmhouse reflects two distinct peri-ods of construction. After the Civil War, farmer Peter McRae erected the symmetri-cal, 2-story house with Italianate brackets and airy, sawnwork entrance porch. In a common pattern, he retained as a rear wing the 1-story, Federal period dwelling built for his grandfather of the same name.

SC 7 Caledonia Methodist Church

1881; N side SR 1614, 0.2 mi. W of US 501, Johns vic.

The customary temple form is enriched with brackets punctuating the eaves, pedimented

portico, and belfry. The congregation, tak-ing the Latin name for Scotland, was orga-nized in 1835 by Methodist minister Allen McCorquedale of Argyle and became mother church of Methodism in the area.

SC 8 John Blue House

1890s; SE side SR 1108 (West Blvd./X-Way Rd.), 1.1 mi W of US 15/401 BYP, Laurinburg vic.; open regular hours

SC 8 *John Blue House*

The multifaceted local historic site centers on the ebullient late 19th-c. residence of farmer and inventor John Blue, a leader in the Scots community. His 2-story frame house is among the most extravagantly deco-rated late 19th-c. farmhouses in the state—an asymmetrical concoction of bays and tower, encircled by lacy, 2-tier galleries, giv-ing the effect of a small resort hotel or a steamboat. During the local cotton boom years, Blue gained fame as an inventor and maker of agricultural machinery, especially for cotton cultivation. His shop, later fac-tory, stood across the road until it burned in 1945. Given to the county by the family in 1976, the house he built has been restored locally.

Three local 19th-c. log dwellings have been moved here, permitting access to the Cape Fear region's venerable and rapidly vanishing log building tradition: the **John McDonald Shaw House** (ca. 1802), the only surviving 2-story log house in the county; the **McNeill Family House** (ca. 1810s), a 1½-story house with the logs skinned, not hewn, before being sheathed; and the **Jones-Litch House** (ca. 1810s), a fine, 1½-story, hall-parlor-plan dwelling with tightly joined hewn logs left exposed inside the house.

SC 8 *Jones-Litch House and John McDonald Shaw House*

SC 9 Masons Crossroads
SR 1128 and SR 1131, SE of Laurinburg

Several well-tended farmsteads compose a picturesque rural neighborhood extending roughly a mile from the junction of SR 1128 and SR 1131. Farmhouses represent popular forms and styles from the mid-19th through the early 20th c. Most visible are the **Jesse Mason House** (ca. 1895; E corner SR 1131 and SR 1128), an asymmetrical residence with Italianate porch; the **W. Frank Wright House** (1908; McColl & Benson, contractors; NE side SR 1131, 0.2 mi. NW of SR 1128), a large, Southern Colonial style house with full-width portico overlapping a 1-story porch; and the **Margaret G. McKenzie House** (ca. 1912; SW side SR 1131, 0.5 mi. NW of SR 1128), a rambling cottage with Ionic-columned porch. The big, gable- and gambrel-roofed frame barns at the Wright and McKenzie farms are among the largest and finest in the county. An unexpected note appears in the **William Mason House** (ca. 1860; end of SR 1103), a Carpenter Gothic cottage with a sharply peaked front gable.

SC 10 Gibson

The community at the South Carolina line began with the mercantile business estab-lished by Noah Gibson in 1846. In 1884 the village gained a depot on a spur of the Raleigh and Augusta Railroad and soon thrived as a cotton trading center serving farmers in both states. The large Gibson family, prominent in the area since the 1740s, continued mercantile and agricultural activities and erected stylish houses along Main St. At the center of town, the **Gibson Depot** (ca. 1884) exemplifies the small-town, board-and-batten depot, here combining passenger and freight functions under one long gable roof. Notable in the commercial district on E. Main St. are the **Z. V. Pate Building** (ca. 1916), a big, 2-story store with a blond brick facade, extending sixteen bays back from the street, and the **Bank of Gibson** (ca. 1916), of Neoclassical Revival style. The **Gibson Methodist Church** (ca. 1885, 1912; 101 Church St.) is a picturesque, L-shaped frame building with touches of Carpenter Gothic on its broad gable and corner tower. The **Thomas J. Adams House** (1902; 4320 W. Main St.) drapes a classically detailed Colonial Revival porch around a towered, asymmetrical, Italianate residence. South of the town center is the **David D. Gibson House** (1875; Joshua Moses Parker, carpenter; 260 McColl St.), one of the largest late 19th-c. houses in the county, with two large blocks linked by a breezeway and adorned with gables, brackets, and fancy porches. It was built for a planter and merchant who was the son of Gibson's founder.

SC 11 John Rhodes Gilchrist Farm

Late 19th to early 20th c.; W side SR 1105, 1.0 mi S of SR 1321, Laurinburg vic.; private, visible from road

The county's largest and most intact late 19th- to early 20th-c. farm complex centers on a farmhouse built in stages from the 1850s to 1920. The front 2-story block was built for John Rhodes Gilchrist. Dominating the farm is a massive, 2-story, frame barn (ca. 1915), its great gable roof sheltering twenty-two stalls and reaching out with a bay to protect the entrance.

Glossary

This glossary has been adapted from lists of architectural terms that have appeared in survey publications on historic architecture in N.C., including especially Dru Gatewood Haley and Raymond A. Winslow, *The Historic Architecture of Perquimans County, North Carolina* (1982); Davyd Foard Hood, *The Architecture of Rowan County, North Carolina* (1983); Peter B. Sandbeck, *The Historic Architecture of New Bern and Craven County, North Carolina* (1988); and Kelly A. Lally, *The Historic Architecture of Wake County, North Carolina* (1994). For analysis of period usages of early architectural terms, including many eastern N.C. references, see Carl R. Lounsbury, *An Illustrated Glossary of Early Southern Architecture and Landscape* (1994).

Adam or Adamesque: See *Federal style.*

Akron plan: A design for Sunday schools developed by an Akron businessman and Sunday school teacher in the 19th c. for maximum efficiency in use of space. A central room for general teaching was surrounded by smaller rooms, opening from it, for smaller class groups. Often an Akron-plan Sunday school was attached to a church with an *auditorium plan,* and in some examples the two could be combined by opening a partition, to provide a larger auditorium for large services.

anta, antae (in antis): *Pilasters* or piers at the corners of a building. Typically these are used at the ends of a colonnade (pair or row of columns) as part of a *portico* set into (rather than projecting from) the building, so that the antae flank the colonnade. This is described as a portico "in antis." Usually the antae are simpler than the columns they flank.

apse: A semicircular or polygonal portion of a building, such as a church or a courthouse.

arcade: A row of arches supported on piers or columns, attached to or detached from a wall.

architrave: The lowest part of a 3-part classical *entablature* (architrave, frieze, cornice). Often used by itself as a casing for a window, door, etc. A single architrave consists of an inner *bead*, a broad band, and an outer raised molding; a double architrave has two bands separated by a molding.

Art Deco: A style of decorative arts and architecture popular in the 1920s and 1930s, characterized by geometric forms and exotic motifs. So called after its popularization at the Exposition Internationale des Arts Décoratifs et Industriels, held in 1925 in Paris.

ashlar: Stonework consisting of individual stones that are shaped and tooled to have even faces and square edges.

auditorium plan: A plan employed in late 19th- and early 20th-c. church architecture, in which the *sanctuary* is treated like the auditorium of a theater, to maximize good sight and hearing of the word preached from the pulpit. Often the floor is slanted down toward the pulpit, which may be in front or in a corner, and pews may be arranged in curved or angled fashion concentrically from the pulpit. Sometimes confused with the *Akron plan,* which was a Sunday school plan often built in conjunction with an auditorium plan sanctuary.

ballast stones: Stones carried by oceangoing vessels for weight. In N.C. ports, such as New Bern and Wilmington, small, rounded ballast stones were unloaded when ships picked up heavy cargoes of timber and naval stores, and these stones were reused locally to build walls and foundations—very convenient in an area without good local building stone.

balustrade (baluster): A series of regularly spaced uprights (balusters) topped by a railing to provide an ornamental and protective barrier along the edge of a stair, roof, balcony, porch, etc. Balusters (and railings) were typically heavy and *turned* in the 18th c. as part of the *Georgian style,* became simpler and slenderer—often extremely delicate—in the *Federal style* of the late 18th and early 19th centuries, grew heavier again in the mid-19th c. with the *Greek Revival* and *Italianate* styles, and gained heft and ornateness with the *eclecticism* of the late 19th c.

bargeboard: A board attached and covering the sloping edge of a *gable roof* or *dormer*. Often sawn in a decorative, curvilinear design when used in the picturesque styles of the mid-19th c., especially the *Gothic Revival*. Also called vergeboard.

bartizan: A small, overhanging turret projecting from a tower, often rounded, sometimes polygonal; a feature of chateauesque, *Gothic Revival*, and *Romanesque Revival* styles, especially on church towers.

bay: (1) An opening or division along a face of a building; for example, a wall with a door flanked by two windows is three bays wide. (2) The space between principal structural members, as in a timber frame, the space between posts. (3) A projection from the *facade* of a building, in particular a polygonal or semicircular projection with windows, called a bay window.

bead: A rounded molding semicircular in section, often used to finish an edge or corner of a wooden element, such as a *weatherboard* or *flush sheathing* board. A bead provides a neat appearance and protects against splitting and wear.

Beaux Arts: A style or school of design characterized by the academic and *eclectic* use of historical—typically *classical*—architectural elements, usually on a monumental scale, as promulgated by the École des Beaux Arts in Paris in the 19th c. The Beaux Arts style attained great popularity in American architecture from the 1890s through the 1920s, especially in public architecture, banks, and mansions. Beaux Arts design stressed rational and hierarchical planning in form, layout, and detail. Beaux Arts classicism produced monumental architecture—epitomized and popularized by the World's Columbian Exposition of 1893 in Chicago—that employed Roman and Renaissance *orders* and forms on a grand scale, with imposing formality and dignity. Through commissions to nationally and regionally active architects, and through the federal government's supervising architect of the Treasury, a number of N.C. towns gained public buildings, especially post offices, in Beaux Arts influenced styles in the early 20th c.

belt course: A projecting horizontal course of brick, stone, or wood used on exterior walls, usually to delineate the line between stories, also called a *string course*.

board and batten: A method of covering a wall using vertical boards, with narrow strips of wood (battens) covering the joints between the boards. Popularized in the mid-19th c. as a suitable covering for modest wooden buildings in the picturesque movement, especially cottages and Gothic churches. The *Carpenter Gothic* style typically employs board-and-batten walls and decorative *bargeboards*.

bond: The pattern in which masonry, particularly brickwork, is laid to tie together the thickness of the wall; specifically, the pattern of the *headers* and *stretchers* seen on the outer face of the masonry. A header is a brick laid through the wall so that only its short end is visible. A stretcher is a brick laid along the wall so that its long side is visible. The principal bonds used in N.C. were *English bond, Flemish bond,* and *common bond.*

In English bond, a row of headers alternates with a row of stretchers, creating a very strong wall. English bond was used from the 17th c. well into the 18th c. but became rare by the end of the 18th c.

In Flemish bond, stretchers and headers alternate in each row and are staggered vertically, with each header centered over the stretcher below, creating a decorative checkerboard effect. Especially in the 18th c. the use of all *glazed headers* emphasized this pattern. (Glazed headers attained a vitrified, dark, shiny surface during firing by being placed toward the heat in the brick kiln.) Flemish bond was used from the 17th c. into the early 19th c. and occasionally into the mid-19th c. It was the predominant bond in the 18th c. Often 18th-c. brick buildings displayed English bond up to the water table and Flemish bond above it.

Common bond (also called American bond) has 1 row of headers to 3, 5, or 7 rows of stretchers. Until the late 18th c., 1:3 bond predominated; 1:5 and 1:7 ratios grew more frequent in the 19th c. Common bond was more economical than Flemish bond, and in some early and mid-19th-c. buildings the principal *facades* were of Flemish bond; the others, of common bond. In the mid-19th c., stretcher or all-stretcher bond came into use, with the outer bricks bonded to interior ones with concealed diagonal bricks. Flemish bond, either as a solid wall or veneer, saw renewed use in *Colonial Revival* architecture.

bracket: A device—ornamental, structural, or both—set under an overhanging element, such as the *eave* of a building. Brackets are especially characteristic of the *Italianate* style. Also, the decorative element attached to the ends of steps in a staircase.

bungalow: A house type and architectural style popular in the early 20th c. Typically defined as a relatively modest, 1½-story dwelling of informal character, the bungalow traced its origins to British colonial dwellings in India, as well as to the Arts and Crafts movement of the 19th c. Popularized through magazines and plan books, the bungalow was promoted as a wholesome, natural, inexpensive, modern, and convenient house. It saw its greatest development in California, which lent sunny associations of an ideal home. Its basic characteristics include a low-slung silhouette with a dominant roof form, usually a gable or clipped gable roof; 1½-story height even in larger examples; deep overhanging eaves; broad porches—engaged or attached—with square, squat brick piers supporting wood posts, which are often tapered; and informal plans emphasizing open spaces and deemphasizing passages. Decorative elements, particularly in bungalows rendered in the characteristic Craftsman style, stressed straightforward expression of construction elements, such as exposed rafter ends, triangular brackets beneath the roof, and natural shingles. Some bungalows incorporated Japanese and other Oriental motifs; a few featured Tudor or Spanish motifs; and in N.C. simplified *Colonial Revival* detailing was also popular. In N.C. bungalows began to appear in the mid-1910s, became wildly popular in the 1920s, persisted through the 1930s, but were seldom built after World War II, when the ranch house dominated the market for unpretentious, modern, convenient houses. The Aladdin Company, which had a factory in Wilmington, N.C., produced thousands of pre-fab bungalows, many of which were erected in eastern N.C., including several in Roanoke Rapids.

buttress: A vertical mass of masonry projecting from or built against a wall to give additional strength at the point of maximum stress. Sometimes wooden buttresses are added to frame *Gothic Revival* style buildings as decorative features.

capital: The topmost member, usually decorated or molded, of a column or *pilaster*. Each classical *order—Doric, Ionic, Corinthian, Composite*, etc.—has its characteristic capital.

Carpenter Gothic: A popular term referring to the mid-19th-c. adaptation of the *Gothic Revival* style to wooden buildings produced by carpenters, typified by *board-and-batten* walls and decorative *bargeboards* and porch trim.

castellated: Featuring elements associated with castles, such as *crenellation* and turrets.

center-passage plan (center-hall plan): A plan in which the hall or passage extends through the center of a house and is flanked by one or more pairs of rooms. A center-passage plan two rooms deep—with four main rooms divided by the passage—became especially popular among large houses in the Georgian period and is sometimes referred to as a Georgian plan (also as a *double-pile* plan). This plan continued in widespread use long past the Georgian period, especially from the mid-19th c. onward.

chair rail: A horizontal board or molding fixed on a wall at or about the height of the top of a chair; often the topmost member or cap of *wainscoting*. Until the mid-19th c. this feature was called a chair board.

chamfer: A traditional method of finishing a post, beam, *joist*, or other element, in which the square corners are beveled (cut away at an oblique angle). Often the chamfer ends in a decorative terminus or chamfer stop, the most common in N.C. being the curved lamb's tongue chamfer stop.

chancel: The end of a church containing the altar and often set apart for the use of clergy by a railing or screen. A chancel may be extended as a distinct architectural unit projecting from the main body of the church.

classical: Embodying or based on the principles and forms of ancient Greek and Roman architecture.

Classical Revival: A general term referring to styles that reuse the principles and forms of ancient Greek and Roman architecture. See *Greek Revival, Beaux Arts, Colonial Revival, Neoclassical*.

clipped gable: A *gable* where the peak is truncated for decorative effect; often seen in *bungalows*.

coastal cottage, coastal plain cottage: A recent, general term for 1½-story dwellings characterized by *engaged* or inset porches, so called because of their predominance in the coastal plain and tidewater areas of N.C. Not a standard architectural term, but useful locally as a shorthand word for a common form.

Colonial Revival: A late 19th- and early 20th-c. American architectural style that drew freely on architectural motifs associated with the American past, including not only elements of the Colonial period but also those of the early national era and even the *Greek Revival* and a host of *classical* designs. The *Southern Colonial Revival* and the *Georgian Revival* were developments of the broader Colonial Revival movement. The popularity of the Colonial Revival, chiefly in residential architecture, paralleled the closely kin

Beaux Arts classicism in public and institutional architecture. In N.C. the Colonial Revival saw occasional use as early as the 1880s, grew in popularity in the mid- and late 1890s—often mixed with the late *Queen Anne* style—and became a dominant residential style in the early 20th c. It has maintained its popularity in various guises throughout the 20th c.

colonnette: A small column, generally employed as a decorative element on mantels, overmantels, and *porticoes*.

common bond: A method of laying brick wherein one course of *headers* is laid for every 3, 5, or 7 courses of *stretchers*. Also called American bond. See *bond*.

common rafter, common-rafter roof: One of a series of rafters of uniform size, spaced evenly along a roof. In a common-rafter roof, the roof is made entirely of pairs of common rafters, which may join at the apex in a ridgepole or be joined in opposing pairs by a lapped joint without a ridgepole. This type of roof was used generally in N.C. from the earliest buildings on. See also *principal rafter*.

Composite order: A classical order characterized by a column whose *capital* combines *Ionic* volutes and *Corinthian* acanthus leaves.

corbel: A projecting brick or stone, used for supporting or decorative purposes in masonry construction. In a corbeled *cornice*, each row projects farther out than those below it.

Corinthian order: One of the five classical architectural orders, developed in the 5th c. B.C. The most ornate of the orders, its column is characterized by a *capital* with acanthus leaves and curled ferns.

corncrib: A building, usually small, for storing shelled corn or ears of corn. Usually a separate structure, sometimes attached to a barn; sometimes built with solid walls, sometimes with spaces between logs or slats for ventilation. A common outbuilding on N.C. farms from the 17th c. into the mid-20th c.

cornerblock: A square element, either plain or decorated with a circular or other design, usually marking the upper corner of a window or door *surround*. Typical of the

Greek Revival style during the mid-19th c.; also widely employed ca. 1890–1910.

cornerboard: A vertical board applied to an external corner of a frame building to finish the *facades* and cover the ends of the *weatherboards*. Often treated with a *capital* and base to form a corner *pilaster*.

cornice: The uppermost part of a 3-part classical *entablature* (architrave, frieze, cornice); also, a horizontal molded element used to crown the wall of a building, *portico*, or doorway. The term is loosely applied to almost any horizontal molding forming a main decorative feature, such as a molding (nowadays often called a crown molding) at the junction of walls and ceiling in a room. When enriched with *dentils* or *modillions*, it is called a dentil cornice or a modillion cornice. A raking cornice extends along a slanting (raking) side of a *gable* or *pediment*. A boxed cornice is a simple treatment with a vertical fascia board and a horizontal soffit board enclosing the ends of the ceiling *joists* where they project at the *eaves*.

crenellation, crenellated: Alternating indentations and raised sections (embrasures and merlons) of a *parapet*, creating a toothlike profile sometimes known as a battlement. In the medieval period these were defensive features of castles. Crenellated rooflines, especially on towers, are most often used in the *Gothic Revival* style.

cresting: Ornamental ironwork used to embellish the ridge of a *gable roof* or the curb or upper *cornice* of a mansard roof.

crossette: A lateral projection of the head of the molded frame (architrave) of a door, window, mantel, or panel; also known as an "ear." The motif is characteristically used in *Georgian style* architecture in the mid- to late 18th c. and recurs in *Greek Revival* and *Italianate* work in the mid-19th c. and in *Colonial Revival* work (esp. *Georgian Revival*) in the early 20th c.

cupola: A small structure, usually polygonal, built on top of a roof or tower, mostly for ornamental purposes, sometimes as an observation point or for ventilation.

dentils: Small, closely placed blocks set in a horizontal row (like little teeth, dim. of *dens*: dentil), used as an ornamental element of a classical *cornice*. Distinguished from *modillions*, which are spaced farther apart. Cornices might have courses of both dentils and modillions.

dogtrot: A plan seen principally in log houses in which two *pens* (log-walled units) are separated by an open *passage*. Relatively rare in N.C. today.

distyle: Having two columns, typically in a portico *in antis*.

Doric order: A classical order characterized by heavy columns with simple, unadorned *capitals* supporting a *frieze* of vertically grooved tablets or triglyphs set at intervals. Renaissance architectural authorities classified the order into the Greek Doric order, in which the column has no base, and the Roman Doric, in which the column stands on a base. The Doric order, often greatly simplified, was popularly used in N.C., especially in *Greek Revival* buildings during the antebellum period.

dormer, dormer window: An upright window, set in a sloping roof, with vertical sides and front, usually with a gable, shed, or *hip roof*. Used to light rooms in a half-story.

double-pen: A plan used in log houses in which two pens, each with its own end chimney, are placed side by side. See *pen*.

double-pile: A plan two rooms deep, most often used to refer to a *center-passage plan* house that is two rooms deep on either side of the passage.

double-shouldered chimney: An exterior chimney the sides of which angle inward to form shoulders twice as it ascends from the base to the cap, accommodating a fireplace in each of two stories. Typically in N.C. double-shouldered chimneys were employed through the 18th c. and into the 19th c. but were gradually supplanted by single-shouldered chimneys in the early 19th c. See *shoulder*.

dovetail: A joint in woodworking, commonly used in furniture and in plank or log building, wherein a piece of timber is cut (like a dove's tail) with two outward flaring sides meant to fit into correspondingly shaped spaces in adjoining members. A half-dovetail has only one edge flared; the other is straight. Various framing members might be dovetailed together. The most frequently noted usage is in construction of hewn or sawn plank (and sometimes log) structures with full- or half-dovetailed corner notches. In eastern N.C. this method continued to be used in small outbuildings from the 18th c. through much of the 19th c.

eave: The edge of a roof, usually above a *cornice*, often overhanging to shed water beyond the face of the wall. Eaves were often flush with the wall at the *gable* ends of 18th- and early 19th-c. buildings. Mid- and late 19th-c. eaves normally extended beyond the walls.

eclectic, eclecticism: An approach to design, including architecture, in which elements are selected from a variety of sources—historical, stylistic—and combined. Often applied to mid- and, especially, late 19th-c. architecture such as the *Queen Anne* style.

ell: A wing or extension of a building, often a rear addition, positioned at right angles to the principal mass.

engaged porch: A porch whose roof is continuous structurally with that of the main roof of the building. Typically in eastern N.C., a double-slope roof shelters an engaged porch. Partial *rafters* are attached to the main rafters of a *gable-roofed* house at a point partway down the gable slope, so that the roof breaks to a gentler slope within the block of the house and continues outward over the porch. *Shed rooms* to the rear may be treated in the same fashion. In an inset porch, the porch is set entirely within the block of the house, under a gable roof composed of a single set of rafters.

English bond: A method of laying brick wherein one course is laid with *stretchers* and the next with *headers*, thus bonding the thickness of brick together and forming a high-strength bond of alternating courses of stretchers and headers. (See *bond*.)

entablature: The upper horizontal part of a classical *order* of architecture, usually positioned above columns or *pilasters*. It consists of three parts: the lowest molded portion is the *architrave*; the middle band (plain or decorated) is the *frieze*; the uppermost molded element is the *cornice*. Variously adapted and simplified entablatures are incorporated into doorways, windows, mantels, and the like.

exposed face chimney: In a frame house, an *interior end chimney* built so that the outside face or "back" of the chimney is exposed rather than covered with *weatherboards*. It may be exposed as far up as the *eave* line or only in the first story. This feature appears in N.C. in New Bern and its environs. It also occurs in other areas along the Atlantic seaboard.

exterior end chimney: A chimney located outside the wall of a building, usually rising at the *gable* end.

facade: The face or front of a building.

fanlight: A semicircular or elliptical window, usually above a door or window, with radiating *muntins* suggesting a fan.

Federal style: A style of *Neoclassical* architecture popular in America in the late 18th and early 19th centuries, reflecting the influence of the *Adam* style, the Roman-inspired mode of Scots architects Robert and James Adam, which emphasized delicate, linear forms, attenuated proportions, and curved forms and spaces. In N.C. the Federal style began to appear along with the continuing *Georgian style* about 1800, and many buildings into the 1810s and even the 1820s show elements of both styles. The Federal style became widely popular in the 1810s and 1820s and continued into the 1830s and, in some areas, the 1840s, despite the growing influence of the *Greek Revival* style. The style is characterized by the use of delicate Neoclassical ornament such as fans, garlands, and sunbursts and by attenuation of such elements as *balusters*, window *muntins*, columns, and *pilasters*. Popularized by English and American builders' guides, it lent itself to individualized interpretation, particularly in lavish *reeding* and gougework, by local artisans.

fenestration: The arrangement of windows on a building.

finial: A vertical ornament placed on the

apex of an architectural feature such as a *gable*, turret, or *pediment*.

Flemish bond: A method of laying brick wherein *headers* and *stretchers* alternate in each course and, vertically, headers are placed over stretchers to form a bond and give a distinctive checkerboard pattern. (See *bond*.)

flush sheathing: A wall treatment consisting of closely fitted boards with tight joints, all laid in the same plane to give a uniform, flat appearance. Boards may be finished with a *bead* on one edge. Used in N.C. in interior finishes but also on the portion of an exterior wall sheltered by a porch, where it gives a smoother, more interior-like character than would lapped *weatherboards*.

flutes, fluted, fluting: Shallow, concave grooves running vertically on the shaft of a column, *pilaster*, or other surface.

foursquare, American foursquare: A popular house form 2 stories tall with a *hip roof*, taking a straightforwardly square shape and generally without elaborate decoration. The type was quite popular in the late 19th and especially the early 20th centuries, amid the Progressive era's emphasis on simplicity and practicality, but the terms "foursquare" or "American foursquare" are recent coinages, not period names.

frieze: The middle portion of a classical *entablature*, located above the *architrave* and below the *cornice*. It may be plain or ornamented. By extension, the term is often used to describe the flat, vertical board used beneath a cornice and above the *weatherboards* of a frame building, and also for the flat board between the *pilasters* and shelf (*cornice*) of a mantel.

gable: The triangular portion of a wall formed or defined by the two sloping sides of a ridged roof.

gable roof: A roof formed with two opposing planes sloping to a common ridge, forming triangular *gables* at the ends. Sometimes called a pitched roof or A-roof. Gable roofs were the most common roof form in N.C. buildings.

gambrel roof: A roof with two pitches rising to a ridge, the upper slope being markedly flatter than the lower one. In eastern N.C., gambrel-roofed houses were built in the 18th c. and continuing into the early 19th c. The form was revived and sometimes called "Dutch" or "Dutch colonial" in the early 20th-c. *Colonial Revival* era.

Georgian plan: See *center-passage plan*.

Georgian Revival: A revival of Georgian architectural forms, both in England and America, and as part of the larger *Colonial Revival* style in America. In N.C. the style became especially popular after about 1910 and often took the form of symmetrical, restrained designs with rich *classical* detail, quite frequently in a Virginia vocabulary. The Georgian Revival was particularly popular for public buildings, churches, and residences, often executed in red brick with contrasting white trim.

Georgian style: The prevailing architectural style of the 18th c. in Great Britain and her North American colonies. Popularly called Georgian style (not a term at the time) after the monarchs who reigned during its heyday, George I, George II, and George III. It is derived from *classical* Renaissance and Baroque forms and was shaped in Britain by architects such as Christopher Wren and James Gibbs. Builders' guides published in England, such as those of Batty Langley, Abraham Swan, James Gibbs, William Salmon, William Pain, and others, made the elements of the style available to craftsmen and clients. As expressed in relatively simple form in N.C., the Georgian style is characterized by symmetrical forms and plans, relatively heavy classical moldings, raised *panels*, robust classically derived ornament, and such motifs as *pediments*, *modillion cornices*, *turned balustrades*, and *crossetted surrounds* on doorways, windows, and mantels. Georgian motifs appeared in a few N.C. buildings in the 1750s, but fully realized examples of the style came only in the late 1760s and thereafter. Use of the Georgian style continued into the early 19th c., often in transitional combinations with the *Federal* style.

glazed header: A brick having a glossy dark

surface, ranging in color from gray green to almost black, formed through direct exposure to flame and intense heat during the firing process. In *Flemish-bond* brickwork this glazed surface is often used for decorative effect by laying the brick so that the glazed ends of headers emphasize the checkerboard pattern in the wall or, in some cases, delineate letters, numerals, or other designs. Such work appeared in the mid-18th c. in northeastern N.C. and in the late 18th and early 19th centuries in the western Piedmont.

Gothic Revival: The revival of the forms and ornament of medieval Gothic architecture, characterized by the use of the pointed arch, *buttresses*, pinnacles, and other Gothic details. Begun in Europe in the late 18th c., the Gothic Revival came into N.C. use in the mid-19th c. (though there were a few early gestures in the style in the 1810s and 1820s, chiefly in work by architect William Nichols). The Gothic Revival style appeared occasionally in residential architecture in picturesque cottages (a few in the 1850s, more in the post–Civil War era) influenced by the publications of Andrew Jackson Downing, but it was vastly more popular in religious architecture. Introduced in the state by the Episcopal Church in the 1830s and 1840s, the Gothic Revival flourished from the 1850s onward as a predominant religious style and has continued in use in church architecture through the 20th c.

graining: A decorative painted treatment on wood, usually used to simulate exotic or costly woods, sometimes stylized to the point of abstraction.

Greek Revival: The mid-19th-c. revival of the forms and ornamentation of the architecture of ancient Greece. The Greek Revival, often much simplified, was the most popular style in N.C. from the 1830s until the Civil War. A few early motifs appear in the 1810s and 1820s in work by architect William Nichols, and in some areas elements of the style persist into the 1870s. Builders' guides by Asher Benjamin and Minard Lafever were widely used sources. The Greek Revival domi-

nated fashionable architecture and was translated by local carpenters into greatly simplified versions. It is characterized by broad, rectilinear, usually symmetrical forms, wide *friezes* and *pilasters*, flat surfaces, doors and window frames marked by *cornerblocks* at the corners, and heavy mantels featuring columns and *entablatures*, or a plain pilaster and frieze format. Porches are often treated as *porticoes*, with the *Doric order* frequently employed—and simplifications thereof often with squared *pillars*. Courthouses and churches were often rendered as gable-fronted temple forms with projecting or recessed porticoes, but this treatment was rare in residential architecture.

hall-parlor plan: A traditional plan consisting of two principal rooms: a larger "hall," often nearly square, and an adjoining smaller "parlor." In most instances the hall was entered directly from the outside and had a fireplace centered on the end wall. It was the room where most domestic activities took place and from which doors led to other rooms and to the stairs. The smaller parlor tended to be used for sleeping. This plan was used from the late 17th c. through the 18th c. in top-quality houses in N.C. and continued into the mid-19th c. in middling and small houses.

header: A brick placed in a wall so that the short end faces outward. Used with *stretcher* bricks to form a *bond* in the wall.

hexastyle: Having six columns, usually referring to a portico.

hip roof: A roof that slopes back equally from each side (usually four) of a building. A hip roof may have a pyramidal form or have a slight ridge. A hip roof on a porch usually has three slopes, the center one being widest.

I-house: A term coined by geographer Fred Kniffen to describe a certain house type commonly seen in states beginning with the letter *I*, but also seen frequently elsewhere, including N.C. Kniffen applied the term to 2-story houses one room deep and two rooms or more wide. The tall, thin profile also suited the term

"I-house." The term is employed as a convenient shorthand for a common form but has no basis in traditional architectural language.

inset porch: See *engaged porch*.

interior end chimney: A chimney positioned inside the end wall of a house.

International style: A term first used by Henry-Russell Hitchcock and Philip Johnson in 1932 to describe the nontraditional architecture that had begun in the 1920s in Europe and was appearing in the United States. Simplified, abstracted forms, rejection of historical allusions, and direct expression of volume and materials were among its characteristics. Before World War II the style was most popular in advanced urban settings and among especially progressive clients. It became more generally used after World War II and continued into the 1970s. The Bauhaus and Miesian styles are related developments.

Ionic order: One of the five *orders* of classical architecture, which was associated with the Ionian Greeks and was used by the Greeks and the Romans. The order is characterized by a column whose *capital* features large volutes (spirals), sometimes enriched with other decoration. The Ionic order was considered to be between the plain *Doric* and the elaborate *Corinthian*.

Italianate: A revival of elements of Italian Renaissance architecture popular during the mid- and late 19th c., influenced by both villas and palazzos. Characterized by the presence of deep overhanging *eaves* and *cornices* supported by ornate *brackets*, arched windows often with heavy hoodmolds, and, less often, square towers placed centrally or asymmetrically. In antebellum N.C., where examples appeared by the 1840s and 1850s, the style was restricted to large towns and progressive rural areas and found favor among elite, relatively cosmopolitan clients. Later in the 19th c. the style found widespread use in commercial and industrial as well as residential architecture.

joist: One of a series of parallel timbers or beams, usually set on edge, that span a room from wall to wall to support a floor or ceiling; a beam to which floorboards, ceiling boards, or plaster laths are nailed. In the 18th c., ceiling joists meant to be left exposed in a neatly finished house were often finished with a *bead* or *chamfer*.

keystone: The central, wedge-shaped stone at the crown of an arch or in the center of a *lintel*.

kitchen: A room or building used for cooking and sometimes eating. In the 17th, 18th, and much of the 19th c., common practice in N.C., especially in the countryside but also in towns, was the use of a freestanding kitchen as one of the domestic outbuldings. This was regarded as a specifically southern practice, variously attributed to keeping the heat, smells, and threat of fire separated from the dwelling house. Kitchens commonly had large chimneys with cooking fireplaces until the late 19th c. Some had one room, some two, with a separate dining room, and many had upper chambers for servants. In the late 19th and early 20th centuries kitchens became more frequently attached to the main house by a breezeway or *passage*, and in more and more cases were incorporated into the main block of the house as cooking technology changed from open fireplaces to cookstoves.

lintel: A horizontal element of wood or stone that spans an opening. In masonry construction it frequently supports the masonry above the opening.

marbling: Painted treatment on wood simulating the color and texture of marble. Now often called marbleizing, but the 18th- and 19th-c. term was "marbling."

medallion: A large, typically circular or oval ornament that adorns the center of a ceiling.

meetinghouse: A place of worship or public gathering, often preferred by dissenting denominations and sects over the word "church" when describing a building. Meetinghouses were typically plain rather than elaborated. They were planned to focus on the word, with emphasis on the pulpit rather than the altar. In a meeting-house plan, typically benches or pews were arranged around the pulpit, which was often on the long side (often the north) rather than in the gabled end. In many cases the main entrance was on the long side opposite the pulpit, and secondary entrances opened on the two gable ends.

Moderne: A general architectural term applied to designs from the 1920s through the 1940s and sometimes the 1950s, defined by stylized forms, often streamlined with smooth curves and flat planes.

modillion: A horizontal *bracket*, often in the form of a plain block, supporting the underside of a *cornice*. Undercut modillions, with an S-curved bottom outline, were used in classically detailed buildings.

mortise and tenon: A joint made by one member having its end cut as a projecting tongue (tenon) that fits exactly into a groove or hole (mortise) in the other member. Once joined in this fashion, the two pieces are often secured by a peg. In traditional framed buildings, many elements are so joined.

muntin: The strip of wood separating the panes of a window *sash*, often molded.

Neoclassical: A general term for an approach to design drawing inspiration from ancient Greek and Roman precedents. It is often used in reference to the revival of Roman, then Greek classical forms in the late 18th and early 19th centuries (the *Federal* and *Greek Revival* styles), and also to the renewed interest in classicism around the turn of the 20th c., though the latter is frequently called Neoclassical Revival or *Beaux Arts* classicism.

newel, newel post: The principal post used to terminate the railing or *balustrade* of a flight of stairs.

order: In *classical* and *Neoclassical* architecture, the basic unit of design, composed of a column with base, shaft, *capital*, and *entablature*, proportioned and detailed according to certain rules codified in the Renaissance and based on observation of ancient Roman examples. Each order—Tuscan, *Doric*, *Ionic*, *Corinthian*—had its own distinctive features and proportions. In N.C. some architects and builders used British, then American, books that explained these rules and illustrated both the elements and how to work out the proportions. Often the motifs of the orders were freely adapted in actual use.

Palladian: An approach to design associated with the buildings and books of the 16th-c. Italian architect Andrea Palladio and popularized by British architectural books of the 18th c. The term is often used to describe buildings with a symmetrical three- or five-part composition, usually consisting of a large central block flanked by (usually smaller) wings. It is also applied to buildings with a central pedimented *pavilion* projecting from the *facade*.

Palladian window: A window design featuring a symmetrical, three-part arrangement with a central arched opening flanked by lower, square-headed openings and separated from them by columns, *pilasters*, piers, or narrow vertical *panels*. Inspired by the work of Renaissance architect Andrea Palladio, who like many of his contemporaries, often used this motif. The period term was "Venetian window."

panel: A portion of flat surface set off by molding or some other decorative device. Generally, *raised panels* were used as well as flat panels in the 18th and early 19th centuries as part of the *Georgian style*. Flat panels became popular with the *Federal style* in the early 19th c. and continued in use throughout most of the century, though slightly raised panels came back into use late in the 19th c. and were reiterated in the *Georgian Revival* style.

parapet: A low wall along a roof or terrace, used as decoration or protection.

passage: An enclosed space leading between rooms, today usually called a "hall" or "hallway." In the 17th, 18th, and much of the 19th c. the term "passage" was employed, and "hall" more often referred to a principal major room.

paved shoulder: In a brick chimney, the treatment of the sloped transition from the wider base to the narrower shaft by a smooth diagonal surface topped with bricks laid flat like pavers on the slope. This treatment was generally used in the 18th c. but was superseded in the early 19th c. by the *stepped shoulder*.

pavilion: A portion of a building's *facade* that projects forward slightly to give architectural emphasis, sometimes accentuated by a *pediment*.

pediment: A crowning element of *porticoes*, *pavilions*, doorways, and other architectural features, usually of low triangular form, with a *cornice* extending across its base and carried up the raking sides. Sometimes broken in the center as if to accommodate an ornament; sometimes open at the bottom; sometimes of segmental, elliptical, or serpentine form.

pen: A rectangular or square structural unit. The term is usually used when referring to log buildings and specifies a structure enclosed by log walls. Most single-pen log houses had only one room in the space enclosed by the logs, but within a single pen there may be partitions dividing the space into smaller rooms, such as a *hall-parlor plan*. Many dwellings in N.C. were single-pen structures. Often these were expanded into two-pen houses following the *double-pen*, *saddlebag*, or *dogtrot* plans.

pent: A single-sloped lean-to or *shed*, typically small, attached to a building, or, such a roof.

piano nobile: The principal story in a building; the term is usually employed when the main story is above the ground story and is taller and more elaborately treated than the story beneath. Characteristic of Renaissance palaces, the treatment appears in N.C. chiefly in public buildings such as courthouses where the courtroom is in the second story.

piazza: An Italian term for a plaza. Used in the 18th, 19th, and 20th centuries in N.C. for a covered porch, pronounced with a short *a*, and usually for a porch large enough to accommodate seating.

pilaster: A shallow pier or rectangular column projecting only slightly from or at-

tached to a wall. Pilasters are usually decorated like columns with a base, shaft, and *capital*.

pillar: A general term for a vertical supporting member, often used interchangeably with pier, post, and column. Commonly used for fairly massive examples, often square in section, as opposed to columns that take a particular *order* and are circular in section.

porte cochere: A projecting porch that provides protection for vehicles and passengers. A common feature of the *Queen Anne*, *Colonial Revival*, and *bungalow* houses of the late 19th and early 20th centuries. Predecessor of the carport.

portico: A roofed space, open or partly enclosed, often with columns and a *pediment*, usually employed as centerpiece of the *facade* of a building and to shelter the main entrance. Typically treated in *classical* fashion.

principal rafter, principal-rafter roof: A member of a pair of large, diagonal framing members composing a truss roof. In a principal-rafter roof, the large principal rafters carry horizontal purlins, upon which rest secondary *common rafters*. This roof type was unusual in N.C. except in especially large or heavily built structures and in Germanic framed buildings in the Piedmont.

Queen Anne: A popular late 19th-c. revival of early 18th-c. English architecture, characterized by irregularity of plan and massing and a variety of textures. In N.C. the style was frequently rendered in wood in residential architecture, with asymmetrical plans, high *hip roofs* with projecting *gables* and *dormers*, and abundant mass-produced, *eclectic* ornament. The style continued into the early 20th c. and was frequently executed with *Colonial Revival* classically inspired detail.

quoins: Ornamental blocks of wood, stone, brick, or stucco placed at the corners of a building and projecting slightly.

rafter: A structural timber rising from the plate at the top of a wall to the ridge of the roof and supporting the roof covering.

raised panel: A portion of a flat surface, as in

the panel of a door or *wainscot*, that is set off from the surrounding area by a molding or other device and is raised above the surrounding area. Raised panels were especially typical of *Georgian* architecture and appeared in N.C. from the 18th c. into the early 19th c.

reed, reeding: Decoration consisting of parallel convex moldings, often vertically applied to a column or *pilaster*, derived from a bundle of reeds.

return: A horizontal portion of a *cornice* that extends part of the way across the *gable* end of a structure at *eave* level.

Romanesque Revival: A 19th-c. revival of pre-Gothic medieval architecture, characterized by round-headed arches, often with heavy stone-faced stone or brick walls, sometimes with foliated *terra-cotta* ornament.

rosehead nail: A handmade, wrought-iron nail having a broad, conical head. Often the heads of such nails have four or five faces or facets formed by the hand hammering process.

saddlebag: A plan in which two single-pen rooms are joined together, separated by a single interior chimney. Especially common in log houses but also applied to small frame houses with two rooms flanking a center chimney.

sanctuary: (1) A term used generally for a church, a holy place, or the main worship space within a church. (2) The portion of the church containing the principal altar, within the *chancel* and east of the choir.

sash: The frame, usually of wood, that holds the pane(s) of glass in a window. It may be movable or fixed. It may slide in a vertical plane or may pivot. Windows with double-hung sash are sometimes described by the number of panes in the upper and lower sash, such as 9/9 (9 over 9), 9/6 (9 over 6), etc. In period documents, however, they were not described in that way, but by the total number of panes (lights), thus, for example, 15 lights of sash.

Second Empire: An *eclectic* style derived from the grandiose architecture of the French Second Empire of Napoleon III,

popularly used in America from the 1860s to the 1880s, especially for public buildings, and characterized by heavy ornament and high mansard roofs with *dormers*. At the time it was frequently called the "French" style. In N.C. the Second Empire style was relatively rare and mainly urban, appearing in residences and a few public and commercial buildings associated with the recovery of wealth after the Civil War.

segmental arch: An arch formed on a segment of a circle or an ellipse.

shed, shed room: (1) A 1-story appendage to a larger structure, covered by a single-slope roof that "leans" (as in "lean-to") against the principal building mass. A shed porch is one with such a single-slope roof. Often a rear shed or shed rooms may be built as a rear, balancing pendant to a front porch of similar form, or as a pendant to an *engaged porch*, in which case the double-slope roof form is usually repeated. (2) A simple, general-purpose outbuilding, often used for storage.

shotgun: A house or house plan one room wide and two or more rooms deep, with the narrow, usually gable-fronted, end toward the street. The entrance opens directly into the front room, and doors lead directly into each successive room proceeding to the rear. This narrow house form was built most often in African American neighborhoods, though not exclusively so, and some writers argue that it had its origins in New Orleans, the West Indies, and ultimately African precedents. In N.C. the form was built most in the rapid urbanization of the early 20th c.

shoulder: The sloping shelf or ledge created on the side of a masonry chimney where the width of the chimney changes. Sometimes called "weathering."

sidelight: A framed area of fixed glass of one or more panes located to either side of a door or window opening.

side-passage, side-hall plan: A plan with an unheated (no chimney) passage along one side and one or (usually) two heated rooms on the other, with the main entrances at the front and rear of the passage. Side-passage plans were especially common in late 18th- and early 19th-c. townhouses, particularly in New Bern, but the plan was also used in rural dwellings, especially in the Albemarle region. In the late 19th and early 20th centuries, many towns, especially New Bern, Elizabeth City, and others along the coast, saw construction of hundreds of side-passage plan houses 2 stories tall with *gable* fronts, especially as working- and middle-class dwellings on narrow lots.

sill: A heavy horizontal timber, positioned at the bottom of the frame of a wood structure, that rests on top of the foundation; also, the horizontal bottom member of a door or window frame.

smokehouse: A small building where meat (mainly pork) is cured by smoking, and subsequently stored, usually hanging from *joists* or *rafters*. A common outbuilding type in N.C., typically built of frame or log without windows and of tight construction.

Southern Colonial Revival: A primarily residential style within the broader *Colonial Revival*, which drew upon themes popularly associated with the antebellum plantation house but included under the broader term "colonial." The typical "Southern Colonial" residence featured a massive, full-height *portico* that overlapped a 1-story porch or terrace that extended across the front *facade* and in some cases around the side(s) of the house. Houses of this style were typically fairly symmetrical, with broad center *passages*, and some examples retained vestiges of *Queen Anne* massing. The style was quite popular from the 1890s to the 1910s in N.C. and appeared in designs by many local and regional architects.

Spanish Colonial Revival, Spanish Revival, Spanish Mission Revival: The revival of designs associated with the Spanish colonial missions in the American southwest and in Mexico and translated loosely in popular architecture into stuccoed buildings with red tile roofs and a variety of motifs such as arched openings, exposed timbers, and towers. The style was rela-

tively rare in N.C. but did appear in a few towns in the 1910s and 1920s, particularly in railroad buildings and residences.

spindle frieze: A row of lathe-turned members (spindles), usually as a decorative feature of a porch below the *cornice*.

stepped shoulder: On a brick chimney, a sloping ledge formed by the successively stepped course of bricks to make the transition from the lower, wider base to the narrower stack. Generally in N.C. stepped shoulders appear in the early 19th c., superseding the *paved shoulders* typical of the 18th c.

stretcher: The long face of a brick when laid horizontally.

string course: A projecting course of bricks or other material forming a narrow horizontal strip across the wall of a building, usually to delineate the line between stories; also called a *belt course*.

surround: The border or casing of a window or door opening, sometimes molded.

terra-cotta: A ceramic material, molded decoratively and often glazed, used for facings for buildings or as inset ornament. Tobacco farmers experimented with terra-cotta blocks for their curing barns in the 1920s and 1930s.

tobacco barn: A building in which tobacco is cured. Typically in eastern and Piedmont N.C. these are flue-cure tobacco barns, built specifically for the purpose of curing bright-leaf tobacco through a carefully regulated process of heating the barn full of tobacco. In some portions of western N.C., burley tobacco is grown and is air cured by hanging it in well-ventilated barns, which may be purpose-built or general-purpose barns. See the Introduction for a discussion of tobacco barn types and usage.

Tower of the Winds: The Horologium of Andronikos Cyrrhestes in Athens, which has columns showing a distinctive variation of the *Corinthian order*, with the *capitals* lacking volutes and having a row of palmlike leaves. The motif was used occasionally in the antebellum era—in N.C. especially in Wilmington—and again in the early 20th c.

transom: A horizontal window unit above a door.

tripartite: Having three parts. Often applied to symmetrical buildings with a principal central feature or block and subsidiary flanking elements.

triple-A: A locally used, nonstandard colloquialism for the roof form especially popular after the Civil War, where a center front *gable* (often a cross-gable, sometimes simply a gabled wall *dormer*) rises from the *facade* roofline. Coined in the mid-1970s by Franklin County health inspector Thilbert Pearce during an architectural survey of Franklin County conducted with the authors of this guidebook, the term is now widely used as a shorthand reference to a common form.

Tudor Revival: A popular style, primarily residential, in the early 20th c., characterized by motifs associated with Tudor and Jacobean English architecture, particularly half-timbered walls (often applied rather than structural), diamond-paned casement windows, steep *gables*, irregular plans, and chimneys with multiple stacks or chimney pots. Rather rarely used in N.C., except among expensive houses, typically interspersed among the more popular *Colonial Revival*, especially *Georgian Revival* styles.

turned: Fashioned on a lathe, as in a *baluster*, *newel*, or porch post.

Venetian window: See *Palladian window*.

Victorian: A general term for a period, the reign of Queen Victoria (1837–1901), and often used broadly to describe the wide variety of *eclectic* revival styles that were introduced in British and American architecture during that era.

wainscot: A decorative or protective facing applied to the lower portion of an interior wall or partition.

weatherboards, weatherboarding: Wood siding consisting of overlapping horizontal boards usually thicker at one edge than the other. More commonly used in N.C. than the term "clapboard." The usual method of covering a frame building in N.C.

Bibliography and Sources of Information

SELECTED BIBLIOGRAPHY

Allcott, John V. *Colonial Homes in North Carolina.* Raleigh: Carolina Tercentenary Commission, 1963. Reprint. Raleigh: Archives and History, 1975.

Arrington, Joel. "From the Ocean's Bed— a Vast and Sandy Plain," *Raleigh News and Observer,* July 14, 1985.

Barefoot, Daniel W. *Touring the Backroads of North Carolina's Lower Coast.* Winston-Salem: John F. Blair, 1995.

———. *Touring the Backroads of North Carolina's Upper Coast.* Winston-Salem: John F. Blair, 1995.

Barnett, Angela. *Pamlico County Imagery.* Bayboro: Pamlico County Historical Association, 1980.

Bishir, Catherine W. *North Carolina Architecture.* Chapel Hill: University of North Carolina Press for the Historic Preservation Foundation of North Carolina, 1990.

———. *The "Unpainted Aristocracy": The Beach Cottages of Old Nags Head.* Raleigh: Division of Archives and History, 1983.

Bishir, Catherine W., Charlotte V. Brown, Carl R. Lounsbury, and Ernest Wood III. *Architects and Builders in North Carolina: A History of the Practice of Building.* Chapel Hill: University of North Carolina Press, 1990.

Bivins, John, Jr. *The Furniture of Coastal North Carolina.* Winston-Salem: Museum of Early Southern Decorative Arts, 1988.

Butchko, Thomas R. *Edenton: An Architectural Portrait.* Edenton: Edenton Woman's Club, 1992.

———. *Forgotten Gates: The Historical Architecture of a Rural North Carolina County.* Gatesville: Gates County Historical Society, 1991.

———. *An Inventory of Historic Architecture: Sampson County, North Carolina.* Clinton: City of Clinton, 1981.

———. *On the Shores of the Pasquotank: The Architectural Heritage of Elizabeth City and Pasquotank County, North Carolina.* Elizabeth City: Museum of the Albemarle, 1989.

Carriker, S. David. *The North Carolina Railroad Map.* Charlotte: Heritage Publishing Co., 1993.

Carson, Cary, Norman F. Barker, William M. Kelso, Garry Wheeler Stone, and Dell Upton. "Impermanent Architecture in the Southern American Colonies." *Winterthur Portfolio* 16, nos. 2/3 (Summer/Autumn 1981): 55–89.

Cheeseman, Bruce. "The Survival of the Cupola House: 'A Venerable Old Mansion.'" *North Carolina Historical Review* 63, no. 1 (Jan. 1986): 40–73.

Cotter, Michael, Kate M. Ohno, and Mary Hollis Barnes. *The Architectural Heritage of Greenville, North Carolina.* Greenville: Greenville Area Preservation Association, 1988.

Crow, Jeffrey J., and Flora J. Hatley, eds. *Black Americans in North Carolina and the South.* Chapel Hill: University of North Carolina Press, 1984.

Dill, Alonzo T. *Governor Tryon and His Palace.* Chapel Hill: University of North Carolina Press, 1955.

Flowers, Linda. *Throwed Away: Failures of Progress in Eastern North Carolina.* Knoxville: University of Tennessee Press, 1990.

Greco, Thomas A. *Historical Architecture of Selma, North Carolina.* Selma: Town of Selma, 1980.

Gunter, S. Carol. *Carolina Heights, Wilmington.* Wilmington: City of Wilmington Planning Department, 1982.

Haley, Dru Gatewood, and Raymond A. Winslow. *The Historic Architecture of Perquimans County, North Carolina.* Hertford: Town of Hertford, 1982.

Hammond, Barbara. *An Architectural*

Inventory of Goldsboro, North Carolina.
Goldsboro: City of Goldsboro, 1987.

Hanchett, Thomas W. "The Rosenwald
Schools and Black Education in North
Carolina." *North Carolina Historical
Review* 65, no. 4 (Oct. 1988): 387–444.

Hill, Michael. *Guide to North Carolina
Highway Historical Markers.* 5th ed.
Raleigh: Division of Archives and
History, 1990.

Hobbs, Samuel Huntington, Jr. *North
Carolina: Economic and Social.* Chapel
Hill: University of North Carolina Press,
1930.

Hood, Davyd Foard, Christopher Martin,
Edward F. Turberg. *Historic Architecture
of New Hanover County, North Carolina.*
Wilmington: New Hanover County
Planning Department, 1986.

Johnson, Guion Griffis. *Ante-Bellum North
Carolina: A Social History.* Chapel Hill:
University of North Carolina Press, 1937.

Johnston, Frances Benjamin, and Thomas
Tileston Waterman. *The Early
Architecture of North Carolina.* Chapel
Hill: University of North Carolina Press,
1947.

Jones, H. G. *North Carolina Illustrated,
1524–1984.* Chapel Hill: University of
North Carolina Press, 1983.

Lane, Mills. *The Architecture of the Old
South: North Carolina.* Savannah:
Beehive Press, 1985.

Leary, Robert, and Associates. *An
Architectural and Historical Survey of
Central Lumberton, N.C.* Lumberton:
City of Lumberton and the Division of
Archives and History, 1979.

Letsinger, Philip. *An Inventory of Historic
Architecture of Maxton, N.C.* Maxton,
N.C.: Maxton Historical Society,
1982.

Little-Stokes, Ruth. "The North Carolina
Porch: A Climatic and Cultural Buffer."
In *Carolina Dwelling,* edited by Douglas
Swaim, 104–11. Raleigh: North Carolina
State University School of Design
Student Publication, 1978.

Lounsbury, Carl R. *The Architecture of
Southport.* Southport: Southport
Historical Society, 1979.

———. "The Development of Domestic
Architecture in the Albemarle Region."
North Carolina Historical Review 54,
no. 1 (Jan. 1977): 17–48. Reprinted in
Carolina Dwelling, edited by Douglas
Swaim, 46–61. Raleigh: North Carolina
State University School of Design
Student Publication, 1978.

———. *An Illustrated Glossary of Early
Southern Architecture and Landscape.*
New York: Oxford University Press,
1994.

Mathews, Donald G. *Religion in the Old
South.* Chicago: University of Chicago
Press, 1977.

Mattson, Richard L. "The Cultural
Landscape of a Southern Black
Community: East Wilson, North
Carolina, 1890–1930." *Landscape
Journal* 11, no. 2 (Fall 1992): 145–59.

———. *The History and Architecture of
Nash County, North Carolina.* Nashville:
Nash County Planning Department,
1987.

Mearns, Kate. *Central City Historic
Buildings Inventory: Rocky Mount, North
Carolina.* Rocky Mount: Central City
Revitalization Corporation, 1979.

Mobley, Joe A. *Ship Ashore!: The U.S.
Lifesavers of Coastal North Carolina.*
Raleigh: Division of Archives and
History, 1994.

Morris, Glenn. *North Carolina Beaches.*
Chapel Hill: University of North
Carolina Press, 1993.

National Register of Historic Places
Nomination Forms, Archaeology and
Historic Preservation Section, and
Archives and Records Section, Division
of Archives and History, Department
of Cultural Resources, Raleigh (originals
at National Park Service, Washington,
D.C.).

North Carolina Department of
Transportation. *North Carolina Scenic
Byways.* Raleigh: North Carolina
Department of Transportation,
1994.

Oates, John A. *The Story of Fayetteville.*
2d ed. Fayetteville: Fayetteville Woman's
Club, 1972.

Ohno, Kate. *Wilson County's Architectural Heritage.* Wilson: County of Wilson, 1981.

Ohno, Kate, and Robert Bainbridge. *Wilson, North Carolina, Historic Buildings Inventory.* Wilson: City of Wilson, 1980.

Powell, William S. *Dictionary of North Carolina Biography.* 6 vols. Chapel Hill: University of North Carolina Press, 1979–96.

———. *The North Carolina Gazetteer.* Chapel Hill: University of North Carolina Press, 1968.

———. *North Carolina through Four Centuries.* Chapel Hill: University of North Carolina Press, 1989.

Power, Scott. *The Historic Architecture of Pitt County, North Carolina.* Greenville: Pitt County Historical Society, 1991.

Preservation North Carolina. *The Complete Guide to North Carolina's Historic Sites.* Raleigh: Preservation North Carolina, [1994].

Robinson, Blackwell P. *The North Carolina Guide.* Chapel Hill: University of North Carolina Press, 1955.

Sandbeck, Peter B. *The Historic Architecture of New Bern and Craven County, North Carolina.* New Bern: Tryon Palace Commission, 1988.

Seapker, Janet K. "James F. Post, Builder-Architect: The Legend and the Ledger," *Lower Cape Fear Historical Society Bulletin* 30, no. 3 (May 1987): 1–7.

Shoemaker, Mary M. *The Historic Architecture of Hamilton, N.C.* Hamilton: Historic Hamilton Commission, 1979.

———. *An Inventory of Historical Architecture in the Town of Smithfield.* Smithfield: Town of Smithfield, 1977.

Simpson, Bland. *The Great Dismal: A Carolinian's Swamp Memoir.* Chapel Hill: University of North Carolina Press, 1990.

Southern, Michael T. "The I-House as a Carrier of Style." In *Carolina Dwelling,* edited by Douglas Swaim, 72–83. Raleigh: North Carolina State University School of Design Student Publication, 1978.

Stick, David. *North Carolina Lighthouses.* Raleigh: Department of Cultural Resources, 1980.

———. *The Outer Banks of North Carolina, 1584–1958.* Chapel Hill: University of North Carolina Press, 1958.

Swaim, Douglas, ed. *Carolina Dwelling.* Raleigh: North Carolina State University School of Design Student Publication, 1978.

Tilley, Nannie May. *The Bright-Tobacco Industry, 1860–1929.* Chapel Hill: University of North Carolina Press, 1948.

Wrenn, Tony P. *Beaufort, North Carolina.* Raleigh: Division of Archives and History, 1970.

———. *Wilmington, North Carolina: An Architectural and Historical Portrait.* Charlottesville: University Press of Virginia, 1984.

SOURCES OF INFORMATION

Division of Travel and Tourism
N.C. Department of Commerce
430 N. Salisbury St., Raleigh, NC 27611
919-733-4171, or 1-800-VISIT NC

Map Section
N.C. Department of Transportation
P.O. Box 25201, Raleigh, NC 27611
919-733-7600

Ferry Division
N.C. Department of Transportation
113 Arendell St., Morehead City, NC 28557
1-800-BY FERRY

Division of Parks and Recreation
N.C. Department of Environment, Health and Natural Resources
512 N. Salisbury St., Raleigh, NC 27611
919-733-4181

Archaeology and Historic Preservation Section
Division of Archives and History
N.C. Department of Cultural Resources
109 E. Jones St., Raleigh, NC 27601-2807
919-733-4763

State Historic Sites
Division of Archives and History
N.C. Department of Cultural Resources
532 N. Wilmington St.,
Raleigh, NC 27604-1147
919-733-7862

Preservation North Carolina
101 St. Mary's St.
P.O. Box 27644
Raleigh, NC 27611-7644
919-832-3652

Photography Credits

Most of the photographs used in this volume are from the collection of the North Carolina Division of Archives and History. The following photographs from other sources are used with permission and acknowledged with thanks.

Durwood Barbour Postcard Collection, private: Wayne National Bank (WY 2).

Division of Travel and Tourism, North Carolina Department of Commerce, Raleigh: Wilmington (pp. ii–iii); Cape Hatteras Lighthouse (Fig. 2): Somerset Place (Fig. 17; p. 152); Iredell House Kitchen (Fig. 18); Cupola House (CO 8); Wessington (CO 16); Iredell House (CO 37); Wright Brothers National Memorial (DR 9); Bodie Island Lighthouse (DR 14); Cape Hatteras Lighthouse (DR 19); Ocracoke Aerial View and Ocracoke Lighthouse (HY 23); Palmer-Marsh House (BF 28); New Bern Academy (CV 48); Fort Macon (CR 18); Cape Lookout Lighthouse (CR 24); Portsmouth Village (CR 25); Bellamy Mansion (NH 10); Wilmington Waterfront (NH 14); Bald Head Lighthouse (BW 4); The Rocks (BW 5); Orton Plantation (BW 7); Hope Plantation (BR 7); Falcon Tabernacle (CD 30).

Duke University Special Collections Library, Duke University, Durham: Atlantic Trust and Banking (Fig. 58); Federal Building, New Bern (Fig. 65); Craven County Courthouse (CV 40); Pitt County Courthouse (PT 1); U.S. Post Office, Greenville (PT 2); Cumberland County Courthouse (CD 13); Hay Street Methodist Church (CD 15).

Historic American Buildings Survey, Library of Congress, Washington, D.C.: First Presbyterian Church (CV 47), Frances Benjamin Johnston Collection.

Elizabeth Matheson Photographs, Division of Archives and History: Bennett's Pond (Fig. 4); The Homestead (CO 6); Bank of Edenton (CO 9).

North Carolina Collection, Wilson Library, University of North Carolina, Chapel Hill: Hauling Cotton, *Harper's Weekly,* 1866 (Fig. 8); Former Slave Quarters, Fayetteville (Fig. 20); St. John's Masonic Lodge and Theater, New Bern (Fig. 25); Wilkinson-Dozier House (Fig. 27), Frances Benjamin Johnston Collection; Tobacco Warehouse, Wilson (Fig. 47): Queen St., Kinston (Fig. 54); W. Nash St., Wilson (Fig. 59); Elizabeth City State University (Fig. 63); Nags Head (Fig. 64); Old Brick House (PK 8), Bayard Wootten Collection; Johnston County Courthouse (JT 1); Prince Charles Hotel (CD 16); Post Chapel, Fort Bragg (CD 25).

Sarah Pope Postcard Collection, private: W. Center St., Goldsboro (Fig. 50); Weil House, Goldsboro (Fig. 53); Goldsboro City Hall (Fig. 57); Middle Street, New Bern (p. 89); Herman Park (WY 12).

Preservation North Carolina: Rosedale, Beaufort Co., with "SWAT" (Save Worn-Out Architectural Treasures) Team at work (Fig. 69).

Index